LIBANIUS

I

LCL 478

LIBANIUS

AUTOBIOGRAPHY AND SELECTED LETTERS

VOLUME I

EDITED AND TRANSLATED BY

A. F. NORMAN

HARVARD UNIVERSITY PRESS

CAMBRIDGE, MASSACHUSETTS
LONDON, ENGLAND
1992

First published 1992

Library of Congress Cataloging-in-Publication Data

Libanius.
[Selections. English & Greek. 1992]
Autobiography and selected letters / Libanius :
edited and translated by A. F. Norman.
p. cm. — (The Loeb classical library : 478–479)
Includes bibliographical references and index.
ISBN 0–674–99527–9 (v. 1)
0–674–99528–7 (v. 2)
1. Libanius—Translations into English
2. Sophists—Correspondence. 3. Orators—Antioch—
Correspondence. 4. Sophists—Biography.
5. Orators—Antioch—Biography.
I. Norman, A. F. (Albert Francis) II. Title. III. Series
PA4227.E6 1992
885′.01—dc20 [B] 91–26316 CIP

Typeset by Chiron, Inc, Cambridge, Massachusetts.
Printed in Great Britain by St Edmundsbury Press Ltd,
Bury St Edmunds, Suffolk, on acid-free paper.
Bound by Hunter & Foulis Ltd, Edinburgh, Scotland.

CONTENTS

INTRODUCTION   1

ABBREVIATIONS AND BIBLIOGRAPHY   44

THE AUTOBIOGRAPHY   51

SELECTED LETTERS   339
  Letters 1–50

CONTENTS OF VOLUME TWO

SELECTED LETTERS
   Letters 51–193

APPENDIX: ADDITIONAL NOTES

CONCORDANCES

INDEX

PREFACE

The *Letters* and the *Autobiography* of Libanius are mutually illustrative. In the present edition of the *Autobiography*, the practice of my Loeb Classical Library edition of the *Orations* has been maintained with reference to the pagination of both Reiske and Foerster, for the reasons outlined there in Volume I. Since the appearance of my earlier edition of the *Autobiography* in 1965 there have been published the translation by P. Wolf, and a new recension of manuscripts by J. Martin together with the commentary by Paul Petit in their joint edition, due note of which has been taken here. The death of Paul Petit has since sadly diminished the study of the later Roman Empire. As an interpreter of Libanius he stood head and shoulders above the rest for nearly a generation, and his inspiration is sorely missed.

The selection of the *Letters* represents one eighth of the total. The text is based on the work of Foerster, whose study of the manuscripts in Volume IX of his edition is, and will remain, fundamental. The letters appear in chronological order, the principle of selection being to present a conspectus of Libanius' activities and attitudes throughout his career, and to introduce the more important of his correspondents. They are accordingly numbered anew; but concordances with Foerster's as well as other recent editions are appended. It should be noted that I cite letters by a system such that *"Letter 25"* designates a letter included in the present collection (with my numeration), *"Ep.* 280" (with Foerster's numeration) one that is not.

The identification of Libanius' correspondents follows the listings by Roman numerals in Seeck, *BLZG* (for this and other abbreviations see the list in the Bibliography), with references to *PLRE* listed by Arabic numerals for amplification and amendment.

This edition claims no independent work on the manuscripts; and the critical apparatus restricts itself to drawing attention to readings that deviate from Foerster's edition.

University of Hull   A. F. Norman
March 1992

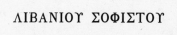
ΛΙΒΑΝΙΟΥ ΣΟΦΙΣΤΟΥ

INTRODUCTION

THE career of Libanius may be established with some precision. Born in A.D. 314 of an old established municipal family in Antioch, he left home at the late age of twenty-two—already decided on a sophistic career—to complete his studies in Athens. There he quickly made a name for himself by his ability and unorthodoxy as a student. In 339/340 he settled as a private teacher in Constantinople and soon was so successful as to ruffle enough official and sophistic feathers to be expelled in the aftermath of the rioting of 342. After a brief stay in Nicaea, he was established as municipal teacher in Nicomedeia, a post which he held with great success from 344 to 349, when he was recalled much against his will to a chair in Constantinople. Disenchanted with what he regarded as the uncouth and parvenu atmosphere of the new capital, he lost no time in trying to get away, and he returned to Antioch for the first time on a vacation visit in 353. A warm reception there and betrothal to his cousin, short-lived though this was since she died in the winter following, occasioned negotiations to succeed to the municipal chair; early in 354 he came back home and within a year was installed as official sophist.

He remained in Antioch for the rest of his life, forming a matrimonial union with a woman of lower status, whom he does not mention until after her death.

His removal from Constantinople had been secured on the somewhat flimsy excuse of ill-health, but the unremitting efforts which he had to apply to consolidate his new position, though productive of startling success, turned these fictitious ailments into real ones. Overwork, gout, and migraine combined to induce a severe depression which by the end of the decade fed upon professional and personal worries so as to bring him close to nervous breakdown. Breakdown, indeed, was to be a feature of his life thereafter, but on this occasion he found relief in the accession of Julian.

Julian's brief stay in Antioch saw Libanius, despite his physical frailties, at the height of his rhetorical powers, and with a congenial atmosphere to work in. He was accepted as spokesman of a regime with which he could at last identify himself, and he could match his heroes of the Second Sophistic in relations with the emperor. Not only had he full scope for his eloquence but he was able to put it to practical effect with arguments on behalf of distressed individuals of whatever persuasion. His eloquence was less successful, however, when he attempted to mediate between his emperor and the mass of his fellow citizens who quickly and constantly expressed raucous dissatisfaction with the aims and conduct of the new regime. For such activities he received precious little thanks after Julian's death. Under the reaction that followed he was a marked man, at worst a target for assassination, at best suspected of disaffection towards the regime, which was no less dangerous. Under such circumstances the composition of the Monody or Lament and the Epitaphios over Julian (*Or.* 17, 18) was an act of loyal consistency and courage, as indeed was that of the original Autobiography nearly a decade later. Except for that work, prudence dictated an enforced silence throughout the reign of Valens.

The advent of Theodosius saw Libanius emerge into the open with a counter-attack in *Oration* 24 upon the recent radical regime, and with a rebuttal in *Oration* 2 of the personal criticisms he had been forced to endure. As a sign of his changed circumstances, he could now at least enunciate such views. He enjoyed enough prestige and support at court throughout the 380s to produce a series of "reform" speeches critical of current policies and social developments, and yet be accorded such marks of imperial favour as the award of honorary office to himself and the privilege of legal inheritance to his bastard son. At the same time, however, relations with the governors on the spot tend to deteriorate, and there is increased opposition, both professional and personal, shown towards him in his own community as friends and supporters die

off. Nervous breakdowns ensue, first on the death of
his brother, and then in 386 with the recurrence of
his old ailments, which become progressively worse
throughout his last years, producing melancholia
and depression verging on paranoia. After the
deaths of his wife and son in 391 his letters harp on
the imminence of death; they, and the additions to
the Autobiography, cease in the middle of 393.

That the child is father to the man is especially
true of Libanius. His upbringing in a close-knit
household which was with difficulty recovering from
the loss of personnel, property, and prestige in
consequence of the arbitrary mass punishments
inflicted by a vengeful emperor was never forgotten.
It had a crucial influence upon his later notions of
the imperial power and its relation to the law. For
him there was no room for the Themistian notion of
the emperor as law incarnate. The emperor had
struck too close to home, and even his provincial
governors were at best a necessary evil (*Or.* 51.3).
Furthermore, the intensity of his adolescent conversion to the study of classical literature brought with
it a devotion to the religion and the ideals in which
that literature was rooted, so that he was
antipathetic to the quick and drastic changes in the
society in which he grew up. His deliberate and
unorthodox extension of his period of study by
repeating the course under the *grammatistes* may
have made him a maturer student and sharpened

his critical faculty and his capacity for memorization, but it ran counter to the material aspirations of his family. The remark of the upwardly mobile Panolbios that here was a sophist in the making was certainly not complimentary. A precocious and prim young man like Libanius stuck out among his contemporaries. This nonconformity throughout his career was exaggerated by an intense local patriotism which grew the stronger with the recognition that Antioch was fast losing ground to the newly founded capital and its uncouth and cosmopolitan society. His sophistic career was not to be just a profession but a way of life conditioned by such personal experience and observation, and consistent enough for him to be saluted as a practical philosopher by Julian, whose own formative years had been affected by experiences somewhat similar.

Libanius was sociable by nature. His near contemporary Eunapius, who was certainly not well predisposed towards him, remarks upon his innate sensitivity and an affability and charm that he claims for himself in *Oration* 2. Whatever his reactions to the doctrines of other persuasions, he remained generously supportive of individuals among them, Manichees, Jews, or Christians, no less than of his pagan co-religionists. In personal relationships he showed a loyal devotion and expected as much in return. In his professional capacity he needed a responsive atmosphere to appear at his best; without it, he tended to freeze, for him the worst of all fates, and to succumb to depression. In this there lay the basic self-contradiction of his career, which was increasingly laid bare by age and infirmity. Background and experience had inculcated in him a wariness of officialdom and its deeds, but for success in the conduct of his profession he needed the consistent approval and support of the great and the influential among these same people. His ideal of a free expression of views was too often impossible of attainment. Hence the sorry tale of collision with so many governors, where fair beginnings end in bitter recriminations. The favour of this class was essential, but he could not and would not disguise his antipathy towards so many of their policies and methods, even where his judgement was not clouded by self-interest, as it was in his last years by his ambitions for Thalassius and Cimon. His failure to resolve this tension goes far to explain the gloom of his later years. So, while aspiring even in his last letters to display his qualities as a panegyrist, he leaves as his last surviving oration an invective. His journal, which had as its starting point the public applause which greeted his eloquence, ends with him in semi-seclusion, gloating incoherently over an imagined divine vengeance exacted in return for a fancied wrong that he had suffered.

The Autobiography

Gibbon tersely dismissed the Autobiography of Libanius as "the vain, prolix, but curious narrative of his own life." Indeed for Gibbon, despite a tepid commendation of some of his orations, the writings of Libanius appear as "the vain and idle compositions of an orator who cultivated the science of words—the production of a recluse student, whose mind, regardless of his contemporaries, was incessantly fixed on the Trojan War and the Athenian commonwealth." Lack of sympathy for the style and of appreciation for the material combine in this damningly influential half-truth.

The Autobiography is not without problems, most obviously as regards its composition. Reiske began his commentary with the observation that the oration was not written as a unitary whole, since Libanius gives a date of writing in his sixtieth year, that is 374 (§ 51), and yet proceeds to mention events that are manifestly later than that. For a century or more there was uncertainty as to where this original oration actually ended, until comparatively recently the line of division has been established at § 155.

This original oration was indeed a single composition, presenting a reasonably consistent sequence of events, as required by the nature of the material, but beginning with § 156 the case is very different. There is no longer any address or reference to an audience, there is less discipline either in pattern or in tone, and the original point of reference of §1, which had been so strongly marked in §155 to conclude the original speech, is gradually lost almost in its entirety. This portion of the work is, in fact, a series of occasional additions some of which are indicated by interim pronouncements (as in §§233, 234, 244), others by doublets (as with the state of his studies, §§213 ff, §234), or by the completion of unfinished business (so Sabinus, §§190 ff, §261; his brother's illness, §§197 ff, and death, §213; Proclus' arrival, §212, and departure, §221 ff). The most recent study of this aspect of composition is that in the late Paul Petit's admirable edition of the *Autobiographie* (pp. 3–7), whose conclusions amplify and correct earlier studies, my own among them. They are:

Addition (1): §§156–162, written just before 380.
     (2): §§163–170, shortly following.
     (3): §§171–204, of 382.
     (4): §§205–215, of 383.
     (5): §§216–234, before harvest 385.
     (6): §§235–250, of 386.
     (7): §§251–261, of 388.
     (8): §§262–277, written in 389/390.
     (9): §§278–285, summer 393.

This scheme seems generally satisfying, but there is still some room for debate. Additions (3–7) can be taken as proven, and 9 as highly probable; but 1, 2, and 8 deserve further scrutiny. In brief, there is a reasonable case to be made out for the merging of 1 and 2, since the reference back in §163 seems to indicate not so much a break in composition as the activities of officials of differing status within a continuing narrative. Conversely, 8 should be split at §270, since the action of Fortune there is very strongly underlined.

The shapelessness of the whole thus becomes more understandable. It was composed at intervals over nearly twenty years and comprises two distinct elements, a completed formal discourse, and private memoirs of different dates, connected to it and to each other in a very perfunctory fashion. Publication of the addenda by Libanius was out of the question: the contents were too self-revelatory, the style too fragmented and unpolished. However, publication of the oration of 374 is clearly indicated. References to the presence of an audience should be taken at face value. In fact, it influences both the contents and the presentation of the address. They were his contemporaries, so that he must not be caught out promoting deliberate falsehoods, though manipulation of material might be justified on stylistic or psychological grounds. Thus the telescoping together of the discomfitures of Eubulus and Zenobius (§§98–104), misleading though it may be, is stylistically justifiable, while pathos dictates the inversion of the sequence of events in §118. Omission is prudently selective, most obviously so of his experiences in the reign of Valens.

However, his denial in *Oration* 2 (12 ff) of any public parading of the material which had been the staple of the Autobiography points to the restricted character of this audience. It was a small but select group of intimates, gathered in a private auditorium, in accordance with the practice of the day. The most extreme example of the practice appears in his account of his funeral oration on Phasganius, where he explains the good reasons for it (*Letter* 64). His hearers could be relied upon to be appreciative and discreet, so that a real but controlled publication could be ensured while the oration remained safely undocumented, which for Libanius in 374 in particular was a matter of considerable importance. The mention of the dangers he ran (§1) is relevant in this context.

The character of the audience interacts with that of the oration itself. The audience was sophisticated, literate, and appreciative of the implications of the terms of reference which he lays down for himself in §1. They knew better than to expect the epideictic approach suited for a wider company. Just as Isocrates, by adopting the form of forensic oratory familiar to the audience of his day, justified himself in the conduct of his career in the Antidosis, Libanius responds to the demands of his particular audience by presenting his theme in the more intimate terms of sophistic discourse. Twenty years earlier he had composed the discourse On Genius

(Περὶ εὐφυίας). This he defines as a *dialexis*, one of
Aristaenetus' favourite types of composition (*Letter*
6.13). It became well enough known for Eunapius
(*V.S.* 497) to notice in some detail. The material of
it was an examination of the abilities of his rival
Acacius, which he developed, according to Eunapius, in no friendly fashion with a result not to his
own advantage. Now in 374 the subject set for
examination is Fortune, the material to be supplied
by his own life. Dressed in terms of good and bad,
the theme broadens to a critique of the human condition, and the need to attain by constant reappraisal a proper appreciation of reality as opposed to
appearance—a topic dear to sophists and Libanius
not least among them, as in the mini-dissertation
Oration 8. With the treatment moralizing and the
conclusion didactic, this composition illustrates
popular philosophizing in sophistic guise.

The title *Bios* may thus be put into its proper
context. Despite the chronological framework
Libanius conceived this oration no more in terms
of the merely autobiographical than St. Augustine
did the *Confessions*. The alternative title has more
to recommend it, though even here there is the
possibility of intrusion by a later hand. His other
moralizing compositions bear general descrip-
tions—insatiability, poverty, slavery, and the like.
Even when dealing with his rival as an individual,
the theme becomes generalized into a discourse on
Genius. In treating a concept so intimate to him-

self, the appropriate formula for his theme is simply Περὶ Τύχης, On Fortune.

No Antiochene, least of all Libanius, was in any doubt as to the role Fortune had to play. Others might consider her as blind chance, fickle jade, or ineluctable destiny, but Antioch was conditioned to regard her in particular as the tutelary goddess of the city. Such a notion was ingrained in Libanius the traditionalist. For him the field of her operations is not to be defined by abstract philosophy nor yet by any novel religiosity. From the terms of reference in § 1, it is self-evident that her activity is confined to the practical field of human conduct where morality has scope for action, and that it is performed in collusion with the gods. Value judgements of good and bad, of right and wrong, must therefore be sure, and the individual, despite her presence, is not absolved of responsibility for choice or the exercise of will. So in his own case, his first interest in rhetoric and the choice of his career were primarily his own (§§ 5, 11); thereafter Fortune can make her first explicit appearance (§ 12), setting the scene so that there is no occasion for misunderstanding and ensuring no excess of good or ill.

This evaluation of the quality of her performance requires repeated and intelligent reappraisal. Her efforts are to be subjected to scrutiny in order to remove misapprehension (as in § 73) or to secure final confirmation, as in the prosopopoeia of § 155. Periodic stock-takings of his circumstances

throughout his career are the means of such evaluation. In § 51 he seems to suggest five-yearly intervals for them, and although this line of argument is
not pursued, on rough and ready reckoning a loose
pattern of such a nature may be observed from 329
to 359. Fortune's care and prescience repeatedly act
as corrective to the vanity of his human wishes and
actions, so that circumstances which at the time had
appeared bad ultimately turn out good through her
agency. Thus his misadventures upon his arrival in
Athens are turned to his advantage (§§ 18 ff), and
his withdrawal from Nicomedeia, much against his
own wish, is her method of securing his protection
(§ 78), but reappraisal is needed for such correct
judgement to be achieved. Libanius is the opportun-
ist, Fortune the embodiment of the long view. He
may be the worker, but she is the supervisor who
arranges the material of his career into a well-
balanced statement of accounts.

Her prescience is optimistic, and her presence
beneficial, both as protector and arranger of the
course of events, but her appearance in the narrative has a further advantage for him in the composition of the work. It acts as a buffer between him and
his audience. The transference of the account from
first to third person absolves him from any criticism
of excessive glorification of his successes such as had
provided the theme of the discourse (§ 1). Direct
narration of his own achievements could be a risky
business for him, as he recognizes (§ 37).

The original Autobiography follows this pattern of repeated balance and counterbalance, with Fortune overtly leaving little room for other deities. Their existence is subsumed by such mentions as the ceremonials of § 23, the local cults of § 48, or the religious revival of § 119, but except for the healing powers of Asclepius (§ 143) no divinities are mentioned as active in real life. The dispensations of the gods, in combination with Fortune, provide material for the theme in § 1, but thereafter Fortune has no rival.

In the second part of the work, the appearances of Fortune are no less frequent, but the pattern in which her activities are presented is relaxed. Only once (§ 181) is the technique of stock-taking introduced with its paradox between the real and the apparent in Fortune's favours. Good and bad are then produced as realities, catalogued but not reappraised, until a halfhearted piece of prosopopoeia appears in § 190. Prescience and protection she may provide as before (for example, §§ 175 f, 190, 217). Her influence upon his rhetorical performances remains (§§ 232, 253), and her scope in other aspects of his life is as wide as ever. She it is "under whom all things lie" (§ 266), who saves him from the powers of magic (§ 250) and from accusation (§ 240), and who, by reversing the outcome of events, compensates him for his discomfitures without any effort on his part (§ 230). In his latest years he was unable to get any such compensation from her.

The private nature of these parts of his journal is reflected in the increasing pessimism and bitterness which, with regard to the treatment of Fortune, is revealed in two ways. First, the role of Fortune herself undergoes a change. She is no longer the consistently forward looking support that she used to be. Her support now tends to come after the event, and to consist of consolation for misfortunes or injustices now irreparable, as in the case of Cimon. From 386, after his breakdown, a more ominous tendency, which had indeed found expression at times in the past (for example, § 194, of 381), is manifested more frequently and with increasing lack of control. Fortune's consolations degenerate into revenge exacted from individuals (§ 270) or from whole communities (§ 285). Time was when he had personally punished a city by his oratory (*Letter* 145). Now his is the passive role. Fortune manifests herself as his avenging rather than guardian angel. She has taken upon herself the attributes of Nemesis.

Moreover, in these activities of his declining years, she no longer has unchallenged supremacy. Zeus acts in concert with her (§§ 270, 285), as do Hermes and the *logioi theoi* (§ 274), in each case to assist him by the exaction of punishment. It may be an expression of a return to a deeper and darker religiosity in his old age, but the gods increasingly act without reference to her in the conduct of his affairs (§§ 259, 260, 273), and they are no less ready to intervene on his account, but, significantly

15

enough, only after the event (for example, Zeus, § 222; Apollo, § 262), until the combination of Zeus, the gods, and Fortune brings his story to its vengeful close.

Three scholars in the past two hundred years have had a lasting effect on the study and establishment of the text of Libanius. Reiske's *Animadversiones* with its mass of conjecture and comment set a pattern for the next century. His flair, and the devotion of his widow in publishing the posthumous four volume edition of the works, pointed the way for a wider and deeper appreciation of Libanius. Foerster's monumental work in the examination and classification of the manuscripts of the entire Libanian corpus was indeed the work of a lifetime, and it has brought the whole range of these studies to a wider readership, so helping to promote the surge in the study of late antiquity. Martin, in a more technological age, is reexamining Foerster's legacy to produce most salutary refinements and amendments with new insights into the text. In textual matters, if Reiske improved on his predecessors by his insight and choice of manuscripts, including A, and Foerster's analyses led to a juster appreciation of the various groupings around manuscripts like A, C, and V, Martin's meticulous reappraisal is vital for the appreciation of interrelationships between manuscripts of different groups and of the importance to be attached to C in the formulation of the text. The only other edition of the Autobiography, my own of 1965, was based on the work of Foerster's recension of the manuscripts, with amendments as I judged required.

The Autobiography survives in sixteen manuscripts. The present text is based on the readings of

A: Monacensis gr. 483 (Augustanus), originally of c. X–XI, but with extensive replacements of c. XIV
C: Chisianus R VI 43: c. X–XI
P: Palatinus Vaticanus gr. 282: c. XIV
V: Vindobonensis phil. gr. 93: c. XIV
L: Laurentianus LVII 20: c. XIV.

Detailed examination of these is to be found in the preface to Foerster's edition of the Autobiography (Vol. i, pp. 10 ff) and in Libanios, *Discours* I, ed. J. Martin, pp. 36–92.

The Letter: Theory and Practice

The picture of Libanius presented by Gibbon in his twenty-fourth chapter has profoundly affected the modern view of the sophist as a literary figure. While giving him due credit for the consistency of character revealed in his relations with Julian, Gibbon yet damns him as a writer with the faintest of faint praise. He may notice the Orations with a measure of approval for their contents, but his pithiest and most memorable comments are those based

17

on the Declamations, so that the reader is left with the indelible impression of Libanius as a mere word-monger, a recluse student whose sole preoccupation was with the glories of a Greece long gone. Of his merits and standing as an epistolographer Gibbon was particularly dismissive, according him but seven words of text supported by a brief but tendentious note, in which the dreaming pedant of Bentley's *Phalaris* is identified, without more ado, with Libanius himself. In this note Gibbon's lack of sympathy is complete, but his wording demands more scrutiny. His total for the number of the letters ("near two thousand") reveals his assumption that the inanities of Zambecari's Latin versions, as reproduced in the edition of J. C. Wolf, were part of the genuine Libanian corpus, while the back-handed compliments to previous literary judgements about the charm of Libanius' style give some cause for suspecting that his assessment of this branch of his work has been influenced as much by a reading of Wolf's accompanying Latin as by the original text. Such suspicion may be reinforced by Gibbon's own account of his late-come and self-taught appreciation of "the beauties of the Latin and the rudiments of the Greek tongue."

This coolness towards Libanius as an epistolographer ran counter to all preceding literary experience. Even in his own lifetime Libanius' mastery of the art was generally acknowledged. As early as 362 he was held to be the model for Julian's epistolary style (*Or.* 13.52, *Ep.* 716.3). Shortly after his death, Eunapius, in a rather hostile account of him, yet acknowledges his virtue as a composer of letters (*V.S.* 496). And within a century his preeminence as a writer of letters was recognized by the publication of that collection of forgeries attributed to St. Basil and himself whereby his name was endowed with an unaccustomed odour of sanctity which, combined with the stylishness of his writings, made him the more acceptable to generations of devout Byzantine scholars.

Yet his reputation was due to no theorizing on his part, nor to any innovation in technique or ethos. He himself was confessedly averse to change for the sake of change (see *Or.* 10.18), and the correspondent's art was by now fenced around with rules of venerable antiquity. These first appear in the brief exposé of the letter contained in "Demetrius" *On Style,* and they had since been developed and refined in successive commentaries, such as the selection in *Epistolographi Graeci* (pp. 1–16). If such as Gregory Nazianzen was loud in praise of the virtues of these rules, Libanius was likely to be the last to reject them, particularly in matters of technique. In fact, all the desiderata of style outlined by Demetrius and the rest appear as a matter of course in his letters. For instance, the clarity demanded by Demetrius (§ 226) is explicitly required by Libanius (*Ep.* 716); harmony of subject and diction, with avoidance of exaggeration (§ 229), appears in *Ep.* 606, while the long-vexed question of the length appropriate to the letter (§ 228) is a regular topic, especially with intimates like Anatolius and Aristaenetus. The final requirement of Demetrius for charm of diction is all-pervasive in the letters of Libanius. In one important aspect, however, Libanius appears as both beneficiary and prime exponent of the tradition. For Demetrius there was no argument but that a decent restrained Attic should be the natural stylistic vehicle for correspondence. But during the intervening centuries, after the bitter dispute with the more florid Asianism, a deliberately and artificially cultivated Atticism had emerged, with a method of training now long formalized. Libanius' own enthusiastic adherence to this, clearly revealed in the Autobiography, made him the foremost exponent of this refined Attic style in his day (Eunap. *V.S.* 496), and earned him an enduring fame for technical expertise, so much so that he could be, according to one manuscript tradition, adjudged to be the author of the technical treatise *Characteres Epistolici* (Foerster Vol. ix, pp. 1–47).

Examination of the ethos of the letter had had an equally long history according to the evidence of Demetrius, where basic concepts appear already defined and discussed, themselves to be continually reassessed in the following centuries. Long before Libanius' time Demetrius' simplistic definitions— that the letter is a kind of gift (§ 224), an expression of the writer's character (§ 227), and a token of friendship drawing its charm from the warmth of that feeling (§ 232)—had been absorbed, amplified, and embroidered by generations of theorists. The universality of the rhetorical education and the formalization of Greco-Roman society and its institutions had produced in the cities of every province a type of educated notable, each of whom was, regardless of place of origin, race, or religion, potentially linked with others of his kind elsewhere by the standard upbringing and associations of the universal literary culture of classical antiquity. Potentiality was transformed into reality by the formal institution of friendship, and the letter became the vehicle for this. It overcame any difficulties of geographical separation and, by harking back to the shared formative experience of a common culture, it became the prime means for the propagation and maintenance of this tie. For Cicero true friendships had been those of the *boni,* and the correspondents of the fourth century had no difficulty in identifying themselves as such. At any rate, for the author of the *Characteres Epistolici* (§ 49: Foerster Vol. ix, p. 34) such a person is the λόγιος ἀνήρ, the ideal correspondent by birth, upbringing, and intellect. In his hands the letter became not merely a communication with absent friends but a communion with them; it was "a written association of people separated from one another ... in it one speaks as though present oneself directly to another person"

21

(*ibid.* § 2; p. 27). Thus by means of the letter physical absence is exchanged for spiritual presence, and so Libanius, himself a practitioner rather than a theorist, can remark as a matter of course (*Ep.* 245.9) "When you look at my letter, think that you are looking at me." In *Ep.* 1225.3 he employs the same conceits and terminology as those of *Characteres Epistolici* 2, emphasizing that such is indeed the special function of correspondence between friends. Similarly he can imagine himself present at and participating in the conversation that ensues between the recipient of his letter and its bearer, where both content and direction are dictated by his own personality (*Ep.* 1428.2).

In letter writing of this kind between private individuals the messenger's role is vital. The composition and despatch of the letter are themselves accidental upon the presence of an appropriate bearer, and not every volunteer for such a job was suitable (*Ep.* 704). In the absence of a regular postal system for all but official despatches, composition was inevitably intermittent, even between the closest of friends, despatch requiring both organization and improvization on the part of the individual writer. In consequence, the value of the letter as a means of exchanging news and views between peers was much reduced, even if it were safe to commit such items to writing, which was not always the case (see *Ep.* 1264, *Or.* 1.175). Instead, emphasis is laid almost overwhelmingly upon the cultural ground common to the correspondents, and the letter becomes a fully developed art form. Incidentally, various Demetrian definitions are also developed. The letter is indeed sent and received as a gift, as Libanius and his friends, such as Anatolius or Hyperechius, admit when they complain of not receiving letters. The vexed question of the length appropriate to any letter is also resolved in practice rather than by theory, since news and confidential messages are conveyed by the bearer orally rather than by writing. Moreover, the receipt of the letter thus producing a conversation between bearer and addressee such as that imagined in *Ep.* 1428, a dialogue is stimulated in which the writer, though absent, plays his part, and a situation is produced reminiscent of Demetrius' comment that the letter is half a dialogue.

If the letter is the vehicle for friendship, the fuel and lubricant is undoubtedly the quality of grace and charm associated with χάρις. In the letters of Libanius this appears as something traditionally and peculiarly Greek, by its association with the divine through myth (for example, *Epp.* 217, 221, 673, 757, 1417) and with artistic creativity through inspiration (*Ep.* 361, *Or.* 22.18), and mention of these connotations is reserved for his dealings with intimates of like culture and attainment such as Bacchius or Andronicus. At the more mundane level of social relationships, however, *charis* is also inescapable, since it was embedded in the language and inextricably woven into the exercise and institutions of patronage by which the world wagged. It was thus inevitable that a large proportion of Libanius' letters should deal with recommendations or intercessions, where he acts as friend and mouthpiece of others. As the institution of patronage had its own conventions, sometimes more honoured in the breach than in the observance, whereby *gratia* in the contemporary Code could become synonymous with graft, so its language had its own etiquette, by which such an imputation could be avoided. The basic appeal was to friendship; presentation of it was based on honour and justice (see, for example, *Epp.* 284, 1053.3); its appearance must be disinterested (*Epp.* 905, 907.2), and its notions adapted to the sensibilities of the recipient (*Epp.* 904–909 and note).

With the letter as an art form, *charis* was essential. Demetrius (§ 235) had reserved its role for diction only, but for the correspondents of a later day, trained as they were in declamatory techniques in their quest for persuasiveness, its presence had become all-pervasive. Libanius in his own day had become renowned as a purveyor of such charm (Eunap. *V.S.* 495–6), and he himself claims to have gained fame as ἐπίχαρις in the conduct of his social relationships in Antioch (*Or.* 2.18). In his letters he deploys his charms to the full (see Eunap. *V.S.* 496), and to each recipient according to his merits, with the devices of classical style and literary and philo-

24

sophical nuances tactfully directed to those who can appreciate them or who, like the egregious Alexander (*Ep.* 1385), merely aspire to do so. Thus Maximus the philosopher receives a letter full of hints of Plato (*Ep.* 694); similarly Themistius. Anatolius (*Ep.* 19), a prefect of literary bent, is treated to a robust lampoon upon his behaviour, with appropriate classical references. The receipt of a comedy on gout elicits a joke in kind from him, as one fellow-sufferer to another (*Ep.* 1301). However, it is with his ex-pupils that the charm of Libanius may be best observed, simply because of the pleasure given and received, as in his letters to Andronicus. In *Ep.* 1221, in particular, this exuberant pleasure elicits a fulsome reply acknowledging his gratification at Andronicus' friendship, his choice of messenger, his letter and the circumstances in which it was received, which combine to become a model of good feeling.

In 380/1, however, Libanius unexpectedly found himself criticized as tiresome and overbearing. His immediate reaction was to compose *Oration* 2, which in fact went some way towards justifying the criticisms, but the scar was slow to heal and any report of such comments thereafter was received with indignant protest (cf. *Ep.* 12). His sophistic status was already under attack and his professional competence impugned, a situation dealt with at length in *Oration* 62, which probably belongs to this same period. He became increasingly valetudinarian (see, for example, *Ep.* 12, *Or.* 1.202 ff and 243 ff) and subject to a growing persecution complex throughout the 380s (*Or.* 1.221 ff, *Or.* 3, *Or.* 36). Thus when he reinstituted his duplicate files in 388, the tone of his letters had changed dramatically. Style remained, but grace and graciousness had departed along with self-confidence. The epithet ἐπίχαρις which he had once enjoyed (*Or.* 2.18) now seems to be something of the past. Mention of the Graces, whether as divine or as inspirational, is absent from his letters, and instead recourse is had to the more sober, less joyous concept of the λόγιοι θεοί (*Epp.* 907.2, 1051.8, 1085.1, 1089.2) imported from his study of the works of another sophistic invalid, Aristeides. The lack of humour for which he was chided (*Or.* 2.19) is also apparent in these years. There are none of the literary jokes he used to share with his peers, for there were fewer to share them with. Any laughter has a wry tone of self-deprecation (for example in *Ep.* 1075) and his wit is bitter, in answer to affronts real or imagined (*Ep.* 1091).

The changed character of his correspondents also affects his approach in these latter years. Only a handful of the educated elite of an earlier day survive, such as Entrechius or Priscus. The minor sophists of the day, including ex-pupils like Firminus and Priscio, receive letters adorned with the customary graces of their profession, but his age and standing make this an unequal friendship, and his expressions appear more stilted in consequence. A rare letter from a visitor to Athens (*Ep.* 962, Sopolis) produces an enthusiastic reply filled with nostalgic religious and scholastic fervour, but his correspondents do not usually venture so far afield. They are more often courtiers, settled in Constantinople, a place he detested, and his distribution of the flowers of his style is tempered by their capacity to enjoy them no less then by his immediate motive in writing. Tatianus, a prefect of literary pretensions, is consistently rewarded with the appropriate classical allusion (for example in *Ep.* 990), as are also the highly educated senior official Eusebius xxvii and the elder statesman Aburgius, in due recognition of their cultivated tastes. The younger generation of officials, however, such as Proclus (*Ep.* 937) or Optatus (*Ep.* 923), receives such tribute only when Libanius has some special objective in mind, and in their particular case, considering the scurrilous account of them both given in *Oration* 42, any classical graces in the letter are utterly divorced from his real feelings, making a mockery of the customary appeal to friendship. His new-found military friends also get the occasional delicate compliment as testimonial to their aspirations to culture, though it may be suspected that this was to him little more than a device of habit and stylistic practice.

In general, the keynote of these last letters is that of a struggle against increasing odds, a far cry from the confident beginnings of *Ep.* 19. The opposition in Antioch is no longer confined to a single family as it had been in 355 (*Epp.* 529.3–4, 537.3, 550), but is now both public and militant. In such an atmosphere at home and in his disappointment in his friendships abroad, it became more and more incongruous for him to deploy his old airs and graces. Learning and culture were channelled into the invectives of his orations, and disillusion culminates in the grateful acknowledgement of any kind attention which inspires the grotesque flattery of his last letters (*Epp.* 1106, 1110–1), and in the classically derived curse called down on false friends with which the Autobiography ends.

Libanius and His Letters

The surviving correspondence of Libanius is for the most part concentrated into two widely separated periods of his life, the first, with some 1250 letters, covering the years 355 (spring) to 365 (summer), the second, with some 270, from summer 388 to summer 393, after which date no more appear. The rest of the collection, numbering no more than a score, are gleanings from the years 353–4 and 365–388. From information provided by Libanius himself (see Seeck, *BLZG* 21) it is clear that the letters surviving from the first period are not all those then written, while in the second there is a gap in the correspondence from winter 388/9 to summer 390. On a rough count the annual density of those of the first period is 120, in the second 70—an output which is in itself a notable achievement of composition and organization, the more remarkable considering the vast bulk of his other literary productions and the afflictions of body and spirit which he experienced in his later years.

The collection clearly owes its origin to the files of duplicates which Libanius kept for his correspondence and mentions quite regularly. Sometimes he uses them as evidence to clear himself from the charge of neglecting to write (*Epp.* 88.5, 1218.2, 1307.1–3); sometimes he even amends the address when there is a risk of offence to the recipient (*Epp.* 915, 933; cf. Seeck pp. 18 f, Foerster Vol. ix, p. 50). Seeck (p. 23) propounded the thesis that Libanius used these duplicate files himself to publish an edited collection of Letters 19–607 (the traditional Books i–vi of the manuscripts Va and Vo) covering the period 355 to spring 361. He justified this as a compliment to Julian whose career had progressed from nomination as Caesar to proclamation as Augustus precisely in that period. This theory, however, was disproved first by Silomon in his examination of the chronology of these so-called six books, and then by Foerster in a convincing summary (Vol. ix, pp. 49–52), that shortly after Libanius' death an edition of his collected letters was published from various sources by some enthusiastic but unknown admirer acting as his literary executor.

29

Even so, questions remain. If, in 364, Libanius refused the request of Aristophanes for copies of the full correspondence that had passed between Julian and himself, thus implying that there had been no publication up to that time (*Ep.* 1264), how could he in July 362 (*Or.* 13.52) publicly assert the affinity between Julian's epistolary style and his own to be a well-known fact? Even taking into account any self-interested exaggeration by the orator, for such a claim to be credible before an audience schooled in the niceties of current literary criticism, the implication is that there must have been at this time some more general acquaintance with the letters of both. Similarly, when Entrechius in 362 is said to be eager for Libanius' letters since "in them he will get everlasting fame" (*Ep.* 773.5), Libanius' renown as an epistolographer obviously is already widely established; yet there is no evidence for any formal publication up to that time. Here the conclusions of Petit with regard to the oral dissemination and the formal publication of the orations of Libanius (*Historia* 5 (1956), 484 ff) offer a pertinent analogy. Private letters between friends and peers get their primary publication individually upon receipt. Throughout his correspondence without exception Libanius summoned gatherings of his friends immediately he received any letter from the great and the good, to read it aloud to them and then to subject it to group discussion and critical appreciation. This was standard practice; his own correspondents did the same with his letters, as he well knew, for reports would come back to him from third parties, sometimes to his acute embarrassment (*Epp.* 476–7). In such closely knit literary circles where memorization was the norm, letters, as pieces of stylistic composition, obtained detailed examination and wide local publicity immediately, to be treasured in family archives thereafter. It was the individual addressee who initially gained the kudos of receiving any missive from a master of the genre. The enhancement of the writer's prestige was secondary, following upon the group analyses and discussions inspired by these initial readings, but cumulative, upon their spread and frequency. Granted this convention, it may be doubted whether in such a social milieu a collection of these miscellaneous letters could have been published by a writer in the lifetime of the recipients. The sole purpose of such an edition would have been the enhancement of the writer's own prestige in a manner that was socially unacceptable, and in addition the basic principle, to which Libanius tenaciously adhered, of the letter passing as a gift between individuals would have been vitiated.

A further point of debate concerns files from the missing years 365–388. There is no doubt that they were missing when the collection was originally established, but clearly Libanius did not take a vow of silence. Correspondence was maintained at some unknown level, for a scatter of letters or fragments survives among the gleanings of *Epp.* 1–17. Significantly enough, this period begins with the revolt of Procopius and ends with that of Maximus, both of whom Libanius was either suspected or accused of supporting. In the meantime, under the reign of terror conducted by Valens in Antioch, Libanius (*Or.* 1.175, 177 ff) relates two occasions when his letters were nearly the death of him. Each time, however, it was the archives of his correspondent that were under investigation. Mere prudence dictated extreme care in writing and retaining letters in times such as these, when communication with anyone suspect or under a cloud was dangerous (see *Epp.* 840, 957.3 ff). The inference must be that the absence of his duplicate files in these years was due to deliberate suppression on his own part. His personal and professional survival depended upon nothing less, for he knew that he was unpopular with Valens.

Hence, it is a matter of conjecture as to why they should begin only in spring 355, a full year after his final removal to Antioch. Some letters from a preceding time survive among the gleanings (for example, *Epp.* 15–16), but these antedate the removal itself. If he had had duplicates of letters written from Constantinople, they must have been lost in this move, but that in itself would indicate that he did not attach particular importance to them, and it leaves this lapse of a year unexplained. Had he so wished, he could have instituted the system at any time between. As it is, when he does resume correspondence with his intimates, he makes up for lost time with an unusually large budget of news, as in *Ep*. 405. The narrative of the Autobiography (*Or*. 1.86 ff) provides the clue. It was the taunts of his rivals in Constantinople, that he would not have the same success in Antioch as he had enjoyed elsewhere, that sets the scene for his final return home early in 354. Once there, his position remained precarious; his removal had been effected by deceit and he lacked official permission for permanent absence. He had no *locus standi* in Antioch and he remained in the unsatisfactory position of private nonestablished teacher for almost a full year. Only when he gained the coveted appointment as sophist of the city after Zenobius' death in early 355 did he have the face to resume formal correspondence with his literary friends and acquaintances, and to confirm it with the institution of these duplicates which are to mark this turning point of his career and the vindication of his Fortune. Hence the part they obviously play in his Autobiography of 374. Items from the earliest duplicates appear there with remarkably little alteration to the information they present (for example, *Epp*. 391, 405) other than the inevitable tailoring to the shape of a rhetorical declamation. Indeed, the whole thrust of the first year's correspondence is towards the academic, to the rallying of friends, the promotion of his new venture, to his literary activities and the recruitment of students. Even opposition, which naturally appears as minimal, is presented in a purely professional context, Eubulus remaining a shadowy figure in the background (see *Epp.* 529, 550).

The confidence and energy displayed in the earliest letters stand in stark contrast to the frustration and disillusion of those of his final years. Those weaknesses which are finally to prove his undoing, vanity and valetudinarianism, are present from the beginning, but are as yet under control. The resilience which enabled him ultimately to resume his career after the deaths of Phasganius and Julian is missing after that of his son, but by then age, infirmity, and disappointment had taken their toll. Sparks of the old fire remain: he obstinately continues with his teaching, even from his bed (*Or.* 1.280, *Ep.* 1075.1); he requests a text that interests him (*Ep.* 1078); he delivers a magisterial reproof to a parent (*Ep.* 1093), and *ex cathedra* demands the reconciliation of two old pupils publicly at odds with each other. Now, however, the practical conduct of his school is increasingly entrusted to subordinates like Calliopius and Thalassius, and his public appearances as sophist are rarer and ill-supported (*Ep.* 1075). He certainly lacked the stimulus of professional peers, and the proportion of literati in the correspondence of these final years slumps noticeably. Instead, his letters are directed increasingly towards courtiers and officials, the more distanced from him as Antioch had come to lose ground to the capital. He had become resentfully aware that he was an odd man out, and his reactions, whether positive, as in his letter to Rufinus, or negative, as in his invective against a governor like Eustathius (*Or.* 54), had become more extreme, with a heightened note of hysteria to be detected in his expressions. The self-confidence that had given life and variety to his earlier letters had gone, and in its place—whether in letters of congratulation, as to Ammianus, of acknowledgement, as to Postumianus, or even of reproof, as to Uranianus—there is a querulous self-pity.

Manuscript Tradition of the Letters

The detailed analyses of the individual manuscripts in Foerster's *Prolegomena* (Vol. ix) are, and will remain, basic for any appreciation of the manuscript tradition of the Letters.

The genuine letters of Libanius number 1544, all of which except three (*Epp.* 18, 1543–4, found in Baroccianus gr. 50, f. 369 and Laurentianus IV.14 respectively; cf. Foerster Vol. ix, pp. 163, 189) are contained in three major codices: Vaticanus gr. 83 (V), Vaticanus gr. 85 (Va), and Vossianus Leidensis gr. 77 (Vo). Other manuscripts, numbering over 250 (*ibid.,* pp. 183, 188–191), contain genuine letters as selections varying in density and textual authority. Of these Berolinensis gr. qu. 3 (Be; *ibid.,* pp. 169 f) is perhaps the most worthy of note because of the scholia it contains. None of the three great collections antedates the eleventh century.

V, placed at two removes from the archetype, contains 1566 letters in all, a total reduced by duplications and false attributions to 1528 genuine compositions. It thus remains the greatest single collection of the letters, but it is not without its problems. Compiled in the eleventh century, it soon sustained severe damage of some kind and its contents were reduced to no more than half the original (V_1). The missing half was replaced within the next century by a copy from a closely related manuscript, and a consistent effort was made to match the two sections together (V_{11}). This desire for tidiness also produced an arbitrary division into five books of 300 letters each, with a sixth book containing the remainder. A table of contents was also appended (Foerster Vol. ix, pp. 52 ff). A final attempt to remedy any remaining faults and deficiencies was made by yet further insertions and recopyings (V_{111}), so that the whole codex now appears as a compilation of various hands and dates, with some complication and inconsistencies of detail in consequence.

Va and Vo together form a related tradition, containing between them almost 450 letters less than V. Even so, neither is preserved in its entirety. Va lacks pages both at the beginning and the end, so that it now begins in the middle of *Ep.* 95 and finishes with *Ep.* 1005, having lost *Epp.* 1006–1112, while Vo has lost *Epp.* 411–498. They are both derived from the archetype more indirectly than V, by four or more removes (Foerster Vol. ix, pp. 70 ff; cf. p. 184 for stemma), in such a manner that any deficiencies in the one may be supplemented from the other. The common derivation of all three manuscripts is indicated by the fact that they all show virtually the same progression of letters. In particular, the immediate transition from *Ep.* 839 (of 363) to *Ep.* 840 (of 388) and that from *Ep.* 914 (of 388/9) to *Ep.* 915 (of 390) are worthy of note.

In both Va and Vo three distinct sections, which in V had been more disguised by loss and replacement, are to be observed: (a) *Epp.* 1–17, gleanings from the years 353–354 and 365–388; (b) *Epp.* 19–607, covering the period 356–361, and in these manuscripts divided into six clearly defined portions formally marked by later Byzantines as books; (c) *Epp.* 615–1112, similarly marked as a new book, the intervening seven letters being no more than fragments here inserted for convenient disposal. The letters of this section cover two widely spread periods, *Epp.* 615–839 the years 361–363, *Epp.* 840–1112 the years 388–393, including the eighteen-month gap already mentioned. Both portions proceed in a recognizable chronological order.

The case is very different with the six books containing *Epp.* 19–607, the contents of which had already secured for Libanius his fame as an epistolographer by 362, and were to be the most heavily worked in antiquity. They form the core of the whole collection, yet the books themselves appear in no readily explainable order, and their constituent letters have also been subject to obvious editorial rearrangement. In chronological order the books run:

Book 5 (*Epp.* 390–493), from spring 355 to spring 356;

Book 6 (*Epp.* 494–607), from summer 356 to summer 357;

Book 4 (*Epp.* 311–389), from summer 357 to winter 358/9;

Book 1 (*Epp.* 19–96), from summer 358 to winter 359/60;

Book 2 (*Epp.* 97–202), from winter 359/60 to spring 360;

Book 3 (*Epp.* 203–310), from spring 360 to spring 361.

These books, though adding nothing to the detail of the text as such, are significant for understanding how and why it was compiled as it has been. If the collection had been presented in the normal chronological order, it would have had an obviously ill-starred beginning, the consolatory *Ep.* 390, and Libanius' insecurity would have been immediately clear to all. Considerations of both style and prestige therefore demanded a more felicitous opening by some more authoritative arrangement. This was to be found in the positioning of the present *Ep.* 19 recognizably out of chronological order as the letter to introduce the collection to a reader. As an example of the *parrhesia* which Libanius prized so much it was deliberately selected as the "keynote" composition, as was shown by Silomon (p. 29), and it was supported by letters which revealed him as the sophist now firmly established in his community.

The books themselves are most obviously explained as six separate batches of his duplicate files. Similar batches may be traced in the third section of Va and Vo, and, less certainly, in *Epp.* 1113–1542 which are preserved only in V. Thus *Epp.* 615–839 (of 361–363) may be interpreted as two more such batches, and *Epp.* 840–1112 (of 388–393) as yet another two. None of these has been subjected to any elaborate reworking before editing, and indeed the eighteen month gap between *Ep.* 914 and *Ep.* 915 may well mark a missing file accidentally lost in Libanius' last years or after his death. As for the letters preserved in V, more confusion exists. One batch of letters covering the year 363 (*Epp.* 1342–1461), probably representing one of his files, may be distinguished from another of the year 365 (*Epp.* 1462–1542). However *Epp.* 1113–1341, which cover the period 363–365, are in total disarray. The copy books upon which this whole section was based had evidently been sadly disturbed by the time they came to hand for editing.

Seeck's hypothesis (*BLZG* p. 18 ff) for the compilation of the text of Va and Vo has remained the chopping block upon which later scholars have shaped their studies. His view was that it was derived from three disparate sources, the first being the six books edited and published by Libanius himself in Julian's day; the second comprising all the remainder except for the gleanings of *Epp.* 1–17, derived from the duplicate files left by Libanius at his death; and the third, these gleanings themselves, externally obtained by his editor and literary executor after his death from the family archives of the individual recipients. Of these views the first was disproved first by Silomon and then by Foerster. No exception can be taken to the second which appears eminently sensible. However, Seeck's view of the provenance of *Epp.* 1–17, which is crucial to his hypothesis, seems highly improbable, for all that it has gained the approval of Foerster and later scholars. One can but wonder at the success of such an individual in opening up the archives of two praetorian prefects and one emperor some fifty years after the writing of some of the letters, and at the meagreness of the results from this literary coup. These letters, some of them little more than scraps, were of course written when Libanius' formally organized duplicate files had not yet been conceived of or else were held in limbo, and the material they contain seems for the most part uncontentious. The obvious conclusion is that these were stray copies retained at random by Libanius himself, in the same way as he retained *Epp.* 608–614 from the period 355–361. These last, scrappy though they might be, could be attached to existing files. The gleanings, however, were retained in his archives separately from the main body since no files for the period existed to which they could be attached.

The hand of Libanius himself may also be deduced from the form in which the rest of the letters survive. Seeck may have gone too far in persuading himself that Libanius formally published an edition of *Epp.* 19–607 in honour of Julian, but it has yet to be proved that he could not and would not have reworked them into their present form. The probability is that he actually did so. The selection and rearrangements point to one intimately acquainted with the contents and circumstances of the letters and whose prime motivation was literary and aesthetic, and Libanius is the obvious candidate. He certainly had them at hand for the composition of the original Autobiography in 374: a comparison of *Epp.* 391 and 405 with *Or.* 1.90 ff indicates that. This composition, it may be suggested, was the occasion when Libanius remodelled this section. He left it as the definitive form for when the time came for publication, and so it remained as the basis of the present text. Publication at the time was of course out of the question. It ran counter to convention and to his own reluctance to produce any edited version at all; and, above all, it was not safe. Prudence dictated that it should remain a private labour of love.

Prudence also dictated the interruption in the formal organization of his duplicates from 365 to 388, but it may equally be the explanation of the confusion of order and the manner of survival of those covering the years 363–365, which are preserved in V. Valens' reign of terror was notorious, and it is not inconceivable that the disorder of these files is due to Libanius' own hurried precautions in scrutinizing and withdrawing any possibly incriminating documents immediately, and then, when times became even more critical, in removing from his archives all correspondence written after the death of Julian. These would be deposited in some place of safety well away from prying official eyes, and there they stayed. This was an act of self-censorship, the prelude to the long period of almost total silence when the files were discontinued. For twenty-five years self-preservation took precedence over all else in the handling of his correspondence, and only when it was safe to do so were the duplicate files reinstituted in 388.

The reactions of Libanius to his immediate circumstances at different stages of his career may thus be interpreted as the determining factor for the survival of his letters in their present format. The archetype was compiled after Libanius' death by his editor, but he went about his task in a very mechanical way. He had easy access to the whole corpus which survives in Va and Vo, since that was to be found at hand in the archives, but by beginning the edition with the random gleanings of *Epp.* 1–17, he ruined the grand opening planned for *Ep.* 19 and Book 1. It was presumably he who unearthed the remaining letters from their hiding place, and dealt with them in the easiest and most obvious way by simply appending them to the already existing corpus. Piety may well have prompted him to reproduce the letters as he found them; any literary presentation had already been effected by the author himself where it was possible and safe to do so.

ABBREVIATIONS AND BIBLIOGRAPHY

Abbreviations

For abbreviations of manuscripts, see Introduction. Designation of persons by roman numerals in the form "Thalassius (i)" refers to the listings in *BLZG*; that by arabic numerals—for example "Cynegius (3)"—to those in *PLRE*.

BLZG	O. Seeck, *Die Briefe des Libanius zeitlich geordnet*, Leipzig 1906, repr. Hildesheim 1967.
Bouchery	*Themistius in Libanius Brieven* (listed under Editions below).
C. Th.	*Codex Theodosianus*, ed. T. Mommsen, 3 vols., Berlin 1905, repr. 1954.
Dig.	*Digesta Iustiniani*, ed. A. Watson, Philadelphia 1985.
ELF	Julian, *Epistulae, leges, fragmenta* (under Historical Sources below).
Ep.	Precedes the number of a letter of Libanius in the edition of R. Foerster, *Epistulae* (under Editions below).
F	R. Foerster 1903–1927 (under Editions below).
F/Kr.	Fatouros and Krischer 1980 (under Editions below).

BIBLIOGRAPHY

Letter   precedes the number of a letter of Libanius
              in the present volume.
Or. 1   Libanius' *Autobiography* (*Oration* 1).
Paroem. Gr. *Corpus Paroemiographorum Graecorum*
              (under Historical Sources below).
PG   J. P. Migne, *Patrologiae cursus completus,
              series Graeca*, Paris 1857–1866.
PLRE   A. H. M. Jones, J. Martindale, and J. Morris,
              Prosopography of the Later Roman Empire,
              vols. 1–2, Cambridge 1971–.
PW   Pauly-Wissowa, *Real-Encyclopädie der
              classischen Altertumswissenschaft*,
              Stuttgart 1894–1979.
Re.   J. J. Reiske 1791 (under Editions below).
Zenob.   W. Bühler, *Zenobii Athoi Proverbia*,
              Göttingen 1978–.

Editions, Translations, Concordance

Libanius, *Epistulae, ed. J. C. Wolf, Amsterdam 1738.*
Libanii Sophistae Orationes et Declamationes, ed. J. J.
    Reiske, 4 vols., Altenburg, 1791 (= Re.).
L. Petit, *Essai sur la vie et la correspondance du sophiste
    Libanius*, Paris, 1866. Includes translation of *Oration* 1.
Demetrius et Libanius, ed. V. Weichert, Leipzig 1910.
Themistius in Libanius Brieven, ed. H. F. Bouchery,
    Antwerp 1936.
Libanius, *Opera*, ed. R. Foerster, 12 vols., Leipzig
    1903–1927; repr. Hildesheim 1963 (= F). Vol. I,
    pp. 10–206: *Oration* 1. Vol. IX: *Characteres epistolici et
    prolegomena ad Libanii epistulas.* Vols. X–XI: *Epistulae.*

BIBLIOGRAPHY

Libanius' *Autobiography (Oration* 1), ed. A. F. Norman, Oxford 1965.

Libanios, *Autobiographische Schriften*, trans. P. Wolf, Zurich/Stuttgart 1967.

Libanius, *Selected Orations*, ed. A. F. Norman, Loeb Classical Library 451 (1969), 452 (1971).

Libanios, *Discours Moraux (Or.* 6, 7, 8, 25), ed. B. Schouler, Paris 1973.

Libanios, *Autobiographie (Discours* 1), ed. J. Martin and P. Petit, Paris 1979.

Greek and Roman Authors on Jews and Judaism, 2: 580–599, ed. M. Stern, Jerusalem 1980.

Libanios, *Briefe*, ed. G. Fatouros and T. Krischer, Munich 1980 (= F/Kr.).

G. Fatouros, T. Krischer, D. Najock, *Concordantiae in Libanium. Pars Prima, Epistulae*, 2 vols., Hildesheim, Zurich, New York 1987.

Libanios, *Discours* 2–10, ed. J. Martin, Paris 1988.

Historical Sources

Ammianus Marcellinus, *Histories*, ed. J. C. Rolfe, 3 vols., Loeb Classical Library, 1935–1939.

St. Basile, *Lettres*, ed. Y. Courtonne, 3 vols., Paris 1957–1966.

Codex Theodosianus, ed. T. Mommsen, 3 vols., Berlin 1905, repr. 1954.

Codex Theodosianus, translated by C. Pharr, Princeton 1952.

Corpus Paroemiographorum Graecorum, ed. E. L. von Leutsch and F. G. Schneidewin, Göttingen 1818–1839, repr. Amsterdam 1965. A new and improved edition by

BIBLIOGRAPHY

W. Bühler (*Zenobii Athoi Proverbia*, Göttingen 1978–) is in progress.

Digesta Iustiniani, ed. A. Watson, Philadelphia 1985 (*Corpus iuris civilis* vol. 1 pt. 2).

Epistolographi Graeci, ed. R. Hercher, Paris 1873, repr. Amsterdam 1965, pp. 1–16.

Eunapius, *Lives of the Philosophers and Sophists*, ed. W. C. Wright, Loeb Classical Library 1922.

Eunapius, *Vitae sophistarum*, ed. J. G. Giangrande, Rome 1956.

John Chrysostom, *Opera*, Migne, *PG* vols. xlvii–lxiv.

Johannes Lydus, *De magistratibus*, ed. R. Wünsch, Leipzig 1903.

Julian, *Works*, ed. W. C. Wright, 3 vols., Loeb Classical Library 1913–1923.

Julian, *Oeuvres Complètes*, ed. J. Bidez, G. Rochefort, and C. Lacombrade, 2 vols. in 4, Paris 1932–1964.

Julian, *Epistulae, leges, fragmenta*, ed. J. Bidez and F. Cumont, Paris/London 1922. (=*ELF*)

Himerius, *Declamationes et Orationes*, ed. A. Colonna, Rome 1951.

Malalas, *Die römische Kaisergeschichte bei Malalas*, ed. A. Schenk von Stauffenberg, Stuttgart 1931.

Socrates, *Historia Ecclesiastica*, Migne, *PG* vol. lxvii.

Sozomen, *Historia Ecclesiastica*, Migne, *PG* vol. lxvii.

Themistius, *Orationes*, ed. H. Schenkl, G. Downey, A. F. Norman, 3 vols., Leipzig 1965–1974.

Zosimus, *Historiae*, ed. L. Mendelssohn, Leipzig 1887, repr. Hildesheim 1963.

Zosimus, *Historiae*, ed. F. Paschoud, 3 vols., Paris 1970–1989.

BIBLIOGRAPHY

Selected Modern Literature

J. Bidez, *La vie de l'empereur Julien,* Paris 1931, repr. 1965.

G. W. Bowersock, *Julian the Apostate*, London and Cambridge, Mass. 1978.

R. Browning, *The Emperor Julian*, London 1975.

G. Dagron, *L'empire romain d'orient au ive siècle et les traditions politiques de l'Hellenisme: le témoignage de Themistios*, Travaux et mémoires 3, 1–242, Paris 1968.

G. Downey, *A Study of the Comites Orientis and the Consulares Syriae*, Princeton 1939.

G. Downey, *A History of Antioch in Syria*, Princeton 1961.

G. Fatouros and T. Krischer, *Libanios, Wege der Forschung* vol. 621, Darmstadt 1983.

A. J. Festugière, *Antioche païenne et chrétienne*, Paris 1959.

A. H. M. Jones, *The Later Roman Empire*, 3 vols., Oxford 1964.

A. H. M. Jones, *Cities of the Eastern Roman Empire*, 2nd ed. Oxford 1971.

A. H. M. Jones, J. Martindale, and J. Morris, see *PLRE* under Abbreviations above.

A. Koskenniemi, *Studien zur Idee und Phräseologie des griechischen Briefes bis 400 n. Chr.*, Helsinki 1956.

J. W. H. G. Liebeschuetz, *Antioch*, Oxford 1972.

J. W. H. G. Liebeschuetz, "The Syriarch in the 4th century A.D.," *Historia* 8 (1959): 113–126 (repr. in Fatouros and Krischer).

K. Malzacher, *Die Tyche bei Libanios*, diss. Strasburg 1918.

H. I. Marrou, *A History of Education in Antiquity* (tr. G. Lamb), London 1956.

BIBLIOGRAPHY

J. Matthews, *The Roman Empire of Ammianus*, London 1989.

J. Misson, *Recherches sur le paganisme de Libanios*, Louvain 1914.

A. F. Norman, "The Book Trade in Antioch," *Journal of Hellenic Studies* 80 (1960): 122–126 (repr. in Fatouros and Krischer).

A. F. Norman, "The Library of Libanius," *Rheinisches Museum für Philologie* 107 (1964): 158–175.

R. A. Pack, *Studies in Libanius and Antiochene Society under Theodosius*, diss. Michigan 1935.

R. A. Pack, "*Curiales* in the Correspondence of Libanius," *Transactions of the American Philological Association* 82 (1951): 176–192 (repr. in Fatouros and Krischer).

P. Petit, *Libanius et la vie municipale à Antioche au ive siècle après J.C.*, Paris 1956.

P. Petit, *Les étudiants de Libanius*, Paris 1957.

P. Petit, "Recherches sur la publication et la diffusion des discours de Libanius," *Historia* 5 (1956): 476–509 (repr. in German in Fatouros and Krischer).

P. Petit, "Les senateurs de Constantinople dans l'oeuvre de Libanius," *L'Antiquité classique* 26 (1957): 347–383 (repr. in German in Fatouros and Krischer).

P. Petit, "Sur la date du *pro templis* de Libanius," *Byzantion* 21 (1951): 285–310 (repr. in German in Fatouros and Krischer).

E. Richtsteig, *Libanius qua ratione Platonis operibus usus sit*, diss. Breslau 1918.

E. Salzmann, *Sprichwörter und sprichwörtliche Redensarten bei Libanios*, diss. Tübingen 1910.

F. Schemmel, "Der Sophist Libanios als Schüler und Lehrer," *Neue Jahrbücher für das klassische Altertum* 20 (1907): 52–69 (repr. in Fatouros and Krischer).

BIBLIOGRAPHY

B. Schouler, *La tradition hellenique chez Libanios*, 2 vols., Lille 1983.

O. Seeck, *Geschichte des Untergangs der antiken Welt*, Berlin 1897–1921, repr. Darmstadt 1967.

O. Seeck, "Libanius gegen Lucianus," *Rheinisches Museum für Philologie* 73 (1920): 84–101 (repr. in Fatouros and Krischer).

O. Seeck, see *BLZG* under Abbreviations above.

G. R. Sievers, *Das Leben des Libanius*, Berlin 1868, repr. Amsterdam 1969.

H. Silomon, *De Libanii epistularum libris i–vi*, diss. Gottingen 1909.

E. A. Thompson, *The Historical Work of Ammianus Marcellinus*, Cambridge 1947, repr. 1969.

J. H. W. Walden, *The Universities of Ancient Greece*, New York 1912, repr. 1970.

P. Wolf, *Vom Schulwesen der Spätantike: Studien zu Libanius*, Baden-Baden 1950.

THE AUTOBIOGRAPHY

(Oration 1)

ΒΙΟΣ Η ΠΕΡΙ ΤΗΣ ΕΑΥΤΟΥ ΤΥΧΗΣ[1]

1. Τοὺς δὲ περὶ τῆς ἐμῆς τύχης οὐ τὰ εἰκότα
δοξάσαντας, οὔθ᾽ ὅσοι με ἀνθρώπων εὐδαιμονέ-
R 2   στατον εἶναί φασιν ἀπὸ τούτων δὴ τῶν ἐπὶ τοῖς
λόγοις θορύβων οὔθ᾽ ὅσοι τῶν ὄντων ἀθλιώτατον
ἀπὸ τῶν συνεχῶν δὴ κινδύνων[2] καὶ πόνων, τού-
τοιν τοίνυν ἑκατέραν ταῖν ψήφοιν τῆς ἀληθείας
ἀπενηνεγμένην ἐπανορθῶσαι πειρατέον διηγήσει
τῶν τε ὑπαρξάντων ἐμοὶ τῶν τε ἔτι νῦν ὄντων,
ὡς εἰδεῖεν ἅπαντες, ὅτι μοι τὰ τῆς τύχης ἐκέρα-
F 80   σαν οἱ θεοὶ καὶ οὔτε εὐδαιμονέστατος οὔτε ἀθλιώ-
τατος ἐγώ, Νεμέσεως δὲ ἡμᾶς μὴ βάλοι βέλος.

2. Πρῶτον τοίνυν, εἰ καὶ τόδε εἰς εὐτυχίαν
φέρει, πόλεως πολίτην εἶναι μεγάλης τε καὶ
ὀνομαστῆς, ἀθρείτω μέν τις τῆς Ἀντιόχου τὸ
μέγεθος καὶ οἷα τις αὐτὴ καὶ πόσην νέμεται γῆν

---

[1] Tit. deest A: Λιβανίου σοφιστοῦ τὰ καθ᾽ ἑαυτὸν λόγος πρῶτος V.

[2] κινδύνων Mss. exc. Vat. 939, Martin: ὀδυνῶν Vat 939,
edd.

THE AUTOBIOGRAPHY

1. Some people labour under a misapprehension in the opinions they entertain about my career. There are some who, as a result of this applause which greets my oratory, assert that I am the happiest of men: there are, on the other hand, those who, considering my incessant perils and pains, would have it that I am the wretchedest man alive. Now each of these verdicts is far removed from the truth, and I must endeavour to correct them by a narration of my past and present circumstances, so that all may know that heaven has granted me a mixture of fortune, and that I am neither the happiest nor the unhappiest of men. And I pray that the bolt of Nemesis may not light upon me.

2. First then, if it is conducive to good fortune to be a citizen[a] of a great and famous city, let us consider the size and character of the city of Antioch, the extent of its territory, the streams which water

[a] Commonplace, from either Simonides (so Amm. Marc. 14.6.7) or Euripides (so Plut. *Dem.* 1). The latter is the more likely here. "Antioch the Great" had now become a stock term (e.g. *Or.* 21.7, *Letter* 101; Amm. Marc. 22.9.14, Auson. *Ord. Urb. Nob.* 4–5).

R 3 καὶ οἴων μὲν πίνει πηγῶν, οἷοις δὲ ζεφύροις
τρυφᾷ, ἔστι δὲ καὶ οὐκ ἰδόντι τὴν πόλιν ἀκοῇ
πάντα ἐπίστασθαι. ποῖος γὰρ ἠπείρων ἢ ποῖος
θαλάττης μυχός, οἳ τὸ κλέος οὐ πεπόρευται τοῦ
ἄστεος; ἐν δὴ μεγίστῃ μεγίστους εἶναι συνέβη
γένος τοὐμὸν παιδείᾳ τε καὶ πλούτῳ καὶ χορη-
γίαις καὶ ἀγῶσι καὶ λόγοις, ὅσοι φοραῖς ἀρχόν-

F 81 των ἀπαντῶσιν.   3. οἴονται δέ τινες τὸν ἐμὸν

R 4 ἐπίπαππον ἐξ Ἰταλίας ἥκειν ὑπὸ λόγου τινὸς τῇ
ἐκείνων γλώττῃ ποιηθέντος ἠπατημένοι. ὁ δὲ
ἄρα τὸ μὲν εἶχε ποιεῖν, ἦν δὲ οὐκ ἄλλοθεν.
ἐκοσμεῖτο δὲ οὐ μᾶλλον φωνῇ τῇ 'κείνων ἢ μαντικῇ, ᾗ δὴ καὶ ἀπολουμένους προῄδει τοὺς υἱεῖς
τοὺς ἑαυτοῦ σιδήρῳ καλούς τε ὄντας καὶ μεγάλους καὶ εἰπεῖν ἱκανούς. τοῦτο ἡμῖν χρημάτων
μεγάλων ἐκένωσε τὸν οἶκον, ὥστε ὁ πατὴρ οὑμὸς
ἀδελφὰς ἐπιγάμους ἐλεούμενος ἔτρεφε. τῷ δ' αὖ
πρὸς μητρὸς πάππῳ τἆλλα τε ὄντι λαμπρῷ καὶ
ῥητορικῷ μόλις διαφυγόντι τὸν ὅμοιον θάνατον ἡ
τελευτὴ συνέβη νόσῳ δύο προμάχοις τὴν βουλὴν
παραδόντι, οἷν ὁ μὲν ἐπ' ἀρχῇ κατέλυσε τὸν
βίον, ὁ δὲ ἀρχὴν ἀπωσάμενος. οὐκοῦν ἐν τούτοις

R 5 τὰ μὲν ἡμέρου, τὰ δὲ οὐ τοιαύτης τύχης.

54

it, and the breezes in which it basks. Even without seeing it, one can have full knowledge of it from hearsay, for there is no corner of land or sea to which the fame of the city has not spread. My family was one of the greatest in a great city—in education, wealth, the provision of shows and games, and in the oratory which opposes itself to the excesses of governors. 3. There is a notion current that my great-grandfather came from Italy—a mistaken idea arising from a speech which he composed in Latin. The fact is that, although he was versed in Latin, he originated from nowhere else but here.[a] Acquaintance with Latin was not his only endowment: he had the power of divination, and it was through this that he foresaw that his own sons would perish by the sword, noble, great, and eloquent though they were.[b] Their execution drained our household of great wealth, so that my father in his compassion maintained his sisters after they had reached an age for marriage. Moreover my maternal grandfather, who was especially preeminent as a speaker, barely escaped a like fate. He died of an illness and left the leadership of the city council to his two sons, of whom one died after holding a governmental office, the other after declining it. So in this, part of my fortune was good, part bad.

[a] The family was of the class of *principales*.

[b] After the revolt of Eugenius in Seleuceia in 303; cf. *Or.* 19.45–46, 20.18–20, 11.158–162. See also §125 below, *Letter* 124.

4. Γήμας δὲ τὴν ἐκ τοιούτων οὑμὸς πατὴρ
τρεῖς παῖδας ποιησάμενος, ὧν ἐγὼ μέσος, ᾤχετο
πρὸ ἀκμῆς μικρὰ ἐκ πολλῶν κεκομισμένος, καὶ
εὐθὺς τῆς μητρὸς ἐπ᾽ ἐκείνῳ ὁ πατήρ. δείσασα
δὲ ἡ μήτηρ ἐπιτρόπων κακίαν καὶ ὑπὸ σωφροσύνης τὰς τοῦ δεῖν εἰς λόγους ἰέναι σφίσιν
F 82 ἀνάγκας αὐτὴ πάντα ἡμῖν ἀξιοῦσα εἶναι τῶν μὲν
ἄλλων εὖ μάλα εἴχετο σὺν πόνῳ, τελοῦσα δὲ
ἀργύριον τοῖς ἐπὶ τοῦ παιδεύειν οὐκ ᾔδει χαλε-
R 6 πῆναι πρὸς καθεύδοντα παῖδα, φιλούσης εἶναι
νομίζουσα τὸ μηδαμῇ μηδαμῶς ἀνιᾶν τὸν ἑαυ-
τῆς, ὥστε τοῦ ἔτους τὸ πλέον εἰς ἀγροὺς ἡμῖν
μᾶλλον ἢ λόγους ἀναλοῦσθαι.   5. τεττάρων δή
μοι τουτονὶ διελθόντων τὸν τρόπον ἐνιαυτῶν
πέμπτου τε ἐπὶ τοῖς δέκα· ἡπτόμην καί με εἰσήρ-
χετο δριμύς τις ἔρως τῶν λόγων· ὥστε ἠμέλητο
μὲν αἱ τῶν ἀγρῶν χάριτες, ἐπέπραντο δὲ περι-
στεραί, δεινὸν θρέμμα καταδουλώσασθαι νέον,
ἅμιλλαι δὲ ἵππων καὶ τὰ τῆς σκηνῆς πάντα
ἀπέρριπτο, καὶ ᾧ δὴ διαφερόντως ἐξέπληξα καὶ
νεότητα καὶ γῆρας, ἀθέατος ἔμεινα μονομαχιῶν
ἐκείνων, ἐν αἷς ἔπιπτόν τε καὶ ἐνίκων ἄνδρες,
οὓς ἔφησθα ἂν μαθητὰς εἶναι τῶν ἐν Πύλαις

4. My father took his bride from such a family and had three sons, of whom I am the middle one.[a] He died before his prime when he had recovered a little of these great losses, and he was followed almost immediately by my maternal grandfather. My mother was a prudent woman and feared the dishonesty of guardians and the litigation which would inevitably arise with them, and so she herself set out to be all in all to us. In general, she succeeded very well by dint of her exertions, but though she paid out fees to schoolmasters for us, she did not have the heart to get annoyed with her sleepyhead of a son, for she thought it was a loving mother's part never never to upset her child. Thus it came about that we spent the greater part of the year in the countryside rather than in the study. 5. Four years passed by in this way, but when I was nearly fifteen my interest was kindled and an earnest love of study began to possess me.[b] Hence the charms of the countryside were put aside: I sold my pigeons, pets which are apt to get a strong hold on a boy; the chariot races and everything to do with the stage were discarded, and I remained aloof, far from the sight of those gladiatorial combats where men, whom you would swear to be the pupils of the three

[a] Libanius was born in 314 (cf. §§ 51, 139, 143 f, below; Sievers, 207 f). His father died in 325.

[b] This conversion occurred in 328, before the *Olympia* presented by his uncle Panolbius.

τριακοσίων. ὁ μὲν δὴ ταῦτα λειτουργῶν ἦν θεῖος
ἐμὸς πρὸς μητρὸς ἐκάλει τέ με ὀψόμενον, ἐγὼ δὲ
ἄρα ὑπὸ τῶν βιβλίων εἰχόμην. λόγος γε τὸν
F 83 σοφιστὴν ἐκεῖνον μαντεύσασθαι περὶ ἐμοῦ πόρρω-
R 7 θεν, ἃ δὴ καὶ τετέλεσται. 6. ποῦ δὴ τὴν ὀρ-
φανίαν θήσομεν; καὶ ἥδιστα μὲν ἂν ἐπεῖδον τὸν
πατέρα ἐν γήρᾳ, εὖ μέντοι τοῦτό γε οἶδα, ὡς νῦν
ἂν ἦν ἐν ἑτέρᾳ ἀτραπῷ βίου τοῦ πατρός μοι προ-
βάντος εἰς πολιάν. ἀντεξετάζων δή τις τὰ νῦν
[τὰ παρόντα] ἐκείνοις, βουλῆς λέγω φροντίσιν ἢ
δίκαις ἢ καὶ νὴ Δία γε θρόνοις ἀρχῶν, οὐ χαλεπῶς ἂν καὶ οὕτω γ' ἀνεύροι, ποτέρωσε τοῦτο
τιθεὶς ὀρθῶς ἂν εἴη τεθεικώς.   7. ἀλλὰ μὴν
τήν γε τῆς μητρὸς σωφροσύνην, ἣ μυρίους ἀπὸ
τῶν θυρῶν ἀπήλασεν, οὐδ' ἂν ὁ σφόδρα ἡδονῶν
R 8 ἥττων τολμῆσαί μοι δοκεῖ μὴ συγχωρῆσαι παίδων εἶναι εὐτυχῶν, εἰ δὴ καλὸν τὸ σὺν παρρησίᾳ
ζῆν, ποιεῖ δὲ ταύτην οὐ τὰ αὐτῷ τινι βεβιωμένα
μόνον, ἀλλὰ καὶ τὰ 'κείνοις ἐξ ὧν ἔφυ, ὡς πολ-
λοί γε ἀμέμπτους σφᾶς αὐτοὺς παρασχόμενοι
γονέων ἐπεστομίσθησαν ὀνείδεσι.

ᵃ Gladiators, only here mentioned in Libanius, were
banned in 325 by Constantine (*Codex Theodos.* 15.12.1),

hundred at Thermopylae, used to conquer or die.[a] My attitude in this caused the greatest amazement both to young and old. The person responsible for the presentation of these shows was my maternal uncle, and though he invited me to the spectacle, I still stayed wedded to my books. The story goes that he, all that time ago, foretold for me the position of sophist that has actually come to pass. 6. In which category, then, shall I put my orphan's state? Gladly would I have beheld my father in his old age, but of one thing I am certain—that if my father had come to a ripe old age, I would now be engaged upon a very different way of life. If you compare the present with the might-have-been—a career in local politics, for instance, or law, or even in the imperial administration—you would have no difficulty in discovering which would be the correct estimate of my fortune. 7. Moreover, not even the most self-indulgent of men would dare deny that we children were fortunate in our mother's goodness, which drove countless admirers from our doors—once it is granted that it is a fine thing to be able to express oneself naturally, and that this is ensured not only by one's own conduct in life but by that of one's parents too. Many people, in fact, who have shown themselves to be personally beyond reproach, have been reduced to silence by the ill-repute of their forebears.

but this was evidently not immediately effective in the provinces.

F 84   8. Πάλιν τοίνυν τὸ μὲν παρ' ἄνδρα πεφοιτη-
κέναι λόγων προχέοντα κάλλος εὐδαίμονος φοι-
τητοῦ, τὸ δὲ μὴ ὁπόσον ἄξιον, ἀλλ' ὁπότε μὲν
ἀφωσιούμην φοιτᾶν, κινοῦντος δὲ ἤδη πρὸς
μαθήσεις ἔρωτος οὐκ ἔχειν τὸν μεταδώσοντα
θανάτῳ σβεσθέντος τοῦ ῥεύματος, τουτὶ δὲ
ἀθλίου. ποθῶν μὲν τοίνυν τὸν οὐκέτ' ὄντα, χρώμενος δὲ τοῖς οὖσιν, εἰδώλοις γέ τισι σοφιστῶν,
ὥσπερ οἱ τοῖς ἐκ κριθῶν ἄρτοις ἀπορίᾳ γε τοῦ
βελτίονος, ἐπειδὴ ἤνυτον οὐδέν, ἀλλ' ἦν κίνδυνος
ἡγεμόσι τυφλοῖς ἑπόμενον εἰς βάραθρον ἀμαθίας
R 9   πεσεῖν, τοῖς μὲν χαίρειν εἶπον, παύσας δὲ τὴν
μὲν ψυχὴν τοῦ τίκτειν, τὴν δὲ γλῶτταν τοῦ
λέγειν, τὴν δὲ χεῖρα τοῦ γράφειν ἓν ἕδρων μόνον,
μνήμῃ τὰ τῶν παλαιῶν ἐκτώμην συνὼν ἀνδρὶ
μνημονικωτάτῳ τε καὶ οἵῳ τῶν παρ' ἐκείνοις
καλῶν ἐμπείρους ἀπεργάζεσθαι νέους. καὶ οὕτω
δή τι αὐτῷ προσεκείμην ἀκριβῶς, ὥστ' οὐδ'
ἀπαλλαττομένου τῶν νέων ἀπηλλαττόμην, ἀλλὰ
καὶ δι' ἀγορᾶς ἐν χεροῖν τε ἡ βίβλος, καὶ ἔδει τι
τὸν ἄνδρα καὶ πρὸς ἀνάγκην λέγειν, ἣν ἐν τῷ
παραχρῆμα μὲν δῆλος ἦν δυσχεραίνων, χρόνοις

─────────────────────────────

ᵃ Ulpianus; cf. Eunap. V.S. 487, PLRE 973. κάλλος cf.

8. Again, I was lucky as a pupil in that I attended the lectures of a teacher with a fine flow of oratory;[a] my bad luck was that my attendance was not as regular as it should have been but occurred only in a most perfunctory fashion, and then, when my desire did spur me on to study, I found none to instruct me, for death had stopped his flow. So, though I longed for my dead teacher, I began to frequent the living, mere shadows of teachers, as men eat loaves of barley bread for want of anything better. However, when I found that I was making no progress but was running the risk of falling into the bottomless pit of ignorance through following blind guides, I had done with them. I restrained my mind from composing, my tongue from speaking, and my hand from writing, and I concentrated upon one thing only—the memorization of the works of classical authors—and studied under a man of prodigious memory who was capable of instilling into his pupils an appreciation of the excellence of the classics.[b] I attached myself to him so wholeheartedly that I would not leave him even after class had been dismissed, but would trail after him, book in hand, even through the city square, and he had to give me some instruction, whether he liked it or not. At the time he was obviously annoyed at this impor-

[a] Hom. *Od.* 22.156.

[b] Unusually, he now gives up the advanced study of rhetoric to repeat the elementary course under the *grammatistes* (Didymus? so Petit).

δὲ ἐν ὑστέροις ἐπήνει.   9. πέντε ταῦτα ἔτη ἦν

F 85 ἀπάσης μοι τῆς ψυχῆς ἐκεῖσε τετραμμένης, καὶ
συνέπραττεν ὁ δαίμων οὐδενὶ νοσήματι τὸν δρόμον ὑποσκελίζων, ἐπεὶ καὶ ὃ προσέπεσε τῇ
κεφαλῇ—ἦν δὲ τοιόνδε· ἐν τοῖς Ἀχαρνεῦσι τοῖς
Ἀριστοφάνους ἦν καθημένῳ τῷ γραμματιστῇ
παρεστηκώς, ὁ δὲ ἥλιος οὕτω παχέσιν ἐκέκρυπτο
νέφεσιν, ὥστ᾽ ἤδη τινὰ νύκτα ἐκείνην τὴν ἡμέραν προσειπεῖν. μέγα δὲ κτυπήσαντος τοῦ Διὸς
καὶ ἅμα κεραυνὸν ἀφέντος ἐπέπληκτο μὲν τῷ
πυρὶ τὰ ὄμματα, ἐπέπληκτο δὲ ἡ κεφαλὴ τῇ
βροντῇ. καὶ ᾤμην μὲν οὐδὲν ἐνιδρῦσθαί μοι δεινόν, ἀλλ᾽ αὐτίκα λήξειν τὴν ταραχήν, ἀπελθὼν

R 10 δὲ οἴκαδε καὶ ἐπ᾽ ἀρίστῳ κατακλιθεὶς βροντῆς τε
ἐκείνης ἐδόκουν ἀκούειν κεραυνόν τε ἐκεῖνον τὴν
οἰκίαν παραθεῖν ἱδρῶτά τ᾽ ἐκίνει τὸ δέος καὶ
ἀναπηδήσας ἐκ τῶν σιτίων ἐπὶ τὴν κλίνην
καταφεύγω. σιγᾶν τε ᾤμην δεῖν τοῦτο καὶ
φυλάττειν ἄρρητον, ἀλλὰ μὴ κοινώσας ἰατροῖς
εἰς φάρμακά τε καὶ τὰ ἀπὸ τῆς τέχνης ἐκ τῶν
εἰωθότων ἑλκυσθεὶς ἀνιᾶσθαι.   10. τοῦτο καὶ
εἰς ῥίζας ἤγαγε τὴν συμφορὰν ἐκβληθεῖσαν ἄν,
ὥς φασιν, ἐν προοιμίοις οὐ σὺν πόνῳ. διὰ τοῦτο
καὶ συναπεδήμησέ μοι τὸ κακὸν αὐξόμενον τὴν

tunity, but in later days he was full of praise for it. 9. For these five years my life was entirely devoted to these pursuits, and heaven helped me by placing no hindrance of illness in my course, and then the incident of the thunderbolt occurred.[a] This was as follows: I was standing by my teacher's chair engrossed in the *Acharnians* of Aristophanes, when the sun was hidden by such a pall of cloud that you could hardly tell the difference then between day and night. The heavens resounded with a mighty crash and a thunderbolt hurtled down, blinding my eyes with its flash and stunning my head with its roar. My first thought was that I had suffered no permanent ill-effect and that the shock would soon settle. However, after I had reached home and was at the lunch table, I seemed again to sense that crash and the thunderbolt hurtling past the house. I broke out into a sweat of fear, and leapt up from the table to the refuge of my bed. I decided that I ought to say nothing of the matter and to keep it secret and not suffer the inconvenience of telling it to the doctors and being dragged from my usual routine to take medicine or undergo professional treatment. 10. This caused the malady which, as the saying goes, could have been removed with no trouble at all in its early stages, to take a deeper root. Hence my affliction was my constant companion

[a] Cf. *Ep.* 727; the accident occurred in 334 when he was twenty.

αὔξην τὴν ἑαυτοῦ δεῦρό τε ἀφίκται πάλιν τροπὰς
μέν τινας τρεπόμενον, οὐ μὴν τοῦ γε ἐλαύνειν
παυόμενον, ἐπεὶ καὶ ὁπότε δοκεῖ χαλᾶν, οὐ
F 86 παντάπασι λήγει—ἀλλ' ὅπερ ἔφην, πλὴν τοῦδε
τηνικαῦτα τἄλλα ἦν ἄνοσος, καὶ οὐδὲ τοῦτο εἶργε
μὴ ἀπολαύειν τῶν παιδικῶν.

11. Συνειλεγμένων τοίνυν εἰς τὴν ψυχὴν τῶν
ὑπὲρ τοὺς ἄλλους κατὰ λόγου δύναμιν θαυμα-
ζομένων ἀνδρῶν ὁρμῆς τέ με ἐπὶ τοῦτον εἰσ-
ελθούσης τὸν βίον—ἦν γάρ τις ἑταῖρος ἐμοὶ
Καππαδόκης, Ἰασίων ὄνομα αὐτῷ, βραδέως
R 11 μὲν ἥκων ἐπὶ λόγους, φιλοπονίᾳ δέ, εἴπερ τις
ἄλλος, ἡδόμενος—οὗτος ὁ Ἰασίων, ἃ παρ'
ἀνδρῶν πρεσβυτέρων Ἀθηνῶν τε πέρι καὶ τῶν
αὐτόθι δρωμένων ἐδέδεκτο, καθ' ἡμέραν ὡς
εἰπεῖν πρὸς ἐμὲ ἐμυθολόγει Καλλινίκους τέ τινας
καὶ Τληπολέμους ἑτέρων τε οὐκ ὀλίγων σοφιστῶν διηγούμενος σθένος λόγους τε οἷς ἀλλήλων ἐκράτησάν τε καὶ ἐκρατήθησαν, ὑφ' ὧν τις
ἐπιθυμία τοῦ χωρίου κατελάμβανέ μοι τὴν
ψυχήν.   12. τοῦτο μὲν δὴ ὕστερον ἔμελλον
ἐκλαλήσειν, ὡς εἴη μοι πλευστέον, τῆς φήμης δὲ
τῶν πόνων οὓς ἐπόνουν κατεχούσης τὴν πόλιν
καὶ τῆς γε ἐν ὥρᾳ σωφροσύνης—λέγω γὰρ

abroad, growing great with increase, and it has returned home with me. There have been some fluctuations, of course, but it never stops worrying me, for even when it seems to abate, it never ceases completely. However, as I have said, except for this, I was untroubled by illness all this time, and even this did not prevent me from enjoying my pleasures to the full.

11. Now when I had committed to memory the works of those who were most renowned for their stylistic abilities, the urge for this way of life came over me. I had as a fellow student a Cappadocian, Iasion by name, and he, though late come to learning, had an infinite capacity for taking pains. This Iasion, almost every day, would tell me the tales he had heard from his elders about Athens and the goings-on there. Names like Callinicus and Tlepolemus were always on his tongue,[a] and he would tell the tale of the rhetorical prowess of many another sophist too and of the orations by which they won or lost their disputations, and as a result of all this a longing for Athens began to possess my soul. 12. Later on I intended to let the news out that I had to go there; in the meantime there spread through the town the report of the labours upon which I was engaged and also of my youthful discretion. I make mention of this discretion with

[a] For Callinicus, *PLRE* 174 (2); Tlepolemus, *PLRE* 920.

οὖν σωφροσύνης πέρι θαρρούντως ζώντων ἔτι
μοι μαρτύρων, οἳ βουλομένων ὑμῶν ἀναστάντες
μαρτυρήσουσιν, ὁρῶ γὰρ αὐτῶν οὐκ ὀλίγους ἐνταυθοῖ καθημένους, ἣν δὲ ἀνάλωτος οὐ φρουρᾷ καὶ
φόβοις παιδαγωγῶν, οὓς ἀσθενεῖς πέφυκεν
F 87 ὀρφανία νέου ποιεῖν, ἀλλὰ προνοίᾳ Τύχης, δι'
ἣν αὐτός τε ἐμαυτοῦ φύλαξ ἦν ἄλλους τε ἐρρυό-
μην παιδιάς τε ἔπαυον ἐπιζημίους, ἐφ' ἃς τοὺς
λόγους ῥίψαντες οὐκ ὀλίγοι τῶν νέων ἐφέροντο—
γεμούσης δὴ τοῦ περὶ ἀμφοῖν τοῖν ἀγαθοῖν
λόγου τῆς πόλεως ἁπάσης οἱ παρθένους τρέφον-
τες πατέρες διὰ τοῖν θείοιν τοῖν ἐμοῖν ᾖεσαν ἐπ'
ἐμὲ πλήθει προικὸς ἕτερος ἕτερον παριόντες,

ἀλλ' ἐμὸν οὔποτε θυμὸν ἐνὶ στήθεσσιν ἔπειθον,

οἶμαι δὲ κατὰ τὸν Ὀδυσσέα καὶ θεῖον ὑπεριδεῖν
ἂν γάμον πρὸς τὸν Ἀθηνῶν καπνόν.   13. ἡ
R 12 μὲν οὖν μήτηρ ἐδάκρυεν οὐδὲ τὸν λόγον ἀνεχο-
μένη τοῦ ἔργου, τοῖν θείοιν δὲ ὁ πρεσβύτερος τῇ
μὲν ᾤετο βοηθεῖν δεῖν, ἐμὲ δὲ ἐκέλευεν ἀδυνάτων
ἀφεστάναι, μηδὲ γὰρ εἰ σφόδρα ἐρῴην, ἐπιτρέ-
F 88 ψειν αὐτόν. τὰ Ὀλύμπια δὲ τοῦ νεωτέρου ποιήσαντος τῷ Διὶ καὶ ἐμοῦ τῆς ἀνάγκης ἡττημένου

confidence, for I have witnesses still alive to rise and testify to it, should you so desire; many of them, indeed, I see seated here. I was incorruptible, not through the vigilance or the deterrents of any attendant,[a] for them the orphan state of their charges tends to make unreliable, but through the providence of Fortune whereby I acted as my own protector and as the rescuer of others besides, putting an end to the harmful pranks to which many youngsters who neglected their studies betook themselves. Well then, when the whole town buzzed with the account of both these virtues of mine, those fathers who had daughters on their hands approached me through my two uncles—one outbidding another in the size of the dowry he offered, 'but never for a moment did they win my heart.'[b] I think that I would have followed Odysseus' example and spurned even marriage with a goddess for a glimpse of the smoke of Athens.[c] 13. My mother was in tears and could not bear even the mention of the matter. Of my uncles, the elder thought that he should support her and he bade me give up this wild-goose chase, for, however much I hankered after it, he would not give his consent. However, after the younger of the two had presented the Olympic festival in honour of Zeus

[a] For the role of pedagogues, see Festugière, *Antioche,* pp. 107 ff.

[b] Homer *Od.* 7.258.

[c] Philostr. *Imagines* 1.15.

ζημιοῖ μὲν ὁ δαίμων τὴν πόλιν, μᾶλλον δὲ πᾶσαν
τὴν γῆν τῇ Πανολβίου τελευτῇ, τουτὶ γὰρ ὄνομα
τῷ πρεσβυτέρῳ τῶν θείων, τῆς μητρὸς δὲ πρὸς
τὸν ἕτερον οὐκέτι τὰ αὐτὰ τοῖς δάκρυσι δυναμέ-
νης, ἦν γὰρ δὴ ὁ Φασγάνιος οἷος οἴκτῳ βλαβερῷ
μὴ ἐνδιδόναι, τὴν μὲν πείθει λύπην οὐ μακρὰν
καρποὺς μεγάλους ὑπισχνουμένην ἐνεγκεῖν, ἐμοὶ
δὲ ἀνοίγει τὰς πύλας.

14. Ἐν τοῖς εἰρημένοις οὐκ ἄδηλον ὅ τι μὲν
εὔδαιμον, ὅ τι δὲ οὐ τοιοῦτον. ἐξεληλακὼς δὲ
ἤδη τότε ἄρα ᾐσθανόμην ὡς δεινῶς πικρὸν ἀπο-
λιπεῖν οἰκείους. ἐφερόμην οὖν σὺν ὀδυρμοῖς τε
καὶ ὀδύνῃ, πυκνὰ ἐπιστρεφόμενος πόθῳ τῆς τῶν
τειχῶν ὄψεως. μέχρι μὲν Τυάνων δάκρυα, ἐντεῦθεν δὲ σὺν πυρετῷ δάκρυα. δυοῖν δὲ ἐπιθυμίαιν
μαχομέναιν ὁ τῆς αἰσχύνης φόβος θατέρᾳ προσ-
γενόμενος ἐκεῖσε ἐποίησε τὴν ῥοπήν, ὥστε ἔδει
νοσοῦντα ὁδοιπορεῖν. τοῦ νοσήματος δὲ ὑπὸ τῆς
πορείας αὐξανομένου διαπλέω μὲν τὸν Βόσπορον
R 13   μικρόν τι νεκροῦ διαφέρων, καὶ οἱ ὀρεῖς δὲ ταὐτὸν
ἐπεπόνθεσαν, ἐν ᾧ δὲ εἶχον ἐλπίδας ὡς βασιλείοις με πέμψοντι παρὰ τὴν Ἀθηνᾶν ζεύγεσιν,
οὗτος μὲν ἐξεπεπτώκει τῆς πολλῆς ἐκείνης
ῥώμης καὶ τἆλλα δὴ προθυμότατα ξενίζων ἐν

and I had yielded to necessity, Fate afflicted the city, or rather the whole world, with the death of Panolbius—as the elder of my uncles was called.[a] My mother could not now prevail so well upon the other by her laments, for Phasganius was not the man to give way before idle tears. He persuaded her to bear her grief, for it would not be of long duration and it gave promise of great returns, and so he opened the door for me.

14. In this account the good luck and the bad are perfectly clear. However, once I had set out, I began to realize at last how terribly hard it is to leave behind one's kith and kin. So I went on my way with weeping and wailing, often turning round in longing for the sight of the city walls. As far as Tyana, I was in tears all the way: from there onwards, I was in a fever as well. I was torn between two desires, but the fear of the shame I would incur was added to the one and weighted the balance in its favour, and so I continued on my way perforce, ill though I was. My illness grew worse with the journey, and I crossed the Bosporus little better than a corpse, with my mules in much the same shape. There the man on whom I relied to send me on to Athens by the Imperial Post had fallen from his previous position of influence. He was most zealous in the other duties of hospitality, but this was the one thing which he said he could

[a] The *Olympia* in Antioch was celebrated in July/ August. Panolbius died in autumn 336.

τοῦτο ἔφη μὴ δύνασθαι.   15. ἐγὼ δὲ εἰς τὴν
θάλασσαν ἔβλεπον ἤδη κεκλεισμένην ὑπὸ τῆς
ὥρας ναυτίλοις, ἐντυχὼν δέ τινι λαμπρῷ κυβερ-
F 89   νήτῃ μνησθείς τε χρυσίου πείθω ῥᾳδίως καὶ
ἐμβὰς τυχὼν τοῦ Ποσειδῶνος ἐκομιζόμην τερπόμενος, Πέρινθόν τε παραπλέων Ῥοίτειόν τε καὶ
Σίγειον καὶ τὴν τὰ δεινότατα παθοῦσαν Πριάμου
πόλιν ἀπὸ τῶν καταστρωμάτων ὁρῶν τόν τε Αἰ-
γαῖον διέδραμον οὐ χείρονι πνεύματι χρησάμενος
Νέστορος, ὥστε μοι κέρδος γενέσθαι τὴν ἀδυνα-
μίαν τοῦ ξένου.   16. καταπλεύσας οὖν εἰς
Γεραιστόν, ἔπειτα εἰς λιμένα τινὰ Ἀθηναίων, οὗ
δὴ καὶ ἐκοιμήθην, τῆς ἐπιούσης ἐν ἄστει τε ἦν
ἑσπέρας καὶ ἐν χερσὶν ὧν οὐκ ἂν ἐβουλόμην,
ἔπειτα τῆς ὑστεραίας ἐν ἑτέρων αὖ χερσὶν ὧν
οὐδὲ τούτων ἐβουλόμην· οὗ δὲ ἦλθον μετασχή-
σων, τοῦτον οὐδ' ὁρᾶν εἶχον ἐν πίθῳ μικροῦ
καθειργμένος, οἷα τὰ 'κείνων εἰς τοὺς ἀφικνουμέ-
νους τῶν νέων. ἐβοῶμεν δὴ διεστηκότες, ὁ σοφι-
R 14   στὴς μὲν ἐμοῦ, 'κείνου δὲ ἐγὼ στερόμενος· τοῖς

---

a Libanius travelled in the closed season for sailing;
hence the need for an official permit for individual use of
the *cursus publicus* (*evectio*), which was strictly regulated
by *Codex Theodos.* 8.5.

not provide.[a]   15. I transferred my attention to
the sea, but it was now closed to seafarers because of
the season. However, I lit upon a well-known sea-
captain, won him over easily enough by the mention
of a fare, embarked, found Poseidon favourable and
went on my way rejoicing. I sailed past Perinthus,[b]
and from the deck I gazed upon Rhoeteum, Sigeum
and the ill-fated city of Priam. I crossed the Aegean
and enjoyed a wind no worse than Nestor did, and so
my host's inability turned out to my advantage.
16. So I made landfall at Geraestus, and then at one
of the harbours of Attica, where I got a bed for the
night. Next night I was in Athens—in the hands of
people I wanted none of; and the day after, I was in
the hands of yet other people, and these I wanted
none of, either. I was unable even to catch a glimpse
of the teacher from whom I had come to learn, for I
was cooped up in a cell about as big as a barrel—
such is the reception they give students on their
arrival. My teacher[c] had lost me and I him, so we
began to set up a hullabaloo from our separate sta-
tions. My captors, however, took no account of our
outcries, but I was kept under lock and key until I

---

[b] Perinthus now was officially called Heraclea. Archa-
ism emphasizes classical piety. For Nestor, Homer *Od.*
3.176 ff.

[c] Epiphanius; cf. Eunap. *V.S.* 495, *PLRE* 280.

ἔχουσι δὲ λόγος οὐδεὶς τῆς βοῆς, ἀλλ' Ἀριστό-
F 90 δημος μέχρι τῶν ὅρκων ἐτηρούμην ὁ Σύρος.
ὀμωμοκότι δὲ ἤδη τοῖς παροῦσιν ἀγαπήσειν ἀνοίγει τις τὴν θύραν, καὶ ἠκροώμην τοῦ μὲν εὐθὺς ἐν
τάξει μαθητοῦ, τοῖν δυοῖν δὲ κατὰ νόμον δὴ τὸν
τῶν ἐπιδείξεων. 17. καὶ ὁ μὲν κρότος πολὺς
εἰς ἀπάτην τῶν τότε πρῶτον γευομένων ἐγειρό-
μενος, ἐγὼ δὲ ᾐσθανόμην ἐπ' οὐδὲν σεμνὸν
ἀφιγμένος τῆς ἀρχῆς τῶν νέων ὑπ' ἀνδρῶν οὐ
πολύ τι νέων διαφερόντων ἡρπασμένης. καὶ ἐδό-
R 15 κουν δὴ πλημμελεῖν τε εἰς τὰς Ἀθήνας καὶ
δίκην ὄφλειν οὐχὶ θαυμάζων τοὺς ἄρχοντας.
μόλις οὖν τὴν ὀργὴν καταπραΰνω σφίσι σιγῇ φήσας θαυμάζειν, κεκωλύσθαι γὰρ ὑπὸ τῶν νοσημάτων τὴν βοήν, διεκνυμένων δὲ ἤδη τῶν ἐμῶν ἔκ
τε γραμματίων καὶ ἄλλως εἰκός τι παθεῖν ἐδόκουν οὐχὶ θαυμασας.

18. Κἂν τοῖς εἰρημένοις δὴ τούτοις ἄξιον
ἐξετάσαι τὴν θεόν. οὐκοῦν αἱ μὲν νόσοι καὶ τὸ
ὥσπερ κατ' ἐμπορίαν πεπλευκότα χείροσι τῆς

---

a Cf. *Ep.* 474, *Or.* 64.83. Originally a θηλυδρίας of Old
Comedy (Cratinus Fr. Kassel-Austin), who as such needed
watching. Libanius contrasts him with himself, a paragon.
b For Diophantus see Eunap. *V.S.* 495, *PLRE* 260.

took the oath, like any Aristodemus,[a] Syrian though
I was. After I had sworn the oath to put up with my
present condition, the door was opened and I began
to attend the lectures of Diophantus[b] as his regular
pupil straightaway and those of the other two[c]
according to the normal practice of public declamation. 17. Though the applause that arose was
enough to deceive those who experienced it then for
the first time, I began to realize that I was present
at nothing out of the ordinary, for the guidance of
students had been monopolized by people who were
little better than students themselves. So my attitude was held to be derogatory towards Athens and
I was held guilty of not respecting my professors. It
was with difficulty, therefore, that I allayed their
anger, telling them that I was listening in respectful
silence, for vocal demonstrations had been made
impossible because of my illness. Finally, I produced some exercises of my own from my notebooks
and the like, and made it appear that my attitude
was satisfactory, despite my lack of enthusiasm.

18. From this narrative you can get a good idea
of my fortune. Thus, my ailments and the fact that,
like a merchant venturer, I found my ports of call to
fall below expectation—highly spoken of but far dif-

[c] Epiphanius and Proaeresius. For the entry and initia-
tion of students, see Walden, *Universities,* pp. 296 ff,
P. Wolf, *Vom Schulwesen,* pp. 1–41.

ἐλπίδος ὁμιλῆσαι λιμέσι δόξαν μὲν ἔχουσι θαυμα-
στήν, πεῖραν δὲ οὐ τοιαύτην τουτὶ μὲν οὐκ εὐτυ-
χοῦς ἀνθρώπου, τὸ δὲ χειμῶνι μὲν οὐδὲν χαλεπω-
F 91   τέρῳ θέρους χρήσασθαι πρὸς τὰ πελάγη,
γενέσθαι δὲ οὐχ ὅπερ ἔσπευδον, ἀλλ᾽ ὡς ἐβεβία-
στο, ταυτὶ δὲ δῶρα Τύχης. ἐοίκατε τὸ μὲν τῆς
εὐπλοίας δέχεσθαι καὶ κατὰ μέλος εἰρῆσθαι
συγχωρεῖν, τὰ δ᾽ αὖ περὶ τὼ σοφιστὰ ἀλλοκότως
εἰρῆσθαι, εἰ δὴ ἅπερ ἠναγκαζόμην, ἐν τούτοις
εὐτυχηκέναι φημί. δεῖ δή με λῦσαι τὸ αἴνιγμα,
καὶ ἐπὶ τοῦτο εἶμι.

R 16   19. Ἀκούων ἔγωγε ἐκ παιδός, ὦ ἄνδρες, τοὺς
τῶν χορῶν ἐν μέσαις ταῖς Ἀθήναις πολέμους καὶ
ῥόπαλά τε καὶ σίδηρον καὶ λίθους καὶ τραύματα
γραφάς τε ἐπὶ τούτοις καὶ ἀπολογίας καὶ δίκας
ἐπ᾽ ἐλέγχοις πάντα τε τολμώμενα τοῖς νέοις,
ὅπως τὰ πράγματα τοῖς ἡγεμόσιν αἴροιεν, ἀγα-
θούς τε αὐτοὺς τοῖς κινδύνοις ἡγούμην δικαίους
τε οὐχ ἧττον τῶν ὑπὲρ τῶν πατρίδων τιθεμένων
τὰ ὅπλα εὐχόμην τε τοῖς θεοῖς γενέσθαι καὶ
ἐμαυτῷ τοιαῦτα ἀριστεῦσαι καὶ δραμεῖν μὲν εἰς
Πειραιᾶ τε καὶ Σούνιον καὶ τοὺς ἄλλους λιμένας
νέων ἐφ᾽ ἁρπαγῇ τῆς ὁλκάδος ἐκβάντων, δραμεῖν δὲ ὑπὲρ τῆς ἁρπαγῆς αὖθις εἰς Κόρινθον

ferent in experience—all this can be placed on the debit side. Yet that my winter sailing weather was no worse than that of summer, and that what occurred was not what I intended but resulted from duress—these are the favours of Fortune. You would probably agree with me on the matter of my voyage and accept my account as consistent with my theme, but for me to assert, with regard to my teachers, that I was lucky in experiencing such compulsion would perhaps seem to you a very queer argument. I must then resolve the riddle, and to this topic I will now proceed.

19. From my boyhood, gentlemen, I had heard tales of the fighting between the schools which took place in the heart of Athens: I had heard of the cudgels, the knives and stones they used and of the wounds they inflicted, of the resultant court actions, the pleas of the defence and the verdicts upon the guilty, and of all those deeds of derring-do which students perform to raise the prestige of their teachers. I used to think them noble in their hardihood and no less justified than those who took up arms for their country: I used to pray heaven that it should be my lot too to distinguish myself so, to go hot-foot to the Peiraeus or Sunium or other ports to kidnap students at their landing, and then go off hot-foot once more to Corinth to stand trial for the kidnap-

κριθησόμενον, δεῖπνα δὲ δείπνοις συνείροντα
ταχὺ τῶν ὄντων ἀνηλωμένων εἰς δανείσοντα

F 92 βλέπειν. 20. εἰδυῖα τοίνυν ἡ θεὸς εἰς τὸν
εὐπρεπῆ με τοῦτον ἐκπεσούμενον ὄλεθρον, ᾧ
τοὔνομα μάλα εὔφημον, ὁ τοῦ χοροῦ προστάτης,
ὑπὲρ ὅτου μὲν ταῦτα ἡγούμην μοι προσήκειν
ὑπενεγκεῖν σοφιστοῦ, τούτου μέν με σοφώτατα,
ὥσπερ εἴωθε ποιεῖν, ἀπήγαγε, φέρουσα δὲ ἑτέρου
ποιεῖ, παρ' ὅτῳπερ ἔμελλον μόνους εἴσεσθαι τοὺς
ὑπὲρ τῶν λόγων μόχθους. ὃ δὴ καὶ ὧδε ἔσχεν.
αὐτός τε γὰρ ὡς ἂν ὑβρισμένος ταῖς ὅρκων

R 17 ἀνάγκαις οὐδὲν ὧν ἔφην ἠξίουν λειτουργεῖν,
ἄλλος τ' ἂν οὐδεὶς ἐπέτατε διὰ τὸ οὐχ ἑκόντα
δεδεκέναι, καὶ ἅμα δέος ἦν μὴ δυσχεραίνων τὸ
φορτίον ἕτερόν τι βουλεύσω πρὸς τὸν ὅρκον ἀπο-
λογησάμενος οἷς προσηναγκαζόμην. 21. ἦν
οὖν ἀτελὴς ἐξόδων τε καὶ στρατειῶν καὶ ἀγώνων, ἐφ' οἷς ἔρχεται Ἄρης, καὶ παρατάξεων, καὶ
δὴ κἂν τῇ μεγάλῃ μάχῃ πάντων συμπεπτωκό-
των καὶ ὅσους ὁ χρόνος ἀφίει, μόνος πόρρω που
καθήμενος ὅ τι ἕκαστος λάβοι κακὸν ἤκουον
πληγῶν τε διεγενόμην καθαρός, ὅσας ὀργαὶ ποι-

ping,[a] give a string of parties, run through all that I had, and then look to someone to make me a loan. 20. Well, Fortune knew that I would be heading for ruin in this specious trap with its high sounding title of head of the school, and so, in her usual wisdom, she withdrew me from the teacher whom I used to regard as the proper recipient of such services on my part, and took me off to be the pupil of some-one else, under whom I would become acquainted only with the labours connected with rhetoric. This, in fact, is precisely what happened. I felt myself outraged by the compulsion of the oath and refused to perform any of the services I have mentioned, and no one else would order me to do them because of my unwilling bondage, and there was also the fear that, in my resentment of the imposition, I might take some fresh line with regard to the oath, basing my case upon the compulsion to which I was subjected. 21. Thus I took no part in the sallies, skirmishes, martial affrays, and pitched battles. In fact, even on the occasion of the great riot, when everyone was involved, even those excused by their age, I alone stayed in my seat far away from it all, hearing of the harm which befell each one and remaining aloof from the blows

[a] The *proconsul Achaeae,* with headquarters at Corinth, supervised order and discipline in the University of Athens. Cases arising from 'Town and Gown' riots and from kidnapping of freshmen, as here, were referred to him; cf. Himer. *Or.* 48.37, Eunap. *V.S.* 483–485.

οὖσιν ἑνὸς πρὸς ἕνα, οὐ δούς ποτε, οὐ λαβὼν οὐδὲ
μελλήσας οὐδέτερον. καίτοι ποτὲ Κρὴς λελουμένος ἐντυχών μοι λουσομένῳ, μέσος δὲ ἐπορευόμην
F 93 δυοῖν, τὸν μὲν ἔνθεν καὶ ἔνθεν ἐπάταξεν ἀσελ-
γαίνων, οὐκ ἀμυνόμενος, ἐμοὶ δὲ οὐδὲ ἀντέβλε-
ψεν, ἐδόκουν δὲ ὅμως ἠδικῆσθαι τῷ ἐν ἐμοῖς τὰ
R 18 τοιαῦτα ὀφθαλμοῖς τετολμῆσθαι. 22. οὕτως
ἅπαντες ἅπαντας ἠξίουν ἐμοῦ παρόντος σωφρο-
νεῖν τοῦ γε οὐδὲ σφαίρας Ἀθήνησιν οὐδεπώποτε
ἁψαμένου τοσοῦτον <τε> ἀποσχόντος κώμου τε
καὶ κοινωνίας τῶν ἐν νυξὶν ἐπὶ τὰς τῶν πενεστέ-
ρων πορευομένων[1] οἰκίας· ἐπεὶ καὶ Σκύλλης
κεφαλὰς ἢ εἰ βούλει γε, Σειρήνων δεινοτέρας
γείτονας, ἑταίρας μελῳδούσας, αἳ πολλοὺς ἐξέδυ-
σαν, μάτην ᾀδούσας ἀπέφηνα.

23. Ἀλλ' ὅθεν ἐξέβην, ἐκείνων τε τῶν πολλῶν κακῶν διὰ τὴν Τύχην ἀπελελύμην, ὥστε
τὴν Κόρινθον εἶδον οὐ φεύγων οὐδὲ διώκων, ἀλλὰ
νῦν μὲν ἐφ' ἑορτὴν Λακωνικήν, τὰς μάστιγας,
ἐπειγόμενος, νῦν δὲ εἰς Ἄργος τὰ παρ' αὐτοῖς

___

[1] πορευομένων conj. Gasda, F.: ποιουμένων Mss., Martin.;
[κεφαλὰς] Wolf.

they dealt each other in their anger, giving none and receiving none, and with no intention of so doing, either.[a] Why, a Cretan coming out from his bath once met me, as I was going in for mine with a companion on either side of me. Without any provocation at all, he brutally clouted one of them on both cheeks, and never even glanced at me; for all that, I felt myself the victim of such an outrage committed before my very eyes. 22. Thus when I was present, everyone made a point of getting all to behave decently, for I never so much as touched a ball all the time I was in Athens, and I kept myself well away from the carousals and the company of those who raided the houses in the meaner quarters at night, and I made it quite clear too that the singing girls—Scylla's heads, or neighbours perhaps more dangerous than Sirens—who have wrecked the career of many a man, sang to me in vain.[b]

23. But to return to my point—from all those disasters I was preserved by Fortune, and so I saw Corinth neither as defendant nor as plaintiff, but only once when I passed through on my way to attend the festival of the Whippings at Sparta, and again when I went to Argos to be initiated in the

[a] For student gang fights, cf. Eunap. *V.S.* 483–485, Himer. *Or.* 69.
[b] For such low life in student society, cf. Isocr. *Antid.* 286 ff; and for a singing girl as Scylla the man-eater, Alciphron *Ep.* 18.

μυησόμενος. καὶ τοῦτο δὲ τοσοῦτον. καὶ κατ᾽
F 94 αὐτοὺς δὴ τοὺς λόγους μιμητὴς ἂν ἐκείνου, παρ᾽
R 19 ὃν ἠρχόμην, γενόμενος, τὸ γὰρ δὴ ἐρᾶν καὶ τοῦτο
ἂν ἔπραξεν, εἱπόμην ἀνδρῶν ἴχνεσιν, οὓς αὐτοὶ
μὲν ἐπίστασθε, σιγᾶσθαι δὲ ἐμοὶ κάλλιον. οἷος
ἂν οὖν ἦν, εἰ ἀνθ᾽ ὧν ὑμᾶς νῦν ἐν τοῖς ἐμαυτοῦ
λόγοις ἀναμιμνήσκω, τοῦ δεῖνος ἀνεμίμνησκον
ταπεινοῦ τινος καὶ πένητος ῥήτορας;

24. Ταυτὶ μὲν οὖν οὕτως εὖ καὶ καλῶς ἐστρα-
τήγηται τῷ δαίμονι. καὶ προσῆν τὸ οἷς ἐχρῆν
ἡγεμόσιν ἀκολουθοῦντα μηδὲν ἰατρῶν ἐν τῷ
σώματι δεδεῆσθαι, ὥστε ὁπόσαι ἡμέραι, τοσοῦτοι
πόνοι, πλὴν ὅσας αἱ πανηγύρεις αὐτῶν ἐποιή-
σαντο, οὐ πολλάς τινας οἶμαι. ἐπεὶ δὲ ἐδόκει
μέγιστον εἶναι θρόνων ἄξιον τῶν παρ᾽ Ἀθηναίοις
κεκρίσθαι, καὶ τοῦτο φροντίσασα ἡ Τύχη δέδωκε
τοῦτον τὸν τρόπον.   25. ἦν τις ἄρχων ἀνὴρ
τῶν ἐξ Ἰταλίας φρονήματός τε πλέως οἰόμενός
τε δεῖν ἁμαρτάνεσθαι μηδὲν ὑπὸ τῆς ἐκεῖ νεότητος. ἐν δὴ μανίᾳ τῶν νέων παύει μὲν τοὺς ποιμένας, ὡς δὴ κακοὺς ποιμένας, τοὺς δὲ ἀντ᾽
ἐκείνων ἄρχοντας ἀνεζήτει τρεῖς ἀντὶ τοσούτων

local mysteries.[a] So much for that. Moreover, with regard to my studies, if I had become an imitator of the man I had set out to attend, for affection would have ensured this happening, I would have followed in the steps of individuals I would prefer not to mention—you know well enough whom I mean. So imagine what I would now be like, if I reminded you of some wretched starveling hack instead of those classic writers who are now the models for my oratory.

24. This, then, was one of the excellent dispositions of Fate. There was the added fact that, as I followed my proper guides, I needed no doctor for my bodily ailments. So I applied myself to study day in and day out, save those reserved for official holidays, and they were not many. Since it was agreed that the peak of a man's career was to be deemed worthy of holding a professorial chair at Athens, Fortune devised this and granted me it in the following manner. 25. An Italian was governor,[b] a martinet who demanded that the students there should not misconduct themselves at all. As a result of rioting by the students, he dismissed their teachers as being no good shepherds, and he began to look around for three others to take their places as

[a] At Sparta, the διαμαστίγωσις at the festival of Artemis Orthia, Eunap. V.S. 483, Synes. Ep. 57; at Argos, the mysteries of Iacchus of Lerna, cf. Or. 14.7. He also visited Delphi, § 35 below.

[b] Proconsul Achaeae, 339; cf. PLRE 1013 (Anon. 46).

R 20 ἐκείνων. ἐπῃνεῖτ' οὖν Αἰγύπτιός τέ τις εἰς τὴν
ἀρχὴν πολίτης τέ τις ἐμός, ἄμφω παρόντε. τῆς
F 95 ἰσορρόπου δὲ αὐτοῖς εὐτυχίας ἀπέλαυον εἰς
πόνους ἔτη πέντε καὶ εἴκοσι γεγονώς, ὁ δὲ Αἰγύ-
πτιος πλείω δέκα, τούτου δὲ ἦν ἅτερος πρεσβύτερος. ἔδει δὴ παρεῖναι καλούμενον. καὶ τῷ μὲν
τὸν θυμὸν ὁ χρόνος ἐκοίμιζε, καὶ εἶχον οἱ σοφισταὶ τὰ αὑτῶν, ἐγὼ δὲ οἷς ᾑρέθην ἐκεκοσμήμην.
μεστὰ δὴ τἀπὶ τούτοις ὑποψίας καὶ οὐκ ἦν οὔτ'
ἐκείνοις οὔτε ἡμῖν καθεύδειν, ἀλλ' ἠνάγκαζε
τοὺς μὲν τὸ ἐπιβουλεύειν ἀγρυπνεῖν, ἡμᾶς δὲ ἡ
τοῦ τι δεῖν πείσεσθαι τῶν ἀηδεστέρων ἐλπίς. οὐ
μὴν οὐδ' ἐνταῦθά με προήκατο θρασύτητι νεωτέ-
ρων ἡ Τύχη, κατεῖχε δὲ αὐτοὺς καὶ μάλα ὀργῶν-
τάς τε καὶ παρωξυμμένους.

26. Φέρε δὴ καὶ ἑτέρας οὐκ ἀγεννοῦς μνησθῶ-
μεν ἀποδείξεως, ὡς ἦν ἐν ἐπιμελείᾳ τῇ Τύχῃ.
ἔμελλέ μοι πεπράσεσθαι τὰ πατρῷα, καὶ τοῦτο ἡ
θεός, οἷα δὴ θεός, προηπίστατο, γνώμην δὲ εἶχον
ἕτερα τέτταρα ἔτη τοῖς ἠνυσμένοις προσθεὶς
οὕτως Ἀθήνηθεν ἀπελθεῖν, ὡς τῆς μοι ψυχῆς
R 21 δεομένης γενέσθαι βελτίονος· καὶ γὰρ εἰ ὅτι
μάλιστα ἀποχρώντως ἐδόκουν τοῖς ἄλλοις ἔχειν,

professors.[a] So an Egyptian and a fellow citizen of my own, both resident in Athens, were recommended. My professional success matched theirs, though I was but twenty-five years old and the Egyptian was ten years older and the other older still. So I was bound to accept the invitation. However, the governor's temper was soothed in the course of time, and the professors retained their posts, but I had been marked for distinction by this choice. After this, the atmosphere was charged with suspicion: there was no rest either for them or for me, for their intrigues caused them sleepless nights, while the expectation of having to undergo some unpleasant experience had the same effect on me. Yet here too Fortune had not abandoned me to the misconduct of the students; rather did she restrain their heightened tempers and vindictiveness.

26. Now let me mention yet another signal proof that I was under the protection of Fortune. My father's estate was going to be sold, and the goddess, naturally, had foreknowledge of this.[b] My intention was to spend another four years additional to those I had already completed and then to leave Athens, since I felt that my intellect needed to be improved still further: however sufficient my ability might

[a] *Or.* 2.14 and *Ep.* 1274 may refer to this invitation, but see on §§ 82–85 below.

[b] Cf. *Or.* 55.15 for a different account of his mother's sale of the property.

ἀλλ' οὐκ αὐτός γε ἐφαινόμην ἐμαυτῷ, δέος δέ με
F 96 ἐξετάραττεν, ὡς περιστάντες οἱ ἑκασταχοῦ σοφοὶ
μυρίᾳ βασάνῳ κατενεγκεῖν ἐθελήσουσι· δεῖν οὖν
ἐπιζητοῦντα[1] μανθάνειν.   27. ἐπὶ δὲ ἀγγελίᾳ
τῇ περὶ τῆς πράσεως Ἀθήναζε ἠκούσῃ πάντως
ἂν αὐτοῦ κατέμενον οὐδέν τι τοῖς κτηθεῖσι χρώμενος, ὃ δὴ πολλοὺς τῶν νέων κατέλαβε θρόνων
τε οὐ δυνηθέντας ἀντιλαβέσθαι τῶν αὐτόθι πρὸς
γῆράς τε μετ' ἀφωνίας ἥκοντας. μηχανᾶται δή
τι τοιόνδε. Κρισπίνῳ μάλα ἐχρώμην Ἡρα-
κλεώτῃ νεανίσκῳ τὸν ἴσον ἐκεῖ μοι διατετριφότι
χρόνον, ᾧ τὸ δύνασθαι λέγειν μετὰ μικρῶν ἡ
φύσις ἐχαρίσατο πόνων, ἡλικιώτης δὲ ὢν ἐμὸς
πατέρα με ᾤετο προσορᾶν καὶ τοῖς ἐμοῖς νόμοις
ἐν μείζοσί τε καὶ ἐλάττοσι πειθόμενος πατρῴας
οὐ κατῄσχυνεν ἀρετὰς ἡγουμένου πάντων αὐτῷ
ῥημάτων ἐρυθήματος. οὗτος οἴκαδε καλούμενος
ὑπὸ τοῦ θείου,—θείου τινὸς ὡς ἀληθῶς ἀνθρώπου
καὶ πλείω γε θεοῖς ἢ ἀνθρώποις ὁμιλήσαντος ἐν
γῇ, καίτοι νόμος γε εἶργε καὶ ἦν ἡ δίκη τῷ τολ-
μῶντι θάνατος, ἀλλ' ὅμως σὺν αὐτοῖς ἐκείνοις

[1] ἐπιζητοῦντα AC, Martin: ἔτι ἐπιζητοῦντα P, F.: ἔτι
ζητοῦντα VL.

seem to other people, it did not seem so to me, and I was harassed by the dread that the pundits, who were everywhere about me, would wish to trip me up by exhaustive examination, and so I must still continue to research and increase my knowledge. 27. If the news of the sale had reached me in Athens, I would certainly be there now, making no use at all of my acquired learning, a fate that has befallen many students who, unable to get one of the professorial chairs there, reach old age with no chance of showing their eloquence. However, Fortune devised the following remedy. I had a close friend in Crispinus from Heraclea,[a] a lad in my own year there who possessed a natural gift of eloquence. He, though of my own age, looked upon me as a father, and in all things great and small he followed my precepts, doing nothing to sully the virtues of his house, for modesty was his guide in his every word. He was summoned home by his revered uncle—revered indeed, for he consorted more with gods than with men on earth: despite the law which banned it and the death penalty inflicted on any who dared do so, he yet went his way through life in the company of the gods, and he laughed to scorn that evil law and its sacrilegious enactor.[b] As I have

[a] For Crispinus see § 54 below, *BLZG* 112.

[b] Anti-Christian polemic. The law is perhaps *Codex Theodos.* 16.10.2. If so, he has, deliberately or not, antedated it by some months.

R 22 πορευόμενος τὸν βίον νόμου τε πονηροῦ καὶ νομο-
θέτου δυσσεβοῦς κατεγέλα—ὡς οὖν ἐκέκλητο καὶ
μένειν οὐκέτ' ἦν, ἡ καρδία οἱ καθ' Ὅμηρον
'μεγάλα στήθεσσι πάτασσε' καὶ μᾶλλόν γε ἢ εἰ
ἤρχετο πολεμίοις συμμίξων· ἐν πολίταις γὰρ αὖ
F 97 δεξιοῖς καὶ περὶ σοφίαν διατρίβουσι μέλλων δεί-
ξειν τὰ Ἀθήνηθεν ἀγωνίσματα νεανίσκος εὐ-
λαβής τε καὶ τοιούτων ἄθλων ἄγευστος εἰκότως
ἐδείμαινε.   28. δεόμενος δὴ συμμάχου τε καὶ
φίλου παραστησομένου τε καὶ θαρρυνοῦντος ἐγγύθεν οὐκ ἔμελλε [τοῦτον] δὴ τὸν τοιοῦτον ζη-
τήσειν ὄντος ἐμοῦ, καὶ εἰπόντος δὴ τό τε αὐτοῦ
πάθος ὅτου τε χρῄζοι, πρὸς μὲν τῆς ὁδοῦ τὸ
μῆκος οἶμαι κατώκνουν, ἐνίκα δὲ ὅμως ἡ φιλία
τὸν ὄκνον, καὶ ἅμα ἐνενόουν, ὡς εἴ του φαινοίμην
ἐν συνουσίαις ἐπιδεής, ἐκ τῆς αὖθις ἐπὶ ταῦτα
R 23 πορείας ἀπολογησόμενος.   29. τουτὶ μέν με
ἐπὶ τὸ ζεῦγος ἀνεβίβαζεν, Ἑρμοῦ δὲ εὐνοίᾳ καὶ
Μουσῶν ἀπὸ Πλαταιῶν ἀρξάμενοι χρῆσθαι οἷς
εἴχομεν ἐπαινούμενοί τε καὶ μακαριζόμενοι τῶν
τε Ἀθηνῶν εὐεργέται προσαγορευόμενοι διὰ
παντὸς ἐχωροῦμεν ἄστεος, καὶ οὐδὲ ὅστις εἰώθει
τοῖς διὰ Μακεδονίας ἰοῦσιν ἐπιτιθέμενος ἐκτα-
ράττειν ἀνὴρ Μακεδὼν ἐτάραξεν· ἐπέθετο μὲν γάρ,

said, Crispinus was called home and could no longer stay, and, as Homer puts it, 'his heart was sore afraid within him'[a]—more so even than if he were going out to do battle against the foe, for that skill in declamation which he had acquired in Athens he was going to demonstrate among his fellow citizens, clever and highly cultured people, and so, being a prudent lad and without experience of such an ordeal, he was not unnaturally alarmed. 28. He needed an ally and friend to stand by him and to be near to encourage him, and such a one was not far to seek when I was there. He told me of his predicament and of his need, and naturally I, considering the length of the journey, hesitated, but friendship overcame my hesitation. I also had the notion that, if my performance before such an assemblage proved at all inadequate, I would excuse myself from any second journey for this purpose. 29. This was the consideration which set me on my way, and by the grace of Hermes and the Muses, from Plataea onwards we began to make the most of our accomplishments, and, in every town through which we passed, we had praises and blessings showered upon us and were entitled benefactors of Athens. Nor yet did the Macedonian, whose habit it was to set upon travellers passing through Macedonia to their discomfiture, cause any discomfort to us. He engaged with us, indeed, but went off, himself for

[a] Hom. *Il.* 7.216.

ἀπῆλθε δὲ ὃ ποιεῖν εἰώθει, πεπονθώς. 30. τούτων οὐδὲν φαυλότερα τὰν τῇ Κωνσταντινουπόλει πολλῶν ἀπανταχόθεν παιδείᾳ διαφερόντων ἐκεῖσε μετοικούντων, οἳ ἐπήνουν τε ἡμᾶς
καὶ ἐπηνοῦντο. διαβάντες δὲ τοῦ Πόντου τὸν
αὐχένα, καθ' ὃν πάλαι ποτὲ τὴν Ἰὼ λόγος ἐν
F 98 εἴδει βοός, ἐλθόντες τε διὰ Χαλκηδόνος διά τε
Ἀστακίας τρίτης τε ἑτέρας πόλεως μικρᾶς μὲν
ἐκ μεγάλης τῆς πρίν, ἐχούσης δέ τι παντὸς
μεγέθους μεῖζον, γέροντα γλώττης ἡδονῇ τῷ
Νέστορι παρισούμενον καὶ αὐτὸ δὴ τοῦτο διὰ
τοῦτο καλούμενον μᾶλλον ἢ ὅπερ ὁ πατήρ τε
αὐτῷ καὶ ἡ μήτηρ ἔθεντο, ἐνταῦθα ξενίων τυχών,
τοῦ Κρισπίνου δὲ ἄρα κηδεστὴς οὗτος ἦν, ἔρχο-
μαί τε εἰς τὴν Ἡρακλέους, ἣν ἔκτισεν ἐκεῖνος
R 24 τοῦ τῶν κάτω θεῶν κρατήσας κυνός, καὶ τὴν
ἀνάβασιν εἶδον. 31. τετελεσμένων δὴ τῷ Κρισπίνῳ πάντων ὑπὲρ ὧν με ἀφῖκτο λαβών, πάλιν
τε ἦν ἀναστρέφων ἐν τῇ τοῦ Κωνσταντίνου
πόλει καὶ καταβὰς εἰς λιμένα τὸν μέγαν ἐγὼ
μέν, ὅστις Ἀθήναζε πλέοι, περιὼν ἐπυνθανόμην, λαβόμενος δέ μου τοῦ ἱματίου τῶν τις

---

[a] Libanius archaizes into myth and history. An Argive

once discomfited. 30. Our experience in Constantinople was no less pleasant, for the many famous men of letters, who come from all over the world to reside there, welcomed us and gave and received their meed of praise. We crossed the Bosporus, that neck of the Pontus where once long ago, so the story goes, Io went in the guise of a heifer,[a] and passed through Chalcedon, Astacus, and a third city which, though small in comparison with its former greatness, possessed something greater than mere size, since there lived there an old man, Nestor's double in the sweetness of his eloquence and therefore called by that name rather than by the one which his parents had given him.[b] There we were duly entertained, for he was father-in-law to Crispinus, and so I arrived at Heraclea, the town that Heracles founded after he had overcome the hound of the gods of the underworld, where I saw the route by which he had returned to earth. 31. After performing for Crispinus everything for which he had taken me, I was in the process of returning and, in Constantinople, was down at the Great Harbour going the rounds with inquiries about sailings to Athens. There I felt a tug at my gown. It was one of

party, searching for Io, are the first founders of Antioch, *Or.* 11.44 ff; the people of Astacus had been transplanted at the founding of Nicomedeia, Strabo 12.4.2 (p. 563). The third city is uncertain, Bithynium (Foerster) or Prusa (Sievers, p. 50).

[b] Perhaps Thespesius, *Ep.* 1032.

διδασκάλων, ἴστε αὐτόν, Νικοκλέα λέγω τὸν
Λακεδαιμόνιον, οὗτός με ἐπιστρέψας πρὸς ἑαυτόν, 'οὐ τοῦτόν σε,' ἔφη, 'δεῖ πλεῦσαι τὸν
πλοῦν, ἀλλ' ἕτερον.' 'καὶ τίνα ἄν,' ἔφην, 'ἕτερον ὁ τῶν Ἀθηνῶν γλιχόμενος ἢ τοῦτον πλέοι;'
'ὅτι, ὦ μακάριε, παρ' ἡμῖν σε,' ἔφη, 'μένοντα
χρὴ κυβερνῆσαι τῶν πολλῶν τουτωνὶ καὶ εὐδαι-
μόνων τοὺς παῖδας. ἔα δὴ τὴν ναῦν καὶ ἐμοὶ
πείθου καὶ μήτε σαυτὸν μήτε ἡμᾶς ἀδίκει μηδὲ
ἀγαθὰ πολλά τε καὶ μεγάλα προσιόντα φεῦγε
F 99 μηδ' ἄρχειν ἐξὸν ἀρξόμενος πλέε· ταυτηνὶ δὲ
ἐγώ σοι παραδώσω τὴν βασιλείαν αὔριον,
τετταράκοντα νέους, τὰ πρῶτα τῶν τῇδε· ἡ
κρηπὶς δὲ εἰ καταβληθείη, πολὺν τὸν ὄλβον
ἐπιρρέοντα ὄψει.' καὶ διηγεῖτο ἃ Βημαρχίῳ τῷ
σοφιστῇ τελέσειεν ἡ πόλις. ἐδεῖτο δέ μου κατα-
πολεμῆσαι δι' ἐμοῦ βουλόμενος ἀνθρώπιον ἐκ
Κυζίκου μιαρόν τε καὶ ἀχάριστον, δι' ἐκείνου
μὲν τῆς πόλεως μετασχόν, κριοῦ δὲ τροφεῖα
κατὰ τὴν παροιμίαν ἐκτίνον. 32. ἐγὼ δὲ
οὕτω μὲν ἔφην ποιήσειν καὶ οὐκ ἀπειθήσειν,
R 25 λαθὼν δὲ ᾠχόμην πλέων. τοῦ δὲ Αἰγαίου κινη-
θέντος τῶν τε ναυτῶν οὐδὲν εἰδέναι τοῦ
πελάγους λεγόντων στὰς ἐγὼ παρὰ τὸν κυβερ-

the teachers there—you know him, Nicocles the Spartan.[a] He turned me round to face him, and, 'That is not the tack for you,' said he. 'There is a different course for you to take.' 'Oh! and what is that, when I am anxious to get back to Athens?' I replied. 'Stay with us here, my dear fellow,' he said, 'and be master of the sons of our many wealthy citizens. To the deuce with your ship! Just you listen to me, and don't put a spoke in your wheel or in mine. Don't try to dodge the many great rewards that will come your way. When you can be in charge yourself, why sail off to be under someone else? Here is your domain, and I will hand it over to you inside twenty-four hours—forty pupils, the cream of the place! Build on these foundations, and you'll see— you are a made man.' Then he went on to tell me of the fee the city paid to the sophist Bemarchius.[b] This request of his was occasioned by his desire to bring down, through my efforts, a nasty, graceless fellow from Cyzicus who had become a citizen through his assistance and then had bitten the proverbial hand that fed him.[c] 32. I agreed and accepted his suggestion, but quietly slipped away by ship. The Aegean was stormy and the sailors said they had never known a sea like it. I stood by the

[a] *Grammatistes,* still alive in 388; cf. *Or.* 32.1, *PLRE* 630.

[b] Official sophist of the city, 340. *PLRE* 160.

[c] Menander *fr.* 804 K., Zenobius 2.31 Bühler.

νήτην ὑπὸ τοῦ κακοῦ νικώμενον εὔχομαι Νηρεῖ
τε καὶ ταῖς Νηρέως κόραις· νύξ τε ἦν ἐν ᾗ
τὰ δεινὰ ταῦτα παρῆν, καὶ ἀνίσχει ἥλιος διὰ
νεφῶν προσβάλλων τὴν θάλασσαν, σημεῖον
μὲν ἀγριωτέρων πνευμάτων, καὶ τὰς τρίχας
ἅπαντες ἐτίλλομεν, ἦν δὲ ἄρα τι τῶν εὐχῶν
ἔργον, καὶ πάντα τὰ λυποῦντα ὀξέως ἐλέ-
λυτο θεῶν θαλαττίων ἡμερούντων τὴν θάλατταν.
33. ἔπλεον δὲ μένειν ὑποσχόμενος οὐ ψεύστης
οὐδ᾽ ἀπατεών τις ὢν οὐδὲ τῷ παρακρούεσθαι
τερπόμενος, ἀλλὰ ὅρκον ἐμπεδῶν, ἐφ᾽ ᾧ τὴν
Ἀθήνηθεν ἐπεποιήμην ἔξοδον, ἐπάνοδον ἔχοντα·
F 100   οὔκουν ἐδόκει μοι χρηστὸν ἔσεσθαι τῇ ἐπιτηδεύσει
προοίμιον ἡ ἐπιορκία. διὰ ταῦτα ἔπλεον. ἐλθὼν
δὴ καὶ οὐκ ἐπιορκήσας ἐπ᾽ ὀχήματος δικύκλου
χειμῶνος ἀρχομένου τῶν τῆς ὥρας ἀνεχόμενος
R 26   ἀνιαρῶν ἤλαυνον, ὅπως αὖθις λόγῳ προσθείην
ἔργον.   34. τοῦτο[1] δὴ τοῦ νέων τε ἐπιστατεῖν
καὶ ἐν τοσούτοις ἔθνεσι τῆς τῶν λόγων ἀπεργα-
σίας οὐκ ὀλίγων δημιουργηθέντων καὶ ὅλως ὧν
τοῦ νῦν ἀπολέλαυκα σχήματος ἓν ἐκεῖνο αἰτια-
τέον, τὴν τῷ φίλῳ μὲν ἐν κοινωνίᾳ τῆς ἐξόδου
δεδομένην χάριν, τὸν ἐμὸν δὲ πρὸς τοὺς ἔξω
τόπους ἀφελοῦσαν φόβον. εἰ γὰρ αὖ μὴ τότε με

helmsman who was overcome by this plight, and offered a prayer to Nereus and his daughters. It was night when these terrors encompassed us about, and when the sun rose, his rays struck the sea through a bank of clouds—a sign of worse weather to come. We all tore our hair, but there was, after all, some result to my prayers, for the gods of the sea calmed the deep and all our troubles were quickly resolved. 33. Now, when I sailed away after promising to stay, I was no liar or trickster, nor did I take any joy in deception. I was bound by oath to return, and that was the condition on which I had set out from Athens. To break my word did not seem the fitting prelude to a teaching career, and that was the reason why I sailed away. So I returned and kept my word, but in early winter,[a] despite the inclement weather, I travelled by fast carriage back to Constantinople, once again to put my words into effect. 34. This then must be accounted the sole cause of my career as a teacher and of the production of the many orations I have composed in so many provinces, in short, of the fruits of the state I now enjoy—that I did a friend a good turn by accompanying him upon his going down, and so rid myself of my fear of places else-

[a] On this journey he first becomes acquainted with Sopater, *Ep.* 762.

---

[1] τοῦτο Mss. exc. P, Martin: τούτου P, F.

ἐξήγαγεν ὁ δαίμων, ἐκράτει ἂν τὸ ἀεὶ δεῖν μέλλειν. 35. ἤδη μὲν καὶ ἄλλον τινὰ ἀνθρώπων
R 27 δι᾽ ὁδοῦ τραχείας ἐπὶ γλυκὺ τέρμα προήγαγεν ἡ
θεός, ἀτὰρ οὖν καὶ ἐμὲ τότε. ὡς γὰρ δὴ ἐνέβαλον εἰς τὴν ἀγοράν, ὁρῶ τινα Καππαδόκην
ἥκοντα ἐπὶ θρόνον βασιλέως πέμποντος, καὶ γὰρ
ἐτύγχανεν ἡ βουλὴ τὸν ἄνδρα ᾐτηκυῖα, ῥήτορα
ἄκρον ἐξ οἶμαί τινος ἀγῶνος ἑνὸς αἰτησαμένη. ὁ
μὲν δὴ σεμνὸς σεμνῶς εἱστήκει, γνοὺς δὲ ἐγὼ
παρά του γέροντος, ὅστις τε εἴη καὶ ὅθεν καὶ
F 101 ὅπως καὶ ἐφ᾽ ὅτῳ παρείη, πληγεὶς τὴν ψυχὴν
τοῖς εἰρημένοις ᾖειν παρ᾽ ἐκεῖνον, ὅς μοι
προὐξενήκει τὴν πόλιν, ὡς δὲ ἀνέμνησα τῶν
λόγων, 'παῖς εἶ,' ἔφη, 'μάλα παῖς, εἰ δὴ ὁπόσον
ἐστὶ καιρὸς οὐκ οἶσθα καὶ ταῦτα ἥκων εἰς Δελ-
φούς. ὑποσχέσεων δὲ ἐκείνων, ἃς τῷ πλῷ
κεκίνηκας, αὐτόν τε σὲ μεμνῆσθαι μάταιον ἕτερόν τε ἀναμιμνήσκειν.' πληγῇ ταύτῃ δευτέρᾳ
R 28 πληγεὶς ἀπεχώρουν Ἀθηνῶν τε ὁμοῦ καὶ ἐλπίδος ἁμαρτών. 36. ἦν δέ τις αὐτόθι Διονύσιος,
ἀνὴρ Σικελιώτης, οὕτω μέγας τε καὶ δυνατὸς ἔκ

---

a Cf. Diog. Laert. 1.4.79 (Pittacus) καιρὸν γνῶθι; Paus.
10.24.1 this is inscribed on the pronaos of the temple at
Delphi.

where. In fact, had not heaven sent me forth at that time, the necessity of making the break would ever be with me. 35. Other men before me have been advanced by Fortune safe to port after passage through stormy seas, and so she treated me then. As soon as I entered the city square, I caught sight of a Cappadocian taking his seat, appointed by the emperor. The city council had asked for him, requesting his appointment as a first-class orator merely upon the result of a single competition, I am sure. There he stood in all his glory, and when I learned from some old fellow who he was and where he had come from, and of the manner and purpose of his coming, I was stricken to the heart at the tale, and approached him who had recommended my coming to the city. I reminded him of his offer, but he replied, 'You really are a simpleton if, even after your visit to Delphi,[a] you have not the wit to take time by the forelock. It is of no use for you to recall those promises or to remind anyone else of them. You put an end to them by sailing away.' Shaken by this second blow, I began to take my leave, cheated both of Athens and of my high hopes. 36. But there was in Constantinople a Sicilian named Dionysius[b] who was great and influential

---

[b] Flavius Dionysius, *PLRE* 259 (11); *consularis Syriae*, 329–335, that is, during Panolbius' tenure of office.

τε τῶν ἐν δίκαις ἄθλων ἔκ τε τῶν ἐν ἀρχαῖς
ἐπαίνων ἔκ τε φιλοξενίας ἔκ τε τοῦ ῥᾳδίως
τὸν λυποῦντα ἐπικλύζειν, ὥστε ἐλυσιτέλει τῷ
τὴν ἀρχὴν ἔχοντι χρῆσθαι Διονυσίῳ. οὗτος ὢν
τε εἴην εἰδὼς ἡνίκα ἐπετρόπευε Σύρους, τῷ τε
Νικοκλεῖ τούτῳ τῶν πρὸς ἐμὲ πρότερον συνεφα-
ψάμενος λόγων ἔκειτο τηνικαῦτα ἀσθενῶν, ᾧ δὴ
μάλιστα ἐβλαπτόμην. ἐπεὶ δὲ ῥαΐσας τὸν
ἅπαντα ἤκουσε λόγον καὶ ὡς χειμαζοίμην, δυοῖν
γὰρ ἕνα οὐκ εἶναι κρατεῖν, οὐδὲ γὰρ τὸν Ἡρα-
κλέα τὴν παροιμίαν λέγειν, ἑαυτῷ τοῦτ᾽ ἔφη
μελήσειν, μὴ χρῆναι δὲ ἀθυμεῖν ἐμέ, καὶ τὸ τοῦ
Πλάτωνος προσέθηκεν, ὡς ὑπ᾽ ἀνδρῶν οὐκ ἂν
ποτε τρόπαιον ἀθυμούντων σταθείη.[a]

37. Τρεπόμεθα δὴ πρὸς τὰ ἀγωνίσματα, καὶ
ἔδει μὲν ἕτερον τὸν ταῦτα διηγούμενον εἶναι,
περὶ ἑτέρου γὰρ ἂν ἕτερος ἀποκεκαλυμμένως
διῄει, λόγοι τε ὁπόσοι παρ᾽ ἑκάστου καὶ οἵτινες
τὰς μορφάς, νικῶντάς τε καὶ νικωμένους, ὅστις
τε ὁ τὴν πόλιν ἐφειλκυσμένος, καὶ ὡς οὐδὲν
ἐλάττωμα εἰς τὸν στέφανον τὸ μὴ τῶν βασιλέως
ἐσθίειν. τοῖς μὲν οὖν ἡ τροφὴ παρ᾽ ἐκείνου

R 29
F 102

---

[a] Plato *Phaedo* 89c; *Paroem. Gr.* 1.140.

because of his successes in the courts, his reputation in office, his ready hospitality and his ability to bring to heel any who fell foul of him—so much so that it paid any governor to be on good terms with Dionysius. He had known my family when he had held office in Syria and had been associated with Nicocles in the previous overtures to me, but at this time he had fallen ill, which was a great misfortune for me. Upon his recovery he heard the whole tale and of the straits in which I now found myself, that by myself I could not get the better of two men—not even Heracles in the proverb could do that[a]—and so he told me to leave things to him and to cheer up. He added, quoting Plato, that no trophies are ever raised by men downcast.[b]

37. So I turned to the public competitions. Really, someone else ought to be telling this story, for he would have no personal axe to grind. He would recount the number and the type of orations each contestant made, who won and who lost, who attracted the favour of the city, and how it was no detriment towards gaining the crown not to be supported by the imperial exchequer. The others, in fact, got maintenance in plenty from it,[c] but the

[b] Plato *Critias* 89c; *Paroem. Gr.* 1.382.

[c] A sophist of the city, appointed and paid by the municipality, also received, if confirmed by imperial nomination, supplementary payment in kind; cf. *Codex Theodos.* 13.3.11 (*annona*, πυροί §110, τροφή *Epp.* 28, 132, σῖτος *Ep.* 800).

πολλή, πατέρες δὲ ἡμᾶς τῶν φοιτητῶν ἔβοσκον
ἄλλοι ἄλλους παρακαλοῦντες, καὶ ἐν οὐ πολλαῖς
ἡμέραις ὑπὲρ τοὺς ὀγδοήκοντα ὁ χορὸς ἐπιρροῇ
τε τῶν ἔξωθεν καὶ ταῖς τῶν ἔνδον ἀποστάσεσιν,
οἵ τε ἐπτοημένοι περὶ τὰς τῶν ἵππων ἀμίλλας
καὶ τὰ τῆς σκηνῆς θεάματα πρὸς τὰς ὑπὲρ τῶν
λόγων μετερρυήκεσαν σπουδὰς δόγματά τε
ἐγράφετο παρὰ τοῦ κρατοῦντος ἐπαγγέλλοντα
τὴν ἐμὴν αὐτοῦ μονήν. ἦν γὰρ δὴ δέος μὴ ἐν
ἐξουσίᾳ τοῦ ἀπαίρειν ὧν μνησθείην τῆς ἐμαυτοῦ.
38. τὼ μὲν δὴ σοφιστὰ ἐπενθείτην, ὁ μὲν οὐδὲ
ἀνθήσας ἀρχήν, ὁ δὲ ἀπηνθηκώς· ὁ μὲν γὰρ
οὐδὲ παρῆλθεν εἰς τὸ δύνασθαι, ὁ δὲ ἐξεπεπτώκει. ἐπενθείτην μὲν οὖν καὶ τἄλλα ἐλοιδορείσθην
βίαιον, πλεονέκτην, ἀκόρεστον, οὐδαμοῦ στῆναι
δυνάμενον, τὰ τοιαῦτα ἀναισχυντοῦντες. οὐ γὰρ
δὴ χειρῶν ἔργον ἦσαν οἱ ἀφιστάμενοι τῶν νέων,
ἀλλ᾽ ἕτερον τὸ πεῖθον. ὥσπερ οὖν τοὺς καλοὺς
οὐκ ἂν γράψαιτό τις βιαίων, εἰ πολλοὶ σφῶν
ἐρῶεν, οὕτως οὐδ᾽ ἡ ἐν λόγοις ὥρα τὸ τῆς
μαγνήτιδος πράττουσα πονηρὸν ἂν τὸν πατέρα
τῆς ὥρας ἐλέγξαι.

39. Οἰμώττουσι δὴ τοῖς ὧδε πεπραγμένοις
ἔρχεται Βημάρχιος σύμμαχος μηνὶ ἑβδόμῳ, μάλα

fathers of my pupils supported me, one encouraging another, and in a few days my class had grown to more than eighty by the influx of students from elsewhere and by the defection of those within the city. People who had been all of a flutter about the chariot races or the theatrical performances had changed to a sudden interest in rhetoric, and a decree was drafted by the emperor enjoining me to stay in the capital, for they were afraid that, if I were at liberty to leave, I would bethink me of home. 38. So both the professors[a] were full of chagrin, one because he had never enjoyed any success at all, the other because he had lost it, for the first had never even had the chance of pre-eminence and the second had been ejected from it. As I have said, they were full of chagrin, and they proceeded to heap abuse upon me, calling me a greedy, insatiate, restless disturber of the peace and other such insulting names. Yet it was through no deed of violence of mine that their students were deserting them; the inducement was something different. You would not prosecute men of good looks for rape if many people transferred their affections to them: in the same way the attraction of perfect oratory would not prove the author of that perfection to be a rogue.

39. So while they were moaning and groaning at their plight, after six months Bemarchius came to

[a] The professors from Cyzicus and Cappadocia.

δὴ τὸν Κωνστάντιον ᾑρηκὼς ἀνὴρ καὶ τῶν περὶ
ἐκεῖνον τοὺς ἀμυήτους ψόφῳ τε καὶ κτύπῳ
παρανόμων ῥημάτων δόξαν ἐπὶ λόγοις ῥωμαλέου
R 31 λαβὼν φίλοις τε τοῖς ἀπ᾽ ἐκείνων ἐτετείχιστο
τῶν χρόνων, δεινοὶ γὰρ δὴ οἱ κύβοι καὶ τὰ μέχρι
μέθης συμπόσια φιλίας ἰσχυρὰς κεράσαι. διέβη
μὲν δὴ τὸν πορθμὸν 'κυδιόων τε καὶ ὑψοῦ κάρη'
ἔχων κρότῳ τε ἐπηρμένος καὶ οἷς εἰργάσατο χρήμασι, λόγον ἕνα μέχρι Νείλου δεικνύων τόν τε
ἐναντία τοῖς θεοῖς τεταγμένον ἐγκωμιάζων,
αὐτὸς θύων θεοῖς, διδάσκων τε καὶ διηγούμενος,
οἷον αὐτῷ τὸν νεὼν ἐγεῖραι Κωνστάντιος. διέβη
μὲν δὴ μειδιῶν, ὡς δὴ οὐδενὸς αὐτὸν ὑπομενοῦν-
τος, ἀλλ᾽ ἀμαχεὶ τά τε αὑτοῦ κομιούμενος καὶ
καταδύσων αὐτόν τε ἐμὲ καὶ ὅ τι ἐμοὶ συνέπνει.
40. πρῶτον μὲν οὖν τὸ μηδεμίαν ἐς αὐτὸν
ἐπάνοδον γενέσθαι τῶν νέων ὠδύνα καὶ ἐκέντει
τὴν ψυχήν· ἔπειτα ἐμοῦ λόγον εἰς σύλλογον εἰσ-
αγαγόντος παρών τε καὶ ἀκροώμενος οὐχ ὡς
ἥδιστα διετέθη, τῶν φίλων δέ οἱ παραινούντων

---

[a] Christian courtiers: Datianus and others; *Or.* 42.24.
[b] Homer *Il.* 6.509.
[c] Christ, never mentioned by name in Libanius. The

their aid. He had been a staunch supporter of Constantius and the profane crew about him,[a] and by the rattle and clatter of his blasphemous oratory he had gained the reputation of a vigorous speaker, and he had hedged himself about with the protection of the friends he had made at that time, for gambling games and drunken orgies are fine things to cement strong friendship. So he crossed the Bosporus, 'glorying in his might, with head held high,'[b] uplifted by the applause and the wealth he had amassed. He had travelled as far as Egypt, delivering just one oration, in which, although he personally was a worshipper of the gods, he spoke in praise of him who had set himself up against them, and discoursed at length upon the church Constantius had built for him.[c] Anyway, over he came all smiles, his idea being that none would withstand him and that he would gain his objective without a struggle and shipwreck me and all my supporters. 40. First of all, the fact that no students returned to him pained him and cut him to the quick. Then, being present when I introduced an oration to a public audience he listened in no very sweet frame of mind. His friends urged him to loose his thunders,

temple is the Great Church in Antioch, begun by Constantine in 327 and dedicated by Constantius in January 341; cf. Downey, *Antioch*, pp. 342 ff. Bemarchius has spent nearly nine months touring the East with this single 'travelling lecture.'

F 104 βροντᾶν καὶ ἀποκρύπτειν λόγῳ λόγον γράψαντα
περὶ ὧνπερ ἐγώ, πάντως δ᾽ ἄν με τῇ πρώτῃ
R 32 κατασῦραι προσβολῇ, πλὴν εἰ μήπου τὴν δύναμιν
ἣν εἶχεν ἀπολώλεκε, τοιούτοις ἀναπτερωθεὶς
ῥήμασι μηνὶ ὕστερον ἧκε κομίζων λόγον, ὃς ἐκεῖνον ᾧ προσεπολέμει καὶ πρόσθεν ἐπαινούμενον
θαυμαστότερον ἀπέφηνεν. 41. ἡττημένος δὴ
τοῦτο οὐδ᾽ ἂν θεοῦ προειπόντος ἐλπίσας ἧκεν
ἀναμαχούμενος τὴν ἧτταν τῷ τὸ πολὺ χρυσίον
πεποιηκότι λόγῳ, καὶ διεξιόντος αὐτοῦ κίονας δή
τινας καὶ κιγκλῖδας ὁδούς τε ὑπ᾽ ἀλλήλων
τεμνομένας ἐμπιπτούσας οὐκ οἶδ᾽ ὅποι, βλέπον-
τες εἰς ἀλλήλους οἱ καθήμενοι, συνεῖναι αὐτὸς
ἕκαστος οὐκ ἔχων, νεύμασι τοὺς ἀφεστηκότας
ἠρώτων εἰ τὸ αὐτὸ πάθοιεν, καὶ ταὐτὸ τοῦτο τοῖς
ἄλλοις ἐγὼ παθὼν σαφηνείας δόξαν οἷς ἐθορύ-
βουν ἐπειρώμην περιάπτειν τῷ λόγῳ χαριζό-
R 33 μενος τῇ φάλαγγι. 42. δευτέρῳ δὴ τούτῳ
τρώσας αὐτὸν λόγῳ λόγον ἐμὸν ἕτερον φανῆναι
διακωλύει τὸν ἄρχοντα πείσας οἷ χαρίσασθαι τὸ
μὴ ἀφικέσθαι μοι. ἦν δὲ ἐκεῖνος οἷος καὶ πεισθῆ-
ναί τῳ. τῆς τοίνυν πόλεως τοσούτῳ μείζόνως
τἀμὰ ἑλομένης, ὅσῳπερ μᾶλλον ἑώρα τῶν
F 105 δικαίων ἀποστερούμενον, εἶδεν ὁ γενναῖος ἐκεῖνος

to write a speech on the theme I had chosen and to put mine in the shade: he would surely lay me low at the first encounter, unless perhaps he had lost any of his former ability. Elated by such remarks, he came the following month with a speech which proved that mine, which he was attacking, was, for all the approval it had gained, even more admirable. 41. After this reverse which he would not have expected even though foretold by a god, he came again to avenge his defeat with the speech which had made his fortune. He rambled on and on about pillars, trellised courts, and intercrossing paths which came out heaven knows where.[a] Meanwhile, the audience looked at one another, and when not a single one of them knew what he was talking about, they nodded and signed to those who were some distance away to inquire whether they were in the same boat. My own feelings were exactly the same as the rest, but, in order to oblige his company, I tried, by my applause, to make it appear that his dissertation was a model of lucidity. 42. Having injured himself by this second speech, he took pains to prevent another speech of mine from appearing, for he got the governor,[b] who was the sort of fellow to follow anyone's lead, to do him a good turn by not attending my declamations. However, the city took

[a] Cf. Euseb. *Vita Const.* 3.50.

[b] Alexander, proconsul of Constantinople, 342: *PLRE* 40 (3).

καὶ πρὸς τῷ Νικοστράτῳ τοῦ Ἰσοκράτους κατα-
φρονῶν, ὅτι λόγοις μὲν οὐκ ἂν ἔτι παρέλθοι
λόγους οὐ μᾶλλόν γε ἢ ποσὶ πόδας τοὺς ἐμοὺς
R 34 τοῖς ἑαυτοῦ, μία δὲ ἀπαλλαγὴ κυρία, εἰ μηκέτ᾽
εἴην.   43. εἰ μὲν δὴ φαρμάκῳ οἷός τ᾽ ἦν ἀπενεγκεῖν, ἐπὶ τὸ ἔκπωμα ἧκεν ἄν, τοῦτο δὲ οὐκ
ἔχων γοήτων ἡττῆσθαι περιιὼν ἐτραγῴδει· ξυν-
εῖναί με γὰρ ἀνδρὶ τυραννοῦντι τῶν ἄστρων, δι᾽
ὧν ἐκεῖνον τὸν μὲν εὖ, τὸν δὲ κακῶς ποιεῖν
ἀνθρώπων, ὥσπερ τοὺς ἐν ταῖς δυναστείαις διὰ
τῶν δορυφόρων· τούτου δὲ εἶναι τὸν ἔλεγχον ἐν
τοῦ βιβλογράφου ταῖς πλευραῖς, Κρητός τινος
ἐπιεικοῦς πολλὰ τῇ δεξιᾷ καμόντος Ἀθήνησί τε
καὶ πανταχοῦ.   44. γνοὺς δέ, ὡς μόνος μὲν
ὑλακτῶν οὐδὲν περαίνοι, δέοι δὲ αὐτῷ καὶ συμμορίας, εὑρίσκει πόνου χωρὶς τοὺς συλληψομένους
πρὸς τοῖς σοφισταῖς τοὺς ἀμφὶ τοὺς ποιητάς.
ἐποίει δὲ αὐτῷ τοὺς συνεργοὺς[1] λύπη τε καὶ
φόβος καὶ φθόνος· τοὺς μὲν σοφιστὰς πάντα,
τοὺς ἄλλους δὲ τὸ φθονεῖν. χρῶνται δὴ καιρῷ τῇ

---

[1] αὐτῷ τοὺς συνεργοὺς VL, F: αὐτὸ CA, Martin.

my side, and all the more so since it saw me robbed of my due. Then our fine fellow realized that he had bitten off more than he could chew,[a] for he could not outstrip me in his oratory any more than he could actually outpace me: there was only one thing for it—to put an end to me.   43. If he could have done away with me by poison, he would have got at my drink, but, finding this impossible, he went around with the fairy tale that he had been worsted by magic. I was intimate, so he said, with an astrologer who controlled the stars and through them could bring help or harm to men[b]—just like a tyrant with his bodyguard: the proof of all this was to be got from the hide of my copyist, a Cretan and a decent fellow whose hand had served me well both at Athens and elsewhere. 44. Yet he realized that he was getting nowhere by setting up this howl all by himself; he required a gang of his own and he found people ready enough to take up the cudgels among schoolmasters and professors. Chagrin, fear, and envy made them his accomplices—all these emotions in the case of the professors, envy in the case of the rest. They made the most of the

[a] Isocrates was proverbially the master orator, Nicostratus an outstanding actor, *Paroem. Gr.* 1.395. A good sophist was required to be both.

[b] Astrology tends to be regarded as magic, and so a treasonable offence. The copyist, as one of the *humiliores,* could be tortured to provide evidence against his master, though himself not involved in the charge.

τοῦ δήμου μανίᾳ, ἣν ὁ μὲν ἄρχων τραυματίας
φεύγων τῷ Περινθίων σῴζεται τείχει, συλλαβόντες δὲ τοὺς συκοφαντουμένους οἱ συνωμόται
καθείρξαντες εἶχον ἀθάνατον ἔσεσθαι τὴν στάσιν
οἰόμενοι.   45. ὡς δὲ οἱ μὲν ἑαυτῶν ἐγένοντο οἱ
παραφρονήσαντες, ὁ δὲ ἄρχων ἐπανῆκεν, ὁ
δεσμὸς δὲ ἦν παρὰ τοὺς νόμους, ὁ μέν, ὡς ἐμοί
τε καὶ τοῖς νόμοις ἔμελλε βοηθήσειν αὔριον καὶ
ὡς οὐ σμικρὰν λήψοιτο δίκην, παρεδήλου, τῶν δὲ
ἐν τρόμῳ τε καταστάντων καὶ ἀλλήλους αἰτιω-
μένων, οἷα ἐβούλευσας, ὦ δαῖμον. περὶ μέσας
νύκτας ἐξέβαλες τῆς ἀρχῆς τὸν Ἀλέξανδρον καὶ
παρέδωκας ἅμα ἡμέρᾳ Λιμενίῳ τὸ ἄστυ, συν-
ωμότῃ μὲν οὐκ ἂν φαίην, ἀνωμότῳ δὲ καὶ τὰ
αὐτὰ βουλομένῳ· θεὸς μὲν γὰρ ἤθελεν εἶναι
δοκεῖν, ἐγὼ δὲ αὐτὸν οὐδὲ σπουδαῖον ἐνόμιζον
ἄνθρωπον, ᾧ γε ἦν ἡ σπουδὴ γελασθῆναι.
46. οὗτος πρὸ τῆς ἀρχῆς ἐν ἀγορᾷ καθήμενος
ᾔτησε παρὰ τῆς Τύχης εἰς τοσοῦτον τὴν ἀρχήν,
ἐν ὅσῳ γένοιτ' ἂν αὐτῷ κτεῖναι ἐμέ. λαβόντος

R 35
F 106

---

[a] For the riots between Orthodox and Arian Christians
in Constantinople in 342, cf. Socr. *H.E.* 2.12–13, Sozom.
H.E. 3.7. Libanius ignores the religious origin and transfers the trouble to the field of scholastic rivalry. Nicocles

opportunity afforded by popular riots,[a] when the proconsul fled wounded and gained the protection of the walls of Perinthus and the conspirators arrested any who were denounced to them and kept them clapped in jail as if the disturbances would last for ever. 45. When the rioters had regained their senses and the governor had returned, my confinement was clearly illegal. He let it be known that on the following day he intended to support the law and myself, and that the punishment he would inflict would be a severe one. They were all in a panic and beginning to make accusations one against another—when what did heaven dispose! About midnight Alexander was deposed from his office, and at daybreak control of the city was handed over to Limenius.[b] I would not go so far as to assert that he was a member of the conspiracy against me, but, even if he were not, his attitude was the same as theirs. He assumed the airs of the almighty, but I did not regard him seriously even as a man—his only serious aim was to play the fool. 46. Before taking up his office, he sat in the city square and prayed Fortune that his tenure would last at least long enough for him to be able to kill me. When he took control of

and the sophists may well have seized the opportunity to attack him; cf. *Letter* 23.2. Eunapius (*V.S.* 495) confines the accusation to one of pederasty, while dismissing it as groundless.

[b] For Limenius as proconsul of the city, cf. *Ep.* 206, *Letter* 23, *PLRE* 510 (2).

οὖν τὸ δικάζειν ἔμενον ὁ ταῦτα εἰδὼς ἐγὼ
πιστεύων εἶναί τι τἀληθές, τοῦ γραφομένου δὲ
οὐκ ὄντος νοῦν γε ἔχων. τῶν ὀμωμοκότων οἱ μὲν
ἐπαινοῦντες ἐκεῖνον λύσιν ἐμαντεύοντο τοῖς
δεδεμένοις, ὡς οὐκ ἂν ἐκείνου παραβάντος τὸν
περὶ ταῦτα νόμον, ὁ δὲ πρὸ τοῦ νόμου τοὺς
κολακεύοντας αἰδούμενος οὐ διώκοντα ὁρῶν, οὐ
φεύγοντα καλέσας ἀρχὴν ἐποιεῖτο τῆς κρίσεως
τοῦ ταλαιπώρου τὴν βάσανον, ἐν ᾗ πρῶτον
ἤκουσα βασανιστὰς ἀπειπεῖν.   47. πρίων δὴ
R 36 τοὺς ὀδόντας καὶ τοῦ γε δευτέρου σώματος
ἀποκρουσθεὶς ἀξιώματι, πῦρ ἠπείλει τῷ κατα-
τετμημένῳ φάσκων οὐ λήξειν πρὸ τῶν αὑτῷ
F 107 φίλων ῥημάτων. καὶ ἅμα ἐμοὶ διὰ τοῦ παρέδρου
παρῄνει πρὸς κέντρα μὴ λακτίζειν, ἀλλ᾿ ἀπελθεῖν εἰ μὴ θανατῴην. ἔδοξέ μοι πολλῆς ἀποπλη-
ξίας εἶναι τηνάλλως ἀποθανεῖν καὶ ταῦτα ἐπὶ
νίκῃ τῇ διὰ τῆς βασάνου.   48. προσπαρεκάλει
δέ με καὶ τὸ χείρονος ἄμεινον ἀντιλήψεσθαι
χωρίον, τὴν Νικομήδους πόλιν, λόγων τροφὸν
τῆς τρυφῇ βαρυνομένης. ὁ δὲ κἀκείνην ἔκλειέ
μοι γράμμασιν, οὐ μὴν εἰς ἅπαν· ἧκον γὰρ

the case, I stayed on, though I knew all this well enough, for I was confident that truth would prevail, and not without reason since there was none to indict me. The members of the cabal who approved of him were full of forebodings that the prisoners would be released, since he would not transgress the law on this matter, but he had more respect for his flatterers than for the law, and though he found no prosecutor and summoned no defendant, he set the case in motion with an examination by torture of the poor fellow, and it was here for the first time that I heard of the torturers giving up from sheer exhaustion.[a] 47. He gnashed his teeth in anger and, balked of a second victim by reason of my standing, he threatened the poor devil with death at the stake, swearing that he would never give up until he had got a statement that satisfied him. At the same time, he warned me, through his assistant, not to waste time resisting, but to be off if I wanted to save my skin. I thought it sheer lunacy to die to no purpose, especially after my triumph in the matter of the examination. 48. I had also received an invitation to change my position for the better, at Nicomedeia, and to exchange a city that was full of self-indulgence for one which was the nurse of eloquence. Through his dispatches he tried to bar me from there too, but he did not succeed entirely. I got

[a] Torture of the copyist produced no evidence for a charge against him, so intimidation follows. Date 343.

ἐκεῖσε διὰ τῆς Διονύσου. Νικαίας γὰρ οἱ οἰκήτορες ἐπειδὴ ᾔσθοντο τὴν ἔξοδον, πρεσβείαις παρ᾽
ἑαυτοὺς ἐκάλουν ἅπασιν ἐπαίνοις ἐν ψηφίσμασι
χρώμενοι. προσκυνήσας δὴ τὸν Διόνυσον εἰπόμην
καὶ αὖθις ὢν ἐν νέοις τε καὶ λόγοις ψηφίσμασιν
ἑτέροις ἐπὶ τὴν τῆς Δήμητρος ἠγόμην τοῦ τῶν Βιθυνῶν ἄρχοντος δεηθεῖσι χαριζομένου. 49. ἐδέοντο
δὲ οὐκ ἀπορίᾳ σοφιστοῦ· πολίτης γὰρ δὴ ἦν τις
σφίσι τῶν ἐπαινουμένων, ὁ δὲ λόγων μὲν οὐκ ἀπείρως εἶχε, θυμῷ δ᾽ ἐδούλευε καί ποτε τὴν βουλὴν
ἅπασαν δούλους τῶν αὑτοῦ πατέρων ἐτόλμησε
προσειπεῖν. τοῖς δὲ ὑπὲρ δίκης βουλευομένοις
καὶ ὅτῳ χρὴ τὸν ὑβριστὴν μετελθεῖν, ἀθανάτῳ
τις εἶπε κακῷ, ὡς τῶν γε ἄλλων οὐ μακρῶν
ἐσομένων· ἐρομένων δὲ τί τοῦτο εἴη τὸ ἀθάνατον
αὐτῷ κακόν, ἐμέ τε ἔφη καὶ τοὺς ἀπ᾽ ἐμοῦ τοῖς
ἀντιτέχνοις μόχθους. 50. ἐδεδίειν μὲν οὖν
μή με ἐντυχὼν δάκῃ, φυλαξάμενος δὲ λέγων
σιγῶντα ἐτρεψάμην ὄντα μὲν οὐδὲ πρότερον
ταχύν, ὀργῇ δὲ βραδύτερος ἐγεγόνει. τῷ δὲ ἄρα

R 37

F 108

---

[a] Dionysus was tutelary deity of Nicaea (*Letter* 153),
Demeter that of Nicomedeia. His tenure there was more
secure than in Nicaea, since it was based not merely upon

there by way of Nicaea, the city of Dionysus.[a] The inhabitants of Nicaea found out that I had left the capital, and sent envoys to invite me there, with all kinds of complimentary references in their decrees; so I paid my respects to Dionysus and went with them, and I was once more engaged with my students and my studies when, by another decree, I was invited to Demeter's city, Nicomedeia, the governor of Bithynia having graciously acceded to their request.   49. This request was not due to any lack of a teacher. One of their own citizens was a sophist of repute, by no means without skill in rhetoric, but the slave of a passionate temper, who was once so bold as to call the whole town council the slaves of his forefathers. They came to consider a fitting punishment and to decide how this scoundrel should be dealt with, and one member suggested that he be visited with endless woe, for none of the ordinary methods would last long enough. When they inquired what form this was to take, in answer he spoke of me and my labours against my rivals. 50. My fear was that at our first meeting he would do me harm, but I took precautions and by my speeches caused him to retire silenced, for though he had not been particularly smart before, his stupidity had increased because of his temper. So, in the end, after my arrival it paid him better to remain

decree of the curia but upon invitation of the governor (the vicar of Pontus) whose authority in his own diocese overrode any ban imposed by the proconsul.

κρεῖττον ἦν, ἐπειδὴ ἀφικόμην, σιγᾶν ἢ λέγειν οὐχ
ὡς οὐ καλὰ ὑφαίνοντι, δεῖ γὰρ τό γε ἀληθὲς
τιμᾶν, ἀλλ' αὑτῷ φόβους τινὰς ἐντεκών, ὡς δὴ
γοητεύοιτο, τοῖς δόγμασι τὴν μνήμην ἐξέπληττε
καὶ ἀπῄει πᾶν μὲν δρῶν, πᾶν δὲ φθεγγόμενος,
ὥστε ὑπ' ἀλλήλοις κρύπτεσθαι τῶν διαλυθέντων
πολλούς, μὴ ζέων ἔτι προσπεσών τῳ διαρπάσαι.

R 38   51. Τοῦτον ἐγὼ τὸν χρόνον, ἔστι δὲ ἔτη
πέντε, τοῦ παντὸς ὃν βεβίωκα, ταυτὶ δὲ σχεδὸν
ἑξήκοντα, ἔαρ ἢ ἄνθος προσειπὼν οὐδ' ἂν οὕτως
εἴην συμμέτρως προσειρηκώς. ἔχω μὲν γὰρ καὶ
ἕτερα πέντε καὶ πάλιν ἕτερα τοσαῦτα ἐπαινέσαι,
τὸ νικᾶν δὲ τούτων ἐστὶ τῶν ὑπὸ τῇ Δήμητρι,
νικώντων τοῖς ἅπασιν, ὑγιείᾳ σώματος, εὐθυμίᾳ
F 109 ψυχῆς, ἐπιδείξεων πυκνότητι, τοῖς ἐν ἑκάστῃ
πηδήμασιν, ὁρμαθοῖς νέων, ἐπιδόσει νέων, νυκτε-
ρινοῖς πόνοις, μεθημερινοῖς ἱδρῶσι, τιμαῖς, εὐνοίᾳ,
φίλτρῳ.   52. τῶν δ' <ἐκεῖ>[1] εἴ τις ἤρετο ὁντι-
νοῦν, ὅτῳ μεγίστῳ καλλωπίζοιτο ἡ πόλις, τὰς
ἐμὰς <ἂν> ἦν[2] ἐν αὐτῇ διατριβὰς ἀκοῦσαι.
ἐκείνη γὰρ αὖ ἡ πρὸς τοσοῦτον ἤκουσα μεγέθους
τε καὶ κάλλους τῶν τε ἄλλων ἀγαθῶν, ὅσα γῆ τε

[1] <ἐκεῖ> ins. Herwerden, F.

112

silent than to speak, though, to give the devil his due, this was not because of any inability of his to compose first rate stuff; but, because of hallucinations that he was bewitched, his memory was affected and off he would go, with all sorts of queer words and actions, so that many of his audience, after his lectures, would hide one behind another for fear that, while still in his frenzy, he would fall upon someone and rend him limb from limb.

51. If I called this five-year period the spring or flower of my life—and I am now nearly sixty[a]—I would not be quite correct, for I can speak as highly of another five-year period and yet another in my life. However, this time which I spent under Demeter's care in Nicomedeia excels them all, winning on every count—health of body and peace of mind, frequent declamations and excited applause at each of them, throngs of students and their progress, study by night and the sweat of my labours by day, honour, kindness and affection. 52. If anyone there were asked what was the city's proudest boast, the answer was that my declamations could be heard in it. Indeed, this town, which had grown to such size and beauty and possessed every other blessing provided by land and sea, in any recital of

[a] The first explicit indication of the date of composition of the original *Autobiography* in 374.

---

[2] ἀν <ἦν> Martin: ἀν Mss., Re.: ἦν F.

καὶ θάλασσα δίδωσιν, οὐδενὸς ἂν ἐν μνήμῃ μεγα-
λαυχίας πρὸ τῶν ἐμῶν ἐμνημόνευσεν, ἐπεὶ καὶ
R 39 πρὸς τὴν εὐδαιμονίαν τῆς πλησίον πόλεως τοῦτο
ἀντεξῆγεν, ὡς ἡ μὲν εὐθηνοῖτο θεάτρων ἡδοναῖς,
αὐτὴ δὲ φορᾷ παιδείας καὶ ὡς ἡ μὲν οὐδὲ φυλάξαι
παρὸν εἰδείη καλόν, αὐτὴ δὲ καὶ ἀπὸν κτήσασθαι. 53. ἐγὼ δὲ ἐῴκειν ἀνδρὶ κατακεκλιμένῳ
πρὸς πηγαῖς τε διαφανῶν ὑδάτων καὶ ὑπὸ δένδρων
παντοίας ὑπεραιωρούντων χάριτας ἐστεφανωμένῳ
τε καὶ συνεχῶς εὐωχουμένῳ κατὰ τὸν Αἰγύπτιον
ἐκεῖνον, ὃς ἐσοφίσατο μακρὸν αὑτῷ τὸν βραχὺν
γενέσθαι χρόνον. ἐποίει δέ μοι τὰς ἡδονὰς οὐ
τὸ ἐσθίειν καὶ πίνειν, τὸ δὲ τὰ τῶν λόγων εὖ καὶ
καλῶς χωρεῖν καὶ τὸ τὰς Ἀθήνας τῆς Βιθυνίας
καταβοᾶν, ὥσπερ γεωργοὶ γεωργῶν ῥύακος ἀρ-
χαίου κωλυθέντος ᾗ πρότερον ῥεῖν. οὕτω τὸν ἐκεῖσε
F 110 δρόμον τῶν νέων παλαιόν τε καὶ ἐξ ὅσουπερ ἐμ-
πορία λόγων, ἥδε ἔστησέ τε ἡ γῆ παρ᾽ αὑτῇ καὶ
ἔπεισε μὴ πόρρωθεν πονηρὰ λαμβάνειν ἐξὸν
ἐγγύθεν ἀμείνω. 54. καὶ μὴν ὅ γε ἀνὴρ ἐκεῖνος

---

[a] For his heartfelt loathing of Constantinople, see for
example, § 48 above, § 215 below.
[b] Mycerinus, cf. Herod. 2.133.

its glories would have prided itself on none of these in preference to my compositions: this was the comparison that it drew with the prosperity of Constantinople nearby,[a] that there they revelled in the delights of the stage, here, in Nicomedeia, in the fruits of learning; there they had not the wit to keep the good things they had, here they knew how to gain possession of those they had not.   53. I was like a man who laid himself down by streams of clear water beneath the pleasant shade of trees of every kind, garlanded and in continual junketing, like that Egyptian who devised a way whereby his short life should become a long one.[b] My pleasures were not those of eating and drinking, but arose from the excellent progress of my oratory and from the hue and cry that was set up at Athens against Bithynia, for all the world like some farmers complaining against others of their kind about the diversion of a watercourse from its original channel.[c] The flow of students to Athens, which was something of long standing and as old as the business of rhetoric itself, was stayed, and the province kept them to herself, persuading them not to go abroad to get inferior stuff when there was better to be found closer to home.   54. Moreover, my friend

[c] Eunapius (*V.S.* 495 f) preserves traces of these unfavourable comments. Proaeresius, his teacher, resented Libanius' success. Himerius had no reason to like him (*Ep.* 742), and Tuscianus of Lydia (*FHG* iv. *fr.* 25) was a hostile critic.

ὁ Ἡρακλεώτης σωροὺς ἐφ᾽ ἁμάξης ἧκεν ἄγων
βιβλίων, ποιῶν με οἷς ἐβουλόμην πλούσιον· ἐπεὶ
R 40 εἰ γῆν τε καὶ ὁλκάδας καὶ συνοικίας ἐδίδου, δοκῶ
μοι τὸν ἄνθρωπον ἂν ἐπαινέσας αὐτὸν κελεῦσαι
ἔχειν. οἷόν τι καὶ πρὸς ἐκεῖνον ἐποίησα τὸν ἐπὶ
δεῖπνόν τε ἅμα καὶ αὐτὴν τὴν θυγατέρα
καλοῦντα μόνην ἐν μεγάλοις αὐτῷ τρεφομένην
χρήμασι, τὴν μὲν γνώμην ἐπαινέσας, κελεύσας
δὲ ζητεῖν νυμφίον, ὡς ἔμοιγε οὔσης ἀντὶ γυναικὸς τῆς τέχνης.   55. περὶ ἣν οὕτω τὴν ἔν-
θεον ἐμεμήνει μανίαν ἡ Νικομήδους πόλις, ὥστε
ἤδη με κἂν ταῖς θερμαῖς κολυμβήθραις τἂν τῷ
διδασκαλείῳ ποιεῖν καὶ μηδὲ ταῦτα ἔξω τοῦ
νόμου τοῖς ἰδιώταις εἶναι δοκεῖν. οὕτως ἡμῖν
ἅπασα ἡ πόλις καθειστήκει μουσεῖον· οἵ γε καὶ
τοὺς προλόγους παραλαμβάνοντες, τἄλλα ἐκβάλ-
λοντες ᾄσματα, ᾄδοντες πανταχοῦ διετέλουν.
56. ἡ μεγίστη δὴ τῶν εἰς εὐφροσύνην ἀφορμὴ τὸ
σαφεῖς κεκτῆσθαι φίλους, ὧν οὐδὲν ὅ τι οὐ λείπε-
σθαι τῶν δοκούντων ἀγαθῶν ὁ Εὐριπίδης φησίν,
F 111 εἰδὼς ὅτι οὗτοι οἱ σαφεῖς οὐκ οὐσίας μόνον ἀπο-
σταῖεν ἂν ὑπὲρ τῶν ἐπιτηδείων ἀλλὰ κἂν ἀποθά-

---

[a] For Crispinus and his cartload of books, with inciden-

116

Crispinus from Heraclea came with a cartload of books and made me rich in what I most desired.[a] Had he offered land, ships, or villas, I would, I feel, have thanked him kindly and told him to keep them. Something of the sort I did do, even with him: he invited me to dinner to meet his only daughter whom he was bringing up in the lap of luxury, but I thanked him for the thought but told him to look elsewhere for a bridegroom: my bride was my art. 55. The city of Nicomedeia was by now visited with such inspired frenzy for it that I gave school lessons even in the swimming baths and this seemed nothing out of the ordinary to the average person. In this way the whole city had become my lecture room, as it were, and those who had learnt my prologues turned their backs upon other people's compositions, continually reciting mine everywhere.[b] 56. The greatest incentive towards happiness is the possession of firm friends. All the blessings a man can think of do not equal this, says Euripides,[c] for he knew that these firm friends would, for their comrades' sake, give up not just their possessions

tal echo of Philostr. *V.S.* 539, cf. Norman, *JHS* 80 (1960), 122 ff. The offer of marriage was refused since the engagement to his cousin, Phasganius' daughter, had already been arranged.

[b] A play on ἄσματα songs, and ᾄδειν rhetorical declamation.

[c] Eurip. *Or.* 1155; a favourite citation of Libanius, cf. *Letter* 24.

νοιεν, ὧν δὴ γενέσθαι καὶ τὸν τῆς Θέτιδος υἱόν,
ὃς ἐπρίατο τῆς ψυχῆς τὴν ὑπὲρ τοῦ Πατρόκλου
δίκην. ταύτης οὐδέν τι νωθροτέρας ἐνταῦθα ἐκ-
τησάμην φιλίας.   57. ὧν εἰ τὴν Ἀρισταινέτου
R 41 φαίην ὑπερφέρειν φιλίαν, οὐδένα ἂν νεμεσῆσαί
μοι δοκῶ τῶν τιθεμένων δευτέρων· ᾧ μοι καὶ ἡ
μήτηρ καὶ εἴ τῳ ἄλλῳ λύπην ἐνεποίουν ἀπών,
εἰκότως ἂν ἐγκαλοῖ. ἐκεῖνος γὰρ δὴ καὶ τὰ τοῦ
'κείνου τρόπου φάρμακα τῶν γλυκέων τούτων
ἐφάνη γλυκύτερα.

58. Καίτοι τίς φιλομήτωρ μᾶλλον ἐμοῦ;
τεκμηρίῳ δὲ μεγάλῳ τοῦτο ἀποδεικνύσθω. γῆν
οὖσάν μοι πατρῴαν ἀπέδοτο, ὁ δὲ ἐωνημένος ἐπ'
Ἰταλίας πορευόμενος δείσας μὴ παρακαλέσας
ὕστερον τὴν συμμαχίαν τῶν νόμων ἢ ζώσης τῆς
μητρὸς ἢ οἰχομένης ἐπιστρατεύσω τῇ πράσει,
λύειν ἤδη ταύτην ἢ βεβαιοῦν ἐδεῖτο. ἠρόμην οὖν
εἰ καὶ αὐτὸς ἐν τοῖς πεπραμένοις εἴην, ὡς οὐδὲ
τούτῳ μαχούμενος· καὶ ὃς τὸ βιβλίον προὔτεινεν
ὡς προσλάβοι ταυτησὶ τῆς χειρὸς γράμματα,

a Homer Il. 18.88 ff.
b For Aristaenetus, PLRE 104 (1).
c Cf. Or. 55.3.
d For the sale of the family property cf. § 26 above, Or.

but their very lives, as, for instance, Achilles, who secured vengeance for Patroclus at the cost of his own life.[a] In this town, I found friendships no less devoted than this.   57. And if I were to state that my friendship with Aristaenetus surpassed them all, none of those who play second fiddle would have held it against me, I am sure.[b] Both my mother and any other person who was pained by my absence would have reproached me on account of him, and with good reason, for he and the charm of his character were more potent than any charms of theirs.

58. For all that, there is no one fonder of his mother than I,[c] and let me demonstrate this with signal proof. She sold my family property,[d] and the purchaser, now on his way to Italy, was afraid that I would later invoke the aid of the law and attempt to invalidate the sale, either during my mother's lifetime or after her death. He asked me either to confirm or to deny the sale now. Well, I asked him whether I too was part and parcel of the items for sale; even so, I would not contest it. He proffered the document, to get my signature written by this,

11.9, 55.15. He was of curial family, but ridding himself of the land would distance him further from the risk of performing the liturgies and buttress the immunity he enjoyed as official sophist, cf. Petit, note *ad loc.* Why the buyer should demand his signature to a transaction already performed in due order is unclear. Possibly he saw it as an added guarantee in case Libanius should try to invalidate the sale later.

καὶ ἡ μὲν ἔγραφεν, ὁ δὲ οἷς ἑώρα διηπίστει.

F 112   59. δεινὰ δὴ δοκῶν ἐμαυτῷ δρᾶν εἰ τὴν οὕτω
R 42 στεργομένην μὴ συνὼν γηροτροφοίην, ὁπότε
ἀκούοιμι φθεγγομένου τοῦ φίλου, δεσμὸς τοῦτο ἦν,
ὥστε καὶ ἡνίκα δεῦρ’ ἐπανήειν, ἐπὶ μόναις ταῖς
παρ’ ἐκείνου τοῦτο ἐπράττετο ἀνάγκαις ἀπει-
λοῦντος ἦ μὴν χείρω με, εἰ τοῦτο[1] ἀτιμάσαιμι
τὸ δίκαιον, νομιεῖν.

60. Πλείοσι τοίνυν καὶ μείζοσιν ἀγαθοῖς τὰ
δυσχερέστερα ἠφάνιζεν ἡ Τύχη, καὶ ἡ λύπη
μικρὰ διὰ τὸ πλῆθος ἦν τῶν ἡδονῶν, μᾶλλον δὲ
οὐδὲν τοσοῦτον ὁπόσον καὶ ἀνιᾶσαι δύνασθαι,
ὥσπερ αὖ καὶ τοῖς ἀριστεύουσιν ἃ πλήττονται
κοῦφα διὰ μέγεθος ὧν δρῶσι. λεγέσθω οὖν καὶ
τὰ χείρω· τῇδε γὰρ ἂν καθαρώτερον φανείη τὰ
βελτίω δεικνυμένων τῶν ὑπ’ αὐτῶν νενικη-
μένων.

61. Ὁ μὲν δὴ παῖς ἄνηβος ἐλπίσιν ἀπατηθεὶς
ὑπὸ τῶν οὓς ἀναπείθουσιν ἀποκτιννύντων πεντα-
κοσίους τε καὶ χιλίους ὑφελόμενος στατῆρας
ᾤχετο, ὡς εἰκός, ἀποθανούμενος μέλλοντός μοι
R 43 δέξεσθαι τοῦ ἄρχοντος λόγον, καὶ ἐπεδεικνύ-
μην κινούμενος τὰ εἰωθότα τῶν ἀκροατῶν τῇ

___
[1] τοῦτο Mss., Martin: τούτῳ F.

my hand, and I signed it—and he could hardly believe his eyes.   59. I felt that I was being most remiss not to attend and support so loving a mother in her old age, but whenever I heard my friend's voice, it was a chain that bound me. Finally, even when I did come home, it was only under compulsion from him, for he swore that he would think the worse of me if I so disregarded what was right and proper.

60. Fortune, then, banished sorrow by the provision of more and bigger blessings. My troubles were small because of my many pleasures; in fact, nothing was enough to cause me distress, just as, with great champions, their mishaps seem mere nothings because of the greatness of their achievements. So let me mention my misfortunes, for good fortune can be more clearly revealed so, if there is an account of what it has overcome.

61. My slave, a mere lad, beguiled by men who murder those they lead astray, decamped, perhaps to his death, taking 1,500 staters with him.[a] I was on the point of delivering an oration before the governor, and though my audience was greatly disturbed by the theft, I proceeded to give my declamation in my customary manner of delivery, so that I

[a] Collusion between slaves and local bandit gangs was common enough. No less so the killing by the gangsters of such collaborators once they had served their purpose. For staters = *solidi,* cf. *Letter* 46 note.

κλοπῇ τεταραγμένων, ὥστε εἶναί μοι διπλοῦν τὰ
θαῦμα, τὸ μὲν ὡς λέγειν ἐπισταμένῳ, τὸ δὲ ὡς τὰ
τοιαῦτα φέρειν· καὶ τρίτον γε ἕτερον προσεγεγό-
νει διωθουμένου μου τὸν ἠθροισμένον ἐκ τῶν πόλεων

F 113 ἄργυρον παριόντα τὸν ἐξεληλυθότα χρυσὸν θεραπεύειν πειρωμένων τοῖς παρὰ σφῶν τὴν βλάβην.

62. Ταυτὶ μὲν ἀφείσθω τὴν ζημίαν ἔχοντα ἐν
χρήμασιν, ἃ δὴ διαπτύσειεν ἂν ἀνὴρ ἐλεύθερος.
ἀλλ᾽ ἐνόσει μὲν ἡ γυνὴ τῷ σοφιστῇ τὰς φρένας,
ὁ δὲ οὐ βουλόμενος ταῦτ᾽ εἶναι τῆς τοῦ σώματος
πονηρίας ἐπ᾽ ἐμέ τε ἦγε τὴν αἰτίαν καὶ κακοῖς
ἑπόμενος παραδείγμασι βιβλιογράφον καὶ αὐτὸς
εἷλκε καὶ οἰχομένης δὴ τῆς γυναικὸς ἀπὸ τοῦ
τάφου μετὰ δακρύων εἰς τὸ δικαστήριον ἐλθὼν
κατήγορος μὲν κατὰ τοὺς νόμους οὐδὲ οὕτως
γίνεται, τοσοῦτον δὲ εὗρε, τὸ δῆσαι τὸν ἄνθρω-

R 44 πον. 63. ἐπὶ τούτοις τὸ πρᾶγμα ἀνέστραπτο
τοῦ μὲν φεύγοντος τὴν κρίσιν, ἐμοῦ δὲ ἐπανα-
γκάζοντος. ὁ δικαστὴς δὲ ἄρα ἐγέλα, εἰ περὶ
γυναῖκα ἐγὼ παρανήλισκον τὸν θάνατον ὑπερβὰς
τὸν σοφιστήν, ὥσπερ ἂν εἴ τις ἀθλητὴς κτεῖναι
ἔχων τὸν ἀντίπαλον τούτῳ μὲν ᾐδεῖτο[1] συμ-

---

[1] ᾐδεῖτο conj. Schenkl, Norman: ᾐρνεῖτο Par. 3016, C
corr., F.: ᾑρεῖτο CPVL, Re.: ᾑρεῖτο <μὴ> Martin.

gave cause for wonder on two counts, by my ability in oratory and by enduring such a loss with equanimity. There was yet a third reason for wonder, for I refused the collection of money made from the cities who tried to repair my loss by their contributions, which exceeded the amount of money stolen.

62. So much for that and the financial loss it involved. A man of breeding would think nothing of it. However, the professor's[a] wife began to suffer from mental illness, and he, refusing to believe that this was due to any physical ailment, tried to pin the blame on to me and, following bad example, he too tried to have my copyist examined. Upon his wife's death, he left her grave in tears and entered the court, but even so his accusation was not presented in any legal form; his sole recourse was to have the man arrested.[b]   63. Consequently, the roles were reversed; he tried to avoid a trial and I insisted that it be held.[c] The governor was amused at the idea that I, having got the better of the professor, should now go to the length of procuring his wife's death; it was just as absurd as for an athlete, who had it in his power to kill his opponent, to refuse to engage

[a] The sophist of § 49 f.

[b] Cf. §§ 43 ff above. The sophist accuses Libanius of magic as a result of his success, and to get proof has the copyist arrested for examination.

[c] Libanius counters by citing *Codex Theodos.* 9.1.7 which required prompt examination of the detainee.

πλέκεσθαι καὶ διέσωζε, τὴν τεκοῦσαν δὲ αὐτὸν
ἥρπαζε διὰ δαιμόνων. τῷ μὲν δὴ ἔργον ἦν φεύγειν, ὁ δικαστὴς δέ, οὐδὲ γὰρ ἀνίην, εἷλκέ τε διὰ
τῶν ὑπηρετῶν καὶ ἐπηνάγκαζεν ἢ λαβεῖν ἢ δοῦναι δίκην, τὸν γὰρ αὖ νόμον οὐκ ἐᾶν κεναῖς αἰτίαις ὑβρίζειν. ὁ δὲ πεσὼν ἱκέτευε μὴ ἄτιμος
F 114 ἀπελθεῖν μηδὲ αὑτοῦ μᾶλλον ἢ τοῦ πένθους
ἐκεῖνα νομισθῆναι.   64. ἐλεεῖ τὸν σοφιστὴν ὁ
δικαστής, καὶ οὐκ ἐμεμψάμην τὸν οἶκτον· ἐμοὶ
γὰρ εἴη τὸν ἐχθρὸν εἰς συγγνώμην καταφεύγοντα
R 45 ἰδεῖν καὶ οὐδὲν ἂν ἑτέρας δέοι δίκης, καὶ δὴ καὶ
φίλον εἶναι βουλόμενον οὐκ ἀτιμάσω· ὅστις δὲ
αἰσχυνόμενον τὸν ἡμαρτηκότα ὁρῶν προσαπολέ-
σαι βούλοιτ' ἄν, θηριώδης τε οὗτος καὶ οὐκ αἰσθανόμενος, ὡς ἀνθρώπῳ γε ὄντι γένοιτ' ἄν ποτε
ἴσως εἰς τὴν τῶν ὁμοίων χρείαν πεσεῖν. ἀλλ'
οὐχ οἱ Βιθυνοὶ πρὸς ἐκεῖνον οὕτως, ἀλλ' ὁ μὲν
ἀπαντῶν ἐξετρέπετ' ἄν, τῷ δὲ πρόνοια μὴ
ἀπαντῆσαι, τὸ δὲ μὴ κεκολάσθαι τοῖς προσήκουσι
τὸν ὑβριστὴν ἤδη τινά τι καὶ ἀπορρῖψαι εἰς
τὸν ἐψηφισμένον καίτοι σφόδρα ἀγαπώμενον
ἠνάγκασε.   65. πιεζόμενος δὴ πολλαχόθεν καὶ
οὐκ ἀποχρώντων οἱ τῶν λόγων ἄλλως τε καὶ τοῦ

124

and to let him go, and then to try to do away with
the fellow's mother by means of magic. He did his
best to escape, but the governor[a] had him fetched by
his attendants, since I maintained my stand, and
gave him the alternative of proving me guilty or
being found guilty himself, for the law forbade the
ill-treatment of anyone on baseless charges. He fell
on his knees and besought that he should not be
dismissed in disgrace, for his grief was to be
regarded as the cause of all this, not he.   64. The
governor took pity on him, and I could not blame
him for it, for I could ever wish to see my enemy
throwing himself on the mercy of the court, with no
need for any other punishment; indeed, I will not
refuse him if he wishes to become my friend, for any
man who sees a sinner shamed and yet wants him
done away with, is a mere brute and without the wit
to realize that he is only human and may sometime
perhaps be brought to such a pass himself. Not so
the Bithynians in their attitude towards him: they
would either get out of his way if they met him, or
take good care not to meet him at all, and the fact
that my assailant suffered no condign punishment
caused people to inveigh against the magistrate who
had given such a decision, even though he was very
popular.   65. So he was crushed completely: his
eloquence availed him nothing, especially as his

[a] Pompeianus, *consularis Bithyniae* 343–348 (cf. *Ep.*
742, *PLRE* 712 (3)) has the accuser arrested to reveal his
proofs (*Codex Theodos.* 9.39.1). The case collapses.

τρόπου προσδιαβεβλημένου τρέπεται ἐπ' ὠνὴν
τῶν νέων, χρημάτων οὐ φειδόμενος πολλῶν οἱ
προσιόντων ἐκ γῆς· οἱ δὲ δέχονται μὲν τὸ διδό-
μενον, σφᾶς δὲ αὐτοὺς οὐ προΐενται, ἀλλ' εἰς

R 46 μέσον τε τὸ ἀπόρρητον ἤγετο καὶ γέλως διὰ τῆς
πόλεως ἐχώρει, οἷα μὲν ἐμεμηχάνητο, οἷα δὲ ἤλ-

F 115 πισεν, οἷα δὲ ἐπεπόνθει. 66. ὡς δὲ αὐτῷ
μόνος Βιθυνῶν συνελάμβανεν ἀνὴρ εἰς ὅ τι ὁρμή-
σειεν ἀπαύστῳ φιλονεικίᾳ χρώμενος φήσας ἐν τῷ
περὶ τουτωνὶ τῶν δώρων λόγῳ τε καὶ ἐλέγχῳ
καὶ γέλωτι μηδὲ τὸ τῆς αὑτοῦ γυναικὸς ὄνομα
σεσιγῆσθαι ὡς δὴ τοῦ τε ἔργου κεκοινωνηκυίας
τῶν τε ἀνηλωμένων, ἐπὶ ζεῦγος ὁρικὸν ἀναβὰς
ἤλαυνεν ἐπὶ Καππαδοκίας παρὰ ἄρχοντα φίλον
εἰδότα χάριτι βλάψαι νόμον, νέω δὲ ἄρα τώδε
πάντα ἀλλήλοιν Ἀθήνησι κεχαρισμένω διὰ
τέλους ἔμελλον τοῦτο ποιεῖν. ὁ δὲ παρασκευῆς
τε αὐτὸν τῆς πρὸς τὸν Περσικὸν πόλεμον ὃς τότε
ἦν, ἑτέρων τε προμηθείας οὐ μείονος ἀξίων
μένειν ἀναγκαζόντων πάντα τὰ μέγιστα μικρὰ

---

[a] For the purchase of pupils by cash cf. Themist. *Or.*
23.290c, and by more dubious offers, Eunap. *V.S.* 490. Cf.
Petit, *Étudiants,* pp. 103 f. For a similar trick played by
Libanius' students in Antioch, cf. *Letter* 85.

general behaviour was held in disrepute. Hence, he had recourse to buying his pupils[a] and spared none of the great wealth that came from his estates, but though they took all he offered, they did not entrust themselves to him. The cat was let out of the bag, and he became a laughing-stock throughout the city because of his trickery, his high hopes, and his disappointment. 66. There was only one Bithynian to take his part, a man of unquenchable rancour in all his undertakings. He alleged that, in the gossip, the inquiries, and the ridicule that arose from these gifts, his wife's name had been bandied about too as a participant in this business and in the bribery.[b] Into his travelling carriage he got and set off for Cappadocia, to his friend the governor, who was quite capable of obliging him by flouting the law, for these two had been students together in Athens and had done each other all kinds of good turns and probably continued to do so thereafter. Though the preparations for the Persian war, which occurred then,[c] and other duties no less deserving of consideration ought to have induced him to stay

[b] The Bithynian *principalis,* in collusion with the sophist, revives the charge of treason by magic, and has recourse to a superior official, Philagrius, vicar of Pontus 348–350 (*PLRE* 694 (5)). His headquarters were at Nicaea, where the accused were transported.

[c] The Persian War and the battle of Singara, 348.

127

LIBANIUS

ἡγησάμενος ἀναστὰς ἐφέρετο γυμνῷ τῷ ξίφει προπέμψας στρατιώτην, ᾧ χρῆν με εἰς Νίκαιαν ἕπεσθαι, τῶν νέων ἄγοντα ἑπτὰ τοὺς ὅτι μὴ σφᾶς αὐτοὺς ἀπέδοντο ἠδικηκότας. 67. Νικομηδεῖς μὲν οὖν ἡμᾶς ἔτι ζῶντας ἐπένθουν, ὥσπερ οὓς εἰς τὸν Λαβύρινθον ἔπεμπον Ἀθηναῖοι.

R 47 σωτὴρ δὲ ἄρα ἡμῖν ἔμελλε τῆς Τύχης βουλομένης Ἡρακλῆς ὁ Διὸς ἔσεσθαι καὶ προὐδήλου γε ὃ ποιήσει καὶ ὡς σβέσει τὴν πυράν, ὀνείρατι· πυρὰν γὰρ δὴ μεγάλην ἐν μέσῃ τῇ Νικαίᾳ τῶν τινα Ἀντισθένους μιμητῶν ἐδόκουν ἐφιζάνοντα σβεννύειν καὶ εἶναι κρεῖττον τοῦ πυρὸς τὸ σῶμα.

F 116 θαρρῶν δὴ τοῖς τε ἀπὸ τῆς ἀληθείας τῇ τε ἐπαγγελίᾳ τῆς ἐπικουρίας ᾖειν· οἱ συνήγοροι δὲ ἡμῖν μέχρι Λίβου μὲν ἧκον, αὐτοῦ δὲ καταδύντες ἀπεσκόπουν ὅπη τὸ πρᾶγμα πεσεῖται, καὶ ἀναφανέντες ἐπὶ τῷ τέλει συνέχαιρον, ὥσπερ οἱ Λακεδαιμόνιοι μετὰ τὴν ἐν Μαραθῶνι μάχην τοῖς Ἀθηναίοις. 68. ἦν δὲ ἄρα κἀκεῖνο Ἡρακλέους τὸ ἔργον, ὃς καὶ ἡμῖν τὸ νέφος ἀπέωσεν·

---

a Obscure. Reiske suggested that Libanius' friend, the sophist Alcimus, had Cynic connections; hence the reference to Antisthenes. As he is also dubbed θεοῦ τινος παῖδα (68), there seems to be a play on names Alcimus/Alcides,

128

where he was, the governor thought all important matters to be mere incidentals; so he got up and came along with bared blade, sending in advance a soldier whom I had to follow to Nicaea with seven youths whose crime was that they had not sold themselves.   67. So the people of Nicomedeia gave us up for dead, as the Athenians did those whom they sent to Labyrinth. However, under the guidance of Fortune, my saviour was destined to be Heracles, son of Zeus, who in a dream revealed to me what he would do and how he would quench the funeral flame;[a] for I dreamed that a disciple of the Cynic Antisthenes mounted a great pyre in the centre of Nicaea and quenched it, and that his body prevailed over the fire. So I went on, heartened by this revelation of truth and the tidings of help. My advocates went as far as Libon, but there they went to ground and watched the outcome of the affair from afar, and when it was all over they emerged to offer their congratulations, as the Spartans did to the Athenians after the battle of Marathon.[b] 68. Yes, that too was a labour of Heracles, and he brought me also from out of the shadow:[c] the

with reference to the saving grace of Heracles. The presence of Alcimus (*PLRE* 38) thus links both aspects in the dream.

[b] Herod. 6.120.

[c] Homer *Il.* 15.668.

ᾖδον μὲν γὰρ ἀλεκτρυόνες καὶ ἐκήρυττον οἱ
κήρυκες, ἐκρούετο δὲ ἡ θύρα καὶ ὅτῳ μέλει τῶν
τοιούτων, ἐβόα καταβαίνειν. ἐκαθήμεθ᾽ οὖν ἐν

R 48 μυροπωλίῳ τινὶ τὸν καιρὸν ἀναμένοντες Ἀλκιμός
τε καὶ ἐγώ (τὸν Ἄλκιμον τοῦτον θεοῦ τινος ἔγωγε
παῖδα ἡγοῦμαι γεγονέναι, μὴ γὰρ ἂν ἐξ ἀνδρὸς
φῦναι τοιοῦτον). σμικρὸν δὴ πρὸ μεσημβρίας
οὐδενὶ κόσμῳ κεκραγὼς ὁ συκοφάντης ἔστειχεν
ἡμιμανὴς κεκρατῆσθαι τῇ βαφῇ καὶ Φιλάγριον
λέγων, ἡμῖν γε οὐ συνετὰ λέγων. 69. καὶ αὐτίκα
ὁ δικαστὴς ἐξῄει, καὶ φαιδροὺς ἑωρῶμεν τοὺς
φίλους ὡς δὴ ἐπ᾽ ἀγαθῷ τῳ, τουτὶ δὲ ὅ τί τε ἦν

F 117 ὅτῳ τε τρόπῳ συμβάν, εἰδέναι οὐκ ἦν, πρὶν δή
τις τῶν ἡμῖν εὔνων πόρρωθεν ἐσήμηνε τῇ χειρὶ
τὸν πολέμιον πεφευγέναι, τῷ δικαστῇ γὰρ
ἀνάγκην ἐξαίφνης τῆς τοῦ νόμου φυλακῆς ἐπι-
πεσεῖν· ἐγνωκότι γὰρ ἐπὶ πρόδηλον εἰσάγειν

R 49 σφαγὴν ἥκειν τινὰ ἄγγελον τῆς Φιλίππου κινή-
σεως καὶ δεῖν ἤδη θεῖν καὶ δέχεσθαι τοῖς ὅροις
τὴν βλοσυρὰν ἀρχήν· καὶ τὸν δείσαντα εἰπεῖν
ἀπολωλέναι τὸν καιρὸν τῇ χάριτι καὶ εἶναι τοῦ

---

a Perfumers, doctors, and barbers, all near the centre of

cocks were crowing and the criers were crying
when there came a knocking at the door and our
jailer shouted to us to come down. Alcimus and I
were lodged in a perfumer's shop awaiting our turn.[a]
This Alcimus, by the way, had something divine
about him, I am sure; such a man could never have
been sired by mortal man. Well, just before noon,
that rascal of an accuser dashed in distraught and
howling that Philagrius too was tarred with the
same brush, an incomprehensible remark as far
as we were concerned.[b] 69. The governor left
immediately, and we saw our friends all smiles, as
though at some fortunate event. Of the nature and
manner of it we had not the slightest idea until one
of our friends gestured to us from a distance that
our enemy had fled, for the governor had suddenly
been confronted with the need to maintain the law.
He had made up his mind to disclose a charge of
murder against me when news arrived of Philippus'
tour of inspection, and he had to go off in a hurry to
receive his grim overlord into his diocese:[c] in a
panic he declared that the time for favours was past

town, were handy for the court room (cf. *Or.* 51.10, Plaut.
Amph. 1011).

[b] The accuser presents his case, is dismissed, and pro-
tests that Philagrius has fallen victim to Libanius' magic.

[c] Philippus, Praetorian Prefect of the East and consul
348 (*PLRE* (7) 696 f), then on tour of inspection, which
required Philagrius' attendance, thus closing the case.

νόμου τὸ κράτος. δεῖν οὖν ἢ γραφὴν ἀπενεγκεῖν
ἢ μὴ ἀγανακτεῖν ὑπὸ ἀνάγκης νικώμενον. διὰ
ταῦτα ἐκεῖνον μεμνῆσθαι τῆς βαφῆς ὡς δὴ μετα-
πεπεισμένου.   70. καὶ ὁ μὲν ὃν θυμὸν κατέδων
ᾤχετο οἴκαδε στένων, ὁ δὲ οἷς ἔδωκεν ἂν ἐρυθριῶν[1] καλέσας ἐμὲ καὶ παρ' αὐτὸν καθίσας ἐν
τῷ δικαστηρίῳ τρίβων τῇ χειρὶ τὸ πρόσωπον διασύρων τε τοὺς ὑπὲρ τοῦ σοφιστοῦ παρὰ τοῦ φίλου
R 50   λόγους ἠξίου με πρᾴως τε ἔχειν τῇ παρ' αὐτὸν
ὁδῷ καὶ μηδὲν οἴεσθαι τῶν πεπραγμένων πεπρᾶ-
χθαι. φήσαντος δέ μου καὶ πρὸ τῶν αὐτοῦ λόγων
ὧδε ἔχειν πίστιν ἀπῄτει τῶν εἰρημένων, εἶναι δὲ
πίστιν, εἰ ποιησαίμην αὐτὸν ἀκροατὴν ἐν μέσοις
Νικομηδεῦσι λόγου τινός. 'καίτοι ὅ γε Φίλιππος,' ἔφη, 'καλεῖ, ταυτὶ δὲ ὅμως προτετιμήσθω.'
71. νεύω καὶ ὑπισχνοῦμαι, καὶ ἦμεν ἐν τῇ Νικομήδους καὶ εἰσῆγον τὴν ἐπίδειξιν. ἔπειτα ἦκέ
F 118   ποθεν, ὥσπερ πνεῦμα, ὁ συκοφάντης ἄγων τὸν
ὑπόπτην ἐκεῖνον καὶ ἔφασκε δεῖν τὸν ἐκείνου
φθάσαι λόγον, πρὶν ὑπὸ κρότου πολλοῦ κατα-
ληφθῆναι τὸν δικαστήν. ὁ μὲν οὖν ἤσχαλλεν,
ἐγὼ δὲ συνεχώρουν. ὁ δὲ εἰσελθὼν ἦν <ὁ>[2]

---

[1] ἂν ἐρυθριῶν Mss., Martin: ἀνερυθριῶν conj. F.
[2] <ὁ> conj. F., Martin.

and the law must prevail: he must either hand in his charge in proper form or reconcile himself to being a victim of necessity. Hence the expression 'being tarred with the same brush,' to explain his sudden change. 70. So my accuser went off home despondently, 'eating his heart out,'[a] while the governor, all blushes for the favour he would have granted, summoned me to him, sat me down by his side in court, wiped his hand across his brow and tried to make light of his friend's remarks on the professor's behalf. He begged me not to be annoyed at my coming to him and to think of the whole incident as though it had never happened. I replied that such was my reaction even before he had begun to speak, but he asked for some guarantee of my words, namely, that I should allow him to attend an oration of mine in the heart of Nicomedeia. 'Philippus summons me, to be sure,' he exclaimed, 'but let this have precedence.' 71. I consented and gave my promise, and there in Nicomedeia I was just introducing my declamation, when my accuser entered like an ill wind with that jealous rival of mine, and asserted that his oration ought to precede mine, before the governor was beguiled by the roars of applause. Though the governor was put out, I was agreeable, and so he entered, but behaved like his usual self although he spoke before an audience of

[a] Homer *Il.* 6.202.

αὐτὸς καίτοι γε λέγων ἐν πεντεκαίδεκα ἀνθρώ-
R 51 ποις αὐτὸς δεηθεὶς τὴν ἐμὴν ἀπεῖναι μερίδα. ὡς
γὰρ εἶδε τὸ στάδιον, ἰλιγγιάσας ἐξενήνεκτο τῆς
μνήμης καὶ ἐβόα μηδὲ τότε πεπαῦσθαι τὸν
γόητα ἐμέ· τοῦ δὲ ἀναγνῶναι κελεύοντος, εἰσελθεῖν γὰρ λόγον, οὐ μνήμην κρίνων, οὐδὲ τοὺς
ὀφθαλμοὺς ἔφη δύνασθαι τὸ αὑτῶν ὑπὸ τοῦ αὐτοῦ
ποιεῖν. 'ἀλλ' ὁ δεῖνα λαβὼν ἀναγνώσεται,' δείξας τῶν ῥητόρων τὸν ἄριστον. ὁ δὲ ὡς τοῦτο
ἤκουσε, ῥίψας τὸ βιβλίον ἀπῄει πιμπλὰς τὴν
ἀγορὰν ἀνοήτων ῥημάτων.   72. τῆς δὲ ὑστεραίας ὁ μὲν ὄχλος ἐν τῷ βουλευτηρίῳ, τοῦ δὲ
ἐγγὺς ἐγὼ τὴν φωνὴν ἀνακινῶν τε καὶ ἀποπει-
ρώμενος, ὁ δὲ ἄρχων περὶ ἔξοδον, ὁ δὲ αἴσχιστα
ἀπηλλαχὼς ἐκεῖνος ἐξ ἀκροπόλεως ἐπὶ τὸ σῶμα
τοὐμὸν ὡπλισμένος παρῆν, καὶ ἐμὲ μὲν αἱ θύραι
ῥύονται τοῦ νεὼ τῆς Τύχης, οὗπερ καὶ ἐκαθήμην.
τὸν ἄρχοντα δὲ καὶ πρὸ τῶν λόγων τῇ 'κείνου
R 52 τόλμῃ κτῶμαι, καὶ σὺν εὐνοίᾳ μὲν εἰσέρχεται,
γενόμενος δὲ ἐραστὴς ἀνίσταται καὶ παραχρῆμα
F 119 γράμμασι συγγενεῖς τε οἳ αὐτῷ παρ' ἄλλοις
διέτριβον φίλων τε παῖδας εἰς ἓν τοῦτο διδασκα-

---

[a] As official sophist he was to lecture in the Town Hall,

but fifteen, having himself requested the with-drawal of my supporters. As soon as he saw the course before him, he grew dizzy and his memory failed him, and he exclaimed that I, the sorcerer, had not even then stopped my tricks. The governor told him to read then; he had come to judge a speech, not a test of memory. His reply was that his eyes could not do their job, either, and for the same reason. 'Then he shall take it and read it,' said the governor, pointing out the best speaker present. On hearing this, he threw aside his script and made off, filling the square with meaningless cries.

72. Next day while the crowd was assembling in the town hall,[a] and I was exercising my voice and testing it nearby, the governor was just about to leave his headquarters, when that madman, who had fled in disgrace, came from the citadel armed against my person. I was saved by the doors of the temple of Fortune where I was seated. Even before my speech I had the governor on my side because of this mad attempt, and he made his entry well disposed towards me. When he rose to leave, he was one of my devoted admirers, and immediately he sent out letters and collected his relatives, who happened to be studying under others, and the sons of his friends, and brought them to my school, and mine

and was practising in the *Tychaeum* (also used for scholas-tic purposes in Antioch, *Letter* 45; cf. §102 below for the use of temples by teachers). The charge of magic is finally ended.

λεῖον ἤθροιζε τῷ λόγῳ τε ὃν ἠκηκόει συνῆν αἰτήσας τε καὶ λαβών, τῷ συκοφάντῃ τε οἵαν οὐχ
ἑτέραν ὀφείλειν ἔλεγε χάριν γνῶναι δόντι ταῦτα
ἃ ἀγνοεῖν ζημία.

73. Ὧν λεγομένων τε καὶ πραττομένων φερο-
μένης τε εἰς ἐκείνους παρ' ὧν ἀπεληλύθειν τῆς
φήμης, οἳ οὐχ ὅτι τὰ ἄστη, ἀλλὰ καὶ τοὺς σμι-
κροτάτους τῶν ἀγρῶν ἀβάτους ᾤοντό μοι ταῖς
διαβολαῖς ἐργάζεσθαι, τίς Τέλλος, τίνες Ἀργεῖοι
νεανίσκοι διὰ τῶν περὶ τὴν ἅμαξαν τῇ μητρὶ
κεχαρισμένοι, τῇ σφῶν αὐτῶν τὴν ἐμὴν εὐδαιμονίαν παρῄεσαν; ὥστε μοι δοκῶ καὶ τῆς αἰτίας ἣν
R 53   ἐπὶ τῇ γενέσει τούτων ᾐτιασάμην τὴν Τύχην
ἀφήσειν τὴν θεόν, εἴπερ ἐκ τῆς βασάνου ταῦτα.
οὐδὲ γὰρ Μέλανθος δήπουθεν ἠτύχει φεύγων
μέλλων ἀντὶ τοῦ Μεσσήνην οἰκεῖν βασιλεύειν
Ἀθηνῶν.

74. Ηὐξημένης δὴ τῆς δόξης μυρίων τε ἡμᾶς
ἐπαινούντων στομάτων ὄντων τε τῶν καὶ τοῦτο
λεγόντων, ὡς συνείην ἀνθρώποις οὓς ἐξέβαλεν ἂν
κατὰ τὸν Ἀρχιλόχου φονέα τοῖς χρησμοῖς ὁ Πύ-

---

[a] Herod. 1.30–31.
[b] Herod. 5.65.
[c] A proverbial reference to the murderers of Archi-

alone. He attended the oration he had heard—a favour which he requested and received, and he declared that he owed an unparalleled debt of gratitude to my accuser for the chance to get to know my work: without it, he would have been so much the poorer.

73. The report of these orations and occurrences reached those from whom I had fled and who thought that by their calumnies they made it impossible for me to live in towns or even in the tiniest villages. Could Tellus or those Argive youths, who blessed their mother by their exploit with the carriage,[a] have had greater happiness than I? I am tempted to absolve Fortune of the charge I levelled against her for causing all this, if such are the results of putting her to the test. Certainly, Melanthus was not unlucky in his exile, since it was destined that instead of being a dweller in Messene he should be ruler of Athens.[b]

74. My reputation had increased and countless were the tongues that praised me, though there were some who asserted that I associated with people whom Apollo would have deemed unworthy— as in his oracle he rejected the murderer of Archilochus.[c] The blameless importuned those who

lochus (Suidas *s.v.*) is regularly applied to the heinous criminal; cf. *Or.* 15.65, *Decl.* 1.180. These critics are extreme pagans, offended by his good relations with Christian potentates at court resulting from his recent panegyric on Constantius and Constans (*Or.* 59).

F 120 θιος, ἐπικειμένων τε τῶν ἔξω τῆς αἰτίας τοῖς ἐν
αὐτῇ γίνονται πρὸς τὸν ὕπαρχον ἱκετεῖαι τῆς
ἐμῆς ἀποδόσεως πέρι· ὡς δὲ ἀδικήσειν τοὺς ὑπο-
δεξαμένους ἔφην καὶ ἅμα ἐδεόμην μή με αὖθις
ἐμβαλεῖν εἰς ἀηδῆ σιγήν, ἀπελθὼν ὡς δὴ οὐκ
R 54 ἐπαναγκάσων, ἀνάγκῃ μεταφέρει μείζονι, βασιλείοις γράμμασιν.   75. ἐγὼ μὲν δὴ τὴν τῶν
αἰχμαλώτων ἐλυπούμην λύπην, οἳ πατρίδα καὶ
ἐλευθερίαν ἀποβαλόντες ἔρχονται ἐν ἀλλοτρίᾳ
δουλεύσοντες. καὶ ἐμὲ τοίνυν κατελάμβανε τὸ
τῶν μὲν ἡδίστων τε καὶ λυσιτελεστάτων στέρε-
σθαι, εἰς δὲ τὰ ἀνιάσοντά τε καὶ ζημιώσοντα
ἄγεσθαι· χρῆν γὰρ δὴ ἢ συμπίνειν τοῖς δυνατοῖς
καὶ περὶ τραπέζας ἡμέρας τε καὶ νυκτὸς διατρίβειν τὸ πλέον ἢ ἐχθρόν τε κεκρίσθαι καὶ πολεμεῖ-
σθαι. ταυτὶ δὲ ὡς ἐναντιώτατα τοῖς τῆς ψυχῆς
ἀγαθοῖς, πᾶς ἄν μοι συμφήσαι μεθύσας τε αὐτὸς
καὶ ἕτερον ἰδὼν τοῦτο πάσχοντα.   76. τὸ μὲν
οὖν δεικνύναι λόγους οὐδὲ ὡς κατέλυσα, καὶ
συνῇεσαν οἱ μὲν ἀκουσόμενοι λόγων, οἱ πλείους
δὲ θεασόμενοι κινούμενον, οἷα δὴ τὰ τῆς βουλῆς
ἐκείνης ἐξ ὅπλων ἢ μουσείων τὸ πλέον. τουτὶ
μὲν οὖν οὐ παντάπασιν εἶχε κακῶς, χορὸς δὲ ὂν

had been at fault, and there followed pleas to the prefect to restore me to Constantinople. I protested that I would be behaving badly toward my hosts and I also pleaded that I should not once more be reduced to awful silence, and the prefect[a] departed apparently with no intention of forcing me to go, but then he had me moved with harsher constraint, an imperial summons.   75. I grieved as prisoners grieve, who have lost land and liberty and go into slavery in a foreign clime. I was fated to lose all my pleasure and profit and to be brought into trouble and distress, for I had either to go drinking with the men of influence and waste the greater part of day and night at the table, or else be regarded by them as an enemy and an object of hostility.[b] That all this is completely opposed to the well-being of the spirit everyone would agree, if he has ever been drunk himself or seen others in that state.   76. For all that, I did not relax in the presentation of my orations. Some came to listen to declamations, but the majority came merely to observe my gestures in delivery, for the Senate there was for the most part drawn from the army rather than from the schools.[c] This activity was not at all unsuccessful, but the

[a] Philippus, as in § 69 above.

[b] On the standing of teachers in Constantinople, cf. *Ep.* 399. He returns in 349.

[c] Expressive of his local patriotism he always criticized violently the Senate of Constantinople with its coarse military element.

ἦλθον ἄγων ὡς τάχιστά μοι διέρρει, τῶν μὲν
ἡδοναῖς γοητευθέντων, οἷς δὲ αἱ γνῶμαι βελτίους, οὗτοι δὲ δείσαντες, οἶμαι, ὡς δὴ πεφυκότα
νέων ψυχὰς διαφθείρειν τὸν τόπον οἱ μὲν εἰς Φοι-
F 121 νίκην ἱστία πετάσαντες, οἱ δὲ Ἀθήναζε ᾤχοντο,
ἐμοὶ δὲ τοὔνομα ἐλέλειπτο, ὥστε ἐδάκρυσεν ἄν
R 55 τις ὑπὲρ ὁπόσων ὁμιλητῶν πρὸς ὁπόσην χιόνα
παραταξόμενος ἐξήειν.

77. Περιῄειν οὖν πενθοῦσιν ἐοικώς, τοῖς τε
παροῦσιν ἀχθόμενος τά τε ἀπόντα ποθῶν, καί μοι
οὕτως ἀκριβῶς ὁ τῶν Βιθυνῶν ἔρως ἐνῴκει μηδὲν
ἕτερον ἐπιτρέπων θαυμάσαι, ὥστε ἐπειδὴ θέρος
ἦν, αὖθις ἐκεῖσε ἐκομιζόμην ἀφιέντος μὲν οὐδενός, ἀπειλούντων δὲ πολλῶν, κρατοῦντος δὲ τοῦ
θεοῦ. λοιμοῦ δὲ ἐλαύνοντος τοὺς ἀνθρώπους
μετασχών πως τοῦ κακοῦ καὶ αὐτὸς παραινέσεσιν
ἰατρῶν πάλιν ἦν, ἐξ ἧς ἐπεφεύγειν. δευτέρου
θέρους ταὐτὰ καὶ ἐτόλμων καὶ ἠναγκαζόμην
λιμοῦ ποιοῦντος ἃ πρότερον ὁ λοιμός. καὶ κατὰ
ταύτην γε τὴν πορείαν ἐν Λιβύσσῃ—σταθμὸς δὲ
ἡ Λίβυσσα τάφῳ τε καὶ λόγῳ τῷ περὶ τοῦ κειμέ-
νου κοσμούμενος—ἐνταῦθα ἐξ αἰθρίας τε ἀκρι-

class I had brought with me promptly began to
disappear, for they were either seduced by pleasure
or, if they were of finer intellect, they became
alarmed, feeling I suppose that the place was naturally ruinous for a student's character. So they
hoisted sail for Phoenicia or went off to Athens,[a] and
only my fame was left to me. You would have wept
to see how few were the students for whom I sallied
forth to encounter all that snow.

77. So I went about as though in mourning,
grieving at my present state and longing for what
was past. My love for Bithynia possessed me so
utterly and allowed me no regard for anything else
that, next summer, I made my way there again,[b]
under the god's direction, though none gave me permission and many threatened me; but there was an
attack of the plague and, having been affected by it
slightly, I returned to the city from which I had fled,
under medical advice. The next summer I ventured
the same once more and was again forced to return,
for famine was the cause, as plague had been before.
On this journey, while I was at Libyssa, which is a
post-station famous for a tomb and the legend of the

[a] The law school at Berytus had been established for
nearly a century. Athens, as an old university town, still
had the advantage over the upstart Constantinople, and
its winter climate was better.

[b] The two vacation visits to Nicomedeia occur in 350 (cf.
Letter 25) and 351.

βοῦς καὶ δριμυτάτης ἀκτῖνος νέφη συνδραμόντα
σκηπτὸν καὶ ποιεῖ καὶ ἀποστέλλει, κὰδ δὲ
πρόσθ᾿ ὀρέων Διομήδεος ἧκε χαμᾶζε, καὶ ἐπε-
R 56 πόνθειν μὲν δὴ ὅσα εἰκὸς ὑπὸ τοῦ τοιοῦδε πυρός.
78. τοῦ δὲ χάριν ἐραστὴν πόλεως ἠδικημένον
F 122 ἀπεκώλυεν ἀπὸ τῶν παιδικῶν ἡ Τύχη; τὸ
πτῶμα ᾔδει γενησόμενον, ὑφ᾿ ᾧ με καὶ αὐτὸν
κεισόμενον. λυποῦσα δὴ τοιαῦτα τὴν σωτηρίαν
ἐπόριζε καὶ ἀποστεροῦσα τόπου τινὸς ἐχαρίζετο
γῆρας, ἐπεὶ καὶ τὸ εἰς τὴν μεγίστην με πόλιν
αὖθις φέρουσα ἐμβαλεῖν οὐ κακοῦν ἐθέλουσα
ἔπραττε, κακὸν δέ τι κἀνταῦθα ἰωμένη. 79. ὁρῶ-
σα γὰρ αὖ τοὺς μὲν κακοηθείᾳ, τοὺς δέ τινας
καὶ ἀγνοίᾳ τὴν ἐκεῖθεν ἀναχώρησιν οὐχ ὅπερ ἦν
καλοῦντας, τιμωρίαν δὲ μετονομάζοντας καὶ
ψῆφον τῆς πόλεως ἀλλ᾿ οὐκ ἐργαστηρίου πονηροῦ τινος ἐπήρειαν, εἶδεν ὡς ἑνὶ μόνῳ τοῦτ᾿ ἂν
ἐξαλειφθείη τὸ αἰσχρόν, εἰ ὑπὸ τῆς πόλεως αὖθις
R 57 θηραθεὶς ἐχοίμην ἐν ἅπασί τε οἷς ἔμπροσθεν εἴην
νέων τέ τινων ἐκεῖ υἱέων περιεστηκότων θεά-

---

[a] Hannibal's burial place; cf. Amm. Marc. 22.9.3,
Eutrop. 4.5.2, Plut. *Flamin.* 20.

[b] Libanius outdoes his Philostratean models. He was
twice so blasted, here with Homeric force (*Il.* 8.134).

man buried in it,[a] from clear sky and bright sunlight a mass of clouds suddenly gathered and sent forth a thunderbolt 'and hurled it to earth before the steeds of Diomede,' and from this flash I suffered my usual trouble.[b]   78. Why, when I loved the city so, did Fortune so misuse me and keep me from my heart's desire? She knew the disaster that was to come and that I too would have fallen a victim.[c] By these afflictions she granted me salvation, and by keeping me from one place she blessed me with old age. In causing me to return to my life in the capital, she acted from no desire to harm me, but here too to provide a remedy for trouble.   79. For here again, she saw that some from malice, others from ignorance, were calling my retirement from the capital what it never was, dubbing the abuse of a wretched cabal a 'punishment' and 'an ordinance of the city.'[d] She realized that the one way for this calumny to be wiped out was for me to be courted once again by the city and to be engaged in all my former activities, with the sons of its inhabitants attending me as students and the theatres filled

[c] An anticipation of the earthquake at Nicomedeia in 358 (§118 below).

[d] Recalls his enforced departure in 343, and hints at the canard of pederasty then levelled against him (Eunap. *V.S.* 495). He needs to be purged of all such taint, and secures this by Senatorial decree and imperial ratification of these extra privileges.

τρων τέ μοι πληρουμένων ὑφ' ἡλικίας ἁπάσης.
80. καίτοι καὶ πλέον τι τὰ τότε εἶχε· τῶν γὰρ
δὴ ἀρχόντων ἀεὶ τοῦ δευτέρου τὸν πρότερον ταῖς
εἰς ἐμὲ σπουδαῖς τε καὶ τιμαῖς παριόντος ὁ
τέταρτος Φοίνιξ ἀνὴρ ὑπὸ Χαρίτων κυβερνώ-
μενος δόγμα ἠμελημένον ἀνανεοῦται τῆς βουλῆς,
καὶ βασιλεὺς συνησθεὶς τῇ πόλει τοιαῦτα ψηφι-
ζομένῃ μυρίαις με κατακοσμεῖ δωρεαῖς, ὧν αἱ
F 123 μὲν ἀξίωσιν, αἱ δὲ πρόσοδον ἔφερον, ὥστε ἄνευ
τῶν περὶ γῆν φροντίδων τὰ τῶν γεωργούντων
ἔχειν. 81. ὃ δὲ δὴ τῶνδε μεῖζον ἔργον τῆς
Τύχης, μᾶλλον δὲ ὅτου τις ἂν φήσειεν ἀνδρὶ
δόξαν τὴν ἀπὸ λόγων οἵωνπερ ἡμεῖς διώκοντι,
R 58 μετὰ γὰρ τὴν τῶν τυράννων κατάλυσιν, ὧν τὸν
μὲν λόγῳ, τὸν δὲ χειρὶ Κωνστάντιος ἔπαυσε,
δωρεῖται μὲν τοὺς Ἕλληνας τῇ Στρατηγίου
πραότητι κόσμον τῆς αὑτοῦ πολιτείας[1] τὴν
ἐκείνου νομίζων ἐν ἀρχαῖς χρηστότητα. 82. ὁ
δὲ οὐκ ἀπείρως μὲν ἡμῶν ἔχων, εἰς πεῖραν δὲ
τῶν Ἀθήνησιν ἐρχόμενος καὶ τὰ μὲν δακρύων,
τῶν δὲ οὐκ ἀμνημονῶν ἐπέπληξεν Ἀθηναίοις, εἰ
ἀξιοῦντες διὰ κάλλη λόγων ἐκεῖσε ἅπαντας

[1] πολιτείας ACP, Martin: βασιλείας VL, F.

with men of all ages. 80. Yet my position then excelled even this. Each successive governor outdid his predecessor by the regard and honour in which he held me, until the fourth of them, a Phoenician motivated by the Graces,[a] revived a neglected decree of the Senate, and the emperor, rejoicing at such a decision by the city, honoured me with countless gifts which increased my prestige and my income, so that I had the revenue of estates without the worry of them. 81. A stroke of luck more important than this—or indeed, than anything you could think of for a man who, as I did, sought a name for eloquence for himself—happened as follows: after the removal of the tyrants—put down by Constantius, one by persuasion, the other by force[b]—he bestowed upon Greece the gentle Strategius, for he considered his uprightness in office to be one of the glories of his government. 82. Strategius was not unacquainted with me, and he went to acquaint himself with affairs at Athens. By his complaints and his account of the situation there he reproached the Athenians for expecting everyone to sail there for excellence in oratory while yet refus-

[a] Strategius, called Musonianus (τῶν Μουσῶν ἐπώνυμον Himer. Or. 62.6), PLRE 611.

[b] For the revolts of Vetranio (τὸν μὲν) and Magnentius, cf. Julian Or. 1 and 2, Zos. 2.44 ff, and Eutrop. 10.12 ff. Libanius adapts directly Julian Or. 1.1 (as does Greg. Naz., Migne PG 35.5C1). This appointment to Achaea is in 353.

καταπλεῖν οὐκ ἐπεισάγουσι τῶν ὄντων σφίσιν
ἀμείνω· 'ἀλλὰ σίτῳ μὲν ἐπεισάκτῳ χρώμενοι
διδάσκαλοι τῶν περὶ τὸν σῖτον αὐτοὶ καταστάν-
τες ἅπασιν οὐδὲν ἡγεῖσθε δεινόν, εἰ δὲ περὶ τοὺς
λόγους τοῦτο δράσετε, τὰ σεμνὰ ὑμῖν οἰχήσεται;
ἐγὼ μὲν οὐδ' εἰ πάντας ὑμῖν κατεχρύσουν τοὺς
νεώς, μᾶλλον ἂν ἦν εὐεργέτης ἢ τοιαῦτα εἰσ-
ηγούμενος.'   83. οἱ δὲ πάλαι μὲν ἔφασαν καὶ
R 59   αὐτοὶ ταυτὶ διανενοῆσθαι, παθεῖν δὲ ὃ πολλοὶ
F 124 πολλάκις, αἰδοῖ βεβλάφθαι, προσλαβόντες δὲ νου-
θεσίαν βελτίους ἔσεσθαι. καὶ αὐτίκα τὸ μὲν ψή-
φισμα ἐγέγραπτο· τοὺς σοφιστὰς δὲ πρὸς σφᾶς
αὐτοὺς διήλλαττεν ὁ φόβος, καὶ πυκναὶ μὲν αἱ
βουλαί, πολλοὶ δὲ οἱ δρόμοι, καὶ ᾗ χρὴ τοὐπιὸν
διενεγκεῖν ἐσκόπουν. τοῦτο οὔπω πρόσθεν Ἀθηναίους ἀκήκοα δράσαντας οὐδ' αὖ ἑτέρῳ τοιαῦτα
εἰς δόξαν παρὰ τῆς Τύχης εὑρημένα. καίτοι καὶ
πρότερόν ποτε λόγοι λόγων ἡττῶντο τῶν παρ'
ἑτέροις οἱ παρ' αὐτοῖς, ἀλλ' ὅμως οὐ φαίνονται
κεκληκότες ἑτέρωθεν ῥήτορα.   84. τουτὶ μὲν δὴ
κεφάλαιον τῶν παρὰ τῆς δαίμονος ἀγαθῶν νομι-
στέον· εἰ γὰρ αὖ καὶ παρ' ἑτέρων κλητὸν Ἀθή-

---

[a] Cf. Or. 62.61, where his ex-pupil Celsus takes the ini-

ing to import anything better than they already had. 'You live on imported corn,' said he, 'and set yourselves up as expert advisers on corn with no compunction at all. But if you do the same with education, will not your pride be humbled? Even if I gilded all your temples, I would be no more of a benefactor than I am by my present suggestion.'[a] 83. They said that they too had long entertained this idea, but, as people often do, they had been misled by a sense of shame; after this admonition, however, they would mend their ways. They drafted their decree without more ado. The professors were reconciled to one another by their fear, and there was much deep cogitation, much coming and going, as they considered how to put up with what was to come. Never before have I heard of such an action on the part of the Athenians, or of such a device of Fortune to increase any man's repute. At other times before this their speakers have been worsted by outsiders, but for all that they have never been known to invite an orator from abroad. 84. This, then, I must consider the chief of the favours of Fortune. It is thought a matter of congratulation for a

tiative with this recommendation and Strategius gives it official backing. Libanius imputes to Strategius an imitation of Dem. *de Cor.* 87, *Lept.* 31. The unusual feature of this suggested appointment is that the holder of an established chair elsewhere is to be translated to a chair in Athens. *Or.* 2.14 must refer to this prestigious invitation, not § 25 above.

R 60 νηθεν ἐλθόντα νέων ἀρχὴν κτήσασθαι μακαρι-
στόν, πηλίκον[1] εὐδαιμονίας τὸ Ἀθηναίους εἶναι
τοὺς μεταπεμπομένους; ἐγὼ δὲ ἥσθην μὲν κατὰ
τὸν Κρῆτα ἐκεῖνον ἐπὶ τὴν κατέχουσαν τὰ πράγματα τῶν λόγων νόσον καλούμενος, οὐ μὴν οὕτω
γε ἐπιλήσμων τις ἦν ὥστ' εἰρήνην τε καὶ ἀσφάλειαν ἐλπίσαι μετὰ τοὺς πολέμους ἐκείνους οὓς
ἐτύγχανον ἑωρακώς, ἐν οἷς τραύματα πόνον πολλοῖς ἰατροῖς παρασχόντα συνέβη.

F 125   85. Ἦν οὖν δεινῆς ἠλιθιότητος τοὺς ἐπ'
ἀλλήλους ὅπλα αἱρουμένους, οἷς ἰσχὺς παραπλη-
σία δι' ἴσου πᾶσι παραγενομένη τοῦ χρόνου, τὸν
ἄρτι ἥκοντα τὰ σφῶν ἐλέγξοντα τούτους οἴεσθαι
μετὰ θυσιῶν τε καὶ αὐλῶν καὶ χορῶν ἐπιστήσειν
ταῖς ἀγέλαις ταῖς αὑτῶν. ἤκουον δέ γε πρὸς οἷς
R 61 ἐτεθεάμην τῷ μὲν Ἀραβίῳ λελουμένῳ τε καὶ
ἐπ' ἄριστον ἰόντι δύο τινὲ μισθωτὼ βορβόρῳ κρύ-
ψαι τὸ πρόσωπον, Παφλαγόνας δὲ τρεῖς ἅπαντα
ἀδελφούς, τὴν φύσιν, τὴν ἀμαθίαν, τὴν τόλμαν,
τοῦ σώματος τὸ πάχος, τὸν Αἰγύπτιον ἀπὸ τῆς
εὐνῆς ἁρπάσαντας ἐπὶ τὸ φρέαρ κομίσαντας
ἐμβαλεῖν ἀπειλῆσαι καὶ μέλλειν, εἰ μὴ ὀμεῖται

[1] πηλίκον ACP, Martin: πηλίκης VL, F.

148

man to be invited from Athens by other people to assume the guidance of students; how deep is the happiness, then, when it is the Athenians themselves who extend such an invitation! I rejoiced like Epimenides of old,[a] since I was summoned to deal with the malady that afflicted the world of letters, but I was not so absent-minded as to expect peace and quiet, after all those battles I had seen and the resulting wounds which provided many a doctor with employment.

85. It was sheer stupidity to expect that those people who took up the cudgels against each other, and who had all enjoyed pretty well the same influence for an equal length of time, should welcome to the head of their own classes with offerings or music or dancing the newcomer who was to reveal their ability for what it was. Besides what I had seen, I heard how two hired roughs had set upon the Arabian professor[b] as he was on his way to dine after his bath, and had rubbed his face in the dirt; and how three Paphlagonians, brothers in everything, character, ignorance, insolence, and physique, had dragged the Egyptian[c] from his bed, carried him to the well and threatened to throw him in—

[a] Epimenides the Cretan (Plato *Laws* 1.642d) was called by the Athenians in obedience to the Delphic oracle to purge the city of the curse that followed the murder of the supporters of Cylon (Herod. 5.71, Thuc. 1.126).

[b] Probably Diophantus.

[c] Cf. § 25.

τὴν πόλιν ἐκλείψειν, καὶ ἐξέλιπεν, ὥστ᾿ εἰς
Μακεδονίαν ἥκων ἕτερόν τι ποιῶν ἐτελεύτησε
τὸν βίον.

86. Τούτοις ἐμαυτὸν κατεῖχον τοῖς λογισμοῖς.
τῶν δὲ οὐκ ἀντεχόντων σοφιστῶν οὐκ ἂν οἴκοι με
ταὐτὰ λεγόντων δυνηθῆναι, χαλεπὸν γὰρ εἶναι
πολίτου τυχεῖν ἐπαινέτου, οἵ γε κἂν σὺν δόξῃ
παρὰ σφᾶς ἀφίκηταί τις περιαιρεῖν τε ἐπιχει-
ροῦσι καὶ πάσῃ τέχνῃ μικρὸν ποιεῖν, καὶ ταῦτα
αὐτοὺς ληροῦντας ἐπιδεῖξαι βουλομένη ἡ Τύχη
R 62 κινεῖ μέν με πρὸς αἴτησιν μηνῶν τεττάρων,
ἐφέντος δὲ βασιλέως καὶ πρὶν ἢ χειμῶνα ἄρχε-
σθαι δεῖν ἐπανήκειν εἰπόντος ὁρῶ μὲν ὁδούς τε
καὶ πύλας τὰς ἐμοὶ φιλτάτας, ὁρῶ δὲ ἱερά τε καὶ
F 126 στοάς, ὁρῶ δὲ τοίχων τῶν ἐμαυτοῦ γῆρας, ὁρῶ δὲ
μητρὸς πολιάν, ὁρῶ δὲ τὸν ἐκείνης ἀδελφὸν
οὔπω ἀφῃρημένον τὸ τοῦ πατρὸς ὄνομα, ὁρῶ δὲ
ἀδελφόν τε πρεσβύτερον ἤδη πάππον κεκλημέ-
νον συμφοιτητῶν τε ἔθνη, τοὺς μὲν ἐν ἀρχαῖς
φανέντας, τοὺς δὲ δικαζομένοις συμμάχους,
φίλους τε πατρῴους ὀλίγους γε ἐρρωμένην τε
πλήθει σοφῶν τὴν πόλιν, ὥστε ἡδόμην τε ὁμοῦ

---

and would have done so too—if he did not swear to leave town: and leave it he did. He retired to Macedonia, took up another occupation, and died there.

86. These were the calculations with which I restrained myself. The teachers, though making no opposition,[a] began to allege that I would not have the same influence in my home town, for 'a prophet is without honour in his own country,'[b] where, even if a man of high renown comes among them, they try to take him down a peg and use every device to deflate him. Fortune, therefore, in her desire to prove that they were talking nonsense in this, spurred me on to ask for four months leave, to which the emperor consented, though stipulating that I must return before winter.[c] So I saw the streets and gates that I loved, the temples, the colonnades, the old walls of my home, my grey-haired mother, her brother who had not yet lost the name of father,[d] my elder brother already a grandfather, all my school-friends, some of them as governors, some as advocates, my father's friends, the few that were left, and my city strong in the number of its learned

of him by foisting him on Athens, now egg him on to try his luck in Antioch, a challenge which he cannot resist. Summer 353.

[b] Cf. Aristotle *Rhet.* 1388a8: τὸ συγγενὲς γὰρ καὶ φθονεῖν ἐπίσταται.

[c] His leave of absence was for the long vacation only.

[d] Phasganius' daughter died in winter 353/4, §95 below.

καὶ ἐδεδοίκειν, τὸ μέν, ὅτι τῆς τοσαύτης τε καὶ
τοιαύτης πολίτης εἴην, τὸ δέ, ὅτι παγχάλεπόν
ἐστιν οὕτω μεγάλην λαβεῖν.   87. ἡ Τύχη δὴ
κἀνταῦθα ἐβοήθει πρός τε τὰ πολλαχόθεν ἐρωτή-
ματα, ἐν ἐργαστηρίοις δὲ τοῦτο ἦν γιγνόμενον,
ἀπαντῶντι καὶ ἐπειδὴ δι᾽ ἀγῶνος αὐτοῖς ἔδει τίς
ποτε ἦν φανῆναι· πρῶτον μὲν γὰρ ἐδεήθησαν
οὐδὲν τῶν σὺν θωπείᾳ συλλεξόντων ἕκαστον,
R 63   ἀλλ᾽ ἐξήρκει γενέσθαι δῆλον ὡς ἐροίην. ἔπειτα
οὐκ ἀναμείναντες ἥλιον ἐνεπεπλήκεσαν τὸ βουλευτήριον, καὶ ἔδοξε τότε πρῶτον εἶναι οὐκ
ἀποχρῶν, ὥστε ἐγὼ μὲν ἐπυνθανόμην εἰ ἥκοι
τις, ὁ παῖς δὲ ἔφη τινὰς καὶ αὐτοῦ κοιμηθῆναι.
88. τοῦ θείου δέ με εἰσάγοντος τρέμοντος μειδιῶν τε αὐτὸς εἰπόμην θάρσος ἐμβαλούσης τῆς
Τύχης καὶ βλέπων εἰς τὸν ὄχλον, ὥσπερ ὁ Ἀχιλ-
F 127   λεὺς εἰς τὰ ὅπλα, ἐτερπόμην, τούτῳ δὲ οὔπω
λέγων ἐκπλήξας πῶς ἂν ἀξίως εἴποιμι περί τε
τῶν ἐπὶ τῷ προλόγῳ δακρύων, ὃν καὶ ἐκμαθόντες
ἀπῆλθον οὐκ ὀλίγοι, περί τε τῆς ἐπὶ τοῖς δευτέροις
βακχείας; οὐδεὶς γὰρ εἷς γε τὸ πηδᾶν καὶ

---

[a] Compare the air of confidence of Polemo (Philostr.
V.S. 537), Libanius' model here.

sons. I was glad, and yet fearful, glad that I was
a citizen of so great and noble a city, and fearful,
since it is most difficult to win over one so great.
87. Here too Fortune aided me, both when I was
the target for questioning from every side, which
happened in the workshops, and when in a declamation I finally had to prove my mettle to them,
for, first of all, they did not require anyone to
call them together with words of flattery for each of
them, but it was enough for them to have the news
that I was going to speak. Then, without waiting for
daylight, they packed the city hall, and for the first
time it proved too small, and the result was that,
when I inquired if my audience had turned up, my
slave told me that some had even slept the night
there. 88. My uncle introduced me with trepidation, but I followed him smiling, for Fortune had
instilled confidence into me.[a] I gazed upon the
throng and rejoiced, as Achilles rejoiced at the
sight of his armour, and in this way I made an
impression upon them before ever I began my speech.
How could I describe adequately the tears that
followed my introductory address, which many had
learnt by heart before they left, or the excitement
which greeted my subsequent oration, for no one—
not even the elderly, the slow or the sick—but
jumped up and applauded enthusiastically? Even the
gouty, who had much ado to stand up, were on their
feet, and when I tried to get them seated again,

ἅπαντα δρᾶν οὐ γέρων ἦν, οὐ φύσει βραδύς, οὐκ
ἀσθενής, ἀλλὰ καὶ οἷς ἔργον ἑστάναι διὰ νόσον
ποδῶν εἰστήκεσαν καὶ ἐμοῦ καθίζοντος αὐτοὺς
οὐκ ἐᾶν ἔφασαν τὸν λόγον, ὃν δὴ καὶ διακόψαν-
τες δεήσεσιν ἐδεήθησαν ἀποδοῦναί με τοῖς ἐμοῖς
βασιλέα.   89. τοῦτ᾽ οὖν ἕως ἀπεῖπον ποιήσαν-
τες αὖθις ἐπὶ τὸν λόγον μετέβαινον μακάριον ἐμέ
R 64   τε καὶ σφᾶς αὐτοὺς ἀποφαίνοντες, ἐμὲ μὲν ὡς
τέχνῃ λέγοντα, σφᾶς δὲ αὐτοὺς ὡς ἀρεταῖς πολί-
των ἡδομένους, καλῶς ἐλέγξαντες ἔργῳ μάταιον
λόγον, ὡς οὐκ ἀνάγκη τοῖς ἀλλήλων ἀγαθοῖς
φθονεῖν τοὺς κοινωνοῦντας πατρίδος. οὐ φαιδρο-
τέραν ἐπεῖδεν Ἀγαμέμνων ἡμέραν ἐν ᾗ Τροίαν
εἷλεν ἢ ἐγὼ ταύτην ἐν ᾗ ταῦτα ἃ διῆλθον ἔλα-
βον. οἵ γε καὶ ἐπὶ λουτρὸν ἰόντι συνηκολούθουν
θιγεῖν ἕκαστος ἐπιθυμοῦντες τοῦ σώματος.

    90. Ἦν δέ τις τῇδε Φοῖνιξ θαυμαζόμενος ἐπὶ
τῇδε τῇ τέχνῃ, σοφιστοῦ μὲν υἱός, σοφιστοῦ δὲ
υἱιδοῦς, καὶ τὸ τιμᾶσθαί γε οὐχ ἧττον ἐντεῦθεν
ἦν ἢ παρὰ τῶν λόγων αὐτῷ. οὗτος νόμῳ μὲν
F 128   τῆς ὡραίας ἐτύγχανεν ἀφιγμένος οἴκαδε, δει-
χθέντων δέ μοι τῶν λόγων καὶ πάντων οἰχομένων γράμματα πέμπεται πρὸς ἐκεῖνον φράζοντα
τὴν ταχίστην ἐπιστῆναι τοῖς νέοις ὡς ᾑρημένοις·

they declared that my speech would not let them be, and they kept interrupting it with clamorous demands that the emperor[a] should restore me to my own folk. 89. This they did, until they stopped from sheer exhaustion. Then they passed on to my speech, and congratulated both themselves and me—me, for my skill in oratory, themselves, for their pleasure in the excellence of their citizens. Thus they fully disproved the idle tale that fellow citizens inevitably envy each other's success.[b] The sun did not shine more brightly for Agamemnon the day he captured Troy than it did for me on the day when I had the reception I have described. Why, they even escorted me as I went to bathe, every one desiring to touch me.

90. There was here a Phoenician,[c] much admired for his ability in this profession. He was the son and the grandson of teachers, and was respected no less on this account than because of his oratory. He had gone home, as was usual, for the summer vacation, but after I had delivered my declamations and all were deserting him, a letter reached him, telling him to come and take charge of his pupils as soon as he could, for they had been filched from him. 'If you

[a] Gallus Caesar.

[b] Herod. 7.237.

[c] Acacius (*PLRE* 6 (6)), as shown by P. Wolf, *Vom Schulwesen,* pp. 93 ff. Cf. *Letter* 90, Petit note *ad loc.* (*Autobiographie*, pp. 228 f).

'εἰ δὲ μελλήσεις,' τὰ γράμματα ἔλεγεν, 'ἐπὶ
κενὸν ἥξεις τὸ διδασκαλεῖον. οὕτως ἅπαντας
ἀπαγαγὼν ὁ Ὀρφεὺς οἰχήσεται.'   91. καὶ ὃς
αὐτίκα παρῆν γυναῖκα καὶ οἶκον θέρους ἀφεὶς καί
R 65   με ὡς εἶδεν ὠχρὸν καὶ ἰσχνόν, ἅ με ἡ νόσος εἰργάσατο—νόσος γὰρ δὴ κατειλήφει <μετὰ>[1] τὴν
ἐπίδειξιν—ἀλγεῖν μὲν ἔφη, πολέμου δὲ ἤρχετο
καὶ ὡς δὴ οὐκ ἐγνωσμένος λέγει τε ὡς περιεσό-
μενος καὶ εἰπὼν ᾐτιᾶτο τοὺς μεταπεμψαμένους.
τοιαῦτα ἠθέριζε, κειμένῳ δὲ ἐπενέβαινεν, ὃς ἀεί
ποτε πρὸς αὐτὸν ἤριζε, καὶ ἐπιλαβόμενος εἷλκε
πρὸς τὸ βασίλειον παλαίειν ἀξιῶν. ἐγὼ δὲ ἰδών
τε τὸν βασιλεύοντα καὶ λόγῳ τιμήσας μὲν ἂν καὶ
μὴ αἰτοῦντα τὸν λόγον, νῦν δὲ ᾐτηκότος ἔφερον
αὖθις ἑτέροις τισὶν ἑστιάσας τὴν πόλιν, ὧν νῦν
κλέος οὐρανὸν ἵκει.   92. καὶ δὴ κλάων κλάον-
R 66   τας ἀπελίμπανον, οἱ δὲ οὐκ ἔκλαον οἱ βέλτιστοι
μόνον, ἀλλὰ καὶ μεγάλα ὑπισχνοῦντο δώσειν εἰ
F 129   διαπραξαίμην τὸ παρὰ σφίσι ζῆν. ἐμοὶ δὲ ὧν
ὑπισχνοῦντο τῶν μεγάλων μεῖζον ἦν τὸ οἴκοι
ζῆν.

---

[1] <μετὰ> τὴν conj. F., Martin.

dally,' so ran the letter, 'you will return to an empty classroom. This Pied Piper will be gone, and all of them with him.' 91. He returned promptly, leaving wife and home in summertime. He found me pale and emaciated as a result of an illness which had affected me after my declamation, expressed his regrets and began hostilities, and, just as though he was not well known already, he gave a speech, sure of success, and after it reproved those who had sent for him. Such were the slights he began to heap upon me, and he tried to trample on me when I was down—he who was always at loggerheads with himself—and he took hold of me and dragged me to the palace, thinking fit to compete against me. I saw our ruler and would have honoured him with an oration, even without his asking. As it was, he did ask for one and I produced it, delighting the city with another discourse, the fame of which has now reached up to heaven.[a] 92. And so I began to take my leave, all of us in tears, but they, fine people that they were, were not just tearful: they promised a big salary if I could manage to come and live among them.[b] But for me, to live at home was a more important factor than all their great promises.

[a] For this panegyric on Gallus, cf. Foerster Vol. xi, p. 617. The triumph is Homeric, *Od.* 9.20.

[b] His objective was thus attained. Negotiations were in train for his translation to Antioch, which he furthers by correspondence (cf. *Letters* 1 and 2).

93. Ἀναβαίνων δὴ τὸ μετὰ τὸν πρῶτον τῶν σταθμῶν ἄναντες, οὗ λόγος κατακαυθῆναι τοὺς Γίγαντας μαχομένους τοῖς θεοῖς, μικροῦ τῇ ῥάβδῳ τοῦ τὸ ζεῦγος ἐλαύνοντος τὸν ὀφθαλμὸν ἐξεκόπην, ὥστε καὶ τοῖν βλεφάροιν τὸ κάτωθεν ῥαγῆναι, τὸν ὀφθαλμὸν δὲ αὐτὸν ἡ Τύχη διέσωσεν. 94. ἀνύσας τοίνυν τὴν πολλὴν ὁδὸν μᾶλλον ἢ πρὶν ἐδυσχέραινον τὸ χωρίον. εἰπὼν δὴ πρὸς τὸν ἄρχοντα ἃ φρονῶ καὶ βοηθεῖν παντὶ θυμῷ δεηθεὶς καὶ πείσας αὐτόν τε καὶ ἰατρούς, τοὺς μὲν λέγειν ὡς τῇ κεφαλῇ μοι φάρμακον μὲν ὁ παρ' ὑμῖν[1] ἀήρ, ἐχθρὸς δὲ ὁ παρ' ἐκείνοις, τὸν δὲ ἁπλῶς οὕτω προσίεσθαι, πείθω πάλιν τῶν τινα ἐν βασιλείοις δυνατῶν τῇ τῶν ἰατρῶν γνώμῃ συναγορεύοντα πεῖσαι βασιλέα μὴ φθονῆσαι τῇ κεφαλῇ· ὁ δὲ ἐβοήθει μέν, ἐβοήθει δὲ οὐ φιλῶν, διειστήκειμεν[2] γὰρ τοῖς τρόποις, ἐνδεικνύμενος δὲ ὡς οὐδὲν ἂν αὐτὸν ἐγχειρήσαντα διαφύγοι. 95. δίδωσι μὲν δὴ βασιλεὺς ἐπανελ-

R 67

[1] ὑμῖν Mss. exc. Vat. 939, Martin: ἡμῖν Vat. 939, edd.
[2] οὐ φιλῶν, διειστήκειμεν Mss., Martin: οὐ φιλῶν μέν, διειστήκει γὰρ edd.

93. As I went inland, up the slope past the first station at Phlegrae where, so the story goes, the Giants were burned to death as they fought against the gods,[a] I nearly lost my eye when the driver's whip struck me. The lower lid was gashed, but Fortune saved the eye itself.   94. After completing my long journey, I disliked Constantinople more than ever. I told the governor[b] of my feelings, and asked for his wholehearted assistance, and I won over both him and my doctors. I got them to report that the climate here was beneficial for my migraine while that in the capital was not, and from him I got full support for this. I also induced a man with influence at court[c] to back the doctors' opinion and to persuade the emperor not to grudge me the treatment my migraine needed. Assist me he did, but through no feeling of affection, for we were very different in outlook, but merely to show that he would succeed in everything he undertook.   95. Even then the emperor did not allow me to return home

[a] Cf. Malal. 202. The *mansio* is named Pagrae (*Letter* 173, Malal. 202) or Phlegrae (*Or.* 5.41).

[b] Anatolius (*PLRE* 59 (3)), proconsul of Constantinople, 353.

[c] Datianus (*PLRE* 243 ff), thanked for these services in *Letter* 7.

θεῖν οὐδὲ τότε εἰς ἅπαξ, λαβὼν δὲ ἐγὼ τὰ γράμματα καὶ συσκευαζόμενος δέχομαι πικρὰν ἀγγε-
F 130 λίαν τεθνάναι μοι τὴν ἀνεψιάν, κεῖσθαί τε τὸν
θεῖον ἐν τέφρᾳ τῆς Τύχης τὴν αὐτῆς διαφθειρού-
σης δόσιν· οὐ γὰρ ἔτ' ἦν μοι βουλομένῳ τὴν
πόλιν ἔχειν μέλλοντί γε ἀντὶ τῆς γυναικὸς τὸν
ἐκείνης ὄψεσθαι τάφον. αἰσθομένου δὲ ἄμφω τοῦ
θείου καὶ ὡς εἴην κύριος ἐπανελθεῖν καὶ ὡς οὐκ
ἐθέλοιμι, καὶ τρίτον γε, διότι, καὶ δακρύσαντός
γε εἰ μηδ' ὃ μόνον αὐτῷ παραμύθιον λείποιτο,
τῆς ἐμῆς ἀκούοι φωνῆς, καὶ κατηγοροῦντος ἐν
γράμμασιν εἰ μὴ κινοίμην, ἔρχομαι μέν, οὐχ
ὁμοίᾳ δὲ καὶ πρότερον τῇ ψυχῇ, ἀλλὰ τότε μὲν
R 68 ἱλαρᾷ τε καὶ εὐθυμουμένῃ, ὕστερον δὲ ἄχους τε
πλέᾳ καὶ διατεθρυμμένῃ.[1]   96. καὶ γὰρ αὖ
πρὸς τοῖς ἰδίοις ζάλη τις κατειλήφει τὸ κοινόν,
ὀργὴ βασιλέως εἰς φόνον προελθοῦσα· καὶ οἱ μὲν

---

[1] διατεθρυμμένη conj. Asmus διατεθυμμένη conj. Cobet, F.:
διατετυμμένη Mss., Martin.

---

[a] The exeat was only temporary, obtained on medical
grounds. He maintains this excuse throughout 355 (*Epp.*
438–441) and 356 (*Ep.* 473). Final official release came
only in 357 (*Ep.* 572). Cf. Petit, *Vie Municipale*, p. 409.

for good,[a] and I had just got the letter of authorization and was making my preparations when I received the grievous news that my cousin was dead and my uncle in mourning—and so Fortune ruined her own gift. Despite my wishes, I could no longer bear to live in the city, for I would see, instead of a wife, only her tomb. My uncle realized both that I had it in my power to return and that I was reluctant to do so, and he also realized why. He lamented that he did not hear my voice, the one consolation left to him, and in his letters he reproached me for not stirring—and so I came, but not in the same frame of mind as before. Then I had been cheerful and in good heart, but now I was full of sadness and dejection. 96. For, besides my own troubles, the whole community was tempest-tossed by the murderous anger of the emperor Gallus.[b] Some were

[b] The chronological sequence in §§96–106 is deliberately distorted to combine the effect of Eubulus' discomfiture with that of the eclipse of Zenobius. Libanius returned in March 354, with the decurions still under arrest. The lynching of Theophilus and the attack on Eubulus follow shortly, before midsummer (Amm. Marc. 14.7.2 ff). Here Libanius postpones this flight of Eubulus to use it as introduction to the account of relations with Zenobius. But, according to *Letters* 4.10 and 6.3 ff, these come to a head almost simultaneously with the opening of his school in autumn 354. Zenobius died in the winter following, leaving the way clear for Libanius' appointment as official sophist in spring 355.

ἔκειντο, τοὺς δὲ ὡς κτείνειεν ἔδησεν, ἅπαντας
ἀγαθούς· ἐν οἷς καὶ τὸν ἐμαυτοῦ διδάσκαλον ἑώ-
ρων· ἦλθον γὰρ δὴ οὗπερ ἐδέδεντο, καὶ τὸν οὐδὸν
ὑπερβὰς πεσὼν ὠλοφυρόμην ἐν πᾶσιν ὀδυρομέ-
νοις. καὶ τῆς ὑστεραίας ἐλέλυντο καὶ ἐγένετο
δόξα συνεισελθεῖν τινά μοι τῶν βελτιόνων δαιμόνων, ὑφ᾽ οὗ στορεσθῆναι τὰ κύματα.   97. τῆς
δὲ ἐπιούσης προσειπὼν τὸν βασιλέα δεύτερον
F 131   αἰτηθεὶς λόγον, ἄκων μέν, φόβῳ δὲ ἐγκωμιάζω
κύκλῳ περιερχόμενος· καὶ παρῆν μὲν ὁ διδάσκαλος οὔπω καθαρῶς ἀναπεπνευκώς, εἰσάγω δὲ
αὐτὸν εἰς τὸν λόγον ὡς δὴ ἐπηνεκότα πρός με
πολλάκις τοῦ βασιλέως τὴν γλῶτταν, ὁ δὲ
ἡσθεὶς ὀρέγει τὴν δεξιὰν τὸ διηλλάχθαι δηλῶν,
καὶ ὁ μὲν κατεφίλει προσκεκυφώς, ἡμεῖς δὲ
ἐβοῶμεν ὁπόσα ἐν τοιούτοις εἰκὸς εἰς βασιλέα
δέους ἠλευθερωκότα διδάσκαλον γέροντα.

98. Τῶν τοίνυν ἐν μέσῳ μοι γιγνομένων ἐπιδείξεων συχνῶν τε οὐσῶν καὶ οἵων ἐφέλκεσθαι
R 69   νέους νεανίσκος πολλὰ δεῖπνα δεδειπνηκὼς ἐπὶ
τῷ σώματι μισθῷ μεγάλῳ παρὰ τοῦτον τὸν βασιλέα δραμὼν δυοῖν γυναίοιν ἔφη με κεφαλὰς ἀπο-
τεμόντα κεκτῆσθαι τῇ μὲν ἐπ᾽ ἐκεῖνον χρώμενον,

dead already, others he had arrested for execution, and all were men of parts. Among them I saw even my old teacher Zenobius, for I went to their prison and, crossing the threshold, I fell on my knees and wept among them as they all lamented. Next day they were released, and the rumour spread that some kindly spirit had entered with me, and by its agency the storm had been stilled. 97. On the day following, I made an address to the emperor, and being asked to deliver another oration, unwillingly and fearfully I gave a panegyric, trying to get round him. My old teacher was there, scarce breathing freely after his ordeal, and I introduced him into my oration, saying that he had often spoken to me in praise of the emperor's eloquence. At this the emperor was delighted and stretched out his hand in token of reconciliation, and he did obeisance and kissed it, while we applauded, as you would expect in such a case when the emperor had freed an old teacher from fear.

98. In the meantime my declamations were numerous and of the kind to attract students. Then a lad, who had earned many a dinner by the favours of his person, was influenced by a large bribe to scurry off to this emperor with allegations that I had cut off the heads of a couple of girls and kept them for use in magic, one against him, the other against

θατέρᾳ δὲ ἐπὶ τὸν πρεσβύτερον. ἦν δὲ τοῦ ψεύ-
δους ὁ μισθὸς συγκοίμησις ὀρχηστοῦ τινος πάντα
πειθομένου τοῖς ἀμφ' ἐκεῖνον τὸν σοφιστήν. εἰ
μὲν δὴ καὶ ἐκομίσατο τὸν μισθὸν ὅ τε λαβὼν ὅ τε
δοὺς οἶδεν, ἐφ' ᾧ δ' οὖν ἐτόλμα ἅπερ ἐτόλμα,
τοῦτο ἦν. 99. ὁ δὲ αὐτὸν ἔπεμπεν εἰς τὸ
δικαστήριον οὐ τοῦτο οἰόμενον, ἀλλ' αὐτός τε
ἐκεῖνος ὕφ' ὧν τε ἐμεμίσθωτο ταῖς αἰτίαις ἤλπι-
ζον ἀκολουθήσειν τὸ ξίφος. οὔκουν ἐδίωξεν, ἀλλ'
ἐν τοῖς ἐσχάτοις τῆς πόλεως περὶ τὰς ὑπωρείας
ἔκειτο συγκεκαλυμμένος. ἐδόκει δὲ ὅμως ὁ βασι-
R 70   λεὺς ὑπὸ ψιλῆς τῆς αἰτίας φαυλότερόν με ἡγεῖ-
F 132   σθαι καὶ τοῦτο πάντως ἐπιδείξειν προπεμπόμε-
νος, οὐδὲ γὰρ βλέμματός με ἀξιώσειν.   100. ὁ
δὲ ἐκ μέσων τῶν ἱππέων ἐπὶ τῆς τάφρου
τὸ χεῖλος οὗπερ εἱστήκειν τὸν ἵππον ἐξελάσας
εἶδέ τε οἷον πρότερον ἐκέλευέ τε μὴ μέλλειν
ἀλλὰ μεμνῆσθαι τῆς Θρᾴκης. ἐγὼ δὲ οὕτω μὲν
ἔφην ποιήσειν, ἐποίουν δὲ τὰ πάλαι δεδογμένα
μένων τε καὶ τῆς πατρίδος ἐχόμενος. καίτοι τῶν
τε ὑποσχέσεων ἔργον οὐδὲν ὅς τέ με ἐπὶ διαδοχὴν

---

[a] Cf. *Letter* 4.10. Sophistic success results in the usual
charge brought by the loser of treason by magic, allegedly

his senior colleague.[a] The reward for this lie was to
bed with a dancer who obeyed my rival the sophist's
clique in everything.[b] Whether he actually got his
reward, only he and the dancer can tell, but that
was the object of this misdeed.   99. Gallus directed
him to the courts, which was the last thing he
expected, for both he and those who had hired him
anticipated that my execution would follow straight
upon the charge. So he did not prosecute me, but
lay in hiding in the outskirts of the city near the
mountain foot.[c] Still, it was believed that the
emperor, as a result of this baseless charge, thought
me disloyal and would certainly show it when he
appeared in public, for he would not spare me so
much as a single glance.   100. But he rode out
from the middle of his escort, cantered up to the
edge of the ditch where I was standing, looked upon
me just as he had done before, and bade me not to
linger but to bethink me of my duties in Thrace.
Though I agreed to do so, I acted upon my earlier
resolve and stayed clinging to my native city. However, the promises I had received were not put into

directed against the Caesar Gallus and Constantius
Augustus.

[b] This clique had, as its political leader, the principalis
Eubulus, opponent of Phasganius. Hence the charge
against Libanius, mouthpiece of the opposing faction.

[c] Mt. Silpius, traditional refuge of citizens in trouble
and of ascetics; cf. § 227 below, Theodoret, *HR* 12, Migne
PG 82.1397.

ἐκάλει τῶν περὶ τοὺς νέους πόνων ὁ Ζηνόβιος
ἕτερος ἐγεγόνει πόνων τε αὐτὸς ἐρᾶν λέγων καὶ
ἐμὲ μὴ δεῖν ἐπείγεσθαι.   101. ὃ δή μοι καὶ
τὰ πράγματα οὐχ ἥκιστα ἔβλαψε, τὸ μὴ εὐθὺς
προσπεσόντα τρέψασθαι τοὺς τεταραγμένους·
καθ' ἡσυχίαν γὰρ τὰ αὐτῶν ἐβεβαιοῦντο, ἐγὼ δὲ
οἴκοι μὲν πεντεκαίδεκα νέοις συνῆν, ὧν ἧκον τὸ
πλέον ἄγων, οὔπω δὲ ἦν ἐν τῷ τοῦ δημοσιεύον-
τος σχήματι, καὶ κατεῖχε μὲν ἀθυμία τοὺς ἐμούς,
κατεῖχε δὲ αὐτὸν ἐμέ, καὶ τῷ ἀργεῖν ὥσπερ ὁ τοῦ
Πηλέως ἀχθόμενος ἄχθος τε ἀρούρης ἐμαυτὸν
ὀνομάζων εἰς τοῦτο ἀπεφερόμην, ὥστε φαρμά-
R 71 κων πόσει διεσωσάμην τὰς φρένας τοῖς μὲν χείροσι τῶν ἐλπίδων χρώμενος, ἐπὶ δὲ τοὺς οὐκ
ἔχων ἄνευ γέλωτος ἐπανελθεῖν.

102. Ἐνταῦθά μοι γέρων τις προσελθὼν οὐδὲν
ἔφη θαυμαστὸν εἶναι μὴ εὖ πράττειν ἐν τῇ κλίνῃ
κείμενον· πλεονεκτεῖν γὰρ δὴ τοὺς ἐν μέσῳ
F 133 καθημένους· 'ἀλλ' εἰ βούλει,' ἔφη, 'μαθεῖν τῶν
διψώντων τὸ πλῆθος, ὅρμησον ἐπί τι τῶν ἱερῶν.'
ἐγὼ δὲ τοῦτο μὲν οὐχ ὑπακούω τῷ γέροντι, τῶν

---

a Letters of 355 make no mention of double-dealing by
Zenobius (for example *Letter* 6.4). He seems to have made
a half-promise to retire after the wire-pulling of *Letters* 1

effect;[a] Zenobius, who invited me to succeed him, changed his mind and said that he was devoted to his work and that there was no need for me to bother. 101. What affected my position most adversely was the fact that I did not attack at once and put them to rout while they were in disorder. Thus they quietly strengthened their position, while I stayed at home attending to my class of fifteen, most of whom I had brought with me.[b] I did not as yet hold the post of publicly appointed professor, and both my friends and I were full of despondency. Like Achilles, I found idleness burdensome and called myself a burden to the earth, and I reached such a pass that I kept my wits only by taking draughts of medicine, since here I was disappointed in my hopes and I could not return to Constantinople without becoming a laughing-stock.

102. At this point an old gentleman came to me and said that it was no wonder I had no success if I lay abed, for those who were in the public eye always got the best of it. 'If you really want to know how many they are who are thirsting for knowledge,' said he, 'just go to any of the temples.' Though I did not take the old fellow's advice in this,

and 2, but changed his mind. Libanius had shown indecent haste, and still had no permission for permanent removal, as Gallus reminded him.

[b] Cf. *Letter* 6.4. He took a nucleus of students with him to Antioch, as he had done from Nicomedeia to Constantinople, and set up as private teacher in the autumn. For his epic disillusion, Homer *Il.* 18.104.

ἀγοραίων δέ τινα μεταστήσας ἄλλοσε τῆς συνοικίας καταβὰς αὐτὸς ἐκεῖσε ἐκαθήμην ψαύων τῆς
ἀγορᾶς, καὶ ἔδρασέ τι τὸ χωρίον προστεθέντων
οἷς ἔφην ἄρτι πλειόνων ἢ τοσούτων νέων, τὸ
Μουσεῖον δὲ τῶν ἄλλων ἦν, ῥοπὴ τοῖς ἔχουσι
μεγάλη. λέγω δὴ πρὸς τὴν Καλλιόπην, ὅτι 'ὦ
Μουσῶν μὲν ἀρίστη, τὴν πόλιν δὲ ἡμῖν ἄγουσα,
τίνων ταύτας σὺ πράττῃ δίκας; τί με ἐδελέαζες
οὖσα θεός; τί τῶν μὲν ἐξέβαλες, τὰ δὲ οὐ δίδως;
R 72 ἀλλ' ὁ μὲν ἠπατηκὼς τρυφᾷ, τὸν ἠδικημένον
δὲ ἀπερριμμένον περιορᾷς;' 103. τοιαῦτα
μὲν πρὸς τὸ ἕδος πόρρωθεν ἀπὸ τῆς στοᾶς
διελέχθην, ἡμέραις δὲ οὐ πολλαῖς ὕστερον ἐγὼ
μὲν οἴκοι τι καθήμενος ἐδημιούργουν, βοὴ δ'
οἵα γίνοιτ' ἂν ἐξ ὄχλου νόμων ὑπερορῶντος
προσέβαλεν, ὥστε με στήσαντα τὴν χεῖρα
τί τὸ ταῦτα ποιοῦν παρ' ἐμαυτῷ σκοπεῖν· ἐν
τούτῳ δὲ ὄντος ἀναβὰς οὑμὸς ἀνεψιὸς ἀσθμαί-
νων τὸν μὲν ἄρχοντα ἔφη τεθνεῶτα ἕλκεσθαι
παιδιὰν ποιουμένων τῶν κτεινάντων τὸν νεκρόν,
Εὔβουλον δὲ σὺν τῷ παιδὶ δρασμῷ τοὺς ἐκείνων
διαφυγόντα λίθους εἰς ὀρῶν ποι κορυφὰς ἀναφυ-

---

[a] For the Museum cf. Malalas 317 ff, Downey, *Antioch*,

I got one of the market people to move to another room in the block and went down and settled myself there, on the fringe of the square. This move was quite successful, for the number mentioned above was increased by as many more, but my rivals had the great advantage of using the Museum for their lessons.[a] Then I addressed Calliope thus: 'Most glorious of the Muses, our city's guide, for what reason do you punish me so? Why do you, a goddess, ruin me? Why have you removed me from one position and refuse me another? While the deceiver flourishes, are you content to see his victim utterly cast away?' 103. So I addressed the temple from afar as I stood in the colonnade, but not many days thereafter, as I sat at home engaged in my craft, there came to my ears a shouting, as of a riotous mob. I stopped writing and began to wonder what could the matter be, and while I was still like that, my cousin came puffing and panting up the stairs and reported that the governor was murdered, his body was being dragged along as sport for the murderers, and Eubulus and his son had fled before their brickbats to seek refuge somewhere on the hilltops, while the mob, cheated of their persons, vented

pp. 622 f. It had been commandeered, probably temporarily, as headquarters of the newly appointed *Comes Orientis* in 335. It is not (as Wolf, *Vom Schulwesen,* p. 95) part of the *bouleuterion* where the official sophist taught, but a temple occupied by the others, like Acacius. The citation (Hes. *Theog.* 79) makes this distinction certain.

F 134 γεῖν, τοὺς δὲ ἁμαρτόντας τῶν σωμάτων εἰς τὴν
οἰκίαν τὴν ἐκείνου ἀφεῖναι τὸν θυμόν. ʻκαὶ
καπνὸς οὑτοσί, τοῦ πυρὸς ἄγγελος, αἴρεται καὶ
ὁρᾶν ἔξεστιν.ʼ   104. οὕτω μὲν ὁ Πάτροκλος
πληγῇ τῆς ψυχῆς ἀπολωλέκει τὰ ὅπλα, τὸν δὲ
R 73 ἀπόντα μὲν καλοῦντα, παρόντα δὲ ἀπωθοῦντα
φεύγειν μὲν ἠνάγκαζεν οὐδέν, νόσος δὲ καταβαλοῦσα μακρὰ τῶν νέων ἀφίστη, καὶ δυοῖν ἐβιά-
ζετο κακοῖν, πυρετῷ τε καὶ λύπῃ πυνθανόμενος
ἱδρῦσθαί με ἐν τῷ βουλευτηρίῳ τοσοῦτόν τε εἶναι
τὸ ποίμνιον ὥστε μὴ οἷόν τε εἶναι, πρὶν ἥλιον
δῦναι, διὰ πάντων ἰέναι.   105. τὸν δὲ καὶ
οὕτως ἔχοντα γνώμης ἐρχόμενος ἐθεράπευον καὶ
οὐκ ἦν εἰπεῖν ἣν οὐκ ἦλθον ἐπισκεψόμενος ἡμέραν. καίτοι που καὶ ἀπηλαυνόμην, ἀλλ' ὅμως
οὐκ ἀνίην, καὶ τελευτήσαντι δέ οἱ δακρύων μετέ-
δωκα καὶ λόγον ἐποίησα.

106. Πρότερον δὲ ἦν ἀφιγμένος ἀρχὴν ἔχων ἢ
τῶν ἄλλων ἄρχει Στρατήγιος πάλαι προειρημέ-

---

[a] For the chronological displacement of the lynchings
and of the arson directed at Eubulus (Amm. Marc. 14.7.6)
see note on § 96 above.

[b] Cf. Homer Il. 16.787 ff. Patroclus is here Acacius,
understudy of the missing Achilles, Eubulus. Zenobius

its wrath against his house.[a] 'There is the smoke rising to mark the fire,' he exclaimed. 'Look, you can see it.' 104. So our Patroclus,[b] sore smitten, had lost his weapons, but as for Zenobius, who summoned me from abroad and rejected me when I came, nothing forced him to take to his heels. Instead, a prolonged illness attacked him and separated him from his students, and he was harried by a double ill—his fever and his chagrin on learning that I was established in the city hall[c] and that I had such a large class that I could not get through them all before sunset.   105. I went to tend him, even though he was in such a frame of mind, nor could you name the day when I did not go to visit him. Though I was even turned away at times, I still did not give up and, upon his death, I gave him his meed of tears and composed a funeral oration.[d]

106. There had previously arrived, in the office of praetorian prefect, Strategius,[e] as had long been

had nothing to do with this riot. The juxtaposition and insinuation of bad faith are exaggerated and malicious.

[c] Libanius had thus usurped Zenobius' schoolroom even before his death. For this extension of his class duties, cf. *Letter* 6.9.

[d] For such punctilio in sick-visiting, cf. *Or.* 2.21 f, 63.4, and for this show of professional piety, with a monody immediately, followed by a full-scale epitaphios, *Letter* 6.9.

[e] Strategius as Praetorian Prefect of the East, ἀρχὴ ἣ τῶν ἄλλων ἄρχει, was charged with the conduct of the enquiry into the disturbances under Gallus, with specific instructions to use clemency (Amm. Marc. 15.13.2).

νον αὐτῷ. προσλαβὼν δὴ φίλον οὕτω μέγαν, οὑ-
F 135 τοσὶ δὲ ἦν ἐκεῖνος ὁ τὰς μὲν Ἀθήνας ἐμοί, ταῖς
Ἀθήναις δὲ ἐμὲ διδούς, κατέστην οὖν ἥκοντος εἰς
τὸ βοηθεῖν ἐκείνοις ὧν ἐδόκουν δεήσεσθαι βοηθῶν. 107. οὐκ ἔτ᾿ οὖν ἡμῖν ὁ λόγος μόνον
R 74 ἔργον ἦν, ἀλλ᾿ ἔδει τὴν μὲν ἡμέραν εἶναι λόγων,
τὴν δὲ ἑσπέραν πράξεων· οἵ τε γὰρ δὴ ὑπὸ
δυνατωτέρων ἀδικούμενοι οἵ τε κατ᾿ ὀργὴν ἐγ-
γραμμένοι, τῆς ἀρχῆς δὲ εἰς ἀπαλλαγὴν δεόμενοι
οἵ τε ἐπιθυμοῦντες ὡς τάχιστα ψήφου τυχεῖν—
πολλὰς δ᾿ ἂν καὶ ἄλλας ἀρχὴ δοίη χάριτας οὐ
λυποῦσα τὸν νόμον—οὗτοι, οἱ μὲν αὐτοί, τῶν δὲ
γυναῖκες, ᾔτουν καὶ ὑπὲρ σφῶν ἐλθεῖν ἐκεῖσε.
108. ἐγὼ δὲ μέχρι μὲν μεσημβρίας ταὐτὸν ἐποίουν τοῖς ἄλλοις διδασκάλοις, ἔπειτα τῶν μὲν οἱ
μὲν εὐθὺς ἠρίστων, οἱ δέ, ἐπεὶ λούσαιντο, ἐγὼ δὲ
ἦν ἐν οἷσπερ πρότερον. σκότους δέ με ἀνιστάν-
τος ἐφοίτων παρὰ τὸν φίλον ἐκ γραμμάτων δή
R 75 τινων ἐν τῇ χειρὶ κειμένων, ὑπὲρ ὧν δεηθῆναι
χρῆν, ἀναμιμνησκόμενος. ὁ δὲ τὰ μὲν ἐπείθετο,
τὰ δὲ οὐ πειθόμενος, ὡς οὐκ ἐῴη τὸ δίκαιον,
διδάσκων ἐξέπεμπε, μᾶλλον δὲ ἐκολάκευε
<κελεύων>[1] ἀναμένειν λουόμενον,[2] ὡς οὐ τῷ

---

[1] δ᾿ ἐκολάκευε κελεύων Re.: δ᾿ ἐκολάκευεν Mss., Norman

172

prophesied for him. He was the one who had recommended Athens to me and me to Athens, and upon gaining so powerful a friend, after his arrival I set about helping those whose help I thought I should need. 107. Thus oratory was no longer my only concern, but while my days were taken up with it, my nights were perforce engaged with business. Those people who had suffered injury at the hands of men of greater influence, those who, indicted in anger, now needed the governor for their deliverance, and those desirous of a speedy trial—and many other favours too a governor can grant without harm to the law—all these, either in person or through their wives, begged me to approach him on their behalf.[a] 108. Until noon my activities were the same as those of other teachers, but then, when they dined, either at once or after they had bathed, I would remain at my previous task. When darkness forced me to rise, I would visit my friend, refreshing my memory from jottings which I took with me, about the people whose cause I must plead. He would either consent or, when he did not, would inform me that justice would not allow it, and so he would dismiss me, or rather he would flatter me by

[a] He here prides himself upon acting as mediator for those accused of complicity in the disturbances. Contrast his later criticism of such εἴσοδοι by others, *Or.* 51 and 52.

(1965): δ' ἐκέλευεν conj. Cobet, F.: δὲ κολακεύ<ων ἐκέλευ>εν Martin.

[2] λουόμενον ACL, Martin: λουσόμενον V, F.: λούμενον Cobet.

λουτρῷ μᾶλλον ἢ τῇ 'μῇ θέᾳ δυναμένων αὐτῷ κουφίζεσθαι τῶν πόνων. ἃ δὴ ἐγὼ γνοὺς ἐχαριζόμην αὐτῷ ταῖς καθ' ἡμέραν εἰσόδοις, ἀνάγκης δὲ εἰργούσης πέμπων ὅ τι τὸ κωλῦσαν ἀνεπυνθάνετο.   109. ἠνία μὲν δὴ καὶ ταῦτα τὸν ἀντικαθήμενον τό τε εὖ πάσχειν οὐκ ὀλίγους τό τε ἀμισθί. τουτὶ γὰρ δὴ καὶ τὸ πολλοὺς εἶναι τοὺς παρ' ἐμὲ καταφεύγοντας ἐποίει τὸ μὴ δεῖν τιθέναι τιμὴν ὥσπερ λαχάνων ἢ κρεῶν. ἤγχετο δὲ διαφερόντως τῷ τῶν ἐπιδείξεων ἀριθμῷ καὶ αὖ πάλιν τῷ ταῖς μορφαῖς διαφέρειν ἀλλήλων καὶ ἠπορεῖτο καθήμενος ὁπότε ἄρα πλάττοιμι τοὺς λόγους, οὐκ εἰδὼς ὅ τί ἐστι καὶ τὸ ὕπνου περιεῖναι.   110. σιγῶν τε οὖν ὠδυνᾶτο, καὶ οὐ σιγῶν ὅτι τὸ σιγᾶν εἴη βέλτιον ἐμάνθανε. μέχρι μὲν δὴ μέσου θέρους ἄκων τε καὶ μόλις, ὥσπερ ἵππος ὑπὸ τοῦ ὁμόζυγος ἑλκόμενος, ἐχώρει, τοῦ καιροῦ δὲ τὸ συνεῖναι παύοντος ἐξῄει μὲν ἐπανήξειν εἰπών, ἀπελθὼν δὲ ἔμενεν, ὡς δὴ ὑπὸ τῆς οὔσης τῷ 'μῷ θείῳ δυνάμεως κεκακωμένος. ἕλκω δὴ τὸν ἄνδρα πρὸς τοὺς ἀγῶνας ἀπειλαῖς τε ταῖς τοῦ ἄρχοντος καὶ ἅμα ἐπὶ πλείους

---

[a] Cf. *Letter* 22.5; contrast *Or.* 52.7.

bidding me wait while he bathed, for he got more relaxation from his labours at the sight of me than from his bath.[a] I realized all this, and obliged him with my daily audiences, and whenever anything happened to prevent it, he would send to inquire what it was. 109. It irked my rival that many received these benefits, and without paying for them. In fact, the reason for the large number of those who sought my aid was that they need not make a set payment as though for meat and vegetables. He was especially dismayed at the number of my declamations, and again at their different types, and he sat puzzling out when on earth I managed to compose my orations, for he had no idea what it was like to burn the midnight oil.[b] 110. So he suffered in silence, and when he did not, he soon found out that silence is golden. Unwillingly and grudgingly, he stayed until midsummer, like a horse forced along by its team-mate, but when the season brought our classes to an end, he went off, saying that he would be back; but, once he was away, he stayed away, alleging that his position had been jeopardized by my uncle's influence. However, I fetched the fellow back to the contests, by means of threats from the governor and also to a bigger allowance, for he knew how to turn things to his

[b] For a list of his output at this time, see Foerster Vol. xi, pp. 617–621. He skates rapidly over later coolness with Strategius (e.g. *Ep.* 506), and moves on to the end of his prefecture in 358. Acacius meanwhile had enjoyed some official favour, cf. Petit, *Autobiographie,* p. 236 note.

πυρούς, ᾔδει δὲ ἀνὴρ κερδαίνειν, καὶ ἐπειδὴ ἧκε,
φίλος ἦν διὰ τοὺς πυρούς, αὖθις δὲ ἀφισταμένων
ὁμιλητῶν καὶ ἑτοιμότερον ἢ πρόσθεν ἤσθιέ τε
ἅμα καὶ ἦν ἐχθρὸς καὶ κατὰ τοὺς λόγους ἀμείνων
μέν, ἀφελών τι τῆς ῥᾳθυμίας, οὐ μὴν ἐφ' ὅσον γε
ἄξιον, ἦρτο.   111. καὶ δή τι καὶ τοιοῦτον γίνε-
ται· ὁ ὕπαρχος τοῦ ἐπαινεῖσθαι ἐπιθυμῶν μᾶλλον
ἢ ἕτερος τοῦ ἄρχειν, χρέος μέ τι τοιοῦτον εἰσ-
έπραττεν, ὡς ἂν ἔχων τὴν ἀρχήν, ἧς ἐπιβάντα
αὐτὸν ὑπεσχήμην ἐπαινέσεσθαι. προσείρητο μὲν
οὖν μοι καὶ φανεὶς εὐθὺς ἐν βραχέσιν, ὁ δὲ αὐτά
τε ἐκεῖνα διεργασθῆναι καὶ τῶν ἐνόντων ῥηθῆναι
σιωπηθῆναι μηδὲν ἐβούλετο.   112. ἐγὼ δὲ ὡς
μὲν οὐχ ὑπεσχήμην οὐκ ἐξηρνούμην, ἔφην δὲ
ἀποδώσειν εἴ μου οἴκοθεν ἐξελθὼν ἐν τῷ βουλευτηρίῳ δέχοιτο τὸν πόνον· καινὸν μὲν γάρ τι
ποιήσειν τὸν ὕπαρχον, ἔσεσθαι δὲ καὶ τοῦτο τοῦ
λόγου μέρος τὸ πρῶτον ὧδε τετιμηκέναι τοὺς
λόγους. ἔφη τιμήσειν, οἱ πολλοὶ δὲ ἠπίστουν· ὁ
δὲ καὶ δὴ παρῆν, δεομένου δὲ τοῦ μήκους αὖθις
αὐτὸν παρεῖναι πάλιν παρῆν, δεομένου δὲ καὶ

F 137

R 77

R 78

---

[a] On first arriving in Antioch Strategius had been
greeted by Libanius with a *prosphonetikos* (*Letter* 6.7).

own profit: when he did return, he was quite
friendly because of this allowance, but his pupils
deserted him even more readily than before, and
then he took the allowance and fell out with me. As
regards his oratory he had improved, for he had rid
himself of some of his slackness, but not nearly as
much as he should have done.   111. Finally, there
occurred the following incident. The prefect was
more desirous of praise than other men were of
office, and he demanded of me a panegyric as repayment of the debt I owed him, since I had promised a
speech in his honour once he had attained his
present office. Immediately after his appointment, I
had made a brief address to him,[a] and now he
wanted the subject elaborated, and none of the possible topics to be passed over in silence.   112. I did
not deny that I had made this promise, but I said
that I would settle my debt if he left his quarters
and came to listen to my oration in the city hall, for
this would be something without parallel for the
prefect to do, and it would form the first part of my
speech that he had honoured eloquence so. He
agreed to do me this honour, though most people
would not believe it, but attend he did; and when
the length of the speech required a second attendance, he did so again, and similarly, a third time.[b]

Now before leaving he demands a full-scale panegyric.
[b] Cf. Philostr. *V.S.* 537, where Polemo has a similar triumph with a marathon performance. For delivery of such
orations by installments, cf. Isocr. *Antid.* 12.

τρὶς οὐδὲ τότε ἀπῆν. καὶ νῦν τοῦτο ᾄδεται περὶ
ἀμφοῖν, τίς καὶ τίνος καὶ τί καὶ ποῦ τῆς πόλεως
ἀκήκοε.   113. βουληθεὶς δὴ τῶν πόλεων εἰς
τὰς ἀρίστας ἀφικέσθαι τὸν λόγον, οὕτω γὰρ ἂν
καὶ ἐπὶ πάσας ἐλθεῖν, τρέπει μὲν ἐπὶ τοῦτο τῶν
βιβλογράφων δέκα.   τούτων δὲ ἑνὶ χρυσὸν
δείκνυσιν ὁ σοφιστὴς καὶ διαφθείρας μετ᾽ ἐκείνου
τὴν παροιμίαν κοινὰ τὰ τῶν ἐχθρῶν ποιησάμενος
καὶ ῥήματα τὰ πολλὰ μὲν εἰς χώραν τὴν ἀλλήλων μεταθείς, σμικρὰ δὲ ἄττα ἐμβαλὼν καλεῖ
μὲν ἐπὶ τὸ αὐτὸ χωρίον παραλυθέντα τῆς ἀρχῆς,
ὡς δὴ τὸ ἴσον οἰσόμενος.[1]   114. τέρατος δὲ
εἶναι τοῦ πράγματος δοκοῦντος χελώνης ἵππου
τάχει χρωμένης μηνύει τις τοῦ λόγου τὴν πρᾶσιν, καὶ ὁ τὸ χρυσίον ἔχων, ὡς εἶδε τὰς μάστιγας, ὁμολογεῖ τε καὶ ἱκετεύει συγγνώμην ἔχειν
αὑτῷ μεγάλης ἡττηθέντι τιμῆς. ὡς οὖν μὴ ὀλίγοι ταῦτα εἰδεῖεν, ἄγω τὸν πρατῆρα τοῦ λόγου
παρὰ τὸν Νικέντιον, οὗ ἦν ἡ ἀρχὴ Σύρων, καὶ ὁ
ἄνθρωπος καίτοι προσδοκωμένης ζημίας ὅμως
ὁμολογεῖ ταῦτα καὶ ἀθῷος ἀπῆλθεν οὐδὲν ἐμοῦ

F 138

R 79

---

[1] οἰσόμενος Mss., Martin: οἰσόμενον F.

[a] An inversion of κοινὰ τὰ τῶν φίλων, *Paroem. Gr.* 1.106,

And now it is on everyone's lips about us both, the
speaker and the auditor, and about the speech and
whereabouts in the city it took place.   113. He
wanted the oration to reach the foremost of the
cities, for by that means it would reach them all,
and so he put ten copyists on the job. To one of these
the sophist offered a bribe and in concert with him
he completely falsified the old proverb, making it a
case of share and share alike between foes;[a] of my
expressions he changed the majority around in their
contexts, and he made minor insertions, and then he
invited the governor, when his term of office was
done, to come to the same place, thinking to get his
due reward.   114. It seemed more than strange
that the tortoise should beat the hare,[b] and information was laid that the speech had been sold. As soon
as he saw the lash, the copyist who had been bribed
confessed and pleaded for pardon for succumbing to
the great temptation. So, in order that all should be
aware of it, I haled the seller of my speech before
Nicentius, governor of Syria,[c] and, for all that he
expected to be punished, the fellow confessed and

266. For Strategius' publicity campaign, cf. *Letter* 27.1.
Plagiarism was not an offence, so the charge is one of bribery brought only against the copyist. It implies, however,
incapacity on Acacius' part, and Libanius, his point made,
parades his clemency.

[b] Cf. *Or.* 62.44. This is an adaptation of χελώνην Πη-
γάσῳ, *Paroem. Gr.* 1.189.

[c] Nicentius, *consularis Syriae,* 358, soon dismissed:
Letter 34, *PLRE* 628 (1).

προσδεηθέντος δίκην λαβεῖν. 115. ὁ δὲ ἀν-
δρειότατος σοφιστῶν ἐκεῖνος οὐδ' οὕτως ἡσύχασεν,
ἀλλ' αὖθις τὰ εἰρημένα ἐμυθολόγευε,[1] καὶ ταῦτα
ἐν τῇ τοῦ Στρατηγίου καταγωγῇ. καὶ ὁ μὲν ἐξ-
ήλασεν, Ἑρμογένη δὲ τὸν τὴν ἀρχὴν ἐκδεξάμενον
F 139 αὐτῷ δεινόν τε καὶ ἄγριον ἦγεν ἡ φήμη καί,
ἦν γὰρ ἡμῖν ἀγνώς, ἐδόκουν οὖν οὐκέθ' ἃ πρότερον ἰσχύσειν. ἦν δὲ ἄρα ὁ Ἑρμογένης βέλτιστος
ἀρχόντων καὶ οὐ πολλοῖς μὲν ὁμιλεῖν ἀξιῶν,
πρᾷος δὲ καὶ λόγῳ μᾶλλον ἢ θυμῷ χρώμενος.
116. οὗτος εὐθὺς μὲν εἰσκαλέσας τὴν βουλὴν
εἰπόντων ὅ τι ᾤετο τῇ πόλει λυσιτελήσειν
ἑκάστου, τὸν θεῖον τὸν ἐμὸν ἀπὸ τῶν λεγομένων
εὑρών, 'οὗτος ἐκεῖνος,' ἔφη, 'Φασγάνιος,'
ὥστε τὸν Εὐβουλόν τε καὶ τὴν ἐκείνου μοῖρα
μικροῦ πεσεῖν. ἔπειτα ἐμὲ καλέσας φίλον
R 80 ἐδεῖτό οἱ γενέσθαι τοιοῦτον, ὥστε μηδὲν
εἶναι πλέον ταύτῃ Ἀρισταινέτῳ καὶ Σελεύκῳ,
παρ' ὧν δὴ καὶ εἰς ἐπιθυμίαν κεκινῆσθαι τοῦ
κτήματος. 'ἀλλὰ δίκαιον μέντοι,' ἔφην, 'τὸν
φιλοῦντα ἐκείνῳ καὶ ὑπ' ἐμοῦ φιλεῖσθαι.'

[1] ἐμυθολόγευε F., (cf. Od. 12.453): ἐμυθολόγει Mss., Re.,
Martin.

got off scot-free, since I did not press for the infliction of the penalty. 115. Not even then did my brave sophist be still, but he tried to tell the tale again, and in Strategius' residence, too.[a] Strategius sent him packing, but rumour had it that Hermogenes, his successor, was a man of stern and unbending character.[b] As he was unacquainted with me, it seemed that I would no longer have my former influence. However, it turned out that Hermogenes was an excellent governor, and, though considering it below his dignity to have a host of intimates, he was of kindly disposition and was guided by reflection rather than by passion. 116. He convened the town council forthwith, and when its members were each making suggestions for the city's welfare, he recognized my uncle as a result of his remarks. 'Why, there's Phasganius,' he exclaimed, and thereupon Eubulus and his clique nearly collapsed. Then he summoned me to him, and begged me to be his friend, as intimate with him as I was with Aristaenetus and Seleucus,[c] by whom he had been inspired with the desire to obtain this boon. 'Well,' said I, 'it is only right that I should be a friend of a friend of theirs.'

[a] Strategius had just left office when Acacius tries again, between June and late August 358.

[b] Praetorian Prefect of the East, 358–360, *PLRE* 423 (3).

[c] Seleucus, a friend of Julian in Bithynia, *Ep.* 13, *PLRE* 818 (1).

117. Ταυτὶ μὲν εὐπότμου, δυστυχοῦς δὲ τὰ ῥηθησόμενα. τὴν γὰρ δὴ πάντ' ἐμοὶ μητέρα καὶ τὸν τῆς μὲν Ἀσίας ὀφθαλμόν, ἐμοὶ δὲ ἀντὶ πύργου, τὸν θεῖον ἥρπασεν ἡ Τύχη, τὸν μὲν πρότερον, ἡ δὲ οὐκ ἐνεγκοῦσα ἐπαποθνήσκει. καὶ οὐδὲν ἔτι μοι τῶν ἡδέων ἡδὺ οὐδ' αὐτό γε τὸ πάντων ἥδιστον, αἱ ἐπιδείξεις· καὶ γὰρ καὶ αὐτὸ τοῦτο ἥδιστον ὑπ' ἐκείνοιν ἐγίνετο, τοῦ μὲν οἷον ἀνηβῶντός τε ἐν τοῖς κρότοις καὶ τῆς αὐτοῦ πληγῆς ἐπιλανθανομένου, τῆς δὲ ὑπερχαιρούσης

F 140 ὁπότε αὐτῇ τὸν ἐκ τῶν ἄθλων ἱδρῶτα κομίσαιμι. 118. μετ' ἐκείνας τὰς ταφὰς καὶ τὴν Εὐσεβίου γε τοῦ πρὸ ἀμφοῖν ἀπελθόντος—ἦν μὲν γὰρ καὶ τὸ Νικομηδείας πτῶμα καὶ ὃν ἡ πόλις ἐκάλυψε

R 81 πεσοῦσα δεινά τε καὶ οἷα λύπην τὴν ἐσχάτην ἐμβαλεῖν, ὑφ' ἧς δὴ καὶ πολιὰς ἐξαίφνης ἔδειξα— κακὰ δὲ προστεθέντα κακοῖς, ταῦτα ἐκείνοις φίλῳ τε φίλος καὶ πόλει φίλη μήτηρ τε καὶ ὁ ταύτης ἀδελφός, πάντα ἐμοὶ δ' ἃ ζῆν βούλοιτ'

---

[a] The order of events is inverted. The chronological sequence is: (1) earthquake at Nicomedeia and death of Aristaenetus, 24 August 358. (2) death of Eusebius (*BLZG*

182

117. Such was my good fortune; I will now proceed to the bad.[a] My mother, who was all in all to me, and my uncle, the light of Asia and a tower of strength to me, Fortune snatched from me—him first, she, heartbroken, dying soon after. No more could I derive any pleasure from my pleasures, not even from the chief of them, my declamations. For during their lifetime, this really was my greatest pleasure, since he, as it were, regained his youth in the applause and forgot his own trouble, while she rejoiced exceedingly whenever I returned to her with the sweat of my labours upon me. 118. With their death, and that of Eusebius also who had died before either of them—and there had also occurred the earthquake at Nicomedeia and the death of Aristaenetus, buried in the ruins of the city, a shocking event and one that caused me such extreme grief that my hair went white all of a sudden—trouble piled upon trouble,[b] one thing followed another, friend after friend died, a city I loved was destroyed, my mother and her brother had passed away, and all that a man could wish to live

ix), 359; cf. *Ep.* 72, 110. (3) death of Phasganius, autumn 359; *Letter* 50. (4) death of his mother, and his monody upon her; *Or.* 2.69, *Ep.* 553.

[b] Other tensions, here unmentioned but prominent in the letters, are the treason trials at Scythopolis in 359 (Amm. Marc. 19.12), where he pleads for friends (*Letters* 55, 70), professional troubles (*Or.* 31) and his cut in salary (*Letters* 65, 89). For his hesitations in 360/1, cf. *Letter* 79.

ἄν τις, ἀποφαίνουσι πικρά, πρὶν δὴ τὴν γῆν
ἅπασαν ἀμαχεὶ παραλαβὼν ὁ παντὸς φιλοσόφου
μᾶλλον ἐν βασιλείοις τὴν σοφίαν ἀγαπήσας
κατήγαγεν ὥσπερ ἐκ φυγῆς εἰς τὸ αὖθις ἀσπάζε-
σθαι τὰ δυσχεραινόμενα.   119. καὶ ἐγέλασά τε
καὶ ἐσκίρτησα καὶ σὺν ἡδονῇ λόγους καὶ συν-
έθηκα καὶ ἔδειξα, βωμῶν μὲν ἀπειληφότων αἷμα,
καπνοῦ δὲ φέροντος πρὸς οὐρανὸν τὴν κνίσσαν,
θεῶν δὲ ἑορταῖς τιμωμένων, ὧν ὀλίγοι τινὲς
ἐπιστήμονες λελειμμένοι γέροντες, μαντικῆς δὲ
εἰς ἐξουσίαν παριούσης, λόγων δὲ εἰς τὸ θαυμά-
ζεσθαι, Ῥωμαίων δὲ εἰς τὸ θαρρεῖν, βαρβάρων
δὲ τῶν μὲν ἡττημένων, τῶν δὲ μελλόντων.
120. οὗτος ὁ σωφρονέστατός τε καὶ δικαιότατος
καὶ ῥητορικώτατος καὶ πολεμικώτατος, ὁ μόνοις
F 141   τοῖς δυσσεβέσιν ἐχθρὸς τῶν μὲν παρ' ἡμῶν
πρέσβεων οὐ μετ' ἐμῶν ὡς αὐτὸν ἡκόντων
γραμμάτων ἤλγησε καὶ 'ὦ Ἡράκλεις,' ἔφη, 'ὁ
τοὺς ἐκ τοῦ γράφειν ὑπομείνας κινδύνους ἐν
ἀσφαλείᾳ σιγᾷ.' τῆς δεῦρο δὲ ὁδοῦ καὶ τοῦτο
κέρδος ὠνόμαζεν, εἰ ἐμέ τε ἴδοι καὶ ἀκοῦσαι
λέγοντος. καὶ ἐπ' αὐτῶν δὴ τῶν ὅρων ἐπὶ τῆς
πρώτης ὄψεως πρῶτον τοῦτο ἐφθέγξατο· 'πότε

for turned to gall for me, until at last there came the
unopposed accession to the throne of the emperor
Julian.[a] He, who in his palace loved philosophy
more than did any philosopher, restored to popular-
ity, as though from exile, the things that had fallen
out of favour.   119. I laughed and danced, joyfully
composed and delivered my orations, for the altars
received their blood offerings, smoke carried the
savour of burnt sacrifice up to heaven, the gods were
honoured with their festivals, which only a few old
men were left to remember,[b] the art of prophecy
came again into its own, that of oratory to be
admired; Romans plucked up heart, and barbarians
were either vanquished or soon to be so.   120. This
emperor, in his prudence and justice, eloquence and
might, enemy to the unbelievers alone, was grieved
when our ambassadors reached him and brought
him no message from me.[c] 'Good heavens,' he
exclaimed, 'Libanius, who has withstood the perils
his writings occasioned, is silent now that he is safe.'
The profit he got from his journey here was simply
this, he said, that he would see me and hear me
speak. Indeed, at the very first sight of me, right at
the city boundary, the first thing he said was, 'When

[a] He makes much of Julian's fortuitously bloodless
elevation to Augustus (*Or.* 12.65, 18.118 f), as also to his
role of philosopher-king and restorer of pagan rituals.

[b] As Julian himself observed in Antioch, *Misop.* 360d ff.

[c] For his refusal to go on this embassy in 362, cf. *Ep.*
697, *Letter* 84.

185

R 82 ἀκουσόμεθα;’ ὁ δὲ ἀνταγωνιστὴς ἐκεῖνος ἤδη
ἦν οἴκοι τεθνηκυίας μὲν αὐτῷ τῆς γυναικός,
θυγατέρων δὲ ὡραίων γάμου τῶν ἐκείνου δεομένων ὀφθαλμῶν, ἐλέγετο δέ, ὡς καὶ ζώσης τῆς
γυναικὸς ᾤχετο ἄν.

121. Ὁ τοίνυν βασιλεὺς προοίμιον μὲν τῶν
λόγων καθ’ ἑκάστην ἐποιεῖτο τὴν ἡμέραν θυσίας
ὑπὸ τοῖς ἐν τῷ κήπῳ τοῦ βασιλείου δένδροις,
πολλῶν δὲ φοιτώντων τε καὶ διὰ τῶν περὶ τοὺς
θεοὺς ἐκεῖνον θεραπευόντων αὐτὸς ἦν οὗπερ ἀεί,
καὶ οὔτε ἐκαλούμην τό τε ἄκλητον ἰέναι μετέχειν
τινὸς ἀναιδείας ὑπελάμβανον καὶ τὸν μὲν
ἄνδρα ἐφίλουν, τὴν ἀρχὴν δὲ οὐκ ἐκολάκευον.
122. ἧκε δέ ποτε εἰς Διὸς Φιλίου θύσων καὶ
τοὺς ἄλλους κατιδών, ἐβούλοντο γὰρ καὶ πᾶν
ἐποίουν ὅπως ὀφθήσονται, μόνον οὐ τεθεαμένος
ἐμὲ τοῖς πολλοῖς ἐμμεμιγμένον δείλης διὰ δέλτου
τινὸς ἠρώτα τε ὅ τι εἴη τὸ κεκωλυκός, καὶ μετὰ
χαρίτων καθήπτετο. ἃ μὲν δὴ ἀπεκρινάμην διὰ
τῆς αὐτῆς δέλτου καὶ ὡς οὐκ ἐδήχθην μᾶλλον ἢ
F 142 τοῦτο ἐποίησα καὶ αὐτὸς σὺν χάρισιν, οἶδεν

ᵃ For a different account of this first meeting, cf. *Letter*
88. Here he adapts to himself and Julian Philostratus’
account of the meeting between Aristides and Marcus

shall I hear you speak?'[a] Meanwhile my rival was still at home, for his wife was dead and his daughters, now of marriageable age, required his supervision; but rumour had it that, even if his wife had still been alive, he would have left.

121. Now the emperor, as a prelude to each day's address, used to sacrifice under the trees in the palace garden.[b] He had many to attend him and flatter him by means of their religious activity, but I stayed where I always was; I received no invitation and I considered that to attend without one was a sign of rudeness, and while I liked him personally, I refused to flatter him because of his position. 122. One day he came to sacrifice at the altar of Zeus Philius,[c] and there he saw the rest, for that was their desire and they would go to any lengths to ensure that they were seen: the only one missing from that throng was myself, and in the afternoon he sent a letter to inquire what had prevented me, his tone being one of delicate reproof. My answer I sent by return, and when he read it, he realized that I was as capable of administering delicate reproofs

Aurelius (*V.S.* 582 f); see *Classical Philology* 48 (1953), 20 ff. As a consequence he produces the *Prosphonetikos* (*Or.* 13). In contrast, Acacius is here mentioned for the last time.

[b] For such exaggerated religious displays, cf. *Or.* 15.79, 18.127, Jul. *Misop.* 346b ff. These soon became grounds for criticism (Amm. Marc. 22.12.6 f).

[c] Sacrifices at the shrine of Zeus Philius in the city, *Or.* 15.79; of Zeus Casius on the mountain (which Libanius did not attend because of ill-health), *Ep.* 739.

ἀναγνούς τε ἐκεῖνος καὶ ἐρυθριάσας. 123. ἀπε-
χομένου δέ μου καὶ μετὰ τὴν δέλτον οὐδὲν
ἧττον τοῦ τε κήπου καὶ τῶν ἐν τῷ κήπῳ δρωμέ-
R 83 νων καὶ ἀπημελῆσθαι δοκοῦντος καὶ οὔτε ἀθυ-
μοῦντος ἐπισταμένου τε ὅστις ἦν ὁ τὴν φιλίαν
διορύξας, Πρίσκος, Ἠπειρώτης ἀνὴρ ὅτι πλεί-
στοις ἐπὶ σοφίᾳ συγγεγονὼς ἀνδράσι, πλημμε-
λεῖσθαι ταῦτα ἡγησάμενος τῷ βασιλεῖ παύει τὴν
ἁμαρτίαν· οἵοις μὲν λόγοις, οὐκ οἶδα, καλοῦμαι
δὲ πληθούσης ἀγορᾶς, καὶ διηπορεῖτό τε καὶ εἰς
γῆν ἔκυπτεν ὁ κεκληκὼς κατηγορῶν οἷς ἔπασχεν
ὧν ἐδεδράκει. 124. μόλις δ' οὖν ποτε αὐτὸν
ἀναλαβὼν καὶ τὸ πολλὰ κατηναγκάσθαι πράττειν αἰτιασάμενος, ἐπειδὴ καλῶν μὲν ἐπ' ἄριστον ἤκουσεν ὡς δειπνοίην, καλῶν δὲ ἐπὶ
δεῖπνον ἤκουσεν ὡς καὶ τοῦτο ἐξὸν ποιεῖν ἡ
κεφαλὴ κωλύοι, 'σὺ δ' ἀλλὰ θαμίζειν ἡμῖν,' ἔφη.
'καλοῦντός γε,' ἔφην· ἄλλως δὲ οὐκ ἐνοχλήσειν.
ὁ δὲ πείθεταί τε καὶ οὕτως ἐποίει. 125. αἱ
δὲ συνουσίαι λόγους τε ἡμῖν τοὺς ὑπὲρ λόγων
εἶχον καὶ ἐπαίνους τῶν εὖ πραττομένων ἐκείνῳ
καὶ μέμψεις τῶν ὠλιγωρημένων, ᾔτουν δὲ οὐδὲν
F 143 οὐ τῶν ἐν θησαυροῖς, οὐκ οἰκίαν, οὐ γῆν, οὐκ
R 84 ἀρχάς, καὶ τὸ τοῦ Ἀριστοφάνους λόγος ἦν οὐκ

188

as I was of receiving them, and he blushed for shame. 123. Even after this message I still held aloof from the garden and the goings-on there, and it seemed that I was quite out of favour. Yet I was not downcast, for I understood who it was who had undermined our friendship,[a] but Priscus of Epirus, who as a philosopher had a large circle of acquaintances, thought the emperor to be at fault in this attitude and checked his error. What his arguments were, I do not know, but one morning I received an invitation. The emperor who had issued it was out of countenance and kept his eyes on the ground, and by his emotions showed how wrong he had been. 124. Anyway, he recovered himself at last with some difficulty and blamed the mass of business with which he had to deal. Then he invited me to lunch, and got the reply that I was in the habit of dining: so he invited me to dinner, but was told that, though I was free to go, my headache prevented me. 'Still, visit me often,' he exclaimed. 'Certainly,' I replied, 'if you invite me. Otherwise I will not trouble you.' He consented and so he began to carry on. 125. Our intercourse consisted of literary discussion, of praise for his successes and criticism of his oversights. I asked for nothing—for none of his treasure, for no villa, estate or office. That business about Aristophanes was an oration to

[a] This unnamed courtier is almost certainly Maximus of Ephesus, *Letter* 80, *PLRE* 583 (21). For Priscus, *PLRE* 730. For these overtures to Libanius, cf. *Letters* 88, 97, *Or.* 5.7.

ἐῶν κακὸν τὸν τοιοῦτον δοκεῖν, καὶ τοῦτο ἐδίδου
τὴν ἀρχήν, ἐγὼ δὲ οὐδ' ἀπολαβεῖν ἠξίουν ὄντων
μοι παππῴων οὐ μικρῶν ἐν τοῖς ἐκείνου κτήμα-
σιν. ὁρῶν δὴ κέρδος τε ἅπαν ὑπ' ἐμοῦ καταπε-
πατημένον ζητοῦντά τε οὐδὲν ἕτερον ἢ ὅπως
ἐκεῖνος ἀποκρύψαι τὰ ὑμνούμενα, τοὺς μὲν
ἄλλους ἔφασκε τὸν αὑτοῦ πλοῦτον φιλεῖν, ἐμὲ δὲ
αὐτόν, καὶ μηδ' ἂν τὴν τεκοῦσαν αὐτὸν ὑπερβα-
λέσθαι τὸ φίλτρον τὸ παρ' ἐμοῦ.   126. διὰ
τοῦτο καὶ τὴν ὑπὲρ τῆς βουλῆς παρρησίαν ὑπέ-
μενεν, ὅτε ἡ γῆ μὲν οὐδὲν ἐδεδώκει στερηθεῖσα
R 85 τοῦ ἄνωθεν ὕδατος, ὁ δὲ ἠξίου γέμειν τε ὠνίων
τὴν ἀγορὰν καὶ μένειν ἐντὸς ὅρων οὓς ἔστησε
ταῖς τιμαῖς· δαίμων δὲ ἄρα ταῦτα ἠνάγκαζε
φθονερὸς ὠθῶν εἰς ὅπερ αὖ καὶ τέλος τὰ
πράγματα ἔωσε. τότε οὖν ὁ μὲν ᾤδει καὶ μάχεσθαι τοῖς ἑαυτοῦ βουλήμασι τοὺς βουλευτὰς ἐβόα
κόλακες δὲ ἔνθεν καὶ ἔνθεν παρεστηκότες ἐρρίπι-
ζον τὸν θυμόν, ἐγὼ δὲ οὐδὲν τρέσας, τὴν δὲ τοῦ
πράγματος ἐξετάζων φύσιν διετεινόμην ἀδικοῦ-

a Oration 14 of early autumn 362. For the post offered
to Aristophanes as a result, cf. Letter 124.3, and Petit
Autobiographie, p. 242 note. For his own disinterestedness, cf. Letters 97 and 124. An honorary quaestorship

ensure that a man who was no rogue should not be regarded as one, and this prompted the offer of an official post to him, but I did not think it proper to accept anything, though a large part of my grandfather's estate was among his possessions.[a] He saw that I spurned all gain and that my sole object was to ensure that he should outdo all the good things said about him, and he asserted that, while other people loved him for his wealth, I loved him for himself alone, and not even his mother's affection could have surpassed mine. 126. It was for this reason that he suffered my frankness on behalf of the city council,[b] when the land had produced no crops because of lack of rain from heaven, and yet he demanded that the market should be full of goods for sale and that they should stay within the price limits he had set. Some spirit of evil, it seems, was at work in this, forcing the march of events towards the crisis that ensued. So then his anger swelled and the flatterers surrounding him on every side inflamed his wrath, but I, with never a tremor, insisted upon examining the facts of the matter and

even if offered by Julian, was certainly not accepted.

[b] For a detailed comparison of this passage and its parallels, *Or.* 15.20, 16.21, 18.195, see Petit, *Historia* 5 (1956), 481 ff. For the famine in Antioch and the crisis caused by Julian's price-fixing ordinance and his quarrel with the curia, Petit, *Vie Municipale,* pp. 109 ff. Interventions on behalf of the curia culminate in *Or.* 15 and 16, for which see *Orations* Vol. i, Intro. xxxii.

F 144 σάν τε οὐδὲν ἀπέφαινον τὴν βουλήν. καίτοι τις
τῶν καθημένων παρρεῖν τὸν Ὀρόντην ἔφασκε
τῷ ποταμῷ με φοβῶν, ἀναξίοις ἀπειλαῖς τὴν
βασιλείαν ὑβρίζων. ὁ δὲ οὕτως ἦν ὡς ἀληθῶς
ἀγαθός, ὥστε κρατῆσαι μὲν ἐπεχείρησεν, ἡττη-
θεὶς δὲ οὐκ ἐμίσησε.   127. μᾶλλον μὲν οὖν ἢ
πρόσθεν ἠγάπησεν ὑπὲρ πατρίδος ὥσπερ ὅπλα
θέμενον τοὺς λόγους, ὕπατον δὲ αὐτὸν ἀποδει-
κνὺς αἰσθανόμενός τε τῶν τε ἤδη παρόντων τῶν
τε ἡξόντων μυρίους σὺν ᾠδαῖς σφίσι παραστησομένους[1] κελεύει μοι τιμῆσαι λόγῳ τὴν ἑορτήν·
ἐγὼ δὲ ἑτέρων εἶναι τοὖργον εἰπὼν κατὰ τὴν
ἑτέραν φωνὴν οὐκ ἤργουν, ὡς μηδένα μηδὲν
ἱερὸν δόξαι λέγειν, μηδ' ὃς λαμπρῶν ἀπολελαύκει θορύβων.   128. καί πως συμβαίνει ἐν τῷ
R 86 προτέρῳ λόγῳ τύχης, οἶμαι, τινὸς τοὺς 'αὖθις'
βοησομένους[2] τε καὶ χαριουμένους ἑτέρωσε πεμ-

---

[1] παραστησομένους Mss., Martin: παραστησομένων edd.:
[σφίσι] Martin.
[2] βοησομένους VL, Martin: βοηθησομένους ACP, F.: post
πεμψάσης lac. ind. Martin.

---

[a] In fact, Julian remained unmoved by his pleas; *Letter*
98, *Ep.* 824.
[b] Jan. 1, 363: Julian Aug. Cos. iv with Flavius Sallus-

showed conclusively that the council was not in the wrong. Yet one of the audience called out that the Orontes was flowing close by, trying to frighten me with the threat of a ducking but merely insulting the royal presence with his unseemly threats. The emperor was so truly good that, though he tried to win his point, he bore no malice on being worsted.[a] 127. On the contrary, his liking for me was more than ever before, after I had presented my oratory in defence of my native city. So, when he designated himself consul,[b] although he saw that of the people already present and of those yet to come there would be thousands who would try to win his support by their songs, he bade me give a speech in honour of the festival. I said that it was a job for someone else, but I began to busy myself with the task in Greek, so that no one, not even he who enjoyed rapturous applause, was thought to have said anything out of the ordinary. 128. Somehow this success was secured for me in the speech which preceded mine, since some fortune, I am sure, diverted to me people

tius. The text is weak, the style allusive; hence the obscurities. The day's panegyrics begin with one in Latin ("someone else", §127). The author, possibly the Carthaginian of *Or.* 12.92, did a reasonably good job, though Libanius could not understand it. Then followed a panegyric in Greek by a visiting speaker which was a resounding failure, diverting the applause elsewhere, i.e. to Libanius who, as sophist of the city, rounded off the proceedings with *Or.* 12.

ψάσης, οἷς ἐλυσιτέλει μὴ τἀμὰ διαβάλλειν· ὁ δὲ
αὑτὸν μὲν ἔνδον οὐδενὸς ἐπαινοῦντος ἐπήνει,
δευτέρῳ τούτῳ παρέχων ἀφορμὴν γέλωτι, τοὺς
δὲ ἐπ’ αὐτῷ γελάσαντας οὐκ ἀνίει λοιδορῶν, οἱ
δ’ ἂν[1] αὖθις ἐγέλων, καὶ τὸ δι’ ἀπάτης πορι-
σθὲν ἐξεκέχυτό οἱ οὐ φωραθὲν ἄν, εἰ τοσοῦτόν γε

F 145 ἠπίστατο, ὅτι δόξαν οὐχὶ δικαίαν ἡσυχίᾳ φυλάττειν δύναιτο ἄν.   129. οἱ μὲν δὴ ἀλλήλοις εἰς
παραμυθίαν ἦρκουν, ὡς δὲ ἀπέδυν ὕστατος αὐτοῦ

R 87 τοῦ βασιλέως ὅπως ὅτι πλεῖστοι συνέλθοιεν φρον-
τίσαντος, τὸν Ἑρμῆν ἔφησαν τοῦ θεράποντος
κηδόμενον τῇ ῥάβδῳ κινεῖν τῶν ἀκροωμένων
ἕκαστον, ὅπως μηδ’ ὁτιοῦν ὄνομα θαύματος ἄμοι-
ρον ἀπέλθῃ. βασιλεὺς δὲ τὰ πρῶτα μὲν τῇ διὰ
τῆς μορφῆς ἡδονῇ μηνυομένῃ συνετέλει, ἔπειτα
τῷ μέλλειν ἀναπηδᾶν, ἔπειτα, οὐ γὰρ δὴ κατεῖ-
χεν αὑτὸν καὶ σφόδρα πειρώμενος, ἤλατο μὲν ἐκ
τοῦ θρόνου, τῆς χλαμύδος δὲ ὁπόσον ἐξῆν ταῖν
χεροῖν ἀνεπέτασεν, ὡς μὲν ἂν εἴποι τις τουτωνὶ

[1] ἂν del. F, Norman (1965).

[a] For general disapproval of such uncontrolled expressions of enthusiasm by the emperor, see *Or.* 18.154 ff (*Orations* Vol. i, p. 380 note). Libanius finds the justification of

who could cry 'Encore' and support me, and who found it paid them not to disparage my work. The previous speaker, since there was none in the company to praise him, spoke in praise of himself, and so provided another cause for ridicule, and he did not cease abusing those who ridiculed him, whereupon they laughed all the more. The fruits of his deceit were lost to him, though he could have retained them, had he realized that, by keeping silence, he could keep his ill-deserved reputation. 129. The others, to be sure, were capable of consoling one another. I was the last to take part, for the emperor himself had so devised it that there should be the fullest possible audience, and people insisted that Hermes, in his care for his servant, stirred every member of the audience with his wand, so that no single expression of mine should pass without its share of admiration. The emperor contributed to this, first by the pleasure which he expressed at my style, then by his tendency to rise to his feet in applause, until finally when he could no longer restrain himself, despite his best efforts, he leapt up from his seat and, with outstretched arms, spread wide his cloak. Some of our boors would assert that in his excitement he forgot the dignity of his position,[a] but anyone who is aware of

royalty to be its encouragement of classical culture; cf. *Or.* 31.36 f, 62.7 ff. He here equates Julian's open support of rhetoric with that accorded to the philosophy of Maximus (*Or.* 18.154).

τῶν ἀγγάρων, ἐκφερόμενος τοῦ σχήματος, ὡς δ᾽
ἂν ἀνὴρ εὖ εἰδὼς οἷς ἂν σεμνὴ βασιλεία γένοιτο,
R 88 ἄρα ἐν τοῖς προσήκουσι μένων· τί γὰρ δὴ βασιλι-
κώτερον τοῦ βασιλέως ψυχὴν πρὸς κάλλη λόγων
ἀνίστασθαι; 130. τῷ δὲ οὐδὲ ἄλλως οἷόν τ᾽
ἦν τὰ τοιαῦτα πάσχειν, πατρὶ πολλῶν λόγων
πρό τε δὴ τῆς ἀρχῆς καὶ ἐν αὐτῇ γεγενημένῳ·
αἱ γὰρ ἀγρυπνίαι τοῦ βασιλέως ἡμῖν λόγους
ἐποίουν, ᾗ δὴ[1] καὶ μᾶλλον ἑτέρων ὑπὸ τῆς ἐν
αὐτοῖς ὥρας οὐδὲν ὅ τι οὐκ ἔδρα.

F 146 131. Τὸν δὴ ἐντεῦθεν μέχρι τῆς ἐπὶ Πέρσας
ἐξόδου χρόνον τοῖς μὲν ἄλλοις ἄλλ᾽ ἄττα, πλέον
δὲ ἐμοὶ παρ᾽ ἐκείνου τὸ φίλτρον, καὶ διετέλει δὴ
λέγων ὅτι ᾽δώσω σοι δῶρον ἐξελαύνων, ὃ οὐκ ἂν
R 89 ὥσπερ τἆλλα φύγοις.᾽ δεδειπνηκότες οὖν, ἐβιά-
σθην γὰρ παρ᾽ αὐτοῦ, ᾽ὦ ἄνθρωπε,᾽ φησίν, ᾽ὥρα
σοι τὸ δῶρον δέχεσθαι.᾽ καὶ ἐγὼ μὲν οὐκ εἶχον ὅ
τι αὖ τοῦτό ἐστιν εἰκάσαι· ὁ δὲ ᾽δοκεῖς μοι,᾽
φησίν, ᾽εἰς μὲν ῥήτορας κατὰ τοὺς λόγους
τέλειν, ἀπὸ δὲ τῶν ἔργων ἐν φιλοσόφοις γεγράφθαι.᾽ καὶ ἥσθην εἰπόντος, ὥσπερ ὁ Λυκοῦργος

---

[1] ἐποίουν, ᾗ δὴ conj. Re., Martin: ἐποίουν ἤδη Mss., F.

what it is that makes kingship an object of reverence would maintain that he stayed within the bounds of what is proper. For what is more royal than that an emperor should be uplifted to the glory of eloquence? 130. It was indeed impossible for him not to be so affected, for he had sired much eloquence both before and during his reign.[a] The emperor's burning of the midnight oil gave us oratory, and consequently his every action was to an unprecedented degree influenced by elegance of style.

131. In the interval from then until his departure for the Persian expedition,[b] his attitude towards others varied but I always received tokens of affection from him. He always used to say, 'When I leave, I will give you a present, which you will not try to avoid, as you do the rest.' So after dinner—for I had accepted his invitation perforce—he told me, 'My friend, it is time for you to receive your present,' and, as I was unable to guess what on earth it might be, he continued: 'It is this. Your eloquence puts you among the rhetoricians, but your actions have enrolled you among the philosophers.' I rejoiced at this statement as did Lycurgus at the god's greeting,

[a] Cf. *Or.* 12.94, 18.178. He composed the *Contra Galilaeos* at this time.

[b] Julian left Antioch for the Persian campaign on March 5, 363. Meantime the quarrel with the curia continued, as did measures against the Christians, coupled with the last minute appointment of the hard-line Alexander as *consularis Syriae*.

ἐπὶ τοῖς εἰς αὐτὸν παρὰ τοῦ θεοῦ· καὶ γὰρ ταῦτα
ὑπὸ τοῦ θεοῖς συνοικοῦντος εἴρητο. 132. προ-
πεμπούσης δὲ τῆς βουλῆς καὶ δεομένων ἀφεῖσθαι
τὰ ἐγκλήματα, Ταρσοῖς, πόλει Κιλίκων δώσειν

R 90 αὐτὸν εἰπὼν ἢν ὁ θεὸς ἀποσῴζῃ, 'καίτοι μοι
δῆλον,' ἔφη, 'τὸ πρὸς ταῦτα γενησόμενον, ὡς ἐν

F 147 τῷ πρεσβεύσοντι τὰς ἐλπίδας ἔχετε, τὸν δὲ καὶ
αὐτὸν ἐκεῖσε μετ' ἐμοῦ δεήσει βαδίζειν.' ἀσπα-
σάμενος δή με δακρύοντα οὐ δακρύων ἤδη βλέπων τὰ τῶν Περσῶν κακά, γράμματα ὕστατα
πέμψας ἀπὸ τῶν τῆς ἀρχῆς ὅρων ἤλαυνε γῆν
τέμνων, κώμας ἁρπάζων, φρούρια λαμβάνων,
ποταμοὺς διαβαίνων, τείχη κατασείων, πόλεις
αἱρῶν. 133. καὶ τούτων ἕκαστον ἤγγελλε μὲν
οὐδείς, τὴν δὲ τῶν ὁρώντων ἡμεῖς ἡδονὴν ἡδό-
μεθα πιστεύοντες, ἃ δὴ καὶ ἐγίγνετο, γενήσε-
σθαι, πρὸς τὸν ἄνδρα ἀποβλέποντες. ἀλλ' ἡ
Τύχη γὰρ τὰ αὑτῆς, κωμάσαντος γὰρ κατὰ Περ-

---

a Such close connection between rhetoric and philosophy is claimed by Themistius for himself and attributed to
Julian by Libanius (*Or.* 12.92). Libanius is here compli-
mented as a practical philosopher, and so superior to mere
theorists. Similarly, in his assessment of the ruler, he

AUTOBIOGRAPHY

for this was uttered by one who consorted with
heaven.[a]   132. When our city council escorted him
on his way with prayers that they might be forgiven
the charges against them, he replied that, if heaven
preserved him, he would favour with his presence
Tarsus in Cilicia.[b] 'Though I have no doubt that you
will react to this,' he went on, 'by pinning your hopes
upon him who will be your envoy, yet he too will
have to go there with me.' Then without a tear he
embraced me in my tears, with his gaze now fixed on
the ruin of Persia. He sent me a last letter from the
frontier of the Empire,[c] and marched on, ravaging
the countryside, plundering villages, taking for-
tresses, crossing rivers, mining fortifications and
capturing cities.   133. There was no messenger to
tell us of any of these achievements,[d] but we rejoiced
just as if we saw them, confident that events would
happen as they did, as we looked to him. But here
Fortune played her usual trick. The army had

eschews the exaggerations of a Pacatus (*Paneg.* 4, *deus
quem videmus*) or a Themistius (e.g. *Or.* 5.64b, νόμος
ἔμψυχος) by immediately amending παρὰ τοῦ θεοῦ into ὑπὸ
τοῦ θεοῖς συνοικοῦντος in the comparison with Lycurgus
(Herod. 1.65).

[b] Cf. *Or.* 15.86, Amm. Marc. 23.2.5. Julian was to be
buried at Tarsus (*Or.* 18.306).

[c] Julian *Ep.* 98 (ed. Bidez-Cumont), written from
Hierapolis.

[d] Cf. *Or.* 15.76. For the Persian campaign, see *Or.*
18.212 ff. Libanius makes great efforts to get information
from eyewitnesses, e.g., *Letters* 115, 120.

σῶν τοῦ στρατοῦ φόνοις τε καὶ τροπαῖς ἀγῶσί τε
γυμνικοῖς καὶ ἱππικοῖς, ἃ κατεθεῶντο ἀπὸ τῶν
ἐπάλξεων οἱ Κτησιφῶντος οἰκήτορες οὐδὲ τῷ
πάχει τοῦ τείχους πιστεύειν ἔχοντες, τοῦ τε Μή-
δου διὰ πρεσβείας τε καὶ δώρων ἐγνωκότος ἱκε-
τεύειν, μηδὲ γὰρ νοῦν ἔχειν πρὸς δαίμονα ἄνδρα
μάχεσθαι, τῶν δὴ πρέσβεων ἐπὶ τοὺς ἵππους
R 91 ἀναβαινόντων αἰχμὴ τοῦ σοφωτάτου βασιλέως
τεμοῦσα τὴν λαγόνα βρέχει τῷ τοῦ νενικηκότος
αἵματι τὴν τῶν ἡττωμένων γῆν καὶ ποιεῖ τὸν
πεφρικότα τῶν διωκόντων κύριον.   134. τῷ
μὲν δὴ Πέρσῃ παρ' αὐτομόλου τινὸς μαθεῖν
ὑπῆρξεν ἐν ὅτῳ εἴη τύχης, ἡμῖν δὲ τοῖς Ἀντιο-
χεῦσιν ἀνθρώπων μὲν οὐδείς, σεισμοὶ δὲ
ἐγίγνοντο τοῦ κακοῦ μηνυταὶ πόλεων τῶν ἐν τῇ
Παλαιστίνῃ Συρίᾳ τῶν μὲν μέρη, τὰς δὲ ὅλας
κατενεγκόντες· ἐδόκει γὰρ ἡμῖν ὁ θεὸς μεγάλοις
F 148 πάθεσι μέγα σημαίνειν. εὐχομένων δὲ μὴ τὰ
ὄντα δοξάζειν πικρὸν διὰ τῶν ὤτων τρέχει τῆς
ἀγγελίας βέλος, Ἰουλιανὸν μὲν ἐκεῖνον ἐν σορῷ
φέρεσθαι, τοῦ δεῖνος δὲ γεγενῆσθαι τὸ σκῆπτρον,

---

a Cf. Or. 18.249 ff, Eunap. fr. 22, Festus, Brev. 28.
b Homer Il. 17.98, emphasized by a τειχοσκοπία from the
walls of Ctesiphon and a ὁρκίων σύγχυσις unique to

revelled in the slaughter and rout of the Persians
and in the athletic competitions[a] and horse races, on
which the inhabitants of Ctesiphon had gazed from
their battlements with no grounds to trust even
their thickness of wall: the Persians had decided
to come as suppliants with prayers and gifts, knowing that it was against common sense for a man
to oppose heaven's will.[b] Then, as their envoys
remounted their horses, a spear pierced the side of
our wise emperor, and with the victor's blood it
drenched the land of the vanquished, and the pur-
suers it delivered into the hand of the fugitive.
134. It was by means of a deserter that the Persians
found out their good fortune, but we in Antioch
discovered it through no human agency: earth-
quakes were the harbingers of woe, destroying the
cities of Palestine Syria either wholly or in part. We
were sure that by these afflictions heaven gave us a
sign of some great disaster, and, as we prayed that
our guess should not be right, the bitter news
reached our ears that our great Julian was being
carried in his coffin, that some nonentity held the

Libanius. Ammianus' account differs greatly from this
(25.3). Libanius' attitude towards Julian's death hardens
over the years. In *Or.* 17.23 the responsibility is divine
and the event accidental. From 365 onwards the deed is
murder and the motives treason (cf. *Orations* Vol. i, Intro.
p. xxxvii). Certainly the Christians in Antioch were over-
joyed (*Letter* 120), as was Gregory Nazianzen (Migne, *PG*
35.531 ff).

Περσῶν δὲ Ἀρμενίαν τῆς τε ἄλλης ὁπόσον ἐβούλοντο γῆς.   135. εὐθὺς μὲν οὖν εἰς ξίφος εἶδον,
ὡς ἁπάσης σφαγῆς ἀλγεινοτέρας τῆς ζωῆς ἐσο-
R 92 μένης. ἔπειτα ἐνενόησα τὸν τοῦ Πλάτωνος
νόμον καὶ ὡς αὐτὸν οὐ λυτέον τὴν τοιαύτην δὴ
λύσιν καὶ ὡς οὕτως ἐλθὼν εἰς Ἅιδου τε καὶ παρ'
ἐκεῖνον ἐν αἰτίαις ἂν εἴην ὧδε τετελευτηκώς·
πάντως γὰρ ἂν ἐμέμφετο μὴ τὰ ἀπὸ τοῦ θεοῦ
περιμείναντι. πρὸς δὲ καὶ ἐδόκει μοι χρῆναι
λόγοις ἐπιταφίοις τὸν ἀπελθόντα τιμᾶν.

136. Τοῦτο μὲν οὖν οὕτω διὰ ταῦτα ἔσχε,
λόχον δέ τινα διαφεύγω βουληθείσης τῆς Τύχης.
οἱ γὰρ αὖ τῶν μὲν πρὸ τοῦ καιρῶν ἐν βασιλείοις
πρὸς ἰσχὺν ἀπολαύσαντες, τότε δὲ τὰ αὑτῶν
ἠναγκασμένοι πράττειν, ὑπὸ Φρυνώνδου τινὸς
R 93 ἀναπεισθέντες ὡς ἐμὲ δεινὰ αὐτοὺς εἰργάσθαι δι'
ἐπιστολῆς εἰς Βαβυλῶνα ἠκούσης, ὑφ' ἧς ἂν
αὐτοῖς δυσμενὴς ἐπανῆκεν ἐκεῖνος, ψηφίζονται
παρὰ συγγενῆ με γυναῖκα εἰσιόντα συλλαβόντες

---

[a] The 'nonentity' Jovian is never mentioned by name in
Libanius, but is bitterly criticized for the disgraceful peace
of Nisibis (*Or.* 18.279, 24.9). On this point Libanius is at
odds with Themistius.

[b] Plato, *Phaedo* 61 d. His grief was sincere and extreme.
He was unable to compose for some time (*Or.* 17.38, *Letter*

throne, and that Armenia, and as much of the rest of the Empire as they liked, was in Persian hands.[a] 135. My first impulse was to look to my sword, for life would be harder to bear than any death. Then I bethought me of Plato's maxim,[b] and that one must not seek such relief, and that if I met Julian in the other world, he would hold me guilty for dying so, for he would have no good word to say for a man who had not waited for orders from heaven. Moreover I felt it my duty to honour the fallen with funeral orations.

136. Such was the position and such the reason for it, when by the will of Fortune I avoided a trap set for me. Those people, who had made the most of their earlier opportunities but who under Julian had been forced to mind their own business, were induced by some blackguard[c] to believe that I had done them serious wrong in a letter to Babylon, as a result of which Julian on his return would have been hostile to them. They decided to kidnap me on my way to see a lady, a relative of mine,[d] to take me

111), and resumed declamations only after New Year (*Letters* 116, 123). He composed the Monody in 364 (*Letter* 133.6), and the Epitaphios by late 365.

[c] Phrynondas was a proverbial scoundrel; cf. *Ep.* 1145.3, Kassel-Austin on Aristoph. fr. 26, *Thesm.* 861, *Paroem. Gr.* 1.376.

[d] Probably Theodora, widow of Thalassius (1), a Christian whose family he had supported under Julian and which had now regained its influence. Libanius was in much danger from this attempt; *Ep.* 1453.1.

εἰς τὸν κῆπον, οὗ τὰς βουλὰς ἐβούλευον, εἰσαγαγόντες κτεῖναι· καὶ γὰρ ἂν δῶρα σφίσι παρὰ τοῦ τὰ σκῆπτρα λαβόντος γενέσθαι.   137. τοῖς μὲν
F 149 δὴ ἡτοίμαστο τὰ ῥόπαλα, τῶν δέ τις ταυτὶ μὲν συνειδότων τοῦ δὲ ἔργου κοινωνεῖν οὐκ ἐθελόντων, πρὸς ἐμὲ δὲ οὐ μάλα οἰκείως ἐσχηκότων, τῆς θεοῦ πεμπούσης, ἀφεκτέον εἶναί μοι τῶν παρὰ τὴν γυναῖκα ἐκείνην ὁδῶν ἔφη, κερδαίνειν γάρ, ὅ τι δὲ ἦν τὸ δεινὸν ἀπαιτοῦντι, τουτὶ δὲ οὐ προσέθηκε. θαυμαζούσης οὖν ὡς οὐ τὰ αὐτὰ ποιοίην τῆς γυναικός, ἀπεκρινάμην ἀφ᾽ ὧν ἠκηκόειν. καὶ ἣ διερευνωμένη νοῦν τε ἔχοντα καταμαθοῦσα τὸν φόβον παύσασά τε ἐξαπατωμένους ἐπῄνεσε τὸν ἐξελόμενον αὐτῇ τοιούτου μύσους τὴν οἰκίαν δαίμονα.

138. Μετὰ ταῦτα τοίνυν ἀνὴρ βάρβαρος ἐξώργιζε τὸν κρατοῦντα ἐπ᾽ ἐμὲ λέγων ὡς οὐ παυοίμην θρηνῶν τὴν τοῦ πεσόντος πληγήν. ὁ δὲ
R 94
ἔμελλε μὲν ἀπολεῖν με κακῶς δίκην ὀδύνης πραττόμενος, ἀνὴρ δέ τις Καππαδόκης ἀγαθός, συμφοιτητὴς ἐμός, παρ᾽ ἐκείνῳ δὲ μέγας, 'καὶ τίνα ἂν ἔχοις,' ἔφη, 'ψυχήν, εἰ ὁ μὲν κέοιτο ἀποθανών, ζῶντες δὲ οἱ λόγοι περιφοιτῷεν [τὴν

to the garden which was the scene of their plot and there to kill me: they would, they were sure, be rewarded by the new emperor. 137. They had already got their clubs ready, when one of the accessories to the plot (who had no desire to participate in the affair but were not on very intimate terms with me) was guided by Fortune to tell me that I should refrain from going to see the lady, as it would be to my advantage. I inquired what was the trouble, but he would tell me nothing further. When the lady began to wonder why I did not visit her as before, I sent her a reply based on the information I had received. She made further inquiries and, finding my fear well founded, she put an end to their plot and praised the powers that had preserved her home from such pollution.

138. Next, however, a barbarian[a] tried to rouse the emperor against me, asserting that I never ceased to bewail the fate of the fallen Julian. The emperor was about to slay me in dishonour as punishment for his resentment, but a Cappadocian, a good fellow and a schoolmate of mine who had great influence with him, exclaimed, 'Now, how would you feel, for him to lie slain, while the living words,

---

[a] Unknown, but certainly a military officer. For the accusation, cf. *Letter* 120.6. The Cappadocian was identified with Fortunatianus (cf. *Ep.* 1425, *PLRE* 369 (1)) by Sievers, p. 131, less probably with Iasion by Wolf (*Autob. Schr.*, p. 194). Libanius' writings critical of Jovian were unpublished, but were he to be executed, his friends would immediately release them.

γῆν] οἱ ἀπ᾽[1] ἐκείνου περὶ τῆς σῆς γεγραμμένοι
φύσεως;' τοσαῦται μὲν αἱ τρικυμίαι, τοσαῦται δὲ
αἱ ἀρωγαί.

139. Τὰ δὲ ἐπὶ τούτοις ἦν μὲν Ὀλύμπια τὰ
παρ᾽ ἡμῖν, ἔτος δὲ ἐμοὶ πεντηκοστὸν ἐπιθυμία τε
τῆς πανηγύρεως ὑπερφυής· παρακύψας δὲ ἐπὶ
τὰ πρῶτα τῆς ἑορτῆς δεσμώτης ἦν, οὐκ ἄρχον-
F 150 τος δήσαντος, ἀλλὰ ποδάγρα τότε πρῶτον
πολλή τις ἐπιπεσοῦσα καὶ χαλεπὴ πυνθάνεσθαι
τῶν εἰσιόντων ἠνάγκαζε ῥώμης τε πέρι καὶ
τέχνης τῶν ἀθλητῶν, ἡ δὲ ὥσπερ ἐν ἐκεχειρίαις
μικρὸν διαλιποῦσα πάλιν ἠκόντιζε καὶ πολλάκις
γε ἑκάτερον.   140. ἰατροὶ δὲ νενικῆσθαι μὲν
ὡμολόγουν, παρεμυθοῦντο δὲ μετατιθέντες ἀπὸ
τῆς κεφαλῆς ἐπ᾽ ἐκείνους τῷ λόγῳ τὴν νόσον·
τὸ γὰρ αὐτὸ ποσὶ μὲν κακόν, τῇ δὲ ἔσεσθαι ἀγα-
R 95 θόν. ἦν δὲ ἄρα τοῦτο φλυαρία, ἐπεὶ τό γε ἐκείνην κατειληφὸς εἴχετο τῶν ἄνω καὶ τοσοῦτόν γε
ἀπέσχον οἱ πόδες ὀνῆσαί τι τὴν κεφαλήν, ὥστε
ὥσπερ ἂν ἀπὸ τῶν ἐν αὐτοῖς κακῶν μοῖράν τινα
ἐκεῖσε πέμψαντες χαλεπώτερα τἀκείνης ἐποίη-
σαν.   141. οὔκουν ἐπὶ τοῖς πρὸ τοῦ φόβοις
ἐταραττόμην μόνοις, ἐν οἷς καὶ τοῦτο ἦν, μὴ τὴν

[1] περιφοιτῶεν τὴν γῆν VL, F.: ἀπ᾽ ACP, Martin: ὑπ᾽ VL, F.

which he has written about you, go everywhere?'
Such was my crisis, such my salvation.

139. The next event to follow this was the Olympia at Antioch, in my fiftieth year.[a] I was more than eager to see it, but after briefly appearing at the start of the festival I was held prisoner, not arrested by any governor but experiencing then for the first time a severe attack of gout, whereby I was forced to learn of the strength and skill of the competitors only by making inquiries of my visitors. It left off for a while—a truce, as it were—and then began to make me its target again, a sequence often repeated. 140. My doctors confessed themselves beaten, but tried to console me with the story that my illness had passed from my head to my feet; what was bad for the feet would be good for the head. This was, of course, arrant nonsense; my migraine remained in possession up above, while my gout, so far from relieving it, made it worse by transmitting to it, as it were, some part of its own affliction.[b] 141. So now I was harassed not merely by my previous nightmares, for example, that a hur-

[a] Cardinal evidence for his date of birth; see note on § 4 above. He supports the Syriarch Celsus in his search for competitors for the games (*Epp.* 1278–1279, 1399–1400). For his health problems at the time cf. *Letter* 138, *Ep.* 1274.4 (of 364).

[b] Cf. *Ep.* 1483 (of 365)

πόλιν ἡμῖν ἁρπάσαντες ἄνεμοι φέροντες εἰς τὸν
Ὠκεανὸν ἐμβάλωσιν, ἀλλ' ἔδεισα μέν, ὦ ἄνδρες,
καὶ τὸν τῶν ἀπαντώντων ὄχλον, ἔφυγον δὲ τὰ
μέσα τοῦ ἄστεος, ἔδεισα δὲ μεγέθη λουτρῶν,
ἔδεισα δὲ οἰκίας πλὴν τῆς ἐμαυτοῦ πάσας, νεφέ-
λης μὲν ἐπὶ τὰ ὄμματα ἐρχομένης, τοῦ πνεύματος δὲ εἰς μικρὸν συστελλομένου, τὴν κεφαλὴν

F 151   δὲ ἰλίγγων κατεχόντων, δόξης δὲ ἀεὶ τοῦ πεσεῖσθαι παρούσης, ὥστε ἑσπέρας ᾔδομεν ἐπ' αὐτῷ
τὴν Τύχην ἐν κέρδει τὸ μὴ πεπτωκέναι ποιούμε-
νοι.   142. ἓν ἐνῆν ἐκείνοις μέτριον, ὅτι μήτε
τοὺς λόγους μήτε τοὺς νέους ἐφεύγομεν· αὐτὸ

R 96   γὰρ δὴ τοῦτο ἦν ἡ παραψυχὴ τὸ ὡς ἥδιστα περὶ
ταῦτα πονεῖν οἴκοι τε ἐπὶ τῆς κλίνης ἐπί τε τοῦ
σκίμποδος ἐν τῷ διδασκαλείῳ· τὸ δὲ ἐφ' ἑκάτερον κομισθῆναι παρακινδύνευσις, αἱ δὲ ἐπιδείξεις
ἐκποδών, ἀηδὴς δὲ φίλος προσιών. ὥσπερ δὲ οἱ
πελάγη διαβάλλειν μέλλοντες καλοῦσι Διοσκού-
ρους, οὕτως ἡμῖν οἴκοθεν ἐξιοῦσιν ἐκαλοῦντο θεοὶ
κωλυταὶ γενέσθαι τῶν ἐν ἐλπίσιν ἀσχημόνων.
143. καὶ ὁ κλύδων οὗτος ἔτη τέτταρα ἐπεκράτει,
καὶ καταφεύγω δι' οἰκέτου πρὸς τὸν ἕτοιμον

ricane would uproot our city and cast it into the sea,[a] but, gentlemen, I was also afraid of meeting a crowd. I avoided the centre of the city, I feared the great baths and every house but my own. A cloud would descend upon my eyes, my breathing would become short, bouts of dizziness would overcome me, and I always felt that I was going to fall—so much so that in the evening I thanked my lucky stars and counted it a blessing that I had not done so. 142. I showed one grain of sense in all this, in that I did not seek to avoid my studies or my students. My consolation lay in the fact that such work was as pleasant as could be; at home I would lie in my bed, in school, upon the couch, but to be carried to either was a risky business, declamations were out of the question, and friends' visits unwelcome.[b] As travellers, before setting out on a journey overseas, call upon the Heavenly Twins, so I, on setting out from home, used to pray the gods to prevent the trouble I expected. 143. For four years I was subjected to the buffets of this sea of troubles, but then with a servant's aid I sought the aid of that ready

[a] Homer *Il.* 6.345 (and Eustath. *ad loc.*). Prophecies of doom abounded in 364 after the disasters of the previous year; cf. *Epp.* 1127.6, 1134.

[b] Cf. Ion of Chios, *TrGF* fr. 56, cited by Plut. *de Tranq. Anim.* 3.466d.

209

ἀμύνειν, τὸν μέγαν Ἀσκληπιόν, καὶ φράσαντος
οὐ καλῶς ἀφεστάναι με τῶν εἰωθότων πίνω τε
οὗ πάλαι φαρμάκου, καὶ ἦν μέν τι κέρδος, οὐ μὴν
παντελῶς γε ἐξελήλατο τὸ κακόν. ἔφη δὲ ὁ θεὸς
καὶ τοῦτο χαριεῖσθαι. ἐγὼ δὲ ᾔδειν μέν, ὡς οὐκ
εὐσεβὲς ἀπιστεῖν ἐγγυητῇ τοιούτῳ, θαυμάζειν δὲ
ὅμως παρῆν εἰ καὶ ταύτης εἶναί ποτε δόξαιμι τῆς
χάριτος ἄξιος. καὶ ἦν μὲν ἔτος ἕβδομον ἐπὶ τοῖς
F 152 πεντήκοντα λῆγον ἤδη, τρισὶ δ’ ἐνυπνίοις ὁ θεός,
ὧν τὼ δύο μεθημερινώ, μέρος οὐ μικρὸν ἑκάστῳ
τοῦ νοσήματος ἀφῄρει καὶ κατέστησεν εἰς τοῦτο,
ὃ μήποτε ἀφέλοιτο.   144. οὕτω δὴ τοῦ βασιλέως ἥκοντος τὴν αἴγλην τήν τε ἀπὸ τῶν ὅπλων
R 97   τήν τε ἀπὸ τῶν δρακόντων ἠχώ τε ὀργάνων
ὑπέμεινα συμμιγῆ, μηδ’ ἂν διηγουμένου πρότερον. καὶ οὐ πολὺ ὕστερον δῶρον αὐτῷ λόγον
εἰσῆγον, ἐφ’ ᾧ πλέον ἢ ὅτε τὰ ἔργα ἔπραττεν
ἡσθῆναι βασιλεὺς ἐδόκει. καίτοι τῶν μειζόνων
γε ἀνήκοος ὢν ἐν Σκύθαις ἐπεδέδεικτο ἐμεμενή-

---

[a] Date 367. He had consulted Asclepius at the shrine at
Aegae by proxy for some years, *Epp.* 706–708 by his
brother (363); *Letter* 137, *Ep.* 1300 by Eudaemon (364).
Health matters allow him to avoid mention of more serious
crises.

protector, the mighty Asclepius.[a] His message was that I had been wrong to give up my usual habits, and so I drank the medicine I had drunk long before, and there was some improvement, though my affliction was not completely removed. Then the god declared that he would grant me this favour too. I knew that it was not right to disbelieve such a promise from him, but I could not but wonder whether I should ever be thought worthy of this boon. However, when I had reached the end of my fifty-seventh year, by each of three visions, of which two occurred in the daytime, the god removed a great part of my ailment, and restored me to this condition, in which, I trust, I will always remain.[b]   144. Thus, when the emperor came to Antioch, I could stand the glint of arms and standards and the raucous blare of trumpets, though previously I could not have borne even the mention of them. Not long afterwards I presented him with an oration, a narration of his achievements, from which the emperor seemed to derive more pleasure than he had done from their performance. Yet he remained unacquainted with the greater part of it, an account of his feats among the Scyths.[c] Half of it was postponed because of its

[b] Summer 371. The final cure comes now, before the arrival of Valens in Antioch, 10 Nov. 371 (Malal. 338). For such interim pronouncements, cf. §§ 233, 244.

[c] The Panegyric on Valens' Gothic wars (for which cf. Amm. Marc. 27.5) was intended to rival that of Strategius in length and importance. He always archaizes by identifying Goths with the Scyths of classical literature.

κει. τοῦ γὰρ δὴ ἡμίσεος διὰ μῆκος ἀναβεβλημέ-
νου δείσαντες οἷς οὐκ ἄμεινον τέρπεσθαι λειμῶσιν
ἀληθινοῖς τὸν βασιλέα Μουσῶν, ἐν τοῖς εἰρημένοις ἱστᾶσι τὴν ἀκρόασιν, λεγόντων δὲ ἑτέρων
φόβος οὐδείς, ταυτὶ δὲ αὐτοῖς τῆς Γοργοῦς φοβε-
ρώτερα. βασιλεῖ γε μὴν καὶ ἀπὸ τούτων οὐκ ἐν
ἀγνοουμένοις ἐγώ.

145. Σὸν ἔργον, ὦ δαῖμον, καὶ τὸ τεθῆναι
νόμον τῶν παίδων τοῖς νόθοις ἐπίκουρον. τὸ μὲν
οὖν ἐπὶ νοῦν τε αὐτὸν τῷ πρεσβυτέρῳ τοῖν βασι-
λέοιν ἐλθεῖν ἕνα τε τῶν κρατούντων τοῖς ἐκείνου
γεγονέναι γράμμασι, κοινῆς τοῦτο ἔστω τῆς τῶν
ἐν χρείᾳ νόμου καθεστηκότων τύχης, τὸ δὲ τὸν
νεώτερον ἥκιστα αὐτὸν ἐπαινοῦντα μάλιστα
ἐπαινοῦντα φανῆναι ποιῆσαί τε κύριον, ἐπειδή με
ἐξουσίας τῆς ἀπ' αὐτοῦ δεόμενον ᾔσθετο, πῶς
F 153   οὐκ ἂν ἐν δίκῃ τῆς ἐμῆς κριθείη τύχης; ἤ με
πολλῆς τε καὶ βαρείας ἠλευθέρωσεν ἀνίας, ὡς
R 98   τῆς αὐτῆς ἡμέρας τελευτὴν μὲν ἐμοί, πτωχείαν
δὲ ἐκείνῳ τὴν ἐσχάτην οἰσούσης.

146. Ἀλλὰ μὴν τό γε ἐχθρούς—καὶ μή με
οἰέσθω τις τὴν Ὁμήρου συμβουλὴν παραβαίνειν

---

[a] Valentinian was older than Valens and his senior as

length, and they who found it better that the
emperor should not enjoy the true fields of learning
stopped my declamation at this point. They felt no
fear if others spoke of this, but such a declamation
from me scared them to death. For all that, I was, in
consequence, now known to the emperor.

145. Fate also helped to enact a law in favour of
illegitimate offspring. Granted that it may be attributed to the fortune shared by all who stood in need
of the law that the senior emperor devised it and
made it valid by his decree, but that his younger colleague, who thoroughly disapproved of it, should yet
be seen to approve it and ratify it—this must rightly
be judged as proper to my own Fortune, since she
saw that I required the privilege it bestowed. Thus
she freed me of great and heavy disquiet—the
thought that the very same day would bring death
for me and utter beggary for my son.[a]

146. Moreover, with regard to my enemies—and
let it not be thought that I go counter to Homer's

Augustus by a month. The law is *Codex Theodos.* 4.6.4 of
371, which allowed partial rights of inheritance to illegiti-
mates, here interpreted by Libanius as a special dispensation to himself. It was abolished by Theodosius (cf. note on
§ 195 below), causing Libanius yet further anxiety. For the
woman's low status cf. § 278 below, *Letter* 188.5. Her son
Arrhabius (later Cimon) was born about the end of 355 and
started his elementary education in 361 (*Epp.* 625, 678).
Julian had intended to grant him a special right of legiti-
mate succession (*Or.* 17.37), and even Jovian had made
some vague promise (*Ep.* 1221.6).

τὴν οὐκ ἐπιτρέπουσαν ἐπὶ κταμένοις ἀνδράσιν
εὐχετάασθαι, οὐ γὰρ ἀπὸ τοιαύτης γε μνησθήσο-
μαι τῆς γνώμης, ἀλλ' ὅπως μηδὲ τοῦτ' ἄρρητον
εἴη τῶν παρ' ἐκείνης δεδομένων—οἱ τοίνυν ἐπ'
ἐμὲ μηδενὸς μὲν λόγου, μηδενὸς δὲ ἔργου, μηδε-
μιᾶς δὲ ἀποσχόμενοι τέχνης, ἀλλ' οἱ μὲν ὀνείδεσι
περιβάλλειν ἀποχρῆν νομίσαντες, οἱ δὲ πᾶν
μικρὸν εἰ μὴ καὶ ἀποκτείναιεν, οἱ δὲ οἷς ἦν ἡδὺ
καὶ ταύρου τὸν νεκρὸν ἐκδήσαντας ἀφεῖναι
R 99   διὰ πετρῶν φέρεσθαι, τούτους τοίνυν τοὺς
πάλαι μὲν πολεμοῦντας, ἐγκαλεῖν δὲ οὐδὲν
σὺν ἀληθείᾳ γε ἔχοντας προαπήνεγκεν ὁ δαίμων ἡμῶν γε ἡσυχαζόντων καὶ οὐδ' ὅσον ἀραῖς
ἀμυνομένων· τί γὰρ δὴ ἔδει καταρᾶσθαι πάντα
ἐπισταμένου τοῦ δαίμονος, τὸν ἀδικοῦντα, τὸν
ἀδικούμενον, τὸν ὀφείλοντα δίκην, ᾧ τὴν δίκην
ὤφειλεν;   147. ἦν δέ τι καὶ πρὸ τοῦ θανάτου
τοῖς πολλοῖς θανάτου παρά γε σώφροσιν ἀνθρώποις δεινότερον τὸ πολλὰ κακὰ ἐπιδόντας εἶτα
οὕτως ἀπελθεῖν· ὧν ἕν τι καὶ τό <τινα>[1] τῶν
αἰδοίων τοῦ μοιχοῦ λαβόμενον τῇ χειρὶ ξυρῷ τὰ
πάντα ἀμῆσαι.

[1] τό <τινα> τῶν Martin.

214

maxim forbidding boasting over the fallen,[a] for it is in no spirit of gloating that I shall mention this; rather my intention is not to leave even this aspect of Fortune's favours unmentioned—my enemies, then, spared no word or deed or wile against me. Some thought it enough to encompass me about with slander; some thought it of no avail unless they also had me killed; there were others who would have enjoyed tying my dead body to an ox-tail and leaving it to be dragged over the rocks. Those people, then, who had long been at odds with me, but who could bring no accusation against me compatible with the truth, destiny made haste to remove, while I remained still and sought no protection, not even that of imprecations, against them. What need was there of imprecation, when the all-seeing eye of destiny saw the just and the unjust, the guilty and the victim? 147. For most of them, before their death, suffered a fate worse than death, for decent people, at least—deep disgrace followed by a disgraceful end.[b] One such instance was the castration and mutilation of an adulterer by the outraged husband.

[a] Homer *Od.* 22.412. This is the sole, and very veiled, reference in this part of the work to his perilous position under Valens when, as a known pagan and supporter of Julian's programmes, he was suspected of sympathizing with Procopius' revolt and participating in later conspiracies.

[b] Homer *Il.* 22.61.

F 154
R 100

148. Τούτοις ἄξιον ἐκεῖνο προσθεῖναι σμικρόν τε καὶ οὐ σμικρόν· ὑμῶν μὲν γὰρ ἴσως τῷ μικρολογεῖσθαι δόξω, δηχθεὶς δὲ αὐτὸς τὴν ψυχὴν οἶδα καὶ ἐπὶ μεγάλῳ τοῦτο παθών. ἦν μοι ἡ Θουκυδίδου συγγραφή, γράμματα μὲν ἐν μικρότητι χαρίεντα, τὸ δὲ σύμπαν οὕτω ῥᾴδιον φέρειν ὥστ' αὐτὸς ἔφερον παιδὸς ἀκολουθοῦντος καὶ τὸ φορτίον τέρψις ἦν. ἐν τούτῳ τὸν πόλεμον τῶν Πελοποννησίων καὶ Ἀθηναίων μαθὼν ἐπεπόνθειν ὅπερ ἴσως ἤδη τις καὶ ἕτερος· οὐ γὰρ ἂν ἐξ ἑτέρας βίβλου ταῦτ' ἂν αὖθις ἐπῆλθον πρὸς ἡδονήν. 149. ἐπαινῶν δὴ πολλὰ καὶ πρὸς πολλοὺς τὸ κτῆμα καὶ εὐφραινόμενος μᾶλλον ἢ Πολυκράτης τῷ δακτυλίῳ κλέπτας αὐτῷ τοῖς ἐπαίνοις ἐπῆγον, ὧν τοὺς μὲν ἄλλους εὐθὺς ᾕρουν, ὁ δέ γε τελευταῖος πῦρ¹ ἀνῆψε τοῦ μὴ ἁλῶναι, καὶ οὕτω δὴ τοῦ ζητεῖν μὲν ἐπεπαύμην, τὸ μὴ λυπεῖσθαι δὲ οὐκ εἶχον. ἀλλὰ καὶ τὸ κέρδος μοι τὸ παρὰ τοῦ Θουκυδίδου μέγα ἂν γενόμενον μεῖον ἤρχετο διὰ τὸ σὺν ἀηδίᾳ γράμμασιν ἑτέροις ὁμιλεῖν· 150. ἀλλὰ καὶ τοῦτο μέντοι τὸ οὕτως ἀνιαρὸν βραδέως μέν, ὅμως δὲ ἰάσατο ἡ Τύχη. διετέλουν μὲν γὰρ πρὸς τοὺς ἐπιτηδείους

---

¹ πῦρ Mss., Martin: πυρὰν Re. (Anim.), F.

148. Another occurrence deserves mention also. Although a trivial matter, it is significant. Some of you perhaps will regard me as a mere pedant, but I, smitten to my very heart, know that my emotion arose because of a calamity great indeed.[a] I had a copy of Thucydides' *History*. Its writing was fine and small, and the whole work was so easy to carry that I used to do so myself, while my slave followed behind: the burden was my pleasure. In it I used to read of the war between Athens and Sparta, and was affected as perhaps others have been before me. Never again could I derive such pleasure from reading it in another copy. 149. I was loud in praise of my possession, and I had more joy in it than Polycrates did in his ring,[b] but by singing its praises so, I invited the attention of thieves, some of whom I caught in the act. The last of them, however, started a fire to prevent capture, and so I gave up the search but could not but grieve at the loss. In fact, all the advantage I could have gained from Thucydides began to diminish, since I encountered him in different writing and with disappointment. 150. However, for this discomfort Fortune provided the remedy, a tardy one, admittedly, but, none the less, the remedy. I kept writing to my friends about it, so grieved was I, and I would describe its size and

[a] For this episode cf. Norman, "The Book Trade in Antioch," *JHS* 80 (1960), 122.

[b] Herod. 3.40 ff.

R 101 γράφων αὐτὸ μετὰ λύπης, τῷ λόγῳ μέτρα τε
διηγούμενος καὶ οἷον μὲν τὰ εἴσω, οἷον δὲ τὰ ἔξω
καὶ ποῦ νῦν ἄρα καὶ ἐν τίνος χερσί. νέος δέ τις,
πολίτης ἐμός, ἐωνημένος ἧκεν ἀναγνωσόμενος,
F 155 καὶ ὁ διδάσκαλος ἀνεβόησε 'τοῦτ' ἐκεῖνο,' τοῖς
γνωρίσμασιν ἑλών, καὶ ἧκεν ἐρωτῶν εἰ μὴ ἁμαρ-
τάνοι δόξης. λαβὼν οὖν ἐγὼ καὶ ποιήσας οἷα ἄν
τις ἐπὶ παιδὶ τὸν ἴσον μὲν ἀφανισθέντι χρόνον,
φανέντι δὲ οὐ προσδοκηθέντι περιχαρὴς ἀπηλλαττόμην καὶ τότε εὐθὺς καὶ νῦν οἶδα τῇ θεῷ
χάριν. γελάτω δὲ ὁ βουλόμενος, ὡς ὑπὲρ φαύλου
μακρολογήσαντος, ἀδεὲς γὰρ δήπουθεν ἀπαιδεύ-
του γέλως.

151. Ἐφ' ᾧ δ' ἂν μάλιστα νομιζοίμην ἄθλιος,
ἤδη φράσω. εἰ γὰρ αὖ πατὴρ ὅστις πολλοὺς μὲν
παῖδας παρέδωκε μνήμασι, πολλαῖς δὲ κλίναις
σώματά γε τούτων φερούσαις ἠκολούθησεν,
R 102 ἄθλιος, πῶς οὐχὶ καὶ αὐτὸς ἂν ἐν δυστυχοῦσιν
ἀριθμοίμην, οὐ πολλοὺς μόνον ἀλλὰ καὶ ἀγαθοὺς
παῖδας τοὺς μὲν αὐτὸς θάψας, τοὺς δὲ ἐν σοροῖς
ξένους νεανίσκους εἰς τὴν οἰκείαν ἀποπέμψας;
152. ὥσπερ γὰρ ὁ Θρασύβουλος τοὺς τῶν ἀστα-
χύων ὑπερέχοντας ἐξέκοπτεν, οὕτως ἡ Τύχη τῶν
ὁμιλητῶν τοὺς ἀρίστους ἥρπασεν, ἀρξαμένη μὲν

what it was like inside and out, and wonder where it was and who had it. Then a student, a fellow citizen of mine, who had purchased it, came to read it. The teacher of the class set up the cry, 'That's it,' recognizing it by its tokens, and came to ask whether he was right. So I took it and welcomed it like a long-lost child unexpectedly restored.[a] I went off rejoicing, and both then and now I owe my thanks to Fortune. Let him who likes laugh at me for making a mountain out of a mole hill. I have no regard for the laughter of boors.

151. I will now recount the chief reason why I should be thought unhappy. Now, if a father is unhappy when he has consigned many sons to the tomb or followed the biers which bore their bodies to the grave,[b] I too must be accounted unhappy, for my pupils who have died were not only many but good. Some I have buried myself, others, students from abroad, I have sent back to their homes in their coffins. 152. As Thrasybulus used to cut off the tallest ears of corn,[c] so did Fortune leave me reft of the best of my pupils. It has been the case, right

---

[a] The text of Thucydides takes on the role of a heroine of New Comedy, experiencing arson (as in Men. *Dysc.* 60), kidnapping, recognition, restoration.

[b] A morbid commonplace (cf. *Or.* 62.28 f, 62.53, 35.25) cloaked with classical allusion (§152) to Herod. 5.92 and the Nekuia of Homer.

[c] Herod. 5.92.

ἀπὸ τῶν ἐν Βιθυνίᾳ διατριβῶν, προελθοῦσα δὲ εἰς
τόδε, ἀεὶ φειδομένη μὲν οἳ οὐκ ἂν ἐξέλαμψαν,
τοὺς δὲ ἤδη τε ἐν δόξῃ καὶ αὖ τοὺς ἐσομένους
ἀφῄρει.   153. λέγω οὖν πρὸς τοὺς οἰομένους τι
λέγειν, ἐπειδὰν ἐρωτῶσι 'τίνας δὲ ἡμῖν ἀπέφηνε

F 156 ῥήτορας;' ὅτι ἐλθόντες εἰς Ἅιδου θεάσαιντ' ἂν οὐκ
ὀλίγους. ὧν οἰχομένων ἐζημίωνται μὲν βουλαὶ

R 103 καὶ διοικήσεις πόλεων, ἐζημίωνται δὲ δίκαι
λόγων τῷ δικαίῳ συμμάχων ἐστερημέναι, ἐζημίωνται δὲ θρόνοι ὧν τοὺς μὲν Ἑρμῆς, τοὺς δὲ
ἐφορᾷ Θέμις.

154. Καὶ μὴν καὶ τόδε δυστυχοῦς ἐν ἀσθενείᾳ
τε καὶ ἀτιμίᾳ καὶ προπηλακισμῷ τῶν λόγων
λόγους διδάσκειν καθήμενον ἑτέρων ὄντων ἐν οἷς
αἱ ἐλπίδες· ἃς εἰ μὲν μὴ ἠπίστασθε, τοῦ διδάξον-
τος ἂν ἔδει· νῦν δὲ ἴστε μὲν οὓς μακαρίζετε·
παρ' οἷς οἱ πλοῦτοι, ἴστε δὲ οὓς ἐλεεῖτε· παρ' οἷς
οἱ λόγοι.   155. εἴποι ἂν οὖν ἡ Τύχη καθάπερ ἐν
δράμασι λαβοῦσα φωνήν, ὅτι 'εἰ καὶ μυρίοις ἐναν-
τιώμασιν ἡ τέχνη σοι πεπολέμηται, τοῦτό γ' ἂν

---

a The chairs of professors of rhetoric and the seats of
provincial governors (iudices) sitting in judgment.

b The peroration of the original work reverts to its open-from my teaching days in Bithynia up to the present time, that always she spares the second-rate and removes those who had made a name for themselves or were just beginning to do so. 153. Some persons think they have a good case when they ask, 'What orators has he turned out for us?' My reply to them is that they would see plenty if they went down to the underworld; and their deaths have inflicted a grievous loss upon the city councils and administration, upon the courts of law, since they have been deprived of the eloquence which is the helpmate of justice, and upon the chairs of rhetoric and the seats of judgement.[a]

154. Moreover, it is also part of my misfortune that I sat giving lessons in rhetoric while rhetoric is sick, disparaged, and reviled and your hopes are pinned on other men.[b] If you do not know what these hopes are, you would need an instructor. As things are, you know well enough those whom you count the lucky ones—the men with the money—and the unlucky ones, too—the men of culture. 155. So Fortune, assuming a speaking part as though in a play,[c] might retort, 'Though your art has met with countless rebuffs, grant me this much, at

ng theme. The disciplines competing with rhetoric for power and prestige are increasingly Latin, law, and the secretarial skills required by an inflated civil service; cf. Or. 62 passim, Petit, *Vie Municipale,* pp. 360 ff, *Étudiants,* p. 179 ff.

[c] As in Menander, *Aspis.*

ὁμολογήσαις, ἐν πολλῶν ἀντάξιον παρ' ἐμοῦ σοι
γενέσθαι, τό τε εἰς πλῆθος ποιῆσαι λόγους τό τε
οὕτω δόξαι τοὺς ποιηθέντας εἶναι καλούς, ὥστ'
ἔτι ζῶντος, ἐν ᾧ καὶ φθονεῖσθαι ἀνάγκη, τὰς τῶν
βιβλογράφων δεξιὰς τὰς πολλὰς ὀλίγας ἐλέγχε-
σθαι τῷ πλήθει τῶν ἐραστῶν. τοιγάρτοι πᾶν
ἐργαστήριον λόγων καὶ τούσδε δείκνυσιν ὁμοίως ἐν
παιδευομένων τε καὶ παιδευόντων χερσί.' καὶ τούτων, ὦ ἄνδρες, οἶδα τῇ Τύχῃ χάριν καὶ αἰτῶ γε
παρ' αὐτῆς ἀεὶ βελτίω παρέχειν τὰ δεύτερα.

F 157   156. Ἀλλὰ γὰρ οὐκ οἶδ' ὅπως με διεφυγέτην
Αἰθέριός τε καὶ Φῆστος, Σύρων μὲν ἄρχων ἑκάτε-
ρος, ἄρξαντες δὲ πρὶν ἢ Βάλεντα δεῦρ' ἥκειν. ὃ
R 104 μὲν οὖν φωνῆς Ἑλλάδος ἄπειρος ἦν, ὁ Φῆστος
παραπαίων ἄνθρωπος, ἀλλ' ὅμως αὐτὸν οὐδὲ
τοῦτο ἔπεισε διώσασθαι τὴν ἀρχήν, ἐλθὼν δὲ δείλης εἰσάγων ὡς ἑαυτὸν Εὔβουλον καὶ συνὼν αὐτῷ
δι' ἑρμηνέως πιστοῦ, ὁ δ' ὡμολόγει τῆς ἐμῆς
ἐπιθυμεῖν τελευτῆς, ὅπως αὖθις εἶναί τι δόξειεν·
ἐπώλει οὖν Εὐβούλῳ τὸ μισεῖν ἐμὲ Φῆστος,
ὧν καθ' ἑκάστην ἤσθιε ἡμέραν· ἦσαν δὲ χῆνε-

***

ᵃ His declamations were accepted as textbooks in his
own lifetime; Eunap. V.S. 496.

least: you have had one thing from me which makes up for them all, your composition of so many orations and their reputation for excellence, so that even in your own lifetime the copyists of your works, many though they may be, have yet proved to be too few for the number of your admirers. That is bound to involve envy. But every school of rhetoric reveals that your works are thumbed by pupils and teachers alike.'[a] In this, gentlemen, I am grateful for Fortune's favour, and I beg of her that she may ever improve my future lot.

156. Yet somehow or other Aetherius and Festus have escaped mention so far.[b] They were both governors of Syria, holding office before Valens came to Antioch. The first of them, Festus, was an ignoramus who knew no Greek, but not even this fact induced him to refuse the office. He arrived, and one evening he gave an audience to Eubulus, and held a conversation with him by means of a trusted interpreter.[c] Eubulus admitted that he was eager for my death, so that he might once again be thought to be somebody. Festus, then, made a bar-

[b] The first addition: a recapitulation of events from 365, previously avoided. For the dating of the governors, cf. Downey, *Comites Orientis and Consulares Syriae*; Norman, "Notes on some *Consulares* of Syria," *BZ* 51 (1958), 73 ff. For Festus see *PLRE* 334 (3); on the identification with the historian, Baldwin, *Historia* 27 (1978), 197–217.

[c] His old enemy, Eubulus, reemerges. Like Phasganius, he knew no Latin.

πίονες ἐκείνῳ καὶ οἶνος ἡδὺς καὶ φασιανοί.
157. ἔβλεπέ τε οὖν με οὐχ ὡς ἥδιστα ὁ Φῆστος
καὶ ὡς περὶ κακοῦ τοὺς λόγους ἐποιεῖτο καὶ
ὁπόσα ἐξῆν ἔπληττε. καί ποτε θέατρον μέν μοι
συνείλεκτο, λῦσαι δὲ τοῦτο πειρώμενος ἐπὶ γράμματα βασίλεια τοὺς καθημένους ἐκάλει, ὡς δὴ
ἐπὶ τῷ τέλει τῆς ἀναγνώσεως ἐξελῶν, καὶ ὑπο-
γραφεῖς ἅμα παρῆσαν γραψόμενοι τὰ τῶν οὐκ
R 105 ἀναπηδώντων ὀνόματα · ᾤετο γάρ με μαχεῖσθαί τε
καὶ οὐκ ἐπιτρέψειν ἀπελθεῖν, τὸ δὲ ἀρκέσειν εἰς
θάνατον. ἐνταῦθα οἱ μὲν ὑπ' ἀνάγκης ἐξῄεσαν
πολλάκις μεταστρεφόμενοι πρὸς ἐμέ τε καὶ
τὰ ῥηθησόμενα, οἷς δὲ ἐξῆν ἀκούειν ἤκουον,
ποθοῦντες δὲ τὴν οὐχ ἑκοῦσαν οἰχομένην μοῖραν.
158. ἐμίσει μὲν οὖν καὶ ἐπεβούλευε, τοῦ μίσους
F 158 δὲ οἶδα τῇ Τύχῃ χάριν, ἥ γέ με οὐκ ἐποίησε φίλον
ἀνδρὶ δείσαντι μετὰ ταῦτα ὕστερον μὴ φθάσῃ
τὸν ἐκείνου σίδηρον ἡ νόσος ἀπενεγκοῦσα τὸν

---

a Festus summons the curia to hear the reading of an
imperial letter; refusal to attend would be treasonable,
and duly punished. This maneuvre removes the cream of
Libanius' audience from his declamation.

b Mention of the execution of Maximus, which occurred
during Festus' proconsulship of Asia in 372/3 (Eunap. fr.
39, V.S. 480, Amm. Marc. 29.1.42) is here brought forward
into his governorship of Syria (365/6), to increase the

gain with him, that for the price of his daily fare he would be my enemy, for Eubulus had plenty of fat geese, sweet wine, and pheasants at his disposal. 157. So Festus did not look very kindly upon me, and he began to speak of me as a villain and to cause me as much annoyance as he could. On one occasion, an audience had mustered to hear me when he tried to dissolve it by summoning them to listen to a letter from the emperor,[a] or he would banish them at the end of this recital. He posted secretaries there to take the names of any who did not immediately rise to their feet, for he thought that I would resist and forbid them to leave, and that that would be excuse enough for my execution. Then some began to go out, forced to do so, turning round again and again towards me and what I had to say, while those who were able to do so, listened to it, but missed the company of those who had made such an unwilling departure. 158. So he hated me and plotted against me, but I thank Fortune for his hatred. At least she kept me from friendship with a man who afterwards was on tenterhooks lest Maximus should die of natural causes before he had the chance to murder him.[b] So the poor deluded fool

odium. This confuses the chronology. Martyrius, otherwise unknown, seems to belong to his time as *magister memoriae*, 369–370, before he left court for Ionia. Martyrius seems to have dabbled in black magic, a treasonable offence, merely to pick the winner. Mention of this less serious matter allows Libanius to avoid direct reference to the notorious conspiracy of Theodorus.

Μάξιμον. ὁ δὲ ὡς ἐνίκησε ταύτην τὴν νίκην,
ἐγάννυτο ὁ κακοδαίμων, οὐ μὴν ἐμέ γε ἴσχυσε,
προσκυνῶ δὲ τὴν Ἀδράστειαν, καίτοι τοῦτό γε
ῥάπτων διὰ Μαρτυρίου, Πισίδου τινὸς ἀνθρώπου
R 106 χαίροντος μὲν ἀθληταῖς ἀμέμπτου δὲ ἄλλως,
δοκοῦντος δὲ τῷ Φήστῳ γόητος διὰ τὸ προσκεῖσθαι
παλαισταῖς. 159. περὶ τούτου μόνος πρὸς μόνον
τὸν Βάλεντα εἰπών, ὡς ἐμέ τε ἂν ἐν αὐτῷ ῥαδίως
καὶ τὸν Εὐτρόπιον ἕλοι, σπεύδων ᾤχετο εἰς
Ἰωνίαν ἐπὶ τὴν ἀρχήν, ὥστε γέλωτα πολὺν ἐν
τῷ δικαστηρίῳ τὸν Μαρτύριον παρασχεῖν οὐκ
ἐχόντων τῶν δικαζόντων μαθεῖν ἥτις ἡ ἀρχὴ τῷ
τοῦτον ἀχθῆναι[1] γένοιτο, τῆς ἀρχῆς τοῦ πράγματος ἐν σκότῳ γεγενημένης. Φήστῳ μὲν οὖν ἆθλον
τῆς κακίας ἐγένετο γάμος, νέα μὲν γυνή, συχνὴ
δὲ οὐσία, καὶ νῦν ἐν πόλεσιν ἃς ἐκένωσε τρυφᾷ.

160. Αἰθέριος δὲ τέθνηκε μὲν πολλὰ δὴ καὶ
μεγάλα πρότερον ἐπιδὼν κακὰ καὶ τό τε λαλεῖν
τό τε ἀκούειν ἀποβαλών. γίνεται δὲ καὶ αὐτὸς
εἰς ἐμὲ κακός, ὥσπερ ἀχθόμενος ὅτι με ἐν Βιθυ-

---

[1] ἀχθῆναι Mss., F., Martin: εἰσαχθῆναι conj. Herwerden,
Norman (1965).

rejoiced at gaining this victory, but he did not prevail over me—praises be!—despite his attempts to do so by means of Martyrius, a Pisidian. This fellow, for all that he had a weakness for athletes, was otherwise of good character, but Festus chose to regard him as a dabbler in magic because of his craze for the wrestling schools. 159. He had a private conversation with Valens about him, telling him that he could easily involve both Eutropius[a] and myself in the business, but then he went off in a hurry to Ionia to be governor there. The result was that Martyrius caused much laughter in court, for the judges could not understand why on earth the proceedings against him should ever have been commenced, since the commencement of the whole affair was veiled in mystery. Well, Festus got the reward for his villainy—marriage with a young bride and a large fortune, and now he rules the roost over the cities which he has bled white.[b]

160. As for Aetherius,[c] he died, but not before he had seen much misery, losing the powers of speech and hearing. He too behaved badly towards me, as though he was sorry that he had relied upon me in

[a] Eutropius (*PLRE* 317 (2)), Festus' predecessor as *magister memoriae* and as *proconsul Asiae,* was embroiled in the conspiracy of Theodorus, but acquitted (Amm. Marc. 29.1.36).

[b] The passage is written before Festus' death on 3 Jan. 380.

[c] Successor to Festus as *consularis Syriae,* probably 366/7, although mentioned before him in §156.

227

νίᾳ προὐβέβλητο καὶ ὁπότε τι δείσειεν ἐπ᾽ ἐμὲ
κατέφευγε. τὰς μὲν δὴ εἰς τοὺς λόγους ὕβρεις
F 159 αὐτοῦ παραλειπτέον, ἐν αἷς ἐχαρίζετο πάνυ
μὲν ἀνδρὶ πλουσίῳ, παῖδας δὲ οὐ κεκτημένῳ.
161. ἀλλ᾽ οὗτός γέ ἐστιν ὁ στήσας με ἐν μέσῳ
πολλῶν μὲν ἡνιόχων, πολλῶν δὲ ἱπποκόμων, οἷς
τε ἔργον ἀναπετεννύναι τοῖς ἅρμασι τὰς θύρας·
ὧν τοὺς μὲν ἔπαιε, τοὺς δὲ ἠπείλει κατακαύσειν,
ἑνὸς δέ τινος ἡνιόχου γέροντος καὶ πλευράς, ἐφ᾽
R 107 ᾧ δὴ καὶ μέγα ἐβόησεν ὁ λεώς, κατέτεμνεν ἐμοὶ
δὲ ἦν πόνος οὐ μικρὸς μὴ τὸ αἷμα ἰδεῖν. καὶ
ταῦτα ἀπὸ ψιλῆς αἰτίας ἀνδρὸς ἐποίει μαινομένου δεικνύντος τὴν μανίαν καὶ[1] τοῖς ἐν αὐτῇ
γιγνομένοις τῇ δίκῃ.   162. οὗτος ἦν ὁ κἀμὲ
κελεύσας εἰσάγειν, ὡς δὴ τῆς Φιλουμένου γοη-
τείας ἐν ἐμοὶ τὸν ἔλεγχον ἔχων· ὁ δὲ ἔλεγχος ἦν,
παρῄνουν αὐτῷ μὴ συκοφαντεῖν ἀλλ᾽ ἀπηλλά-
χθαι πραγμάτων. καὶ τοῦτο ἦν ἐφ᾽ ᾧ παρεκαλούμην.[2] τῷ δὲ οὐδὲν ἐδόκει δεινὸν ἐμὲ ἐφ᾽
οὕτως ἀνοήτοις εἰσελθόντα ἑστάναι. καὶ ἐγὼ μὲν
ἐξῄειν ἐλεῶν τὸν δικαστήν, ὁπόσον ἀπέχων νοῦ
δικάζειν ἠξίου, τῶν δὲ φίλων πολλοὶ συνέρρεον

[1] καὶ ACVL, Re., Martin: κἄν P, F., Norman (1965).

228

Bithynia and had recourse to me whenever he was
at all afraid. I must leave aside his insults to my
oratory—insults by means of which he tried to
curry favour with a rich man who had no children.
161. But it was he who set me in the middle of a
crowd of drivers, grooms, and starters, whom he used
either to beat or to threaten to burn alive. One old
driver he lashed about the ribs, and the populace set
up a loud outcry, while it was all I could do to avoid
the sight of blood. And all this was due to the baseless charges of a madman who revealed his madness even in the actual course of the trial. 162. It
was he who haled me into court, thinking to find in
me the proof of the charge of magic brought against
Philumenus.[a] And his proof? Why, that I advised
him not to concoct slanderous charges, but to keep
out of trouble: and that was the only reason for his
summons to me. He thought it nothing out of the
way that I should be fetched into court and stood up
there for such a stupid purpose. I left the court
room, pitying the governor for the perversity with
which he saw fit to govern, while many of my friends

---

[a] Assistant teacher to Libanius in 363; cf. *Ep.* 1355.
Petit (note *ad loc.*) canvasses the possibility that this accusation belongs to 371, but Libanius would not have got off
so easily then (cf. §172 below).

---

[2] ᾧ παρεκαλούμην Re. (Anim.), Martin: —οῦμεν Mss. exc.
Par. 3016: ᾧπερ ἐκαλούμην Par. 3016, F., Norman (1965).

ἄλλος ἄλλο τι πρὸς παραμυθίαν ἐσκεμμένος.
ἐποίουν δὲ οὐδὲν αὐτοὺς δεῖσθαι τουτωνὶ τῶν
σκεμμάτων. οὕτως οὐκ ἐτετρώμην.

163. Φιδήλιος δὲ ἦν μὲν Φήστου πολίτης,
ἄγριος ἄνθρωπος, ἀρχὴ δὲ αὐτῷ τῶν βασιλέως
F 160 ἐπιμελεῖσθαι χρημάτων, φιλία δὲ πρὸς τὸν Εὔ-
R 108 βουλον ἀφ' ὧνπερ καὶ τῷ Φήστῳ. ἔχων τοίνυν
αὐτὸν πειθόμενον ἐκ πολλῶν δώρων[1] τε καὶ συμ-
ποσίων κινεῖται ἐπ' ἐμὲ καὶ συνεβούλευε δίκην
λόγου λαβεῖν. τὸν δὲ λόγον, τοῦ τυράννου μὲν
ἐγκώμιον, γεγράφθαι, κεῖσθαι δὲ παρ' ἐμοὶ τῷ
συγγραφεῖ. ῥᾷστον δὲ εἶναι δι' ὑπηρετῶν ἑλεῖν.
164. ἔδοξεν οὖν ἐκείνῳ κάλλιον εἶναι τὸν στρα-
τηγὸν ἐπὶ τοῦτο προσλαβεῖν, πολλοῦ μὲν ἄξιον
Ἰουλιανῷ γενόμενον, πολλοῦ δὲ ὄντα τότε τῷ
Βάλεντι, φοβερὸν μὲν πολεμίοις, φοβερὸν δὲ τῶν
οἰκείων τοῖς κακοῖς, αἰδούμενον δὲ καὶ σοφίαν καὶ
λόγους, λόγου δὲ ἐν σοφῶν συνουσίαις οὐκ ἀπο-
ροῦντα· τουτὶ δὲ αὐτῷ παρὰ τῆς φύσεως ἦν.
165. οὗτος ὁ Λουπικῖνος αὐτὸν μέν με οὐδεπώ-

---

[1] δώρων Mss. exc. Vat. 939, Martin: δόρπων Vat. 939,
edd.

---

[a] *PLRE* 337 dates Fidelius from 365 to 370. Mention of
Lupicinus and his consulship seems to point him to late

flocked round me to console me with all kinds of reflections. But I ensured that they had no need of them, and so it was that I came to no harm.

163. Then there was Fidelius.[a] He was a fellow citizen of Festus and a brute of a man, and he held the post of imperial finance officer. He struck up a friendship with Eubulus for the same reason as Festus had done. Eubulus dined him and wined him and got him under his thumb, and then set him upon me, counselling him to have me punished for a speech of mine. This speech, a panegyric upon the usurper Procopius, had, according to him, been composed by me and remained in the possession of the composer—me. It was the easiest thing for him to lay his hands on it through his agents. 164. So Fidelius decided that it would be better to bring the military commander into the plot. He had served with distinction under Julian, as he did under Valens at this time, for he was a terror both to the enemy and to the wrongdoers among his own people: he revered wisdom and eloquence, and was never at loss in the company of the wise—such was his natural gift. 165. This man, Lupicinus,[b] had

366/367. Libanius (§165) denies that he composed any panegyric on Procopius, but the company he had kept made him suspect. Significantly, his correspondence of 363/5 is in disorder and then ceases; see Intro, "Libanius and His Letters."

[b] *Magister equitum* under Julian in Gaul and Britain, and under Valens against Procopius. Consul 367. *PLRE* 520 (6).

ποτε ἰδών, παρὰ φήμης δὲ ἴσως τινὸς περὶ ἐμοῦ
τι δεξάμενος πρὸς μὲν τὸν εἶπε· 'σίγα, ὦ φιλό-
της, καὶ ἐν ἡμῖν ταῦτα ἱστάσθω.' μεταπεμψάμενος δὲ ἐμὲ ποιεῖταί τε φίλον καὶ ἐπαγγέλλειν
εἴ του δεοίμην ἐδίδου παρεκάλει τε τοὺς τῶν
ἑδῶν τούτους καταγελῶντας, τοὺς τοῦ Οὐρανίου[1]
κληρούχους, ἀφέντας ἃ ἀλαζονεύονται τἀμὰ
ζηλοῦντας ὁρᾶσθαι. τοιαῦτα μὲν ἀνέσεισεν ὁ
δαίμων, τοιαῦτα δὲ καὶ ἐκοίμισεν, οὐχ ὡς πεπ-
ποιημένου μοι τοιοῦδέ τινος λόγου, ἀλλ' ὅτι τῆς
πρώτης πείρας ἁμαρτὼν ὁ Φιδήλιος προὔβαινεν ἂν
ἐπιβουλεύων ἕως ἔργου τύχοι. 166. ὑπῆρξε δέ
μοι καὶ ἀμείψασθαι τὸν οὐχ ὑπαχθέντα ἄνθρω-
πον· παρὰ μὲν γὰρ τοῦ κρατοῦντος ἦν αὐτῷ τὸ
ἐν ὑπάτοις εἶναι, παρ' ἐμοῦ δὲ <....> Ἀρχέ-
λαος.[2] καὶ ἐτιμώμην ἄλλοις τε οὐκ ὀλίγοις καὶ δὴ
καὶ ᾠήθη δεῖν ἐλθὼν ὡς ἐμὲ προσειπεῖν πατὴρ
γινόμενος τῆς τιμῆς, οὐ γὰρ ἦν ὃν ἐμιμεῖτο, ἀλλ'
ἐγὼ τοῦτο αἰσθανόμενος φθάσας ἐδεήθην ἔν τι,[3]
προελέσθαι μεῖναι τὸν γέροντα, τὸν δὲ χρὴ νομί-

---

[1] Οὐρανίου Mss., Re., Martin: οὐρανοῦ conj. Wyttenbach, F., Norman (1965).
[2] Post δὲ lacunam ind. VL Par. 3016, Re., Martin.
[3] Post τι lacunam ind. Martin.

never seen me, but he had perhaps heard some report about me, for he replied, 'Hush, my friend. Don't let this go any further than me.' Then he sent for me, made me his friend and offered to provide any service I required, and he called upon those persons who make mock of our temples, these fee-holders of god above,[a] to cease their vaunting and to look on me in emulation. Such were the storms which destiny conjured up and laid to rest—not that I had ever composed a speech of that sort, but Fidelius, after an initial failure, might have continued his plots until he attained his object. 166. I was able to make some return to Lupicinus too for not being led by the nose, since, although his appointment as consul depended upon the emperor, he depended upon me <...> Archelaus.[b] From Archelaus I received many tokens of esteem; in fact, he felt that he should visit me for an interview as a mark of such esteem—an unprecedented course for him to take—but I got wind of it and forestalled it by simply requesting the old man to stay where he was. His nephew, however, I must admit was my visitor.

[a] Obscure and textually suspect. Martin (note *ad loc.*, p. 255) pertinently distinguishes κληροῦχοι, the Christian clergy, from κληρονόμοι, Christians en masse.

[b] Obscure and lacunose. For the visit of the Archelai cf. *Or.* 2.9 (written within a year or two of this passage). The uncle had held office in the East under Constantius, the nephew was *comes sacrarum largitionum* at the time of the visit, which is thus to be dated to 369.

LIBANIUS

ζειν ἀφῖχθαι. 167. Προτάσιον ἐνέπλησαν μὲν
τῶν κατ᾽ ἐμοῦ λόγων ἄνδρες ἐν οὐδενὶ μὲν λόγῳ
πρότερον ὄντες, κτησάμενοι δὲ ἰσχὺν ἐκ τῆς Ἰουλιανοῦ σφαγῆς. οὗτοι τοῦτον ἐφόβουν ὡς
αἴσχιστα ἂν ἄρξειεν εἰ μὴ ἀπελαύνοι με τῶν
θυρῶν, καὶ παρέζευξάν οἱ τῶν ἐκ τῆς συμμορίας
κοινωνὸν τῆς πορείας τηρήσοντα ἐν ἐκείνῳ τὸν
φόβον. ᾔει μὲν οὖν ὡς ποιήσων με μικρόν, νόσῳ
δὲ πιεζόμενος ἐβάδιζεν αὐξομένης τῇ πορείᾳ τῆς
νόσου. καὶ ἧκέ γε εἰς τὴν καταγωγὴν νυκτὸς
οὐδενὸς τῶν ἐν τῷ νόμῳ τυχών, οὐ γὰρ εἴα τὸ
νοσεῖν. 168. ὡς δὲ πολλῶν ἰόντων αὐτῷ μόνος
ἀπελιπόμην, λέγει πρὸς τὸν Ζήνωνα, ᾧ μάλιστα
ἐχρῆτο, τοὺς κατ᾽ ἐμοῦ λόγους ἐξελεγχθαι τοῖς
ἔργοις. τὸν γὰρ δὴ λεγόμενον ἐνοχλεῖν τοὺς ἄρχοντας ἥκιστα προσιέναι. ὁ δὲ καὶ πάνυ ταῦτα
ἐλπίζειν ἔφη· οὐ γὰρ ἰέναι μᾶλλον παρ᾽ αὐτοὺς
ἢ καὶ τοὐναντίον· χαρίζεσθαι μὲν γὰρ ταύτῃ τοῖς
ἐρῶσι· τοὺς δὲ οὐκ ἐρῶντας οὐδὲ ἐπίστασθαι.
ταυτὶ μὲν ἤκουσε, δῆλος δὲ ἦν ἀτιμάσων, οὐ μὴν
ἐπέτρεψέ γε ὁ θάνατος.

169. Ἕτερος Προτάσιος τά γε πρὸς ἐμὲ ῥᾷσθ᾽

a *Consularis Syriae,* Christian, otherwise unknown. He

234

167. As for Protasius,[a] he had his ears filled with accounts of my misdeeds by men who had been of no account in time past, but who had gained influence as a result of Julian's murder. They sent him into a panic, asserting that he would be a really bad governor if he did not bar his doors to me, and they appointed one of the members of their clique to accompany him on his journey here and to keep his panic alive within him. So he made his way here to bring me down, but, as he came, he fell ill and his illness increased with his journey. He reached his headquarters one night, with no formalities of welcome because of his illness. 168. Since he had many visitors and I was the only absentee, he remarked to his close friend Zeno[b] that the worth of the assertions made against me had been shown by the facts: I, who had a name for annoying the governors, would never show my face at his audiences. Zeno's reply was that he was not a bit surprised, for it was not my way to visit them any more than theirs to visit me: only to my well-wishers did I pay such a compliment, and those who did not wish me well I ignored completely. He listened to this but still was clearly bent on my disgrace, but death forestalled him.

169. His successor[c] was, in his attitude to me,

evidently entered office before the arrival of Valens' court in Antioch in 371.

[b] Otherwise unknown.

[c] A Christian *consularis,* name unknown.

οὗτος ἧκεν, ὃς καθάρμασι μὲν συνῆν, παρ' ὧν δ'
ἄν τι καὶ ἐμάνθανεν, ἄβατον ἐποίει τὴν καταγω-
γήν. καὶ ᾤετο μὲν ζημιοῦν, ἐγὼ δὲ ἐκέρδαινον.
καὶ κλῆσιν μὲν τὴν ἐπὶ τοὺς λόγους ἤλπιζεν,
ἐγὼ δὲ ἄλλους ἑστιῶν διδάσκων αὐτὸν ὅτι οὐ
λίαν αὐτοῦ δεοίμην. ὁ δὲ ᾖδει τούτοις γε τὴν
καρδίαν, ἔδειξε δὲ ἔν τινι κατηγορίᾳ νέοιν· οἶν
δέον, εἴπερ ἠδίκουν, ἐπιθεῖναι δίκην, ὁ δὲ τὸ
διδασκάλων ἐσαγήνευεν ἔθνος οὐχ ἅπασιν ἐγκαλῶν, ἀλλ' ὅπως ἐν τῷ παντὶ κρύπτοιτο αὐτῷ τὰ
πρὸς ἐμέ.   170. καὶ τὼ μὲν νέω γυμνώ τε
ἤστην καὶ μετεώρω πρὸς πληγάς, παρεκάθητο
δέ τις Ὀλύμπιος. τοῦ δὲ οὐ μετεῖχον ἐγώ, ἠδι-
κεῖτο δὲ ὁ νόμος. ὁ δ' οὕτω δή τι ξυνετὸς ἦν,
ὥστε οἷς ἐφθέγξατο μὴ μαστιγοῦν ἐκεκώλυτο.
φρόνημα δὲ τὸ θράσος καὶ ἡγούμενος καὶ ὀνομάζων ὅπλα ἀνταράμενος τῷ στρατηγῷ γνῶναί τε
R 113   αὐτὸν ἠναγκάσθη καὶ συνεσταλμένος ἔκειτο, καὶ
τοῦτό οἱ τῆς ἀρχῆς πέρας.

236

just another such. He associated with the scum of
the earth, but made his headquarters out of bounds
to everyone from whom he might have learned
something. He thought to do me harm, but it was
clear profit for me. He used to expect an invitation
to my declamations, but I reserved this feast for
others and gave him to understand that I had no
great need of him. At this his anger swelled, and he
displayed it in charges made against a couple of students. If they were guilty, he should have punished
them both, but instead he cast his net over the
whole teaching profession, not with any accusation
to level against the whole body, but, by actions
which affected them all, seeking to conceal his personal hostility towards me.   170. The two lads
were stripped and hoisted up for the flogging, while
a man named Olympius[a] was in attendance. I was
not acquainted with him, but the law was being
flouted. Olympius showed such sound sense that,
because of his outcries, the governor was prevented
from carrying out the flogging, but, proceeding to
regard and describe his outrageous conduct as
sound policy, he took up the cudgels against the military commander, was forced to his senses, and
reduced to eating humble pie. And that was the end
of him.

[a] An assessor to the *consularis,* otherwise unknown,
but certainly not (as in *PLRE* 643) Olympius (3). The
general is likewise unknown, perhaps still Lupicinus, but
more probably Julius (2); cf. *Or.* 2.9.

171. Ἀλλ' ἐπάνειμι δὴ πρὸς τὸν Βάλεντα·

F 163 ὃν ἔδειξε μὲν χρηστὸν τὸ μὴ τῷ τυράννῳ τοὺς τοῦ τυράννου φίλους ἐπαποκτεῖναι· ἐπεὶ καὶ ὁ Ἀνδρονίκου τοὐμοῦ φίλου θάνατος Ἱερίου μᾶλλον τῆς ἀλώπεκος ἔργον ἢ τοῦ παρακρουσθέντος ἦν. ἀσφάλειαν δὲ τῆς πρᾳότητος ἐωνῆσθαι νομίζων εὗρεν ἕτερον λόχον, Φιδούστιόν τε καὶ οὓς ἐκεῖνος ἐπανέστησε τῷ σκήπτρῳ, καὶ ἐχώρει μὲν διὰ τῶν ἠδικηκότων ὁ βασιλεὺς τὴν ἀρχήν, προσετίθετο δέ τις καὶ τῶν οὐδὲν τοιοῦτον ἐπισταμένων. μάντις τε ἅπας ἐχθρὸς ὅτῳ τε ἐδέησε τῆς τέχνης διδάσκεσθαί τι περὶ τῶν ἰδίων τῶν αὑτοῦ παρὰ τῶν θεῶν βουλομένῳ· χαλεπὸν γὰρ δὴ ἐδόκει εἶναι παρόντος μάντεως μὴ ἄν τινα καὶ ἐπὶ τοῖς

R 114 μείζοσι χρήσασθαι τῷ ἀνδρί. 172. τὴν ἐκείνου δὲ ὁρμὴν οἱ συκοφάνται λαβόντες πάντα ἐκύκων ἐπὶ πάντας ἰόντες. δόξα τε ἦν παρὰ τῷ Βάλεντι, φθόνου τὴν δόξαν πεποιηκότος, πάντως

---

[a] Second recapitulation of the events of 365–371, recognised by Petit as beginning another addition. Libanius' assessment of Valens' repression of the revolt of Procopius as clement both here and in Or. 19.15 ff, 20.25 f, while akin to Themistius Or. 7, is flatly contradicted by pagans and Christians alike; cf. Zos. 4.8.5, Amm. Marc. 26.10.6, Socr. H.E. 4.5.

171. But to return[a] to Valens—the fact that, after Procopius' death, he did not execute Procopius' friends too argued that he was a decent person. The execution of my friend Andronicus was more the work of that sly fox Hierius than of the emperor whom he deceived.[b] Yet just when he thought that, by his clemency, he had bought himself security, he found more treason in Fidustius and those whom he roused to conspire against the throne.[c] So the emperor proceeded at first against the culprits, but there were added to the list names of men completely innocent of such a crime. Every soothsayer was his foe: so was any who, in his desire to learn from heaven something of his own fortunes, had recourse to this art, for it was hard to believe that, with a soothsayer handy, his services would not be employed on matters of greater moment. 172. This tendency of his the informers fastened upon, attacking everyone and setting everything in turmoil. Valens had an idea, and my enemies had

[b] For Andronicus, *Or.* 62.56, *PLRE* 64 (3). For Hierius, *PLRE* 430 (3). In 360 Libanius had introduced Hierius to Andronicus, *Letter* 67.

[c] A direct leap from the revolt of Procopius, 365–366, to the so-called conspiracy of Theodorus in 371, which resulted in an official reign of terror (Amm. Marc. 29.1 ff). Ammianus confirms Fidustius' prominent part in the affair, and similarly the roles of Irenaeus and Pergamius (§§172, 176).

ἂν εἰς ἔλεγχόν με πεσεῖν δι᾽ ἑνός γέ του τῶν ὑπὸ
τὴν βάσανον ἀγομένων. λέγεται δὲ καὶ αὐτὸς
ἐρέσθαι τὸν Εἰρηναῖον εἰ μετεῖχον τοῦ ἐπιβουλεύ-
ματος, θαυμάσαι τε οὐ μετασχεῖν ἀκούσας.
173. καὶ μαντικῇ μὲν οἶδα χάριν, ἥ μοι τὴν
κεφαλὴν ἐν πρᾳοτέροις κατέστησεν, ὅτῳ τε χρη-
στέον καὶ ὅτῳ μὴ φράζουσα, τὴν κεφαλὴν δ᾽ ἂν
ἀπετεμνόμην, ὡς δεινότερον ὂν τοῦ ἀπολωλέναι
F 164 τὸ ταύτῃ σεσῶσθαι, ᾗ[1] τις ἧκεν ἐπὶ τὸν Ἀδελ-
φεῖον, ὃς θεῖον μέν τι τὴν φιλίαν ἡγεῖτο, καρτε-
ρεῖν δὲ πρὸς ἀνάγκας οὐκ εἶχε καὶ ὡμολόγει γέ
τοι τοῦτο καὶ ὁμολογῶν ᾐσχύνετο.   174. ἐδεῖτο
οὖν ἡμῶν αἰτεῖν αὐτῷ παρὰ τῆς Τύχης τὸν
R 115 θάνατον, οἷοι πολλοῖς ἐξαίφνης ἐπῆλθον. οἱ μὲν
δὴ ἄλλοι πάντες εὔχοντο, ἐμοὶ δὲ ἡ τῶν δεινῶν
ἐλπὶς ἧττον εἶναι κακὸν τοιαύτης εὐχῆς ἐφαίνετο. σιγῇ τοίνυν ἐδάκρυον. ὁ δὲ λουσάμενός τε
καὶ δειπνήσας ὕπνον τε ὁμοῦ καὶ θάνατον δέχεται, ὥστε ἕωθεν ἡμεῖς μὲν παρῆμεν ἐπὶ τὴν ἐκ-
φοράν, ἐκ δὲ τῶν βασιλείων τινές, ὡς ἐκεῖνον
δήσοντες. ὁ δὲ αὐτοὺς διεπεφεύγει πτηνῷ τάχει.

[1] ᾗ τις conj. Norman: ἥ τις Mss., Norman (1965), corruptum indic. F: εἰ τις conj. Schmidt, Martin.

fostered it, that I would certainly be implicated by
the statements of one of those subjected to examination. It is said that he personally asked Irenaeus
whether I was party to the plot and was surprised to
hear that I was not.[a] 173. I am grateful to the
soothsayer's art for relieving the suffering of my
head and for telling me which course to adopt and
which not, but I was in fair way to losing my head
altogether, for it was more dangerous to have been
preserved by its help than to have succumbed, as in
the attack upon Adelphius.[b] He regarded friendship as something sacred, but could not steel himself against torture, as he admitted and was
ashamed of his admission. 174. Thus he begged
us to pray fortune for his death—such a death as
suddenly befalls many a man. All the others offered
up this prayer, but for me such a terrible prospect
was less of an evil than this prayer, and so I silently
wept. He bathed, dined, and welcomed sleep and,
with it, death: and next day, at dawn, we were
attending his funeral when people from the palace
arrived to arrest him, but he had escaped them on

[a] A persistent tradition has Libanius participating in
similar practices of divination (ἀλεκτορομαντεία, Zonar.
13.16, Cedren. 548, *PG* 121.597), so that Valens' question
to Irenaeus becomes more pointed. The dangers of employ-
ing such practices for private purposes were great; cf.
§ 177, Amm. Marc. 29.2.26.

[b] Adelphius is otherwise unknown. The statements he
would make under examination by torture would serve to
incriminate his friend Libanius, the real suspect.

175. σπινθήρων τοίνυν ἐξ ἐπιστολῶν, τῶν μὲν παρ' ἐμοῦ πρὸς ἑτέρους, τῶν δὲ ἐμοὶ παρ' ἄλλων ἀφιγμένων, ἐν αἷς ἀδικία μὲν οὐδεμία, λαβαὶ δ' ἂν ἐγένοντο συκοφάνταις ἀνθρώποις, ταύτας δὴ τὰς ἀφορμὰς μάλα εὐπετῶς ἀνεῖλεν ἡ Τύχη, ὥστε ἐν μυρίοις γράμμασι μὴ εἶναι γράμμα ἐμόν.

176. Τῆς αὐτῆς θεοῦ καὶ τὸ περὶ Περγάμιον πολὺ πρὸ τῶνδε τῶν κακῶν ἐγκαλέσαντά τι, ψεῦδος μέν, ᾤετο δὲ ἠδικῆσθαι. τοῦτο δὴ πείσας αὐτὸν ἐχθρὸς ἦν. εἰ δὲ οὐκ ἦν, κἂν ἐξελάλησέ τι R 116 τῶν οἰσόντων ἐμοὶ ζημίαν. καὶ τὴν Αὐξεντίου δὲ περὶ τούτων πρός με σιωπὴν τῆς Τύχης δῶρον νομιστέον, ὅτι οὐδὲν εἰδέναι ἀξιῶν ἄνθρωπος, ὃ μὴ καὶ ἐμὲ δεῖν, τοῦτό γε ἄρρητον ἐποιήσατο.

F 165 177. ὁ μὲν δὴ βασιλεύς, ὥσπερ τις θηρατὴς ἁμαρτάνων θηρίου, δεινῶς ἤχθετο, κινεῖται δὴ κίνδυνος ἐκ χαλεπότητός τε δεσπότου καὶ λύπης οἰκέτου. ὑπογραφεὺς μὲν ὁ οἰκέτης ἦν, οἰωνιστὴς δὲ ὁ δεσπότης. τοῦτον δέ ποτε δι' ἐπιστο-

---

[a] Fortune's favour was supported by human intervention. He had suppressed his correspondence files.

[b] Pergamius had been praised in letters of 364 (*Epp.* 1206, 1210–1211, 1214, 1216); for his indiscretion, see Amm. Marc. 29.1.25. Auxentius of Tarsus corresponds with Libanius in 361–363; *BLZG* 92 (ii).

the swift wings of death.   175. Yet there was some
cause for misgiving owing to the correspondence
which had passed between some of my friends and
myself. There was nothing wrong in it, but it could
have provided a handle for informers, but, by the
favour of Fortune, this menace was removed quite
easily, and in all the mass of correspondence there
was not a single letter of mine.[a]

176. By her aid also the business with Pergamius was settled.[b] Long before this trouble he had
made some complaint against me, and, false though
it was, he reckoned himself the injured party. Anyway, he had convinced himself of this and was my
enemy. Had he not been, he would have blurted out
some statement which would have got me into
trouble. Also the silence which Auxentius maintained towards me in this matter must be regarded
as one of Fortune's gifts, for though he wanted
acquaintance with nothing which I too should not
know, this at least he kept secret from me. 177. The
emperor, like a hunter balked of his quarry, was in a
towering rage.[c] Then I experienced some danger
owing to the harshness of a master who practised
divination from birds, and the resentment of a slave,
his secretary. I had once written to him, inquiring

[c] For Valens' rages, cf. Amm. Marc. 29.1.18 ff. Libanius
dramatizes his own importance, but was justifiably
suspect. Though an appendage to the major inquisition,
this episode must precede *Codex Theodos.* 9.6.1–2 of March
376, which was severe upon slaves who brought unsuccessful charges.

λῶν ἠρόμην φαρμάκου τινὸς πέρι, τοὺς μὲν θεοὺς
οὐκ εἰπών, ἰατρῶν δὲ μνησθεὶς ἀσφαλείας εἵνεκα.
ταῦτα ὁ μὲν οὐ κατέκαυσε τὰ γράμματα, ὁ
δὲ κτησάμενος ἐφύλαττεν ὅπως, εἴ τί ποθ᾽
ὕστερον ἐπίοι δεινόν, σώζοιτο ταῖς ἐπιστολαῖς.
178. ὡς οὖν ἐκάκου τε καὶ ἐδίωκε τὸν δεσπότην
ἐπὶ τοῖς οἰωνοῖς, ἐν τοῖς γράμμασι τούτοις εἶχε
τὴν πίστιν· συνήσειν γὰρ δὴ τὸν δικαστὴν ὅ τι
ἐδήλουν οἱ ἰατροί· ἐμπεσόντι δὲ εἰς τὸ δίκτυον
ὁπωσοῦν ἐπέκειτ᾽ ἂν εὐθὺς κεκραγὼς ὁ βασιλεύς.
πολλαὶ μὲν δὴ παραινέσεις ἀπὸ πολλῶν πρὸς τὸν
οἰκέτην μὴ τὸν εὐεργέτην ἀδικεῖν, εὐεργέτην δέ
με ἐπεποιήκεσαν αὐτοῦ μέμψεις τε καὶ ὀργαὶ καὶ
ἐπιτιμήσεις αἷς τὸν δεσπότην ἐπειρώμην ἀνείρ-
R 117   γειν, ὁ δὲ οὐκ ἀγνοεῖν μὲν ταῦτα, ἔλεγε δὲ οὐ
μεγάλα νομίζειν, προέσθαι δ᾽ ἂν αὐτὸν μετὰ τῶν
ἐπιστολῶν. ἀπράκτων δὲ τῶν πολλῶν συμβού-
λων ἀπελθόντων δαίμων αὐτὸν ἃ μηδεὶς ῥητόρων
ἔπειθε, καὶ τὰ γράμματα ἀποπέμψας εἰσελθὼν
ἡττᾶτο τῶν ἰσχυρῶν ἐστερημένος.   179. καὶ
τὰ μὲν περὶ τὴν πυρὰν ἐκείνην ἐλελωφήκει, τῆς
F 166   Θρᾴκης ἐφ᾽ ἑαυτὴν τὸν ἄρχοντα καλούσης, Σκυ-
θῶν ἅπαντα πλὴν τειχῶν κατασυρόντων, γενομένης δὲ τῆς μεγάλης μάχης καὶ τοῦ πολλοῦ

of some remedy, with no mention of the gods but guardedly referring to physicians. He did not burn this letter and the slave got hold of it and kept it, so that, if any trouble arose in future, he could protect himself with the letters. 178. So when he began to abuse his master and to prosecute him for his auguries, he placed his reliance upon this correspondence, for the governor would know exactly what 'physicians' meant, and the emperor would in any case set up a hue and cry against anyone so entrapped. Many were the entreaties, and many they who entreated the slave not to harm his benefactor, for the reproaches and angry censures with which I had striven to restrain his master had made me such. He replied that he was well aware of all that, but did not attach much importance to it: if he gave away the letters, he would be giving himself away too. Many who went to him with advice came away unsuccessful, but then destiny succeeded in doing what none of the advocates could do, and made him change his mind. He returned the letters, carried on with the case and lost it, since he had lost the evidence to corroborate it. 179. This crisis had now passed when the presence of our ruler was demanded in Thrace, since the Scyths were ravaging the whole district save the fortified places.[a] The

---

[a] The battle of Adrianople and death of Valens, 9 Aug. 378. Shortly afterwards, Hypatius is nominated Prefect of the City of Rome, and assumes the insignia while still in Antioch.

φόνου καὶ πεσόντος ἐν μέσῳ τοῦ προθυμίᾳ μᾶλλον ἢ τέχνῃ συμβαλόντος, ἔρχεται Ῥωμαίοις ὕπαρχος ἐν ὑπάρχου σχήματι τῇδε φανούμενος, ἀρέσκοντα Ῥωμαίοις οὕτω ποιήσειν ἡγούμενος. 180. πᾶς δὴ μικροῦ λόγον ἐποίει, μία δὲ πᾶσιν ὑπόθεσις ὁ ἤπιος ἐκεῖνος. τὰ μὲν δὴ τῶν ἄλλων ἐδέδεικτο, Ἀνδρόνικος δὲ ὁ ποιητὴς μέλλων ἀεὶ λέξειν εἰπὼν οὐδὲν ἀπῆλθεν. ἐμὲ δὲ ὁ καιρὸς εἰς τὸ μέσον ἐκάλει. καὶ ὁ μὲν εἷλκεν οὗ κατήγετο τὸν λόγον ἐν ὀλίγοις τοῖς ἀκροαταῖς φανούμενον, ἐγὼ δὲ τὸν ἄνδρα εἰς τὸ βουλευτήριον, ὡς πολυάνθρωπον. ὁμολογήσαντος δὲ γίγνεταί τι τὸ διακωλῦον, καὶ ὁ πόνος ἡμῖν, ὡς ἐδόκει, ζημία. 181. εὐθὺς μὲν οὖν βοή τε πολλὴ καὶ ἀθυμία, καὶ ἀπὸ τῆς φαυλοτέρας τύχης τῷ πράγματι τοὔνομα, μικρὸν δὲ ὕστερον ἐπηνεῖτο τὸ δαιμόνιον πολέμου μεγίστης πόλεως ἐξελόμενον τὸν ποιητήν. ἃ γὰρ δὴ εἶχεν ἀνάγκην τῷ ἐπαινέτῃ διελθεῖν, τῷ λόγῳ μὲν τὸ εἰκὸς ἐφύλαττε, πόλιν δὲ οὐ ῥᾳδίαν ἐνεγκεῖν ἐποίει πολεμίαν. οὕτω τὸ

ᵃ For Andronicus, *PLRE* 65 (5).

ᵇ Hypatius (*PLRE* 448 (4)) had lived in Antioch since 371 at least, and was there regarded as one of their own. Panegyrics upon his elevation would inevitably mention

great battle occurred and great losses were sustained, and he fell, delivering his attack with more ardour than skill. Then for Romans a prefect came, to appear here in prefect's guise, thinking to please Romans by such a course. 180. Practically everyone began to compose orations: his clemency was the sole topic for all. All the other addresses had been delivered, but Andronicus the poet,[a] who all the time was going to give his recital, left without a word. The occasion thus called me to the fore. The prefect was eager for the speech to be given at his lodging, in front of a select audience, but I wanted him to come to the city hall where the audience would be larger. To this he consented, but something happened to prevent it, and all the trouble I had gone to seemed so much wasted effort. 181. At the time there was much alarm and despondency, and the incident was accounted part of my misfortune, but a little later my luck was commended, since it had saved me, the author, from incurring the hostility of a great city. The statements which a panegyrist was bound to make, though maintaining the tone of the speech, would tend to exasperate a city which was not easy to win over in any case.[b] So what was, at first

his imminent translation to Rome and so Antioch's loss of one of its local luminaries. This would cause some offence in Antioch which was sensitive about its own importance, and so would have roused resentment against Libanius, who would be rubbing salt into the wound.

δοκοῦν κακὸν ἀγαθὸν ἀπεφάνη.

182. Οὐ μὴν ὅ γε ἐρῶ τοιοῦτον, ἀλλὰ κακὸν
F 167 καὶ δοκοῦν καὶ ὄν, κακῶν τὸ μέγιστον. τέτταρες
R 119 ἄνδρες οἰκιῶν τῶν πρώτων, λαμπροὶ μὲν ἐν
διδασκαλείοις, λαμπροὶ δὲ ἐν ἀρχαῖς, ἦν δὲ ἐν
ταῖς ἐλπίσι τὸ μειζόνως ἐκλάμψειν, οὗτοι οἱ τέτταρες ἐν μησὶ τοσούτοις ἐτάφησαν, καὶ τοῦτο
βασιλεὺς ἀγνοῶν ἔπεμπεν ἀρχὰς τοῖς κειμένοις.
183. τούτους ἔτι μοι πενθοῦντι τὸ περὶ τὸν πόδα
τὸν δεξιὸν συνέβη· περὶ οὗ ποία πόλις οὐκ ἀκήκοε τῶν ἐν ἠπείροις ἢ νήσοις; ὡς ἀπῄειν μὲν
δειπνήσων λελουμένος, παύειν δέ τινα μάχην
ἐπιχειρῶν ἐν μαινομένου τε ἀνθρώπου χερσὶν ἦν
καὶ χαμαί. καὶ περιτειχισθεὶς ὁ ἵππος ὑπὸ τοῦ
ὄχλου κατηναγκάσθη τῇ ὁπλῇ γυμνῶσαι τὸν
πόδα τοῦ δέρματος. τούτῳ δὲ ἐπηκολούθησεν ὁ
πολὺς ῥοῦς ἐπὶ πᾶν ὁμοίως μέλος χυθείς, ὥστε
οὐδεὶς ἦν ὃς οὐκ ἐπέπειστό με αὐτίκα ἀποθανεῖ-
σθαι τῶν γε παρόντων, τοῖς ἀποῦσι δὲ καὶ ἐτε-
θνήκειν.   184. καὶ τοῦτο μεταξὺ συνεβεβήκει
θανάτοιν παιδίου τε καὶ ἀνδρός, ἀνδρὸς μὲν ὅς
μοι συνεῖχε τὸ ποίμνιον διακονίᾳ τε καὶ πόνοις,
παιδίου δὲ ὅ μοι τὰ ἀπὸ τοῦ καμάτου λῦον μετὰ
ῥώμης πάλιν ἐπὶ τὸ κάμνειν ἦγε. τὰ μὲν δὴ

sight, bad luck turned out well.

182. However, the next part of the story is nothing like this, but an evil both apparent and real—in fact, the greatest of evils. Four men of the leading families, renowned in the schools and in their tenures of office, whose fame we expected to increase still further, were dead and buried in as many months, and the emperor, in all ignorance, sent their promotions when they lay in their graves. 183. I was still in mourning for them when I sustained the accident to my right foot, news of which has reached every city of continent and island. I had been to bathe and was leaving for dinner when, in trying to stop a brawl, I found myself in a maniac's grip and hurled to the ground. My horse, hemmed in by the crowd, could not but trample on me and strip the skin from my foot. A severe bleeding ensued, and this spread over every limb, so that everyone present was convinced that I would soon be dead, and as for those who were not actually there—well, I was dead already.[a] 184. This accident occurred in the interval between the death of the man who worked and slaved to keep my flock together, and that of the slave who relieved me of the drudgery and enabled me to undertake fresh

[a] For this accident, dated to early 380 by the *Olympia* which follow, cf. *Or.* 38.3.

R 120 Ὀλύμπια ἐποιεῖτο τῷ Ὀλυμπίῳ Διί, λόγος δὲ ὁ
ποιηθεὶς εἰς τὴν πανήγυριν ἔκειτο, ἐμὲ δὲ τά τε
ἄλλα ἔτηκε καὶ ἀγρυπνία. 185. διὰ πικροῦ δὴ
τοῦ θέρους τοῦδε οἶδα ἐλθών. σκληρὸν δέ μοι καὶ
F 168 τὸ ἐπὶ τούτῳ. παιδίον γὰρ ἕτερον, ὃ σὺν ἐκείνῳ
τέ με ἐκούφιζε καὶ μετ' ἐκεῖνο τὸ αὐτοῦ μέρος
παρείχετο, γάμων εἵνεκα ἐλθὸν εἰς ἀγρόν, ἐν ᾧ
καῦμά τε οὐ φορητὸν ὕδωρ τε πονηρὸν συνέλεξαν
νόσον, ἐπανῆκον θνήσκει. ἐπὶ δὴ τούτοις πολλάκις ἤκουσαν οἱ θεοὶ τὸ 'ὦ θεοὶ' βοῶντος.

186. Τὴν Τύχην δὲ αὖθις ἐπηνέσαμεν Καρ-
τέριόν τε καὶ τοὺς ἐπ' αὐτὸν καταφυγόντας
καταγελάστους ποιήσασαν. ὁ μὲν γὰρ ὡς ἐγκατα-
στήσων ἐνταυθοῖ διδάσκαλον τὸν λοιμὸν Γερόντιον
γνώσει βασιλέως ἀναλαβὼν ἦγεν εἰς Θρᾴκην
μέγας ἐλπίζων ἐν βασιλείοις ἔσεσθαι, τῆς ἀνοίας
δὲ αὐτοῦ πολλαχόθεν ἐξελεγχθείσης, δι' ἣν οὐδὲ
ὑβρίζειν ὤκνει τοὺς βασιλεῖ τιμίους, ὁ μὲν ὠθού-

---

[a] The freeman, Maximus, his secretary in 364 (*Ep.*
1217), was succeeded by Thalassius (*Or.* 42.3 ff). The slave
was a valet and masseur (so Reiske).

[b] This episode has been discussed most recently by
Martin (*Discours,* Vol. ii, pp. 4–7, 59–60). He contests the
identification of Carterius with a *consularis* (*BZ* 51 (1958),
75; 57 (1964), 1–5) and, less probably, that of Gerontius

tasks.[a] It was the occasion of the Olympia in honour
of Zeus Olympius, but the speech I had composed for
the festival was put aside and I was racked with
pain, especially insomnia.   185. So this summer
passed, and a wretched one it was, I know. Then
another disaster befell me. A second slave, who
along with the first used to assist me and who, after
the other's death, did his best for me, went off into
the country to get married. There intolerable heat
and bad water brought on a sickness, and on his
return he died. At this the gods time and again
heard me lament, 'Alas, ye Gods!'

186. However, I had occasion to thank my stars
once more for making a laughing-stock of Carterius
and his toadies.[b] He had it in mind to set up that
plaguy Gerontius as teacher here at the emperor's
command, and he went off to Thrace, with him in
his train, fully expecting to be a power at court, but
he made a complete fool of himself, even going to the
length of insulting persons who enjoyed the imperial
favour, so that he was dismissed, boarded ship for

with the sophist of Apamea (*PLRE* 393 (3)). However, Carterius is certainly linked with Neoterius, Praetorian Prefect of the East, 380–381, and influential enough to try to
supplant Libanius as sophist. This implies a position as
governor (cf. § 255 for a similar attempt). Gerontius, *pace*
Martin, must be the sophist of Apamea, who begs forgive-
ness from Libanius here and is his friend later (*Ep.* 863).
Here Libanius interprets, with much exaggeration, Carterius' return home to Italy as a disgrace, and Gerontius'
reappearance in Antioch as exclusion from Apamea.

LIBANIUS

R 121 μενος ἐμβὰς εἰς πλοῖον ἐπ᾽ Ἰταλίας ἔπλει τῆς
ἀτιμίας τῆς ἑαυτοῦ μηνυτής. 187. ὁ δὲ ὀρχη-
στῇ μισθώσας ἑαυτὸν ὁ σοφιστὴς εὐημερίας
πραττόμενος χρυσίον, τελευτῶν φεύγων τοὺς
ἀντιτέχνους τοὺς τὸν μισθὸν οὐ διδόντας εἰς
Σελεύκειαν κομίζεται καὶ δεῦρ᾽ ἀναβὰς ἐν σκότῳ
διὰ δέος ἐπὶ τὴν κεκλεισμένην αὐτῷ πατρίδα
ψηφίσμασιν ὑπ᾽ ἀνάγκης ἔρχεται τὸν τὸν ἠδικημένον ἱκετεύσων ῥήτορα. 188. ἐνταῦθα ἔφη
τις μέλειν ἐμοῦ τε καὶ τῶν ἐμῶν τῇ Τύχῃ. ἡ δὲ
ἐπεισήνεγκε τῇ ἑορτῇ πένθος ἡλίκον οὐ πρότερον, Εὐσεβίου τελευτήν· ὁ δὲ ἦν τῶν ἐμῶν
ἀγαλμάτων τὸ κεφάλαιον, ὥστε ὤμωξε μὲν ἡ γῆ
τεθνεῶτος, ὤμωξαν δὲ αἱ νῆσοι· καὶ γὰρ ἀφῖκτο
F 169 πανταχοῖ λόγος τρόπων τε πέρι τῶν ἐκείνου καὶ
λόγων ἡγοῦντό τε οὐδένα ἐκείνῳ προσόμοιον ὑπὸ
τῆς ἀκτῖνος ἐφορᾶσθαι τοῦ θεοῦ. 189. καὶ
διείλεγμαι δέ, ἴσως οὐ φαύλως, περὶ αὐτοῦ λόγον
R 122 ἀπελθόντι ποιήσας, ὥστε εἶναι τοῖς ἔπειτα μανθάνειν οἷός τις ἦν. τὸ δ᾽ οὖν τῆς λύπης μέτρον
ἐξεπίσταται Εὐμόλπιος, ὅς μοι παρακολουθῶν
ἐπανήγαγε τὸν νοῦν ὑπ᾽ αὐτῆς ἐξελαυνόμενον

252

Italy, and sailed away to bear the news of his own disgrace. 187. The sophist, meanwhile hired himself out to a dancer and made hay while the sun shone, but in the end he fled from the dancer's rivals who refused him any pay of theirs, and he landed at Seleuceia. From there he came up here at dead of night, in fear of returning to his own city which had barred her gates against him by her decrees, and he was compelled to approach me, the teacher whom he had wronged, and to beg my assistance. 188. Hence I and mine were described as the darlings of Fortune. Yet she brought a new cause of grief to the festival—such a one as had never occurred before—for Eusebius died.[a] Of my pupils he was my pride and joy, so that the whole wide world bewailed his passing, for the report of his character and eloquence had spread far afield, and it was thought that the light of day beheld not his peer. 189. I have delivered, and not badly perhaps, an oration composed in his memory, so that future generations may know what manner of man he was. At any rate, Eumolpius[b] is well aware of the measure of my grief, for he attended me and, when I was well nigh distraught with sorrow, restored me to

[a] Martin (*Discours,* Vol. ii, p. 5) interprets, with Reiske, ἑορτή as his recent triumph over Carterius, but in this work the word seems to signify only religious celebrations—here the *Olympia* of 380. Seeck's identification of Eusebius (*BLZG* xx) is merely a possibility.

[b] *PLRE* 295. Recipient of *Or.* 40. *Consularis Syriae* 384.

διεξιὼν ὁπόσον τι ἀνθρώπῳ τὸ παραφρονεῖν
κακόν.

190. 'τί δέ; τὰ περὶ τὸν Σαβῖνον οὐ καλά;'
τάχ' ἂν ἔροιτο ἡ Τύχη· πάνυ γε. ὁ δὲ ἦν μὲν
ἀεὶ κακὸς πᾶν ἂν χρημάτων εἵνεκα γινόμενος,
ἥδιστ' ἂν παρὰ βασιλέως εὑρόμενος ἐξεῖναί οἱ
πλοῦτον ἀπὸ τάφων ἀγείρειν· ἐξηπατήκει δὲ
τοὺς πολλοὺς καὶ ἦν ἐν δόξῃ τὰ πρῶτα βελτίονι,
ὥστε καὶ ἦσαν οἳ περιῄεσαν τὰ κάλλιστα αὐτῷ
τῶν ὀνομάτων ἀνατιθέντες.   191. ὁ δὲ οὐκ
ἄρα ἦν ἀγαθὸς ἥ τε σοφία αὐτοῦ πιστευθέντα
ἀδικῆσαι τὰ μὲν τέχνῃ τὰ δὲ καὶ ἀναιδείᾳ, ὥστε
ἤδη τι λαβὼν ὡς ἀποδώσων ἐν μέσῳ μυρίων
ὀμμάτων, εἶτα ἠρνήσατο ἐπί τε δικαστὴν ἧκε
τῶν ἅπαντα εἰδότων ἀποθαυμαζόντων, λόγου δὲ
ἀπορῶν, οὐκ ἔχων κρατῆσαι τοῦ δικαίου, πλασάμενος σκοτοδινίαν, ἐξελθὼν ὡς δὴ εὐθέως ἥξων
F 170 αὖθις ἐπὶ τὴν δίκην, ἀναβὰς ἐπὶ τὸν ἵππον ἔρ-
ρωτό τε καὶ ἤλαυνε καὶ λαβόμενος τῆς κλίμακος
ἐπὶ τραύματα τοὺς οἰκέτας ἔταττεν.   192. ἀλλ'
ὅμως οἱ κολακεύοντες καὶ ὡς ἦσαν κόλακες
R 123 καὶ ἐφενάκιζον, μέχρι δὴ καὶ ἐπ' αὐτοὺς ἐκείνους
τραπόμενος ἐχρήσατο καὶ ἐνταῦθα τῇ φύσει,

sanity by recounting how great an affliction madness can be for a man.

190. 'Well,' Fortune may rejoin, 'did not that business with Sabinus turn out all right?' Certainly it did.[a] He was always a rogue who would turn his hand to anything for money and would cheerfully have wangled an imperial permission to make a fortune out of graves. Yet he had most people hoodwinked, and at first he enjoyed a pretty good reputation, and as a result there were even some who went about speaking of him in most complimentary terms. 191. However, he turned out to be no good after all. His speciality was fraud, no matter whether by subterfuge or by brazen impudence. Why, in full view of a crowd of witnesses he obtained a loan upon promise to repay: then he denied the whole transaction and went to law about it, to the astonishment of those who knew the facts. He had not a shred of a case and was unable to override the course of justice, so he pretended to faint, left the court—he would, of course, return to the case immediately!—mounted his horse, suddenly recovered and was away, reached his house stairs and deployed his servants against assault. 192. Yet still his toadies, true to type, fawned upon him and truckled to him until he turned upon them too, consistent as

[a] The passage is reexamined by Martin, *Discours,* Vol. ii, pp. 6–7, 59–60. Petit (note *ad loc.*) sees Sabinus as a grasping *principalis* who eagerly bought up the property of his bankrupt fellows, graveyards and all (cf. *Or.* 18.289).

ὥστε καὶ οἵδε συνεχώρουν εἶναι ἀνθρώπων Σαβῖνον ἀδικώτατον, καὶ νῦν ταὐτὸν ἀπὸ γλώττης
ἁπάσης ἐστὶ λεγόμενον νενικῆσθαι τὸν Εὐρύβα-
τον. οὐκοῦν οἷς ὀφείλει δίκην μείζω δέδωκε νῦν
ἢ εἰ ἐτεθνήκει. δεινότερον[1] γὰρ παρά γε ὀρθῷ
κριτῇ ἢ μηκέτ' εἶναι ζῆν[2] ἐν ὀνείδεσιν. ἀλλ' οὐ
Σαβίνῳ γε φαίης ἄν. 193. οὐκοῦν καὶ τοῦτο
δίκη. χθές τις ἧκε στρατιώτης γράμματα βασιλέως κομίζων ὀργῇ δικαίᾳ γεγραμμένα, καὶ ἦν
ἐν τοῖς γράμμασιν ἄτιμόν τε αὐτὸν εἶναι καὶ
ἀποτῖσαι διπλάσιον, τοῦ πρώτου δὲ αἰσθομένου
R 124 πολλοὺς εἰδέναι ποιήσαντος ἡδονὴ μισθὸν ἐποίει
τῷ στρατιώτῃ, καὶ ἦν εὐεργέτης. 194. τοῦτό
μοι πολλῶν δίκη παραμυθουμένου με τοῦ δαίμονος. καὶ τοῦτο μὲν ἀντὶ τῶν εἰς τὸν ἐμὸν μὲν
ἀνεψιὸν ἕνεκεν, αὐτοῦ δὲ κηδεστήν, ὃν ἐξέβαλε
F 171 τῶν ὄντων, ὥστε εἶναι τὸ δεῖπνον ἐκείνῳ φακῆν,
τοῦτο δὲ ἀντὶ τῆς ἐν ἀγρῷ τῆς γυναικὸς τελευτῆς, ᾗ μία μὲν νύξ, μία δὲ ἀπέχρησεν ἡμέρα.
ᾔδει καὶ τὰ περὶ τὴν τοῦ νεκροῦ κεφαλὴν ἡ
Τύχη, ἣν ἀπεκάλυψέ τε Σαβῖνος καὶ ἐμὸν ἔργον

---

[1] δεινότερον Mss., Martin: ποθεινότερον conj. F.: ἐλεεινότε-
ρον Norman (1965).

256

ever. Even they began to agree that Sabinus
was the greatest villain alive, and now everyone
tells the same tale, that he would beat the devil
at his own game.[a] So in his punishment his
present fate is worse than death, for death is prefer-
able to a life of dishonour, so any right-minded man
would think. But not for Sabinus! 193. So this too
is his punishment. A day or two ago there came a
military courier with dispatches from the emperor
written in righteous indignation. Therein it was
stated that he was disgraced and subjected to double
the fine.[b] The first man to hear of this spread the
news to others besides, and their joy provided the
courier with his reward, for he was a benefactor
indeed. 194. This, so destiny consoles me, is the
punishment for the many wrongs he has done me.
This is his reward for his behaviour towards my
cousin, his father-in-law, whom he robbed of his possessions so that he had but a bowl of lentils to eat.
This is the reward for the death of his wife down on
his farm: twenty-four hours were enough to do away
with her. And Fortune was also aware of the business about the head of the corpse which Sabinus

[a] Eurybatus, like Phrynondas (§136 above), a proverbial villain; see Wankel on Dem. de Cor. 24.

[b] The punishment is in respect of the frauds of §191
above.

---

[2] ἢ μηκέτ' εἶναι ζῆν conj. Festugière, REG 78 (1965)
p. 630: μηκέτ' εἶναι ἢ ζῆν Mss., F.: τοῦ μηκέτ' εἶναι τὸ ζῆν Re.
(Anim.).

οὖσαν ἐπειρᾶτο δεικνύειν, ἐπιστολῇ ψευδεῖ τοῦτο
μηχανώμενος. καὶ ᾤετο μέν με πτήξαντα κεχω
ρηκέναι[1] εἰς σπονδάς, συμπλακέντος δὲ μάλα
γενναίως ἔξω τε ἦν αὐτοῦ καὶ ἱκέτευε.

195. Καὶ τούτου οὖν ἰστέον τῇ Τύχῃ χάριν καὶ
R 125 πρὸ τούτου γε ἐκείνου· καὶ γὰρ αὖ πρὸ τοῦδε
γέγονεν. ὁ νόμος ἐπολέμει τῷ νόθῳ κληρονομεῖν
οὐκ ἐῶν, ἀνελὼν παλαιὸν νόμον ποιοῦντα κλη
ρονόμον. φίλων μὲν οὖν ἦν ἀφθονία μοι δικαίων,
οἳ δώσειν ἃ λάβοιεν ἔμελλον, τοὺς δὲ τοῖς ὧδε
δρωμένοις ἐπιθησομένους ἦν οὐ ῥάδιον διαφυγεῖν
γραφομένους τὴν ὁδὸν τῆς κτήσεως, ὡς ἀδικοῖ
F 172 τὸν νόμον.   196. χρηστῷ δὴ βασιλεῖ τῆς ἡμε
τέρας βουλῆς εἰς τοῦτο χρησαμένης τῶν τε βασι
λεῖ φίλων αἰτησάντων[2] ἐπαινεσάντων τὴν χάριν
νεύει τε ὁ καθήμενος, καὶ ἠνείχετο τῆς δωρεᾶς ὁ
νόμος, ᾧ τε μάλιστα τὴν ψυχὴν ἐβαρυνόμην ἐλέ
λυτο τῶν ἐμῶν εἰς τὸν ἐμὸν ἐλευθέρως τε ἡξόν
των ἐν βεβαίῳ τε μενούντων. ταυτὶ δὲ πεπεισ

---

[1] κεχωρηκέναι PA corr.: πεσεῖσθαι V, Martin: om. rel. mss.:
χωρήσειν conj. F.
[2] [αἰτησάντων] Martin. Num ἐπαινεσάντων <τε> τὴν?

---

[a] Cf. §145 above. *Codex Theodos.* 4.6.4 had since been
rescinded by Theodosius (*ibid.* 4.6.5, 'genitoris nostri').

258

produced and then tried to make out, by means of a forged letter, that it was some of my work. He had the notion that I had given up in alarm and come to terms with him, but when I tackled him spiritedly, he was disconcerted and began to plead with me.

195. So I must thank Fortune for that, and for something else that had occurred before it.[a] There was a law that was detrimental to my natural son, for it banned him from becoming my heir, so rescinding a previous law that had allowed it. Now, though I had plenty of good friends who would be sure to hand over to him anything they received in trust, it was not easy to escape the attentions of people who would attack such a transaction and indict this method of acquiring the property as illegal. 196. Our city council approached our good emperor on the matter and, with the backing and favour of some of his friends, the governor consented, and the legality of the grant was upheld. The law which caused me the greatest worry was rescinded, and my property will go to my son

Now, about 381–382, the curia, always eager for a potential recruit of substance, suggested the transfer of Libanius' property to Cimon *inter vivos*; and with the support of his friends at court, a dispensation was obtained in his favour. This was confirmed by the *consularis*, a much safer procedure than the unofficial transfer to trustees just outlined.

μένον ἀφεῖναί τε τὴν ψυχὴν ἐλθεῖν τε εἰς Ἅιδου
R 126 πῶς οὐκ ἂν εὐδαίμονος εἴη;

197. Ἐν οὖν τῇ ἀπὸ τούτων εὐφροσύνῃ διά-
γοντι πνεῦμα πολέμιον ἐπελθὸν ἐκβάλλει μὲν
τὴν ἡδονήν, ἀντεισάγει δὲ τραῦμα οἷον οὔπω
πρότερον. ἦν μοι ἀδελφὸς νεώτερος οἰχομένου
τοῦ πρεσβυτέρου, μέσος γὰρ δὴ ἦν ἐγὼ κατὰ τὸν
τόκον ἀμφοῖν. οὗτος πρό τε τῆς ἀποδημίας μοι
συνέζη, καὶ ἐπειδὴ παρὰ Βιθυνοῖς ἐκαθήμην,
ἦλθεν ἵππον ἐλαύνων μέγα ποιούμενος ἰδεῖν ὑπ᾽
ἐμοῦ νεμομένους παῖδας. 198. ἔπειθ᾽ ὁ μὲν
ἐπανῆλθεν οἴκαδε, ἐγὼ δὲ ὑπ᾽ ἀνάγκης τῆς τοῦ
κρατοῦντος ἦν αὖθις ὅθεν δὴ καὶ ἀπῆλθον· οὗ δὴ
πάλιν ἀδελφὸς ἀναφαίνεται καὶ χρόνου δὴ προϊ-
όντος λόγοις τε πολλοῖς καὶ παρακλήσεσιν ἀνα-
στήσας ἄγει τέ με οἴκαδε καὶ συνέζευκτο. καὶ
ὁπότε δὴ κάμνοι τὰ ἄρθρα, πικρά μοι τὰ τῆς
F 173 τραπέζης ἦν. 199. οὗτός ποτε συνδειπνῶν
ἀρχομένου χειμῶνος πληγεὶς μεταξὺ ῥεύματι τὴν
κεφαλήν, βοήσας οἷα εἰκός, χερσὶν οἰκετῶν ἄγε-
ται πρὸς τὸ δωμάτιον, καὶ ἅμα ἡμέρᾳ ἧκέ
τις ἀγγέλλων τοῖν ὀφθαλμοῖν αὐτῷ τὸν ἕτερον
οἴχεσθαι ῥυέντος ἐπ᾽ αὐτὸν ἀπὸ τῆς κεφαλῆς
R 127 ὕδατος, ἔπειτ᾽ οὐ πολλαῖς ἡμέραις ὕστερον ἐπι-

without let or hindrance and will remain firmly in his possession. Happy indeed is the man who departs this life with such an assurance.

197. I was still basking in contentment as a result of this when the advent of some hostile spirit cast out my joy and, in its stead, inflicted such a wound as I had never known before. I was the middle one of three brothers: my elder brother was now dead, but the younger was still alive. He had lived with me before I went abroad, and, when I held my chair in Bithynia, he travelled overland, eager to see pupils under my care.[a] 198. Then, after his return home, I was constrained by the emperor to return to Constantinople, the place from which I had started. There too my brother made an appearance, and, as time went on, by his arguments and pleas he got me to move and brought me home. Here we lived together, and if ever he fell ill with gout, the pleasures of the table were soured for me. 199. One day early in winter,[b] as we were dining together, he was suddenly afflicted with a discharge from the head: he uttered a cry, as you would expect, and was carried by the slaves to his room. Early next morning I was told that one of his eyes was blinded, as a result of matter discharging over it, and not many days

[a] He seems to have been Phasganius' emissary to Libanius in Constantinople before the final removal of 354, cf. § 95 above.

[b] Winter 381/2.

κλύζεσθαι καὶ τὸν δεξιὸν ἤκουον.   200. καὶ ἦν
πάντα τὰ πρὸ τοῦ δοκοῦντα ὑπέρδεινα μικρά τε
καὶ κοῦφα πρὸς τοῦτο ἐξεταζόμενα, καὶ οὐδὲν ὧν
ἔπραττον ἄνευ δακρύων ἐπράττετο, ἐπεὶ καὶ
λόγων μοι δεικνυμένων, ἦν γὰρ ἀνάγκη, μετὰ
τῆς φωνῆς ἔρρει τὰ δάκρυα, καὶ ἐθαύμαζέ γε οὐδείς, οὐδεὶς γὰρ ἦν ὃς οὐχ ὅθεν ταῦτα ἦν
ἠπίστατο. δάκρυα ἐν λουτρῷ, συμβουλὴ γὰρ ἦν
ἰατρικῆς λουτρόν, δάκρυα ἐν δείπνῳ· τοῦ γὰρ δὴ
πρὶν συνδειπνοῦντος ἀπεστερήμην συνόντος ἐπὶ
τῆς κλίνης, παρὰ τῆς ἐν τῇ ἡμέρᾳ νυκτὸς τῇ
νυκτὶ παραδιδομένου.   201. πολλαὶ μὲν δὴ χεῖρες ἰατρῶν, μυρία δὲ φάρμακα, πλείω δὲ
περίαπτα. ἔπειτ' ἔδοξε τὰ μὲν ἄλλα χαίρειν
ἐᾶν, καταφεύγειν δὲ ἐπί τε βωμοὺς καὶ ἱκετείας
καὶ τὴν τῶν θεῶν ἰσχύν· οἳ δὴ καὶ αὐτὸς οἰχόμε-
νος ἔκλαιον, καὶ τοῦτο ἡσυχῇ, οὔτε γὰρ οἷός τ'
F 174   ἦν ἰδεῖν οὔθ' ὅλως χρῆσθαι λόγῳ πρὸς τὰ ἀγάλ-
ματα, τοῖς γόνασι δὲ τὼ χεῖρε περιθεὶς καὶ ἐπ'
αὐτοῖν τὴν κεφαλὴν βρέξας θοἰμάτιον τοῖς
R 128   δάκρυσιν ἀπῄειν. τὸν δὲ οὔτε ὁρᾶν οὔτε μὴ ὁρᾶν
φορητὸν ἐγίγνετο νῦν μὲν τοῦ πόθου, νῦν δὲ τῆς
ὄψεως τοῦτο ποιούσης.   202. καί ποτε δείλης
βιβλίων ἐγγύς μοι κειμένων καὶ ἰατροῦ γέροντος

thereafter I heard that the right eye had gone too. 200. All the previous experiences which I thought so terrible proved trifling details as compared with this. Everything I did, I did in tears. Even at the lectures, which I was bound to deliver, a flow of tears accompanied my voice, and no one wondered at it, for there was no one who was unaware of its cause. I shed tears while bathing, for bathing was prescribed by the doctors, and I shed tears while dining, for I missed the presence at table of my former companion who was now consigned from the darkness of his day to the darkness of night. 201. We had physicians in plenty, cures beyond number, and charms without end. Then I decided to have done with the rest, and to betake myself to the altars, to supplications and to the power of the gods.[a] There I would go in person and mourn—and that silently—unable either to look upon the images or to utter a single word to them. I would clasp my hands around my knees, bend my head upon them and drench my gown with my tears, and so depart. As for my brother, I could not bear to see him, so much was I affected by the sight of him, or not to see him, so much did I miss him. 202. And one afternoon, when I had my books by my side and an old physician seated nearby, I began to ask what I

[a] He carefully abides by the restrictions of the religious legislation recently passed (*Codex Theodos.* 16.10.7, Dec. 381, *'castis deum precibus excolendum'*).

παρακαθημένου ἐρόμενος ὃ ἠπιστάμην, εἰ τυφλός
μοι γέγονεν ἀδελφός, τῶν φρενῶν τε ἐξώσθην
καὶ οὐκέτ᾽ εἶχον οὐδὲν ὧν τέως ᾔδειν εἰδέναι
οὔτε οὗ κατεκείμην οὔθ᾽ ὅ τι εἰρήκειν οὔθ᾽ ὅ τι
χρὴ ποιεῖν οὔθ᾽ ὅ τι μή.   203. πειρωμένου δέ
με ἐπανάγειν τοῦ γέροντος καὶ αὖθις ποιεῖν ὑγιαίνειν, λόγῳ γε ὃν ἐτύγχανον συντιθεὶς κελεύσαν-
τος προσθεῖναί τι, τὸ γραμμάτιον ἀναιροῦμαι μὲν
καὶ ἐνεχείρουν, εἰς ἄγνοιαν δὲ τῆς ὑποθέσεως
καταστὰς ἀπ᾽ οὐδενός τε τῶν γεγραμμένων ἐμαυτὸν ἔχων διδάξαι τί ποτε ἦν μοι βουλόμενος ὁ
λόγος, τὸ μὲν ἔρριψα, πρὸς δὲ τὸν ἰατρὸν εἰπὼν
ὡς οὐδὲν ἔτ᾽ εἴην, ἐκείμην ῥᾴων καὶ οὐκ ᾐσχυνό-
μην ἐπὶ τοῖς τοιούτοις μανείς.   204. οὐ γὰρ
οἶδ᾽ ὅ τι ἂν τούτῳ παρεξετάσας κακόν, καίτοι
μυρίοις βεβλημένος, ἢ μεῖζον ἢ ἴσον εὗρον ἄν.
ὥστε καὶ ᾐτιώμην τοὺς δαίμονας ὅτι μὴ θάνατος
ἀντὶ τοῦ παρόντος ἐπῆλθεν. οὐδὲ γὰρ τῶν μοι
γενομένων ἀγαθῶν ἔσθ᾽ ὅ τι ἂν ἀντίρροπον αὐτοῦ
δόξειε. ποία γὰρ ἐπιδείξεις; τίνες εὐφημίαι; τίς
κρότος; τίνες ἐκ βασιλέων τιμαί; πλοῦτος μὲν
γὰρ οὐκ ἐγένετο, καὶ τὸν Γύγου δὲ νικῶν ἡττᾶτο
ἂν τοῦ πάθους.

F 175
R 129

really knew, whether my brother had gone completely blind, when suddenly I lost my senses and could no longer recognize any of the things with which I was familiar—where I was, what I had said, what I must or must not do.   203. The old fellow tried to restore me to my senses and to health once more, and so he bade me continue with the speech I was composing. I picked up my notebook and set to work, but I had completely forgotten my theme and could not discern from anything I had written what on earth my speech was about, so I cast it aside, told the physician that I was done for, and lay back without compunction, raving unashamedly under such a blow. 204. Now, though I have been afflicted with innumerable woes, I know of none that, in comparison, could equal or exceed this. I cursed heaven that I had not died instead of suffering the fate I did, for none of my previous good fortune could ever be found to counterbalance this—not my declamations, not the applause, not the congratulations, not the honours bestowed by the emperors.[a] I was not rich, and yet a man richer than Gyges would have bowed before this disaster.[b]

[a] Refers to the recent dispensation in favour of Cimon (§ 196 above). On his honorary office, see below § 219 note.

[b] Gyges (Herod. 1.14) was, like Croesus, the historical example, Cinyras (§ 273 below) the mythical example of the millionaire in Greek literature.

205. Καίτοι καὶ ἐν αὐταῖς ταύταις ταῖς τοῦ πάθους ἡμέραις ἀπ' ἔργου τοῦδε θαυμαστὸς ἐδόκουν εἶναι καὶ ἅμα μακάριος. ἀπολελαύκει μὲν οὐ χρηστοῦ τοῦ χειμῶνος ἡ γῆ, μετριωτέρα δὲ οὐδὲν ἡ μετ' ἐκεῖνον ὥρα. καρπῶν δὲ τῶν μὲν οὐδ' ἀναφύντων, τῶν δὲ ὡς ὀλιγίστων καὶ οὐδὲ αὐτῶν ὑγιῶν, ἐκεκίνητο μὲν ἐπὶ τὴν βουλὴν ὁ δῆμος οὐδενὶ δικαίῳ, οὐ γὰρ δὴ ὄμβρων ἡ βουλὴ κυρία, σῖτον δὲ οἱ ἄρχοντες πανταχόθεν ἐκάλουν, αἱ τιμαὶ δὲ τοῖς ἄρτοις ἐπὶ τὸ πλέον ἦκον. 206. Φιλάγριος δέ, ἀνὴρ ἐνδοξότατος, ἐπὶ τὸν μείζω θρόνον ἦκων, κρείττω μὲν οὐκ ἔχων τὰ πράγματα ποιῆσαι, ἀγαπῶν δὲ εἰ μὴ φαυλότερα, παρεκάλει μὲν τὸ τῶν σιτοποιῶν ἔθνος εἶναι δικαιοτέρους, ἀνάγκας δὲ οὐκ ᾤετο δεῖν ἐπάγειν, δεδιὼς τὴν ἐπὶ πλεῖον ἀπόδρασιν, ᾧ ἂν εὐθὺς ἐβαπτίζετο τὸ ἄστυ, καθάπερ ναῦς ἐκλιπόντων τῶν ναυτῶν. 207. ἐνταῦθα οἱ τῇ δόξῃ τῶν ἐν ταῖς ἀρχαῖς ῥηγνύμενοι τὸν ἄνδρα ὁρῶντες ἰσόθεον νομιζόμενον αἰτιῶνται οἱ δυσσεβεῖς, τὴν περὶ τὸ πρᾶγμα σοφίαν οὐ σοφίαν εἶναι λέγοντες,

R 130

a On the food crisis in Antioch, which lasts until at least 386, cf. Petit, *Vie Municipale,* pp. 105 ff, 118 ff; Downey,

205. Yet even in this very time of disaster I won admiration and blessings from the following act.[a] The countryside had experienced a bad winter, and the following summer was no better. Part of the corn had not even germinated, the rest was sparse, and even this was blighted. In consequence, the populace created disturbances against the city council, quite unreasonably since the council could not control the weather. Though the governors tried to get corn from every possible source, the price of bread rose higher and higher.   206. The renowned Philagrius, having reached a higher office,[b] though unable to improve the situation, was content if it got no worse. He kept urging the bakers' corporation to be more reasonable, but was reluctant to enforce his demands, for he was afraid of the increasing desertion, which would have left the city ship-wrecked, abandoned by its crew.   207. Hereupon, that irreligious crew, who burst with envy at the governors'

[a] *Antioch,* pp. 419 ff. In summer 382, the damage was already done. The harvest of 381 had been poor (*Or.* 2.68), and the winter of 381/2 unfavourable. The curia and the bakers' corporation were held to blame, with allegations of hoarding and profiteering, as under Gallus and Julian. Hereafter Libanius consistently prides himself upon this support of the bakers, for example in *Or.* 29.6, 34.4.

[b] Philagrius, *Comes Orientis, PLRE* 693 (2). For this term distinguishing the *Comes* from the *consularis,* cf. *Or.* 27.6, 33.27, 45.31; Petit, *Vie Municipale,* pp. 254 f. The bakers' corporation was an institution of Valens' time, and unknown to Julian.

πρᾶσιν δὲ ὀφειλομένης ὀργῆς. ἐγὼ μὲν οὖν
αὐτός τε ἐγέλων ἐκεῖνόν τε ἠξίουν. ὁ δὲ τὴν
πρώτην πειθόμενος ἐπειδὴ χωροῦσαν ἑώρα τὴν
ἀπάτην, πάσχει τέ τι καὶ ἧκεν ἐπὶ μάστιγας, οὗ
F 176 πλεῖστοι τοῦτο ἔμελλον ὄψεσθαι.   208. ὁ μὲν
δὴ ἐπὶ τοῦ ζεύγους καθήμενος ἠρώτα παίων ἅμα,
τῇ περὶ τίνα ἀνθρώπων δαπάνῃ τοιοῦτοι περὶ
τὸν ἄρτον ἀναγκάζοιντο εἶναι. τῶν δὲ οὐδὲν εἰπεῖν ἐχόντων προβεβήκει μὲν ἐπὶ σῶμα ἕβδομον,
οὐδὲν δὲ εἰδὼς ἐγὼ προσῄειν τὰ εἰωθότα πορευό-
R 131 μενος, κτύπου δὲ πληγῶν αἰσθόμενος τῷ δήμῳ
κεχαρισμένων ὃς ἐκεχήνει πρός τε τὸ αἷμα καὶ
τὰ νῶτα, θέαμα ἐπιστὰς εἶδον πικρόν τε καὶ τοῖς
ἐμοῖς οὐκ ἀνεκτὸν ὄμμασιν, οὐ μὴν εἰς ἀνα-
βολήν· ἀλλ᾿ εὐθὺς ταῖς ἐμαυτοῦ χερσὶ διατεμὼν
τὸν ὄχλον σιγῇ μὲν μεμφόμενος μέχρι τοῦ τροχοῦ
προσῄειν, ἐκεῖ δὲ λόγοι τε πολλοὶ καὶ οὐκέτι
σιωπῇ τοῖν δυοῖν ἁπτομένου χρόνοιν,[1] ὡς οὔτε

---

[1] χρόνοιν Mss., Re., Martin: μόνοιν F.

---

[a] The commons, egged on by the Christians, according
to Libanius, and by the theatrical claque (*Or.* 41.18; cf.
Browning, *JRS* 42 (1952), 13 ff), is presented as lacking

renown, saw this man with his immortal reputation and began to bandy accusations against him.[a] The prudence he had shown in this affair was no prudence at all, they alleged: there had been bribery, and it ought to be punished. Now I just poured scorn on this, and advised him to do the same. So he did at first, but then, when he saw that the slander was gaining wider currency, his attitude changed and he had recourse to floggings at a place where many people would be likely to witness them.[b] 208. He sat there in his carriage and inquired at every stroke how much had gone in bribes and to whom, for them to charge prices like this for bread. They had no reply to make, and he had already reached his seventh victim, when I approached in all ignorance, following my usual path. I heard the sound of the lash, so dear to the common folk who were all agog at the sight of the bleeding backs, and I saw a painful spectacle, unbearable to my eyes, but it did not deter me. Straightway I parted the crowd with my own hands, and advanced to the wheel, silent and reproachful. There I spoke long and loud, concentrating upon two points of time, first, that those whom he was

both humanity and reason. He undoubtedly misrepresents the humanitarian efforts which the Christians normally provided as indicating a faction against a pagan governor.

[b] Evidently near the agora. Libanius was passing on his way to school in the *bouleuterion*. For his revulsion to bloodshed see §161 above.

ἠδικήκασιν οἱ ἐν ταῖς πληγαῖς εἴ τε οὐ λήξει τὸ
τῆς ὀργῆς ὄψεταί τις ἡμέραν τὴν ἐπιοῦσαν οἵαν
οὐκ ἂν βούλοιτο.   209. ταυτὶ δὲ δίκαια μὲν καὶ
λυσιτελοῦντα τῷ τε ἄρχοντι τῇ τε πόλει, θάνατον δέ, ὡς ἡ κοινὴ δόξα τῶν παρόντων, ἔχοντα
τῷ λέγοντι μαχόμενά γε τῇ τοῦ ὄχλου βουλήσει.
καὶ γὰρ δὴ λίθοι ἦσαν οὐκ ἐν ὀλίγων χερσὶν εἴ τις
ἐξαιτήσεται· οἳ ὅπως οὐκ ἐπὶ τοῖς πρώτοις ἐπέ-
τοντο ῥήμασι, θαῦμα ἦν.   210. ἔπειτα θαῦμα
ἕτερον, ὅπως οὐ καὶ συνεῖπον οἱ οὕτως ἡσυχάσαν-
R 132 τες. τουτὶ δὲ ἔργον ἀνθρώπων μὲν οὐδενός, θεοῦ
δέ τινος καὶ Τύχης, ἀφ᾽ ὧν καὶ θαλάττης μανία
κοιμίζεται. ἐντεῦθεν εὐεργέτης ὠνομαζόμην τῶν
F 177 τε οὐ βασανισθέντων τοῦ τε ἐπὶ τῆς ἀρχῆς τῶν
τε ἐνοικούντων τοῦ τε τῆς πόλεως σώματος, τῶν
μὲν οὐ πεινασάντων, τῆς δὲ οὐ κατακαυθείσης,
τοῦ δὲ σχοινία διαφεύγοντος.

211. Οὓς δὲ ταῦτα ἀπέπνιγεν ἐπένθουν.
κακὸν δὲ αὐτοῖς οὐ τόδε μόνον ἀλλὰ καὶ ἕτερα
μυρία τιμὴν ἔχοντα μεγάλην, ἐπεὶ καὶ τοῦ νόμου
κατεβόα μὴ διδόντος οἱ βαδίζειν οἴκαδε ὡς ἐμέ·
ᾧ πολλῷ μὲν ἐχρῆτο ὁ Ἠπειρώτης ἐκεῖνος,
πλείονι δὲ ἢ ἐκεῖνος ὁ ἐκ Κύρου· τῷ μὲν ὄνομα
Πελάγιος, Μαρκελλῖνος δὲ τῷ προτέρῳ. πλεῖστα

flogging had done no wrong, and second, that if he did not abate his wrath, he would see a morrow such as he would not wish to see.[a]   209. My arguments were justified and in the best interests of both the governor and the city, but meant death to the author of them—such was the opinion of all present—for they ran counter to the will of the populace. And, in fact, many of them had stones in their hands, in case anyone tried to present any plea for these people, and it was a marvel that they were not hurled at me when I first began to speak. 210. Then followed another marvel, brought about by some divine power and by Fortune who can lull even the raging sea, that those who had been so recently appeased did not themselves join in supporting my advocacy. As a result it was I who was called the benefactor of all—of the victims who were rescued from the lash, of the governor who escaped a lynching, of the citizens who did not starve, and of the fabric of our city, since it did not go up in flames.

211. Lamentations arose from that group which was green with envy at this. However, this was not their only trouble, but there were many other incidents which raised my prestige. The governor even protested against the law which forbade him making personal calls upon me, as Marcellinus of

[a] In time past, the bakers had "done no wrong." In the future there would be riots and lynchings, as there had been under Gallus (§ 103).

R 133 ἀνθρώπους εὖ ποιήσας τόνδε οἶδα τὸν χρόνον τῶν
μὲν ἐν χρείᾳ φαρμάκων ὄντων ἐπ᾽ ἐμὲ καταφευ-
γόντων, ἐμοῦ δὲ αὐτοῖς διὰ τῶν ἐπὶ τῆς ἀρχῆς
ἰωμένου τὰς πληγάς.

212. Πρόκλου δὲ μνησθεὶς χειμῶνός τε μέμνη-
μαι καὶ αἰγίδος καὶ πληγῶν καὶ αἵματος. ἦν
μέντοι τι καὶ ἐνταῦθα ἀγαθὸν ἐμοί, τὸ τοῖς δρωμένοις τούτοις καὶ ἄχθεσθαι καὶ δοκεῖν· οὐδὲ γὰρ
ᾔειν ὡς αὐτόν, ὃ πρὸς οὐκ ὀλίγους ἐπεποίητό μοι
τῶν ἐπὶ τῆς αὐτῆς τάξεως. ηὐδοκίμουν οὖν τῷ
μίσει τῷ τε ἐμῷ πρὸς ἐκεῖνον τῷ τε ἐκείνου πρὸς
F 178 ἐμέ, τῷ μὲν ἐμῷ φανερῷ, τῷ ᾽κείνου δὲ βουλομένῳ μὲν λανθάνειν, ἀδυνατοῦντι δέ.

213. Καὶ συμβαίνει δὴ τελευτῆσαί μοι τὸν
ἀδελφὸν ἐκεῖνον, ὃν ὥσπερ νέον τε καὶ εὐδαιμονίας ἐστερημένον ἐπένθουν οὐκ ἀνεχόμενος τῶν
ἐκ τῆς περὶ τὰ ὄμματα τύχης φερόντων τὴν
παραμυθίαν. 214. κακὸν δὲ ἕτερον σεισμὸν

ᵃ For Pelagius, *PLRE* 686 (1); Marcellinus, *PLRE* 546
(10). They were *consulares* in 382 and 383 respectively.
For visits made by officials to Libanius in Valens' time, see
Or. 2.9 and §166 above. If such visits are now formally
banned by law, this unknown enactment must have been

Epirus and Pelagius of Cyrus had done with ever increasing frequency.[a] Throughout this period I know that I was of the greatest service to people, for those in need of relief took refuge with me, and I would cure their distress by my influence with the governors.

212. However, when I call Proclus to mind, I call to mind storm and tempest, flogging and blood.[b] Yet even here there was some advantage for me, in that I was annoyed at his actions and was seen to be so, for I refused to approach him as I had done so many of his predecessors in office. Thus I acquired a good name from our mutual dislike, but whereas mine for him was open and above board, his for me he tried to keep dark, but without success.

213. The next occurrence was the death of my poor brother.[c] I mourned for him as though he were a young man taken off in his prime, and I could not bear people trying to console me by mention of his blindness. 214. Another trouble arose which was

recent and presumably applicable only to those above the rank of *consularis,* in view of Philagrius' protest. More likely, νόμος is to be interpreted as a hardening of convention.

[b] Proclus (*PLRE*, Proculus (6), 746), *Comes Orientis* 383/4. An interim pronouncement, cf. §§ 221–224 below. For his brutality cf. *Or.* 26.30, 28.13, 29.10. His relations with Libanius are most recently examined by Martin, *Discours,* Vol. ii, pp. 205–211.

[c] In 383.

ἐπενεγκὸν τῇ τέχνῃ φυγὴ μὲν ἀπὸ τῆς τῶν Ἑλλήνων φωνῆς, πλοῦς δὲ ἐπ' Ἰταλίας ζητούντων
κατ' ἐκείνους διαλέγεσθαι· τοὺς γὰρ δὴ λόγους

R 134 τῶν λόγων γενέσθαι δυνατωτέρους καὶ εἶναι μετ'
ἐκείνων δυνάμεις τε καὶ πλούτους, ἐν δὲ τοῖς
πλὴν αὑτῶν οὐδέν. οὐ μὴν ἐπειθόμην γε ταῖς
περὶ τοῦ με δεῖν λιπεῖν τὴν τάξιν παραινέσεσιν,
ἀλλ' οὐκ ἠγνόουν μὲν οἷ τὸ πρᾶγμα ἀφῖκται, δί-
καιος δὲ ὅμως ἠξίουν εἶναι περὶ αὐτό, οὐδὲ γὰρ
μητέρα ἀτυχοῦσαν ἀφεῖναι ἂν ἔρημον, τοῦτο δὲ
οὐκ ἀτιμότερον.   215. καὶ ἐν αὐτῷ δὴ τῷ τῆς
κακοπραγίας χρόνῳ διδάσκαλοι παρ' ἡμῖν ῥητορικῆς ἐξετράφησαν, ὧν πολλοὶ μὲν διασπαρέντες
κατέσχον τὴν Ἀσίαν, εἷς δέ τις τὸ τῆς Εὐρώπης
ἄκρον, ἐφ' οὗ ᾤκισται ἡ μεγάλη τρυφῶσα
τῷ Βοσπόρῳ.

216. Τῆς δ' αὖ τῶν θεῶν ἐπικουρίας καὶ τὸ
ῥηθησόμενον ἀπόδειξις. ἐξιόντι μοι τοῦ βουλευ-
τηρίου μετὰ τοὺς εἰωθότας πόνους ἐπὶ τοῦ ἵππου

R 135 τοῦ μικροῦ φερομένῳ πρός τε τὴν θύραν ἀναβε-
βηκότι τὴν νέαν ἀπαντᾷ ζεῦγος ὀρέων εἰς ἀνα-

F 179 στροφὴν περιαγομένων, καὶ ὁρῶν τὸ ζεῦγος ὁ
ἵππος ἔδεισε μικρὸν δὴ γενέσθαι σφίσι τῶν

274

a great shock to my profession. This was the flight
from Greek and the migration to Italy of those
whose object it was to learn to speak Latin.[a] It was
common belief that Latin was of increasing importance and brought power and wealth, but that
Greek had nothing extra to show for itself. I refused
to heed the advice that I should desert my post, but I
was well aware how critical the situation was. I
thought it but proper to remain loyal to my profession: I would never have left my mother alone and
in distress, and this was something deserving of no
less respect.   215. Yet even in those lean years, I
produced teachers of rhetoric.[b] Many of them have
gone and spread far and wide over Asia, while one of
them is now in Europe, in the capital, where it
stands lording it over the Bosporus.

216. Another demonstration of divine assistance
is the following. I was leaving the City Hall after
my usual day's work and I was going on my pony up
New Gate, when I was confronted by a pair of mules
which were being turned round.[c] Upon seeing

[a] Cf. §154 above; for the lean years for rhetoric under
Constantius, *Or.* 62. 8 ff. He sees no improvement under
Theodosius.

[b] Cf. *Or.* 62.27 ff.

[c] The New Gate, not otherwise mentioned, is evidently
near the *bouleuterion*. For the topography, cf. Downey,
Antioch, pp. 632 ff; the colonnades, *Or.* 11.196, Festugière,
Antioche, pp. 23 f, 39 f; Downey, *PAPS* 103 (1959), 652 ff.

προσώπων τὸ μέσον, καὶ οὔτ᾽ ἀναστρέψαι ἦν τῷ
ἵππῳ διὰ τὴν στενότητα οὔτε ἐξελθεῖν διὰ τὸν
φόβον. λοιπὸν οὖν κατὰ τῶν νώτων κατενε-
χθέντα τὸν ἵππον ἔχειν ὕπτιον ὑπὸ τοῖς νώτοις
ἐμὲ καὶ τὸ μὲν ἄλλο ὧδε κεῖσθαι, τὴν κεφαλὴν
δὲ ἔξω τοῦ ἵππου πεσοῦσαν καὶ τοῖς ἐν μέσῳ τῶν
κιόνων λίθοις ἐνραγεῖσαν δεικνύναι τὸν ἐγκέφα-
λον. 217. ἦν οὖν βοὴ τῶν τε ὀρεωκόμων τῶν
τε ἐν τῷ βουλευτηρίῳ, τῶν μὲν ὡς ἐπ᾽ ἀκουσίῳ
R 136 τῷ κακῷ, τῶν δὲ ἀλλήλους ἀμύνειν παρακαλούν-
των· καὶ οἱ μὲν ὄπισθεν ἀνεῖχον τοὺς πόδας
χερσὶ πολλαῖς, ὁ δὲ οὐ κατὰ τὴν ἑαυτοῦ φύσιν
τάς τε χεῖρας ἀνέσχε καὶ ἡσύχαζε τρέμων.
ἄμφω δὴ τούτω θεοῦ νομιστέον, τό τε τῶν ἀνθρώπων τό τε τοῦ ἵππου.

218. Χειμῶνος δὲ ἀρχομένου πολλαί τε πολλαχόθεν ἀγγελίαι τελευτὰς ἑταίρων μηνύουσαι
καὶ παρ᾽ ἡμῖν ἐκφορὰ νεανίσκου λύπην ὁπόσην
τῷ πατρὶ πολλοῖς ἐνεγκοῦσα καὶ πολιτῶν καὶ
ξένων κατά τε τὴν αὐτοῦ τοῦ τεθνεῶτος καλο-
κἀγαθίαν καὶ τὴν εἰς ἅπαντας τοὺς ἐν ταῖς
F 180 χρείαις τοῦ οἴκου χρηστότητα. 219. νοσοῦντος δὲ ἔτι τοῦδε Ῥιχομήρης ἔρχεται στρατηγός,
ἱεροῖς τε καὶ θεοῖς προσκείμενος ἄνθρωπος,

276

these, my horse suddenly panicked at the narrowness of the gap between him and them. He could not turn back, because of the lack of room, nor could he get through, because of his fright. Consequently, he would have reared up backwards and pinned me flat on my back beneath him. With my body lying so, my head would have fallen clear of the horse and dashed against the cobbles between the porticoes, so badly gashed as to expose the brain. 217. Well, there was an outcry, both from the muleteers and from those in the City Hall, as they shouted that it was all an accident or cried to one another for help. While they, from behind, with willing hands kept his feet away from me, the horse, quite contrary to his usual habit, kept his forelegs up and stood quiet and trembling. The behaviour both of the men and of the animal I must ascribe to the favour of Fortune.

218. Early that winter there came news from all quarters telling me of the deaths of pupils of mine. Here in Antioch there took place the funeral of a lad whose death inflicted upon many a man—citizen and foreigner alike—as much grief as it did upon his father, such was the nobility of the deceased and the generosity of his family to all who were in need.[a] 219. While the lad still lay sick, Richomer arrived to take over the military command. He was a man deeply attached to the religion of the gods and, as I

---

[a] Identity unknown. For similar examples of curial philanthropy see *Or.* 63.9, 53.4, *Letter* 22.

LIBANIUS

ὃς ἦρα μέν μου καὶ πρὶν ἰδεῖν, ὡς τότε
ἐδιδασκόμεθα, ἰδὼν δὲ πάντα τἆλλα ἀφεὶς
εἴχετό τε καὶ ἐδεῖτο φιλεῖσθαι καὶ εἰ τοῦδε τύχοι
R 137 τοῦ μεγίστου ἂν ἡγεῖσθαι ἔλεγε τετυχηκέναι.
γενομένης δὲ ἡμῖν φιλίας τοῖς οὐ φιλοῦσιν ἡμᾶς
ἀνιαρᾶς ἔρχεταί τε ὡς βασιλέα καὶ μέλλων
τελεῖν εἰς τὸν τῶν ὑπάτων χορὸν διπλοῖς με ἐκάλει γράμμασι, τοῖς μὲν αὐτοῦ, τὸ τῶν ἄλλων
ποιῶν, τοῖς δὲ τοῦ βασιλέως, ὃ οὔπω πρόσθεν
ἐγεγόνει.   220. ἐγένετο δὲ αὐτῷ καὶ παρ᾽
ἡμῶν λόγος ἐπαινεῖν αὐτὸν βουλόμενος, εἰ μέν τι
πλέον τῶν παρὰ τῶν ἄλλων ἔχων, οὐκ οἶδα, οἷς
δ᾽ οὖν εἶχον καὶ αὐτὸς ἐτίμων τὸν στρατηγόν.
λέγεται δὲ καὶ ἐρωτώμενος ὑπὸ τοῦ χρηστοῦ
βασιλέως ὅτῳ δὴ μάλιστα τῶν τῇδε ἡσθείη, τοὐμὸν εἰπεῖν ποιῆσαί τε ἐρῶντά μου τὸν ἄνδρα
μᾶλλον ἐρᾶν φάναι τε καὶ τῆς δεῦρο ἐπιθυμεῖν
ὁδοῦ ἐμοῦ χάριν.

---

a Richomer, *PLRE* 765, *magister militum per Orientem*
in autumn 383 when he was designated consul for 384,
while in Antioch. This letter of Theodosius in early 384
secured for Libanius the honorary office (prefecture, so
Petit, "Sur la Date du Pro Templis," *Byzantion* 21 (1951),
291–294), which according to Eunapius *V.S.* 496 and

found out later, an admirer of mine even before he had seen me. Thus when he did see me, he put everything else aside and took me and begged me to be his friend: if he were to obtain this, he said, he would think that he had everything he wanted. So we became friends and he frowned upon any who were not friends of mine. When he returned to the emperor to be appointed consul, he summoned me by two dispatches, one from himself—something others had done—but the other from the emperor—something quite without precedent.[a] 220. He received a speech in his honour from me too. Whether it was more effective than those of others, I cannot say, but at least I honoured him with all the means at my disposal. The story goes that when our good emperor asked him what had given him the greatest delight here, he replied that it was I, and so he caused the emperor, already an admirer of mine, to be even more enthusiastic and to express his desire to visit us here just on my account.[b]

[a] Libanius himself (*Or.* 2.8) he had previously refused. Recently, however, Martin in the note to *Or.* 2.8 (*Discours,* Vol. ii, pp. 248–250) identifies this honour now accepted with the honorary quaestorship, a title attributed to him in the Mss. of his declamations and Julian's letters. The prefecture must then have been offered and refused at some time between 363 and 380, a notion hard to accept considering his unpopularity with the government in these years.

[b] Invitations to the emperor to visit Antioch, though never accepted, were part of the stock flattery and a sop to local pride; see for example *Or.* 20.44.

221. Τοῦτο μὲν δὴ τοσοῦτον. εἰ δὲ καὶ τὸ
εὐχῆς τυχεῖν εὐτυχές, εὐξάμην λῆξαι Πρόκλον
τῆς ἀρχῆς ἣν τυραννίδα ἀπέφηνε. καὶ οὐ μάτην

R 138 γε εὐξάμην, ἀλλ᾽ οἱ θεοὶ τοῦτό τ᾽ ἔδοσαν καὶ
προσέθεσαν τὸ καὶ σὺν ἀσχημοσύνῃ. δραπέτης

F 181 γὰρ δὴ ἦν, αὐτὸς ἑαυτὸν ἐλαύνων· τοιαῦτα
ἑαυτῷ συνῄδει.   222. καὶ ὁ Ζεὺς ἐρρύετο τῶν
ὀφθαλμῶν ἐκείνου τὴν ἑορτὴν ἑαυτοῦ. καὶ γὰρ
ἐτύγχανεν αὐτῷ τὴν δάφνην φόνῳ τε πολλῷ καὶ
αἵματι μιάνας. καί μοι ἐδόκουν αὐτὸν ὥσπερ
κύνες ὑλακτοῦσαι φεύγειν καταναγκάζειν αἱ τῶν
αὐτοῦ πεσόντων ψυχαί, δόξαν ἀεὶ παρέχουσαι δή-
ξεσθαι. τούτων οὐχ ὑπῆρξέ μοι τῶν Ὀλυμπίων
μετασχεῖν, ὅτε δὴ καὶ τὸν λόγον ὃν ὕφηνα μέν,
οὐκ ἐπέδειξα δέ, φέρων ἀνέθηκα τῷ Διί, στύρα-
κος ἅμα ὀσμῇ θεραπεύσας τὸν θεόν.   223. τὸν
μὲν δὴ τῆς ἀρχῆς ἐκείνης χρόνον πάντα ἐπεβου-
λευόμην ὑπὸ τῶν αὐτῷ χρωμένων, αὐτὸς οὐ χρώμενος, ἐδόκουν δέ τισιν εἶναι φιλοκίνδυνος οὐ
δεδιὼς τοὺς ἐκείνου κεραυνούς, θεῶν δὲ οἶμαι
βοηθούντων, ὑπ᾽ ἐκείνων τε δεινὸν οὐδὲν σὺν

---

a Proclus relinquished office as *Comes* in summer 384
before the *Olympia,* which allows Libanius to assert,

221. So much then for that. If it is a matter of good fortune to have one's prayers fulfilled, I prayed that Proclus should lose the office he had turned into a tyranny, and my prayers were not in vain. Heaven granted his dismissal, and a dismissal in disgrace too,[a] for he deserted his post and decamped—all as a result of his own guilty conscience. 222. Zeus kept his festival intact from the fellow's eyes, after he defiled his grove with much slaughter and bloodshed.[b] It seemed to me that the spirits of the men he had murdered there, like howling dogs, caused him to flee under the constant delusion that they were ravening at his heels. I could take no part in this celebration of the festival. I composed an oration but did not deliver it: instead, I took it and offered it to Zeus, at the same time worshipping the god with the scent of incense. 223. During the whole period of his office, I was the object of plots contrived by his associates. I refused to associate with him myself, though I appeared foolhardy to one or two people, but I had no fear of any bolt that he could hurl. With heaven's aid, therefore, nothing serious came from their contrivances, and I maintained my independence,

entirely falsely, that he was dismissed in disgrace.

[b] The grove is the suburb of Daphne. The major events of the *Olympia* were held in the stadium there. Its fame had earlier served to distinguish Antioch from other cities of the same name. Cf. Strabo 15.1.73 (p. 719), 16.2.4 (p. 749), Pliny *NH* 5.18.

παρρησίᾳ τε ζῶντες καὶ τῶν πραττομένων ἐπι-
λαμβανόμενοι πλείοσιν ἢ καὶ πρόσθεν ἠγωνισά-
μεθα λόγοις, οὐδοτιοῦν εἰς Πρόκλον ἀνηλωκότες
R 139 χρόνου, πολὺν δέ γε ἕτεροι παρεστῶτες, παρα-
καθήμενοι, κολακεύοντες, αἰτοῦντες, λαμβάνον-
τες, χρηματιζόμενοι· ὧν οὐδὲν ἐμοὶ ποιοῦντι
ποιεῖν τε ἐνεγίγνετο λόγους φέρειν τε εἰς συλλό-
γους.   224. καίτοι πολλαὶ μὲν ἐγίγνοντο
πρεσβεῖαι περὶ εἰρήνης, πολλαὶ δὲ ὑποσχέσεις,
F 182 ἀλλ' οὐ προυδίδουν γε αὐτοῖς ἐμαυτὸν οὐδὲ ἀνε-
πειθόμην. τοιγαροῦν ἐπηνούμην τε καὶ ἀνὴρ
εἶναι ἐδόκουν ἔν τε ἠπείροις καὶ νήσοις, δεῖγμα
τρόπου βελτίονος ἐκφέρων τὴν ἀπὸ τῆς ὁμιλίας
τῆς ἐκείνου φυγήν.

225. Δοῦσα δὲ ἡμῖν ἄρχοντα ἀγαθὸν ἀντὶ
κακοῦ τὸν Θεοδώρου τοῦ οὐ δικαίως ἀποθανόντος
ἡ Τύχη ἔδωκε μὲν σωτηρίαν, ἔδωκε δὲ ἐλευθερίαν, ἔδωκε δὲ ἀναπνεῦσαι λυπήσασα μόνους
τοὺς σοροπηγούς. ὁ δὲ Μουσῶν τε ἦν τρόφιμος
καὶ τὴν ἀρχὴν ἆθλον εἶχεν ἐπῶν λέγειν τε ἐκ

---

[a] For example *Or.* 10 (On the Plethron), composed in
Proclus' period of office and criticizing his extensions to the
Plethron, where part of the Olympic festival took place.

attacked their activities, and held my own with more orations than before. I never wasted a single second on Proclus: he had time enough wasted on him by others, with their visits and attendance, their flatteries and petitions, their greed and business dealings. I had no use for this sort of thing, and so I could compose my orations and deliver them to my audiences.[a]   224. Though I received many overtures of peace and many promises, I would not surrender to them nor would I relent. So I earned respect and on continent and island I was held to be a man of worth, since I provided an example of virtue by avoiding his company.

225. But when Fortune granted us a good governor in the person of Icarius, son of that Theodorus so foully slain, she granted salvation, freedom, and respite, vexing only the undertakers.[b] He was a nursling of the Muses, and held his office as a reward for his poetry.[c] By virtue of his position he

---

[a] Libanius' story here is at best tendentious. He did in fact attend Proclus' official audiences, as he was obliged to do (*Or.* 2.3).

[b] Icarius, *Comes Orientis* 384/5 (*PLRE* 455 (2)), son of the Theodorus of the conspiracy of 371 (§171 above), and the subject of *Orations* 26–29. Relations with him go from good to bad or worse, as shown by the progress from advice in *Or.* 26, to protest in *Or.* 27, and demand for dismissal in *Or.* 28.

[c] The poetical qualifications here commended are derided in *Or.* 26.6, 28.2.

τῆς ἀρχῆς κεκωλυμένος λεγόντων ἀπολαύειν
ἤθελε ταῖς τε εἰς ἐμὲ τιμαῖς παῖδα ἐμὸν ἑαυτὸν
ἐπεποιήκει, ὥστ᾽ εἶναί μοι καὶ σὺν ὀργῇ φθέγγε-
σθαι ὃ καὶ Θεοδώρῳ ἄν, εἴπερ ἐτύγχανε ζῶν.
226. οὗτος ἐν λιμῷ κατειλήφει τὴν πόλιν. τοῦ-
R 140 τον μείζω τὸν λιμὸν ἐποίουν αἱ κατὰ τῶν σιτοποιῶν ἀπειλαί. εἶθ᾽ οἱ μὲν ἀποδράντες ἔσωζον
ἑαυτούς, ἄρτος δὲ οὐδαμοῦ, πυροῦ δὲ ἐλπίδες, καὶ
κακῶς δ᾽ ἂν ποιήσειε τὸ πεινῆν. ἡ μὲν οὖν
πόλις οὐδὲν διέφερε χειμαζομένης νεώς, ἐγὼ δὲ
εἰσδραμὼν παρὰ τὸν ἄρχοντα μετὰ πόνου μέν,
παύω δ᾽ οὖν βλαβερὰν φιλονεικίαν. ἀπιστία δὲ
εἶχε τοὺς σιτοποιούς, ὡς οὐχ ἁλώσονται φανέν-
τες, καὶ ἅπασαι ὑποσχέσεις ἀσθενεῖς πλὴν μιᾶς
F 183 τῆς ἐμῆς.   227. ὡς δὲ εἶπον δεῖν θαρρεῖν ἐκ-
βαλόντας τὸ δέος καὶ ἧκεν οὗτος εἰς τὰ ὄρη τε
καὶ τὰς νάπας ὁ λόγος, ἦσαν πρὸ ἑσπέρας ἐν
τοῖς αὑτῶν ἕκαστος, καὶ πρᾶγμα οὐκ ἂν ἐλπισθὲν
ἕωθεν ἑωρᾶτο, δρόμος οὐδεὶς ἐπ᾽ ἄρτους· αἴτιον
δὲ τὸ πλῆθος αὐτῶν. τοῦτο μετὰ τῆς Τύχης πε-
πρᾶχθαί μοι φαίην ἄν. διὸ τῶν λελειτουργηκό-
των χρησιμώτερος ἐκεκρίμην τῇ πόλει· τοὺς μὲν
γὰρ ἐν σωζομένῃ πεποιῆσθαι τὴν δαπάνην, ὑπ᾽

was prevented from giving orations, but he wanted to make the most of those who did do so, and in his respect for me he had become almost a son to me, so that I could speak to him in anger in exactly the same terms as Theodorus would have done, had he been alive.   226. He found the city in a state of famine, and this was made worse by threats directed against the bakers.[a] They began to decamp to save their skins: there was no bread at all, corn was merely a fond hope, and famine would have run riot. Our city was like a storm-tossed ship, when I hurried to the governor and quelled this disastrous rancour, though not without difficulty. The bakers were suspicious that if they emerged from hiding they would be arrested, and they placed no reliance in any promise save mine alone.[b]   227. I told them that they must be of good courage and cast out their fears, and this report went over hill and dale, so that before evening every one was back in his shop, and next morning a sight was seen that passed all expectations—no queue for bread, since there was so much of it. I venture to assert that, with Fortune's aid, it was I who brought this to pass. Therefore I was judged to have been of more service to the city than its high magistrates, for while they went to expense upon a city that was intact, I had

[a] These famine conditions had lasted since 381 without a break.

[b] The bakers had fled to Mt. Silpius; cf. § 99 above.

ἐμοῦ δὲ αὐτὴν σεσῶσθαι. 228. πάλιν τοίνυν βουλῆς κακῆς ὑπ' ἀνθρώπῳ μεθύοντί τε καὶ ὀλέθρῳ θείσης τοὺς σιτοποιούς, ὃς ὁμοῦ μὲν ἔτυπτεν, ὁμοῦ δὲ ἔμελλε καὶ οὐ τούτους δὲ μόνον ἀλλ' ἔθνος ἅπαν, καὶ τρίτον ἐπῆν κακόν, τὸ γεγυμνω-

R 141 μένοις τοῖς νώτοις ἄγεσθαι διὰ τοῦ ἄστεος. τού-τοις ἐγὼ μὲν ἤλγουν, ὁ δὲ ἔχαιρε καὶ κατ' αὐτό γε τοῦτο τὸ ἀλγεῖν ἐμέ. 229. τὴν ἀρχὴν δὲ ἦσαν οἳ ὀρθῶς ταῦτα τῇδε πράττεσθαι ἔπειθον καὶ ὡς εἴ τις ἐκεῖνον ἀφέλοι χείρω ποιήσει τὴν ἀγοράν. ἦν οὖν ὁ μὲν ἐν τῷ τοῦ νενικηκότος σχήματι καὶ αὐτός τε ἤσθιεν οἵ τε ταῦτα ἐπαι-νοῦντες, ἡμῖν δὲ κεκρατῆσθαί τε συνέβαινεν ἔχειν τε πλὴν ἀθυμίας οὐδέν. 230. τῇ Τύχῃ δέ, ὡς ἔοικεν, αἰσχρὸν εἶναι ἐφαίνετο τοιαύτην νίκην τε καὶ ἧτταν περιορᾶν, καὶ τὸ πρᾶγμα μετέθηκεν οὐδὲν ἡμῶν πραγματευσαμένων· ὁ γὰρ δὴ ἀεὶ

F 184 οἴνου γέμων ἐκεῖνος ἐξέωστό τε τῆς περὶ τὰ τοι-αῦτα ἐξουσίας οἴκοι τε καθῆστο ἐγκεκαλυμμένος πεποιημένης τε τῷ Ποσειδῶνι ἱπποδρομίας περὶ τῇ οἰκίᾳ τῇ αὑτοῦ δεδιὼς ἔτρεμε· τοσοῦτο κῦμα παίδων ἐπ' αὐτὴν ἐφέρετο, κελεύοντες ἐξεμεῖν[1] ἃ ἐδηδόκει κακῶς, καὶ αἱ δᾷδες ἐν χεροῖν. ταπει-

---

[1] ἐξεμεῖν conj. Wyttenbach: ἐμεῖν Mss., edd.

been instrumental in saving it.   228.   However, evil counsel once more placed the bakers under the control of a villainous sot[a] who began to make indiscriminate use of threats and floggings, not just against the actual bakers,[b] but against the whole corporation. Yet another injustice was perpetrated when they were paraded through the city with backs bared. At this I was grieved, but he was cock-a-hoop, and all the more so because of my grief. 229. At first, some people tried to maintain that such actions were justified and that, if he were removed, conditions in the market would get worse. So he appeared to be on the winning side and, while he and his adherents had food in plenty, we were the losing party and had nothing but disappointment.   230.   However, it seems that Fortune considered it a shabby trick to turn a blind eye to a victory and a defeat of this sort, and so, without any intervention on my part, the whole aspect of affairs was changed, and he, ever the sot, was ousted from his position of authority and sat at home with covered face, and when the horse race had been run in honour of Poseidon, he was all fear and trembling for his own home, such a torrent of lads bore down upon it, torch in hand, calling upon him to disgorge

[a] Candidus, a *principalis*, was appointed *epistates* of the bakers by Icarius. For his venality see *Or.* 27.9 ff.

[b] A contrast is drawn between the actual bakers and all the others employed on the city's food supply.

νὸν δὲ ἦν καὶ ὅσον αὐτῷ συνύβριζε πρότερον, ὅ
τε ἐξηπατημένος αὐτὸν ἀπῄτει δίκας διὰ τῶν ἐν
τῇ κεφαλῇ τριχῶν.

231. Ἧκε δὲ ἐν ταῖς αὐταῖς ἡμέραις ἡμῖν καὶ
τοῦ ὑπάρχου γράμματα πολλαῖς καὶ μεγάλαις τι-
μῶντα εὐφημίαις· ἐν αἷς καὶ πάνυ μ' ἐθέλειν ἰδεῖν
R 142 ἐνεγέγραπτο, ὥστε[1] τοῖς νύκτωρ ἐκτεθεικόσιν
ἐκεῖνα τὰ γράμματα (ὅτου μὲν ἦν οὐκ ἔλεγεν,
ὅσα δὲ ἐσυκοφάντει) πένθος εἶναι τὴν ἐπιστολήν.   232. ὀλίγαις δὲ ἡμέραις ὕστερον ὃν
ἐποίησα λόγον αἰτήσαντι στρατηγῷ, καὶ γὰρ
τοῦτό μοι παρὰ τῆς θεοῦ τὸ εἶναι τοὺς τὰ τοιαῦτα αἰτοῦντας, τοῦτον οὖν τὸν λόγον δεικνύων
εὐδοκίμουν, καὶ ἦν παραμύθιον ὁ κρότος τελευτῆς ἀνδρός, οὗ τὰ γράμματά μοι πρὸς ἐπιδείξεις
συνέπραττε βελτίω τε ὄντα τῶν ἐμῶν ἃ ταῖς
ὠδῖσιν ὑπήκουε, καὶ παρέχοντα τρέχειν τοῖς
ὀφθαλμοῖς δι' αὐτῶν. ἐπὶ τούτοις ἐβοήθουν

---

[1] Lac. ante ὥστε posuit F., perperam.

---

a Candidus was deposed at the end of 384. The festival
of Poseidon occurs early in the New Year, with horse races
and torchlight processions, always an opportunity for high
spirits, riot, and arson for a volatile populace.

all that he had unjustly consumed.[a] His former associates in arrogance were but broken reeds, and he, thoroughly undeceived, tore his hair in mortification.

231. About the same time, there arrived from the prefect[b] letters full of praise and commendation for me. For instance, he wrote that he was very eager to meet me, so that for the underhand publishers of those lampoons—they didn't say who wrote them, but what slander they contained!—his letter was a source of pain. 232. A few days afterwards, the military governor[c] asked me for the oration I had composed—yes, I owe it to Fortune that there were people to make such requests—and when I delivered it, I received high praise. The applause consoled me for the death of my secretary, whose writing assisted me greatly in my declamations, since it was much better than my own notes compiled in the process of composition, and allowed me to run through them at a glance. After this, I helped various

[b] Cynegius (*PLRE* 235 (3)), Praetorian Prefect of the East, is now, in early 385, touring the East on his mission to restore the curiae (cf. *Or.* 52.40). A play on the meanings of γράμματα has caused confusion here: (i) the prefect's letter, (ii) anonymous graffiti and lampooning placards concocted by Libanius' opponents against him.

[c] Ellebichus (*PLRE* 277), *magister militum* 383–388. He was to be one of the commissioners after the Riots of the Statues. For this panegyric, *Or.* 32.2. Libanius' interventions here are connected with Cynegius' policy of forced recruitment to the curiae, then in full swing.

F 185 φίλοις γονεῦσι παίδων παιδευομένων ὀργήν τε
ἄρχοντος ἐξαιρῶν καὶ λύων τινὰ δεσμῶν καὶ
παρέχων οἴκαδε ἀπιέναι.

233. Τὴν δὲ ἀπὸ τοῦ λιμοῦ καὶ ἅμα ἀπὸ τοῦ
λοιμοῦ λύπην, ἐξ ὧν πολὺ τὸ θνῆσκον, οὐδ᾽ ἂν
εἰπεῖν ὅση μοι κατέσχε τὴν ψυχὴν δυναίμην. ὅτε
φόβος ἠνάγκαζε πατέρας καλεῖν τοὺς αὑτῶν παρ᾽
ἑαυτοὺς ὥσπερ ἐκ πυρός, οἱ μὲν δὴ ὑπήκουον,
μεῖον δὲ ἐμοὶ τὸ ποίμνιον, ἐγὼ δ᾽ ἔχαιρον σωζομέ-
νων ἄλλοσε ἰόντων. πάντα μέντοι τὸν χρόνον τοῦτον ἄνευ γέλωτος διῆγον ἱκετεύων θεοὺς δοῦναι
μὲν καρπούς, δοῦναι δὲ ὑγίειαν. καὶ τὸ μὲν ἔδοσαν, καὶ ὁ λοιμὸς ἔστη, καρποὺς δὲ ἐλπίζειν μὲν
ἔνι, τύχοι δὲ ἡ ἐλπὶς τοῦ τέλους.

234. Ἀλλὰ τά γε τῶν ἡμετέρων λόγων νῦν
R 143 πλέον ἢ πρότερον ἥττηται τῶν ἑτέρων, ὥσθ᾽ ἡμῖν
καὶ φόβον ὑπὲρ αὐτῶν γενέσθαι μὴ ἐκκοπῶσιν
ὅλως, νόμου τοῦτο ποιοῦντος. γράμματα μὲν οὖν
καὶ νόμος τοῦτο οὐκ ἔπραττεν, ἡ τιμὴ δὲ καὶ τὸ
τῶν τὴν Ἰταλὴν ἐπισταμένων γενέσθαι τὸ δύνασθαι. θεοῖς δὲ ἄρα τοῖς δοῦσι τούσδε τοὺς λόγους
καὶ ὑπὲρ τῆς νίκης ὧν ἔδοσαν μελήσει καὶ τοῦ τὸ
κράτος ὅ ποτε ἦν ἐν αὐτοῖς κομίσασθαι.

235. Παρὰ τούτων δὲ ἄρα τῶν θεῶν ὑπῆρξε καὶ

friends of mine, parents of boys in my charge, by assuaging the governor's anger, and I even got one released from prison and enabled him to return home.

233. I could not possibly recount the distress caused by plague and famine.[a] Many people died: parents were induced by fear to summon home their sons as though from the dead: they obeyed, and my flock diminished, but I was glad that they found safety by leaving me. All this time I spent joylessly, in prayer to the gods to grant us food and health. Health they granted, for the plague abated; as for food, we can but hope, and I pray that our hope may be fulfilled.

234. Moreover, as regards my studies, they had now lost ground to Latin even more than before, so that I am afraid that they may, through the agency of law, become completely superseded.[b] Yet it is not law or edicts that have brought this about, but the honour and power reserved for those acquainted with Latin. However, the gods have granted this eloquence, and will in the end ensure that what they have granted will emerge victorious and regain the influence it once held.

235. Indeed, I myself have been preserved by

[a] Cf. *Or.* 27.8 (summer 385).
[b] Cf. § 214 above; *Or.* 43.4–5. Only in 439 was Greek admissible in official legal procedures, *Nov. Theod.* 16.

ἐμοί ποτε σωτηρία πολλοῖς μὲν πρότερον ἔτεσι,
λεγέσθω δέ, εἰ καὶ μὴ πρότερον, ἀλλὰ νῦν, ὁ λόγος
δὲ παρὰ τὸν χρόνον οὐδὲν ἀδικήσεται. παρεφρόνει
τις χειροτέχνης καὶ τοὺς μὲν πόρρωθεν ἐτάραττεν,
ἔστι δ' ὧν καὶ ἥπτετο, χαλεπώτατος δὲ ἦν
ἐμοί, καθάπερ τι πεπονθὼς κακόν, καὶ ὁπότε ἴδοι
με, λίθους ἀφίει καὶ ἐπεθύμει κτεῖναι βαλών.
236. τὸ δὲ αἴτιον οὔτε τότε ᾔδειν νῦν τε εὑρεῖν
οὐκ ἔχω. πρὸς δὲ τὰς βολὰς βοαὶ μὲν τῶν ὁρώντων ἦσαν, οἵας ἂν ποιήσειαν ὑπὲρ τοιούτων φόβοι,
χεῖρες δὲ ἔδρων οὐδέν, αἱ δὲ τῶν θεῶν καὶ πάνυ,
δι' οὓς ἅπας λίθος μάταιος, τῶν μὲν οὐκ ἐφικνου-
μένων, τῶν δὲ ὑπερπετομένων. 237. καί ποτε
θέρος μὲν ἦν καὶ μεσημβρία, καὶ ἐκαθήμην ὑφ'
ᾧπερ εἰώθειν κίονι, τῷ Δημοσθένει προσκείμενος,
παρῆν δὲ οὐδείς, οὐκ ἐλεύθερος, οὐ δοῦλος. ὁ
δὲ ἦλθέ τε ὡς ἐμέ, καὶ ὁ λίθος ἐν τῇ δεξιᾷ. προσελθὼν δὴ ταῖς μεγάλαις θύραις αἳ οὐκ ἐκέκλειντο
καὶ δι' ὧν ἦν τἄνδον ἰδεῖν, ἐπειδὴ εἶδεν ἔνδον
ὄντα οὐδένα, ἀπῆλθε τὴν αὐτὴν μετὰ τοῦ λίθου,
καὶ ταῦτα αὐτὸς ἑώρων οὐ κινηθείς, ὁ δὲ οὐκ
ἤνεγκεν ἐπ' ἐμὲ τὸν ὀφθαλμὸν θεῶν τοῦ κεκωλυκό-

---

[a] Demosthenes was staple for the rhetorical education,

these same gods many a long year ago, but let me acknowledge it now, even if I have not done so before, for the account will take no harm, as regards the chronology. One of the artisans began to go mad, and he would annoy other people from a distance or would even manhandle them, but it was for me that he showed the greatest hostility, just as though I had injured him in some way. Whenever he saw me, he would hurl stones at me, and he threw intending to kill. 236. The reason I neither knew then nor can discover now. Whenever he threw, an outcry would arise from the onlookers who were, naturally, alarmed at such conduct, but no one ever lifted a finger to help. It was by divine providence that every stone missed me and either fell short or passed overhead. 237. One summer's day at noon, I was seated at the foot of my usual pillar, engrossed in Demosthenes,[a] with not a soul in sight, free or slave, when this fellow approached with a stone in his hand. He came closer and peered through the big gate, which was open and gave a view of the interior, but saw no one there, and retired the way that he had come, still clutching his stone. I saw this for myself, without moving a muscle, and his eye did not light upon me, since some divine power prevented it. Otherwise there

but particularly so for Libanius, author of the 'Hypotheses' and dubbed Demosthenes the Second by the Byzantines; cf. Foerster Vol. i, p. 74.

τος. ἢ οὐκ ἂν πληγῆς εἰς θάνατον ἐδεήθην
δευτέρας, τοσοῦτος ἦν ὁ λίθος. 238. τὸν τοίνυν
ἐκεῖθεν εἰς τήνδε τὴν ὥραν χρόνον δόσιν θεῶν
F 187 λογίων νομιστέον. ἐφρόντισα μέντοι καὶ τοῦ
φρονῆσαι τὸν ἄνθρωπον δῆσαί τε αὐτὸν τῷ πατρὶ
συμβουλεύσας καὶ μετενεγκεῖν ἐφ' ὕδωρ ἀπ'
οἴνου, καὶ γὰρ δὴ καὶ ἐπεπύσμην οἴνῳ νοσῆσαι τὸν
ἄνθρωπον.

R 145 239. Ἀλλ' ἐπάνειμι δή· τῶν τις ἡμῖν πεπλησιακότων ἀνὴρ ἀεί τινας ἑστιῶν καὶ τούτῳ χαίρων
ὧν τέ τις ἐν τῷ μεγάλῳ συνεδρίῳ, κιβδήλοις ὀνεί-
ρασιν ἐξαπατηθεὶς ὑπισχνουμένοις τὰ οὐκ ἐσό-
μενα, γελῶν ἅμα πρὸς πολλοὺς ἅττα ἴδοι ἔλεγε.
τοῦτο προϊὼν ὁ χρόνος ἐποίησε κίνδυνον. καὶ ἀδικεῖν ἐδόκουν, ὁ μὲν οἷς εἶπεν, ὁ δὲ οἷς ἤκουσεν.
240. ὧν εἷς τις ἐν τῷ δικαστηρίῳ καὶ ἐμὸν ὑπο-
γραφέα κεκοινωνηκέναι τῆς ἀκοῆς ἔφασκεν, ὁ δὲ
ἄρα ἐτεθνήκει, καὶ τοῦτο ἀκούσας ὁ δικαστὴς ἐξέβαλε τὸν λόγον. πάλιν ἐν τούτῳ τῷ θανάτῳ
βασάνου μὲν ἐκεῖνος, ἐγὼ δὲ ὁδοῦ τε καὶ θορύβων
καὶ πόνων οὐ φορητῶν ἀφείθην. ὁ γὰρ δὴ ἐπὶ
τεθνεῶτα ἥκων τίς ἂν ἦν ζῶντος; ἔλεγε δὲ

---

[a] Identified by Sievers (p. 169) with the offender of

would have been no need for a second blow, so big was the stone. 238. The period from that time up to the present, therefore, I must regard as the gift of the gods of learning. However, I took good care to have the fellow brought to his senses: I advised his father to keep him under restraint and to get him off wine on to water, since I had discovered that he was a chronic drunkard.

239. But to resume—one of my ex-pupils was a man who always derived great pleasure from entertaining people.[a] He was a member of the Senate, and had often been deceived by silly dreams that made promises impossible to fulfil, and he would humorously describe his visions to people at large. As time went on, this proved a risky business, for both he and his hearers were held to be guilty of an offence, he because of his story, they because they listened to it. 240. One of them alleged in court that my secretary had been implicated in the business, but as he was dead, the governor rejected the charge. Here again, by his death my secretary was spared the torture,[b] and I the long journey and unbearable clamours and toils, for what trouble would not have been started if the man who attacked him after his death had attacked him in his lifetime? The motive behind this allegation was

Themist. *Or.* 19.229d (of 385). He was a Senator of Constantinople (ἡ μεγάλη βουλή; cf. *Ep.* 1327.3).

[b] A second providential release, similar to the incident of Adelphius (§173).

ταῦτα οὐχ ὡς τὸν νεκρὸν παραδώσων τοῖς νόμοις,
ἀλλ᾽ οἶμαί τι προσεδόκησε, τοῖς οὐ μετ᾽ αὐτοῦ δεδεμένοις τοῦ μὴ δεδέσθαι φθονῶν. τύχης τοίνυν
F 188 ἀγαθῆς τὸ μὴ κακωθῆναι συκοφαντίας ὀδοῦσιν,
ἀλλὰ τοῖς ἡδίστοις τε καμάτοις καὶ εἰωθόσιν ἀντὶ
τῶν οὐκ εἰωθότων διὰ τοῦδε ἐλθεῖν τοῦ χρόνου.

241. Ἐκείνῳ μὲν δὴ τῷ χειμῶνι πέρας ἐπιεικέ-
στερον ἐπέθηκε βασιλεὺς οἷον οὐκ ἂν ἕτερον, ἐμοὶ
δοκεῖν. θανάτῳ μὲν γὰρ οὐδένα, φυγῇ δὲ δύο,[1]
R 146 πληγαῖς δὲ οὐ πολλαῖς ἐποίησε τοὺς ἄλλους βελ-
τίονας, ἐμοὶ δὲ γίγνεταί τις ἑτέρωθεν ταραχὴ τῆς
ἐν τῷ διασκαλείῳ νεότητος οὐ πάσης ἐν τῇ τάξει
μενούσης, ἀλλ᾽ ἐν σωφρονοῦντι τῷ πλείονι μοίρας
τινὸς θρασυνομένης, τῷ λυπεῖν φιλοτιμουμένης
καὶ ἐνδεικνυμένης ὡς εἰ ἐθελήσουσι καὶ πλέον τι
δράσουσιν. 242. ἐμοὶ δὲ μὴ ἀλγεῖν μὲν οὐκ ἦν,
σιωπᾶν δὲ ἠξίουν ἕως αὑτῶν ἀδικεῖν καταγνόντες
ἦσαν ἐν τοῖς προτέροις. τῆς γνώμης δὲ οὐκ ἀρ-
κούσης εἰς πίστιν προσεγένετό τι τὸ τὴν ἀνάγκην
ἔχον, ὥστε μηδὲ βουλομένοις ἀπεῖναι ἐξεῖναι. ὅ τι

[1] Post δύο lac. indic. Re., Martin.

not to deliver the dead man up to justice, but he had something else in view, I suspect, since he bore a grudge against anyone who had not suffered arrest with him just because he had not been arrested. Thus it was by good fortune that I was not harmed by the fangs of envy, but passed this time in my usual congenial labours rather than in most unwelcome toils.

241. The emperor put a fitting end to that winter,[a] none more fitting, to my mind, when, refraining from inflicting the death penalty, he imposed a sentence of exile on a couple of people and corrected the rest with a few floggings. However, a disturbance of different origin affected me, when not all the students in the school kept the rules of discipline. The majority behaved properly, but a certain section misconducted themselves and made a point of being a nuisance, showing that, if they once took it into their heads, they would go to even greater lengths. 242. I naturally felt aggrieved, but I decided to remain silent until they recognized their misconduct and returned to their former station. However, their attitude gave no grounds for confidence, and so some compulsion was applied, so that they could not leave even if they wished. What

[a] Double entendre on χειμῶνι: (i) winter (of 385/6), (ii) the charge of magic. For Theodosius' clemency here cf. *Or.* 19.21, Themist. *Or.* 19.230b, 231d.

δὲ τοῦτο ἦν, ἔδοξέ μοι μὴ λέγειν.

243. Τὸ δὲ πάθος ἐκεῖνο τὸ τῆς κεφαλῆς τὸ
ἀρχαῖον, ὃ βροντῆς ἔργον ἐγεγόνει, διαλιπὸν ἑκ-
καίδεκα ἔτη πάλιν ἐνέκειτο καὶ ἦν χαλεπώτερον
ἀρξάμενον εὐθὺς μετὰ τὴν μεγίστην ἑορτήν, ἥ γε
κοινὴ τῶν ὑπὸ Ῥωμαίοις ὄντων, δέος τε ἦν μὴ
κατενεχθείην ἐπὶ συνουσίᾳ τῶν παίδων καθήμε-
F 189 νος, ἦν δὲ καὶ ἐπὶ κλίνης κειμένῳ δέος, ἡμέραι τε
ἅπασαι πικραί, νυξὶ δὲ χάριν ᾔδειν τοῦ ὕπνου,
φανεῖσα δὲ ἡμέρα τὸ κακὸν ἐκόμιζεν ὥστε
καὶ ᾔτουν παρὰ τῶν θεῶν ἀντ' ἄλλου τινὸς ἀγαθοῦ
τὸν θάνατον, καὶ πιστεύειν μὲν οὐκ εἶχον ὡς οὐ
διαφθερεῖ μοι τὸν νοῦν ἡ νόσος. 244. οὔπω δὲ
τοῦτο ὅτε ταῦτα ἔγραφον ἐπεπόνθειν, θαρρῆσαι
δὲ ὑπὲρ τοῦ μέλλοντος οὐ παρῆν. καὶ αὐτὸ
δὲ τοῦτό μοι τὸ μήπω παρὰ τῶν θεῶν οἳ διὰ
μάντεώς με αἷμα οὐκ εἴων ἐξάγειν φλέβα
R 147 τεμόντα, καίτοι σφόδρα γε ὡρμηκότα. ἔλεγε
δὲ ὁ ἰατρός, εἰ τοῦτο ἐγεγόνει, διὰ τοῦ ῥυέντος
αἵματος ἰσχὺν λαβόντος τοῦ πνεύματος[1]

---

[1] πνεύματος Mss., Re., Martin: ῥεύματος conj. Gasda, F.

[a] Cf. Or. 43 (De Pactis), esp. 9–10. Libanius proposes
the banning of student transfers and desertions, a ban
regarded as comparatively recent in Or. 36.13 of 386. Why

this was exactly, I think it better to leave unmentioned.[a]

243. My old migraine, originally caused by the thunderbolt, began to trouble me again after sixteen years of respite.[b] Commencing straight after the great festival of New Year, in which all Roman subjects share, it became worse, and I feared that I would collapse when seated in front of my class or even as I lay abed. Every day was painful: every night I was thankful for sleep: when day dawned, back came my affliction with it; and I prayed heaven for death in preference to any other boon, and was convinced that the malady would affect my reason. 244. At the time of writing, this has not yet occurred, but I can have no confidence with regard to the future. Yet the very fact that it has not occurred is heaven's work for, through the agency of a soothsayer, I was forbidden to open my veins for bleeding, eager though I was to do so. The doctor's opinion was that, if this had occurred, my breathing would have quickened with the flow of blood, my head would have been affected, and that would have

he refuses to give details is unknown. For indiscipline in the schools in the 380s see *Or.* 3.26–28, 58 *passim.*

[b] New Year 386: gout and migraine, dormant since 371 (§143 above) recur, with the regular symptoms of depression, neuralgia, vertigo; attacks in spring and autumn (§247). For medicine, divination, and magic, cf. Barb, "The Survival of the Magic Arts," in *The Conflict between Paganism and Christianity,* ed. Momigliano, 1963, pp. 100–125.

ἡττηθεῖσαν τὴν κεφαλὴν πάντως ἄν με καὶ
καταβαλεῖν.   245. ἐν τούτοις δὲ ὄντι μοι γίνεται
ὄναρ τοιόνδε· ἐδόκουν μοί τινες θύσαντες δύο
παῖδε τοῖν νεκροῖν τὸν ἕτερον θεῖναι ἐν ἱερῷ Διὸς
ὄπισθεν τῆς θύρας, ἀγανακτοῦντος δέ μου τῇ τοῦ
Διὸς ὕβρει φάναι τινὰς μέχρι τῆς ἑσπέρας τοῦθ'
οὕτως ἕξειν, ἠκούσης δὲ δοθήσεσθαι τάφῳ. φάρμακα δὲ καὶ μαγγανεύματα καὶ πόλεμον ἀπὸ γοήτων ἀνδρῶν ταῦτα ἐδόκει δηλοῦν.   246. καὶ
εἵπετο δὲ τὸ ἔργον, φόβοι τε ἐκεῖνοι καὶ πλὴν τελευτῆς οὐδενὸς ἐπιθυμία. ἀλλὰ περὶ τούτου λόγοι
τε πρὸς τοὺς ἀεὶ παρόντας εὐχαί τε πρὸς θεούς.
ἐχθρὸς μὲν ὁ λουτροῦ μεμνημένος, ἐχθρὸς δὲ ὁ δεί-
πνου, καὶ φυγὴ ἀπὸ βιβλίων ἐν οἷς οἱ τῶν ἀρχαίων
πόνοι, φυγὴ δὲ ἀπὸ γραφῆς τε καὶ ποιήσεως
F 190   λόγων, κατελέλυτο δὲ τὸ λέγειν, καὶ ταῦτα τῶν
νέων βοαῖς τοῦτο ἀπαιτούντων. ὁπότε γὰρ δὴ
πρὸς αὐτὸ γιγνοίμην ἀπεφερόμην ὥσπερ ἀκάτιον
ἐναντίῳ πνεύματι, καὶ οἱ μὲν εἶχον ἀκροάσεως ἐλπίδας, ἐγὼ δ' ἄν[1] ἐσίγων. ἰατροὶ δὲ τὴν τούτων
ἴασιν ἄλλοθι ζητεῖν ἐκέλευον, ὡς οὐκ ὄντων σφίσι
R 148   τῶν τοιούτων ἐν τῇ τέχνῃ φαρμάκων.   247. ἐδόκει δὲ καὶ τούτοις καὶ τοῖς ἄλλοις ἀπὸ τοῦ αὐτοῦ
καὶ τὸ δίς, ὃ μήπω πρότερον, νοσῆσαί μοι τὰ

been the end of me.   245. While I was in this condition, I had the following dream. I saw two boys sacrificed, and the dead body of one was put in the temple of Zeus, behind the door. On protesting at this sacrilege, I was told that this would be the position until evening, but that, when evening came, he would be buried. This seemed to portend spells, incantations, and the hostility of sorcerers. 246. And so it turned out in actual fact, when all those fears obsessed me and I desired nothing save to die. This was the sole topic of conversation with each fresh visitor and of my prayers to heaven. Any man who mentioned baths or dinner, I detested. I avoided all the books containing the works of the classics, and the writing and the composition of my orations, and my eloquence was undone, even though my students loudly demanded it. Whenever I ventured upon it, I was carried off course, like a boat in a contrary wind, so that, while they kept expecting a discourse, I would fall silent. My doctors bade me seek the cure elsewhere, for there was no remedy for such maladies in their art. 247. They, and others with them, also attributed to this same cause a double visitation of gout, both winter and summer—which had never occurred

---

[1] ἂν Mss., Re., Martin: αὖ F.

ἄρθρα χειμῶνός τε καὶ θέρους, δοῦναί τε τοῖς
ἐπισκοπουμένοις ἀεὶ λέγειν ὡς τῆς ἐπιούσης
οἰχήσομαι. ταῖς δὲ δὴ ἄλλαις πόλεσι καὶ ἐδόκουν
τεθνάναι, καὶ τὰς πολλὰς δὴ ἠρώτων πρεσβείας
εἰ τοῦτο ὧδε ἔχοι. 248. ἦσαν μὲν οὖν τῶν φίλων
οἳ ἐμέ τε καὶ σφᾶς αὐτοὺς ἐπί τινας ἐκίνουν οἷς
δόξα τούτων εἶναι τεχνίτας, ἐγὼ δὲ οὔτ' αὐτός τι
τοιοῦτον ἔπασχον ἐκείνους τε κατεῖχον, εὔχεσθαι
δεῖν εἰπὼν μᾶλλον ἢ τινας ἕλκειν ὑπὲρ τῶν ἐν
R 149 σκότῳ συντεθέντων. 249. καίτοι χαμαιλέων ἀνα-
φανείς, οὐκ οἶδ' ὁπόθεν, ἐν τῷ τῶν λόγων χορῷ,
πολὺς μὲν τούτῳ τῷ χαμαιλέοντι χρόνος καὶ
μηνῶν ὁ νεκρὸς οὐκ ὀλίγων, πόδων δὲ ἐν μέσῳ
τῶν ὀπίσω κειμένην ἑωρῶμεν τὴν κεφαλήν, τῶν
δὲ ἑτέρων ὁ μὲν ἦν οὐδαμοῦ, τὸ στόμα δὲ ἅτερος
εἰς σιωπὴν ἔκλειεν. 250. ἀλλ' ὅμως οὐδ' ἐπὶ
F 191 τηλικούτοις τοῖς ἀποκεκαλυμμένοις ὄνομά τινος
ὑπῆγον τῷ φανέντι, δέος μέντοι μοι ἐδόκει τοὺς
R 150 αὐτοῖς τι συνειδότας εἰσελθεῖν καὶ τοὺς μὲν ὑφεῖ-
ναι τῆς συνεχείας, ἐμοὶ δὲ αὖθις ἐγγενέσθαι κινεῖσθαι. τύχης τοίνυν εὐμενεστέρας ἃ κατωρώρυκτο

---

[a] Cf. *Or.* 36.15 for his depression; *Or.* 33.24 for news
from envoys; *Or.* 23.17 ff for this illness and the bitter
cures.

before. The result was that observers kept prophesying that I would be dead before morning, and, in fact, in other cities it was said that I was dead already, and they inquired of our many envoys whether this was really so.[a] 248. Thus some of my friends kept urging me, and each other too, to prosecute certain individuals who were rumoured to be responsible for this, but I did not share their attitude myself, and I restrained them, telling them to offer up prayers rather than to have folk arrested for secret machinations. 249. However a chameleon turned up in the classroom from somewhere or other. It was an old specimen and had been dead for several months, and we saw the thing with its head tucked in between its hind legs, one of its front legs missing, and the other closing its mouth to silence it.[b] 250. Nevertheless, not even after such a revelation did I name anyone as responsible for its appearance, but it seemed to me that the guilty parties were overcome by panic and relaxed their pressure, so that I was able to move about again. Anyway, it was a stroke of good fortune that what had been buried deep should lie above ground,

[b] See *Or.* 36 (*De Veneficiis*), tr. Festugière, *Antioche,* pp. 453–458; Barb, in Momigliano, *Conflict between Paganism and Christianity,* p. 230; Campbell Bonner, "Witchcraft in the Lecture Room of Libanius," *TAPA* 63 (1932), 34–44. This spell is intended to render Libanius lame with gout (the missing forefoot) and speechless (as in § 246).

κεῖσθαι ὑπὲρ γῆν τοῖς βουλομένοις ὁρᾶν.

251. Ἧκεν ἐπὶ τούτοις ἄρχων ἥκιστα τὸν αὑτοῦ πάππον ἐν τοῖς πρὸς ἐμὲ μιμούμενος. ὁ μὲν γὰρ οὐκ ἐπαύσατο τιμῶν, οἷα ἀνὴρ ἐπιστάμενος λέγειν, ὁ δὲ οὐκ ἐβουλήθη με εἰδέναι, ἐν αἰτήσει τε χάριτος δικαίας τε καὶ οὐ μεγάλης ἐξελεγχθεὶς ἀνόητός τε εἶναι δοκῶν. καὶ τῶν μὲν ματαίων ἐπιμελῶς, τῶν δὲ ἀναγκαίων ἀμελῶς ἤρχετο,[1] διαμένων ἡμετέρων ἄγευστος λόγων· οὐ γάρ μοι τοῦδε τοῦ γέρως ἄξιος ἐφαίνετο. μία μὲν ἥδε δίκη, ἑτέρα δέ· πρὸς τὰ τέρματα τῆς ἀρχῆς ὑπάρχου πέμποντος ἥκων, ἐν ἐρημίᾳ τε καθῆστο καὶ ἡλίῳ φλέγοντι διψῶν τε ἀεὶ καὶ πίνων.

252. ἕτερος ἄρχων, ἐφ' οὗ τὰ δεινότατα πολέμῳ πονηρῶν δαιμόνων δόξαντα κεκινῆσθαι, λίθοι τε ἐπὶ τοὺς ἐν ταῖς γραφαῖς βασιλέας ἐκ χειρῶν ἐρχόμενοι, καὶ ἦν πολὺς ὁ ψόφος, χαλκαί τε εἰκόνες διὰ γῆς ἑλκόμεναι ῥήματά τε ἐπὶ τοὺς

R 151

F 192

---

[1] ἤρχετο Mss.: ἦρχε conj. Re.: εἴχετο conj. Gasda, F., Martin.

---

[a] Tisamenus, consularis Syriae 386 (PLRE 916), attacked by Libanius in Or. 33 and 45 (Orations Vol. ii, pp. 155–233); cf. Pack, Studies.

[b] He was sent by Deinias, Comes Orientis (PLRE 246),

exposed for all to see.

251. After this there came as governor Tisamenus,[a] whose behaviour towards me was very different from that of his grandfather. He had always treated me with respect, as befitted a man of eloquence, but Tisamenus refused to have anything to do with me. He showed himself in his true colours and proved himself a complete fool over a request I made for a trifling but perfectly proper favour. He began by being careful about trifles, and inconsiderate of matters of importance, and he stayed unacquainted with my oratory, for I did not think him fit for such a privilege. Anyhow, this was one of his punishments. He endured another on the frontiers of his province, where he was sent by his superior.[b] There he settled in the wilderness under the blazing sun, ever thirsting, ever bibbing.

252. Another governor followed.[c] Under him, it seemed that evil spirits were at war with us. Terrible things occurred: stones were thrown at the portraits of the emperors and rattled loudly against them. Their bronze statues were dragged along the ground, and insults more hurtful than any stone

to the Euphrates for the collection of corn with orders to stay there until Deinias' return with Cynegius from Egypt (*Or.* 33.6 ff).

[c] Celsus, *consularis Syriae* 387 (*PLRE* 194 (5)). For the Riots of the Statues in February 387, see *Or.* 19–23 (*Orations,* Vol. ii, pp. 235–407), John Chrysostom, *Homiliae de Statuis* (Migne, *PG* 49). Cf. Petit, *Vie Municipale,* pp. 238 ff.

τῶν ὅλων κυρίους πικρότερα παντὸς ἀφιέμενα
λίθου· δι᾽ ἃ πολλαὶ δὴ μεταναστάσεις, ὡς οὐκ ὂν
μένοντι σωθῆναι, καὶ ὁ φεύγων τὸν οὐ φεύγοντα
ἐθρήνει. ἐν μὲν οὖν ταῖς ἐλπίσι κατασκαφαί,
τὸ δὲ ἐλπίδος ἔξω σωτηρία. 253. τούτου
δὲ καὶ αὐτὸς αἴτιος εἶναι ἐδόκουν· λόγοις
τε ἡμερώσας καὶ δάκρυσι τοὺς ἐπὶ τὴν κρίσιν
R 152   ἥκοντας γραμμάτων ἐρᾶν ἔπειθον, καὶ ἐν οὐ
πολλῷ χρόνῳ πανταχοῦ γράμματα. καὶ τοῦτο
ἔργον ἡγώμεθα τῆς Τύχης καὶ προσέτι γε τοὺς
πολλοὺς λόγους περὶ μὲν τὴν αὐτὴν πεποιημένους
ὑπόθεσιν, μορφὴν ἄλλην ἄλλος ἔχων, δόξαντας
δὲ εὖ ἔχειν. 254. θέατρα δὲ ἡμῖν οὐχ οἷα
πρότερον, ἄρχων τε καὶ οὓς τότε συνῆγε πολλοὺς
ἀπὸ πολλῶν τῶν ἐθνῶν. τὸ δὲ αἴτιον, ἐν μὲν τῷ
δουλείαν ἐνεώρων, τὸ δ᾽ εἶχεν ἐλευθερίαν, καὶ
R 153   τὸ μὲν φίλους, τὸ δὲ καὶ οὐ φίλους, ζημίαν τῷ

---

[a] The progression is from attacks on the imperial portraits painted on wooden panels to those on their bronze
statues, cf. Browning in *JRS* 42 (1952), 15, 20. The final
paradox is explained by *Or.* 23.1–9; the hopeful refugees
fled the city to their deaths, the forlorn remainder in
Antioch were spared by Theodosius' clemency.

were hurled at the rulers of the Empire. Thus many people fled, and it was the exile who bewailed the fate of him who stayed. Yet in hope lay ruin; despair became salvation.[a] 253. But for this salvation I personally was held responsible. With orations and tears I soothed the members of the newly arrived commission of investigation and began to induce in them an eagerness for petitions, so that in a little while petitions came thick and fast.[b] Let me regard this as the work of Fortune, and also the success of the numerous orations, each with its own variation of style, composed by me on the same theme. 254. My audiences were not now, as they used to be, formed of the governor and the great numbers he used to bring from the many provinces. The reason was that here I saw independence, there subservience involved; here I had an audience of friends, there one in which the unfriendly appeared also, and that put a blight on my oratory.[c]

[b] Caesarius and Ellebichus, the commissioners, readily received γράμματα, pleas and petitions (in *Or.* 21.7, λόγους), while the Senate of Constantinople petitioned for clemency (*Or.* 20.37).

[c] Deinias, the *Comes,* was Christian, as was his anonymous successor. At a time when Christians claimed the credit for saving the city from worse punishment through Bishop Flavianus' intervention (Jo. Chrys. *De Anna* 1.1, Migne *PG* 54.634), so competing with Libanius' claims to have done the same, the presence of such hostile elements at his recitals was harmful to his oratory. Libanius here makes a virtue of necessity.

F 193 λέγοντι. 255. ἄλλος δέ τις ἀντὶ τοῦ οὐκ εἰδότος θεούς, εἰδὼς οὐδ᾽ αὐτὸς θεούς, παραλαβὼν τὴν ἀρχὴν τρυφῇ μὲν εἰς σάρκας ἐπιδούς, οἷα ἐκ πολλῆς οὐσίας, ἡ δὲ ἀδικίας ἔργον ἦν, ᾧ[1] τοῦδε ἀνοητότερος, ἀκούσας μὴ χείρω ποιεῖν τὴν Δάφνην μηδὲ ἐπιφέρειν κυπαρίττοις σίδηρον ἐχθρός τε ἦν καὶ ἐπειρᾶτο τἀμὰ καθελεῖν, πρῶτα μὲν Ἰταλῶν φωνῇ, μετὰ ταῦτα δὲ καὶ Ἑλλάδι, καί τινα ἀσθενέστατον ὡς δὴ ἰσχυρότατον ἀποδύσας ἐκέλευε θεῖν. 256. ὁ δὲ ἄρα ἐπεπέδητο καὶ ἦν ἄφωνος εὐθὺς ἐν προοιμίοις, κερδαίνων μὲν ἐν τῇ σιωπῇ, κινεῖν δὲ ὅμως γλῶτταν ἀποθανοῦσαν

R 154 πειρώμενος. ἡ δὲ ἔκειτο, καὶ ἀχλὺς ἐν ἑκατέρου τοῖς ὄμμασι, τοῦ μὲν ἀπιόντος, τοῦ δὲ καθημένου. ταύτης τῆς δίκης οὐδ᾽ ἂν τὴν διὰ θανάτου προτέραν ἐποιησάμην.

257. Περὶ δὲ τοὺς χρόνους τούτους ὑποψία μέν τις ἄδικος τῶν τινα ἐμοὶ πεπλησιακότων ἐξέμηνεν ἐπ᾽ ἐμέ, καὶ προσπεσὼν ὕβριζε μόνον οὐχ ἕλ-

---

[1] ᾧ CV Martin: ὁ L: om. Par. 3016: ὧν Re., F., Norman (1965).

---

[a] The anonymous *Comes* (*PLRE* 1015 (61)) actively promotes Cynegius' second objective, the suppression of pagan temples. Libanius had just protested at this in *Or.* 30.42 f, emphasizing, as here, that they are imperial property.

308

255. The successor of this ungodly fellow was another unbeliever himself. He took up his office and began to run to fat through his self-indulgence, as being a man of property, but his property was the fruit of his wickedness. He was more stupid than the other in that, upon my telling him to do no damage to Daphne and to lay no axe to its cypresses, he became my foe and tried to bring me down through teachers, first of Latin, then of Greek.[a] Why, there was one weakling whom he groomed like a champion and bade throw down the gage to me. 256. But this fellow was tongue-tied immediately and fell dumb at the very start; he was better off for his silence, but he still tried to wag his failing tongue—and yet it remained speechless. A mist came over the eyes of the speaker as he retired and of the governor who stayed seated there. Even death, to my mind, could not have been a worse punishment than this.

257. About this time an unwarranted suspicion enraged one of my ex-pupils against me. He fell upon my son, insulted him and practically had him dragged into court.[b] Nor did I escape his attentions,

Felling of cypresses in Daphne was already subject to imperial control; cf. *Codex Theodos.* 10.1.12, of 379, *Codex Justinianus* 11.78.1–2. The *Comes'* other misdemeanours were the establishment of a chair in Latin (cf. *Or.* 58.21 f, 38.6) and the encouragement of a rival Greek sophist.

[b] Thrasydaeus; cf. *Or.* 32. Early in 388 he tried to get Cimon drafted into the curia as the possessor of curial property (cf. §196 above).

κων τὸν ἐξ ἐμοῦ. διέφυγον δὲ αὐτὸν οὐδὲ ἐγὼ καὶ
ταῦτα ἀπὼν λέγοντά γε ἀδικεῖν με τῇ ἀτελείᾳ
τὴν βουλήν, ἥ μοι μετὰ συχνῶν ὑπῆρχε παρὰ τοῦ
νόμου.   258. καὶ πρεσβεύων μὲν ἐπὶ τούτοις
ᾤχετο, ταῖς δ' εἰς ἐμὲ τοῦ βασιλέως τιμαῖς ταπει-

F 194 νωθεὶς ἐπανήρχετο, καὶ ἧκέ τις μετὰ τῶν συμ-
πρέσβεων βασίλειον ἡμῖν κομίζων ἐπιστολὴν
αὔξουσαν τὸν δεξάμενον, ηὐξημένον πως καὶ τοῖς
Εὐσεβίου, τῶν πρέσβεων δὲ καὶ οὗτος ὁ λόγος, ὧν
τῷ μὲν τὸν πατέρα, τῷ δὲ ἐκόσμησε τὸν υἱόν,
ὥστε τοὺς Ἀθήνηθεν ἀντὶ τοῦ ἐρίζειν θαυμάζειν

R 155 αὐτόν τε ἐκεῖνον καὶ ἐμέ, τοῦ δοῦναι μὲν ἐμέ, τοῦ
λαβεῖν δὲ ἐκεῖνον.

259. Γνοίη δ' ἄν τις κἀντεῦθεν τὴν περὶ ἐμὲ
τῶν θεῶν εὔνοιαν. ἐπανήειν ποτὲ λελουμένος
ἑσπέρας· ἵπποι δὲ ἐοικότες μὲν θηρίοις, τοῦτο δὲ
οὐ δοκοῦντες, εἱστήκεσαν περιμένοντες τοὺς
δεσπότας, οἱ μὲν εἰς τοὺς κίονας ὁρῶντες, οἱ δ' εἰς
τὸν τοῖχον τετραμμένοι. καὶ ἦν οὐδὲν κακὸν εἰκά-
σαι, τὸ δ' ἄρα ἦν μέγα. χωροῦντι οὖν μοι διὰ

─────────

a The embassy was formed only with great difficulty,
under pressure from Ellebichus (Or. 32.2–7, 12). It consisted of three decurions, including Thrasydaeus, and
Libanius' protégé, the sophist Eusebius (xxii; PLRE 305

even though I was not present, for he alleged that I was guilty of misconduct towards the city council by reason of the immunity which I lawfully enjoyed along with many others. 258. Thereupon he went off on an embassy, but returned humbled by the honours which the emperor bestowed upon me, and there came one in the company of his fellow envoys with a letter from the emperor which increased the prestige of myself, its recipient.[a] My prestige had already risen through speeches by Eusebius, such was the information brought by our envoys, in one of which he praised the father, in the other, the son. Thus the products of the Athenian schools, instead of becoming his rivals, became admirers of him and of me too, of me for what I gave, of him for what he received.

259. From the following incident also one can recognize the favour of heaven towards me. When I was returning from the baths one evening, the horses, contrary to all appearances, were like wild beasts. They stood waiting for their masters, some facing the colonnade, others with their heads turned to the wall. There was no sign of any trouble, great

(24)). Eusebius delivers panegyrics on Theodosius (in his decennial year) and Arcadius, and so provides Libanius with a rhetorical triumph by proxy. The other envoys meantime had insinuated at court that Libanius had favoured the usurper Maximus, but Theodosius' letter freed him of this suspicion; cf. *Letter* 146. For this embassy cf. Pack, *Studies,* pp. 121 ff, Petit, *Vie Municipale,* pp. 418–419.

μέσου τοὺς ὀδόντας ἐδείκνυσαν ἀντὶ βελῶν τοῖς ποσὶ χρώμενοι, τὸ δ’ ἤρκεσεν ἂν εἰς θάνατον. νῦν δ’ ὁ ἱπποκόμος με ἐξαρπάσας, μεθεὶς ὃν ἦγεν ἵππον, φέρων εἰς ἀσφάλειαν κατέστησε. τοῦ ἱπποκόμου μὲν αἱ χεῖρες, τὸ βούλευμα δὲ τῶν θεῶν· 260. οἳ δὴ καὶ πόλεως γείτονος ἐξήλασαν ἄνθρωπον ὀλίγα μὲν εἰδότα, πολλὰ δὲ φάσκοντα, χρώμενον δὲ αὐτοῖς οἷς εἶχεν ἐπὶ τὸν δόντα, ἐφ’ ᾧ τις ἀλγήσας νεανίσκος τῶν μὲν ἠπατημένων τὴν ἀχλὺν ἀφεῖλε, τὸν δὲ ἐλέγχοις ἐξέβαλεν.

261. Ἐξεβέβλητο δὴ καὶ Σαβῖνος οὐ πόλεώς
F 195 τινος ἀλλ’ αὐτοῦ τοῦ ζῆν, εἰς κομιδῇ βραχύ τι συσταλεὶς οὕτως ὥσθ’, ὁπότε ἀμείβοι κλίνην, ἐξαρκεῖν χεῖρα μίαν εἶναί τε αὐτῷ δεινὸν τὸ μὴ τεθνάναι. καίτοι δεσπότην αὐτὸν τῶν ἐμῶν ἐπεποιήκει πολλάκις τὴν αὐτὴν ἡμέραν ἐμὲ μὲν εἰς
R 156 Ἅιδου λέγων ἄξειν, αὑτὸν δὲ εἰς τὴν οὖσάν μοι γῆν.

262. Ἀρχὴ πικρὰ τοῦ μεγίστην ἔχοντος τὴν γαστέρα, δι’ ἀπάτης παρωξυμμένου. ἦν δὲ ἡ

---

[a] Cf. §§ 190–196 above. Even before his condemnation he had been foiled in his ambition to acquire, as a member of the family, the estate of Libanius. The curia's recom-

though this turned out to be. Thus, as I made my way between them, they bared their teeth and lashed out with their hoofs, and that would have been the death of me. However, the groom let go the horse he was leading, snatched me away and set me in a place of safety. The hands were those of the groom, the will that of the gods. 260. The gods also expelled from a nearby city a man who, though of little wit, had much to say for himself. What ability he had, he used against me, the man who had helped him, at which one youth in anger removed the veil from the eyes of those he had hoodwinked, proved him a rogue and had him expelled.

261. Sabinus too had been expelled, not just from any city but from his very life.[a] He had been reduced to such utter destitution that, whenever he changed his sleeping quarters, one hand was enough to do it, and his misfortune was not to be dead. Yet he had ear-marked my estate for himself many a time, saying that one and the same day would bring me to my death and him into my property.

262. The rule of our pot-bellied governor was a harsh one, for his wrath had been kindled by a piece of deceit.[b] He had decided to lay the axe to the

mendation had ensured that, and Sabinus now dies disgraced.

[b] Reverts to the anonymous *Comes* of § 255, who has continued with his ravaging of Daphne. Apollo is both protector of Daphne (*Or.* 60.5) and, as in *Iliad* 1.284, the avenger.

ἀπάτη, κυπαρίττοις μὲν ἐν τῇ Δάφνῃ σίδηρον
ἐπενεγκεῖν ἐγνώκει, τουτὶ δὲ εἰδὼς ἐγὼ τῷ τέ-
μνοντι τελευτῆσον οὐκ εἰς ἀγαθόν, πρός τινα τῶν
αὐτοῦ συμποτῶν ἔλεγον ὡς οὐ παροξυντέον τὸν
Ἀπόλλω διὰ τῶν κυπαρίττων, καὶ ταῦτα αὐτῷ
τῆς οἰκίας ἀφ᾽ ὁμοίας πεπληγμένης αἰτίας, καὶ
παρακαλέσειν δὲ ἔφην τὸν βασιλέα πρόνοιαν τῆς
Δάφνης ἔχειν, μᾶλλον δὲ μείζω ποιῆσαι τὴν
οὖσαν· εἶναι γὰρ δὴ καὶ νῦν.   263. οὗτος ὁ ἄνθρωπος ψευδέσι γράμμασιν εἰς Φοινίκην ἐλθοῦσιν,
ἀπειλῆσαι γὰρ δή με ἔλεγε κινήσειν τὸ σκῆ-
F 196 πτρον ἐπὶ τὴν τοῦδε κεφαλήν, τοῖς οὖν οὐκ ἀλη-
θέσι τούτοις ὀργὴν ἐν αὐτῷ φυτεύσας ἦγεν ἐοικότα
R 157 συὶ θήγοντι τὸν ὀδόντα. καὶ οὔτε ἀπόντα ἐπόθει
παρόντα τε εἶδεν ἂν ἡδέως ἀπιόντα.   264. καὶ
πολὺ πανταχοῦ τοῦτο τὸ τὸν ἄρχοντα ἐκπεπολε-
μῶσθαί μοι. ὃ δὴ καὶ γέροντί τινι καταπεπωκότι
μὲν πολλὴν οὐσίαν αὐτοῦ τε καὶ ἀδελφῶν, ἐν
δὲ συκοφαντίᾳ τῆς τροφῆς ἔχοντι τὰς ἐλπίδας
θάρσος τε ἐνέβαλε καὶ κατήγορον ἐποίησεν.
R 158 265. ἔπειτα καὶ ἦν τῆς αὐτοῦ κατηγορίας κατή-
γορος· οὕτω σφόδρα ταῖς πίστεσιν ἔρρωτο. καὶ ὁ

cypresses in Daphne, and I, realizing that such a
course would bring no good to any who chopped
them down, advised one of his boon companions that
he should not incur the anger of Apollo because of
the trees, especially since his temple had already
been afflicted by similar misdeeds. I told him that I
would invite the emperor to show concern for
Daphne, or rather to emphasize the concern he
felt already, for he was not without it, as it was.
263. This fellow sent a letter full of fabrications
to his superior in Phoenicia,[a] saying that I had
threatened to bring down upon his head the emperor's
displeasure, and by this false report he roused his
wrath and caused him to return like a boar whetting
its tusk. He did not miss him when he was away,
and he would have been glad to see the back of him
when he did come. 264. The tale spread like wildfire
that the governor and I were at loggerheads, and this
caused an old fellow, who had run through his own
and his brothers' fortunes in drink and now found
his hopes of a living in the informer's trade, to take
heart and lay an accusation against me.[b] 265. But
then he was hoist with his own petard, so much was

[a] The *Comes* was touring his diocese. His return is
Homeric (*Il.* 11.416).

[b] The old informer first resurrects the matter of
Libanius' immunity raised by Thrasydaeus, and then,
egged on by the *Comes,* the charge of supporting Maximus.
The charges are referred to in *Epp.* 845, 855.

μὲν ἐπ' ὄνομα κατέφευγεν εἰσφορῶν, ὁ δ' αὐτὸν
ἐν τοῖς ὑπὲρ[1] βασιλέως ἐγκλήμασι καθίστη τοῦτον
εἶναι ἐθέλων ἀλλ' οὐκ ἐκεῖνον τὸν γέροντα. καὶ
αὐτίκα γράμματα ᾖει, τὰ μὲν ὡς τὸν ὅλων κύριον,
τὰ δὲ ὡς πρὸς τὸν πρῶτον τῶν μετ' ἐκεῖνον, καὶ
ἀνέγνωσάν τε ἄμφω τὰ γράμματα κατεγέλασάν
τε ἄμφω τοῦ τρόπου τοὐμοῦ τὴν αἰτίαν ἀποκρουο-
μένου. τῷ δὲ τοῦτο ἦν λύπη μείζων ἢ εἰ νόσημά
τι τῶν ὡρῶν τὰς ἐν τῇ γῇ διεφθάρκει Τυρίων οἴνου μητέρας αὐτῷ.   266. τὸ οὖν μηδὲ κρίσει τό
F 197   γε τοιοῦτον δοῦναι, κεκρίσθαι γὰρ καὶ πρὸ δικα-
R 159   στηρίου τῇ τοῦ δικαστοῦ μωρίᾳ, μεῖναί τέ με κατὰ
χώραν διαφυγόντα μακράν τε ὁδὸν καὶ χαλεπὴν
τῶν τε ἡδίστων ἐμοὶ μὴ στερηθῆναι διατριβῶν, θεῶν τε ἔργον καὶ ὑφ' ᾗ τὰ πάντα, Τύχης.
267. ὁ μὲν οὖν αὐτὸν τιμωρίαν εἰσπραττόμενος,
ἐννοῶν οἷος εἰς οἷον γεγένηται, ᾤχετο ποιήσων
ἑτέρους κακῶς, ὁ πλούτῳ μὲν εἰσελθὼν εἰς τὴν
ἀρχὴν ἀπειρίᾳ δὲ λυμηνάμενος ταῖς πόλεσιν. ὁ δὲ
δὴ μετὰ τόνδε χρόνος, τιμαὶ μὲν εἰς ἐμέ, τιμαὶ δὲ
εἰς λόγους. καὶ ἐδείκνυντο κατὰ τὸν παλαιὸν
νόμον τῆς ἀρχῆς μοι δεχομένης τοὺς λόγους,

[1] ὑπὲρ Mss., Re., Martin: om. F., Norman (1965).

the reliance placed upon his evidence. So he had recourse to a trumped-up charge of tax evasion, but the governor made him appear in a charge concerning the emperor, since it was the emperor he wanted as my accuser and not that old fellow. Letters went posthaste, one to the emperor, another to his chief administrator:[a] both read them and laughed them to scorn, since my conduct sufficed to repel the charge. He was more discomfited by this than if some blight of the season had destroyed his vines down on his estate in Tyre.[b]   266. Thus the fact that the case never came up for judgement, for even before the trial its issue had been prejudged because of the governor's stupidity, and the fact that I stayed where I was, avoided a long and difficult journey, and was not deprived of the declamations I so much enjoy—all this is the work of the gods and of Fortune, under whose control all things are.   267. So he, in mortification and realizing that he had caught a tartar, departed to do his worst upon others—he who had reached his high position through his wealth, and besmirched the province through his incompetence. In the period after this, both I and my oratory were in high esteem. My declamations were held, in the time-honoured fashion, before the

[a] Regular circumlocution for Praetorian Prefect of the East (at this time Tatianus); cf. Zos. 2.23.2, Joh. Lyd. *de Mag.* 2.5 (p. 59).

[b] The *Comes,* like the *consularis* Eustathius (§ 274 below; *Or.* 54.18), had invested in the vineyards of Tyre: 'mothers of wine' (Eur. *Alc.* 757; Aesch. *Pers.* 614).

ἀνδρὸς μὲν εὖ εἰδότος δικάσαι δίκην, πλέον δὲ
πραότητι δυνηθέντος ἢ ἕτεροι ξίφεσι, πείσαντος
δὲ ἐρᾶν αὐτοῦ καὶ ἄνδρα καὶ οἰκίαν καὶ πόλιν καὶ
ἔθνος βουλάς τε καὶ δήμους καὶ ὧν αἱ χεῖρες περὶ
τὴν γῆν.   268. τοῦτον δὴ τὸν χρόνον τὰ μὲν
τῶν εἰωθότων ἡμῖν πολεμεῖν τόξα ἦν ἐν παττά-
λοις, ἡ κεφαλὴ δὲ ἰσχυρῶς ἐπολεμεῖτο τῷ παλαιῷ
κακῷ. καὶ δὴ καὶ τοῦ καταπεσεῖσθαι ὁ φόβος
οἴκοι παρῄνει μένειν χαίρειν εἰπόντα τῷ περὶ
τοὺς νέους ἔργῳ. ἀλλὰ κἀνταῦθα θεῶν τις χεῖρα
ὑπερέσχε δι᾽ ἀγαθοῦ μάντεως λύσας ἐλπίδι τὸν
φόβον· μᾶλλον δὲ ὁ μὲν προσέπιπτεν, ἡ δὲ
R 160   ἐμάχετό τε καὶ ἐπειρᾶτο νικᾶν.

269. Ἄρχων ἕτερος, ὀργή, θυμός, δεῖμός τε
F 198   φόβος τε, ὕβρις, ἀσέλγεια, πᾶν μὲν φθέγξασθαι,
πᾶν δὲ τολμῆσαι, τὰ τυράννων ἐν νόμοις ἐργάσα-
σθαι. οὗτος οὐ δοκεῖν μὲν τολμᾶν ἐβούλετο, πᾶν
δὲ τοὐναντίον ἔπραττεν, ἐν ἑτοίμοις ὑποσχέσεσι
πανταχοῦ ψευδόμενος, ὥστε μετά τινας ἡμέρας

---

[a] This *consularis* was identified by Sievers (pp. 156,
189) with Timocrates of *Or.* 41. Another possibility is
Jullus (*Epp.* 935, 1038).

[b] Homer *Od.* 21.53 rounds off a story of scholastic
success.

governor.[a] He was a man well able to dispense justice fairly, and his authority, based on clemency, was more effective than that of others who relied on executions. He inspired affection in all—individuals and families, cities and provinces, councillors, commons and peasantry alike. 268. All this time, then, my usual enemies had hung up their weapons,[b] but my migraine affected me badly with its old trouble. In fact, my fear of falling was recommendation enough for me to stay at home and give up my teaching, but here too, one of the gods stretched out his hands over me and, by the agency of a good soothsayer, he relieved my fear with hope. My fear continued to attack, but hope opposed it and tried to win the day.

269. Then there arrived another governor, and with him raging temper, fearful panic, wanton brutality, utter recklessness in word and deed, and tyrannical administration of the law.[c] He wanted not to get a name as a trouble-maker but his every action was to the opposite effect; everywhere he broadcast falsehoods with his easy promises, so that in a few days it reached the point that I was the sub-

---

[c] Lucianus (*PLRE* 516 (6)), *consularis Syriae* 388. Cf. Seeck, "Libanius gegen Lucianus," *Rh. Mus.* 73 (1920) (repr. Fatouros and Krischer, *Libanios,* 26 ff); Pack, *Studies,* Appendix. Libanius criticized him in the invective of *Or.* 56, condemning his violence, a criticism here repeated in Homeric terms (*Il.* 11.37, 15.119).

καὶ τοιαύτην ἐπ᾽ ἐμὲ δόξαν ἐλθεῖν, πλάττοντα
λόγους ἔξω κομίζειν, ἀκηκοότα οὐδέν.   270. αἰ-
τοῦμεν δὴ παρὰ τοῦ Διὸς ἀπαλλαγήν, ὁ δὲ ἤκουσέ
τε καὶ ταχέως ἔδωκε προσθεὶς τὸ μετ᾽ αἰσχύνης.
R 161 καὶ γὰρ ἤγχετο καὶ εἵλκετο, καὶ φυλακαὶ καὶ
ὕπνος νικώμενος, ἔκειτό τε τὸν πανδοκέα πριάμε-
νος, οἱ θηραταὶ δὲ καὶ οὗτοι τῶν λόγων ᾑρήκεσαν,
ἔν τε τῇ μεγάλῃ πόλει μέσος ὢν πρακτόρων ἐπὶ
μέσης ἀγορᾶς σφαίρας δίκην πανταχοῖ πανταχόθεν ἐπέμπετο. τούτων δὲ τὰ μὲν ὁρῶν, τὰ δὲ
ἀκούων ἐγὼ προσεκύνουν τὴν Τύχην, δι᾽ ἣν οὐκ
ἔστιν ὅτε μοι δίκης ὀφειλομένης ἐστερήθην.

271. Τὰ δ᾽ αὖ μετὰ τοῦτον, ἀνὴρ τὴν ἑαυτοῦ
μὲν ἐκλιπών, ἑτέρωσε δὲ οἰκῶν, κέρδεσι δὲ τοῖς ἐν
τρίσιν ἀρχαῖς ἐκ πενίας εἰς πλοῦτον ἐλθών, καὶ
λογογράφος ἥκιστα μὲν ὤν, πάνυ δὲ εἶναι νομίζων
F 199 εὔχετο μὲν τήνδε παραλαβεῖν τὴν ἀρχήν, 'ὅπως,'
ἔφη, 'διδάσκαλος γενοίμην τοῖς ἄρχουσιν ὁποίους
τινὰς εἶναι χρὴ πρὸς τοὺς διδάσκοντας λέγειν.'

---

[a] Lucianus was deposed in summer 388 before the
Olympia, recalled in disgrace, sent back to Antioch in the
governorship of Eustathius (probably to be publicly
paraded for evidence to be collected against him, as in *Or.*
14.52 ff; *Codex Theodos.* 8.1.6; Petit, "Recherches sur la
publication," p. 502), returned to Constantinople for the

ject of the following story, that I was inventing accounts and circulating them, since I was out of touch with everything. 270. So we prayed Zeus for deliverance, and he heard our prayer and quickly granted it, and a dismissal in disgrace into the bargain.[a] He was harried and badgered, watched and allowed no rest, and he lay low after bribing his landlord, and the examiners of *his* accounts got hold of him: in the capital he was dunned on every side and chased around from pillar to post in the main square. Some of this I saw myself, the rest I learned by hearsay, and I gave thanks to Fortune through whose aid I have never been robbed of any vengeance which is my due.

271. His successor as governor was Eustathius,[b] who had abandoned his native city and settled elsewhere, and had advanced from poverty to riches by the gains he had made from three official posts. He had no literary gifts, although he thought he had, and he prayed to obtain this province so that he could, as he put it, teach governors how to behave

financial investigators to deal with him, condemned and fined. Libanius uses the language of Old Comedy for his own purposes: θηραταὶ τῶν λόγων, with double entendre of λόγοι, his invectives (§ 269) and their financial enquiries (Aristoph. *Clouds* 258), σφαίρας δίκην Antiphanes *fr.* II.125 K (Athenaeus 1.26).

[b] Eustathius, *consularis Syriae* 388/9 (*PLRE* 311 (6)); cf. *Or.* 44, *Or.* 54 *passim.* A Carian (*Or.* 44), settled in Tyre (§ 279 below; *Or.* 54.4, 18). His literary pretensions, though commended in *Or.* 44, are ridiculed in *Or.* 54.81.

καὶ λέγων ταῦτα συνῆν τε τὸ πλέον τῆς ἡμέρας
καὶ τῆς νυκτὸς οὐκ ὀλίγον ἀνήλισκε, καὶ εἴ τῳ
διακωλυθείη, ζημία τοῦτο ἦν.   272. ὁ δὴ τὰ τοιαῦτα ὑπὲρ τῶν τοιούτων παρὰ τῶν ὅ τι ἂν ἐθέλωσι
δοῦναι κυρίων αἰτῶν, λαβὼν καὶ ἔχων οὐκέτ᾽ ἦν ὁ
αὐτός. ἀλλὰ πέντε μὲν ἢ μικρῷ τῳ πλείους ἡμέρας μόλις κατέχων αὐτὸν οὐκ ἐγυμνοῦτο. ἔπειτά
ποτε ῥημάτων ὑπ᾽ ἐμοῦ ῥηθέντων τῶν πειρωμένων ἀμύνειν ὀρφανίᾳ τε καὶ πενίᾳ καὶ νεότητι
μαθητοῦ τινος ἡμετέρου πῦρ ἐν καμίνοις δημοσίᾳ
τρέφοντος, τότ᾽ οὖν θυμῷ καλυφθεὶς[1] καὶ τώ τε
ὀφθαλμὼ κινήσας τήν τε ῥῖνα χειρὶ πιέσας μέγα
φθεγξάμενος, ῾ἔα με,᾽ εἶπεν, ῾ἄρχειν, ὡς νῦν γε
οὐκ ἐᾷς.᾽ τῷ δ᾽ ἄρα καπηλεύειν ἐδέδοκτο καὶ τα-
λάντων ἔμελεν, ᾧ τὴν ἐμὴν ᾔδει φύσιν ἐναντιωσο-
μένην.   273. ἐγὼ μὲν οὖν αὐτὸν εἴων ἄρχειν καὶ
γίγνεσθαι Κινύραν, ὁ δὲ τοιαύτην κρηπῖδα βαλό-
μενος ἐπῳκοδόμει, πᾶσι μὲν οἷς ἐνῆν ὑβρίζων,
μηχανώμενος δὲ καὶ θάνατον, ξίφος μὲν οὐκ ἀναι-
ρούμενος ἐπ᾽ ἐμέ, ὃν δ᾽ ᾤετο πεινῶντα συκοφαν-
τήσειν, πεινῆν ποιῶν. ἧκε δ᾽ ἡ ᐸδίκηᐳ[2] παρὰ τῶν

R 162

F 200

---

[1] καλυφθεὶς Mss., Re., F. (text): ἐκκαλυφθείς conj. Schenkl,
Martin: καταληφθεὶς F. (Vol. iii, p. xxv).

[2] δίκη inser. post ἡ F., post θεῶν Martin.

towards teachers. With this remark, he attended me for the greater part of the day and part of the night besides, and anything which happened to prevent it, he found distasteful. 272. But although he made such demands for such an object from those who were able to provide him with anything they liked, once he had got them, he was no longer the same man. For five days or so he restrained himself from stripping off the mask, though with difficulty. Then, when I had spoken to him in support of a pupil of mine, a poor orphan boy,[a] who had the duty of providing the fires for the public baths, then he was overwhelmed with anger. His eyes blazed and he rubbed his nose and shouted, 'Leave me to govern. You don't give me a chance now.' He had, it seemed, decided to haggle for bribes and he began to have an eye on the money bags, and he knew that I would naturally object to that.[b] 273. So I let him get on with his governing and make himself a millionaire,[c] and he, after laying this foundation, built upon it, insulting me with all possible means, and even plotting my death. In this he made no actual use of force against me, but he reduced to poverty Romulus who, he thought,

[a] Domninus, *Or.* 54.38.

[b] *Or.* 54.42 ff.

[c] Cinyras, legendary king of Cyprus, one of the proverbial millionaires, like Gyges (§ 204 above).

θεῶν πάλιν, καὶ οὐκ ἀπερρίμμην ἀλλ' ἀπεδεικνύ-
R 163 μην ὧν αὐτοῖς ἐν ἐπιμελείᾳ. 274. τὸ γὰρ σκότος
ἀφελόντες πως τῆς δωροδοκίας ὑπ' αὐγὰς ἤγα-
γον τὴν μισθαρνίαν, χρυσόν, ἄργυρον, ἐσθῆτα· ὧν
τὰ μὲν εἰς χεῖρας αὖθις ἧκε τῶν παρακεκρουσμέ-
νων οὐ ῥᾳδίως ἀλλὰ βοῇ τε καὶ ἀπειλαῖς, τὰ δ'
ἦλθεν εἰς Τύρον, ἧδος τῷ κεκτημένῳ. ὁ δ' ἦλθεν
ὡς ἀναψυχῆς αὐτόθι τευξόμενος, γενόμενος δὲ ὑπὸ
χεῖρα Τυρίοις, τοὺς λίθους μόλις διαφυγών, κλεί-
σας τὰς θύρας ἐπολιορκεῖτο, χρήμασι δὲ αὐτοὺς
διαλλάξας τὴν πολιορκίαν ἔλυσε, τὰς ὀφρῦς ἐκείνας κατενεγκών. ἐδίδου δὲ ἐν Τύρῳ Τύρῳ τε
αὐτῇ δίκην καὶ Ἑρμῇ τῶν λογίων θεῶν ταῦτα
πρυτανευόντων ἄγαν[1] ἀγανακτούντων τῇ κατὰ
τῶν λόγων ὕβρει, καλοῖς αἰσχρῶν ἐπιθεμένων διὰ
τὴν τοῦδε παροινίαν.

275. Ἔτι δὲ τοῦδε ἄρχοντος Ὀλύμπιος τελευτᾷ, πάνυ μὲν φίλος εἶναι δοκῶν, διὰ παντὸς δὲ
τοῦ χρόνου γονεῦσιν ἀκολουθῶν· ἐπεὶ κἀκεῖνος

[1] [ἄγαν] Re., F. om. Norman (1965).

---

[a] Romulus (Or. 54.39 ff, 62) has the sitegia forced upon
him by Eustathius to blackmail him into preferring a
charge of divination against Libanius; cf. Ep. 844. Liba-

324

would act as informer against me through poverty.[a]
Yet once again vengeance came from the gods and I
was not utterly cast away, but was revealed as
under the protection of heaven.   274. Somehow
they stripped the veil from his bribery, and all this
trafficking in gold, silver, and raiment was brought
to light. Part of the loot was restored to his victims,
no easy matter indeed, but only after threats and a
hue and cry: the rest found its way to Tyre, to
delight him in his possession of it. He went there to
enjoy some repose, but once the Tyrians found him
within their reach, he barely escaped a stoning. He
barred his doors and began to stand a siege, which
he only raised after appeasing them with money and
abating his insolence. In Tyre he was punished by
Tyre and by Hermes, for the gods of eloquence so
brought it about, greatly angered at his insolence
towards eloquence, since by his reckless folly good
discourse was attacked by the bad.[b]

275. While he was still in office Olympius died, a
very close friend of mine who all his life maintained

nius however continues to support him; *Epp.* 889–891.

[b] Eustathius, dismissed under a cloud, retires to his
estates in Tyre, where the curia seeks financial redress,
probably by an action for extortion in respect of earlier
misdeeds as governor of Phoenicia (*Or.* 54.4, so Petit). His
insults to Libanius in his professional capacity (*Or.*
54.75 ff) induce the reference to Hermes and the *logioi
theoi*.

R 164 †τῶν ἐμῶν ἁμαρτὼν δὲ†[1] οὐκ οἶδ' ὅπως τῇ τιμῇ,
F 201 γράφει μὲν γὰρ κληρονόμον, ὃ τὸν φθόνον ἤγειρε,
δώσειν τε φίλοις καὶ οὐ φίλοις εἶπεν ἔνδον οὐκ ὀλίγοις, ἐν οἷς ἦν καὶ δυσμένεια. καὶ χρυσὸς καὶ
ἄργυρος ἐν τοῖς γράμμασι διερριπτεῖτο πολύς,
ἥξων[2] ἐπὶ κεφαλὴν ἐμήν· χρήστας μὲν γὰρ ἐδόκει
καταλελοιπέναι χρημάτων, τοῖς δὲ ὑπῆρχε πολλαχόθεν ἀντειπεῖν, καὶ ἦν ὀνόματα ταῦτα χρεῶν,
R 165 οὐ χρέα.   276. ἐγὼ μὲν οὖν τὴν ἐμαυτοῦ πορευόμενος καὶ ἅμα τοῦ πράγματος παραινοῦντος
χαίρειν ᾤμην δεῖν τὸν κλῆρον ἐᾶν, οἱ δὲ σεμνο-
λογούμενοι πλείους ὄντες καὶ πιθανώτεροι στένον-
τες, εἰ ἄτιμος Ὀλύμπιος κείσεται φυγόντος ἐμοῦ
τό τε ὄνομα τό τε ἔργον. καὶ προσῆν τις ἐλπὶς
εἶναί τι ἐν τοῖς δανείσμασιν ἰσχυρόν, ἣν δὲ οὐδὲν
οὐδαμοῦ.   277. ἐμβαίνω τοίνυν εἰς τὴν πυράν,
καὶ πολὺ τὸ ξυροῦν καθ' ἡμέραν ἐπέρρει, καὶ ἐξε-
πεπτώκειν δὲ τῶν ὅρων τῶν ἐμαυτοῦ διατρίβων μὲν
οὐκ ἐν ἐμοῖς χωρίοις, διατρίβων δὲ ἐν ἀλλοτρίοις

---

[1] τῶν ἐμῶν om. L: post ἐμῶν lac. pos. Wolf, Martin. ἁμαρτών <ἥμαρτε> δὲ F., Norman (1965).

[2] ἥξων F.: ἥξειν Mss. exc. L Par. 3016, Martin: om. L Par.
3016: post πολὺς lac. indic. Martin.

this family tie.[a] Now he ... with some mistaken idea of honouring me, named me his heir, which aroused envy: but he privately promised gifts to many persons, whether friends or not, and that aroused enmity too. In his correspondence he had been lavish with gold and silver, and all that was going to come back upon me. He had, it seemed, left plenty in his debt, but they were able to deny it on many grounds, and these remained nominal not actual debts. 276. Thus, since I was set on my own course and warned by the facts of the matter, I thought that I should give up the inheritance, but they out numbered me with their high-flown sentiments and were more plausible with their complaints, that Olympius would be dead and dishonoured if I gave up both the title and the duty. Moreover, there was some hope that reliance could be placed on the loans, though there was none at all, as things turned out. 277. So I went like a lamb to the slaughter; I had many a close shave every day. I was out of my proper sphere, spending my time on unfamiliar ground and on speeches foreign to me, wherein I begged the judges[b] to revere the right and

[a] For the death of Olympius and the doubtful blessing of his inheritance, cf. *Or.* 63 *passim, Ep.* 953, 958, 1030; *PLRE* 643 f (3). On the morass of litigation see *Or.* 63.6, 11; *Or.* 54.82.

[b] The *consulares,* Eustathius and his successor Eutropius (*PLRE* 318 (3)).

R 166
F 202

λόγοις,[1] εὐχομένοις δικαστὰς ἐν αἰδοῖ τὴν Θέμιν
ἔχειν καὶ πολλὰ ταῦτα τὰ οὐκ ἐμά, καὶ ἐδάκρυσα
ὡς δὴ μετακεκινημένου[2] μοι τοῦ βίου καὶ τῆς τέως
περὶ τοὺς λόγους σπουδῆς ἐπ᾽ ἄλλα μεταβάσης.
278. καὶ τοῦτο μὲν δὴ τοιοῦτον, πολλὰ πωλεῖν[3]
ἐπαναγκαζόντων τῶν ἀπὸ τῆς διαθήκης ὁρμωμέ-
νων ἐπὶ τοὔνομα πηδώντων οὐδὲ ἀναπνεῖν διδόν-
των, ἕτερον πολὺ μεῖζον εἰς λύπην, ἐξ ἧς ἐτύγχανον
πεπαιδοποιημένος νόσῳ μακρᾷ τελευτή, γυναικὸς
πολλῶν ἀνταξίας διακόνων. ἀντὶ τοῦ τὴν δραμου-
μένην ἔχειν ἐλείπετό μοι βοᾶν. τῇ δὲ ἦν μὲν
ἀνιαρὰ τὰ γενησόμενα, καὶ γὰρ εὖ ᾔδει, ἦν δὲ τὸ
μὴ τὸν υἱὸν ὁρᾶν.   279. ὁ δ᾽ ἄρα ἦν ἐν Θρᾴκῃ τε
καὶ Θρᾴκης πόλει τῇ τῶν ἄλλων πόλεων τρυφώσῃ
τοῖς ἱδρῶσι. κατηγόρουν τε τῆς ὁδοῦ καὶ προδιδο-
μένης ὕπνῳ φιλίας, ὕβρεών τε κατακλυζόμενος[4]

---

[1] Post λόγοις punct. Mss., post ἀλλοτρίοις F., Norman
(1965).

[2] μετακεκινημένου Re., edd.: μέγα περὶ μὲν οὖν Mss.

[3] πωλεῖν Mss. (exc. P), F., Norman: καὶ ζητεῖν P, γρ. ζητεῖν
in marg. V.: πωλεῖν καὶ ζητεῖν Martin.

[4] κατακλυζόμενος Mss., Martin. —ομένης F., Norman
(1965). Post ῥεύματι lac. stat. Martin.

---

[a] For the status of Cimon's mother, cf. Letters 169.2,
188.5. This is the only time Cimon is called υἱός in this

so on, which is not my line at all. I was grieved, since the whole course of my life was changed and my previous devotion to rhetoric had given way to other considerations.   278. Such was one aspect of the matter, but as people set upon me as a result of the will, forcing me to sell much of the property and impugning the title and allowing me no respite, another event occurred which caused me even more pain, the death after long illness of the woman who was mother of my son and to me worth many a servant.[a] Instead of having a woman who would run to my side, now I could only call. Her illness was to cause her dreadful suffering, of that she was well aware, but so did the fact that she could not see her son.   279. He, meanwhile, was in Thrace,[b] in that city which grows fat on the sweat of the others, and I cursed his journey there, and the friendship which was being betrayed by sloth, for I

work, and then only in relation to his mother.

[b] Cimon, *PLRE* (Cimon Arabius) 92 f. See note on §§145, 195 above. In 390, desperate to escape impressment into the curia, he left for Constantinople, aspiring to senatorial rank through nomination to a governmental post. He obtained the nomination, but this was cancelled when the Senate, led by Proclus PVC refused to coopt him (for the procedure see Petit, "Senateurs de Consantinople," *Ant. Class.* 26 (1957) 358 ff), on the grounds of his illegitimacy (*Letter* 189). His petition was finally dismissed in 391, after which Libanius, while claiming not to have approved of the venture (*Epp.* 1000, 1003; *Letters* 179, 187), continually rails at his 'false friends.'

R 167 ῥεύματι <...> πονηρὰ[1] μέν, καὶ ταῦτα δὲ τύχης
F 203 ἔργα, ἐπεὶ δὲ[2] τῆς ἀπήνης ἐξέπεσεν ἡ περὶ τὸν
πόδα ζημία, χρηστῆς δὲ καὶ βελτίονος οἰκία τε τῶν
Κιλίκων ἀδελφῶν ἀνεῳγμένη τῷ πάθει πλῆθός τε
ἰατρῶν, ἐκείνων [συναγόντων][3] εἰσαγόντων, περὶ
τὴν κλίνην καθημένων οὐκ ἐώντων τι ποθεῖν
F 204 εἰς ἴασιν,[4] πολλῶν τε πόνων ἔστιν ἃ λελυμένα.[5]
280. ἐμοὶ δὲ ἀκούοντι ταῦτα καὶ μετὰ ταῦτα
ὁρῶντι δεῦρο κεκομισμένον περιειστήκει μὲν ὁ
R 168 τῆς τοῦδε μητρὸς θάνατος, περιειστήκει δὲ τὸ
μηδὲ ἐπὶ κλίνης [τὸ γένος] ἐξεῖναι [ἀπ' ἐκείνης]
κινεῖσθαι.[6] πόδες τε καὶ χεῖρες, εἴπερ ποτέ, ἀπειρή-
κεσαν. θεῶν δὲ δωρεαί, λόγοι[7] ἔμενον ἐν τῷ
στόματι [τόποι][8] ὁποῖοι πρότερον, καὶ τοῦτ' ἦν τὸ
μὴ παρασχὸν τοῖς πολεμίοις λαμπρῶς ἤδη παιανί-

---

[1] πονηρὰ μέν, καὶ Mss., Martin: πονηρᾶς μὲν καὶ Re., F.,
Norman (1965).

[2] ἐπεὶ δὲ Mss., Martin: ἐπειδὴ F., Norman (1965).

[3] ἐκείνων συναγόντων εἰσαγόντων CPV: εἰσυναγόντων L Par
3016: [συναγόντων] F., Martin.

[4] οὐκ ἐώντων τι ποθεῖν εἰς ἴασιν, conj. Wyttenbach, F.:
οὐκεντων τίποτινην ἴσασι CP: lacuna in VL Par. 3016.

[5] πολλῶν τε πόνων ἔστιν ἃ λελυμένα conj. Norman: πολλῶν
τε ὦον ἐστι τὰ ἀλίμενα CPL, om. V: πολλῶν τε λόγων τὰ λειπό-
μενα conj. Wyttenbach: λόγων τε ἐστιάματα conj. F.

[6] τὸ μηδὲ ... κινεῖσθαι corruptum indic. F: τὸ μηδὲ ἐπὶ κλίνης τὸ γένος ἐξεῖναι ἀπ' ἐκείνης κινεῖσθαι Mss. (exc. L Par.

was overwhelmed by a stream of insults ... Bad this
was, but it was the work of fortune, as was the
injury to his foot when he fell from his carriage, and
also (when she was kinder) the opening of their
house to him in this plight by the Cilician brothers,[a]
and the many doctors they summoned, who sat
around his bed and saw that he lacked nothing for a
cure, and the relief of some of his great distress.
280. Upon hearing this news, and afterwards, when
I saw him carried home,[b] I felt the full force of his
mother's death and of the fact that I could not even
be moved on my bed. My hands and feet had failed
me as they had never done before, but by the grace
of heaven, my oratory stayed upon my lips as before,
and this was what prevented my enemies setting up
a howl of triumph. Though I was unable to appear

[a] Apolinarius and Gemellus of Tarsus (*PLRE* 83 (2);
388 (2)); cf. *Letters* 179, 187. The text collapses utterly at
intervals in these final paragraphs. Here the translation
is that of Wyttenbach's conjecture followed by that of Norman.

[b] Cimon is brought home injured and soon dies; *Ep.*
1026.

3016): [τὸ γένος], [ἀπ' ἐκείνης] secl. Martin: τὸ μηδὲ ἐπὶ (lac.)
γένος ἀπ' ἐκείνης ἐξεῖναι κινεῖσθαι L Par. 3016: τὸ μηδὲ ἐπὶ
γένος ἐξεῖναι ἀπὸ κλίνης κινεῖσθαι Festugière, *REG* 78 (1965)
p. 630.

[7] λόγοι VL, Martin: λόγων CP, Re., F.

[8] στόματι τόποι ὁποῖοι Mss. [τόποι] secl. Re., Martin τύποι
F.

ζειν. θεάτροις μὲν οὐκ ἦν χρῆσθαι, ἃ δὲ πρὸς τοὺς
ἐν τῷ μανθάνειν, ἐπληροῦτο κατὰ τὸν νόμον.
281. πολλῶν δὲ ἀπὸ πολλῶν φερομένων πηγῶν
δακρύων ἀσθενέστερός τε ἄτερος γίνεται τοῖν
ὀφθαλμοῖν καὶ παρεῖχε δέος οἰχήσεσθαι τελέως.
τουτονὶ μὲν οὖν οἱ θεόντων[1] ἀστέρων ἅπαντα
ἐξαρτῶντες οὐκ ἀπολεῖσθαί φασιν Ἄρεος εἰς
διαλλαγὰς ἐλθόντος, τὰ δ' ἄλλα προσεγένοντο
μὲν ὁμιληταὶ πολλαχόθεν, λόγοι δὲ ἐργασθέντες
ἔμειναν εἴσω θυρῶν. 282. ἄρχουσι δὲ οὐ
μάλα συνεγενόμην, τὸν μὲν ὁρῶν ὄντα κάπηλον
καὶ οὐδὲν ὅ τι οὐ πωλοῦντα, τὸν δὲ ἀναπετά-
F 205　σαντα τὴν καταγωγὴν καὶ περιφόβους οἷς ἦσαν
δίκαι ποιοῦντα <...> τοῦ δὲ ἁμαρτάνων,
†τὸν Μούσαις ποιητὸν ἐν λόγῳ†[2] καὶ τὸν διὰ

---

[1] θεόντων ἀστέρων Martin: θεῶν (corr. θεὸν CP) τῶν ἀστέρων
Mss.: [θεῶν] Re., F., Norman (1965): θεώντων conj. Gasda.
[2] Locus desperatissimus. Post ποιοῦντα lacunam stat.
Norman. τὸν (τοῦ C) μούσαις ποιητὸν CPV: τοὐμὸν ποιητὸν
Par. 3016: τοὐμὸν ποιητῶν L.

---

[a] He was still working in his schoolroom in 392 (*Ep.*
1046, *Letters* 190, 191), despite the joy of his enemies at his
eclipse (*Ep.* 1039).

[b] His weakened eyesight, *Ep.* 1039, *Letter* 184 (written

in the lecture room, I duly fulfilled my duties towards my students.[a] 281. As many a tear welled up in my eyes, the sight of one of them became weaker and I feared that it would go completely. However, the astrologers who make everything depend upon the courses of the stars, declare that the sight will not be lost since Ares has moved into a more favourable position.[b] In addition, pupils came from many quarters, my declamations being composed and delivered at home. 282. With the governors I did not have much to do, for I saw one to be a mere huckster,[c] who would do anything for money, while the other made his headquarters free for all and tried to frighten any man involved in court actions. . . . When he failed in this, he saw this so-called nursling of the Muses(?) for what he was, a

13 months after Cimon's death), *Letter* 189. Mars, in conjunction with the Moon and Saturn, could induce blindness (Ptol. *Tetr.* 3.12), and, in Leo, impaired sight (ps.-Manetho, 2.353; cf. Firm. *Mat. Math.* 6.31.39).

[c] The huckster was identified by Downey (*Comites Orientis,* p. 20) with Eutropius, *consularis* 389. However, for all the textual difficulties, the narrative has proceeded in chronological order up to 391/2, and here he certainly deals with 392/3. The Severus of *Or.* 57 is a possibility. *Pace* Petit, he is not a fictitious character; Libanius did not have the Latin for such a play on names. The 'other' is certainly Florentius (*PLRE* 364 (9)), younger brother of Lucianus (Seeck, "Libanius gegen Lucianus," pp. 91 ff).

τῆς γαστρὸς οὐσίαν ὡς πλείστην ἀνηλωκότα,
ζῶντα δὲ ἐν λύσσῃ τῇ κατ᾽ ἐμοῦ†[1] ἐλέγχων
R 169 ἀπήλασεν, ὥστε ἐκεῖνον ταπεινωθέντα μηκέτ᾽
εἶναι ἐν τοσαύτῃ μανίᾳ. κἂν τοῖς ἐπαίνοις
τοῖς εἰς τὸν Ἴβηρα τοῦτο ὡς μέγιστον ἥδετο
αὐτός τε αὐτῷ συγχαίρειν ἔφασκε τούτων δὴ
τῶν πρὸς ἐμέ, καὶ ταῦτα αὐτῷ τῆς τραπέζης
ἐντεῦθεν οὐδὲν ἐπιδούσης παρ᾽ ἄλλων τοῦτο
ἐχούσης. 283. ἔστω δὴ καὶ τοῦτο τῆς ἀγαθῆς
τύχης, ἔστω δὲ κἀκεῖνο τῆς αὐτῆς. καίτοι με
πρὸς τὸ μέγεθος τοῦ δοθέντος ὄκνος ἔχει τὸν
λόγον. ἀλλ᾽ ὅμως, ὡς μὴ ἀδικοῖμεν τῇ σιωπῇ
τὴν δοῦσαν, τολμητέον εἰπεῖν. κατηφείας γὰρ
κατεχούσης τοὺς φίλους ἐνθυμουμένους τῆς
παροινίας τῆς περὶ τὸν Κίμωνα, καθ᾽ ἣν αὐτοῦ
τοῖν χεροῖν ἡρπάσθη τὸ γραμμάτιον ὃ αὐτὸν
F 206 ἐφίστη τῇ Κύπρῳ, ἐλθὼν οὖν τις[2] καὶ αὐτὸς τῶν
ἐπιτηδείων εἰδὼς τήν τε ἀχθηδόνα καὶ ὅθεν ἔφυ,
᾽ἀλλ᾽, ὦ ἄνδρες ἄριστοι, λήξατε,᾽ ἔφη,[3] ᾽τῆς λύπης,

---

[1] Post κατ᾽ ἐμοῦ CP ins. λερευτὰ: om. VL Par. 3016: del.
F., e scholio ortum.

[2] τις Martin: τε Mss., edd.

[3] ἔφη Mss. exc. V, Re., Martin: ἔφην V, F., Norman
(1965).

glutton who had run through a vast fortune in his gluttony and was rabid in his fury against me, and he sent him packing, so that he was humbled and no longer indulged in such craziness.[a] In all the panegyrics of Spain, this was what pleased him most, and he rejoiced, he said, in the emperor's attentions towards me, even though his table was provided with no contribution from me, though plenty from others. 283. So let that be attributed to good fortune, and also the following, though, considering the munificence of the gift, I hesitate to speak of it. However, I needs must, so that I may do full justice to the fortune that bestowed it.[b] My friends were full of despondency when they considered the disgusting treatment of Cimon, whereby his credentials of appointment to Cyprus had been snatched from his hands. Well, there came someone—one of my friends, in fact—and fully knowing their dejec-

[a] Obscure and textually corrupt, but it certainly refers to the visit of Rufinus Praetorian Prefect of the East to Antioch in winter 392/3 and to the deposition and punishment of Florentius then (see Seeck, "Libanius gegen Lucianus"). The panegyric on Spain celebrates Theodosius and his family, and the compliment to Libanius here is supplemented by the flattering treatment of him recorded in *Ep.* 1111 and *Letter* 193 of summer 393.

[b] Fortune's final favour is to provide vengeance (as in §270), upon Constantinople and the false friends there who had betrayed him and Cimon. For the retraction of this appointment to Cyprus, cf. §278 above, *Ep.* 1011.

ἔχοντες ὃ παύειν πέφυκε λύπην, τοῦτο δὲ τῇ δίκῃ,[1]
ἣν μείζω ποιεῖ τὸ διὰ τῶν θεῶν αὐτῆς τυγχάνειν
τὸν πεπονθότα. 284. ἴστε,[2] οἷόν τι τὸ τῶν εἰς
Κρήτην ἀγομένων Ἀθήνηθεν δεῖπνον ἐσομένων
τῷ ἐν λαβυρίνθῳ τέρατι. περὶ δὲ τοῦ βέλους τοῦ
κεκομικότος τοῖς Ἀχαιοῖς τὴν νόσον καὶ παρὰ
τῶν πρώτων τῆς Ἰλιάδος ἠκούομεν, ὡς ἀντὶ τῆς
εἰς ἕνα ὕβρεως πολλῶν ἔδει πυρῶν τοῖς Ἕλλησιν
εἰς τοὺς ἀποθνήσκοντας. καὶ ἦν μακάριος ὁ Χρύ-
σης τοσούτῳ κακῷ τιμώμενος. 285. ἕτερος τοίνυν οὗτος ἱερεὺς θεῶν[3] λιμῷ μεγάλῳ τιμᾶται.
Δήμητρος, οἶμαι, τοῦτο ἔργον οὐδὲ ἀρᾶς κατ’
αὐτῶν γεγενημένης, ᾧ τότε Ἀπόλλων ἐκινήθη·
καὶ ἡ μὲν ἡμέρων ἐννέα, μῆνας δὲ οὑτοσὶ τέττα-
ρας ἀναλίσκει τὴν πόλιν. εἰ δὲ καὶ ἀνὴρ δοὺς
δίκην μέγα παραμύθιον τῷ τετρωμένῳ, πόσον ἄν
τι πόλεως καὶ τηλικαύτης εἴη;’

---

[1] λύπην, τοῦτο δὲ τῇ δίκῃ ACP, Re., Martin: λύπην. τοῦτο δέ
ἐστι δίκη VL, F., Norman (1965).
[2] ἴστε Re., F: ἴσως Mss.: ἴστε ἴσως Martin.
[3] ἱερεὺς θεῶν Re., F.: ἱερῶν Mss.: ἱερεὺς Martin.

tion and its source, 'Be troubled no more, gentlemen,' he said. 'In vengeance you have a possession which always soothes troubles, and if the victim gets it through the agency of the gods, then it is all the greater. 284. You all know what happened when the Athenians were sent to Crete to become a meal for the monster in the Labyrinth. Of the bolt which brought plague upon the Achaeans we read in the first book of the *Iliad,* that because of an insult to one man, the Greeks needed many funeral pyres for their dead.[a] Chryses was indeed blessed that he was avenged with such an affliction. 285. But here and now another priest of the gods is being avenged with great famine.[b] This is surely Demeter's work, even though no curse has been invoked against them, such as happened when Apollo was moved to wrath. That plague lasted for nine days: this famine has been wasting the city for four months now. If it be a great consolation to the victim that one man should be punished, think what it would be for so great a city to be so visited!'

[a] The Athenians and the Minotaur, Plut. *Thes.* 15.1. For Chryses, Homer *Il.* 1.43 ff.

[b] Libanius, like Chryses, is a ἱερεὺς θεῶν, and the insult to him by the Senate of Constantinople is repaid by the famine that afflicts the city, a vengeance of more than epic character since it is unsolicited. It seems likely that this final passage was written before December 393, since the execution of Proclus (3 Dec.) remains unmentioned.

SELECTED LETTERS

1. Ζηνοβίῳ

Σιγῇ τὴν σιγὴν ἔγνωμεν ἀμύνασθαι. καίτοι γε ἠπιστάμην λειπομένην τῶν ἀδικημάτων τὴν δίκην. οὐ γὰρ ἴσον ἦν ἐμὲ σῶν ἀποστερεῖσθαι γραμμάτων καὶ σοὶ <τὰ>[1] παρ' ἡμῶν μὴ φοιτᾶν. ἀλλ' ὅσῳ καλλίω τὰ σά, τοσούτῳ μείζων ἡ βλάβη τῆς τιμωρίας.

[1] τὰ inser. Re.

---

[a] For Zenobius see *BLZG* 315 (i), *PLRE* 991.

In summer 353 Libanius was encouraged in his project of returning to settle permanently to teach in Antioch by a promise of appointment to the municipal chair, since the present holder, his old teacher Zenobius, indicated a

2. Θαλασσίῳ

1. Ἦν μὲν καλὰ καὶ ὅσα παρών σοι συνῄδειν, ἃ δ' ἀκούω, φιλοσοφίας ἐγγὺς ἥκει, γλῶττα ἐλευθέρα καὶ τρόπος μισοπόνηρος καὶ τῶν σπουδαίων ἔρως καὶ τὸ μετ' ἀνδρείας τοὺς μὲν εὖ ποιεῖν, τοὺς δὲ ἐλαύνειν, καὶ δὴ καὶ τὸ μέγιστον, χρυσὸς κατα-

1. To Zenobius

I am resolved to punish silence with silence. Yet I am well aware that the punishment fails to fit the crime: there is no comparison between me being deprived of your letters and mine not reaching you. But the finer yours are, so much the greater is the harm you do me than my retaliation.[a]

willingness to retire. He then returned to Constantinople and began to pull strings to secure his release from his appointment there. Meanwhile, his uncle Phasganius used his influence on the city council of Antioch to smooth the way. Zenobius, affronted by this indecent haste, withdrew his half-promise and retained his official chair. The estrangement between master and pupil elicited from Libanius this polite reproof and also the following letter to Thalassius to ensure his return.

2. To Thalassius[a]

1. Even those characteristics which I recognized in you on personal acquaintance were fine enough, but those of which I learn by hearsay approximate to true philosophy—independence in speech, a character that shuns evil, a love of things noble, courage in benefiting some and rejecting others and, last but not least, a contempt for gold, which for all its most

[a] *BLZG* 289 (i), *PLRE* 886 (1) and stemma (p. 1141).

φρονούμενος, ὃς μέγιστον ἐν ἀνθρώποις ἰσχύων ἥττηται.[1] 2. Γοργονίου δὲ τοῦθ' ἓν ἀκούσας, ὅτι σε θαυμάζει, πρὸς θαῦμα κατέστην. οὐ γὰρ ἄν, εἰ μή σοι προσόμοιος ἦν, οὕτως εἶχε. 3. πρᾶττε οὖν ἡμῖν δι' ἐκείνου, ἃ καὶ πυνθάνομαι, τὴν ἐπάνοδον· ἐπιθυμῶ γὰρ ἰδεῖν ἃ πυνθάνομαι.

[1] <σοῦ> ἥττηται coni. Re.

---

[b] The terms of this commendation are tempered by Ammianus (14.7.9), who speaks of an arrogant nature.
[c] Chamberlain of the bedchamber to Gallus; *BLZG* 165 (i), *PLRE* 399 (3).

3. Ἱεροκλεῖ

1. Εἰ τὸ τῆς δυνάμεως ἐλάττω ποιεῖν ἑκόντα ῥαθυμεῖν ἐστι, πόρρω τῆς αἰτίας ἐγώ. βραχύτερα μὲν γὰρ ἢ ὁ καιρὸς ἀπῄτει γέγραφα, πλείω δὲ οὐκ εἶχον ὑπ' ἀρρωστίας. 2. τὴν μέντοι συμβᾶσάν σοι πρὸς τὸν ἄνδρα τουτονὶ ταραχὴν ἴσθι μακρὰν ἡμῖν γεγονέναι συμφοράν. τὸ γὰρ οὓς εἰκὸς ἦν μάλιστα συμπνεῖν, τούτους ὁρᾶν ἐν στάσει καὶ τῷ

---

[a] *BLZG* 176 (i), *PLRE* 431 (3), F/Kr. 4.
This letter, the earliest to survive following Libanius'

potent influence among men has been overcome.[b]
2. On hearing from Gorgonius[c] only of his admiration for you, I have come to admiration for him, for unless he were a kindred spirit to yourself, he would not be so affected. 3. Ensure for me then by his agency—which indeed I hear you are doing—my return, for I am desirous of seeing what I hear.[d]

[d] Thalassius, husband of Libanius' cousin and praetorian prefect in attendance upon Gallus at the time, is urged to speed up Libanius' return to Antioch. Though he might have been ready to assist in this, he was dead by the end of 353 (Amm. Marc. 14.7.9).

3. To Hierocles[a]

1. If laziness consists of a wilful refusal to do as much as one can, I am far from being blamed for it, for although my letter was briefer than the occasion warranted, I could not write more because of illness.[b] 2. Yet be assured that the ill-feeling you have come to entertain for this man is a great blow to me. For to see people who should be in complete harmony at odds with one another, and to be pained

settlement in Antioch, develops (3–12) into a miniature consolatory speech on the death early in 355 of Hierocles' nephew and son-in-law Chromatius. No more is known of Chromatius than is given here.
[b] Illness had been the pretext for his removal to Antioch, but in 355 he was ill in earnest with head pains, dizziness and nephritis (*Ep.* 473.3 f).

γιγνομένῳ μὲν ἀλγεῖν, παῦσαι δὲ αὐτὸ μὴ δύνασθαι πῶς οὐκ ἐμοί τε καὶ τοῖς σοῖς ἀδελφοῖς καὶ πᾶσιν οἷς εὔνοια πρὸς τὰ σὰ νομίζοιτ' ἂν συμφορά; 3. ὃ δέ γε τούτου δεινότερον, οἴχεται Χρωμάτιος, ὦ Ζεῦ καὶ θεοί, καὶ πάλιν ἐρῶ Χρωμάτιος, ὃς ἐκόσμει μὲν τὴν Παλαιστίνην τῷ φῦναι αὐτόθι, ἐκόσμει δὲ τὰς Ἀθήνας εὖ τἀκεῖθεν δεξάμενος. 4. ἦν δὲ τῷ γένει μὲν κλέος, τοῖς φίλοις δὲ λιμήν. μόνος δὲ ὢν ἴσμεν μάλιστα μὲν ἐθαυμάσθη, ἥκιστα δὲ ἐφθονήθη. τοῖς λόγοις μὲν ἐξέπληττε, τῷ τρόπῳ δὲ ἔθελγεν αὐτὸς ὢν καὶ ῥήτωρ δεινὸς καὶ ἀνὴρ χρηστός. 5. τί πρῶτον ἐννοήσω καὶ διὰ τί πρῶτον ὀδύρωμαι; ὡς ἓν ἡμᾶς οἴκημα εἶχεν Ἀθήνησιν; ὡς τράπεζα μία; ὡς τοῖς αὐτοῖς ἐχαίρομεν; ὡς ταὐτὰ ἐφροντίζομεν; ὡς ἠκονῶμεν ἀλλήλους ἀλλήλοις ὄντες κριταί; 6. ἀλλ' ὅτε ἐπανῆκον τὴν προτέραν ἐπιδημίαν, τίνας οὐ παρῆλθε κρότῳ τε καὶ τοῖς ἄλλοις, ἃ σοφιστῶν ὠφελεῖν σχῆμα δοκεῖ; καὶ μὴν ὅπως μὲν αὖθις ἐπανέλθοιμι προὔτρεψεν, ἐγένετο δὲ ἀντὶ πολλῶν ἀφιγμένῳ. 7. καὶ ταῦτα ἔπραττεν εἰδὼς ὅτι

---

c Hierocles, a pagan, was brother to Libanius' close friend the pagan Demetrius and to the Christian Julianus (for whom see *Letter* 124).

at the occurrence without being able to stop it is obviously to be accounted a disaster by myself, your brothers,[c] and all who entertain goodwill towards you.   3. But even worse than this is the death of Chromatius, by Zeus and the gods[d]—I repeat, of Chromatius. He was a credit to Palestine, by reason of his birth there, and to Athens, by reason of his ready acceptance of its learning.   4. He was a glory to his family, a haven of refuge to his friends. Of all the men I know he gained most admiration and least envy. He startled with his eloquence, and attracted with his character, for in himself he was both an able orator and a good man.   5. What should I first call to mind? what should be the first reason for me to lament his passing? Our sojourn under the same roof at Athens? the way that we shared a single table, the same enjoyments, the same deliberations? or how we acted as whetstone to each other by our mutual criticism?   6. But at the time of my first homecoming,[e] he excelled everyone in the applause and other marks of appreciation which are thought to be of service to the professorial station. Moreover, he urged me to return home again, and upon my arrival was worth many a supporter.   7. And this he did, though he knew that,

[d] The imprecation is a reminiscence of Dem. *de Cor.* 285.

[e] In summer 353.

λυπήσει τινὰ βέλτιστος ὢν εἰς ἐμέ. ἀλλ' ὅμως
οὐκ ἀπέστησεν αὐτὸν τῆς ὑπὲρ ἡμῶν ἀνδρίας τό
τινα μέμψιν παρὰ τοῦ δεῖνος ἀκολουθήσειν, ἀλλ' ὃ
δίκαιον ᾤετο ἐλευθέρως ἐποίει, καὶ τοὺς ἀξιοῦντας
αὐτὸν αὐτοῖς χαριζόμενον ἀδικεῖν ὡς οὐ σφόδρα
ὑγιαίνοντας ἀπεσείετο. 8. τοιαῦτα ἡμῖν βοηθῶν
ἠσθένησε καὶ τοσούτῳ κακῷ πιεζόμενος ἐκαρτέρει
σιγῇ. ἔπειτα ἀναστὰς ὥρμησε μὲν ἐπὶ Κιλικίας,
ὥρμησε δὲ εἰς Ἅιδου. καὶ τὸ χωρίον, οἷ[1] μετέστη,
πρότερον δοκοῦν ἥδιστον πῶς, οἴει, κέκριται χαλε-
πόν; 9. ἐγὼ δὲ εὐθὺς μὲν ἀκούσας ἄφωνος ἦν
ὡς ἐπὶ πλεῖστον· ἐπεὶ δὲ ἠδυνήθην ῥῆξαι φωνήν,
ἀφῆκα πρώτην, ὡς ἄρα τὸ κάλλιστον τῶν ἐπὶ γῆς
ἀπελήλυθεν, ἀνὴρ σωφρονέστερος μὲν Πηλέως,
θεοφιλὴς δὲ οὐχ ἧττον ἢ Σοφοκλῆς, δεινὸς εἰπεῖν,
ἀμείνων κρῖναι, φίλος σαφής, οὐδέν τι χείρων
ἐκείνων τῶν Συρακουσίων οἷς ἐπίδειξις ἐγένετο τοῦ
πράγματος ἐν τῇ Διονυσίου τυραννίδι. 10. καὶ
ταῦτα ἐγὼ διῆλθον, Ἱερόκλεις, δακρύων. ἔπειτα
ἐξ αὐτῶν ὧν ἐδάκρυον ἐνεθυμήθην πως ὅτι

---

[1] οἷ F. οὗ Wolf (Mss.)

f The Caesar Gallus, who disapproved of Libanius' stay
in Antioch.

g Cf. *Letter* 95.1. *Paroem. Gr.* 1.123.

through his devotion to me, he would annoy a certain person;[f] but for all that, it did not distract him from his courageous support of me that some reproach from someone or other would surely follow, but he generously acted as he thought was just, and those persons who expected him to oblige them by acting unjustly he shook off as being of not very sound disposition.   8. During such efforts on my behalf he fell ill, and though oppressed by such affliction, he endured it in silence. Then he rose from his bed and set out to Cilicia—and to his death. And the place to which he had removed, and which previously seemed so pleasant, now, as you can imagine, I felt to be utterly unfriendly.   9. When I first heard the news, I was struck dumb for a very long time, and when I could utter a word, the first words I uttered were that the noblest being on earth had passed away, a man more prudent than Peleus,[g] no less dear to god than Sophocles,[h] able in speech, better in judgement, a true friend,[i] in no way inferior to those Syracusans who gave testimony to their fidelity in the tyranny of Dionysius.[j] 10. Such was the story I told, Hierocles, amid my tears. Then in consequence of the very cause of my

[h] Cf. *Vita Sophocl.* 12, γέγονε δὲ καὶ θεοφιλὴς ὁ Σοφοκλῆς ὡς οὐκ ἄλλος.

[i] Eurip. *Or.* 1155, a favourite citation of Libanius.

[j] Damon and Phintias, Pythagoreans in the tyranny of Dionysius I: cf. Cic. *de Off.* iii.10.45, *Tusc.* v.22.63, Val. Max. iv.7.1.

347

ἆρα οὐ χρὴ δακρύειν. τὸ γὰρ οὕτω βεβιωκέναι καλῶς εἰς τὴν τελευτὴν παραμύθιον. ὃ μὲν γὰρ ἔπαθε, κοινόν· ἐφ' οἷς δὲ ἐπαινεῖται, ταῦτα οὐ κοινά. 11. καὶ δὴ καὶ σὲ δεῖ μᾶλλον χαίρειν ὅτι τοιοῦτον ἀδελφιδοῦν ἐκτήσω καὶ κηδεστὴν ἢ τῷ συμβεβηκότι πλήττεσθαι. λογίζου δὲ ὅτι θεῶν μὲν γνώμῃ πάντα πράττεται, θεοὶ δὲ τὸν ὧδε ἔχοντα ἀρετῆς οὐκ ἄν τι κακὸν ἔδρων. δίκαιοι γὰρ καὶ οὐκ ἂν ὃν τιμᾶν ἐχρῆν ἐκόλαζον. 12. οὐκ ἄρα ὅπως τι δεινὸν εἴη πεπονθώς, ἀπέθνησκεν, ἀλλ' ἐπὶ τῷ βελτίονι. δοκοῦσι γάρ μοι νομίσαντες τὸν ἄνδρα κρείττω μὲν ἢ διατρίβειν ἐν γῇ, τῷ δὲ αὐτῶν πρέπειν χορῷ μετενεγκεῖν ἐνθένδε εἰς οὐρανόν. οὕτως αὐτόν τε σὲ δεῖ φρονεῖν καὶ τὴν θυγατέρα πείθειν καὶ οἴεσθαι τῆς ἐκείνου παιδείας ἄξιον εἶναι τὸ ὑμᾶς ἐπίστασθαι φέρειν. 13. καὶ περὶ μὲν τῆς τελευτῆς τοῦ ἑταίρου πλείω μὲν ἔνι λέγειν, δεῖ δὲ οὐδέν, εἰδότι γὰρ ἂν λέγοιτο. τὴν δὲ ἐνθάδε ταραχὴν ἡμεῖς τε ὅπως καταστήσεται φροντίζομεν σόν τε μέρος οὐ μικρόν. οἱ μὲν γὰρ τοιοῦτοι καιροὶ φρονίμου δέονται, σὺ δέ, εἴπερ τις ἐπὶ τῷ φρονεῖν δόξαν ἔχεις. 14. ὥσπερ οὖν εἰ κυβερνήτης ἐτύγχανες, ἠξίουν ἄν σε ἐν χειμῶνι

tears, I somehow came to consider that there was, after all, no need for tears, for to have lived a life of such nobility is consolation for his death. His fate is common to all men, but the objects for which he is praised are not. 11. Indeed you should rather rejoice at having had such a nephew and son-in-law than be shocked at his death. Reflect that everything happens by will of the gods, and that gods would never harm a man of such virtue, for they are just and would never punish one whom they ought to honour. 12. He died, surely, not in order to suffer some dire fate, but for better things. It seems to me that they regarded him as too good for a life on earth and as fitted for their own company, and so translated him from here to heaven.[k] That is the way you must think of it too, and persuade your daughter to do the same, and you must believe that your ability to endure this is fitting tribute to his high qualities. 13. I could say more too upon the death of my companion, but there is no need, for it would be a tale told to one who knows already. As regards the disturbance here, my care is to have it allayed, and your part is no small one. Such occurrences require sound sense, and you, if anyone is, are renowned for sense. 14. Then, just as I would call upon you, if you were a helmsman, to

[k] Cf. Julian's reproof to the mourners at his death-bed, Or. 18.296.

δεικνύναι τὴν τέχνην, οὕτως, ἐπειδὴ συνέσει
νικᾷς, ἄνδρα ὀργιζόμενον διάλλαξον.

4. Ἀνατολίῳ

1. Ἐγὼ τοὺς ὄντας μοι φίλους βουλοίμην, ἄττα
ἂν λέγωσιν, ἀληθῆ δοκεῖν λέγειν. σὲ δὲ ἐν πρώτοις τε γράφομαι τῶν ἐπιτηδείων καὶ ὅπως πόρρω
εἴης τοῦ ψεύδεσθαι ποιῶ. 2. τούτου οὖν, ὦ
'γαθέ, κηδόμενος ἐσίγων τὸν ἄχρι τοῦδε χρόνον.
ἔδει γὰρ εὐθὺς μὲν ἐμοῦ γράφοντος ψεύστην εἶναι
σέ, μὴ γράφοντος δὲ καθαρεύειν τῆς αἰτίας, ὥστε
σε ἐκόσμησα τῇ σιγῇ. σὺ δὲ ὡς ἠδικημένος ἐγκαλεῖς ἐπαινεῖν ἀφείς. αἴνιγμά σοι δοκῶ λέγειν.
ἄκουε δῆτα σαφῶς. 3. σὺ τὴν πρώτην ἐκείνην
γράφων ἐπιστολὴν σκώμμασί τε ἡμᾶς ἔτρωσας
οὐκ ὀλίγοις καὶ τελευτῶν ἐπέθηκας ὡς κατασύ-
ραις ἡμᾶς ἐν τοῖς γράμμασι, καὶ ὅρκος ἐπῆν.
4. ἐσκόπουν οὖν, ὅπως ἄν σοι τοῦτο ὀρθῶς εἰρῆσθαι

a *BLZG* 61 (i), *PLRE* 59 (3) give the received account of
Anatolius' career.
For an alternative view which accepts the accuracy of

show your skill in time of storm,[1] so, since you hold the palm for your tact, reconcile one who is angered.

[1] Cf. Plat. *Protag.* 344d.

4. To Anatolius[a]

1. I could wish that the friends I have should, in all they say, be thought to speak the truth. You I account among the foremost of my intimates and so behave that you should be far removed from deceit. 2. In my concern for this, my friend, I kept silence until the present time, for the immediate consequence was that, if I wrote, you would be a deceiver, while if I did not write, you would purge yourself of the charge: thus I did you honour by my silence. Yet you refrain from commending me and accuse me as though I have wronged you. You think I talk in riddles. Then let me make matters clear. 3. In writing your first letter you touched me to the quick with several jesting remarks and ended with the postscript that you had wiped the floor with me in what you had written, and you gave your word for that. 4. So I began to ponder how you had con-

the dates given in *Cod. Th.* and the evidence of Eunapius in his life of Proaeresius, so distinguishing Anatolius Azutrio as prefect in 340's from the present Anatolius in the 350's, cf. Norman, "The Illyrian Prefecture of Anatolius," *Rheinisches Museum für Philologie* 100 (1957): 253 ff.

δοκοῖ[1] καὶ νικῶν φαίνοιο καθαρῶς. νίκη δὲ σαφὴς
τὸ μηδ' αὐτὸν τὸν ἡττημένον ἀναισχυντεῖν, ὡς
ἄρα οὐ κεκράτηται, ὃ δὴ μὴ γράφων ὁμολογεῖ
νενικῆσθαι τῷ μὴ ἔχειν ὅ τι γράψειεν.   5. ἔχεις
οὖν καὶ τουτονὶ τὸν στέφανον ἐπ' ἐπείνῳ τῷ διὰ
δικαιοσύνην σοι δεδομένῳ. καὶ δύο νίκας ἡμῖν ὁ
καλὸς Ἀνατόλιος ἀνῄρηται, τὴν μὲν ὡς ἄριστος
δικαστῶν, τὴν δὲ ὡς κράτιστος σοφιστῶν, τὸ μὲν
ἁπάντων ᾀδόντων, ἐμοῦ δὲ τὸ δεύτερον, ὃ σὺ
φαίης ἂν οὐκ εἶναι φαυλότατον.[2]   6. ὁρᾶν δοκῶ
σε γελῶντα καὶ ἀκούειν βοῶντος καί τινα ἀφιέντος ῥήματα τῶν εἰωθότων. οὐ γὰρ ἂν σύ γε τοῦτο
τὸ μέρος ἄνευ τοῦ ταῦτα ποιεῖν ἐπέλθοις.   7. τὸ
μὲν οὖν τῆς παιδιᾶς ἐνταῦθα ὡρίσθω, πάντως δὲ
δεῖ καὶ ἐπιστέλλοντι παίζειν ὡσπεροῦν συνόντι,
τὴν δὲ οὖσαν αἰτίαν ὑφ' ἧς βραδέως ἐπιστέλλω
νῦν ἀποδώσω.   8. ᾔδειν ὅτι μέγα τι περὶ ἡμῶν
ἐθελήσεις ἀκοῦσαι πρέπον μὲν τῇ πόλει πρέπον δὲ
ταῖς ἐλπίσιν, ὑφ' ὧν κινηθεὶς ἧκον. ἕως μὲν οὖν
οὔπω τοῦτο ἀπῆντα, μέλλειν ᾤμην δεῖν· ἐπεὶ δὲ
ἔστι τι καὶ τοιοῦτον, γράφω.   9. τὸ μὲν γὰρ

----

[1] δοκοῖ F.   δοκῇ Wolf (Mss.)
[2] φαυλότατον Wolf (Va Vo Vind.)   φαυλότερον F (SD, V
corrected).

vinced yourself of the correctness of your remarks and obviously felt that you had won your point. But an obvious win is for the loser himself not to brazen it out that he has not lost, and if he does not write that, then he concedes defeat by having nothing to write about.   5. So you have this prize, besides that which you have won for your justice. Our noble Anatolius has gained two victories over us, the first that he is the best of governors, which is what is on everybody's lips, the second that he is the best of sophists, which is my confession—and this you might say was not least important.   6. In my mind's eye I see you laughing and hear you calling and making one of your usual remarks; for you would never undertake this kind of thing without doing so.   7. So let there be an end to fun here; by all means one should poke fun at a correspondent as though present, but now I will pay you back with the real reason for my dilatoriness in writing.   8. I knew that you would want to hear something high-faluting about me, befitting our city and the ambitions by which I was inspired to return home. Well, while ever this had not yet supervened, I thought I should delay, but since something of the sort has actually occurred, I now write.   9. To begin with, I

LIBANIUS

πρῶτον εἰσήλθομεν εἰς ἄνδρας οὐ πιστεύοντας ὅτι
βιώσονται. καὶ ὅπως μὴ εἴπῃς· 'τί οὖν εἰσῆλθες ;'
οὐ γὰρ ἀκίνδυνον ἀναστρέφειν.   10. ἔπειτα τοῦ
φοβοῦντος ἀπελθόντος διαφυγὼν ἐγὼ θάνατον, ὃν
ἀκήκοας, ἐπὶ πολλοῖς λόγοις, οὓς τὸ θέρος
ἐδέξατο, διδασκαλεῖον ἀνέῳξα καὶ ὁ φθόνος ἔπνει
λαμπρός. εἰδὼς δὲ ὅτι οὐκ ἔστιν αὐτὸν ἄλλως ἢ
λόγοις καταχῶσαι, τοῦ σώματος μὲν ἠμέλουν καὶ
ὅσοις τοῦτο ἥδεται, χαίρειν εἰῶν, τοῦ δὲ ὅπως μηδὲν ἀνήσω λέγων, ἐφρόντισα.   11. τοῖς βελτί-
στοις δὲ ἡμῶν πολίταις τὰ πολλὰ οὐ πολλὰ
ἐδόκει, ἀλλ' ἐγὼ μὲν αὐτοὺς ἡγούμην ἠνωχλῆ-
σθαι, οἱ δὲ ἀγεύστοις ἐῴκεσαν. νέοι δὲ οἱ μὲν
οὔπω πρότερον ὡμιληκότες σοφισταῖς, οἱ δὲ οἷς
ὡμίλουν ἀφέντες ὑφ' ἡμῖν ἐτάττοντο, οἱ μὲν ἐνθένδε προσιόντες, οὐκ ὀλίγοι δ' ἐπῆλθον.   12. ἀλλ'
οὔπω πάντα εὐδαιμονία σοῦ γε ἀπόντος· οὐ
παρόντος ταῦτά γε ἦν ἂν μείζω. καὶ αὐτό γε τὸ
παρεῖναί σε πάσης τῆς περὶ ταῦτα εὐπραξίας
ἄμεινον.   13. παρεμυθεῖτο δέ με τὸ κεκλῆσθαί σε

---

[b] Because of the victimization of the decurions by
Gallus, the riots and the lynching of Theophilus and the
flight of Eubulus (*Or.* 1.103, *Ep.* 386, Amm. 14.7.2).
  [c] Gallus was recalled in summer 354. Before then

came among people who had no confidence in their survival.[b] And don't ask me, "Why did you go, then?", for to return was not without its dangers. 10. Then after the departure of the oppressor and my escape from death,[c] of which you have heard, after many declamations given during the summer season, I opened a school and envy erupted into flame. Realizing that I could not smother it save by declamations,[d] I disregarded my body and took leave of the pleasures it enjoyed, and considered means whereby I should not relax from the delivery of declamations. 11. My worthy fellow citizens regarded this quantity as a mere nothing; and though I thought I surfeited them, they were like men who had never had a taste. Young men, some who had never yet attended any lectures, others who left those whose lectures they did attend, enrolled under me, some from here in Antioch, and not a few coming from abroad.[e] 12. But my cup of happiness is not yet full while ever you are absent. Were you here, then it would be fuller. Indeed the very fact of your presence would exceed all such success. 13. My consolation was that you had

Libanius was accused of treason before him, and got off. The order of events here is more accurate than that of the dramatic narrative of *Or.* 1.93 ff, twenty years later.

[d] Cf. Plat. *Gorg.* 512c.

[e] For another contemporary account of his setting up school in Antioch, cf. *Letter* 6.

πρὸς ἀρχήν, ἢ κεφάλαιον ἀρχῶν εἶναι δοκεῖ, καὶ
μεγαλαυχούμεθά γε Σύροι Ῥωμαίοις παρέχοντες
ἄνδρα³ δεινὸν κοσμῆσαι πόλεων πράγματα.
14. τὸ δ' ὡς φεύγεις τοῦτον τὸν πόνον, ἀκοῦσαι
μὲν ὑπῆρξέ μοι, πιστεῦσαι δὲ ἥκιστα, οὐχ ὅτι σε
οἴομαι σπουδαρχίδην, ᾧ γὰρ αἱ ἀρχαὶ πενίας ἀφορ-
μαί, πῶς ἂν τὸ ἄρχειν διώκοι; ἀλλὰ διεστάναι δή
φασι τὴν Ῥώμην καὶ τοὺς πολλοὺς δυσκόλως
ἔχειν πρὸς τὴν βουλήν, σὲ δὲ τοῦτο δεῖσαι λογιζό-
μενον ὡς ἢ τὸν δῆμον ἢ τοὺς βελτίστους ἀνιάσεις.
15. τοῦτον ἐγὼ τὸν φόβον οὐ πείθομαι τῆς σῆς
εἶναι ψυχῆς. καὶ γὰρ καὶ τῶν ἡνιόχων τοὺς ἄκρους
ὁρῶ θαρρούντως ἀναβαίνοντας ἅρμα ἵππων ἀπειθε-
στέρων εἰδότας ὡς ἰσχυροτέραν κέκτηνται τέχνην
τῆς ἐκείνων κακίας. ἤδη δέ τις καὶ κυβερνήτης
ἐγηγερμένης θαλάττης λύσας ἀνήχθη πιστεύων
περιέσεσθαι τῇ τέχνῃ τῆς ζάλης. 16. σὲ μὲν οὖν
ἵλεως πέμψειε βασιλεύς, ἵλεως δὲ Ἀθηνᾶ δέξαιτο
καὶ μετὰ ταῦτα ἡμεῖς λαμπρὸν ἀπὸ λαμπρῶν
ἔργων· ἐμὲ δὲ ἕλκει πάλιν ἡ πόλις ἡ παρόντι μὲν

---

³ καὶ ... ἄνδρα cited by Thomas Magister s.v. μεγαλαυχῶ.
παρέχοντας ἄνδρα F. (Va Vo, V before correction) ἄνδρα διδόντες
Wolf (S Vi Vind D, V corrected) διδόντες ἄνδρα Thom. Mag.

been summoned to an office that is held to be the peak of an administrative career, and we Syrians boast the fact that we provide the Romans with a man well capable of embellishing the fortunes of cities. 14. It has come to my ears that you are trying to avoid this task, but I utterly disbelieve it—not that I regard you as a place-hunter,[f] for when offices have been the cause of financial losses, how could one pursue office? But it is said that dissension is rife in Rome, with the commons at odds with the Senate, and that that is what you are afraid of, since you reflect that you will annoy either the commons or the nobles.[g] 15. I am convinced that this fear does not form part of your make-up. Why, I see first-class drivers confidently mounting their chariots, although their horses are recalcitrant, for they know that they have gained a skill that can overcome their viciousness; and helmsmen before now have set sail and put out to sea, however tempest tossed, confident that by their skill they will survive the storm. 16. So may the emperor send you with gladness, and Athena, and thereafter we, welcome you with gladness, a man ennobled by his noble deeds. As for me, the capital—which did not employ me when I was there, but seeks me when I am not—

[f] Cf. Ar. *Acharnians* 595.
[g] In 355 Anatolius was offered and refused the prefecture of the city of Rome; cf. *Ep.* 423.

οὐ χρωμένη, ζητοῦσα δὲ ἀπόντα. 17. σὺ δ᾽ ὅ τι ἂν ἔχῃς βοήθει καὶ παῦε τὸν θυμὸν καὶ ὡς ἀρρωστῷ λέγε. καὶ οὐ ψεύσῃ λέγων· φάρμακά τε γὰρ πεπώκαμεν, ἃ ἐν μεγίστῳ κακῷ πίνεται φλέβα τε ἐτμήθην οὐκ εἰωθώς, ὃ προσιοῦσαν ἐκώλυσε τελευτήν.[4]

[4] τὴν τελευτήν. F (SD)

---

[h] Constantinople, where he was still being paid as an appointed sophist. Throughout 355 and 356 he pleaded ill

5. Ὑγιεινῷ

1. Ἔμελλεν ἄρα ὁ περὶ τῆς κεφαλῆς μοι λόγος, ὃν ἐπλαττόμην, εἰς ἔργον ἥξειν παιδεύοντος, οἶμαι, τοῦ θεοῦ μὴ τὰ τοιαῦτα κομψεύεσθαι. ὡς γὰρ ἀφικόμην, ἡμέρᾳ δεκάτῃ μοι προσέβαλεν ἴλιγγος καὶ παρῄνει Δαμάλιος πίνειν φάρμακον. 2. ἐγὼ δὲ οὐκ ἐνεγκὼν αὐξῆσαι ἐν τῷ θέρει τὸ κακὸν τοῦ φθινοπώρου πίνω Μαρκέλλου δόντος ἱερὰν αὐτήν, οἶμαι, καλεῖτε. καὶ ἔπινον ἐκείνης,

---

[a] BLZG 180, amended PLRE 445.
The letter relates to Hygieinus, a doctor in Constan-

is trying to drag me back.[h]   17. Assist me by all means in your power. Allay their anger, and tell them I am ill. If you do so, you will not be telling a lie. I have drunk the potions that are taken in times of severe crisis, and I have had a vein cut, which has never been my habit, and that is what prevented the approach of death.[i]

health, and with good reason, but his resignation was not finally accepted until 357. Cf. *Ep.* 572, Petit, *Vie Municipale*, 409.

[i] The full medical history is given to a doctor friend in *Letter* 5.

5. To Hygieinus[a]

1. It seems that the story which I invented about my head was bound to come true in the end,[b] since the god schools me not to be too clever about such things.[c] Ten days after my arrival, I had an attack of vertigo, and Damalius[d] advised me to drink a cure.   2. I could not stand the increase of the ailment in the summer, and so early in the autumn I drank the potion Marcellus gave me—you call it the

tinople, Libanius' state of health from early summer 354 until the time of writing, spring 355.

[b] Cf. *Or.* 1.94.

[c] Cf. Plat. *Laches* 197d.

[d] Damalius, Marcellus, Olympius, and Panolbius are doctors in attendance upon Libanius in Antioch. The last two are not to be confused with his friend or his uncle.

ἧς γενομένων[1] ἑτέρων ἐταραττόμην, καὶ τοσαύ-
την ἐπικουρίαν δεξάμενος μετὰ φόβου θαυμαστοῦ
τὸν χειμῶνα διῆλθον Ὀλυμπίου τὸ πεπωκέναι τε
ἐπαινοῦντος καὶ κελεύοντος αὖθις ἦρι πιεῖν.
3. ἄρτι δὲ ὑπολάμποντος πόνος ἰσχυρὸς προσέπεσε
τοῖς νεφροῖς βρόχον ἀναγκάζων ζητεῖν. ἔπειτα
μῆνα διαλιπὼν προσέπεσε πικρότερος καὶ ἐποίησεν ἀνάγκην πράγματος, ὃ διετέλουν ἀναβαλλό-
μενος. Πανόλβιος γὰρ τῶν ἄλλων ἐλαίῳ τὰς
ἀλγηδόνας ἀξιούντων κοιμίζειν τέμνει μοι φλέβα,
καὶ ῥάων μὲν εὐθὺς ἐγενόμην, θαρρεῖν δὲ ὑπὲρ τοῦ
παντὸς οὐκ ἔχω.   4. τῷ τοίνυν ἐνταῦθα ὄντι
κακῶν, πῶς ἂν ταῦτα διαφύγοι, λέγε. σοφιστὰς
δὲ ἑτέρωθεν μεταπέμπου. καὶ ὥσπερ ἐγὼ σὲ βού-
λομαι παρεῖναι τῷ βασιλεῖ, οὕτως ἐμὲ σὺ νοσεῖν
παρὰ τοῖς οἰκείοις, ἐπειδὴ νοσεῖν ἀνάγκη.

---

[1] γευομένων conj. Seeck, F. (S Vi).   γενομένων Wolf (V Va
Vo D).

sacred draught,[e] I think. Anyway, drink it I did, though I used to be alarmed when other people tasted it; and after obtaining such assistance I passed the winter in dire trepidation, although Olympius recommended my taking it, and bade me take another dose in the spring.   3. But just as spring put in an appearance, a fierce pain attacked me in the kidneys—enough to make me look for a rope to hang myself. Then after a month's interval, there came a fiercer attack, which forced me to undergo a treatment which I consistently tried to postpone. Other doctors advised the use of oil for the relief of the pains, but Panolbius cut a vein, and I immediately felt better, though there is no guarantee of confidence for the future.   4. Tell a man so beset by troubles how he may escape them, and summon your sophists from somewhere else.[f] Just as I wish for you to attend the emperor, let your wish for me be that I should ail among my own folk, since ail I must.

[e] Cf. Lucian *Tragopod.* 170.
[f] To fill the vacant chair which Libanius had left behind at Constantinople.

6. Ἀρισταινέτῳ

1. Καὶ ὅτε ἀσθενεῖν σοι τὴν γυναῖκα ἠκούομεν, συνηλγοῦμεν ἐννοοῦντες ὡς εἰκός σε διακεῖσθαι καμνούσης, καὶ ἐπειδὴ τὴν τελευτὴν ἐπυθόμην, ἀνῴμωξα δεινόν τι ποιούμενος Ἀρισταίνετον εἶναι ἐν πένθει, οὗ τῇ φύσει πανηγύρεις πρέπουσιν. 2. ὁρμήσας δὲ παραμυθεῖσθαι λόγοις ἀνέσχον δείσας μὴ πάνυ σε δοκῶν εἰδέναι ἔπειτα ἀλοίην ἀγνοῶν. οἷς γὰρ ἔμελλόν σε κουφιεῖν, τούτοις δὴ τοῖς Πινδάρου καὶ Σιμωνίδου, καὶ ὅσα ἐκ τραγῳδιῶν εἰώθαμεν φάρμακα λύπῃ προσάγειν, πάντα ἐδόκεις μοι πάλαι τε εἰδέναι κἂν πρὸς ἄλλους εἰπεῖν. 3. ἐλογιζόμην οὖν ὅτι, εἰ μὲν οἷά τε κατακοιμίζειν ἀθυμίαν, αὐτὸς ἰάσῃ σαυτόν, εἰ δ' οὐχ οἷά τε, καὶ παρ' ἄλλου μάτην ἂν λέγοιτο. διὰ ταῦτα τοῦ μὲν ἀφίσταμαι, τὴν διήγησιν δέ σοι τῶν πραγμάτων ἀποδίδωμι, ἃ τοῦ χειμῶνος συνέβη. 4. ἠρξάμεθα τῆς συνουσίας μετὰ προλόγου καί τινος ἁμίλλης πρός τι τῶν Δημοσθένους. ἦν δὲ ὁ

---

[a] *BLZG* 85 (i), *PLRE* 104 (1).

Aristaenetus was Libanus' closest and most influential friend in Bithynia. No fewer than 36 letters were written

6. To Aristaenetus[a]

1. When I heard of your wife's sickness, I sympathized as I reflected how you were sure to feel about her illness, and on learning of her death I groaned aloud for I grieved that Aristaenetus, for whom festivals are more fitting,[b] should be in mourning. 2. I set out to console you with an oration, but then I stopped myself, for I was afraid that, though seeming to know you through and through, I should then be found not to know you at all. For the words with which I intended to console you, those quotations from Pindar and Simonides and all the passages from the tragedians which we normally adduce as a cure for grief, all these, it seemed to me, you knew long ago and would repeat them to other people. 3. I reflected, then, that if these were the means to assuage your grief, you would be your own physician, and if not, then for someone else to utter them would be labour in vain. Hence, I put this aside, and give you a report of the events which have occurred during the winter. 4. I began my teaching with a prologue and a competitive passage against a bit of Demosthenes. The first was a plea

to him between now and his death in the earthquake. For this letter, cf. Festugière, *Antioche* pp. 428 ff. Its detailed account of Libanius' settlement in Antioch and his rhetorical activities in his first year amplifies that of *Letter* 4.

[b] In particular, the oratory that was part of such festivals.

μὲν Τύχην μονὴν[1] αἰτῶν βεβαίαν, τῇ δὲ ἁμίλλῃ
πολλαὶ μορφαί. καὶ προσῆλθον, ἐπειδὴ ἀνέστην,
ἑπτακαίδεκα νέοι. Πλάτων δέ, οἶμαι, ἠσθένει
Ζηνόβιος ὁ χρηστός.   5. ἔπειτα ἐγὼ μὲν τοῦ
διδάσκειν εἰχόμην, τὰ δὲ ἐπέρρεεν ἔθνεα, πολῖται
καὶ ξένοι καὶ ταύτῃ ὅστις εἴην εἰδέναι ἐθέλοντες.
τὸ μὲν γὰρ εἶναί με μὴ κακῶν[2] λόγων δημιουργὸν
συνεκεχώρητο, θάτερον δὲ ἐδοκιμάζετο.   6. καὶ
ἔδοξα τοῖς μὲν οὐκ εἶναι ταύτῃ χείρων, τοῖς δὲ καὶ
βελτίων, ὥστ' ἐν οὐ πολλαῖς ἡμέραις πεντήκοντα
νέων ἦν ὁ χορός. ἀριστᾶν δὲ οὐκ ἦν, ἀλλ' ἔδει
πονεῖν εἰς ἑσπέραν καὶ ἐθαυμάζετο μετὰ τῶν
ἄλλων καὶ τὸ τῆς γαστρὸς κρατεῖν.   7. ἧκεν ὁ
Στρατήγιος,[3] καὶ ἐδεξάμην τὸν ἄνδρα λόγῳ,
μικρῷ μέν, οὗτος γάρ, οἶμαι, προσφωνοῦντι νόμος,
ῥηθέντι δὲ κατὰ νοῦν αὐτῷ τε καὶ τοῖς ἄλλοις.
ὁ δὲ ἀντίτεχνος, καλῶ μὲν γὰρ αὐτὸν ὃ καὶ αὐτὸς
ἑαυτόν, ἠπείλησεν ἐρεῖν. καὶ τοῦτ' ἦν ἐπίδειξις ἡ

[1] Τύχην μονὴν F. (Vi) μονὴν om. D.   εὐχὴν μόνην Wolf (other
Mss.)   εὐχὴ μονὴν Re.

[2] κακὸν conj. Re.

[3] Στρατήγιος Seeck, F. (S Vi)   στρατηγός Wolf, Re. (other
Mss.)

to Fortune for my stay here to be confirmed, while the competitive piece contained many variations. When I set up in practice, seventeen students attended me.[c] "Plato, I believe, was ill"[d]—the good Zenobius, that is.   5. Then I settled down to teaching, and they came in droves,[e] citizens and strangers and those who wanted to know what I was like at this job too, for it had been agreed that I was a composer of no bad orations, but now this other aspect was under examination.   6. Some people thought that in this I was no worse, others that I was better even, and in consequence in a few days my class numbered fifty. I had no time for lunch, but had to work on until evening, and it was a source of surprise, besides everything else, that I controlled my belly.   7. Strategius arrived,[f] and I welcomed him with a short speech—normal procedure, to my mind, in an address of welcome—but it gained his approval when delivered, and that of others too. My rival[g]—I give him the description which he gives himself—threatened to deliver a speech, but his discourse went no further than his

[c] These he had brought with him from Constantinople; *Or.* 1.101.

[d] Plat. *Phaedo* 59b.

[e] Homer *Il.* xi.724.

[f] Strategius Musonianus, praetorian prefect from July 354. *BLZG* 282 (i), *PLRE* 611. Cf. *Or.* 1.106 f.

[g] Acacius. See *BLZG* 39 (ii), *PLRE* 6 (6), amended by Wolf, *Schulwesen* 73 f, Libanios, *Autobiographie* ed. P. Petit, 228 f. Cf. *Or.* 1.90 f, 109 f.

365

ὑπόσχεσις. 8. ἰδὼν δὲ τοὺς παιδαγωγοὺς ἰσχύοντας ἀπὸ τοῦ πωλεῖν τοὺς νέους καὶ τὸν ἐν μουσείοις κόσμον ἀπολωλότα συμβουλεύω τοῖς ἐμαυτοῦ πολίταις μὴ ταῦτα περιορᾶν, ἀλλ' ἀγανακτῆσαί τε καὶ κωλῦσαι. καὶ ἐγένετό τις ὀργὴ κατὰ τῶν ἀδικούντων οὐ μικρά. ὁ δὲ ἀντίτεχνος ἠπείλει συνερεῖν αὐτοῖς. καὶ τοῦτ' ἦν ἐπίδειξις ἡ ὑπόσχεσις. 9. τελευτᾷ Ζηνόβιος καὶ ἐμονῴδουν ἀπελθὼν τοῦ τάφου. καὶ μικρὸν ὕστερον ἐγκωμιάζω τὸν διδάσκαλον μακροτέρῳ λόγῳ καὶ ἔδοξεν οὐ φαύλους κεκομίσθαι μισθούς. ὁ δὲ ἀντίτεχνος ὑπέσχετο λέξειν, ἢν ὁ πατὴρ αὐτῷ ἀποθάνῃ. ὁ δ' ἔτι ζῇ. τούτων γιγνομένων οἱ σφόδρα ἐγνωκότες ἀναισχυντεῖν, ἦσαν δὲ τρεῖς ἀντὶ τραπέζης λαμπρᾶς οἱ τοῦτο ποιοῦντες, ἐνέδοσαν. 10. ἐγὼ μὲν οὖν ἀναπαύλης ἐδεόμην, τῷ θείῳ δὲ οὐδὲν ἄρα ἧκει. καὶ Κυρῖνος δὲ ἦν τῶν οὐκ ἀνιέντων παρ' ἡμῖν τε ἔχων τὸν υἱὸν καὶ μιμούμενος σὲ μὲν εἰς τἀμά, ἐμὲ δὲ εἰς τὰ σά. 11. ἀγωνίζομαι δή τινα ἀγῶνα τῶν ἐν τοῖς πλάσμασι τούτοις, οἱ δὲ

---

h Here Libanius' procedure is the same as he was to follow after Julian's death, a monody (a personal lament popularised by Aristeides) immediately, and an *epitaphios*, a more extended eulogy, later.

promise. 8. Then, seeing that the pedagogues ruled the roost from the sale of their students and that discipline in the schools had been ruined, I counselled my fellow citizens not to turn a blind eye to this, but to resent and stop it; and no little anger was directed against the culprits. My rival threatened to speak in their support. Here too his discourse went no further than his promise. 9. Zenobius died, and after his funeral I composed a monody; and a little later I produced a eulogy of my teacher in a longer speech, and it was felt that he had won no little reward.[h] My rival promised to deliver a speech if his father died—but he is alive still. At this, those who had firmly made up their minds to be stubborn as mules— there were three who behaved so in return for his lavish hospitality—finally gave in.[i] 10. Although I began to be in need of a rest, my uncle[j] would have none of it, it seemed; Quirinus[k] too was one of those who kept me up to scratch. His son is a pupil of mine, and he is like you in his attitude towards me, and like me towards you. 11. I took part in a declamation on one of those contrived topics, and they

[i] Cf. *Ep.* 504.4. The leader of these three hostile decurions was presumably Eubulus, who headed a pressure group opposed to the clique of Phasganius and his nephew. Acacius seems to have been in collusion with him.

[j] Phasganius: *BLZG* 234.

[k] *BLZG* 250 (i), *PLRE* 760. His son was Honoratus (ii): *BLZG* 180 (ii), *PLRE* 439 (3).

ὠρχοῦντο ἅτε ἐν αὐτοῖς τεθραμμένοι καὶ ἐδέοντό
μου κατὰ μέσον γενομένου τὸν λόγον μετὰ τῆς
ἴσης τέχνης καὶ τὴν ἀντιλογίαν γράφειν. καὶ
γράψας ἐπῆλθον ὅτι τάχιστα. καὶ ἦν ἀδελφὸς ὁ
λόγος τοῦ προτέρου καὶ διεσέσειστο τῶν πολεμίων
τὰ πράγματα.   12. δείσας δὲ μὴ γυμνωθείη
εἰσῆλθε μὲν ὡς καθέξων τὰς ἀποστάσεις, ἐκίνησε
δὲ καὶ τὰς οὐκ ἄν, εἴπερ ἐσίγα, συμβάσας. ἐν γὰρ
τοῖς προοιμίοις ἐδεῖτο ἐφεθῆναί⁴ οἱ τὸ τέλος
εἰπεῖν, Κυρίνου δὲ οὐ διδόντος ὑπερπηδᾶν αὐτὸς
αὑτῷ τοῦτο ἔδωκε. καὶ ἀπ᾽ ἐκείνης τῆς ἡμέρας
κάθηται μόνος, ὅρκοι δὲ καὶ ἀνάγκαι πᾶσαι καὶ
δεσμοὶ καὶ ὅσα ἐπιστεύετο τηρήσειν τοὺς νέους,
ἐπατεῖτο καὶ μετέρρεεν.   13. ἐπὶ τούτοις γράμματα βασιλέως ἀφικνεῖται κελεύοντά με ἀναστρέφειν, πρὸς ἃ ἀπεκρίνατο τό τε τῆς κεφαλῆς καὶ τὸ
τῶν νεφρῶν νόσημα, ὡς οὐκ ἂν δυναίμην. τοῦτο
δὲ οὕτω θέμενος δείκνυμι λόγον περὶ εὐφυΐας,
τύπος δὲ τῆς διαλέξεως, τὰ σὰ παιδικά. καὶ δευ-

---

⁴ ἐφεθῆναί F.   ἐμὲ φθῆναί Wolf (Mss.)   ἐμοῦ ἐφεῖναί Re.

¹ Rhetoric took many of its terms from drama: the class
is a χόρος, the lecture room a θέατρον, and of the declamatory
exercises the declamation becomes the ἀγών, the introduction the προαγών. Libanius' demonstration of the ἀντιλογία is
the delivery of a thesis followed by antithesis.

began to dance for joy, since that is what they had
been brought up in, and when I reached the middle
of the oration they began to ask me to write its
rebuttal too with the same technique. I did so, and
produced it as soon as I could.[1] The oration was twin
to the previous one, and my enemies were shaken to
the core. 12. In fear that he would be stripped of
everything, he entered the lists with the idea of
checking the flow of desertions, but he actually
caused some that would never have happened, had
he kept quiet.[m] For in his introduction he begged
permission to relate his conclusion, but Quirinus
refused, so he gave himself permission to jump this
gap. And from that day, he has sat there alone, and
the oaths, and all the constraints and bonds and
everything else he relied upon to retain his students, have been trampled upon and melted away.
13. After that, a despatch from the emperor arrived,
summoning me to return, to which I replied that,
owing to migraine and kidney trouble,[n] I could not.
Having so settled this, I delivered an oration "On
Genius," a kind of diatribe, the sort of thing you
adore.[o] It needed a second day for its delivery, and

[m] Cf. *Or.* 1.110. The *locus classicus* for such desertions
by students is *Or.* 43.

[n] Cf. *Letter* 5.

[o] Eunap. V.S. 497. This diatribe Libanius dedicated to
Acacius, much to the credit of his rival. In summer 355
Libanius made strong efforts to conciliate his rival, as he
tartly remarks later (*Or.* 1.110). Only after Acacius moved
to Caesarea did the feud between them die down.

τέρας ἐδέησεν ἡμέρας, ἧς ἐκοινώνει Κλημάτιος. 14. τὴν μὲν οὖν ἐπ' αὐτῷ κίνησιν οὐκ ἐμὸν εἰπεῖν· ἐκεῖνο δὲ ἐμόν τε ἦν εἰπεῖν καὶ ἐβοᾶτο, ὅτι τούτων μέντοι διδάσκαλος Ἀρισταίνετος καὶ δὴ καὶ τῶν ἄλλων ὅσα ἂν ἔπαινον δέχηται.

7. Δατιανῷ

1. Ἐπειδὴ πάλαι τῆς βοηθείας ἦρξω, καθ' ἣν ἐκομισάμην τὴν ἐμαυτοῦ, βραχὺς ἀρκέσει μοι λόγος· πείθοντι μὲν γὰρ μακρῶν ἂν ἔδει, κινοῦντι δὲ τὸν πεπεισμένον οὐδὲν ἂν δέοι πολλῶν. 2. χεῖρα ὄρεξον, ὦ ἄριστε, τήρησον τὴν σαυτοῦ γνώμην, δὸς διὰ τέλους τὴν χάριν, μή με περιίδῃς ἀποσπώμενον ἀτυχοῦντος θείου καὶ πενομένων ἀδελφῶν καὶ μητρὸς ὑπὸ γήρως κειμένης μηδὲ

---

[a] *BLZG* 113 ff, *PLRE* 243 (1).

This is one of a batch of 14 letters delivered in summer 355 by the doctor Olympius (*BLZG* 222 (i), *PLRE* 644 (4)), en route to court at Milan. Datianus, chief purveyor of influence at the court of Constantius, was to become consul in 358. He was both *notarius* and Christian.

[b] Cf. *Or.* 1.94, where Datianus is the notable who assists his removal to Antioch. Libanius always addresses him with fulsome courtesy and covert dislike, as the elaborate care of this letter exemplifies.

Clematius[p] participated in that.   14. It is not my place to speak of his emotion at it. But *this* I *could* say and it was widely reported, that Aristaenetus had been my tutor in this, and indeed of all else that merited praise.

[p] *BLZG* 110 (ii), *PLRE* 213 (2): *agens in rebus* and very friendly with Libanius (cf. *Letter* 11, *Ep.* 435).

7. To Datianus[a]

1. Since you long ago began the assistance whereby I regained my own home town,[b] a brief recital will suffice me; for if I were trying to persuade you, there would be need for a long discourse, but in encouraging one already persuaded, there would be no need for much.   2. Stretch out a protecting hand, good sir; maintain your own resolution, grant me your favour to the end, and do not close your eyes to my separation from my unfortunate uncle,[c] my penniless brothers,[d] and my mother,[e] burdened with age, nor yet to my forced

[c] Phasganius' only child, affianced to Libanius, had died the year previously, just before his return to Antioch; cf. *Ep.* 95.

[d] For Libanius' brothers cf. *Or.* 1.4, 86, 197–201, 213. 'Penniless' is a very relative term as applied by Libanius, especially to himself and his own family; see Petit, *Vie Municipale,* Appendix iii.

[e] She died after Phasganius in winter 359 (*Or.* 1.117).

371

ἐμὲ μὲν ἑλκόμενον εἰς γῆν ξένην, ἐκείνοις δὲ
πικρὰν τὴν πατρίδα γινομένην.   3. ποιεῖ δέ σοι
τοὺς ὑπὲρ ἡμῶν λόγους εὐσχήμονας τὰ ἐμὰ κακά.
ἥ τε γὰρ κεφαλή μοι κατείληπται νοσήματι, δι' ὃ
πλέον οἴνου πίνω φάρμακον, οἵ τε νεφροὶ τῇ κλίνῃ
δεδώκασιν ἡμᾶς, ἃ δὲ ἥδιστον ποιεῖ τὸ ζῆν, τούτων ἀποκεκλείσμεθα.   4. μάρτυς δὲ ἡμῖν τῶν
παθῶν ὁ παλαίσας τοῖς πάθεσιν Ὀλύμπιος, ὁ σός
τε ἑταῖρος καὶ Ἱπποκράτους καὶ Πλάτωνος.
οὗ δεδεήμεθα λαβέσθαι σου τῶν γονάτων καὶ
ἐπιδακρῦσαι καὶ μηδὲν ἱκετείας εἶδος ἀφεῖναι.
5. τούτοις σε παρακαλῶ, πρὸς δὲ ἄλλον οὐδὲν ἂν
γράψαιμι τοιοῦτον λογιζόμενος ὡς ἐθελήσας μὲν
ἀρκέσεις καὶ μόνος, οὐ βουληθέντος δὲ σοῦ καὶ
τἆλλα μάταια.

8. Ἀρισταινέτῳ

1. Ἀκούω σου κεκρατηκέναι τὴν λύπην καὶ
εἶναί σοι περὶ τὸ μνῆμα τὴν διατριβήν. ἐγὼ δὲ
ὥσπερ μὴ λυπούμενον ᾐτιώμην ἄν, οὕτω σφόδρα
λυπούμενον οὐκ ἐπαινῶ. τὸ μὲν γὰρ οὐ τῆς σῆς
φύσεως, τὸ δὲ οὐ τῆς σῆς παιδεύσεως.   2. εἰ δ'

removal to a foreign land and the bitterness they feel for their native soil.   3. My troubles lend credence to your pleas on my behalf. My head is afflicted with a malady that causes me to drink more medicine than wine, my kidney trouble has sent me to my bed, and I have been barred from all that makes life worth living.   4. A witness to my afflictions is Olympius, who has combated my afflictions, a companion of yours, of Hippocrates, and of Plato.[f] I have begged him to clasp you by the knees, tearfully, and to leave no form of supplication untried.   5. So I exhort you, though I would write nothing of this sort to anyone else, for I realize that if you consent, you will suffice, even by yourself, but if you refuse, all else is labour in vain.

[f] Such an erudite companionship is most flattering to Datianus, who began life as the jumped-up son of a bath attendant and advanced as an ill-educated shorthand writer (*Or.* 62.24 f). There is malice in this flattery.

8. To Aristaenetus

1. I am told that your grief has got the better of you and that you spend all your time at her grave.[a] If you were not in mourning I would reprove you; similarly, now that you mourn so excessively, I do not approve. That would have been out of keeping with your character; this is out of keeping with your upbringing.   2. So if you need some consolation

[a] For the death of Aristaenetus' wife cf. *Letter* 6.

373

οὖν δεῖ τινος καὶ παρ' ἄλλου παραμυθίας, πληρώσει ταύτην Ὀλύμπιος ἀμφότερα ὢν ἀγαθός, ψυχάς τε καὶ σώματα νοσημάτων ἐλευθεροῦν.

9. Ἀρισταινέτῳ

1. Οἷον πρᾶγμα νῦν λήψεται τὴν ἀρχὴν δίκαιον ὂν ἀρχαῖον εἶναι· νῦν Σπεκτάτος Ἀρισταινέτῳ ξένος ἔσται. πρὸ τοῦδε οὐ σφόδρα, ταχὺ δὲ ὑμῖν[1] ἐκ τοῦ κέρδους ἡ ζημία φαίνεται καὶ θαυμάζοντες ἀλλήλους τὸν προειμένον[2] αἰτιάσεσθε χρόνον. 2. ἃ μὲν οὖν οὗτος ἤκουσε περὶ σοῦ, τοιαῦτά ἐστιν ὥστε ἐρῶν ἔρχεται· ἃ δὲ εὑρήσεις ἐν τούτῳ σύ, τοιαῦτά ἐστιν ὥστ' ἀπιόντος οὐκ οἴσεις. 3. ἄξιον δὲ τὴν ἀρχὴν τῆς πρὸς τὸν ἄνδρα φιλίας πέρας σοι γενέσθαι τῆς λύπης, ἣν ἐπὶ τῇ γυναικὶ τρέφεις. τὸ μὲν γὰρ Ἡρακλέους οὐ ποιήσει — οἶμαι

[1] ὑμῖν F., conj. Wolf.   ἡμῖν Mss.
[2] προειμένον F. (correction in V)   προιέμενον Wolf (Va, V before correction).

[a] *BLZG* 281, *PLRE* 850 (1).
Libanius' cousin, son of Panolbius, and member of the

from someone else besides, Olympius[b] will provide it. He is good at freeing both souls and bodies from their ills.

[b] Olympius, bearer of this and the preceding letter, had attended Libanius during his ailments of the past year; cf. *Letters* 5.2 and 7.4.

9. To Aristaenetus

1. What a state of things will have its beginning now; it should have happened long since. Now Spectatus[a] is going to be friend of Aristaenetus. There was not much indication up to now, but very soon from your profits your losses become obvious, and in your admiration for each other you will regret the misspent time that's past.   2. He has heard such things of you that he comes to you your devoted admirer. You will find in him such qualities that you will not endure his departure.[b]   3. It is proper that the beginning of your friendship with the man should be the ending of the grief which you still feel for your wife.[c] He will not perform that

Christian and office holding branch of the family; cf. *PLRE*, Stemma 18, p. 1141. Now active in court service as *agens in rebus,* he appears in 358 as tribune and notary (Amm. Marc. 17.5.15).

[b] It is taken for granted that this introduction by Libanius will be the beginning of a friendship.

[c] Cf. *Letters* 6 and 8. This letter, written after the start of the new school session of 355, will have found Aristaenetus in mourning for the best part of a year.

δέ, οὐδ᾽ Ἡρακλῆς ἐποίησεν, ἀλλ᾽ ἡ Ἄλκηστις ἀνιοῦσα μῦθός ἐστιν — ὅση δὲ ἀνθρώπῳ δύναμις, εἰς παραμυθίαν οὐδὲν ἐλλείψει.

10. Ἑορτίῳ

1. Περιεργάζομαι μὲν ἴσως πατέρα παρακαλῶν ἐπιμελεῖσθαι παιδὸς ἀμελεῖν ἐγνωκότα, δακρύοντα δὲ ἰδὼν Θεμίστιον μᾶλλον ἐδεξάμην ἐκεῖνο δόξαι ἢ τοῦτο παριδεῖν.   2. ἔλεγε τοίνυν τραχὺ μὲν οὐδέν, ὡς δὲ λήθη σέ τις αὐτοῦ λάβοι, ἐγὼ δέ, εἰ μὲν ἠπόρεις, ἠξίουν ἄν σε παρὰ τῶν φίλων ἀγείροντα τῷ παιδὶ βοηθεῖν· ἐπεὶ δὲ εὖ ποιῶν ἐν πρώτοις εἶ τῶν εὐπόρων, παραινῶ τι τῶν ὄντων εἰς τὸ τῶν ὄντων σοι τιμιώτατον ἀναλῶσαι. 3. ἴσως μὲν γὰρ οὐδὲ πεῖνα σφόδρα νέῳ χρήσιμον, ἔστι δὲ νῦν οὐ περὶ τῆς γαστρὸς ὁ λόγος, ἀλλ᾽ ὅπως ᾖ τῷ νεανίσκῳ βιβλία· ὧν ἀπόντων ὅμοιος ἔσται τῷ πειρωμένῳ τοξεύειν ἄνευ τόξου μανθάνειν.

---

a *BLZG* 171. Cf. Festugière, *Antioche* p. 107.

b *BLZG* 307 (iii), *PLRE* 894 (2).

labour of Heracles—though Heracles didn't either, I am sure: Alcestis' return from the grave is just a fairy tale—but, as far as is humanly possible, he will leave nothing undone for your consolation.

10. To Heortius[a]

1. I am perhaps playing the busybody in exhorting a father who has made up his mind to neglect his son to have some concern for him, but when I saw Themistius[b] in tears I preferred to be thought to do so than to ignore this.   2. Well, without using any harsh word, he told me that some forgetfulness of him had come over you. If you were a poor man, I would ask you to get contributions from your friends and assist your son, but since fortunately you are one of the foremost men of fortune, my advice is that you spend some of your possessions on the most precious of your possessions.   3. Hunger perhaps is not particularly advantageous for a student either, but the question now is not about the lad's belly but about his books.[c] If he has none, he will be like a man learning archery without a bow.

[c] The purchase of books is a normal item of his students' budget (cf. *Or.* 35.12) and he often, as here, reproves parents and friends who are too mean with their allowances to enable them to do so (e.g. *Epp.* 23, 1352). A subvention of 100 solidi by Anatolius as prefect is described as paltry (*Letter* 46.7).

11. Ἀρισταινέτῳ

1. Ἡ μὲν λέξις τῶν ἐπιστολῶν ἔπειθεν ἡμᾶς ὡς σύνει τῷ Πλάτωνι, τὸ δὲ ἀκμάζειν ἐν σοὶ τὴν ἀθυμίαν ἔτι καὶ τὴν τρίχα πρὸς πένθος ἀνεῖσθαι καὶ τὴν οἰκίαν ὡς ἐπὶ χθὲς τῇ τελευτῇ συμβάσῃ διακεῖσθαι, ταῦτα οὐκέτι πάνυ προσκειμένου τῷ Πλάτωνι. καίτοι πολὺ βέλτιον ἂν ἦν, εἰ τὴν γνώμην μᾶλλον ἢ τὴν γλῶτταν ὤνησο. 2. σὺ μὲν οὖν οἴει σύμφωνα ταῦτα ποιεῖν οἷς περὶ ζῶσαν ἔπραττες, εὐφραίνειν γὰρ δὴ καὶ νῦν ὥσπερ καὶ τότε· δοκεῖς δέ μοι ζῶσαν οὐδὲν λυπήσας πάνυ τοῦτο δρᾶν εἰς ἀπελθοῦσαν. εἰ γὰρ ὅπως σαυτὸν διαφθείρεις αἴσθοιτο, μέγα ἂν στενάξαι τοσούτῳ κακῷ διδοῦσα ἀφορμήν. 3. ἀλλ' ὑπὲρ μὲν τούτων εἰ μὴ σαυτῷ διαλέξῃ, τά γε παρ' ἄλλου μάταια· ἐγὼ δὲ ἃ νοσεῖν πλασάμενος ἔφυγον ἥνπερ ἔφυγον πόλιν, ταῦτα ἐνθάδε νοσῶ. καὶ οὕτως ἄρα ἡδὺ πατρίς, ὥστε ἄμεινόν μοι τῇδε πονεῖσθαι ἢ παρ' ἐκείνοις ὑγιέστερον εἶναι Κρότωνος. 4. τὸ κακὸν δὲ πάλαι μὲν ἐπέκειτο τῇ

---

[a] He continues with the bracing reproofs of *Letters* 6 and 8 concerning the excessive grief shown by Aristaenetus at his wife's death.

11. To Aristaenetus

1. The style of your letter induces me to believe that you are a pupil of Plato, but the continued growth of your despondency within you, your hair let down in sorrow, and the appearance of your household, as though your wife's death occurred but yesterday—all this is certainly not like a devotee of Plato. Indeed, it would be far better if you attended more to your attitude than to your eloquence. 2. You believe that your present behaviour is in harmony with your attitude towards her while she was alive, and that this is as pleasing to her now as that was then. Yet it seems to me that, though you never gave her cause for pain during her life, you are certainly doing so now after her death; for if she saw how you are ruining yourself, she would deeply lament that she gave occasion for such misfortune.[a] 3. But on such a subject, unless you take yourself to task, arguments from another are in vain. As for me, the illness I invented so as to make my escape from Town, I now suffer here in good earnest. And yet my home town is something so dear to me that I would rather suffer this distress here than enjoy all the good health in the world back there.[b] 4. My trouble had long ago affected

[b] *Paroem. Gr.* 1.169, a favourite proverb of Libanius (cf. *Letter* 28.8, *Ep.* 383.3). Croton was noted for its health fanatics; Menand. fr. 263 Koerte, Strabo 6.262.

379

κεφαλῇ, νῦν δὲ εἰς τοὺς νεφροὺς κατέβη, μᾶλλον
δέ τούτους μὲν ἰσχυρῶς πιέζει, τὴν δὲ οὐ τελέως
ἠλευθέρωσεν, ἀλλ' ἐκεῖ τε μένει καὶ τούτους ἐπεί-
ληφεν. 5. ἦρι μὲν οὖν ἄνωθεν ἐρρύη, παντὶ δὲ
ἐνέβαλε σθένει· φάρμακα δὲ πάντα ἠλέγχετο καὶ
ἰατροὶ τὴν μὲν ὑπερβολὴν ἐθαύμαζον, κωλύειν δὲ
οὐκ εἶχον. καὶ διετελέσαμεν ἐνναίοντες[1] αὐτῶν
ταῖς χερσὶ καὶ οὐδὲν ὅ τι οὐκ ἀνεχόμενοι.
6. θεῶν δὲ ἄρα τις ἡμῖν εὔνους, ὅστις, ἐπειδὴ
χρῆν με καμεῖν, ἔδωκε παραμύθιον τὴν Κλημα-
τίου παρουσίαν. ἐλθὼν μὲν γὰρ εὐθὺς ἀκροάσεως
μετέσχεν, ὃ ἦν ἐκείνῳ τε πάμμεγα ἐμοί τε οἷον
οὐκ ἄλλο. 7. ἔπειθ' ὁ μὲν ὑπὲρ τὸν Εὐφράτην
ἐλθὼν τὰ Περσῶν σκεψόμενος, ἐπειδὴ ἐπῄεσαν,
ἀναστρέψας ὀξέως παρεσκεύασε Στρατήγιον
πρᾶξαι ταῦτα ἀφ' ὧν ἐκεῖνοι ταχέως ἀπῆλθον·
ἐμοὶ δὲ ἐνέβαλον ἀλγηδόνες, αἳ τῆς κλίνης ἐξ-
ανιστᾶσαι περιτρέχειν ἠνάγκαζον. 8. ταυτὶ μέν,
ὁπότε οἴκοι μένοι Κλημάτιος, παρακαθημένου
δὲ καὶ τούτων ἐδυνάμην κρατεῖν· οὕτως ἰσχυρό-

---

[1] ἐνναίοντες F.   ἐννέοντες Wolf (Mss.)

---

[c] Clematius' summer mission, on behalf of the praetorian prefect Strategius, had been an intelligence gather-
ing operation concerning Persian movements on the

my head, but now it has gone down to the kidneys—
or, more precisely, while causing them severe pain,
it has not entirely cleared from my head, but it stays
up there, and at the same time subjects them to
attack. 5. Well, in spring down it came from
above and attacked with full force. Cures of all
kinds were tried and found wanting, and the doctors
were amazed at its intensity but could not stop it,
and I continued dwelling under their ministrations
and enduring every kind of discomfort. 6. But
after all one of the gods is kind to me; if I have to
suffer, he has given me the consolation of Clematius'
presence. For as soon as he arrived he participated
in a lecture of mine, and that was a very great thing
for him, and quite incomparable for me.[c] 7. Then
he crossed the Euphrates to observe the activities
of the Persians, and when they advanced, he turned
back and quickly primed Strategius to actions of
which the consequence was their speedy withdrawal.
As for me, I suffered bouts of pain which got me up
from my bed and made me pace to and fro. 8. That
was the case when Clematius stayed at home, but
when he sat in attendance on me I was able to
control even them. He was so much more effective

Eastern frontier. He remained in Antioch until the beginning of winter 355, when he travelled back to headquarters
at Milan in the company of two envoys from Antioch (*Ep.*
447). Between them they took at least 23 letters of
Libanius, of which this is one.

τερος ἦν φαρμάκων πείθων φέρειν, συναχθόμενος,
παίζων, σπουδάζων ἀναμιμνήσκων τῶν ἀρχαίων,
χρηστόν τι προλέγων. 9. τὸ πολὺ δὲ τῶν
λόγων Ἀρισταίνετος ἦν καὶ μετ' ἐκεῖνον Ἄλκιμος,
καὶ παντὶ τῷ παραπίπτοντι τὸ σὸν ὄνομα ἐπει-
σήγετο. εἴτε γάρ τις εἰς ἡμᾶς ἐφάνη ῥάθυμος,
'ἀλλ' οὐκ Ἀρισταίνετός γε τοιοῦτος' ἐλέγετ'
ἄν, εἴτε ὄντως φίλον ἐπήνει, 'ἀλλ' οὐκ Ἀρισταινέτῳ γε παραπλήσιος οὗτος' προσετίθετο ἄν.
10. ὡς δὲ ἐγένετό μοι καὶ θυρῶν ἔξω φανῆναι,
παρά τε τὸν Στρατήγιον ᾖμεν[2] καὶ ἐπὶ λουτρὸν
ἐκεῖθεν, ὁ μὲν λουσόμενος, ἐγὼ δὲ αὐτὸν τῶν
Ὁμήρου τι περιέμενον ᾄδων. διὰ δὲ τὸ σφόδρα
ἀλλήλοις συνεῖναι θαῦμα ἦν ἅτερος[3] ἐπ' ἀγορᾶς
ὁρώμενος, καί τινα σκώμματα ὑπεμένομεν ὡς ἂν
ἐξ ἀλλήλων ἠρτημένω. 11. τὸν θεῖον δέ μου
φιλῶν τε ὥσπερ ἐμὲ καὶ νομίζων περὶ σὲ γνώμης
ἔχειν ὥσπερ ἐγὼ δίκαια ἂν ποιοίης. ὃς εἰς τοῦτο
ἥκει τοῦ πεπεῖσθαι κρατεῖν σε πάντων ἀρετῇ,
ὥστε πρὸ τοῦ μὲν ταῦτα ἀκούων ἥδετο, νῦν δὲ ἐν
τοῖς <φάσκουσιν>[4] ἀριθμεῖται. 12. Κλημάτιος
δὲ αὐτὸν ὡς μὲν νοῦν ἔχοντα πάλαι ἐθαύμασεν,
νῦν δὲ καὶ φιλεῖ, διότι σὲ ἐκεῖνος. καὶ δὴ καὶ <ἃ>[5]

than medicines, as he encouraged me to endure it,
sympathized, joked or spoke in earnest, reminding
me of time past, and foretelling something good to
come. 9. The burden of our talk dealt with
Aristaenetus and, after him, with Alcimus, and your
name acted as the introduction to every fresh topic.
Should anyone show himself to us as a slacker,
"Not like Aristaenetus" he would say; and if he
praised a true friend, "Not a patch on Aristaenetus,
though," he would add. 10. As soon as I could
make my appearance out of doors, we went to visit
Strategius and thence to the bath, he to bathe
while I waited for him reciting a bit of Homer. On
account of our close association with each other, it
was a matter of surprise if just one of us was seen in
the city square, and we put up with some jokes about
us being the inseparables. 11. If you have as
much regard for my uncle as for me, and believe
that his feelings towards you are the same as mine,
you would be right. He has become so convinced of
your superiority in virtue over everyone else that,
whereas previously he enjoyed hearing this said,
now he is counted as one of those who say it.
12. Well, Clematius has long admired him for his
good sense, but now he is firm friends with him,

---

² ἦμεν F.   ἦμεν Wolf (Mss.).

³ ἅτερος F., conj. Re.   ἄστερος Mss.   ἀστέρος Wolf.

⁴ φάσκουσιν F., conj. Re.

⁵ <ἃ> Norman,   <ὡς> Re.

αὐτὸν ἐκ Ῥώμης ἥκοντα ἤρου φάσκοντα ἀνδράσιν
ἐντυχεῖν ἀγαθοῖς αὐτόθι, διηγήσατο πολλάκις·
ἔλεγε δὲ ὡς αὐτὸς μὲν ἥκων ἐπαινοῖ τὴν ἐν Ῥώμῃ
βουλὴν ἐπὶ φρονήσει, σὺ δ᾽ εἰ Φασγανίῳ τις
προσόμοιος, πύθοιο. 13. τοῦτο δὲ ἡμῖν ἐντιμότε-
ρον ἢ εἰ Πινδάρῳ πολλὰ εἰς τὴν ἡμετέραν οἰκίαν
ἐγέγραπτο. Κλημάτιον δὲ τὸ μὲν ἐρώτημα ἀπαγ-
γείλαντα καὶ ὡς ἠπόρησεν ἀποκρίσεως ἐπαινῶ,
μέμφομαι δὲ ὅτι με βουλόμενος ὑγιαίνειν ἔσθ᾽ ὅτε
καὶ ἀρρωστοῦντος ἥδετο. εἰδὼς γὰρ ὡς μὴ
νοσοῦντος μὲν ἀπεκλείετ᾽ ἂν ὑπὸ τῶν βιβλίων,
ἀσθενοῦντι δὲ ἔχει λαλεῖν, ὁπότε ἐθέλοι, λαβών με
ῥᾴω ποτὲ τοῦτο ἐξελάλησεν, ὡς ἄρα τι αὐτῷ καὶ
χαρίσαιτο ἡ νόσος. 14. σὺ δ᾽ αὐτὸν ἢ ἐν Νικαίᾳ
κατέχειν, ἕως ἂν πάντα ἀκούσῃς — ὡς πολλήν γε
κομίζει διήγησιν — ἢ συνοδοιπορεῖν εἰς Νικομή-
δειαν ὑπὲρ τῆς ἀκοῆς.

since he is so with you. Indeed, he has often told of the questions you put to him when he came from Rome with his tale of all the good fellows he had met there. He said that when he, on his arrival, spoke in praise of the Senate in Rome for its intellectual gifts, you wanted to know whether there was anyone at all to match Phasganius. 13. This is a greater source of pride to me than anything Pindar might have composed upon my family. I approve Clematius for his report of your question and of his inability to answer it, but I have one complaint against him: for all his desire to bring me to health, there were times when he was quite pleased to find me ill. He knew that if I were not ill, access to me would be barred by my books, whereas if I were, he would be able to talk to me whenever he liked, and once when he found me better he exclaimed that my illness, after all, did him a good turn. 14. So either keep him in Nicaea until you hear all he has to tell—for he is bringing a whole budget of news— or accompany him on his way to Nicomedeia for the hearing of it.

12. Θεμιστίῳ

1. Συνήσθην φιλοσοφίᾳ τε καὶ τῷ βασιλεῖ· τῷ μέν, ὅτι τὸ κάλλιστον ὧν ἔδοσαν ἀνθρώπῳ θεοὶ τιμᾶν ἐπίσταται· τῇ δ᾽, ὅτι καὶ παρὰ τῶν ἐν ἐξουσίαις θαυμάζεται. σοὶ δ᾽ ἂν ἔχοι χάριν αὐτή τε καὶ ἐκεῖνος· σὺ γὰρ ἀμφοῖν αἴτιος τούτων τυχεῖν. 2. ἐγὼ δὲ καὶ πρὶν ἐπιστεῖλαί σε[1] πρὸς ἐμὲ ταῦτα ᾔδειν ἐκ τῶν πρὸς τὸν ἄριστον ἡκόντων Στρατήγιον γραμμάτων. ἔδωκε γὰρ ἅ τε σὺ πρὸς αὐτὸν καὶ ἃ περὶ σοῦ πρὸς τὴν βουλὴν ὁ πάντα ἀγαθὸς ἔγραψε βασιλεύς. ἃ δὴ δι᾽ ἑρμηνέως ὅ τι εἴη μαθόντες ὑπερεχαίρομεν. ἐγένετο δὲ καὶ τούτων τῶν γραμμάτων πρεσβυτέρα φήμη καὶ οὐκ ἠπιστήθη, ταχὺ δὲ προσετέθη καὶ τὰ γράμματα. 3. κάλλιστον δὲ τῶν πεπραγμένων τὸ δι᾽ ὧν μὲν

---

[1] ἐπιστεῖλαί σε F., conj. Re.   ἐπιστείλεις Va.   ἐπιστείλοις Wolf (V. before correction into -λης)

---

[a] *BLZG* 291 (i), *PLRE* 889 (1).   Bouchery pp. 51 ff. Dagron, pp. 20, 60 ff. F/Kr. 57.

In recognition of his preeminence as a philosopher, Themistius was granted citizenship of Constantinople and Senatorial rank by the *Demegoria* sent to the Senate in Constantinople by Constantius (still absent in Italy) on 1 Sept. 355. The grateful Themistius responded with his Oration 2 (November 355): cf. Themistius, *Orationes* edd. Schenkl, Downey, Norman, Vol. iii, pp. 122 ff, Vol. i,

12. To Themistius[a]

1. I rejoiced for philosophy[b] and for the emperor—for him because he knows how to honour the greatest gift the gods have given man, and for it, because it is admired even among the powers that be. Both it and he should be grateful to you, for you are responsible for them both achieving this. 2. Before ever you wrote to me I knew of it from the letters which reach our noble Strategius, for he gave me your letter to him, and that with which our most excellent emperor addressed the Senate about you. I learned of its contents by means of a translator and was highly delighted. But even these letters were preceded by rumour—nor was she disbelieved—and very soon the letters arrived as confirmation.[c] 3. Your finest achievement is that,

pp. 28 ff. Dagron, p. 20.

[b] Cf. Plat. *Lysis* 213d; a delicate compliment to Themistius.

[c] News of Themistius' elevation comes first by rumour; then by a letter sent by Themistius to the praetorian prefect Strategius, together with the Latin text of the Demegoria, which is translated in Antioch for Libanius' benefit; and finally by personal letter from Themistius to Libanius, to which this is the reply. This therefore is dated to late November at the earliest ("around the beginning of winter," *Ep.* 491.1). Seeck (*BLZG* 295 n.) wrongly deduced that Themistius himself translated the Latin text of the *Demegoria* into the present Greek text. Themistius admits elsewhere (*Or.* 6, 71c ff) that he did not know enough Latin for such a task.

ἦν μετασχεῖν τῆς βουλῆς μὴ ἀτιμάσαι, τὰ δὲ τὸ
κέρδος φέροντα ἐμμελῶς διώσασθαι. τοῦτο γὰρ ἦν
αὐτόν τε τιμῆσαι καὶ τὸ δικαίως ὑπ' ἐκείνου τετιμῆσθαι δεῖξαι.   4. τὸ δ' ἐμὸν οὕτως ἔχει· τὰ τοῦ
σώματος ἀρρωστήματα παραινεῖ μοι μένειν. εὖ δὲ
ἴσθι, κἂν εἰ σφόδρα ἦν ὑγιής, ἐμαυτῷ σύμβουλος
ἂν ἐγενόμην μένειν. τῇδε μὲν γὰρ ἀγέλαι² νέων
εὐπορία,³ τὸ δὲ παρ' ὑμῖν διδάσκειν λόγους ἀρχὴ
Σκυρία.

² ἀγέλαι Wolf (Mss.)   ἀγέλαις F., conj. Re. Bouchery,
Fat./Kr.
³ εὐπορία F.   εὐπορίαι Wolf (Mss.).

13. Δατιανῷ

1. Ἴσως μὲν ἐμοὶ καὶ πρὸς τὰ παρόντα βοηθεῖν
ἐθελήσεις ἐμέ τε σώζων διὰ τέλους καὶ τὰς ἔμπροσθεν εὐεργεσίας· εἰ δέ με δεῖ καὶ τοῦτο ἀτυχῆ-
σαι τὸ τὴν σὴν γνώμην ἑτέραν γεγονέναι, τάς γε
πρὸ τοῦ βοηθείας οὔποτε ἐκβαλοῦμεν τῆς ψυχῆς,
ἀλλ' ἐκείνας μὲν τῇ σῇ φύσει λογιούμεθα, τὴν δ'
αὖ μεταβολὴν δαίμονι δυσκόλῳ.   2. καίτοι πρὸς
τῶν πόνων, οὓς ἐπόνησας ὑπὲρ Ἑλλήνων τε καὶ
φίλων, θὲς μὲν ἐρρῶσθαί μοι τὸ σῶμα, βελτίω δὲ

while not disdaining the means whereby you became a member of the Senate, you have deliberately repulsed all that brings financial gain, for this means personal distinction for yourself and clear indication that you have been duly honoured by him.[d]   4. My own situation is as follows; my physical ailments bid me stay here, but you may be sure that, however well I might be, I would have counselled myself to stay, for here the flocks of students provide results in plenty, whereas the teaching profession among you in Town is utter misery.[e]

[d] The grant was accompanied by a rise in salary, which was refused (Them. *Or.* 2.26a).

[e] ἀρχὴ Σκυρία—Scyros was proverbially rocky and unproductive: cf. *Paroem. Gr.* 1.11.

13. To Datianus

1. You will perhaps be ready to assist me in the present situation also, by continuing to maintain me and your previous kindness. However, if I must needs be unfortunate in this too, that your feelings have changed, I shall never expel from my mind the memory of your former assistance,[a] but that I shall ascribe to your own character, and any change to the intervention of an envious spirit.   2. Yet in the name of all the labours you have undertaken on behalf of Greeks and friends, you must know that I

[a] Cf. *Or.* 1.94. *Letter* 7 and note.

τήνδε ἐκείνης ἡγούμενόν με φεύγειν ἐκείνην, τὸ
βελτίω δὲ ὅπως ἀκούσῃ πρὸς τὰς τῶν νέων συνουσίας. 3. ἔπειτα ἐροῦ τὸν βασιλέα, δύνασαι δὲ
σωφροσύνῃ τε καὶ εὐνοίᾳ διηνεκεῖ τὴν δύναμιν
κεκτημένος· 'ὦ βασιλεῦ, ἀνὴρ ἐκεῖνος, ὃν κελεύ-
εις εἰς Θρᾴκην ἐλθεῖν, ἐλθὼν μὲν ἐκεῖσε προσόμοιος ἔσται γεωργῷ πλέοντι καὶ ἐν νηὶ ζῶντι συνεχῶς. 4. οὔτε γὰρ ἐκείνῳ τὴν θάλατταν ἔστιν
ἀροῦν οὔτε τούτῳ σπείρειν εἰς νέους τῶν πολιτῶν
μὲν πρὸς ἕτερα τεραμμένων, τῶν ξένων δὲ ὑφορω-
μένων τὸ χωρίον καὶ νομιζόντων διδασκαλεῖον
εἶναι τρυφῆς. 5. ἡ Συρία δὲ Μουσῶν ἐργαστήριον πολὺν ἤδη χρόνον δημιουργοῦσα ῥήτορας, ὧν
εἷς οὗτος Καλλιόπιος, ᾧ χαίρεις, καὶ πολλὴ
πολλαχόθεν νεότης θήγουσά τε παιδευτὴν καὶ
αὐτὴ λαμβάνουσα ἐφ' ὅπερ ἥκει. πότερον οὖν
βούλει σοι τὸν βουκόλον ἀπορεῖν βοῶν ἢ περὶ
συχνὴν ἀγέλην χρῆσθαι τῇ τέχνῃ;' 6. ταῦτ'
ἀκούων ἀποκρινεῖται σοῦ μειδιῶντος καὶ ἐν τῷ
βλέμματι πρὸς τὸ δεύτερον ἐνάγοντος· 'βόες

---

[b] Now, at the beginning of winter 355/6, Constantius
was holding court at Milan.

[c] His disparagement of Constantinople as a boorish and

am in good health, but that I left town in the
thought that living here is better for me than there,
and please understand "better" as applying to my
classes with my students.   3. And tell the
emperor,[b] as you can, since you have won your position of influence by your tact and consistent kindliness, "Sire, this fellow, whom you are bidding come
to Thrace will if he comes here, be like a farmer
afloat, all at sea always.   4. As the farmer cannot
plough the sea, he cannot sow his seed among the
young, since the citizens have devoted themselves to
other things and visitors disdain the place and
regard it as a school for scandal.[c]   5. Syria however is a factory of the Muses:[d] for a long time now
it has fashioned orators, one of them being Calliopius here,[e] with whom you are well pleased, and
there is a mass of students from many quarters that
sharpens a teacher and itself gets what it has come
for. So do you prefer your herdsman to have no
stock or to employ his skill upon a large herd?"
6. On hearing this, as your smiling glance directs
him to the second alternative, he will answer, "Let

uncultivated place is best expressed in *Or.* 1.75 f; he constantly inveighs against the luxury of the capital, e.g. *Or.*
1.48, 279; *Letter* 4.16.

[d] Cf. *Or.* 11.181 ff.

[e] *BLZG* 99 (i), *PLRE* 174 (2). A companion letter (*Ep.*
442) is addressed to him. He had a position in which he
handled imperial correspondence (*Ep.* 410.4).

ἔστωσαν τῷ βουκόλῳ.' 7. εἰ δέ με οἰήσῃ ῥαψῳ-
δεῖν καὶ μύθους ταῦτα ἡγησάμενος ἀμελήσεις,
ἀλλ' ἔγωγε ἀποσπώμενος βοήσομαι ὅτι με τῆς
Ἀντιοχείας ἀνέπεισεν ἔχεσθαι Δατιανὸς καὶ τὸ
κάλλος, ᾧ Δατιανὸς τὴν πόλιν ἐλάμπρυνε, λουτρὰ
τὰ μὲν τετελεσμένα, τὰ δὲ ἀνιόντα, στοὰ τετα-
μένη τε εἰς μῆκος καὶ εἰς ὥραν ἀνθοῦσα τοσοῦτον
ἔχουσα ἐν τῇ πόλει, ὅσον ὁ τοῦ Πέλοπος ὦμος ἐν
τῷ σώματι τοῦ Πέλοπος. ὅρα οὖν εἴ σοι λίαν ἀδεὲς
ἕλκεσθαί με.   8. ταύτην μὲν οὖν τὴν παιδιὰν
ἵλεως οἶδ' ὅτι δέξῃ, κοινὴν δὲ ἡμῖν ἴσθι πεποιηκὼς
ἑορτήν, ἃς Πομπηιανῷ παρέστησας ἐλπίδας. ὁ
γὰρ ἀνὴρ οἷος εὖ πράττων πολίτας εὐφραίνειν.
9. ἦν μὲν γὰρ καὶ ἐκ νέου μέτριος καὶ τὸ ἄλυπος
εἶναι μελετῶν, ἐπήσκησε δὲ τὸν τρόπον εἰς σέ τε
βλέπων καὶ πειρώμενος αὐτὸν ἄξιον τῆς σῆς δια-
νοίας δεικνύναι. διὸ δὴ καὶ νῦν ὑπὸ κοινῶν εὐχῶν
στέλλεται πάντων ἐπιθυμούντων ἔγκαρπον αὐτῷ
καταστῆναι τὴν ὁδόν.   10. εἰ δὲ γένοιτο τῷ μὲν

---

[f] Plat. *Gorg.* 523a.

[g] For Datianus' public works in Antioch see *Ep.* 435.6,
Or. 11.194.

[h] Pelops, as a child, was cut up and cooked by his father

the herdsman have his herd." 7. If you think that I am waxing lyrical and regard this as a mere fairy tale[f] and so ignore it, then when I am being dragged away, I shall cry aloud, "I was induced by Datianus to cleave to Antioch, and the beauties with which Datianus glorified our city, the baths, both those completed and those still going up, that long and extensive portico with its gleaming perfection,[g] that fulfils in our city the function that Pelops' shoulder did in the body of Pelops."[h] So see whether it is quite safe for you that I should be haled away. 8. I know that you will take this joke well, but be assured that you have made it a red-letter day for us all by the expectations you have aroused in Pompeianus,[i] for he is the sort of man who succeeds in obliging his fellow citizens. 9. From his youth up he has been well balanced, concerning himself not to give offence, and he has cultivated this talent by observing you and trying to show himself worthy of your approval. Hence he is even now speeded on his way by the prayers of all, since all desire his journey to be a fruitful one for him. 10. Should he

as a feast for the gods. Demeter absent-mindedly ate one shoulder, after which Pelops was replaced in the pot and brought back to life in perfect beauty, his missing shoulder being replaced with one made of ivory; cf. Pind. *Ol.* 1.24 ff.

[i] *BLZG* 241 (ii); he was one of the Antiochene envoys sent to court simultaneously with Clematius (*ibid.* 323), presumably on the occasion of Julian's elevation to the rank of Caesar. Libanius' plea on this matter produces no result (cf. *Letter* 38).

τὰ πατρῷα, ἡ μονὴ δὲ ἐμοί, παιᾶνα εἰς τοὺς
αἰτίους ᾀσόμεθα.

14. Φασγανίῳ

1. Ἐρωτᾷς ὅπως ἔχει μοι τὰ πράγματα, τὸ σὸν
δὲ ὅπως σοι σῶμα πέπραγεν οὐ μηνύεις ὥσπερ οὐ
πλείονος οὔσης ἡμῖν ὑπὲρ ἐκείνου φροντίδος ἢ σοὶ
περὶ τούτων. ἄκουε δὴ οὖν.   2. γράμμα οὐδὲν
ἥκει μοι φοβερόν, Σπεκτάτος δὲ καὶ χρηστὸν
ἐπαγγέλλεται. ὁ δὲ μάργος ἐκεῖνος καὶ τὴν
Μεγάλην φθείρων πόλιν ἥν τε ἐκαρπούμην ἐκ τῆς
πόλεως τροφὴν εἰς ἑτέρους μετέθηκε γνώμῃ βασιλέως χρησάμενος καὶ χρυσὸν εἰσπράττει δή με
πρὸς τὸν ἄρχοντα ἐπιστείλας.   3. ἐφ' οἷς οὕτως
ἠγανάκτησε Στρατήγιος, ὥστ' οὐ πώποτε τηλι-
κοῦτον ἀνεβόησε. καὶ δὴ καὶ ταῦτα ἡμῖν εὔνουν
τὸν ἄνδρα ποιεῖ· τὸν γὰρ ὑπ' ἐκείνου μισούμενον
οἴεται προσήκειν εὖ πάσχειν ὑφ' ἑαυτοῦ.   4. τὰ
δὲ περὶ τοὺς νέους τὰ μὲν ἄλλα ᾗ πρὸ τοῦ, Ἰούλιος
δὲ ὁ γραμματιστὴς ὑπὸ λύπης οἴχεται, καὶ γνοὺς

obtain his family possessions and I permission to stay, we will raise a paean of praise to those responsible.

14. To Phasganius[a]

1. You inquire how things are going on with me without telling me about your physical condition, as if I were not much more concerned about your health than you could ever be about my affairs. Well then, just listen. 2. No letter has reached me to cause me alarm, and Spectatus forecasts good news even. But that fathead who is ruining the capital has made use of an imperial decree to divert to others the emoluments I received from the city, and is even dunning me for gold in his letters to the prefect.[b] 3. Strategius was so annoyed at this that he has never protested so forcefully. Indeed, this brings me into favour with him, for he thinks it right that I, the object of that fellow's dislike, should be kindly treated by him. 4. As regards the students, things are generally as they were, but Julius

[a] *BLZG* 234: uncle of Libanius and of Spectatus (for whom see *Letter* 9), unusually absent from Antioch at this time, evidently on private business.

[b] Libanius' salary in Constantinople was still being credited on him. The payment was made in kind, but the proconsul of the city (Photius) was pressing for repayment in gold, and so informed the praetorian prefect.

Εὐδαίμων ὡς οὔπω πάντα αὐτῷ ῥᾴδια, Σεβαστια-
νὸν πείθει δεηθῆναί μου νεῖμαί τι προνοίας αὐτῷ.[1]
5. τῷ δὲ Εὐβούλῳ δῆλός τε ἐγενόμην ἡδέως ἂν
ἰδὼν Ἀκάκιον ἐνθάδε καὶ ἐποιήσατο περὶ τούτου
πρὸς τὸν ἄρχοντα λόγον προσθεὶς ὡς ἄρα ἀρέ-
σκοντά μοι ποιοῖ. ὁ δὲ οὐ μάλα προσέσχεν οὐκ οἰό-
μενος δεῖν ἄκοντα ἕλκειν τὸν ἄνθρωπον, ἐκ δὲ
Παλαιστίνης ἀφιγμένοι τῶν γνωρίμων τινὲς
λέγουσί τε ὡς αὐτοῦ μένει[2] καί τινα ἐπίδειξιν
ἀπαγέλλουσιν οὐκ εὐτυχῆ. 6. ὁ δὲ Ἡρωδιανὸς
προσιὼν ἐμέ τε αὐτοῦ ποιεῖται κύριον καὶ ἐφ' οἷς
Οὐράνιος ζῆν ἀξιοῖ. καὶ πολλὰ τὰ σοῦ χρῄζοντα,
τὰ μὲν ἐμά, τὰ δὲ κοινά.

---

[1] αὐτῷ F. αὐτῷ Wolf (Mss.).
[2] μένει Wolf (Mss.) μενεῖ F.

---

[c] Julius, *BLZG* 193 (i), and Eudaemon, *BLZG* 131 (ii),
PLRE 289 (2), were both teachers in Antioch who saw
Libanius as a dangerous rival upon his removal there.
Eudaemon, however, became his firm friend in later years.

[d] *BLZG* 271 (ii), *PLRE* 812 (2). At this time (winter
355/6) he was passing through Antioch. Soon afterwards
he is found as *dux* in Egypt.

[e] Eubulus, *principalis* of Antioch and long-standing
opponent of Phasganius and of Libanius, was identified by
Foerster (Vol. x, 760 f) as Libanius' rival in his first years

the grammarian is dying of chagrin and Eudaemon,[c] realizing that all is not plain sailing for him yet, is persuading Sebastianus[d] to prevail upon me to show him a bit of consideration.   5. I made it clear to Eubulus that I would be glad to see Acacius here,[e] and he gave an address on the subject to the governor, adding that this met with my approval. However he paid no particular attention since he did not think it necessary to have the fellow fetched back against his will.[f] Some of the notables who have arrived from Palestine say that he is staying there, and they report an unsuccessful declamation of his. 6. Herodianus has approached me and puts himself at my disposal, and asks to live on the same terms as Uranius.[g] There are many things that require your presence, some personal to me, others public.

in Antioch (cf. *Or.* 1.90 ff). However, the interpretation of Wolf (*Schulwesen* 93 ff) and Petit (*Autobiographie*, 228 f) is obviously correct: Acacius was the sophistic rival of *Oration* 1, Eubulus his sponsor and support in the curia. They acted together as propagandist and politician in opposition to the threatened family caucus of Phasganius and Libanius. Eubulus, himself praised after his death as a foremost orator of the curia, continued to show hostility to Libanius long after the death of Phasganius and the departure of Acacius (cf. *Or.* 1.156). The relationship between Libanius and Acacius between 354 and 361 is explained in detail by Petit (236 f).

[f] Cf. *Or.* 1.110.

[g] For these and other assistant teachers of Libanius, see Wolf, 66 ff.

15. Γοργονίῳ

1. Ἥκει σοι καιρὸς παρέχων εὖ ποιῆσαι ἅπαν τὸ Ἑλληνικόν. Ἰμερίῳ γὰρ βίος μέν ἐστι παιδεύειν, τόπος δὲ τῆς συνουσίας Ἀθῆναι, κτήματα δὲ ἐν Ἀρμενίᾳ.   2. τιμῆς δὲ τῆς μὲν ἄκρας ἄξιος ἀνήρ, τυγχάνει δὲ οὐδὲ μικρᾶς, ἀλλ' ἐπιθέμενοι Λυκοῦργοί τινες ἐλαύνουσι τὸν Διόνυσον καὶ γέγονεν αὐτῷ τἀκεῖ Μυσῶν λεία. καίτοι τῷ μὲν εἰς χρήματα ἡ βλάβη, οἱ δὲ εἰς τὸν θεὸν ὃς ἔδωκε λόγους ἀσεβοῦντες οὐκ αἰσθάνονται.   3. σοὶ τοίνυν πρέπει τῶν ταῦτα κωλυόντων, οὐ τῶν ποιούντων ἕνα γενέσθαι. ῥᾴδιον δέ σοι παρεδρεύοντι καὶ κοινωνοῦντι τῆς ἀρχῆς.   4. δεῖξον δὴ τοῖς ἐχθροῖς τῶν Μουσῶν ὅτι εἰσί τινες καὶ φίλοι ταῖς Μούσαις τῶν ἐχθρῶν δυνατώτεροι, καὶ πράξει μιᾷ χάρισαι μὲν θεοῖς Ἑλληνίοις, χάρισαι δὲ τῷ τε

---

[a] *BLZG* 165 (iv), *PLRE* 399 (4): assessor in Armenia (§ 3) and father of Libanius' pupil Aquila (§ 4). Evidently pagan.

Although Libanius regarded rivalry as the norm, he was generous in cooperation and assistance toward those who posed no professional threat. Other examples of this

15. To Gorgonius[a]

1. The opportunity has come allowing you to be a benefactor to the whole Greek world. Himerius'[b] livelihood is teaching; the location of his classes, Athens; his property in Armenia. 2. The man deserves the utmost respect, and enjoys no little of it, but some people harry him, as Lycurgus did Dionysus,[c] and his possessions there have become a free for all.[d] Yet, while his is a financial loss, they disregard their act of sacrilege towards the god who has granted eloquence. 3. So it becomes you to be one of the preventers of such acts, not of the performers of them: and it is easy for you, since you are an assessor and associate of the governor. 4. Then show the enemies of the Muses that the Muses have their friends too, more influential than their enemies, and by one and the same action confer favour on the gods of Greece, upon the writer

are found in his support of a kinsman of the Christian sophist Proaeresius (*Letter* 73), and even of his rival Acacius, for whom he secured an increased allowance (*Ep.* 274.5, *Or.* 1.110).

[b] The famous Bithynian sophist, *PLRE* 436 (2). Cf. Himerius, *Orationes* ed. Colonna (Rome, 1951); T. D. Barnes, "Himerius and the Fourth Century," *Classical Philology* 82 (1982): 206.

[c] Cf. Hom. *Il.* 6.130 ff, Lib. *Or.* 18.8.

[d] Proverbial: cf. *Or.* 12.40, *Paroem. Gr.* 1.122.

ἐπιστέλλοντι καὶ περὶ οὗ τὰ γράμματα, δίδαξον δὲ τὸν υἱὸν Ἀκύλαν ὡς οὐκ ἄτιμον οἱ λόγοι.

16. Θεμιστίῳ

1. Ὁμολογῶ μὴ πυκνὰ γράφειν. ἡ δὲ αἰτία παρ' ὑμῖν. ὥστε καὶ νῦν ὅτι γέγραφα θαυμάζω. τί οὖν ἀδικοῦντες ἠναγκάσατε[1] σιγᾶν; ἢν ἂν ἐπιστολὴν λάβητε, τοῖς ἐνταῦθα εὐθὺς ἔγνωσται. καὶ προδιδόντες τὸν Φίλιον ἐν τῷ Καρὶ κινδυνεύειν οἴεσθε. 2. εἶθ' ὑμεῖς μὲν ἐπ' ἀγορᾶς δείκνυτε τὰ γράμματα, πνεῦμα δὲ ἐκεῖθεν ἀρθὲν καὶ δεῦρο ἐμπεσὸν κύματα ἡμῖν ἐγείρει καὶ ποιεῖ ταῦτα ἃ Μακεδόνιος εἰδώς, εἴ τις ἔροιτο, διδάξει. 3. τὴν μὲν οὖν πληγὴν ἐκείνην οὐκ ἂν ἰάσαιτό τις, δέομαι δὲ ὑμῶν μὴ προσθεῖναι δευτέραν. ὅταν δέ μοι παραινῇς μὴ τῷ πράττειν εὖ τῶν φίλων ἀμνημονεῖν, αὐτὸς ἐπιλελῆσθαι φαίνῃ τῶν φίλων. 4. ἐμὲ γὰρ ὅτι τούτων δὴ τῶν τοῖς πολλοῖς δοκούντων

---

[1] ἠναγκάσατε VVa (Vind.)   ἠναγκάσατε μὴ Wolf (S)   ἠναγκάσατέ με F., conj. Re.

---

[a] Bouchery pp. 63 ff. The letter is conveyed by the sons of Bassus (Epp. 482, 483). Themistius is reproved for broadcasting in Constantinople the contents of Libanius' letter. When news of it was reported back to Antioch,

and the subject of this letter, and teach your son Aquila that eloquence is not a thing without honour.

16. To Themistius[a]

1. I agree that I do not write very much, but the reason lies with you, so much so that even now I am surprised that I have written at all. So what wrong have you done me that you have forced me to silence? Just this—that any letter you get is immediately known to people here. You betray Zeus of friendship and think to put me in the firing line instead.[b] 2. So you in the city square display my letters; wind of it rises there, rushes here and creates storms for me, with consequences that Macedonius[c] knows and will describe on request. 3. So though that particular damage is perhaps beyond curing, I beg you—no more of the kind. When you advise me not to forget my friends in my success, you yourself seem to me to have forgotten your friends. 4. You have long known that none

trouble had arisen between himself and the prefect Strategius. Strategius had plans for Themistius also to remove to Antioch, a scheme which Themistius refused.

[b] The reference to Caria in the Greek is proverbial: cf. Plat. *Lach.* 187b and schol., *Paroem. Gr.* 2.404 f. (*Apostol.* vii.39). Carians were mercenaries and cheap, and so more suitable than citizens to be placed at risk.

[c] *BLZG* 199 (vi): a regular emissary and informant between Themistius and Libanius in the years 355–359 (cf. *Ep.* 463.1, 83–86).

ἀγαθῶν οὐδὲν οὐδεπώποτε ἐπῆρε, πάλαι μὲν
ᾔδεις, νῦν δὲ οὐ βούλει καίτοι μοι πολλάκις ἐπιτι-
μῶν ὅτι τὰς τῶν ἀρχόντων δυνάμεις οὐκ ἠξίουν
θεραπεύειν, ὃ τοσούτῳ νῦν πλέον φυλάττεται, ὅσῳ
προστίθησιν εἰς τὸ θαρρεῖν ἡ πατρίς. 5. καὶ μὴν
εἰ καὶ σφόδρα οὕτως εἶχον ὡς τοῦτο εὐτυχίαν
ἄγειν, ἑτέρων γε νῦν τὸ δύνασθαι τῶν καὶ ἡμᾶς
ἀφῃρημένων τὸ δύνασθαι. ζήτει οὖν, ὅστις σοι
πράξει τὰς διαλλαγάς· ὡς ἔγωγε δέδοικα μὴ τοῦ
πράγματος ἁπτόμενος Ἀκεσίας γένωμαι.

17. Ἀνδρονίκῳ

1. Οἷον ἔδρασας, Ἀνδρόνικε; σοὶ μὲν ἐγὼ
γέγραφα, σὺ δὲ ἑτέροις ἔδειξας, οἱ δὲ εἰς τοὺς
ἐνθάδε ἐξήνεγκαν, καὶ γέγονας ἡμῖν ἀρχὴ πολέμου. εἶτα τοιαῦτα ἁμαρτὼν ἀφεὶς παραιτεῖσθαι
ἐγκαλεῖς. καὶ πονηρὸν ἴσως καλεῖς, ὅτι σοι τὴν
δι᾽ Ἅρματος γράφω δέον θαυμάζειν ὅτι σοι γρά-

---

a BLZG 71 (ii), PLRE 64 (3).

Like Themistius, Andronicus published abroad a
private letter from Libanius, causing him to incur the
displeasure of Strategius. Andronicus is at odds with his
uncle who, as is proved by Bouchery (pp. 63 ff), is Strategius (not Nebridius, as in BLZG 73 and PLRE 65) over (i)

of these so-called blessings of ordinary folk has ever
had any attraction for me, but now you will have
none of it. And yet you reprove me for not deigning
to cultivate the influence of the governors—it is a
practice that is now maintained proportionately to
the support provided by my native city. 5. Indeed, however much I am disposed to regard this as
a mark of success, the influence now lies with other
people, those who have robbed even me of my
influence. So look for someone to effect your reconciliation, for I am afraid that, if I put my hand to the
business, I will do more harm than good.[d]

[d] Cf. *Ep.* 316.2, *Paroem. Gr.* 1.21.

17. To Andronicus[a]

1. What have you done, Andronicus? I write a
letter to you, you show it to somebody else, they
report it to people here, and you leave me with a
fight on my hands. And then, after such misconduct
as that, so far from begging my pardon, you level
accusations at me. You call me a rascal perhaps

a friendship with Cleomenes, of which Libanius also disap-
proves, and (ii) property demanded by his uncle, to which
Libanius thought he should accede for the sake of peace
and quiet.

φειν ἐτόλμησα.   2. εἰ μὲν οὖν ἀλλὰ νῦν Ἀττικοὶ
τὰ Ἐλευσίνια, πάλιν ἐπιστελοῦμεν· εἰ δὲ προθήσεις[1] πρόσθε τῶν Ἐπωνύμων τῷ βουλομένῳ
μαθεῖν, ὁμολογήσεις τῆς σιωπῆς ἡμῶν ἐρᾶν.

[1] προθήσεις F., conj. Re.   προσθήσεις Wolf (Mss.).

---

[b] The proverb τὴν δι' Ἅρματος ἀστραπήν is explained by
Strabo 9.2.11: a district of Attica where omens were regularly looked for and seldom came. Cf. *Ep.* 607.3.
[c] Cf. *Paroem. Gr.* 1.39, 188. At the Eleusinia Athenians
alone were present and the proceedings were secret.
[d] Cf. Demosth. *Timocr.* 18, 23.   Before an ecclesia any

18. Στρατηγίῳ

1. Ἠλγήσαμέν τε ὡς οὔπω πρότερον καὶ ἤσθη-
μεν ὡς οὐκ ἄλλοτε· τὸ μέν, ὅτι σοι ἔκαμνεν ἡ
γυνή, γυνὴ τὰς ὑμνουμένας ἀρετῇ νικῶσα, τὴν δὲ
εὐθυμίαν ἐποίει τὸ τὴν νόσον εἶξαι τοῖς ἰατροῖς. εὖ
δὲ ἴσθι, καὶ μὴ παρόντων ἰατρῶν ἐσῴζετ' ἂν ὀφει-
λόντων σοι τῶν θεῶν χάριν ἀντὶ τῆς περὶ πάντα
δικαιοσύνης.   2. ἡ πόλις δὲ ἡμῖν ἐν χορείαις τὸ
νῦν καὶ πρόφασις μὲν οἱ γάμοι, τὸ δὲ ἀληθές, ὑπὸ

---

[a] Although a Christian, Strategius, with his official
nickname Musonianus, could receive without qualms this

404

because I write to you now and then,[b] but you ought to be surprised that I pluck up courage to write to you at all.   2. Well, if you tell me, "All right! I'll keep mum,"[c] I will write to you again. But if you go and blazon it abroad for all and sundry,[d] when anyone wants to pick up a bit of gossip, you will be confessing that you desire my silence.

Athenian who wished to propose new legislation had to publish a draft before the statues of the Eponymous heroes. Only if Andronicus is discreet in handling correspondence will he continue to receive letters on such private matters from Libanius.

18. To Strategius

1. I have experienced such sorrow and such elation as never before—sorrow at the illness of your wife, a lady who excels in virtue all the heroines of legend, elation induced by the fact that her illness has yielded to her doctors. Rest assured that, even had not doctors been there, she would be safe, for the gods are indebted[a] to you for your utter incorruptibility.   2. Our city is in festive mood; the reason they adduce is the marriage,[b] but the truth is

pagan compliment, knowing that the Muses are among these gods.

[b] Strategius' daughter had recently been married in Antioch (*Ep.* 478.1). In his time in Constantinople Libanius had delivered an oration in her honour (*Letter* 25.2).

τοῦ πεπαῦσθαι τὸν φόβον εἰς τοῦτο κεκίνηνται. εἰ δέ, ὃ μάλιστα ποθοῦμεν, προσθείης καὶ φανείης ἄγων μετὰ τῆς μητρὸς τὰ παιδία, διπλῆν ἑορτὴν ἐργάσῃ. 3. καὶ οὐκ ἀγνοῶ μὲν ὅτι με παρόντα χρῆν τῶν τε ἐλπίδων κεκοινωνηκέναι καὶ τῶν νῦν ἀπολαύειν καὶ ταῦτα ἀντὶ τοῦ γράφειν ἀπὸ στόματος λέγειν· ἀλλ', ὦ ἄριστε, τῆς μὲν παροιμίας ἀκούω στείχειν ἀξιούσης παρὰ τοὺς φίλους τοὺς τηλοῦ φίλους· τὸ κακὸν δὲ ᾧ μοι τὸ σῶμα πιέζεται, πείθεσθαι τῇ παροιμίᾳ κωλύει. μία γάρ μοι σωτηρία τὰ πολλὰ διάγειν ἐπὶ τῆς εὐνῆς, κίνδυνος δὲ ἤδη καὶ τὸ ἀγοράζειν, καὶ πολλάκις ἐκεῖ δεξάμενος προσβολὴν ἐλαυνόμενος ἀπῆλθον. 4. ἀλλ' οἷς ἔξεστιν ὁρᾷς ὡς θέουσιν ἄλλοι τε πολλοὶ καὶ Κληματιος, ᾧ πάντα γέγονάς τε καὶ ἔσῃ, ὃς τοσοῦτον ἔστη[1] παρ' ἡμῖν, ὅσον ἐρέσθαι καὶ μαθεῖν, ὅπως ἔχοι σοι τὰ πράγματα. γνοὺς δὲ ὡς ἄμεινον οὐδ' αὐτὸς ἡγεῖται τοῖς αὑτοῦ πράττειν ἔτι κακῶς. 5. καίτοι τῶν χειμῶνι κεχρημένων ἀνήρ, ἀλλ' ὅμως ἐκ τῶν σῶν εἰς τὰ αὑτοῦ κουφίζεται· οὕτως ἅπασι καταφυγὴ μία Στρατηγίῳ τῷ χρηστῷ σῶν εἶναι τὸν οἶκον.

---

[1] τοσοῦτον ἔστη Wolf (V Va S)   τοσοῦτόν ἐστι F. (Vi D).

that they have been so inspired by the removal of their fear. If you would add to that what we particularly desire, that you appear among us with your children and their mother, you will double our festivities. 3. I am not unaware that I ought to be with you to have shared their hopes, to enjoy the present situation, and to utter this aloud, instead of putting it in writing. Yes, my dear sir, I know the proverb that says that far-off friends must visit friends, but the trouble that affects me physically prevents me obeying it. My own salvation is to spend most of my time abed. Even to go into town is a risky business, and I have often suffered attack there and retired in disorder. 4. But you see that all who can flock towards you—Clematius[c] in particular, to whom you have been and will be all in all. He was with us long enough to inquire and to learn how things are with you. Upon realizing that they are improving, he does not regard himself as too badly off either. 5. Yet he is a man who has experienced some buffetings, but, for all that, he takes comfort for his own position from your own; the sole recourse for everyone lies in the preservation of the household of Strategius.

[c] Recently returned from another journey to court in Milan.

19. Βασιλείῳ[1]

1. Ὦ χρόνων ἐκείνων, ἐν οἷς πάντα ἦμεν ἀλλήλοις. νῦν δὲ διῳκίσμεθα πικρῶς, ὑμεῖς μὲν ἔχοντες ἀλλήλους, ἐγὼ δὲ ἀνθ' ὑμῶν οἷοί περ ὑμεῖς οὐδένα. 2. τὸν δὲ Ἄλκιμον ἀκούω τὰ νέων ἐν γήρᾳ τολμᾶν καὶ πρὸς τὴν Ῥώμην πέτεσθαι περιθέντα σοι τὸν τοῦ συνεῖναι τοῖς παιδαρίοις πόνον. 3. σὺ δὲ τά τε ἄλλα πρᾷός τις καὶ τοῦτο οἴσεις οὐ χαλεπῶς, ἐπεὶ καὶ ἡμῖν τοῦ μὴ γράψαι πρότερον οὐκ ἔσχες χαλεπῶς.

[1] τῷ μεγάλῳ before Βασιλείῳ V S Vind; after Βασιλείῳ Va.

---

[a] *BLZG* 31 ff, 94. F/Kr. No. 68. Petit, Étudiants 125 ff. The identity of this Basil, and that of *Letter* 70, has been much debated and is linked with the problem of the authenticity of the whole collection of correspondence between Libanius and St. Basil the Great, which is reproduced after the *pseudepigraphae* in Foerster Vol. xi, pp. 572–597. Seeck (*BLZG* 30–34) sought to prove that substantial elements of this collection in addition to these two letters were genuine. Laube (*De litterarum Libanii et*

19. To Basileius[a]

1. Ah, for those days when we were all in all to one another. Now we are sadly separated: you have each other, while I have none like you to take your place.   2. Alcimus,[b] I hear, has the venturesomeness of youth in his old age, and takes flight for Rome, investing you with the task of teaching his urchins.[c]   3. But you are a good natured fellow, and you will not take this amiss either, for you didn't take it amiss that I have not written to you before.

Basilii commercio, Diss. Breslau, 1913) denied any authenticity at all. Foerster (*Prolegomena,* Vol. ix. 197 ff), though believing that Basil was indeed a pupil of Libanius, denied that this Basil could be St. Basil himself. Petit came to the very reasonable conclusion that this Basileios is indeed Basil the Great. Hence it is at least possible and at best very probable that Basil taught at Nicomedeia at this time and introduced students to Libanius in 361 (*Étudiants* 126, notes 167–8).

[b] Cf. *Ep.* 397.

[c] This is the only evidence of Basil as a schoolteacher in Nicomedeia. Considering Basil's eminence in the tradition of the Eastern Church, it is difficult to interpret this as the invention of a forger.

20. Ἀνατολίῳ

1. Παρεκαθήμην τῷ θείῳ καὶ διελεγόμην, καί τις ἐπιστὰς ἔδωκεν ἐπιστολὴν ἐκείνῳ, καὶ τὸ δοθὲν ἕλκει μου τὼ ὀφθαλμὼ πρὸς αὐτό, καὶ τὸ σὸν ὄνομα ἐφαίνετο. 2. ἠρόμην οὖν αὐτόν· 'ποῦ δὲ τὰ πρὸς ἐμὲ γράμματα;' νομίζων οὐκ ἂν σε ἑτέροις γράφοντα μνήμην ἡμῶν μὴ λαβεῖν· ὁ δὲ 'ποῖα' ἔφη 'γράμματα; σοὶ γὰρ ἔρχεται δι' ἡμῶν οὐδέν.' 3. ἐνεθυμούμην οὖν ὅτι πλάσμα ἦν ἅπαν ἐκεῖνο καὶ ὁ σὸς ἔρως λόγος ἦν, οὐκ ἔρως. εἰ γὰρ δὴ φῇς ὅτι αὐτὸν οὐκ ἐπιστείλας ἔπαυσα ἐγώ, τούτῳ δεικνύεις αὐτῷ τὸ μὴ πολὺν ἐν σοὶ γενέσθαι τὸν θεόν. εἰ γὰρ ἦν, ὃ πολλάκις ἔλεγες, πολύς τε καὶ ἰσχυρός, οὐκ ἄν ποτε ἐκινήθη φαύλῃ προφάσει. 4. νῦν οὖν ἄνω ποταμῶν· σὺ μὲν ὑπερορᾷς, ἐγὼ δὲ ἐρῶ. καὶ μεταπεσόντος ὀστράκου φεύγεις, ἐγὼ δὲ ὁ διώκων εἰμί. 5. παραμυθεῖται δέ με τὸ μετὰ πολλῶν μὲν ἐθνῶν, πολλῶν δὲ πόλεων, πλείστων δὲ ἀνθρώπων ὑβρίζεσθαι. εἰ γὰρ οἱ μὲν εὔχονταί σε λαβεῖν ἡνίοχον, σὺ δ' ἐξὸν ἄρχειν οὐκ ἐθέλεις, ἀλλὰ μᾶλλον τρυφᾶν

---

a Written in midsummer 356. Anatolius was at court in

410

20. To Anatolius[a]

1. I was sitting by my uncle's side conversing with him, when someone came up and handed him a letter. The offering attracted my eyes to itself, and your name was to be seen on it.   2. So I asked him, "Where is the letter for me?" For I believed it impossible, if you wrote to others, that you would never have a thought for me. But replied he, "What letter? I have got nothing for you."   3. I began to think that all that was mere make-believe, and that your love for me was words, and no love at all. You see, if you say that I, by not writing, have put an end to it, by this very fact you show that the god had no great hold over you.[b] If he had, as you often used to claim, a good strong hold, he would never have been expelled on such a paltry pretext.   4. As it is now, everything is topsy-turvy:[c] you are the one to be finicky, I the one to love; and the case is altered:[d] you are the defendant, I the plaintiff.   5. My consolation is that I am slighted in the company of many provinces, many cities, and a multitude of men: for if they pray to have you at the reins and you refuse, though you could be governor, preferring

Milan at the time after refusing the City Prefecture of Rome.

[b] Cf. Eurip. *Hipp.* 1.

[c] Cf. Eurip. *Med.* 410 ἄνω ποτάμων ἱερῶν χωροῦσι παγαί, and see Aeschylus fr. 335 Radt.

[d] Cf. Plat. *Phaedr.* 241b. The Greek metaphor, from dice, becomes proverbial; cf. *Paroem. Gr.* 1.285.

ἢ πονεῖν, καὶ καθεύδειν ἢ εὖ ποιεῖν, πῶς οὐ πάντα
μικρά σοι νενόμισται; 6. ἀλλὰ γὰρ οὐ καλῶς
ἔοικα ῥητορεύειν, εἰ δυσχεραίνων σου τὴν ὑπερ-
οψίαν ἀφ' ὧν ἔσται μείζων λέγω· τοιοῦτον γὰρ τὸ
φάσκειν εἰς σὲ κεχηνέναι τοσούτους. 7. ἵν' οὖν
μὴ τοῦτο ᾖ, μάνθανε ὡς οὐ πᾶσιν ἀρέσκεις. οἷς
γὰρ αἱ τῶν ἄλλων συμφοραὶ πρόσοδοι, κἂν ἀποτε-
μόντες σε φάγοιεν ἂν ἡδέως, θαυμαστὸν δὲ ἴσως
οὐδέν. καὶ γὰρ οἱ λύκοι μισοῦσι τοὺς κύνας.

21. Ἀνδρονίκῳ

1. Ἢ παίζειν ἔοικας ἐν τοῖς γράμμασιν ἢ τὸ
πᾶν ἀγνοεῖν, πρῶτον μέν, εἰ νομίζεις τὸν σαυτοῦ
θεῖον θείου τι πρὸς σὲ ποιήσειν· ἔπειτα, εἰ δι'
ἡμᾶς.[1] ἐμοὶ γὰρ οὑτοσὶ χαλεπώτερος γέγονε τῶν
παρ' ὑμῖν[2] χαλεπῶν καὶ κακῶς ὅσα δύναται ποιεῖ·
δύναται δὲ πολλὰ καὶ πλουτεῖ· τὸ δ' ὅθεν, ἴστε.
2. ἔσχε δὲ πρὸς ἐμὲ δυσκόλως ἀπὸ τοῦ μὴ παρὰ
σοῦ τυχεῖν ὧν ἐπέταττεν. ἐγὼ μὲν γὰρ οὐδ'
οὕτως ἐπαυόμην φιλῶν, ὁ δ' ὅτι σε μὴ μεταβαλὼν

---

[1] ἡμᾶς F, Bouchery; conj. Re. ἡμῶν Wolf (Mss.).
[2] ὑμῖν Bouchery (V Va Vo)   ἡμῖν F (S Vi Vind.).

a life of luxury to one of labour, dozing to doing good, then obviously nothing means much to you. 6. However, I feel that I am not putting my case at all well if, in my annoyance at your arrogance, I make statements which will cause it to increase, for that is implied in the assertion that so many people are agog for you. 7. So, to avoid this, be assured that you do not please everyone: those who batten on the misfortunes of others would gladly chop you up and eat you—and no wonder, perhaps. Wolves hate the hounds that hunt them.[e]

[e] Cf. *Ep.* 1365.3.

21. To Andronicus[a]

1. In your letter it seems that you are either joking or else a complete ignoramus, in the first case if you think that your uncle[b] will treat you as an uncle should, in the second, if you think of it happening through me. He has become more of an enemy to me than all my enemies among you, and he does me all the harm in his power—and his power is great; so is his wealth, and you know the source of that. 2. He conceived a grudge against me because he failed to get from you what he required. Even so, I did not stop feeling friendly to him, but because I

[a] Cf. Bouchery 85 ff. This letter answers Andronicus' reply to *Letter* 17.

[b] Strategius.

ἐμίσουν, μισεῖν ᾠήθη με δεῖν. 3. σὺ δ' εὖ τι παθεῖν παρ' ἐκείνου ζητῶν λύκου πτερὰ ζητεῖς·[c] ἐπεὶ καὶ νῦν ὁ Θεμίστιος, ᾧ τί παραπλήσιον εἴποις ἄν; οὗ φθεγγομένου κἂν Σκύθαι γένοιντο ἥμεροι, τί μὲν οὐκ εἶπε, τί δὲ οὐκ ἔδρασε; ποίαν δὲ οὐκ ἦλθε πειθοῦς ὁδόν;

τῷ δ' ἄλληκτόν τε κακόν τε
θυμὸν ἐνὶ στήθεσσι θεοὶ θέσαν εἵνεκα κούρης.

4. δοκεῖ γάρ μοι πρὸς τὸ θυγάτριον βλέπων καὶ τὰ Κινύρου μικρὰ νομίζειν, ὥστε πανταχόθεν ἁρπάζειν, κἂν αἰτήσας μὴ λάβῃ, ἐχθρὸς εὐθέως ὁ μὴ δοὺς καὶ κακῶς οὐκ ἀκήκοεν, ἀλλὰ πέπονθεν. 5. ἢ οὖν ἀποστὰς ὧν αἰτεῖ λῦσον τὸν πόλεμον ἢ τῶν σαυτοῦ κρατῶν ἀνέχου τοῦ πολέμου.

---

[c] λύκου πτερά—an impossibility. Compare *Paroem. Gr.* 1.270.

[d] Themistius had at last visited Antioch in late 356. Libanius had been unsuccessful in acting as mediator between Andronicus and his uncle; Themistius had had no more luck.

did not change my attitude and begin to hate you, he thought that he had to hate me. 3. If you look for any kindness from him, you are on a wild goose chase.[c] Now, for instance, Themistius[d]—and what can you mention to bear comparison with him? When he speaks even the Scyths would be tamed[e]—what has he left unsaid or undone? What avenue of persuasion has he left unexplored? "But into his heart the gods put anger harsh and intractable on account of the maid."[f] 4. It seems to me that, in his regard for his daughter, he considers even the wealth of Cinyras[g] a mere nothing, and in consequence he grabs from everywhere, and if he does not get what he asks for, the person who refuses him becomes his foe straightaway and is the recipient not just of harsh words but of harsh treatment. 5. So either give up what he asks for and cease campaigning or keep possession of what belongs to you and keep up the campaign.

[e] Hints at the proverbial Σκύθων ἐρημία, but also at the contemporary identification of Scyths with Goths.

[f] Hom. *Il.* 9.636-7, but the 'maid' is Strategius' daughter, recently married, whom he wished to see richly endowed.

[g] One of the proverbial millionaires of Greek literature; cf. *Paroem. Gr.* 1.449.

22. Ἀνατολίῳ

1. Ἧκεν ἡμῖν ἐξ Ἰταλίας γράμματα δηλοῦντα σοφιστοῦ τινος ὑποξύλου φληνάφους καὶ σὸν γέλωτα μὲν εἰς ἐκεῖνον, ἔπαινον δὲ εἰς ἐμέ. καὶ παρῄνει δὴ τὰ γράμματα γράφειν σοι καὶ νομίζειν ἀνδρῶν σε εἰς ἐμὲ βέλτιστον εἶναι. 2. ἐγὼ δέ σε ἀνδρῶν μὲν ὅλως εἶναι βέλτιστον πάλαι δὴ ψῆφον ἐθέμην, θαυμάζω δέ σου τὸ ἐπειδὴ ἦρξας, τοῖς μὲν ἄλλοις, ᾗ πρόσθεν, ἐπιστεῖλαι, πρὸς δὲ ἐμὲ τοῦτο δὴ τὸ εἰωθὸς μὴ τηρῆσαι. 3. ἀπορῶν δὴ τὸ πρῶτον νῦν ἀπορῶν ἐπαυσάμην· εὑρηκέναι γὰρ οἶμαι, πόθεν ἡ σιγή. ὁρᾷς τῶν σοφιστῶν τοὺς πολλούς, ὅταν τις τῶν αὐτοῖς ἐπιτηδείων εἰς ἀρχὴν εἰσέλθῃ τοιαύτην, οἵαν καὶ σὺ νῦν, τρέχοντας παρὰ τὸν ἄρχοντα μετὰ λόγου καὶ βαλαντίου καὶ τὸν μὲν δεικνύντας, τὸ δὲ διδόντας καὶ δι' ἐκείνου πληροῦντας. 4. ἔδεισας δὴ μὴ γένωμαι καὶ αὐτὸς τῶν ἐπὶ τοῦτο τρεχόντων, καὶ διὰ τοῦτο δὴ τοῦ γράφειν ἀπέστης ἀφαιρούμενός με τὸ θαρρεῖν. πρὸς δὲ καὶ ᾔδεις ὀφείλων μοι χιτωνίσκον, ὃν ὑπέσχου μὲν ἐν Θρᾴκῃ, δέδωκας δὲ οὐδαμοῦ.

---

[a] A letter of congratulation to Anatolius upon his appointment in 357 as praetorian prefect of Illyricum, and

22. To Anatolius[a]

1. A letter has reached me from Italy informing me of some drivelling pseudo-sophist[b] and of your ridicule of him and praise of myself. And the letter reminded me to write to you and regard you as the best of people towards me.   2. My verdict has long been that you are absolutely the best of people, but I am surprised at you, that since taking office you have written to others as before but have not maintained this customary procedure with me. 3. Though puzzled at first, I have now ceased to puzzle, for I believe I have found the reason for your silence. You see the usual run of sophists, when one of their friends attains such an office as your present one, trotting off to the governor with oration and purse, delivering their oration and proffering their purse and filling it with his help. 4. So you were afraid that I too would be one of those trotters to such an end, and thus you gave up writing, depriving me of any grounds for presumption. Besides, you knew that you owed me a jacket, which you promised me in Thrace[c] and have never yet

also to introduce the Antiochene envoy Letoius. It is introduced (§§1–4) by a σκῶμμα—a passage of jesting abuse appropriate to close friends.

[b] A good example of Libanius' choice of comic diction, for which he was famous (cf. Eunap. V.S. 496).

[c] That is in Constantinople, before Libanius' removal to Antioch.

τοῦτο δεύτερον ἔδεισας μή σε ἥκων εἰσπράττοιμι. καὶ πρὸς τὸ μένειν με μίαν εὗρες ἀνάγκην τὴν σιωπήν. ἀλλ' ἐγώ σου καὶ ταύτην ἐλέγξω τὴν τέχνην· ἥξω γάρ.   5. ταυτὶ μὲν οὖν ἐν παιδιᾶς δέξῃ μέρει· πάνυ δὲ ἥσθην ἀκούσας ἃ προσεδόκων. ἤκουσα δὲ ἐν Στρατηγίου λέγοντος αὐτοῦ. ἑσπέρα μὲν ἦν, προσεσιστήκειμεν δὲ τῇ δεξαμενῇ. καὶ λόγος ἦν τις ὑπὲρ ἀρχόντων ἀρετῆς, ἐν ᾧ μὴ τὸ σὸν εἶναι ὄνομα οὐκ ἐνῆν.   6. εἰπόντος δέ του τῶν παρόντων μηδὲν μὲν εἶναι τῶν σῶν μικρόν, ἓν δὲ καὶ δὴ πάνυ μέγα, 'ποῖον' ἔφην 'τοῦτο τὸ μέγα;' Στρατήγιος οὖν εὐθὺς 'μέλλων,' ἔφη, 'παρὰ τοῦ βασιλέως ἀπιέναι μετὰ πολλὰ καὶ καλὰ προσέθηκεν ὅτι, ὦ βασιλεῦ, τῶν ἀδικούντων οὐδένα οὐδὲν ἀξίωμα ῥύσεται, ἀλλὰ κἂν τῶν δικαζόντων τις, κἂν τῶν ἐπὶ ταῖς δυνάμεσι παραβαίνῃ τοὺς νόμους, οὐκ ἀνέξομαι ἀμελεῖσθαι.'   7. ταῦτα σὲ μὲν ἔλεγεν ἀπειλεῖν, τὸν δὲ ἐπαινεῖν τε καὶ ἐπιτρέπειν καὶ σοὶ τὸν λόγον εὐθὺς εἰς ἔργον ἐλθεῖν. τῶν γάρ τινα στρατηγῶν δειλὸν γενόμενον πρὸς τοὺς βαρβάρους δεδέσθαι.   8. παρ' ἐκείνου μὲν ἐγὼ ταῦτα ἤκουσα πέντε παρόντων, παρ' ἐμοῦ δὲ οὐδεὶς ὅστις οὐκ ἀκήκοε, καὶ κρότος ἦν καὶ

given me. This was your second fear—that I would come and dun you for it, and the one means you found of getting me to stay here was silence. But this device of yours too I will set at nought, for come I shall. 5. Well, so much by way of fun.[d] I was very pleased to hear what I expected. I heard it in Strategius' headquarters from his own lips. It was evening[e] and we were standing near the bath, when a conversation arose about the excellence of governors, and there your name could not fail to appear. 6. One of those present remarked that though nothing you had done was on a small scale, there was one thing that was on a really grand scale. "What was this, then?" said I. Strategius then straightaway said, "Just as he was going to leave the emperor's presence after making many a fine profession, his final remark was, 'Sire, rank will not rescue any wrongdoer. Even if it be a governor, civil or military, who transgresses the laws, I shall not suffer it to be ignored.'" 7. This was the threat he said you made, and the emperor gave approving consent, and your words were immediately translated into action, for one of the military commanders who showed cowardice against the barbarians was arrested. 8. There were five of us present when I heard him tell this story, but everybody has heard me repeat it: it was applauded

[d] Plat. *Resp.* 4.424d.

[e] A playful allusion to Dem. *de Cor.* 169: the receipt of the portentous news of the taking of Elatea.

οὐδεὶς εἶχεν ἀπιστεῖν. τῆς γὰρ σῆς φύσεως ἐφαίνετο τὸ ἔργον. 9. ἐγὼ δὲ οὕτως ἔχαιρον, οὐχ ὡς λέγων περὶ ὧν σὺ ποιεῖς, ἀλλ᾽ ὡς αὐτὸς ὢν ὁ ποιῶν, ἐπεὶ καὶ σὺ περὶ τοὺς ἐμοὺς λόγους ἴσον τι πέπονθας· σαυτοῦ τοὺς ἐμοὺς ἡγῇ. οὐκοῦν καὶ τοὺς ἐμοὺς φίλους σαυτοῦ νομίζειν εἰκός. 10. εἰ δὴ τοῦτο οὕτως ἔχει, φίλος σοι Λητόιος οὗτος τῶν οἰκείων οὐδὲν λειπόμενος εἰς ἐμέ, τινὰς δὲ καὶ παρελθών, ἐπεὶ καὶ τὸ τὰ κοινὰ πράττειν ἀφεὶς ἡσυχίας ἐπιθυμίᾳ πάλιν αὐτῶν ἐμὴν χάριν ἀνθήψατο τοῦ τοῖς ἐμοῖς πράγμασιν ἀπὸ μείζονος τῆς δυνάμεως συμμαχεῖν. 11. οὗτος, ἂν μὲν ἐμοί τι χρηστὸν ᾖ, καὶ φαιδρός, ἐν δὲ τοῖς ἑτέροις τῷ λυπεῖσθαί με νικᾷ. καὶ τὰ ὄντα κοινά μοι κέκτηται, κἂν μὴ παρ᾽ ἡμέραν τι πέμψας λάβω, δεινὰ πεπονθέναι φησί. 12. νέων δὲ ὅσοι πένητες, διὰ τοῦτον οὐ πένητες· τὰς γὰρ ἐνδείας τῶν περὶ τοὺς λόγους ὅπως τε μὴ ἀγνοήσει ποιεῖ καὶ ὅπως λύσει φροντίζει. 13. πρεσβεύειν δὲ οὐκ ἐγνωκώς, ἤδη γὰρ ἐντετυχήκει τῷ βασιλεῖ μέλλων θήσειν τὰ Ὀλύμπια, τὸν θεῖον τὸν ἐμὸν

---

f *BLZG* 197 (i): *principalis* of Antioch.

g Cf. *Ep.* 550. Another example of such generosity by a private individual is that of Procopius (*Ep.* 319). Anatolius

and none could disbelieve it, for the action was so obviously in keeping with your character. 9. My pleasure was not that of the narrator of your actions but of their actual performer, since you too have something of the same feeling towards my oratory, thinking it to belong to yourself. Thus it is natural for you to think that my friends too belong to yourself. 10. If this is the case, the bearer Letoius[f] is your friend, since in his attitude towards me he is not outdone by my kinsfolk, and he even surpasses some. After giving up his civic duties in his desire for retirement, he has once again resumed them for my sake so as to support me from his position of higher influence. 11. If things go well with me, he is even radiant; if they do not, he outdoes me in his chagrin. His possessions are at my disposal: if I do not send and take some every day, he says that he is aggrieved. 12. Because of him any poor students are no longer poor. He ensures that he is not ignorant of the needs of those engaged in study, and concerns himself to resolve them.[g] 13. Although he had made up his mind not to act as our ambassador, since he had already had audience with the emperor just before he presented the Olympia,[h] he relieved my uncle of

himself, as prefect, makes a grant of 100 solidi to Optatus, which Libanius complains is too little.

[h] He had shared in the presentation of the Olympia of 356, an expenditure which is employed as commendation for him in *Epp.* 556–9.

ἀπαλλάττων τοῦ πόνου τὸν πόνον ὑπέστη. 14. οἷς
ἂν οὖν ἐχρήσω πράγμασιν ὑπὲρ ἐκείνου ποιῶν
αὐτῷ συμμάχους τοὺς ἐν τέλει, ταῦτα τούτῳ δὸς
ἄγειν· ὡς, ἂν οὗτος ἐκεῖ πράξῃ κατὰ νοῦν, ἡμῖν
ἐνθάδε μέγα φρονεῖν ὑπάρξει.

---

[i] An embassy to court entailed considerable personal
expense and inconvenience for the envoy. The embassy

23. Μυγδονίῳ

1. Ἴσον τι πεποίηκε Σπεκτάτος ὅτι με φιλεῖς
ἐπιστείλας, ὥσπερ εἰ πρὸς ἐμὲ ἔλεγες.[1] σὺ γὰρ
Ἀθήνησί τε[2] τὰ γονέων ἐπλήρωσας εἰς ἐμὲ καὶ
διὰ τοῦτο[3] πρῶτον[4] μόνῳ ἐθάρρησα σοὶ μάλιστα,[5]
ἐπειδή τε[6] διῆγον ἐν Βιθυνίᾳ τὸν σκηπτὸν ἐκεῖνον
ἐκφυγών, σὺ τοῖς ἐκβαλοῦσιν ἐπὶ Θρᾴκης ἐμάχου
μόνος ἐν μέσῳ πολλῶν ὑπὲρ τῶν δικαίων βοῶν.

[1] ἔλεγες F, conj. Re.   ἔλεγε Wolf (Mss.).
[2] τε Wolf (Mss.)   γε F.
[3] After τοῦτο, edd. insert μὲν (Va Vo S): om. V.
[4] πρῶτον F   πρώτῳ Wolf, Re. (V Vo S).
[5] σοί, μάλιστα <δέ>, F.
[6] ἐπειδή τε V   ἐπειδή, ὅτε edd. (Va Vo S).

the task and took it upon his own shoulders.[i]   14.
So grant him the privilege of enjoying the same
treatment as you would have accorded my uncle by
securing him the support of influential officials, for
if he completes his business there to his liking, it
will give me here cause for great satisfaction.

was to go to Rome to congratulate Constantius upon his
Vicennalia and his visit to the capital.

23. To Mygdonius[a]

1. Spectatus, by writing of your friendship for
me, has affected me almost as though you addressed
me yourself. For at Athens[b] you it was who behaved
like a father to me, and for this reason first you were
the only one I especially trusted, and when I was living in Bithynia after escaping that bitter blow, you
were the only one in Thrace to take issue with my
persecutors by publicly proclaiming the cause of

[a] *BLZG* 219, *PLRE* 614: a courtier of long standing and
much influence as *castrensis sacri palatii*.
[b] From 336 to 340; cf. *Or.* 1.16–25.

2. ὥστε σε καὶ Νικοκλῆς ἐκ τῆς ὑπὲρ ἡμῶν
ἀνδρίας ἐποιήσατο φίλον μισῶν μὲν ἐμέ, τότε δὲ
σὲ θαυμάσας ὅτι με οὐ προὔδωκας ὅπως ἐκείνῳ
χαρίσαιο. καὶ δὴ καὶ ὅτε πρὸς τὸν ἀγρὸν ἐπλεῖτε,
κατιδών με ἐπὶ τῆς ἠιόνος οὐ πόρρω Χαλκηδόνος
κελεύσας τὸν ναύτην ἔχειν οὗπερ εἱστήκειν, ἐκβὰς
ἠσπάζου Νικοκλέους ὁρῶντος ἀπὸ τοῦ πλοίου.
3. τί οὖν θαυμαστὸν εἰ ᾧ πέπρακται ἐκεῖνα, τὸν
ἄριστον οὑτοσὶ Μουσώνιον πείθει τι δοξάζειν περὶ
ἡμῶν ἄμεινον; μιμῇ γὰρ τῶν δρομέων τοὺς ἀγα-
θούς, ὧν ἀεὶ τὰ δεύτερα βελτίω. 4. πρόσθες
δὴ καὶ τοῖς τότε πόνοις καὶ τοῖς νῦν ἐπαίνοις τὴν εἰς Λητόιον τουτονὶ προθυμίαν, ὃς
ἔχων φιλοτιμεῖσθαι καὶ γένους ἐπιφανείᾳ καὶ
λειτουργιῶν λαμπρότητι καὶ τῷ δύνασθαι λέγειν

---

[c] In 342, after teaching in Constantinople for two years,
Libanius was expelled by the proconsul Limenius (ἐκείνῳ
§ 2), on the occasion of rioting, for which see *Or.* 1.44–7;
T. D. Barnes, "Himerius and the Fourth Century," *Classical Philology* 82 (1982): 206. By ignoring the conflict at the
time between Christian groups, Libanius makes this solely
a matter of sophistic rivalries and suggests that the puni-
tive action taken by the authorities after these riots was
action in support of himself. Eunapius (*V.S.* 495) also
speaks of allegations of pederasty levelled at him.

justice.[c]   2. Hence even Nicocles[d] became your friend in consequence of your courageous stand on my behalf, since for all his dislike of me he then felt admiration for you because you did not betray me to oblige that fellow. Indeed, when you were sailing to your estate, you saw me on the beach not far from Chalcedon and bade your boatman to stay where he was, and you disembarked and embraced me, with Nicocles looking on from the boat.   3. So what wonder then that, when such a man has behaved so, he induces the excellent Musonius[e] to entertain some kindlier feeling towards me? You are like a good runner whose second lap is always the better one.[f]   4. Now, cap your previous efforts and your present commendations by supporting the bearer Letoius.[g] He can pride himself upon illustrious family, the magnificence of his public services and his oratorical ability, but he would rather be thought

[d] Nicocles (*BLZG* 221, *PLRE* 630) had originally invited Libanius to join him in Constantinople (*Or.* 1.31) but had fallen out with him and was one of the opposing cabal in 342. Afterwards they became reconciled. The meeting here related occurred when Libanius had become established as sophist in Nicomedeia.

[e] *BLZG* 218 (i), *PLRE* 612 (1): *magister officiorum*. As such, one of his duties was arranging the reception of embassies—hence the plea for Letoius (*Ep.* 558).

[f] For the proverb cf. Plat. *Legg.* 4.723d; *Paroem. Gr.* i.62. Libanius here transfers it from its origin, in sacrifices, to athletics.

[g] Cf. *Letter* 22.10.

βούλοιτ' ἂν ἀπὸ τρόπων ἢ ὧν εἶπον εἶναί
τις δοκεῖν. 5. τοῦτον οὔτε εὐτυχία πώποτε
ἐπῆρεν ἐν δυσκολίᾳ τε οὐκ ἔπτηξεν Εὐριπί-
δου μεμνημένος. φίλος δὲ τοιοῦτος ὁποῖος καὶ σύ,
θᾶττον ἂν δεξάμενος τελευτὴν ἢ κακὸς εἰς ἑταῖρον
γενέσθαι, τοῦτο δὴ τὸ σόν, ἀλλὰ μὴν ἥ γε πρὸς
ἐμὲ σπουδὴ τοσαύτη ὥστε οὐκ ἂν μείζω ζητήσαις.
6. ἔχω δὲ τὸν ἄνδρα ἀντευποιεῖν, εἰ βουληθείης.
τούτῳ τε γὰρ ἀντὶ πάντων, εἰ Μουσώνιος αὐτὸν
εὐμενῶς ἴδοι, σοί τε ἐκεῖνον καταστῆσαι τοιοῦτον
ῥᾷστον ἁπάντων. μαθέτω δὴ ὅτι, παρ' ὅσων
κομίζει γράμματα, ταῦτα μάλιστα αὐτὸν ὤνησεν
ἃ παρ' ἡμῶν τῶν ἐν τῷ τρίβωνι φέρει.

24. Ἀρισταινέτῳ

1. Τὸν Ἱμερίου μὲν υἱόν, Σωπάτρου δὲ ἀδελφιδοῦν, Ἰαμβλίχῳ δὲ ὁμώνυμον, ἐμὸν δὲ καὶ συγγενῆ καὶ φίλον ἔχων εὐθὺς ἡγοῦ καὶ σαυτοῦ φίλον
καὶ μὴ κατὰ βραχὺ συγκεράννυ τῷ νεανίσκῳ σαυτόν, ἀλλ' ἐπὶ τοῖς γράμμασιν ἀναπέτασον αὐτῷ
πάντα τὰ πράγματα μὴ τῇ ἡλικίᾳ κρίνων τὸν
τρόπον, ἀπὸ δὲ τοῦ τρόπου τὸν νέον τιθεὶς εἰς
γέροντας. 2. οὗτος ἐμὲ φιλεῖ μὲν ὥσπερ ἡ

somebody not so much for these qualifications as for his personal character. 5. Prosperity has never made him arrogant, nor does he hark back to Euripides[h] and cower down in disappointment. He is such a friend as you are yourself, one who would sooner die than be disloyal to a friend—your own attitude precisely—and besides his enthusiastic support of me is such that you would never find surpassed. 6. I can make some return for his kindness, should you consent. He regards it as all-important that Musonius should look kindly upon him. For you it is the easiest thing of all to induce that frame of mind. Let him then learn, that of all the letters he delivers, those he takes from us wearers of the scholastic gown are most to his advantage.

[h] Cf. Plut. *Consol. ad Apoll.* 4 (Mor. p. 102 F). Eurip. fr. 963 N.

24. To Aristaenetus

1. The son of Himerius, nephew of Sopater, namesake of Iamblichus,[a] my kinsman and friend both, regard as your friend too at first meeting. Do not unite yourself with the lad by degrees, but after my letter display everything to him: do not judge his conduct by his age, but from his conduct class the youth among the aged. 2. He loves me like a

[a] *BLZG* 184, *PLRE* 451 (2). A Cameron, "Iamblichus at Athens," *Athenaeum* 35 (1957); 143–53. This is one of a batch of nine letters of commendation for Iamblichus to various addresses on his way to and at court.

μήτηρ, αἰσχύνεται δὲ ὥσπερ υἱός, φοβεῖται δὲ ὡς ἂν οἰκέτης. τὸ δὲ μέγιστον τῶν ἐν αὐτῷ, νομίζων τὴν μεγίστην ἀνάγκην εἰς ἀρετῆς ἄσκησιν εἶναι θεοὺς τιμῶν δέξαιτ' ἂν Ἶρος γενέσθαι μᾶλλον ἢ μὴ τιμῶν Κινύρας. 3. κληρονομήσας δὲ πατρῴας οὐσίας καὶ φίλων τὸ μὲν τῶν φίλων ηὔξησε μέρος, τὸ δὲ ἐκείνης οὐκ ἠξίωσεν, ἀλλ' ἐπαινῶν Εὐριπίδην λέγοντα νοῦν ἔχοντος εἶναι φίλον πρίασθαι χρημάτων πολλῶν σαφῆ, τοῦτο τὸ κτῆμα κτώμενος ἀναλίσκει τῶν ὄντων. 4. ἀκούσας δὲ τίς μὲν αὐτὸν ὁ καλῶν, ἐφ' ὃ δὲ καλούμενος τίνι γνώμῃ πορεύεται, θαυμάσῃ μὲν αὐτοῦ τὸ μὴ θαυμάσαι πλοῦτον, ἐπαινέσῃ δὲ τὴν σοφίαν, ᾗ πειρᾶται διαφεύγειν ἃ μὴ νομίζει καλά, μακάριον δὲ ἡγήσῃ τῆς περὶ τὰ θεῖα κρίσεως. 5. ξενίσας οὖν τὴν γενναίαν φύσιν καὶ συνευξάμενος αὐτῷ λυθῆναι πέμπε ἐπ' Ἰταλίας, μᾶλλον δὲ ἐπὶ Συρίας.

mother, reverences me like a son and fears me like a slave. His foremost characteristic is that he regards the gods as the chief impulsion towards the practice of virtue,[b] and would prefer to honour them and be a beggar rather than dishonour them and become a millionaire.[c]   3. As the heir to his father's fortunes and friends, he has increased his inheritance as far as friends are concerned, but has not deigned to do so as regards his fortune: instead, he commends the dictum of Euripides, that a sensible man buys a trusty friend at much cost,[d] and on the acquisition of this prize he expends his all.   4. On hearing who it is that summons him, the purpose for which he is summoned, and the reactions with which he sets out, you will admire him for his lack of interest in riches, commend him for the wisdom with which he tries to avoid what he thinks ignoble, and account him blessed for his attitude towards religion.   5. So entertain this noble spirit, join him in praying for his release, and send him on his way to Italy—or better still, Syria.[e]

[b] Cf. *Ep.* 578.5.

[c] Cf. *Or.* 18.140, *Letter* 60. Irus is the beggar of the *Odyssey,* Cinyras one of the proverbial millionaires as in *Letter* 21.4.

[d] Eurip. *Or.* 1155 f, a favourite quotation of Libanius.

[e] That is, back home to Apamea, where his family was of high curial status. It seems that he was at this time being considered for office, a plan which proved abortive.

25. Ἀρισταινέτῳ

1. Εἶχον μέν[1] σε ἐλέγχειν ἐκείνως ἐπεσταλ-
κότα καὶ οὐ τὸ μὴ πολλάκις λαβεῖν, ἀλλὰ τὸ μὴ
μακρὰς αἰτιώμενον· ἵνα δὲ μὴ πόλεμος ἐκ μικροῦ
σπινθῆρος ἀφθῇ καὶ βάλλωμεν ἀλλήλους γράμμασιν ἀντὶ τοῦ τέρπειν ἐπιστολαῖς, δεδόσθω σὲ μὲν
τιμᾶν τὰ τῆς Λακεδαίμονος, ἐμὲ δὲ οὐκ ὀρθῶς
ἐγκαλεῖν. καὶ νίκα τὴν νίκην ταύτην ἡττημένων
ἡμῶν ἑκόντων.   2. βιβλία δὲ ὅτι μὲν ὑπέσχου
μοι, ἐμὸν ἀναμνῆσαι, ὅτι δὲ οὐκ ἔδωκας, σὸν
εἰπεῖν. ὅτε γὰρ ἐν τῇ Μεγάλῃ πόλει τὴν νόσον
τὴν μεγάλην διαφυγὼν ἀνεγίνωσκόν σοι λόγον,
ἔπαινον τῆς Στρατηγίου θυγατρός, βιβλίον τι
παλαιὸν εἰς κάλλος γεγραμμένον ἐθαυμάσαμεν
ἰδόντες καὶ διελέχθημεν ὡς ἦν ποτε κάλλος γραμμάτων, νῦν δὲ οὐκ ἔστιν.   3. ἐνιδὼν δή μοι σὺ
τῶν τοιούτων ἐπιθυμίαν ἔχειν ἔφης πολλὰ καὶ

[1] εἶχον μὲν F., conj. Re.   εἴχομεν Wolf (Mss.).

---

[a] This follows up comments about the length or short-
ness of letters exchanged between Aristaenetus and
Libanius, as reported in *Ep.* 561. Excess in either direction was regarded as a fault by the Greek literary critics
(e.g., Gregory Nazianzen, *Letter to Nicobulus* 1, Demetrius,
On Style 228, in Hercher, *Epistolographi Graeci* pp. 15,

25. To Aristaenetus

1. I could censure you for writing in those terms and for complaining not that you receive infrequent letters but short ones.[a] But lest the blaze of war should be kindled from a little spark[b] and we pelt each other with our writings instead of enjoying our letters, let it be conceded that you respect the Spartan model[c] and that my censures are without foundation. I give you best in this, for I am a willing loser. 2. As for the promise of books which you made me, it is up to me to remind you of it, and to you to confess that you have failed to provide them. When I fled the great plague in the capital,[d] I was reading you a speech, a panegyric on Strategius' daughter,[e] and we both looked in admiration at an old book written in a fine hand; in conversation we remarked that there used to be fine hands in the past but not now. 3. When you saw me so enthusiastic for such things you told me that you had plenty, got from your grandfather,[f] and you said

13). Libanius in the same letter (§ 7) had also requested books of classical authors already promised by Aristaenetus (§ 2 below).

[b] Aristoph. *Peace* 608 ff.

[c] βραχυλογία Λακωνική (Plat. *Protag.* 343b) was proverbial.

[d] In 350 and 351 Libanius made two return visits to Nicomedeia. This was the first; cf. *Or.* 1.77.

[e] Cf. *Letter* 21.3.

[f] On this passage cf. Norman, *JHS* 80 (1960) 124.

κτῆμα παππῷον καὶ πέμψειν ἀπὸ τῆς Νικαίας.
εἶτα ἐγένου Φίλιππος ὑπισχνούμενος Ἀθηναίοις.
καὶ ἀγροὺς μὲν ὑπὲρ ἡμῶν ἄλλοις οἶσθα δοῦναι,
βιβλία δὲ ἡμῖν οὐκ οἶσθα.   4. 'διὰ τί δή;' λέγοις
ἄν. ἢ κἀνταῦθα τὸν Φίλιππόν μοι καιρὸς εἰπεῖν·
'οὐ δίδωσιν Ἀρισταίνετος βιβλία τοῖς φίλοις, ἵνα
μὴ διαβληθῇ πρὸς τοὺς Ἕλληνας;' πάλιν δή σοι
λέγω ταῦτα, ὡς, ἂν μὴ πέμψῃς ἐκείνων, οὐ λήψῃ
τούτων, ἐν οἷς καὶ αὐτοῖς εὑρήσεις πολιάν. οὐ γὰρ
κατὰ τὸν Ἰόλεων ἐκ γέροντος ἐγὼ νέος· οὐχ οὕτω
μοι φαῦλον οἱ νόμοι.

---

g Although Aristaenetus normally resided in Nicomedeia, his family home was at Nicaea.

26. Ἀρισταινέτῳ

1. Χάρις γε σοὶ προσθέντι τὸ ὅτι ὑγίανας τῷ
ὅτι ἠρρώστησας καὶ τοῖς γε μὴ προσαγγείλασιν
ἡμῖν, ἡνίκα ἠσθένεις, χάρις· ἄνευ γὰρ τῆς τοῦ
κακοῦ λύσεως αὐτὸ τὸ δυσχερὲς οὐκ ἂν ἐβουλόμην
εἰδέναι.   2. ἔχω δὲ οὔτ' ἀπιστεῖν μὴ ταύτην
εἶναι τῇ σιγῇ πρόφασιν οὔτ' αὖ πάνυ πιστεύειν.
τὸ μὲν γὰρ ὁ λέγων ποιεῖ· πῶς γὰρ ἔστιν ἀπιστεῖν Ἀρισταινέτῳ; παλιν δὲ πιστεύειν Ἀρισται-

that you would send them from Nicaea.[g] Then you turned into a Philip with his promises to the Athenians.[h] You are capable of giving estates to other people on my account, but books to me no! 4. "Oh! How's that?" you may ask. Here too have I not occasion to compare you with Philip? "Aristaenetus refuses books to his friends to avoid unpopularity among the Greeks."[i] Well, I repeat: unless you send me some of them, you will get none of mine—and you will find a venerable antiquity in them too. I am not like Iolaus, changing my age for youth.[j] The laws of nature are not of such little moment for me.

[h] Dem. *Phil.* 2.23.

[i] [Dem.] 7.35.

[j] Iolaus was granted youth by Hebe, but this decision was rescinded; Ovid, *Met.* 9.398–431.

26. To Aristaenetus

1. I am grateful to you for adding to the news of your illness the postscript that you had recovered, and grateful too to the people who did not give me the news when you were ill. I would not have liked to know of the actual ailment without knowing of its cure. 2. I cannot disbelieve that this was the reason for your silence, but cannot believe it completely, either. Scepticism is dispelled by the thought that it is impossible to disbelieve Aristaenetus, but I am restrained from belief by the

νέτου κωλύει γράμματα Στρατηγίῳ μὲν ἐλθόντα,
δοθέντα δὲ ἡμῖν ὑπ' ἐκείνου γελῶντος ἅμα οἷς δή
τι καὶ σκῶμμα παρέγραψας, ὡς ἄρα τρίτος ἐγὼ
φθονοίην τῷ πρώτῳ.   3. καί μοι δοκεῖτε σύ τε
κἀκεῖνος, δι' ὃν πρῶτος μὲν οὐκ ἐγένου, μένεις δὲ
ἐν δευτέροις, οὐ γάρ με ἔλαθες οὔπω τῶν δευτέρων
ἐκβάς, πλείω τοῦ δέοντος παίζειν. δῆλον γὰρ ὡς
ὅπερ ἐγὼ πρὸς ἐκεῖνον ἀπέρριψα, σοὶ τοῦτο ἐκεῖνος ἐμήνυσε.   4. πρότερον μὲν οὖν ἤκουόν σε
μέλλειν ἐκεῖσε τρέχειν, καὶ πολὺ τοῦτο ἦν, ὡς
μέλλεις, νῦν δ' ἀκούω σοι τὸ μένειν ἀρέσκειν.
5. ἐδόκεις οὖν μοι τότε μέν, εἰρήσεται γάρ, ἐκπε-
πλευκέναι σαυτοῦ, νῦν δὲ ἐπανήκειν εἰς σαυτόν.
οὐ γὰρ ἐν τοσαύταις ἀρχόντων νιφάσι σὲ μόνον
ἰδιωτεύειν δεινόν, ἀλλ' εἰ νῦν ἄρξεις, ἐν ᾧ τοσοῦτοι, τοῦτο οὐκ ἀνεκτόν.   6. ἐλθεῖν μὲν οὖν σε
παρὰ φίλον, εἰ καὶ μὴ μέτριον τοῦτο ἄλλῳ φίλῳ,

---

[a] In *Ep.* 316.3–5 Libanius had paid an elaborate compliment to Acacius, that he was the best orator of the
Greeks. Acacius had passed this on to Aristaenetus, a
mutual friend. He in turn joked of it to the praetorian prefect Strategius, yet another mutual friend.

[b] Acacius: *BLZG* 43 (iii), *PLRE* 6 (7), of Cilicia,
corresponding until 365 at least.

letter of Aristaenetus which arrived for Strategius and which he handed over to me laughing at the joke in the postscript, that I am an also-ran and would envy the winner.[a] 3. Now both you and he[b]—because of him you still are not the winner, only lying second: it has not escaped me that you have not come out in front yet—you both seem to be making more than enough of the joke, for clearly he has told you of the remark I made to him. 4. Now previously I heard that you were intending to go there,[c] and all the talk was about this intention, but now I hear that you are content to stay where you are. 5. Well, frankly, it seemed to me that at that time you had gone on the wrong tack[d] but now you are back on course. There is no harm done if, in all these showers of governmental appointments,[e] you alone remain an ordinary citizen, but for you now to become a governor when such a host of others do so is intolerable. 6. So there is some point in your visiting a friend, even if it is not particularly pleas-

[c] Anatolius, praetorian prefect of Illyricum, in 357 invited Aristaenetus to become his assessor, an offer which was after hesitation refused. In 358 he got his advancement to the newly created vicariate of *Pietas,* which meant that he did not have to leave home.

[d] Cf. Herod. 3.155. To take leave of one's senses.

[e] In 357/8 all prefectural and palace departments were being reorganized, so that Anatolius was able to offer this post to Aristaenetus. It would be undignified for a provincial dignitary like him to agree to take part in this scramble for the security of an official post.

435

παρ' ὃν οὐκ ἦλθες, ἔχει τι σχήματος, γενέσθαι δέ σε δῆλον ἀρχῆς εἵνεκα Νίκαιαν ἐκλιπόντα οὐκ ἴσον. ἰδού, ποταμῶν ἄνω. συμβουλεύω μὲν ἐγώ, σὺ δὲ ἃ πράττων ἀμείνων ἔσῃ, μανθάνεις.

27. Ἀκακίῳ

1. Δέδεικται μὲν ἅπας ὁ λόγος καί τις ἐγένετο θόρυβος καὶ κρότος, καὶ ὅτῳ κόσμος ἦν ὁ λόγος, πέμπειν αὐτὸν ἔγνωκε πολλαχοῖ τῆς γῆς· οὕτως ἥσθη τῷ δώρῳ· ἐμοὶ δὲ μικρὰ μὲν οὐδὲ ταῦτα, τὸ δὲ μεῖζον οὐκ ἐγένετο. τοῦτο δὲ ἦν ἐν τῷ θεάτρῳ σὲ φαίνεσθαι ποιοῦντα ὅπερ εἰώθεις, προεκπηδῶντα. ὥστε καὶ πρὸς τὸν Εὐσέβιον, ὁπότε γίγνοιτο βοή, πολλάκις ἐφθεγγόμην· 'τί δ' ἂν ἦν τὰ νῦν ἐκείνου παρόντος;' σὲ δὴ λέγων. 2. ἀλλὰ τούτων μὲν λήψομαι παρὰ σοῦ δίκην, ἐπειδὰν αὐτὸς μὲν ᾖς ἐν τῷ λέγειν, ἐγὼ δὲ ἐν τῷ ψηφίζεσθαι· τὸν δὲ Τιτιανὸν ἴσθι ζῶντα, ὡς ἂν εὔξαιο, καὶ θέοντα μᾶλλον ἀκέντητον ἢ τὸν Ἱέρωνος ἵππον. φύσις δὲ ἀρίστη προσλαβοῦσα πόνων ἐπιθυμίαν ὁπόσον τι γίγνεται, τεκμαίρου.

---

a Cf. *Letter* 26 note.

b The date of the letter is Jan./Feb. 358. The oration is

ing to another friend whom you have not visited, but for you to be seen to desert Nicaea just for the sake of an official post is not proper. Just look! everything is topsy-turvey.[f] I give the advice; you are told of the action to be taken for your improvement.

[f] Cf. *Letter* 20.4.

27. To Acacius[a]

1. The whole oration has been delivered, to be greeted with some clamorous applause. He, in whose honour it was given, has decided to send copies of it far and wide, so pleased was he with the gift.[b] Though this means a good deal to me, I missed something more important, namely to see you in the lecture room behaving as usual and leaping forward in applause. So whenever a cheer arose I kept on saying to Eusebius[c] too, "What would it be like now if he were here"—meaning you. 2. But I shall get my own back on you for this when you yourself are engaged in giving an oration and I in criticizing it. As for Titianus,[d] rest assured that he is living as you would desire, and racing along with even less need for the whip than the horse of Hieron.[e] You can deduce the progress he is making with his combination of fine natural talent and eagerness for

the celebrated panegyric on Strategius of *Or.* 1.111.

[c] *BLZG* 140 (ix). He died in 359; *Or.* 1.118, *Ep.* 72.

[d] Acacius' son, a pupil of Libanius.

[e] Pindar *Ol.* 1.22.

3. τούτων δέ σοι καὶ Τουσκιανὸς ἄγγελος ἥξει λόγων δημιουργός τε καὶ κριτὴς ἀγαθός, ὃς ἥκων ὡς αὐτὸν δείλης ἀπαιτήσων τὸ σκέμμα ἀπέβη θαυμάσας.

28. Βάσσῳ

1. Τὰ μέγιστα ἡμᾶς ἀφελόμενος ἔδωκας, σμικρὰ μὲν οὐκ ἂν φαίην, οὐ μὴν ἡλίκα γε ἀφείλου· τὸν γὰρ υἱὸν μεταπεμψάμενος ἔπεμψας ἡμῖν ἐπιστολήν. ἦν δὲ ἐκεῖνος μέν μοι παρὼν τοσοῦτον ὅσον καὶ σὺ συνών, τὰ γράμματα δὲ ἡδὺ μέν, δεύτερον δὲ ἐκείνου. 2. Καλλιόπιος μὲν οὖν ἀγαθῶν τύχοι διδασκάλων καὶ διασώσαιτό γε τὴν ἐντεῦθεν κρηπῖδα· νῦν δὲ σὲ χάριν αἰτοῦμαι, ἣν οὐκ ἂν ἠβουλόμην αἰτεῖν ἠναγκά-σθαι. 3. Κυρίνῳ παῖς ἐστιν Ὀνωράτος, ὁ δὲ Κυρῖνος ἀπὸ μὲν τῶν ἀρχῶν, τρεῖς δὲ αὗται, πενέ-στερος ἀπῆλθε, ῥητορικῆς δὲ πρὸς τοσοῦτον ἧκεν ἐφ' ὅσον ἄν, εἰ παρὰ τὸν Ἑρμῆν ἐτύγχανε φοιτή-σας. 4. οὗτος πολλῶν γεγονὼς πατὴρ νῦν ἑνός ἐστιν Ὀνωράτου καὶ εἴη γε καλοῦ τε ὄντος καὶ ἀγαθοῦ καὶ κοσμοῦντος οὕτω γενναῖον πατέρα.

study. 3. Tuscianus[f] too will come to inform you of this. He is a craftsman in rhetoric and a good critic: he approached him in the afternoon to ask for an example of his work and left full of admiration.

[f] *PLRE* 926 (2): assessor to Anatolius.

28. To Bassus[a]

1. In taking from me something most precious you have given me something which, though not to be described as unimportant, is certainly nothing like what you have taken, for when you sent for your son, you sent me a letter. His presence means as much to me as association with you, but your letter, pleasing as it is, rates second to him. 2. So I trust that Calliopius[b] will have good teachers and maintain the foundations he laid here. But now I ask a favour of you which I could wish not to be forced to ask. 3. Quirinus has a son, Honoratus.[c] Quirinus left his official posts, three in number, poorer than he went in, but he attained such a peak of eloquence as he might have done had he been a pupil of Hermes' own. 4. He has been father of many children, but now of Honoratus alone—and may he continue to be, for the youngster is a gentleman and a

[a] *BLZG* 96 (i), *PLRE* 151 (5): *primicerius notariorum* in 358.

[b] *BLZG* 102 (iii): Bassus' son.

[c] *BLZG* 180 (ii), *PLRE* 439 (3), a pupil at the time. The career of Quirinus (cf. *PLRE*) is outlined in *Ep.* 366, which repeats this request to Bassus.

5. τούτῳ δὴ τῷ βελτίστῳ νέῳ νόσημα ἐμπεσὸν καὶ προβὰν εἰς μῆκος, μὴν γὰρ οὑτοσὶ δέκατος, πολλὴν μὲν ἐν πολλῷ χρόνῳ σοφίαν ἰατρῶν ἐνίκησε, καὶ ἦν ἡ πόλις ἐν ἀγρυπνίᾳ τε καὶ φόβῳ· κτῆμα γὰρ ἡμῖν Ὀνωράτος κοινόν. 6. νῦν δὲ ἔκλινε Μάρκελλος ὁ χρηστὸς τὸ κακόν, καὶ χρῆσθαι τοῖν ποδοῖν Ὀνωράτος ἄρχεται. τοῦτο δὲ ἦν κρεῖττον ἐλπίδος. 7. τί δὴ ταῦτα διῆλθον; οὐκ ἀνιᾶν σε βουλόμενος, ἀλλ' ἐπεὶ τοὺς ὑπὸ σοὶ πάντας ἀκούομεν ἐκεῖσε κεκλῆσθαι, ὧν εἷς οὗτος, διδάσκειν σε ἐθέλων ὡς οὔπω εὖ πράττομεν. 8. καίτοι θῶμεν τὸν νέον ὑγιέστερον εἶναι Κρότωνος· οὐκ ἂν ἦν μοι καὶ τότε λόγος πειρωμένῳ κατέχειν, ὅτι, 'ἀνδρῶν ἄριστε, Βάσσε, λόγων τὸν Ὀνωράτον ἐχόμενον καὶ μίαν ὄντα γονεῦσι παραμυθίαν ἐν ἡλικίᾳ δεομένῃ τῶν τοῦ πατρὸς ὀφθαλμῶν ἄφες ἡμῖν καὶ νῦν μὴ κίνει, καί, ὅτε βέλτιον, ἥξει;' ταῦτα οὐκ ἂν ἐπένευες εἰπόντος; 9. ὃς οὖν τότε ἂν ἔδωκας τὴν χάριν, νῦν οὐ λογιῇ τὴν ἀνάγκην; οἶμαί γε. κἀκεῖνο δὴ μαντεύομαι θαρρῶν, ὡς καὶ ἀπὼν τεύξομαι ὧν οἱ παρόντες ἀπολαύουσι Βάσσου τοῦ θαυμαστοῦ μέγα ποιουμένου Κυρῖνον εὖ

credit to such a noble father.   5. This fine young
fellow has been afflicted with an illness of long duration, ten months in fact, and in this long period it
has beaten all the skill of doctors and kept the city
in alarm and suspense, for Honoratus is a treasure
for us all alike.   6. Now the excellent doctor
Marcellus[d] has halted the trouble, and Honoratus is
just beginning to get on his feet—something more
than we dared hope for.   7. This account arises
not from the wish to cause you annoyance but—now
that I hear that all your subordinates, of whom he is
one, have been summoned to you—from the desire
to inform you that we are not yet well enough.[e]
8. However, suppose that we get the lad as healthy
as can be. Could I not then argue, in my desire to
keep him with me, "My dearest Bassus, Honoratus
is engaged in his education in rhetoric; he is the sole
consolation of his parents and he is of an age that
needs to be under his father's eye. Release him to
us, and do not upset him now: he will come when
the time is ripe"? If I said this, would you not agree?
9. So if you would have granted the favour then,
will you not take note of our predicament now? I am
sure you will. I confidently predict that, even in
absence, I shall obtain what those present enjoy
from the admirable Bassus, since he is most con-

[d] Physician in Antioch, who had also attended Libanius
(cf. *Letter* 5).

[e] This letter is occasioned by the summons issued by
heads of departments of provinces in 358, noted in *Letter*
26, note e.

ποιεῖν καὶ ἐμέ, παρ' ὧν αὐτῷ δῶρον οὐ φαῦλον τῶν ἔργων ἔπαιναι.

29. Ἀρισταινέτῳ

1. Νικέντιον μὲν τὰ σὰ γράμματα φίλον ἡμῖν ἐποίει, Μόδεστον δὲ ὄντα καὶ πρὸ τοῦ φίλον μᾶλλον ἢ πρότερον ἐποίει τὰ γράμματα. 2. τὴν μὲν οὖν πόλιν ἡμῖν εὔφρανε τῇ περὶ ἐμὲ σπουδῇ, ἐμὲ δὲ τῇ περὶ σοῦ μνήμῃ. τὸ γὰρ ὑπὸ τῶν καλῶς σε εἰδότων ᾀδόμενον καὶ αὐτὸς ἐφθέγγετο· οὔπω τοιοῦτον εἶδον. 3. καὶ διεξῄει πολλὰ τῶν σῶν προστιθείς, ὡς οὐκ ἂν πάντα εἰπεῖν ἔχοι. εἶτ' ἐκαλεῖτο μὲν ὑπὸ τῆς ἑσπέρας ἐπὶ λουτρά, κατείχετο δὲ ὑπὸ τῆς ἡδονῆς ἐν τῷ λόγῳ. 4. καὶ ὁ μὲν ἐπῄνει τὰ σά, Φουρτουνατιανὸς δὲ ἐκεῖνον, ὅτι ἃ χρῆν ἐπῄνει. τί οὖν ἐγώ; σιγῶν ἠρυθρίων ὡς ἂν αὐτὸς ἐπαινούμενος. εἰσάγω δὴ τὸν ἄνδρα εἰς τὸ βουλευτήριον, οὗ λόγων ἀγῶνες ἡμῖν. καὶ ἴσως οὐκ ἠνίασα λέγων. 5. λαβὼν δὴ παρὰ σοῦ δύο ἄρχοντας φίλους ἑνὶ γέμοντι σοφίας ἀμείβομαί σου

ᵃ *BLZG* 220 (i), *PLRE* 628 (1). As incoming governor he judged the case of the copyist charged with accepting

cerned to oblige Quirinus and myself, from both of whom he gains no small gift of praise for his deeds.

29. To Aristaenetus

1. Your letter made Nicentius[a] my friend, and Modestus,[b] already my friend, even more my friend than before.   2. Well, he has delighted our city with his support for me and me with his references to you, for he too echoed the sentiments expressed by all who know you well—that they have never yet seen anyone like you.[c]   3. He continued to tell us much about you, adding that he could never tell the whole of it. Then, though the coming of evening invited him to the baths, he was detained by the pleasure he found in the discussion.   4. He sang your praises and Fortunatianus[d] sang his for giving credit where credit was due. What about me, then? I never said a word; I blushed just as though I was the one being praised. I took him to the City Hall which is the scene of my rhetorical exercises,[e] and probably I did not discomfort him with my address. 5. Now that I have through you gained two governors as my friends, I return your kindness with one person crammed full of learning. The bearer is

bribes for interfering with the text of the panegyric on Strategius (*Or.* 1.114).

[b] *BLZG* 213, *PLRE* 605 (2). Friendly with Libanius, his career spans the next 20 years.

[c] Homer *Od.* 4.269.

[d] *BLZG* 159 (i), *PLRE* 369 (1).

[e] Cf. *Or.* 1.104.

τὸ δῶρον. Ἀρποκρατίων γὰρ οὑτοσὶ καὶ ποιητὴς
ἀγαθὸς καὶ παιδευτὴς ἀμείνων, δεινὸς μὲν ἐνθεῖ-
ναι τὰ τῶν παλαιῶν νέοις, δεινὸς δὲ ἐκείνοις παρι-
σωθῆναι, βεβιωκὼς δὲ συνεχῶς ἐν βιβλίοις ἥκιστα
μετέχει κομψείας[1] ἁπλοῦς τις ὢν καὶ γενναῖος καὶ
οὐκ ἂν ἁλοίη φρονῶν μὲν ἕτερα, λέγων δὲ ἄλλα.
6. οὗτος Εὐδαίμονι κοινωνήσας καὶ τροφῆς καὶ
μουσείων πάλαι μὲν ἐν τῷ φοιτᾶν, νῦν δὲ ἐν τῷ
παιδεύειν καὶ μικροῦ τῷ φίλῳ συμπεφυκὼς ὑπὸ
τῆς ὑμετέρας ἀπερράγη δυναστείας. καὶ νῦν δια-
κριθέντες, μετὰ δακρύων πορεύεται μὲν αὐτός,
κάθηται δὲ ἐκεῖνος.   7. Εὐδαίμονα μὲν οὖν ἐγὼ
παραμυθήσομαι, σὺ δ' Ἀρποκρατίωνι γίγνου
τοῦθ' ὅπερ ἡμεῖς Εὐδαίμονι.

[1] ἥκιστα μετέχει κομψείας F, conj. Re.   ἥκιστα μὲν εἶχε κομψείας V S   ἥδιστα μὲν εἶχε κομψείας Va Vo Vi   ἡδίστην μὲν εἶχε
κομψείαν Wolf (Vind.).

30. Ἰουλιανῷ

1. Διπλῆν ἀνήρησαι νίκην, τὴν μὲν ἐν ὅπλοις,
τὴν δὲ ἐν λόγοις, καί σοι τρόπαιον ἔστηκε, τὸν μὲν
ἀπὸ τῶν βαρβάρων, τὸ δ' ἀπ' ἐμοῦ τοῦ φίλου.

Harpocration,[f] a good poet and a better teacher: he is clever enough to instil the works of the classical authors into students, and to bring himself to the same level as those authors. His life has been spent uninterruptedly among books, and he is quite without affectation. He is a straightforward, genuine person, and you would never find him thinking one thing and saying something else.[g] 6. He has been an associate of Eudaemon[h] both in upbringing and in the schools, in times past as a pupil now as a teacher, and though almost of one flesh and blood with his friend,[i] he has been torn away by your irresistible attraction. And now they have separated, and he proceeds tearfully on his way, while his friend simply sits there.   7. I shall console Eudaemon, but you must treat Harpocration as I do Eudaemon.

[f] Harpocration (*PLRE* 408) is also introduced to Themistius, and went on to teach in Constantinople (*Ep.* 368).

[g] Plat. *Resp.* 2.361b, Homer *Il.* 9.313.

[h] Cf. *Letter* 14.

[i] Plat. *Resp.* 9.588b.

30. To Julian

1. You have gained a double victory, one in arms, the other in eloquence, and your trophies are raised, one over the barbarians, the other over me, your

2. τουτὶ δὲ τὸ τρόπαιον ἡδὺ τῷ κεκρατημένῳ. πᾶσι γὰρ δὴ πατράσιν εὐχῆς μέρος παίδων ἡττᾶσθαι, καὶ σὺ παρ' ἐμοῦ λαβὼν τὰς εἰς τὸ γράφειν ὁδοὺς οἷς ἔλαβες τὸν δόντα παρήνεγκας. 3. περὶ δὲ τοῦ μέτρου τῆς ἐπιστολῆς δεῖ δήπου με ἀπολογήσασθαι τῷ στρατηγῷ τὸν ῥήτορα, μᾶλλον δέ, τῷ λέγειν οὐχ ἧττον ἢ μάχεσθαι μαθόντι. 4. ἐπειδή σε βασιλεὺς ἐκάλεσεν εἰς κοινωνίαν τῆς ἀρχῆς, ᾠήθην δεῖν ἀφελεῖν τῆς παρρησίας καὶ μὴ ποιεῖν ἃ πρὸ τοῦ πρὸς ἄνδρα τοσοῦτον γεγενημένον. δεινὸν γάρ, εἰ σκιαμαχοῦντες μὲν ἐν ταῖς τῶν ἀγώνων μελέταις εἰσόμεθα, πῶς Περικλεῖ καὶ Κίμωνι καὶ Μιλτιάδῃ διαλεκτέον, ἐπὶ δὲ τῆς ἀληθείας παροψόμεθα τὸν νόμον. 5. αὐτὸ γὰρ τοῦθ' ὃ σὺ φῄς, ὡς αἱ τῶν στρατηγῶν ἐπιστολαὶ βραχεῖαι διὰ τὸ πράττειν, ἔπειθέ με καὶ αὐτὸν συστέλλειν τὰ γράμματα εἰδότα ὡς ὅστις ὑπ' ἀσχολίας οὐκ ἔχει μακρὰ ἐπιστέλλειν, κἂν ὑπ' ἄλλου μακρὰ γράφοντος ἐνοχληθείη. 6. νῦν οὖν

---

[a] To the emperor Julian, early in 358, a letter of congratulation upon his military success in the previous year, and also upon the excellence of his panegyric on Constantius. Julian had sent him a copy with a covering letter now lost (cf. Julian *ELF* no. 6); it is alluded to in § 5.

friend.[a]   2. To me in my defeat this trophy is pleasing, for it is part of the prayers of all parents to be worsted by their sons, and you, after getting from me the first steps towards writing, have excelled me, the donor, in what you have got.[b]   3. For the brevity of my letter I the orator must certainly make my excuses to the general, or rather, to one no less well versed in oratory than in warfare.[c]   4. When the emperor summoned you to share in his government, I thought I had to abate my independence and not to behave towards a man who had been so exalted as I had done previously.[d] If we, in our mock battles in the contests of declamation, know how to address Pericles, Cimon, and Miltiades, it would be scandalous for us to neglect the rules in real life.   5. Your own comment that letters from generals are short because of their life of action induced me too to compress my letter, for I know that anyone prevented from writing at length by pressure of business would be upset by the receipt of a long letter from someone else.[e]   6. Now that

[b] So Hector, Homer *Il.* 6.476 ff. Libanius claims to be parent to Julian in his literary style: *Or.* 1.130, 18.12–15; 15.7.

[c] Cf. *Or.* 13.51.

[d] This is the first letter from Libanius since Julian's elevation to the rank of Caesar. The one previous letter to Julian (*Ep.* 13) was written from Constantinople while Julian was in Nicomedeia.

[e] On the ideal of length and brevity in letter writing, cf. *Letter* 25.

ἐπειδή με παρακαλεῖς εἰς μῆκος, ὑπακούσομαι. καί σοι συγχαίρω πρῶτον μέν, ὅτι τὰ ὅπλα ἔχων ἐν χεροῖν οὐκ ἐξέλυσας τὴν περὶ λόγους σπουδήν, ἀλλὰ μάχῃ μὲν ὡς οὐδὲν ἄλλο δρῶν, ζῇς δὲ ἐν βιβλίοις ὡς ἀφεστηκὼς μάχης· ἔπειθ' ὅτι τῷ μεταδόντι τῆς ἀρχῆς οὐ παρέσχες μετάμελον, ὅτι μετέδωκεν, ἀλλ' ἡγούμενος τὸν αὐτὸν ἀνεψιόν τε εἶναί σοι καὶ συνάρχοντα καὶ δεσπότην καὶ διδάσκαλον οἷς τε πράττεις ἐκεῖνον ἐπιφημίζεις καὶ πρὸς τοὺς ἐναντίους πίπτοντας λέγεις· 'τί δ' ἂν ἐπάσχετε βασιλέως φανέντος;' 7. ταῦτα ἐπαινῶ καὶ τὸ μὴ μετὰ τῆς ἐσθῆτος ἀμεῖψαι τὴν γνώμην μηδ' ὑπὸ τῆς ἐξουσίας ἐκβαλεῖν τὴν μνήμην τῶν φίλων. καί σοι πολλὰ ἀγαθὰ γένοιτο, ὅτι με τὸν ἐπαινοῦντα τὴν σὴν φύσιν οὐ ψεύστην ἀπέφηνας, μᾶλλον δέ, ὅτι ψεύστην ἀπέφηνας οὐδὲν εἰπόντα τοσοῦτον ὁπόσον ἔδειξας. 8. ἐκεῖνό γε μὴν σὸν ἀτεχνῶς καὶ ἐξ οὐδενὸς παραδείγματος ὁρμηθέν. τῶν γὰρ ἄλλων ὁμοῦ τῇ βασιλείᾳ δεχομένων καὶ χρημάτων ἔρωτα καὶ τῶν μέν, εἰ καὶ μὴ πρότερον ἐπεθύμουν, ἀρχομένων ἐρᾶν, τῶν δ' ἐπιτεινόντων προενοικοῦν τὸ πάθος σὺ μόνος ἐν δυναστείᾳ

---

[f] Cf. *Or.* 18.72 ff, Amm. Marc. 16.5.3 ff.

you invite me to spread myself, I will obey. First, I
congratulate you upon the fact that, though you
have your hands full with fighting, you have not
relaxed your interest in oratory, but you fight as if
that were your sole object and yet spend your life
among books as if divorced from warfare.[f] Secondly,
I congratulate you that you have given your colleague in empire no cause to repent of his gift of it,
but regard him alike as your cousin, fellow ruler,
master, and teacher, and by your actions you
increase his fame, and say to his enemies as they
fall, "And what would your fate be if the emperor
were present?"[g]   7. All this I applaud, as well as
the fact you have not changed your attitude along
with your attire nor cast off the recollection of your
friends as a result of your position of power. And
may much blessing light upon you for proving me
no liar in praising your talents—or rather for
proving me a liar in saying nothing to equal the
talents you showed.   8. That indeed is something
quite peculiar to yourself, originating from no
model. Others gain along with supreme power a
love of money also: some of them begin to feel this
desire, even if they never did before, while others
emphasize the feeling if it previously resides in
them: but you alone when promoted to supreme

[g] Such commendation of Constantius was prudent for
both Libanius and Julian, since the imperial agents would
inevitably read these letters and report.

κατστὰς τῶν πατρῴων ἀπέστης τοῖς γνωρίμοις
τῷ μὲν οἰκίαν διδούς, τῷ δὲ ἀνδράποδα, γῆν
ἑτέρῳ, χρυσίον ἄλλῳ, καὶ διεδείχθης ἰδιώτης
μᾶλλον ἢ βασιλεὺς εὔπορος.   9. καὶ μή με οἴου
τῶν φίλων ἐξελαύνειν ἐμαυτόν, ὅτι μὴ τῶν εἰλη-
φότων εἷς καὶ αὐτός. ἔχω γὰρ εἰπεῖν, ἀνθ' ὅτου
μόνος οὐκ ἔχω. σὺ ταῖς πόλεσι τά τε ἄλλα βού-
λοι' ἂν εἶναι, δι' ὧν εὐδαιμονοῦσι πόλεις, καὶ δὴ
καὶ λόγων ἰσχὺν εἰδὼς ὅτι, τούτους ἂν σβέσῃ τις,
εἰς ἴσον ἐρχόμεθα τοῖς βαρβάροις.   10. ἔδεισας
οὖν μὴ λαβόμενος εὐπορίας φύγω τὴν τέχνην, καὶ
δεῖν ᾠήθης ἐν πενίᾳ με φυλάττειν, ὅπως καὶ
αὐτὸς φυλάττοιμι τὴν τάξιν. οὕτω μοι μαντεύ-
εσθαι βέλτιον. οὐ γὰρ ἐκεῖνό γ' ἂν εἴποις, ὡς
ἄλφιτα μὲν Καπανεύς τε καὶ Ἀμφιάραος, ὁ δεῖνα
δὲ οὔτ' ἐν λόγῳ οὔτ' ἐν ἀριθμῷ.   11. ἀλλ' ἔστι
τὸ μὴ δοῦναι κηδομένου τῶν ὅλων. τοιγαροῦν ἐν
ἀπορίᾳ χρημάτων πλουτοῦμεν ῥημάτων, τοῦτο δὴ
τὸ σόν, καὶ τὴν ἀρχὴν ἣν ἄρχομεν ἴσως οὐ καται-
σχύνομεν, ὥσπερ οὐδὲ σὺ τὴν μεγάλην.

ʰ Cf. *Or.* 18.201 f.

ⁱ Cf. *Or.* 1.119. Libanius stresses his disinterestedness
in the reign of Julian repeatedly, cf. *Or.* 1.125, 51.30; *Letter*
124.

power gave up your family property to your
friends—a house to one, slaves to another, land
to this one, gold to that—and you revealed yourself
wealthy as a subject rather than as a prince.[h]
9. And do not think that I exclude myself from the
number of your friends because I too am not one of
the recipients. I can give the reason why I am not
one of them. You want the cities to have everything
which promotes the happiness of cities, in particular
the force of oratory, for you know that, if this is
quenched, we are put on the same level as the
barbarians.[i] 10. So you were afraid that with the
accession of wealth I might desert my profession,
and you thought that you should keep me in poverty
so that I too might keep my post. This is the correct
way for me to interpret it; for indeed you would not
say that Capaneus and Amphiaraus are worth their
keep[j] while this fellow is not of any account or in the
reckoning.[k] 11. It is due to your concern for the
universal welfare that you have made no such gift.
Anyway, in our lack of wealth I am rich in eloquence—just as you are—and perhaps I do not disgrace the office I hold any more than you your great
office.

[j] These two heroes had died smitten by thunderbolts in
the attack of the Seven against Thebes. Libanius had suffered the same visitation: in his case the consequence was
his migraine.

[k] A favourite proverb for Libanius, e.g., *Or.* 31.27, *Ep.*
1170; see Zenob. 4:275.

31. Παύλῳ

1. Καὶ γὰρ ἦν εἰκός, ὦ φίλε Παῦλε, μὴ τὸν νόμον ἀνελεῖν, ὃν αὐτὸς ἔθηκεν ἐκεῖνος. ἦν δὲ οὗτος ὁ νόμος τῷ[1] μεμνῆσθαι προστιθέναι τὸ γράφειν. οἷς δ' ἂν ἔλθῃ τι παρὰ θεῶν ἀγαθόν, οὐκ ἐκείνοις δεῖ μόνον, ἀλλὰ καὶ τοῖς ἱερεῦσιν εἰδέναι χάριν. 2. σὺ τοίνυν ἡμῖν ἐν ἱερεῦσι τεταγμένος μετέχεις ὧν ἐκείνους εἰκός. οὐ γὰρ ἀγνοῶ τοῦθ' ὅτι ὤτρυνας σπεύδοντα καὶ αὐτόν, καὶ ὡς ὁ μὲν ὥρμητο γράφειν, σὺ δὲ ἐπῄνεις τὴν ὁρμήν. πιστεύω τοίνυν ἀμφοτέρους ἐμμενεῖν οἷς πεποιήκατε, σὲ μὲν προτρέψειν, ἐκεῖνον δὲ ἐπιστελεῖν.[2]

[1] τῷ inser. F, conj. Re. om. Wolf.
[2] ἐπιστελεῖν F, conj. Re.   ἐπιστέλλειν Wolf (Mss.).

---

[a] *BLZG* 233 (ii), *PLRE* 683 (4), Constantius' chief inquisitor, nicknamed *Catena*. As such he was at Julian's headquarters in early 358 to observe and report; it was

32. Καλυκίῳ

1. Ἡμῖν τοῖς οὐ μετασχοῦσι τῶν γαμικῶν

---

[a] *BLZG* 103. In early summer 358 Calycius, son of Hierocles and Libanius' pupil of three years standing, had just married the daughter of Acacius (iii). Libanius, in *Epp.* 371 and 373, had already suggested to Acacius the

31. To Paulus[a]

1. My dear Paulus, it was natural not to do away with the custom which he[b] personally instituted— namely, to round off one's remembrance with a letter. When people get some blessing from the gods, they must be grateful not to them alone but also to their priests. 2. Now we count you one of the priests, and you share in the prerogatives normal to gods, for I am not unaware that you encouraged him to this course, eager as he was,[c] and that, while it was his inclination to write, you commended his inclination. So I am confident that you will both continue on the course you have adopted, you of encouragement, he of correspondence.

mere prudence for Julian to begin corresponding with his friends with Paulus' full cognizance.

[b] Julian. Libanius flatters Paulus by insinuating that he had actually given permission for Julian to write, and this flattery is rather daringly conveyed in the full pagan terminology of classical literature.

[c] Cf. Homer *Il.* 8.293.

32. To Calycius[a]

1. Since I had no share in your wedding feast, a

possibility that Calycius should return to Antioch to finish his schooling. Now he approaches Calycius himself; his arguments are similar to those elaborated in the oration to Anaxentius (*Or.* 55).

δείπνων γράμματα γοῦν ἐχρῆν ὑπὲρ[1] τῶν γάμων
ἐλθεῖν παρὰ σοῦ δηλοῦντα ὡς τὰ μὲν ἔχει σοι
καλῶς, τῶν δὲ λόγων νῦν μὲν ἐπὶ σαυτοῦ φροντί-
ζεις, μικρὸν δὲ ὕστερον αὖθις σὺν ἡμῖν.   2. σὺ δ'
ἔοικας ἡμῶν ἐπιλελῆσθαι καὶ δέδοικα μὴ μεθ'
ἡμῶν καὶ τῶν λόγων. ἀλλ' οὐ δίκαιον, ὦ βέλ-
τιστε καὶ ἐξ ἀγαθῶν νεανίσκε. λογίζου γάρ, τίς
μέν σοι πατήρ, τίς δέ σοι κηδεστής. οὐκοῦν Ἱερο-
κλῆς μὲν οὗτος, Ἀκάκιος δὲ ἐκεῖνος, ἄμφω λαμ-
πρώ;   3. τί οὖν αὐτοὺς ἐποίησε μεγάλους; ἆρα
ἰσχὺς σώματος ἢ ποδῶν τάχος ἢ πλῆθος χρημάτων; οὐ μὰ Δία, ἀλλ' ἔν τι γενναῖον, οὗ καὶ Μίδα
βέλτιον ἂν ἦν μετασχεῖν ἢ σχεῖν ὁπόσον δὴ λέγεται χρυσόν. λέγειν γὰρ δυνηθέντες εἰς τοῦθ' ἧκον,
ἐν ᾧπέρ εἰσι.   4. πῶς οὖν οὐ δεινὸν Κίμωνα μὲν
τὰ ἐν τοῖς ὅπλοις ζηλῶσαι τοῦ πατρός, σὲ δὲ
χείρω φανῆναι τῆς τοῦ πατρὸς ἐν δικαστηρίοις
ἰσχύος, καὶ φιλοτιμεῖσθαι μὲν τῷ θυγατρὶ ῥήτορος
συνοικεῖν, ὅσον δὲ κέκτησαι ῥητορικῆς προέσθαι
παρὸν ὁπόσον ἄπεστι προσλαβεῖν;   5. παραινῶ
δή σοι τῷ θέρει μὲν τὰ ἀπελθόντα τῆς μνήμης
αὖθις εἰσάγειν, τοῦ χειμῶνος δὲ πλάττειν λόγους

[1] ὑπὲρ Mss.   περὶ F.

454

letter at least should have reached me from you about it, telling me that things go well with you and that, though you now concern yourself with your studies by yourself, you will resume them with me in a little while. 2. But you, it seems, have forgotten me, and I am afraid that you have forgotten your rhetorical studies along with me. But that is not right, my finest of lads, son of fine parents. For reflect who is your father and who your father-in-law. Is not Acacius this last, Hierocles the other, both men of note? 3. Well, what was it that made them great? Physical strength? fleetness of foot? store of wealth? No indeed! none of these, but one noble quality which Midas too would have done better to have rather than the possession of the masses of gold he is credited with.[b] It was by their capacity for eloquence that they have reached the position they now hold. 4. So it is a crying shame that, while Cimon emulated his father in feats of arms,[c] you should fall short of your father's proficiency at the bar, and that you should be eager to have the daughter of an orator as your wife and yet reject the oratory already acquired when it is in your power to acquire also what you do not yet possess. 5. My advice is for you in summer to reintroduce yourself to all that has slipped from your mind, and during the winter to come and practise oratory under me. Your wife will

[b] Cf. *Or.* 55.20.
[c] Cf. Plut. *Cimon* 5.1.

ὑφ᾽ ἡμῖν. ἡ γυνὴ δὲ πάντως ἕψεται παρακαλοῦσα καὶ συνευχομένη γενέσθαι σοι τὸ διὰ λόγων κάλλος ἢ τὸ Νιρέως.   6. σὺ δὲ μήτοι νομίσῃς αἰσχρὸν ἐπὶ γάμῳ κοινωνεῖν μουσείων. τὸ γὰρ δὴ φύσει καλὸν οὐκ ἔστιν ὅτε οὐκ ἔστι καλόν, καὶ μείζων ἔπαινος ἀφειμένον παρὰ τοῦ νόμου προθυμίᾳ μετιέναι τὴν θήραν. ἀφ᾽ ἧς εὐφρανεῖς μὲν φίλους, φοβήσεις δὲ δυσμενεῖς, καὶ τοὺς μὲν ἕξεις ὠφελεῖν, τοὺς δὲ κατασύρειν.   7. ἐνθυμοῦ δὲ ὅτι καὶ Σωκράτης σοφὸς ὤν, ὥς φησιν ὁ θεός, τὰς ἐν γήρᾳ μαθήσεις οὐκ ἔφευγεν ἀεὶ καιρὸν εἶναι νομίζων μανθάνειν. οὐδὲν δεινὸν ἐγκεῖσθαι βιβλίοις παρούσης γυναικός, τοῦτο μὲν οὖν ἥδιστον παρ᾽ ᾗ βούλοιο ἂν εὐδοκιμεῖν, καὶ ταύτης ὁρώσης καλόν τι ποιεῖν.   8. καὶ μὴν εἰ μὲν οὐ κινεῖ σε πρὸς ταῦτα ὁ πατὴρ οὐκ οἰόμενός σε ἀναστήσειν, κρείττων φάνηθι τῆς ἐλπίδος ἐκείνου· κινοῦντος δὲ εἰ μὴ προσέχοις, ἀνάγκη λυπεῖν τε καὶ λυπεῖσθαι. τοῦτο δέ ἐστι ζητοῦντα ῥᾳστώνην ἐν ἀηδίᾳ ζῆν. 9. ἀλλ᾽, ὦ φίλτατε, λογισάμενος, ἡλίκην ποιήσεις πανήγυριν καὶ γονεῦσι καὶ κηδεσταῖς καὶ τῷ πάντα ἀρίστῳ θείῳ καὶ τῇ χρηστῇ γυναικὶ καὶ

---

[d] Cf. *Letter* 96.1; Homer *Il.* 2.671.
[e] Cf. *Epp.* 652.1, 1171.2: Diog. Laert. 2.5.32, and 37.

certainly follow you, with encouragement and prayers that you may gain rather the beauty of eloquence than that of Nireus.[d] 6. Do not regard it as at all a disgrace to participate in school activities after marriage. For what is naturally good must invariably be good, and there is all the more credit if one who is released by convention should voluntarily engage in its pursuit. By means of it, you will give your friends cause for rejoicing, your enemies cause for fear, and you will be able to help the former and demolish the others. 7. Reflect that even Socrates, a wise man, as the god affirms, did not try to avoid learning in old age, since he thought that any time was time for learning.[e] There is nothing wrong in applying oneself to books while one's wife is present. It is, in fact, the nicest thing to engage upon some noble action under the eyes of her whose good opinion you wish to have. 8. Moreover, if your father is under the impression that you will not budge and so does not urge you to it, rise superior to what he expects of you. If he does urge you and you pay no attention to him, you are bound both to cause and to feel pain. That is, that in your search for leisure, your life will be without pleasure.[f] 9. But, my dearest boy, consider how much joy you will give your parents and your wife's family, your peerless uncle,[g] your good wife, and myself

[f] Cf. Or. 55.31 ff.
[g] Demetrius. See stemma, PLRE 1139.

ἐμοὶ τῷ πολλὰ περὶ σὲ πεπονηκότι, νῦν μὲν ἔμπλησον σαυτὸν παλαιῶν συγγραμμάτων, γεωργῶν δὲ ἤδη τῶν περὶ τὰς ληνοὺς πεπαυμένων αὐτὸς ἥκειν δεῦρο τύχῃ ἀγαθῇ.

33. Εὐφημίῳ

1. Τί τοῦτο νομίσαι χρή; πότερον ἀλογίαν ἢ δυστυχίαν ἢ πέρας αἰνίγματος; Ἀντωνῖνος ἐκεῖνος ὁ τῶν πατρῴων τοῖς ὡς εὐπορεῖ λέγουσιν ἀποστάς, μᾶλλον δὲ τοῦ μηδενὸς αὐτοῖς ἀποστάς, οὐ γὰρ ἦν οὐδέν, αὖθις ἠνάγκασται σιγηγεῖν. καὶ σὺ ταῦτα γράψαι ὑπέμεινας οὐκ ἐνθυμηθεὶς ὅτι τοῖς σαυτοῦ μάχῃ; 2. τοιγαροῦν ὁ μὲν φεύγει τοῦ τὴν μητέρα ὁρᾶν ἐστερημένος, τουτὶ γὰρ ἦν αὐτῷ πλέον οἴκοι μόνον, ὡς τά γε ἄλλα οὐδὲν ἀμείνων ἡ πατρὶς τῆς ἀλλοτρίας, Οἰδίπουν δὲ περιόντες ζητοῦμεν, ὅστις ἡμᾶς τῆς ἀπορίας ἀπαλλάξει. 3. ἀλλὰ γὰρ οὐδὲν Οἰδίπου δεῖ τοῖς

---

a *BLZG* 136 (i), *PLRE* 298 (2). His office is not known precisely, but he certainly held a fiscal court and was presumably a deputy of the *comes sacrarum largitionum.*

b Despite *BLZG* 78 (iii) and *PLRE* 74 (4), this must be the celebrated renegade of Amm. Marc. 18.5.1 ff. There is nothing in this letter to indicate that he was a fugitive

LETTERS

who have laboured much upon you, and now fill
yourself with classical literature, and when the
farmers have ended their work on the vintage, come
back here in person, and blessings light upon you.

33. To Euphemius[a]

1. What must I make of this? Absurdity? misfortune? an utter riddle or worse? Antoninus[b]—he
who gave up his paternal possessions to those who
allege that he is rich, or rather, he who gave up
nothing to them, since there was nothing to give—
he has again been saddled with the duty of supplying corn. And did you allow this registration
without considering that you are opposing your own
interests? 2. Anyway, he is in exile, deprived of
the sight of his mother, which was the only thing
left to him at home, for in all else his home town is
no better than a foreign land, while we go round in
search of an Oedipus to get us out of our quandary.[c]
3. Yet there is no need of an Oedipus, nor yet of a

decurion, only that he was a landowner. As Silomon (p. 42)
indicated, this dates the letter to 358; Petit (*Vie Municipale* 160 f) agrees. This letter relates the beginnings of the
scandalous treatment of Antoninus, which led to his defection to the Persians in 359.

[c] Referring to the riddle of §1, and to Oedipus solving
the riddle of the Sphinx.

παροῦσιν οὐδέ γε Τειρεσίου. ἀλλ' ἡμάρτομεν
ἡμεῖς, ἡμάρτομεν οὐ δεηθέντες τοῦ τὰ τοιαῦτα
στρέφοντος, ὃς τὸν μὲν ἔλυσε, τὸν δὲ ἐνέδησε. τοῦ
γὰρ κράτος ἐστὶ μέγιστον. ἀλλ' ἐπεὶ ἀασάμην,
ἰδού, τὸν ἄνθρωπον ἱκετεύω διὰ σοῦ.   4. καίτοι
τοῦτο μεῖζον ἢ ὁ τότε πορευόμενος Αἴας ἐπὶ τὰς
διαλλαγάς. ἀλλ' εἰξάτω καὶ μὴ φιλονεικείτω.
πάντως, κἂν μὴ τοῦτο τοῖς αὑτοῦ φίλοις ὑπουρ-
γήσῃ, πολλαχόθεν ἄλλοθεν χαριεῖται· πάρεστι
γάρ.

---

[d] Ursulus, *comes sacrarum largitionum*—so Ammianus. The use of his summary powers is perhaps described
as a tragic *peripeteia,* cf. Arist. *Poetics* 1452a27.

34. Ἀρισταινέτῳ

1. Πρότερον μὲν ἐθαύμαζον τὸν κράτιστον
Ἑρμογένην ἀπὸ τῆς φιλοσοφίας ἧς ἤκουον αὐτῷ
μέλειν, νῦν δὲ δὴ καὶ φιλῶ τὸν ἄνθρωπον, διότι δὴ
πόσου τε καὶ τίνος ἄξιος εἶ γινώσκει. λέγεται γὰρ
ἄνδρα τέ σε ἀγαθὸν ἡγεῖσθαι καὶ τὸ συνεῖναι μέγα
ποιεῖν καὶ τὸ μὴ συνεῖναι βαρύ.   2. τοῖς μὲν οὖν
ἄλλοις ἔπεισι σοὶ συγχαίρειν, ἐμοὶ δὲ ἀμφοῖν· σοὶ

Teiresias for us here. But I was wrong, I was wrong in not making my request of him who can effect such a reversal, who frees one man and binds another.[d] "For his might is all powerful. But since I have been blind"[e]—look, I make my plea to him through you. 4. This request is more than that of Ajax at the time when he went to effect a reconciliation;[f] but let him give way and not bear malice. In any case, even if he does not render this service to his friends, he will oblige them by many other means, for he has the power.

[e] A combination of Homer *Il.* 2.118 and 9.119.

[f] Cf. Homer *Il.* 9.623 ff, where Ajax and Odysseus are sent to effect a reconciliation of the Greeks with Achilles, but without success.

34. To Aristaenetus[a]

1. In times past I used to admire the most excellent Hermogenes[b] for the philosophy which, I was told, is his interest. Now, however, I really love him for recognizing your worth and quality. The news is that he regards you as a man of parts, and that he prizes association with you and deplores the lack of it.   2. Well, it will occur to most people to congratulate you, but I congratulate both of you—

[a] Now vicar of *Pietas,* midsummer 358 (cf. Silomon, p. 19).

[b] *BLZG* 173 (iv), *PLRE* 423 (3) and (?9): praetorian prefect in succession to Strategius.

461

LIBANIUS

μέν, ὅτι σοι πρόσκειται τοσαύτη δύναμις, τῷ δ', ὅτι φιλῶν ὃν ἐχρῆν εὐδοκιμεῖ τῇ κρίσει. 3. δεῖ δή σε φιλούμενον ὅσα ἂν ἐξῇ ἐν ταῖς παραινέσεσιν ὠφελεῖν ἐκεῖνον μὴ κατοκνεῖν· ἔξεστι δὲ νῦν ὑπὲρ ἀδικουμένου φίλου κωλῦσαι φίλον ἁμαρτάνειν. Νικέντιον γὰρ τὸν καλόν, ὃν σὺ πρὸς ἡμᾶς ἐπῄνεις ἐν γράμμασι, καὶ τὸ γράμμα γε ἐκεῖνο φιλίαν ἡμῖν εἰργάσατο, τοῦτον δὴ τὸν ἄνδρα, δι' ὃν ἐπιδημεῖ μὲν ἡ δίκη, βία δὲ οἴχεται, πανήγυρις δὲ ἡμῖν ἡ πόλις, εὐφημίας ἐλπίζοντα περιέστηκε ζημία λυποῦσα μὲν καὶ τῇ βλάβῃ, πένης γὰρ ἡμῖν ἐπὶ τοσαύταις ἀρχαῖς ὁ Νικέντιος, ἔχουσα δέ τι πικρότερον τῆς βλάβης τὴν ἀδοξίαν. ἡ γὰρ καταδίκη ζημία τίς ἐστι κατεγνωκυῖα κακίαν. 4. τοῖς μὲν οὖν ἀδικοῦσιν Ἑρμογένης ἐπαγέτω δίκην, ἐγὼ πρῶτος ἐπαινῶ τὴν ὀργήν, κἂν παύσηται τῆς ἐπὶ τοῖς τοιούτοις ὀργῆς, καὶ ἐγὼ τῶν ἐπαίνων, τὸ νῦν δὲ τοῦτο παραγωγή τίς ἐστι καὶ ἔργον ἀπάτης, οὐ τῆς Ἑρμογένους φύσεως. 5. ἄκουε δέ· σταθμός τίς ἐστι περὶ τὸν Εὐφράτην, Καλ-

---

ᶜ Consularis Syriae 358; cf. Letter 29. Owing to the demands of the Persian campaigns, the governorship of Syria was a risky responsibility in these years. Not only

you because you have such influence to support you, and him because, in choosing the friend he should, he gains credit for sound judgement. 3. You then, the object of his affection, must not hesitate to help him to the best of your powers by your advice, and you may now, by taking up the cause of a friend who is wronged, prevent a friend from falling into error. Our good friend Nicentius[c] whom you used to commend to me in your letters—in fact, that letter of yours formed the basis of the friendship between us—Nicentius, I repeat, who has caused justice to dwell among us, expelled violence, and made our city merry, has been visited with a fine, when he expected acclamation for his services. This fine causes him financial embarrassment, for Nicentius is a poor man for all his career in office, but it involves something worse than the embarrassment, namely disgrace. The imposition of such punishment implies condemnation for misconduct. 4. Now, let Hermogenes inflict punishment on the guilty: I would be the first to praise his righteous indignation, and should his indignation cease in such cases, my praises would also. But in this present case there is some mistake. It stems from deception, not from Hermogenes' character. 5. Now listen! There is a post station near the Euphrates called Callinicus,[d] the

was Nicentius broken, but his successors Sabinus and Tryphonianus were dismissed under a cloud.

[d] Amm. Marc. 23.3.7.

λίνικος ὄνομα αὐτῷ· Καλλινίκου γὰρ ἐνταῦθα
ἀποσφαγέντος ὁ σοφιστὴς γίνεται προσηγορία τῷ
τόπῳ, οἷα πολλὰ μὲν ἐν γῇ, πολλὰ δὲ ἐν θαλάττῃ
πάλαι.   6. τοῦτο δὴ τὸ χωρίον ἔχει στρατιὰν
ἱδρυμένην, ἣν δεῖ τρέφεσθαι παρ' ἡμῶν οὐκ ἐκεῖσε
κομιζόντων, ἀλλ' ἑτέρωσε τὴν τροφήν, ἐκεῖθεν δὲ
εἰς Καλλίνικον ἄγειν νόμος τὸν ἄρχοντα τῶν περὶ
τὸν Εὐφράτην. Νικέντιος δὲ τὰ αὑτοῦ διακονήσας
ὧν ἐπλημμέλησαν ἕτεροι δίκας δίδωσι, τοῦτο δὴ
τὸ ἐν Αὐλίδι.   7. ἴσως μὲν οὖν οὐδ' αὐτὸς διηγη-
σάμην κακῶς, εἰ δ' οὖν τι καὶ ἐξηνέχθην, Νικέν-
τιός σε διδάξει καλῶς. σὺ δὲ βοήθησον δυοῖν
ἄρχουσι τὸν μὲν ἐξελόμενος βλάβης ἀδίκου, τὸν
ἐλάττω, τὸν δ' ἀποστήσας ὀργῆς οὐ δικαίας, τὸν
κρείττω.   8. εἰ δὲ παιδὸς ἡγεῖται τὴν μεταβο-
λήν, τὴν μὲν ἐπὶ τὰ χείρω νομιζέτω φαύλην, τὴν
δὲ τῶν φαύλων τι λύουσαν ἀγαθήν, ἄλλως θ' ὅτε
τὸ μὲν τίμημα τηρεῖν ἂν ἔχοι, τὸν δ' ἔξω τῆς
αἰτίας ἀφιέναι.   9. τὸ γὰρ χρυσίον εἰσπραττέτω
μέν, εἰσπραττέτω δὲ παρὰ τῶν λελοιπότων τὴν
τάξιν καὶ προσέτι γε τῶν ἐξηπατηκότων, οἳ
σφίσιν αὐτοῖς χαριζόμενοι τὰ οὐκ ὄντα ἔφρασαν.
10. ἐπειδὴ γὰρ θυμὸς μέγας διοτρεφέων ὑπάρχων,

place name being derived from that of Callinicus the sophist who was murdered there—the sort of thing for which there have been plenty of examples in the past on land and sea.   6. This place has a standing garrison, which has to get its supplies from us, though we do not deliver to it direct but to a depot elsewhere, from which it is the job of the governor of Euphratensis to convey it to Callinicus.[e] Nicentius did his part of the job but is being punished for other people's mistakes—just like what happened at Aulis.[f]   7. Well, perhaps I have not made a bad job of explaining the facts myself, but if I have veered off course at all, Nicentius will put you right. Please help the two governors, by relieving the junior of them of an unwarranted punishment, and by causing the senior to abate his unwarranted anger.   8. If he thinks it childish to change his mind, let him consider that to do so for the worse is a fault, but to do so by removing some fault is good, especially when he can still maintain the fine and yet release him from the charge.   9. Let him press for the gold, but from those who have deserted their post and, what is more, deceived him by lying tales to serve their own advantage.   10. Since "great is the

[e] Cf. Liebeschuetz, *Antioch* 163; Petit, *Vie Municipale* 256, n.2.

[f] As with the sacrifice of Iphigeneia, Nicentius is being punished for the sins of others.

μὴ ἔστω τοῖς φενακίζουσιν ἄδεια, ὅπως τῆς ἀληθείας κρατούσης μηδεὶς ἀδίκως κολάζηται. λύων
δὲ τὴν αὐτοῦ ψῆφον ἐννοείτω τὸν βασιλέα Κρη-
τῶν τὸν παῖδα Διός, ὃς εἰς τὸ ἄντρον δι' ἐνάτου
πορευόμενος ἔτους ὢν ἐτεθείκει νόμων[1] οὐκ ἠσχύ-
νετο κινῶν ὃν κρεῖττον ἦν κινεῖσθαι.

[1] ὧν ... νόμων F.   ὃν ... νόμον Mss.   οὓς ... νόμους Wolf.

35. Ἀρισταινέτῳ

1. Ἐπανήκων ἡμῖν ὁ Σπεκτάτος ἀπὸ τῆς
πρεσβείας πολλοῖς ἔδοξεν εὐδαίμων εἶναι, τοῖς
μέν, ὅτι πολλὴν εἶδε γῆν καὶ ὄρη καὶ ποταμούς,
τοῖς δ', ὅτι τὴν Περσῶν δίαιταν καὶ ἔθη καὶ
νόμους ἐν οἷς ζῶσιν. οἱ δὲ τὴν αὐτοῦ τοῦ δυνα-
στεύοντος θέαν καὶ τῶν λίθων οἷς ἐκεκόσμητο
μέγα ἦγον, τοῖς δὲ σεμνὸν ἐδόκει τὸ δόντα δῶρα
λαβόντα ἀπελθεῖν.   2. ἐμοὶ δὲ καὶ ταῦτα μὲν
ἔχειν τινὰ χάριν ἐφαίνετο, κάλλιστον δὲ τὸ δεί-

[a] This is the last letter written to Aristaenetus (cf.
Silomon, pp. 14, 19). He died in the earthquake at
Nicomedeia, 24 August 358 (Amm. Marc. 17.7.6). The
letter was probably composed in the interval between the
event and the news of it reaching Antioch, and was carried
by Spectatus, who had stopped briefly in Antioch on his

wrath of Zeus-born"[g] prefects, let there be no immunity to tricksters, so that truth may prevail and no one be unjustly punished. Should he rescind his own verdict, let him bear in mind the king of Crete, son of Zeus, who travelled to the cave after a nine-year interval and had no scruples in altering one of the laws he had ordained which was better altered.[h]

[g] Cf. Homer *Il.* 2.196.

[h] Cf. Plat. *Legg.* 1.624b, *Minos* 319d-e; Homer *Od.* 19.178.

35. To Aristaenetus[a]

1. Spectatus has returned from the embassy; some people regard him as fortunate in that he has seen vast lands, mountains and rivers, others that he has seen the manner of life of the Persians, their civilization, and the laws under which they live. Others again think the spectacle of the monarch and the jewels that adorned him to be of great moment, while yet others consider it noteworthy that, after presenting gifts, he should come away in receipt of gifts. 2. This too, I admit, had some passing attraction for me, but the finest thing of all was that he should return after demonstrating his force as an

return from the embassy to Persia, which had left in 357 (*Ep.* 513, Amm. Marc. 17.5.15), and returned in 358. Libanius presents the negotiations on the Roman side as a *tour de force* of classical rhetoric on the part of his cousin Spectatus.

ξαντα ῥήτορος δύναμιν ἐν Σούσοις ἐπανελθεῖν. καίτοι γε ᾤμην αὐτὸν ἀποβεβληκέναι τουτὶ τὸ σθένος πολὺν ἤδη χρόνον ἀπὸ τῶν βιβλίων μετενηνεγμένον ἄλλοσε, τῷ δ' ἄρα ἐνέμενεν ἐπὶ τοῦ ἤθους ἡ δεινότης. 3. ὡς γὰρ ἐχρημάτιζεν ὁ Πέρσης καὶ ὁ λόγος ἦν περὶ τῶν διαφορῶν καὶ πολὺς ἐνέκειτο τοὺς παππῴους ἀπαιτῶν[1] ὅρους καὶ πολλάκις ἐρωτῶν εἰ μὴ δίκαιον εἰς τοὺς παῖδας τὰ τῶν προγόνων καταβαίνειν, τὰ μὲν παρὰ τῶν ἄλλων ἐνταῦθα παλάισματα Σπεκτάτος ἀπαγγελεῖ, τοῦ γέλωτος ἦν οἷός τε γένηται κρατεῖν· οἷς δὲ οὗτος ἐχρήσατο, πάνυ γενναῖα καὶ διασείοντά γε τοὺς εὐπροσώπους τοῦ Πέρσου λόγους. 4. ἔφη γάρ· 'εἰ μέν, ὦ βασιλεῦ, Κωνστάντιός σου τῆς γῆς[2] ἀποτέμνεται, τῶν ὅπλων ἔχου, μέχρις ἂν ἐκεῖνος τοῦ πλεονεκτεῖν· εἰ δ' οἷς μὲν ἐγκαλεῖς πάλαι τεθνᾶσιν, ὁ δὲ μεθ' ὧν εἰσῆλθεν εἰς τὸν πόλεμον, ταῦτα ἔχων καταθέσθαι τὸν πόλεμον ἐθέλει, σκόπει μὴ πλεονεξίαν ἐγκαλῶν αὐτὸς τοῦτο ποιῶν ἐλεγχθῇς.' 5. ἐπὶ τοιούτοις ἐνέδυ, φασί, τὴν λεοντῆν, ὥστ' ἐκεῖνον βλέποντα

[1] πατρῴους ἀπαιτῶν καὶ παππῴους Vi.
[2] γῆς F, conj. Re.   ἀγάπης Wolf (Mss.).

orator in Susa. You see, I believed that he had cast away this power, since he has been diverted elsewhere from his books for such a long time now,[b] but the skill has seemingly remained ingrained in him. 3. For as to how the Persian began the negotiations, and turned the talk to the matters in dispute and forcefully pressed his demands for the return of his ancestral frontiers,[c] repeatedly asking whether it was not right that the possessions of the forefathers should pass down to their sons—Spectatus will report the arguments of the others on this issue, if only he can keep himself from laughing. But the arguments he himself used were very sound and sadly shook the specious pleas of the Persian. 4. They ran as follows: "Sire, if Constantius is appropriating parts of your territories, then maintain yourself under arms while ever he maintains his aggression. However, if those whom you accuse are long since dead, and he wants to put an end to hostilities on terms of the status quo, be careful that, for all your complaints of aggression, you yourself be not proved the aggressor." 5. In this way he bearded the lion,[d] as the saying goes, and the

[b] For Libanius, a scholar who enters imperial service wastes his natural talents and his schooling. These are better put at the disposal of his home city.

[c] In particular, Mesopotamia and Armenia; cf. Amm. Marc. 17.5 and 14.

[d] Cf. Plat. *Crat.* 411a, *Paroem. Gr.* 1.75. The proverb is from Heracles donning the lion skin.

μὲν εἰς τὴν ἡλικίαν, ἐξετάζοντα δὲ τὸν λόγον οὐκ
ὀλιγάκις σεῖσαι τὴν κεφαλήν. καὶ διὰ τὸν σὸν
ἐρώμενον ὁ συκοφαντῶν ἡμῖν τὸν βασιλέα σεσίγη-
κεν. 6. ἄλλῳ μὲν οὖν συνεῖπε λαμπρῶς, αὐτὸς
δ' ὑπὲρ αὑτοῦ τί ποτ' ἂν καὶ λέγοι προθυμότερον
ὡς σὲ παρ' ἡμῶν τρέχων ἢ παρ' ἡμᾶς ἐκ τῆς
Περσίδος;

36. Ὑγιεινῷ

1. Οὐκ ἠμνημόνησα τῶν συνθηκῶν αἳ ἦσαν
ἡμῖν περὶ γραμμάτων, ἀλλ' ἐκωλύθην τὰς συνθή-
κας ἐμπεδῶσαι κακοῖς μυρίοις. 2. πρῶτον μὲν
γὰρ ἡ κεφαλή με καταβαλοῦσα εἶχεν αὐτὴ δεξα-
μένη πλῆθος ἰλίγγων καὶ οὐκ ἦν οὔθ' ἡμῖν οὔτε
τοῖς ἰατροῖς θαρρεῖν. εἶτ' ἐκεῖθεν ἐπὶ τὴν κοιλίαν
τὸ δεινὸν καταβὰν ῥεύματα ἐμιμεῖτο ῥυάκων, τὸ
δὲ ἐπισχῆσον οὐκ ἐφαίνετο. καὶ τούτοις τοιούτοις
οὖσι προσετέθη Λήμνιά φασι κακά, μᾶλλον δέ,
μικρόν τι εἶπον τὸ πτῶμα Νικομηδείας δηλῶσαι
βουληθεὶς τοῖς ἐν Λήμνῳ κακοῖς. 3. διὰ τοιούτων τὸ θέρος ἐλθόντες νῦν φαρμάκου πόσει τὸ
σῶμα κουφίσαντες ἐπιστέλλομέν σοι τῆς μὲν
σιγῆς τὰς αἰτίας ἀποδιδόντες, κινεῖν δέ σε πρὸς

result was that, on looking at his youth and mulling over his argument, he just kept shaking his head. And so, through him you admire so much, the traducer of our emperor was reduced to silence. 6. So, after so signally succeeding in his advocacy for another, what more spirited argument could he present on his own behalf when he goes from us to you than that which he put when he came to us here from Persia?

36. To Hygieinus[a]

1. I have not forgotten the agreement we made about writing, but I have been prevented from ratifying it by countless troubles. 2. First of all, my head has kept setting me down. It has been affected with bouts of giddiness, and neither the doctors nor I could feel any confidence. Then the trouble went down from there to my belly, and it behaved just like floods of water. Nothing appeared to stop it. On top of troubles like these there came the final straw,[b] or worse—for that is an understatement to describe the disaster at Nicomedeia. 3. That is the way I have passed the summer, but now that I have gained physical relief by taking my medicine, I am writing to you with an explanation of the reasons for my silence. I do not expect you to put your-

[a] Cf. *Letter* 5.
[b] Cf. Herod. 6.138, from which 'Lemnian deeds' become proverbial for horror stories.

471

τὰ ἡμέτερα τόν γε οἴκοθεν ὡρμημένον οὐκ ἀξιοῦντες, ὡς ὅστις τινὰ παρακλήσεσιν ἐπεγείρει, κατε-
γνωκὼς ἀργίαν τοῦτο ποιεῖ. 4. σὺ δ' οὐχ ὅπως
αὐτὸς ῥᾳθυμεῖς, ἀλλὰ καὶ ἄλλον ἂν ἐξοτρύναις
εἶναι πρόθυμον εἰς ἡμᾶς, ἴσως μέν τι καὶ ἐν ἡμῖν
ἄξιον εὐνοίας εὑρών, πλέον γε μὴν ἐκεῖνο σκοπῶν,
ὅπως δόξεις ἀκολουθεῖν τῷ πατρί. 5. καὶ γὰρ
ἐκεῖνος ἑώρα τέ με ὡς ἥδιστα καὶ μετεδίδου
λόγων τε καὶ βιβλίων. καὶ ὁ δοὺς ἀρχὴν ἡμῖν εἰς
τὴν ἀμείνω δόξαν ἐκεῖνος ἦν. καὶ νῦν, εἴπερ ἦν,
εἷς ἂν μοι πολλῶν ἦν ἀντάξιος. 6. ἃ σὺ λογιζόμενος ἐπιχειρεῖς μοι δεικνύειν ὡς, εἰ καὶ Δουλκί-
τιος τέθνηκεν, ἀλλ' οὐχ ἥ γε πρὸς ἐμὲ σπουδὴ τῆς
ὑμετέρας τέθνηκεν οἰκίας. 7. ταύτην μὲν οὖν
ζῶσαν ἀεὶ παρέξεις, τοὺς δὲ ἀνεψιοὺς ἴσθι σοι τῇ
μὲν ἄλλῃ καὶ σφόδρα ἐπαινεῖσθαι, λυπῆσαι δὲ ἑνὶ
τούτῳ τοὺς γείτονας· μεγάλῃ γὰρ ἀεὶ φωνῇ τοὺς
λόγους συλλέγοντες τὸν ὕπνον ἀφαιρούμενοι τῶν
πλησίον οἰκούντων τοὺς μὲν ἐξήλασαν, τοὺς δὲ
ἐπέτριψαν.

self out to leave home and come and see me, for whenever anyone encourages people with exhortation, by so doing he declares them guilty of idleness. 4. Not that you are negligent yourself; you would be more likely to spur on someone else to support me, possibly because you find in me something that deserves your kindness, but more probably your intention is to be thought of as following your father's lead.[c]   5. He indeed looked upon me with the greatest kindness and allowed me to share in both his oratory and his books; and he it was who gave a start to the increase of my fame. If he were alive now, he alone would count for as much as an army of supporters.[d]   6. Bearing this in mind you are trying to show me that, even if Dulcitius is dead, the support given me by your family is not dead. 7. So this lives on and you will always provide me with it. As for your cousins, you may be assured they are in general highly praised, but in this one particular they annoy the neighbours. They are always rehearsing their declamations at the top of their voices and deprive their next door neighbours of sleep, so that some they have caused to move, others to have a breakdown!

[c] Dulcitius (cf. § 6).

[d] In Constantinople, 340–2. Evidently he was a doctor, like his son. The Homeric reference is *Il.* 11.514.

37. Δημητρίῳ

1. Αὐτήν τε ταύτην ἐθρήνησα τὴν πόλιν ἣν ἥδιστα μὲν εἶδον, ἄκων δὲ ἐξέλιπον, ἐπόθουν δὲ καὶ οἴκοι καθήμενος, πρό τε τῆς πόλεως τὸν ὑπ' αὐτῆς τε καὶ μετ' αὐτῆς οἰχόμενον τὸν γενναῖον Ἀρισταίνετον. 2. νομίζω δὲ τῶν θρήνων μηδέτερον μὲν ἐμόν, ἀμφοτέρους δὲ εἶναι τῆς Λύπης. ἐν ᾧ γὰρ ἐξειστήκειν τε ἐμαυτοῦ καὶ φόβον παρεῖχον τοῖς οἰκείοις ὡς οὐκ ἀντισχήσων τῷ κακῷ, τότε ἐκείνη λαβοῦσά μου τὴν χεῖρα ἔγραψεν ὅ τι ἤθελεν. 3. οἷς δὲ ἑκάτερον ἔδειξα, τέτταρες ἦσαν, οὐ γὰρ ἦν ὁ καιρός μοι θεάτρου, πρὸς μὲν τῷ θείῳ Πρισκιανὸς ὁ ῥήτωρ, ἐπὶ δὲ τούτῳ Φιλοκλῆς ὁ καλὸς καὶ ὅ γε φιλεῖν μεμελετηκὼς Εὐσέβιος. Σαβῖνος δὲ ἄρα ἦν ἐπ' ἀγροῦ. 4. οὗτοι μὲν ἐμοῦ, τούτων δὲ οὐδεὶς ὅστις οὐκ ἤκουσεν ὡς ἀκούσει· καὶ αὐτίκα με περιειστήκεσαν ἀνάγκαι κελευόντων ἢ ἀναγινώσκειν ἢ ὁμολογεῖν ἀδικεῖν.

---

[a] For Libanius' monody on Aristaenetus see Foerster vol. xi, pp. 623–4; that upon Nicomedeia survives (*Or.* 61). See § 5 below.

[b] The orator was reluctant to give a public declamation unless it had been tested first with a select audience. For the encomium on Phasganius privacy was, however, more

37. To Demetrius

1. I have lamented the fate of that very city which I saw most gladly, left unwillingly, and yearned for, even now I am settled at home, and before the fate of the city, I have lamented that of the noble Aristaenetus, who died by it and with it.[a] 2. Neither of these laments do I consider my own: rather, both are peculiar to Grief, for while I was out of my mind and caused my intimates to fear that I would not survive the disaster, Grief then took my hand and wrote as she willed. 3. My audience for the recital of both speeches was but four, for it was not, I felt, a proper occasion for a public performance.[b] Besides my uncle, there were the orator Priscianus,[c] the noble Philocles,[d] and Eusebius[e] who is practised in the arts of friendship. Sabinus,[f] by the way, was down at his estate. 4. They heard from me, and everybody heard from them, that they were going to get a hearing, and straightaway there was a hue and a cry, as people told me either to give a recital or else confess my villainy.

for reasons of personal security.

[c] *BLZG* 244, *PLRE* 727 (1).

[d] Cf. *Ep.* 732. Evidently closely connected with the Cilicians Demetrius and Acacius.

[e] *BLZG* 140 (ix). He died in 359, to Libanius' distress (*Or.* 1.118).

[f] *BLZG* 262 (i), *PLRE* 791 (5). *Consularis Syriae* at this time, winter 358/9.

ἔδωκα τὸ βιβλίον, οἱ δὲ παραλαβόντες οὐ πολλοὺς
ἀνηκόους ἀφῆκαν. ἐξέστω δὲ καὶ σοὶ μόνῳ τε
ἐντυχεῖν, εἰ βούλοιο, καὶ σὺν ἄλλοις, εἰ τοῦτ' ἀρέ-
σκοι.   5. δοκεῖς δέ μοι καὶ αὐτὸς εἰργάσθαι τι
τοιοῦτον εἰς τὸν ἀδελφόν· οὐ γὰρ ἦν τοῦ σοῦ στόματος σιγῇ θάψαι τὸν ἄνδρα ἐκεῖνον. πέμπε οὖν
ὡς καὶ αὐτῷ μονῳδίαις οὐκ ἀηδῶς συνόντι μετὰ
τὸν σεισμὸν ἐκεῖνον. θαυμάζω δὲ εἰ νῦν τοιούτων
ἀπολαύοντες τῶν βοτρύων τὴν παροῦσαν ὥραν
χειμῶνα καλεῖν τολμήσετε.

38. Ἰουλιανῷ

1. Ἀλλά σοι τὸ μὲν σῶμα, ὡς ἐμήνυες, διὰ
τέλους ἔχοι, τῇ λύπῃ δὲ φάρμακον ἔλθοι παρὰ τοῦ
θεοῦ, μᾶλλον δέ, τὸ μέν τι τῆς λύπης δεῖται θεοῦ,
τὸ δὲ ὑμεῖς ὑμῖν αὐτοῖς παῦσαι κύριοι. τὸ μὲν γὰρ
ἀνορθῶσαι τὴν πόλιν ἕτοιμον, εἰ βουληθείητε, τῆς
δ' ἐπὶ τοῖς τεθνεῶσιν ἀθυμίας ἐξ οὐρανοῦ ποθεν
ἔλθοι παραμυθία.   2. μακαρίζω δὲ ἔγωγε τὴν
Νικομήδους καὶ κειμένην. ἔδει μὲν γὰρ ἑστάναι,
τετίμηται δὲ ὅμως πεσοῦσα δάκρυσι σοῖς. τοῦτο

---

a After the earthquake at Nicomedeia, Julian had written to Libanius, mourning the death of friends and

So, I handed over the text, and they took it and allowed very few to remain unacquainted with it. You too may make its acquaintance—alone, if you like, or in the company of others, if you so prefer. 5. I believe that you too have composed something similar upon your brother,[g] for it would not suit one of your eloquence to allow a man like him to go to his last resting place in silence. So send it me, since I too have formed a not altogether displeasing association with monodies after that earthquake. I am surprised that, while you enjoy such grapes now, you yet dare to give to the present season the name of winter.[h]

[g] Hierocles, recently dead (*Ep.* 26). Demetrius composed a monody on him (*Ep.* 30).

[h] The winter of 358/9 was a mild one, so that Demetrius had sent grapes, probably a New Year present.

38. To Julian[a]

1. May your physical condition continue to be such as you tell me, and may a cure for your grief come from God, though to be accurate, only part of your grief requires God's aid; the rest it is in your own power to stop. It is possible for you, if you so wish, to restore the city, but for your despair for those who died may consolation come from somewhere in heaven. 2. I congratulate Nicomedeia even in her ruins. She should be standing yet, but

acquaintances there; cf. Julian, *Oeuvres Complètes* I.ii.4; *ELF* 7.

δὲ οὐ μεῖον οὔτε τῶν θρήνων, οὓς ἐπ' Ἀχιλλεῖ
Μούσας ἐγεῖραι λόγος οὔτε τῆς ἠμαγμένης ψεκά-
δος, ἣν ἐπὶ Σαρπηδόνι μέλλοντι τελευτήσειν ἀφῆ-
κεν ὁ Ζεὺς παῖδα φίλτατον τιμῶν.   3. τοῦ μὲν
οὖν τὴν πάλαι πόλιν αὖθις γενέσθαι πόλιν ὑμῖν
μελήσει, Ἐλπίδιος δὲ ἦν μὲν καὶ πρότερον ἀγαθός, νῦν δὲ ἡ τῶν τρόπων ἐπίδοσις ἀξία θαυμάσαι.
καὶ οὐκ ἄρα μόνον τὸ τοῦ Σοφοκλέους

σοφοὶ τύραννοι τῇ σοφῶν συνουσίᾳ,

ἀλλὰ καὶ βασιλέως σοφία τοῖς συνοῦσιν ἂν εἰς ἀρετὴν ἡγοῖτο.   4. οἷα καὶ σὺ τουτονὶ τὸν ἄνθρωπον
ὤνησας οὐ μᾶλλον εὐπορώτερον ἢ βελτίω δείξας.
καὶ γὰρ εἰ καὶ νεώτερος Ἐλπιδίου, σὺ γέγονας
τῶν γε καλῶν τούτων Ἐλπιδίῳ διδάσκαλος τῷ
πρεσβυτέρῳ, τῆς ἐπιεικείας, τῆς προθυμίας τοῦ
ποιεῖν εὖ τοὺς φίλους, τοῦ ποιοῦντα χαίρειν, τοῦ
πρᾴως τοῖς ἀγνῶσιν ἐντυγχάνειν, τοῦ τὸν ἐντυγ-
χάνοντα κατέχειν. ὅσοι γὰρ αὐτῷ προσελθόντες
προσεῖπον, τοσοῦτοι τὸν ἄνδρα ἐθαύμασαν, εἶτα
εὐθὺς ἐφίλησαν καὶ μᾶλλόν τι τὴν σὴν κατεθεά-
σαντο γνώμην ἐν τοῖς ὑπὸ σοῦ πεπιστευμένοις.

b Homer *Od.* 24.60 ff.

478

still in her fall she has been honoured by your tears. This is no whit less than the laments the Muses are said to have uttered over Achilles,[b] or the drops of blood which Zeus rained down at the imminent death of Sarpedon, in honour of his dearest son.[c] 3. It will be your concern that the city of old shall become a city again. As for Elpidius,[d] he was a good man even before this, but now the maturity of his character deserves admiration. So not only is Sophocles' maxim true, that "Wise lords are formed by converse with the wise,"[e] but also an emperor's wisdom may, for his associates, be an incentive to virtue. 4. Such are the benefits you have conferred on him by revealing him as not so much a richer as a better man. Indeed, even though younger than Elpidius, you have become instructor to Elpidius, your senior, in these noble arts at least, in kindliness, in eagerness to assist friends, in pleasure at so doing, and in courteous treatment of persons not of his acquaintance, and by that treatment in retaining their affection. For all who have approached him and addressed him have first been struck with admiration for the man, and then straightaway with affection, and, to be more precise, have observed your own attitude in the duties you

[c] Homer *Il.* 16.459 ff.

[d] Helpidius *BLZG* 170 (ii), *PLRE* 415 (6). He had lately (winter 358/9) returned to Antioch from Gaul, bearing the letter from Julian.

[e] Sophocles Fr. 14 Radt.

5. ἐμοὶ δὲ καὶ τούτῳ πυκνοὶ μὲν οἱ πρὸς ἀλλήλους λόγοι, πάντες δὲ περὶ σοῦ τε καὶ τῆς γνώμης ἣν ἔχεις καὶ τῶν πραγμάτων ἐν οἷος ὢν ὅστις εἶ πρὸς αὐτά. καὶ οὕτως ἐγγὺς ὢν πράττεις ἐπὶ τῆς διηγήσεως ἦν, ὥστε σοι μικροῦ διελεγόμην ὡς ἂν παρόντι.   6. κάλλιστον δὲ ὧν ἤκουον τὸ ἐλαύνειν σε[1] τοὺς βαρβάρους καὶ τὰς νίκας εἰς συγγραφὴν ἄγειν καὶ τὸν αὐτὸν ὄντως ῥήτορά τε εἶναι καὶ στρατηγόν. Ἀχιλλεῖ μὲν γὰρ Ὁμήρου ἔδει καὶ Ἀλεξάνδρῳ πολλῶν Τιτήνων, τρόπαια δὲ τὰ σὰ μνήμης τεύξεται τῇ τοῦ στήσαντος φωνῇ· τοσοῦτον ἔφθης τοὺς σοφιστὰς οὐ τὰ ἔργα μόνον πόνον αὐτοῖς προθείς, ἀλλὰ καὶ τὴν πρὸς τοὺς λόγους οὓς ἐπὶ τοῖς ἔργοις ἐποίησας ἅμιλλαν. 7. πρόσθες δὴ τοῖς τροπαίοις καὶ τὸ Πομπηιανὸν τῶν δικαίων τυχεῖν καὶ νόμισον καὶ ταύτην οὐ φαύλην τὴν παράταξιν. ὁ δὲ ἀνὴρ οὗτος ἐκεῖνός ἐστιν, ὅν ποτε ἐνθένδε πρεσβεύοντα ἡδέως εἶδες ἐν Βιθυνίᾳ καὶ μαθὼν ὧν ἀπεστέρητο κατέστησας

---

[1] σε F, conj. Re.   τε Wolf (Mss.).

f For Julian's account of the battle of Argentoratum see *ELF* 160 (p. 212 f), Lib. *Or.* 13.25.

g Obscure, and thus a fertile field for conjecture (ἐπαινετῶν Asmus, τοιούτων Wolf). F. refers to the proverb Τιτᾶνας βοᾶν· ἐπὶ τῶν κεκραγότων τινὰς εἰς βοήθειαν, *Paroem. Gr.* 1.314.

have entrusted to him.   5. The conversations
between him and myself are frequent, and all about
you, your resolution and your reactions to the various important affairs with which you deal: and in
the narration I followed your actions so closely that
I practically conversed with you as though present.
6. The finest piece of news I heard was that of your
defeat of the barbarians and your transference of
your victories into writing,[f] and your revelation of
yourself as being truly orator and general. Achilles
needed a Homer, Alexander many a Titan,[g] but your
trophies will be remembered by the eloquence of
yourself who erected them. You have far outdone
the sophists by proposing to them not just your
achievements as their topic, but also the emulation
of the discourse which you have composed upon your
achievements.   7. Add to your trophies then that
of restoring Pompeianus[h] to his rights, and regard
this too as no minor engagement. He is the man
whom once you were glad to see in Bithynia when

Suidas (s.v. Τιτανίδα γῆν) embroiders this, with references:
the Titans helped mortals at their call. However, the most
likely source is Hesiod *Theog.* 617, where the three
Hecatoncheires are summoned to assist the gods in their
struggle against the rest of the Titans.

[h] *BLZG* 241 (ii). In 355 Pompeianus as ambassador is
commended to Datianus (*Letter* 13) and to friends along
the route (*Epp.* 444–9). The loss of his family property is
mentioned in *Letter* 13.10 also. But here Julian had made
his acquaintance in Nicomedeia, which he had left in 351,
and the reference is to an earlier embassy, probably in 348
(Petit, *Vie Municipale* 415).

εἰς ἐλπίδας, ὡς ἄρα κομιεῖται τὰ αὑτοῦ. τούτων μοι μεμνῆσθαι τῶν ὑποσχέσεων, ὦ βασιλεῦ.

39. Στρατηγίῳ

1. Οὔπω με καθαρῶς ἀπαλλαγέντα τοῦ ἐν τῇ κεφαλῇ κακοῦ μεῖζον ἕτερον ἔλαβε κακόν, ὃ τὴν ψυχὴν ἐνέπλησε ζόφου καὶ δι' ὃ πολλοὶ τῶν φίλων πολύν μοι παρεκάθηντο χρόνον πάσαις ἐπῳδαῖς πειρώμενοι διασῶσαί μου τὰς φρένας. 2. τίνα γὰρ οἴει με γενέσθαι πυθόμενον ὡς ἡ φιλτάτη πόλις ἐπὶ τοῖς φιλτάτοις πέπτωκεν ἀνδράσιν; ἠμέλησα μὲν σιτίων, ἔρριψα δὲ λόγους, ἀπεωσά- μην δὲ ὕπνον, σιγῇ δὲ ἐπὶ πλεῖστον ἐκείμην, δάκρυα δὲ ἡμῶν ἅμα μὲν ἐπ' ἐκείνοις, τῶν δὲ ἐπι- τηδείων ἐπ' ἐμοί, πρὶν δή τις παρήνεσεν ἐν λόγοις θρηνῆσαι τήν τε πόλιν καὶ τὸν οὐ τοιαύτης ἄξιον, ὦ Ζεῦ, τελευτῆς. ᾧ πεισθεὶς καὶ τοῦ πάθους τι μέρος ἐπὶ τῆς γραφῆς ἐκβαλὼν ἤδη πενθῶ σωφρονῶν. 3. εἰ μὲν οὖν μὴ καὶ σοὶ τεταράχθαι

---

a Strategius was now (winter 358/9) in retirement after his prefecture. Libanius' account of his own distress, both

he acted as our ambassador. You learned of what he had lost and gave him grounds to hope that he would, after all, recover his own. Please bear these promises in mind, Sire.

39. To Strategius[a]

1. I was not yet clear of the trouble in my head when a second and greater trouble took hold of me, and it filled my soul with gloom and caused many of my friends to sit by me for a long time trying by incantations of every kind to save my reason.   2. How do you think I felt when I learned that the dearest of cities had fallen in ruin over the dearest of men? I took no thought for meals, tossed my oratory aside, refused sleep[b] and lay for the most part in silence. My tears flowed for them, my friends' tears for me, until it was suggested that I compose an oration of mourning for the city and for him who, God knows, deserved no such death. I agreed to this, and now that I have expended some part of my emotion in the writing of it, I grieve with a sound mind.   3. So did I not think that you too were dis-

mental and physical, is summarised elsewhere (*Letters* 36–7, *Or.* 1.118). His reaction to the news of the disaster at Nicomedeia is reminiscent of the breakdowns he later suffered upon the death of Julian, his brother's blindness (*Or.* 1.202 ff), and the loss of Cimon (*Or.* 1.280).

[b] Cf. Plat. *Resp.* 9.571e.

τὴν γνώμην ἡγούμην ἐστερημένῳ φίλου δείξαντος
ἔργοις τοὔνομα, ἐδεόμην ἄν μοι παρὰ σοῦ φοιτᾶν
παραμυθίαν· ἐπεὶ δὲ ἡ πληγὴ κοινή, λείπεταί μοι
στένειν, ὃ δὴ καὶ ποιῶ.

40. Ἀνατολίῳ

1. Ἀνέγνων τοῖς φίλοις τὴν ἐπιστολὴν τὴν
μακρὰν ἐκείνην, ἐκέλευσας γὰρ καὶ οὐκ ἦν ἀπει-
θεῖν τοσαύτῃ δυνάμει. 2. ἡ μὲν οὖν ἀνάγνωσις
ἐκίνει γέλωτα τοσοῦτον ὅσον ἐβούλου, πολλοῦ δὲ
ἄρ' ἐπεθύμεις, ὡς δὲ διεπαυσάμην, τῶν τις
ἀκροατῶν ἤρετό με, πότερόν σοι φίλος ὢν ἢ
δυσμενὴς τυγχάνω. φήσαντος δέ μου καὶ μάλα
φιλεῖν Ἀνατόλιον τὸν καλὸν 'εὖ ἴσθι τοίνυν,' ἔφη,
'τὰ δυσμενοῦς ποιῶν δεικνὺς τὴν ἐπιστολήν, ἣν
ἀφανίζειν ἔδει.' καὶ ἐτίθετο δὴ τοῖς γράμμασιν
ὄνομα. βούλει μαθεῖν ὅ τι; ἀλλ' οὐκ ἐρῶ γε τοῦτο
ὃ καὶ ἀκούων ἠχθόμην. 3. ἀφέντες οὖν ἐκεῖνον[1]
ἐξετάζωμεν τὰς αἰτίας, καὶ σύ τε φέρειν, ἂν

---

[1] ἐκεῖνον Wolf (Mss. except C D)   ἐκεῖνο F (C D).

---

[a] Silomon (pp. 19, 24) demonstrates that this was written in winter 358/9. Anatolius, ensconced as praetorian
prefect of Illyricum, had written to Libanius, in joking
style but with serious intent, criticising him for not doing
full justice to Spectatus in the eulogy composed for him

traught at the loss of a friend who earned the name by his deeds,[c] I would beg you to send some consolation to me. But since the blow is one that affects us both, all that is left for me is to grieve, and that indeed I do.

[c] Aristaenetus. For his friendship with Strategius, cf. *Letter* 26, *Epp.* 537, 561.

40. To Anatolius[a]

1. I read that long letter of yours out to my friends; so you bade me, and I could not disobey such great authority. 2. Well, the recital excited as much laughter as you wanted, and obviously your desire was for it to be plenty, but when I had stopped, one of the audience asked me whether I was friend or foe of yours.[b] I replied that I was particularly friendly with the noble Anatolius, to which he retorted, "Well, rest assured that you are behaving like an enemy of his in disclosing the contents of this letter. You should have suppressed it." And he went on to put a name to what you wrote—and would you like to know what? I am not going to tell you: I was upset even to listen to it. 3. So, let us leave him aside and go on to examine the charges. You must accept responsibility if you are proved a

after his return from the embassy to Persia the previous summer (see *Letter* 35). Libanius replies in kind.

[b] Reminiscent of the intervention of Thrasymachus in Plat. *Resp.* 1.336b.

φανῇς συκοφάντης, ἐγώ τε οἴσω, κακὸς εἰ δει-
χθείην.

4. Ἔφης Σπεκτάτον μέγαν ὄντα τοῖς ἔργοις
μικρὸν γεγενῆσθαι τοῖς παρ' ἐμοῦ λόγοις, αὐτὸς
δέ γε ἐκεῖνος ἥδετο τοῖς παρ' ἡμῶν ἐπαίνοις· εἰ
μὲν οὖν εὖ φρονῶν, ψεῦδος τὸ σόν· εἰ δὲ οὐδὲν
εἰδὼς τῶν περὶ λόγους, τόλμησον εἰπεῖν καὶ
πάντα ἐγὼ φαῦλος. 5. οὑτωσὶ δὲ σκόπει, ὅπως
σαυτῷ δόξῃς ὁμολογεῖν, ὅς,[2] ὃν ᾐτιάσω τὰ μεγάλα
μικρὰ ποιεῖν, τοῦτον ἔφης τῇ ῥώμῃ τῶν λόγων
αἴρειν τὰ φαῦλα. παραινῶ δή σοι τοῖς μὲν τῶν
βαρβάρων βουλεύμασι πολεμεῖν, σαυτῷ δὲ μή.
6. ζηλοτυπῶν μὲν οὖν τοὺς ὑφ' ἡμῶν κοσμουμέ-
νους εὖ ποιεῖς, οὐ γὰρ κακῆς φύσεως σημεῖον
ἐπαίνων ἐπιθυμεῖν, μέγα γὰρ εἰς ἄσκησιν ἀρετῆς
πολλάκις ζηλοτυπία· μεμφόμενος δὲ τό τινας
τετιμῆσθαι λόγοις ἀντὶ τοῦ φανεροῦν τὴν εὐφη-
μίαν, ποικίλον ἀλλ' οὐ γενναῖον ἔργον ποιεῖς.
7. καὶ προφέρεις δὴ ἐμοὶ τὸ πολλοὺς ἐπαινεῖν,
ἐγὼ δὲ σοὶ τὸ πάντας ψέγειν. οὐκοῦν ἀκρισία μὲν
ἐν ἀμφοῖν, ἔχει δέ τινα τοὐμὸν φιλανθρωπίαν.

[2] ὅς F, conj. Re.   ὥσθ' Mss.   ὥστ' Wolf.

---

[c] Spectatus, during his short stay in Antioch after his

humbug: I shall, if I should be proved in the wrong.

4. You asserted that Spectatus, despite the eminence which he has attained by his acts, has been denigrated by words of mine, though he at least was pleased with eulogies of mine.[c] Now, if his judgment is right, then the falsehood is yours: but if he knows nothing about oratory, just dare to say so—and I shall be utterly worthless. 5. Look at it this way, if you want to appear consistent: you have accused someone of denigrating greatness and yet assert that this same man, by the force of his oratory, elevates the worthless. My advice to you, then, is to do battle against the plots of the barbarians, not against yourself. 6. So you do well to envy those who are honoured by me,[d] for the desire for praise indicates no base character. Envy often is a great incentive to the practice of virtue. But when, instead of declaring your appreciation, you level the reproach that certain people have been honoured by my oratory, your behaviour is underhanded, not that of a gentleman at all. 7. You allege against me the fact that I sing the praises of many people: I tell you that you censure everybody. So both of us display a lack of judgement, but my attitude does have some generosity. Nor is there anyone I have

return from Persia, had received this eulogy from his cousin, who had sent a copy to Anatolius.

[d] Cf. Plat. *Sympos.* 213d.

μᾶλλον δέ, οὐκ ἔστιν ὅντινα ἐπήνεσα τὰ οὐκ ὄντα
προστιθείς, ὥσπερ ὁ μῦθος ἀλλότρια τῷ κολοιῷ
πτερά. ἀλλ᾽ ᾧ χρῶμαι νόμῳ περὶ τοὺς ἐπαίνους,
ἄκουσον.   8. ἂν ᾖ τις κρείττων μὲν χρημάτων,
ἥττων δὲ ἡδονῶν, ἐκεῖνο μὲν ἐπαίνου τεύξεται,
τοῦτο δὲ ἐν σιγῇ κείσεται. καὶ γὰρ εἰ γῆν ἐπήνουν, οὕτως ἂν ἐποίουν. οἷον εἴ μ᾽ ἐχρῆν ἐπαινεῖν
τὰ Κύθηρα, τὰ δὲ Κύθηρα νησός ἐστιν ἐπικειμένη
τῇ Πελοποννήσῳ, τὸν οὖν λόγον ἐργαζόμενος
διελθὼν ἂν ὡς εὔβοτος καὶ πολύοινος εὐλίμενός τέ
ἐστιν ἢ καὶ ὕλη κομῶσα, τὴν εἰς πυροὺς φορὰν οὐκ
ἂν ἐπήνουν, ἐψευδόμην γὰρ ἄν, οὐδὲ γὰρ ὅστις
ἐγκωμιάζει τὴν Ἀττικήν, καὶ τοῦτ᾽ ἂν εἰπεῖν
ἔχοι, κωλύει δὲ οὐδὲν ἐξ ὧν ἔξεστιν ἐπαινεῖν.
9. θαυμάζω τὸν Ἀχιλλέα, διότι τοὺς Τρῶας
ἤλαυνε, θαυμάζω τὸν Παλαμήδην ἀπὸ τῆς σοφίας.
ὁ δὲ ὅτι μὴ παρ᾽ ἑκατέρῳ ταῦτ᾽ ἦν ἀμφότερα
ψέγειν ἀξιῶν ἀδικεῖ. 10. φέρε, εἰ σοὶ λόγον
ἐποίουν καί με τοῦτ᾽ ἔπεισας δεηθείς, ἆρ᾽ ἂν οἴει
τῷ δημιουργῷ πανταχόθεν προσελθεῖν τοὺς ἐπαίνους; σὺ μὲν ἴσως οἴει, τὸ πρᾶγμα δὲ οὐ τοιοῦτον,
ἀλλ᾽ εἶπον μὲν ἂν ἐπιμέλειαν, ἀγρυπνίαν, πόνους,

---

[e] Cf. Perry, *Aesopica* p. 361 no. 101.

praised by attributing to him something he does not have, like the jackdaw's borrowed plumes in the fable.[e] Just listen, and I will explain my methods of panegyric.   8. If there is anyone who is impervious to money but subservient to pleasure, then I will give due credit for the first and draw a veil over this last. In fact, if I were speaking in praise of a country, I would do the same. For instance, if I had to speak in praise of Cythera, Cythera being the island lying off the Peloponnese, in composing my oration I would describe its rich pastures and vineyards,[f] its fine harbour and its crown of trees, but I would not commend it for its production of corn; if I did, I would be lying. Nor yet in any oration in praise of Attica could this be said either, but there is nothing to prevent us praising it with the means at our disposal.   9. I admire Achilles for routing the Trojans, and Palamedes for his wisdom.[g] Anybody who regards it as a reproach that both commendations are inapplicable to either of them is wrong. 10. Look! If I compose a speech for you, supposing you had prevailed upon me to do so, do you think that the topics to be commended would present themselves to the composer from all points of the compass? You might think so, but the case is very different. I would refer to your industry, your vigilance, your exertions, your correct judgement,

[f] Homer *Od.* 15.406.

[g] The inventor of the alphabet; cf. Eurip. *Pal.* fr. 578–90 Nauck, Aristoph. *Thesm.* 768 ff.

ψῆφον ὀρθήν, πρόνοιαν <τοῦ>³ μέλλοντος, φρόνημα δίκαιον, γνώμης ὀξύτητα, γλώττης ἰσχύν,
πολλὰ δ' ἕτερα, καλὸν δὲ καὶ μέγαν οὐκ ἂν εἶπον·
οὐ γὰρ ἔνι σοι ταῦτ' ἐν τῷ σώματι.   11. μεμνημένος δὲ χρημάτων κλοπῆς μὲν ἄν σε πλεῖστον
ἔφην ἀφεστάναι, μισθὸν δὲ μὴ ἔχειν τῆς ἀρετῆς
οὐκ ἂν ἰσχυρισάμην, ἔχεις γὰρ τὰ βασιλέως δῶρα
καί σοι τῆς ἀρχῆς ὁ χρόνος τὰς οἰκίας πεποίηκε
πόλεις ἀδικοῦντι μὲν οὐδένα, λαμβάνοντι δέ.
πολὺ δ' ἂν ἦσθα βελτίων μηδαμόθεν λαμβάνων,
ὡς λαμπρότερόν γε κιόνων οὓς δίδωσι βασιλεὺς τὸ
χρῆμα τῆς δόξης ἣν ἡ πενία φέρει.   12. καὶ μὴν
κἀκεῖνό γέ σου τραχὺ καὶ οὐχ ἥμερον τὸ κακίζειν
Σευῆρον, ὅτι δὴ ζώνης ἐδεήθη δέον φιλοσοφεῖν. εἰ
μὲν γὰρ φιλοσοφίας ἁπτόμενος ἀπεφέρετο τοῦ
σχήματος καὶ ἦν ἐν προσηγορίᾳ φιλοσοφίας κάπη-
λος, εἰκότως ἂν ἐμισεῖτο· εἰ δὲ τὸ μὲν ἡγεῖται μεῖζον αὑτοῦ, ζητεῖ δέ τινα καταφυγήν, ποῦ πλημ-
μελεῖ μὴ φιλοσοφῶν; ἢ καὶ σὺ μᾶλλον ἄρχων ἢ
φιλοσοφῶν ἀδικεῖς;   13. ἐπεὶ δὲ πολὺς ἔγκεισαι
κωμῳδῶν ἡμᾶς, ὅτι πρὸς σὲ ἐμνήσθημεν ἀξιώμα-

³ <τοῦ> F, conj. Re.

your foresightedness, your upright character, keen intellect, powerful eloquence, and so on; but I would never call you handsome and tall. Your physical characteristics are not like that. 11. If I mention money, I would say that you are far removed from peculation, but I would not assert that you enjoy no reward for your ability, for you possess gifts from the emperor and your long period of office has made your villas into towns! You have done wrong to no one, but you do gather things to yourself. You would be a much better man if you had not, for the acquisition of a fame brought by poverty is more splendid than all the pillars granted by a prince. 12. Moreover, another aspect of ungentle harshness in you is your abuse of Severus[h] for requesting an official position when he ought to be practising his philosophy. If it were the case that in embracing philosophy he was turning his back on what it entailed, if he were under the title of philosopher a mere huckster,[i] there would be good grounds for disliking him. If, however, he thinks it beyond him and looks for some other recourse, how is he in the wrong if he is not a philosopher? Are you too in the wrong for being a governor rather than a philosopher?

13. And again, when you set about me and

[h] *BLZG* 275 (v), *PLRE* 832 (9). He was unsuccessful in his present attempt to enter imperial service (ζώνης ἐδεήθη), and despite his claim for sophistic immunity, he was to be called upon for curial duties twice in the next five years.

[i] Cf. Plat. *Prot.* 313e.

τος, ἴσθι τὸ πᾶν ἀγνοήσας. ἔσχε δὲ ὡδί. ἐμοὶ
σχῆμα μὲν ἀρκοῦν οἱ λόγοι, δι' οὓς οὐδεπώποτε
ταπεινότερον ἐμαυτὸν ἡγησάμην ὑμῶν, ὧν ἡ λαμ-
πρότης ὅρκος τοῖς κόλαξι· πρὸς δὲ τὸν βίον ἀφορ-
μαὶ τὰ παρ' αὐτῶν τῶν λόγων μικρὰ μικρῶν δεο-
μένῳ.   14. τίς οὖν ἦν ὁ νοῦς ὧν ἐπέστελλον;
Ἰσοκράτης παραινεῖ πεῖραν ποιεῖσθαι τῶν φίλων
οὔπω παρούσης ἀνάγκης ὥστε ἀτυχήσαντι μὴ
εἶναι βλάβην καί φησι δεῖν μὴ δεόμενον προσποι-
εῖσθαι τὸ δεῖσθαι.   15. τοιοῦτον ἦν τι καὶ τὸ
παρ' ἐμοῦ· μὴ χρῄζων ἐπήγγελλον. τοιγαροῦν σὺ
μὲν οὐκ ἐδίδους, ἐγὼ δὲ ἐγέλων καὶ ζημιούμενος
οὐδὲν εὕρισκόν σου τὸν τρόπον.   16. οὐ μὴν
πάντα γε εἶ ῥᾴθυμος, ἀλλ' εἰς τὸ γένος, εἴπερ τις,
ἕτοιμος, καὶ τῶν σῶν οἰκείων ἰδιώτης οὐδείς. εἶτ'
ἐπὶ μὲν τῶν ἄλλων τιμᾷς τὴν ἀρετήν, κἂν ὁ ταύτης ἄμοιρος ἄρχῃ, κέκραγας μᾶλλον ἢ οἱ τεμνόμε-
νοι· τὸ γένος δὲ οὕτω σοι φίλτατον ὥστε ἄρχειν
δεῖ πάντα οἰκεῖον καὶ ἀπεῖναι βάσανον. τοῦτό σοι
παραίτησις ὧν περὶ τοὺς φίλους ἀμελεῖς.   κἂν
ἐκεῖνό τις κατηγορῇ, τοῦτ' ἀντιτιθεὶς ἀφαιρῇ

scoffed at me for mentioning my position to you, you should realise that you have completely misunderstood the matter. The fact is that my oratory gives me position enough, and because of it I have never regarded myself as more humble than you people whose high-and-mightiness is such that your flatterers take their oath by it. The small rewards actually to be gained from oratory are sufficient means of life for one whose needs are small. 14. Then what was my intention in writing? Just this. Isocrates recommends us to put our friends to the test[j] before ever an emergency arises, so that, if unsuccessful, no harm is done. He says that we should pretend to be in need although we are not. 15. My request too was something of this sort: I put it forward, though I was in no need of it. So when you refused, I shrugged it off with a smile; without actually suffering loss, I discovered the sort of man you are. 16. To be sure, you are not completely lackadaisical. You are ready to assist your family, if ever a man was, and none of your relations remains an ordinary citizen. Again, you respect ability in others. If anyone who does not possess it attains office, you shriek more loudly than people on the operating table, and yet your family is so very dear to you that every connexion of yours must needs hold office, without a word being said against him. This is your excuse for ignoring your friends. If anyone accuses you of that, you bring this for-

[j] Isocr. *ad Demon.* 24.

⟨τὸ⟩[4] τῆς μέμψεως.   17. ἆρά σοι δοκῶ καὶ
αὐτὸς εἰδέναι τοξεύειν ἢ πάσχειν ἐπιτήδειος εἶναι
μόνον; μᾶλλον δέ, εἰ μὲν ἔτρωσας, καὶ τέτρωσαι·
εἰ δὲ παίζοντος ἐκεῖνα ἦν, οὐδὲ ταῦτα σπουδάζον-
τος.   18. δίκαιον δέ, εἴτε ἡσθείης τοῖς γράμμασι,
τῷ φέροντι τὴν χάριν ἔχειν, εἴτε δηχθείης, παρὰ
τοῦ φέροντος τὴν δίκην λαβεῖν. ἐγνωκότα γάρ με
ἡσυχάζειν πάσαις ἀνάγκαις Ἰανουάριος ἐνήγαγεν,
ἀνὴρ πανταχόθεν αἰδέσιμος τῇ πόλει λυπήσας μὲν
οὐδὲν οὐδένα ὧν οὐκ ἔδει, δοὺς δὲ χάριτας ἐν αἷς ἡ
τοῦ δικαίου μερίς, φρουρήσας μὲν ἱκανῶς ἐφ' ᾧπερ
ἐτέτακτο, τῶν δὲ ἐπειγομένων οἷς ἄξιον συλλα-
βών, ὀλίγα λαλῶν, πρᾶξαι δεινός, τῶν γιγνομένων καρπῶν ὑπερορῶν τὸ πλέον, προσήκων μὲν
μείζοσι, στέργων δὲ τὰ παρόντα, τὴν ἐπιείκειαν
ἐν πράγματι τηρήσας οὐκ ἀνεχομένῳ χρηστότη-
τος. ἓν δέδοικα μὴ μέμψῃ τὸν ἄνθρωπον, ὅτι μοι
πάντα ὑπούργησεν.

[4] ἀφαιρῇ ⟨τὸ⟩ F.: ἀφαιρῇ V, corrected from -οῖ S: ἀφαιρεῖτο Vi:
-οῖτο C Vind. D: ἀφαιρεῖται Wolf (Vo).

ward and rid yourself of the reproach. 17. Well, then! Do you think that I too have some skill as a marksman or am I fit just to be a target? To put it another way, if you inflict a wound, you have been wounded yourself, but if your remarks were in jest, mine are not in earnest, either. 18. It is right and proper for you, if you are pleased with this letter, to show your gratitude to the bearer and, if you are annoyed, to punish him. You see, I had made up my mind to keep quiet, but Januarius[k] prevailed upon me by all the means at his disposal. He is universally respected in the city; and has never caused any annoyance to people who do not deserve it; the favours he dispenses are justified, and he is pretty careful in the performance of his duty. When people demand his assistance, he helps those it is right to help. He says little, and is efficient in action; and generally ignores the profits which accrue. He is fitted for greater things, but is content with what he has, and maintains a correct attitude in a situation which allows no scope for virtue. The one thing I am afraid of is that you will disapprove of him for his invaluable services to me.

[k] *PLRE* 454 (4). Evidently in imperial service. He is recommended also in an earlier letter to Aristaenetus (*Ep.* 20.3 ff).

LIBANIUS

41. Μοδέστῳ

1. Ἀκούω τοὺς φόβους εἰς ἀκμὴν ἥκειν καὶ τῷ Πέρσῃ γεφύρας γεγονέναι καὶ τὴν διάβασιν ἐν χερσὶν εἶναι. σοὶ δὲ τοῦτο μεῖζω μὲν ποιείτω τὴν πρόνοιαν, ἀπέστω δὲ τῆς προνοίας ταραχή. τοῦτ᾽ αὐτὸ γὰρ ποιήσει καὶ τὸ δύνασθαι προνοεῖν, ὡς ἐν τῷ τεταράχθαι τοὺς λογισμοὺς ἀνάγκη τυφλοῦσθαι.   2. θαρρυνέτω δέ σε πρῶτον μὲν τὸ μὴ πρώτην αὐτῷ ταύτην τολμᾶσθαι τὴν εἰσβολήν, ἀλλ᾽ ἀεὶ μὲν αὐτόν, ἐξ οὗ πολεμεῖ, διαβῆναι πειρᾶσθαι, παθόντα δὲ ἀεὶ κακῶς αὐτῷ μέμψασθαι τῆς ἐλπίδος.   3. ἔπειτα οὐ τοῖς πλείοσι πανταχοῦ τὸ νικᾶν ἀκολουθεῖ, ἀλλ᾽ ὡς τὰ πολλὰ τὴν πολυχειρίαν ἡττᾶσθαι τῆς σοφίας συμβαίνει. εἰ δὲ τὸ πλέον ἰσχυρότερον ἦν, ἔδει δήπου τὸν τούτου πρόγονον κτήσασθαι τὴν Ἑλλάδα. νῦν δὲ οἶσθα ὡς ἐστράτευσε μὲν ἐκείνης ἐπιθυμῶν, φεύγων δὲ ἐκεῖθεν ἐπεθύμει σωθῆναι. οὐ γὰρ τῶν αὐτῶν ἦν ὄρη τε διορύττειν καὶ ἀνδρῶν κρατεῖν ἀρετῆς.   4. ἐντεύξεται δὴ καὶ οὗτος νῦν βουλεύμασι στρατηγῶν, οἳ αὐτὸν διδάξουσιν ὡς ἄρα κάλλιον ἦν

---

a To Modestus, Comes Orientis, just after the start of the campaigning season of 359. The Comes, unusually for

41. To Modestus[a]

1. I hear that our fears have come to a climax, that the Persian king has got bridges and that the crossing is in his hands. Let this increase your concern, but let there be no panic in your concern. This is the very thing that will enable you to think ahead, since amidst panic the faculty of reason must needs be blinded. 2. Let it be of encouragement to you, first, that this is not the first time he has ventured upon invasion, but from the beginning of hostilities it is always he who attempts the crossing and always he who receives a mauling and reproaches himself for his hopes. 3. Secondly, victory does not always attend the big battalions; for the most part superior numbers are overcome by intelligence. If numbers always won the day, then obviously the ancestor of the present king[b] would have been bound to gain possession of Greece. As it is, you know that he began the campaign with that ambition, but in his flight from Greece his ambition was to save himself. It is by no means the same thing to cut canals through mountains as to overcome the courage of men. 4. So the present king too will contend with the strategy of generals who will teach

[a] a civilian official, had some military functions to perform on the frontier.
[b] Both Persian and Roman maintain the fiction that Xerxes was the ancestor of Sapor; cf. Amm. Marc. 17.5.

ἐλάφοις μάχεσθαι. καὶ γὰρ ἂν τὸν Τίγρητα
διαβῇ, τῶν μὲν τειχῶν ἥττων ἔσται, γῆν δὲ οὔτε
κακοῦν οὔτε καρποῦσθαι δυνήσεται, δεδῄωται γάρ,
πόλεις δὲ τὰς ἐπ᾽ Εὐφράτῃ ζητῶν μὲν λαβεῖν
διατελέσει, λαβὼν δὲ οὐ φανεῖται. τειχίζει γὰρ
αὐτὰς ἡ βασιλέως Τύχη.   5. ταυτὶ μὲν οὕτω χρὴ
προσδοκᾶν ἀποβήσεσθαι, τῶν δὲ σῶν πραγμάτων,
ἃ τῶν Ἑρμογένους ἐδεῖτο γραμμάτων, οὐκ ἠμε-
λήσαμεν, ἀλλ᾽ ἡμεῖς οἱ μύες μᾶλλον ὑμᾶς ὠφελεῖν
πειρώμεθα τοὺς λέοντας ἢ ὑμεῖς ἡμᾶς οἱ λέοντες.

---

c Cf. the proverbial ἐλάφειος ἀνήρ of *Paroem. Gr.* 1.73,
itself derived from Homer *Il.* 1.225.

42. Θεμιστίῳ[1]

1. ᾽Αλλ᾽ εἴη ταύτην γέ σοι τὴν γαστέρα κλη-

[1] Schol. Be: Ζητοῦντος τὸν Θεμίστον τοῦ Λιβανίου τόκους καινοὺς
οὓς ἔτικτεν ἐν Κωνσταντινουπόλει βασιλεύοντος Ἰουλιανοῦ ἐδήλωσεν ἐκεῖνος περὶ τοῦ γάμου καὶ τῆς γυναικὸς αὐτοῦ, ὡς ῾οὐκ ἔστι νῦν ἐμοὶ καιρὸς τοῦ
τίκτειν λόγους ἀλλὰ παῖδας ἐκ γυναικός, ἣν ἀρτίως γήμας ἐλπίζω καὶ
πατὴρ ἔσεσθαι παιδων. ταῦτα γὰρ ἐπαγγέλλεταί μοι τῆς γυναικὸς γαστὴρ
ἐπειγομένη τεκεῖν, πρὸς ὃ καὶ συνεύχου ἡμῖν.᾽ ταῦτα γράψαντος Θεμιστίου
εὔχεται ὁ Λιβάνιος· ῾ἀλλ᾽ εἴη γέ μοι τὴν γαστέρα τῆς γυναικός.᾽

---

a Seeck places this letter in autumn 360, Silomon
(p. 43) to sometime between 357 and 361, Bouchery
(p. 125) to summer 359. This is the only fragment of
Themistius' letters to survive.

him that he would do better to do battle against deer.[c] For if he crosses the Tigris, he will not succeed against the fortified towns, and he will be unable to harm or harvest the countryside, since it is ravaged already[d] and, as for the towns in the Euphrates valley, he will continue in his efforts to take them but will never be seen to do so, for our emperor's Fortune walls them around. 5. This is what we should expect the outcome to be, but with regard to your personal affairs, which required the confirmation of a letter from Hermogenes,[e] I have not been idle. We mice try to help you lions rather more than you lions try to help us.[f]

[d] By the scorched earth policy of the Romans, Amm. Marc. 18.7.4.

[e] Praetorian prefect. These negotiations are mentioned in *Epp.* 55, 58.

[f] Cf. Aesop. *Fab.* 256, Babr. *Fab.* 107, *ELF* 188 (377d).

42. To Themistius[a]

1. I trust that this womb[b] will bear you heirs,

[b] Scholiast on Berolinensis: "Libanius asked Themistius for the new offspring he was producing in Constantinople in the reign of Julian. In reply, referring to his marriage and his wife, he declared, 'now is not the time for me to produce orations, but children from my wife. I have recently married her and hope soon to be the father of children. That is what my wife's womb promises me, for it is eager to give birth. Please join me in praying for this." This is Themistius' second wife (§ 2), a Phrygian.

ρονόμους τεκεῖν καὶ μὴ μόνον τῆς οὐσίας, ἀλλὰ
καὶ τῆς σοφίας, ἣν δὴ λειμῶνος ποικιλωτέραν δεικνύων πάλαι κρατεῖς, εἰ μὲν καὶ τοὺς ταὐτό σοι
καλουμένους οὐκ οἶδα, οἱ ῥήτορες δὲ ἡττήμεθα.
2. τέως μὲν οὖν τῇ Φρυγίᾳ συνέχαιρον, ἣ καὶ σὲ
καὶ τοὺς γάμους ἐδέξατο, νῦν δὲ τῇ Μεγάλῃ πόλει
σέ τε ἀπολαβούσῃ καὶ προσλαβούσῃ τὴν νύμφην,
μακαρίζω δὲ καὶ τὸν οὐκ ἀπόντος σου τὴν Μεγάλην ὀψόμενον πόλιν, ὅτι αὐτὴν ὄντως ὄψεται
μεγάλην. 3. τὸν μὲν οὖν τῶν πραγμάτων πόνον
ἀνεθήκαμεν Κλεάρχῳ, παρὰ σοῦ δὲ Εὐστόχιος
τιμηθήτω τῷ νομισθῆναι τοῦτο ὅπερ ἐστίν. ἔστι
δὲ καλὸς κἀγαθός, κἂν τοῖς πράγμασιν ἃ φίλον
σαφῆ ζητεῖ πάντες ἐπ' αὐτὸν ἐρχόμεθα. 4. τίμα
δὲ αὐτὸν καὶ τῷ μείζονι, καλῶ δὲ μεῖζον τὸ σῶν
ἀκοῦσαι λόγων· οὓς εἰ μὲν καινοὺς δεικνύεις, καινῆς[2] θοίνης μεταλήψεται τὸ μέρος· εἰ δ' οὐκ ἐν
τούτῳ νῦν εἴης, τοῖς παλαιοῖς αὐτὸν ἑστία,
μᾶλλον δέ, πάντως αὐτὸν ἑστιάσεις καινοῖς· ὅ τι
γὰρ ἂν φθέγξῃ, τοῦτο τῶν γεγραμμένων οὐ
χεῖρον.

[2] καινῆς Fabricius, F.   κοινῆς Wolf (Mss.).

---

[c] Cf. *Or.* 13.45, [Plat.] *Axioch.* 371c.
[d] Eustochius (see below).

and not only to your estate but also to the philosophy wherein, by revealing it more verdant than any meadow,[c] you have long been preeminent—whether over those who go by the same title as yourself I cannot say, but we orators are outdone.   2. For some time, then, I congratulated Phrygia for welcoming both you and your nuptials, but now I congratulate the capital for reclaiming you and gaining your bride also, and I also count as lucky the man[d] who will see the capital at a time when you are not absent, for he will see it a capital in very truth.[e] 3. The actual performance of the business we have entrusted to Clearchus,[f] your job is to honour Eustochius,[g] by regarding him as what he is. He is a true gentleman, and in such business as requires a true friend we all have recourse to him.   4. Invest him with an even greater honour, namely, allow him to hear your orations. Should these be fresh ones which you deliver, he will partake of a fresh feast. Should you not at present be so engaged, regale him with your old ones, though in any case you will regale him with something fresh, for any words of yours will not be inferior to your writings.

[e] Seeck and *PLRE* assume that this refers to 360, when Themistius had relinquished his post as proconsul of the city. This compliment, however, seems more appropriate to a time when he actually held the office (i.e. before Dec. 359).

[f] *BLZG* 108 (i), *PLRE* 211 (1). Closely associated with Themistius, he held some unknown post in Constantinople in 359/60, at the beginning of his career.

[g] *BLZG* 149 (i), *PLRE* 313 (3).

43. Θεμιστίῳ

1. Ὑπὲρ μὲν τῶν ἄλλων σε παρακαλῶν ἐκείνοις ᾤμην διδόναι χάριν, Ὀλυμπίῳ δὲ εἴ τι πράξαις κεχαρισμένον, λήψεσθαί σε μᾶλλον ἢ δώσειν ἡγοῦμαι χάριν. οὗτος γάρ ἐστιν ὁ τὴν μὲν Μακεδονίαν εὐδαίμονα ποιήσας ἄρτι παίδων ἐξελθών, τὸ δὲ ἄρχειν μετὰ ταῦτα πλέον φυγὼν ἢ ἐζήτησαν ἕτεροι. 2. τῷ δικαίῳ δὲ οὕτως αὐτὸν δέδωκεν ὥστε ἀδικούμενος μὲν πᾶς ἐπὶ τοῦτον καταφεύγει, τοὺς νόμους δὲ ἐκβαίνων τοῦτον δέδοικε, τοῖς δὲ ἄρχουσιν ἡμῶν μία σπουδὴ τὴν παρὰ τοῦδε ψῆφον λαβεῖν. 3. ἐγὼ δὲ καὶ αὐτὸς πατρικὴν διαδεξάμενοι φιλίαν, ὁ μὲν πάντα ὑπὲρ ἐμοῦ πονεῖ, παρ' ἐμοῦ δὲ ἔπαινος εἰς τὴν προθυμίαν· πρᾶξαι γὰρ οὐδὲν ἂν δυναίμην ἴσον. ἀλλὰ σύ γε τὸν ἄνδρα ἀμείβου, μᾶλλον δὲ μικρὰ ἀντὶ μεγάλων ὑπὲρ ἡμῶν ἀντίδος. 4. οὗτός γε εἰς τὴν ὑμετέραν μετέστη βουλὴν ἀπὸ τῆς μείζονος, συγγνώσῃ δὲ εἰ μείζω καλῶ τὴν Ῥωμαίων σὲ τῆσδε ἐχούσης. γενέσθω τοίνυν αὐτῷ παρ' ὑμῶν ἃ παρ'

---

[a] Bouchery 137 ff. Themistius, as proconsul of the city of Constantinople, was busily recruiting new senators, bringing the numbers up from 300 to 2000 (Them. Or. 34.13).

43. To Themistius[a]

1. When I approached you on behalf of others, I thought that I was doing them the favour, but if you should act in Olympius'[b] favour, I believe that you will be receiving rather than granting it. He is the one who, when he had barely left boyhood, brought prosperity to Macedonia and thereafter avoided office more sedulously than others seek it.[c] 2. He has so devoted himself to justice that every victim of wrongdoing flies to him for protection, every transgressor of the laws holds him in fear, and our governors' sole ambition is to win his approval. 3. He and I have inherited a friendship from our fathers, and he makes every effort on my behalf,[d] while from me comes commendation for his zeal, for no action of mine could come up to it. But do you, at least, give the man his due, or rather on my behalf make some small return to him for his great services. 4. He has been transferred to your Senate from the superior one—and you will pardon me for calling the Roman Senate superior when yours has you in it. So let him have from you what he had

[b] *BLZG* 223 (ii), *PLRE* 643 (3); Libanius' lifelong friend, cf. *Or.* 63. Olympius' case is discussed by Petit, "Les Senateurs de Constantinople," *Ant. Class.* 26: 366–70.

[c] This office was held before 356. The difficulties which arose from it explain his reluctance to proceed further on a career of office (*Epp.* 581, 256.9).

[d] Cf. *Letter* 53.2.

ἐκείνων. τί οὖν; ἐκείνοις ἦρκει τοὔνομα αὐτοῦ
παρ᾽ αὐτοῖς ἐγγεγράφθαι. 5. μᾶλλον δὲ μήτε
τοῦτο δῶτε μήτε μείζω τῆς δυνάμεως ζητεῖτε. ἐν
μὲν γὰρ ἐξετάσει τῶν ἀρίστων πρῶτος Ὀλύμπιος,
οὗ δὲ εἰσενεγκεῖν δεῖ, πάντων ὕστατος. γνῶναι δέ
σοι ῥᾷστον τῆς οὐσίας τὸ μέτρον παρὰ τῶν ἐπὶ
τούτῳ τεταγμένων. 6. δεῖ δή σε παρατηρεῖν,
ἡνίκα ἂν δέῃ χρήματα φέρειν, ὅπως μὴ ἀδική-
σητε, καὶ ἔτι γε πρότερον, ἡνίκα ἂν καλῆτε τοὺς
βουλευτάς, ὅπως ἐνθένδε μὴ κινήσητε. 7. μήτηρ τε γὰρ αὐτῷ ζῶσα ἐν ταῖς τοῦδε χερσὶ καὶ
ζῶσά γε διὰ τοῦτο, ὅτι ἔξεστιν αὐτὸν ὁρᾶν, τοὔνομα δ᾽ οὐκ ἂν ἀποδημίας ἐνέγκαι, καὶ τὰ πράγματα, εἴ τι γένοιτο τοιοῦτον, οἰχήσεται. ταῦτα
δὲ οὐκ ἂν σὺ διαφθαρῆναι δέξαιο. 8. πείσας δὴ
σαυτόν, ὡς ἡμῖν τε ἐκ τῶν αὐτῶν βοηθήσεις καὶ
τῇ φιλοσοφίᾳ προσήκοντα πράξεις, καθαρὰν ἡμῖν
παρασκεύασον τὴν ἄδειαν.

---

[e] As senator of Rome, Olympius had obtained exemption from the entry payment (the *follis*), cf. *Ep.* 252.1. His
situation was complicated, so Libanius asserts (*Ep.* 251
§ 6), by the mistake of the officials in Constantinople who
confused him with another Olympius and saddled him
with the obligations of the other.

[f] The *censuales,* whose duty it was to decide into which

from them.[e] And what then is this? They were satisfied with the registration of his name with them. 5. Or—better—neither grant him this nor seek of him what is beyond his power to give; for in an examination of the best men, Olympius will come first, but where a monetary contribution is involved, he will be the last man home. You can very easily get to know his financial situation from the officers in charge of that department.[f] 6. You must indeed be careful, whenever there is any need of a monetary contribution, that you inflict no injustice, and—still more important—that when you convene your senators, that you do not uproot him from here.[g] 7. He has a mother living in his care, and living only because she can see him. She could not bear the mention of his departure from home, and should such a thing happen, his position will be ruined. You would not wish such a disaster to occur. 8. Then, in the conviction that you will simultaneously be assisting us and acting in a manner befitting philosophy, ensure for us that his immunity remains unimpaired.

of the three classes of senator the candidate was to be placed following an assessment of his property.

[g] Senators at Rome were compelled to reside in the Capital (*Dig.* 1.9.11). Olympius seems to have managed to secure exemption from this, but this exemption had to be renegotiated both with Themistius as proconsul and with the prefect who succeeded him. For details, cf. Petit in *Ant. Class* 26: 347–383.

44. Θεμιστίῳ

1. Οὐκ ἄρα διὰ σπουδῆς μόνον πληροῖς τὸ βουλευτήριον βουλευτῶν, ἀλλ᾽ ἤδη καὶ εὕδοντι κύρτος. Κέλσος γὰρ ὁ τῶν μὲν παρ᾽ ἡμῖν ἄριστος, τῶν δὲ ἐκεῖ μετὰ σὲ τοῦτο ἀκοῦσαι πρέπων, αὐτόματος ἐπ᾽ ἀγαθῶν συνέδριον ἀγαθός. 2. καίτοι πάντα ἡμῖν κεκίνηται τοῦ τὸν ἄνδρα τῶν παρ᾽ ἡμῖν προστῆναι πραγμάτων. ὁ δὲ ἔφασκε χώραν διώκειν ἣν ἐπήνεσε Θεμίστιος. καὶ τὸ σόφισμα οὐκ ἀγνοῶ. 3. οἱ μὲν γὰρ ἄλλοι Βόσπορον ἰχθυόεντα ποθοῦντες ἐκεῖσε τρέχουσι, τῷ δὲ τῆς μὲν ἀρχῆς οὐ μέλει, νομίζει δέ, εἰ πολίτης ὑμέτερος γένοιτο, μετὰ σοῦ βιώσεσθαι. τοῦτο δέ ἐστιν ἐν φιλοσοφίᾳ βιῶναι, ἧς οὐκ ὀλίγον ἐν Σικυωνίᾳ μετασχὼν μάλιστα προσδοκᾷ μετασχήσειν παρὰ σοί. 4. ἐμοὶ μὲν οὖν ἕξει τοὐμὸν ἐπιτήδευμα χεῖρον τοῦ παραβοηθοῦντος ἀπόντος, καὶ πρὸς ὃν ἐκφέρων τὰ λυποῦντα ῥᾴων ἐγιγνόμην, τοῦτον ἐγγὺς οὐκ ἔχων ἀνιάσομαι, γιγνέσθω δὲ ἀγαθόν τι

---

[a] Bouchery 142 ff. The letter dates to early autumn 359 (so Bouchery), when Themistius as proconsul was still recruiting his new senators. Celsus—BLZG 104 (i), PLRE 193 (3), with stemma, 1139—had been officially nom-

44. To Themistius[a]

1. You do not, after all, simply use conscious effort to fill the Senate with senators: the fish now land themselves while you snooze.[b] For Celsus, the best of those among us, and deserving of being so called among you—second to yourself—of his own volition comes to you, a good man to a council of good men.[c]   2. Yet we left no stone unturned to put the man in charge of our affairs, but he replied that he sought the place praised by Themistius. Nor am I unaware of the attraction.   3. For all the rest, in their desire for the "Bosporus rich in fish"[d] scurry there, whereas he has no interest in office, but believes that, if he becomes a citizen of yours, he will live his life with you—that is, live it in philosophy. In Sicyon[e] he gained no small part of that, but he expects to gain the greatest part with you. 4. Though my own way of life will be the worse with the departure of my supporter, though I shall be grieved not to have by my side him who gave me comfort when I revealed my troubles to him, let

inated, and now requests a three-month delay before taking up residence in the capital (a necessary qualification) and a moderate entry fee. The letter is delivered, together with *Epp.* 84–5, by Macedonius.

[b] Proverbial: cf. *Ep.* 1385.4, Plat. *Legg.* 7.823e, *Paroem. Gr.* 1.231.

[c] Cf. Plat. *Sympos.* 174b, with Scholiast.

[d] Herod. 4.88.

[e] Cf. Them. *Or.* 23.295b–296a.

Κέλσῳ καὶ τἀμὰ ὅπῃ βούλεται χωρείτω. πάντως
ἐκ τῶν τοῦδε παραμυθία τοῖς ἐμοῖς. 5. νῦν μὲν
οὖν αὐτὸν ἥ τε μήτηρ καὶ ἐγὼ καὶ πολλοὶ κατέχο-
μεν ὡς ἐνὸν πρὸ τοῦ χειμῶνος ἡμῖν τε χαρίσασθαι
καὶ παρ' ὑμᾶς ἐλθεῖν, ἔφθη δὲ αὐτὸν ἡ περὶ αὐτοῦ
δέλτος, ἐφ' ᾗ τὰ εἰωθότα πράξεις παρατηρῶν
ὅπως μέτριον ἔσται τὸ ἀνάλωμα. ἐδόκει γὰρ ἡμῖν
εἶναι χαριέστερον ἤδη πολίτην αὐτὸν γεγενημένον
ἢ γενησόμενον αὐτὸν[1] ἰέναι.

[1] αὐτὸν om. F (Vi W Vind.).

45. Λεοντίῳ

1. Ἔλαβόν σου καὶ τὴν προτέραν ἐπιστολήν,
οὐδ' ἂν εἰκάσαις, ὅπως ἡδέως. ἦν δὲ ἥδιστον
αὐτῆς, ὅτι ἀκούσας ὡς γράψοιμί σοι, τὰ γράμματα
δὲ ἔχων οὔπω τοῦτο ἐποίησας, ὅπερ ἦν εἰκὸς τὸν
ἔχοντα. 2. ὁ μέντοι δοὺς ἐμοὶ τὰ παρὰ σοῦ δοὺς
ἐπ' ἀγορᾶς καὶ φήσας αὐτίκα ἥξειν εἰς τὸ βουλευτήριον, οὗ διατρίβω — τὸ γὰρ τῆς Τύχης ἱερόν, ὦ
καλὲ Λεόντιε, μετὰ τῆς ἄλλης αἴγλης καὶ τῶν

---

[a] A fellow sophist in Armenia: *BLZG* 194 (iv), *PLRE*
500 (9). Libanius here assumes a serio-comic tone to
examine what later turns out to be a comedy of errors, for
in *Ep.* 94 the missing messenger makes his long-delayed

Celsus enjoy his good fortune and let mine go as it likes. Certainly from his fortunes there will come some consolation for my own. 5. Hence his mother and I, and many besides, now try to keep him with us, believing it possible for him, before winter comes, to grant us this much favour and still reach you. The letter[f] about him comes in advance of him, and in consequence of it, do as you usually do and ensure that his expenditure is moderate. We believed it to be nicer for him to come as a citizen already made rather than as one in the making.

[f] The δέλτος is his official nomination; cf. Petit in *Ant. Class* 26:347–383.

45. To Leontius[a]

1. I have received your earlier letter too, and my pleasure at so doing you would never guess. The most pleasing part of it was that, on hearing that I was going to write to you, even though you had not yet received my letter, you behaved just as though you had. 2. However, the bearer of your letter to me gave it to me in the city square, and told me that he would come presently to the city hall,[b] where I do my teaching. You see, my dear Leontius, the temple

reappearance to collect the reply, having in the meantime taken himself off to Phoenicia.

[b] The location of Libanius' school since his appointment as official sophist after the death of Zenobius. This was to be so for the rest of his life.

ποιμνίων ἅ ποτε ἔτρεφεν ἐστέρηται καὶ ἔστιν ἡμῖν
ἀφορμὴ δακρύων, ὁπότε παρίοιμεν — εἰπὼν οὖν
ἐκεῖνος, ὡς ἥξει, καί τινα προθυμίαν ἐνδειξάμενος
ὥσπερ ἁρπασθεὶς ὑπ' ἀνέμων οὐκ ἔτ' ἐνέτυχέ μοι.
3. κἀγὼ ᾤμην αὐτὸν ἄκοντα ἀπενηνέχθαι, ὁ δ'
ἄρα ἐνταῦθα ὢν ἀπεδίδρασκε. τὸ γὰρ ὡς ἐνταῦθά
ἐστιν ἤκουσα παρὰ τοῦ τὰ δεύτερα δόντος. καὶ
ἴσως συνεγένετο συμμορίᾳ κολάκων, οἷς τὸ μὴ
παρ' ἐμοῦ γράμματα λαβεῖν κεχάρισται. εἰ δὲ
ἐκείνοις ἐντετυχήκει πρότερον ἢ ἐμοί, πάντως
ἂν αὐτοῖς ἐχαρίζετο καὶ τὸ μὴ τὰ σὰ δοῦναι.
4. ἐθαύμασα δέ, ὅπως οὐδ' οἷς νῦν ἔγραψας ἔδειξας ὡς κομσαίό μου τὴν ἐπιστολήν. καὶ πανταχῇ τὸ
πρᾶγμα στρέφων οὐκ ἔχω τὴν αἰτίαν εὑρεῖν. τὸ
μὲν γὰρ ἐλθεῖν ὡς ὑμᾶς Εὐμάθιον δηλοῦται τοῖς
παρ' Ἰφικράτους δεῦρ' ἐλθοῦσι γράμμασιν,
ἥκοντα δὲ παρ' ὑμᾶς οἶμαι μὴ δοῦναι λόγον οὐκ

---

^c As part of the programme of secularisation since the
time of Constantine pagan temples had been given over to
other purposes. Thus the Museum in 335 was requisi-
tioned for the *Comes Orientis* (Malal. 318.23), and other
temples became the location for schools (*Or.* 1.102). These
included the Tychaeum: in 363, the tradespeople gathered
there to present their grievances (cf. *Letter* 110.4). Julian
is critical of this in *ELF* no. 176.

of Fortune has been robbed not just of the rest of its glory but also of the classes it once nurtured, and gives me cause to weep every time I pass it.[c] Anyway, he told me that he would come and expressed considerable eagerness, but he did not meet me again. It is just as though he has been carried off by a whirlwind. 3. I thought that he had been taken off against his will, but it appears that he was here all the time and had deserted, for the bearer of your second letter informed me that he was here. Perhaps he fell in with a gang of flatterers, whom he obliged by not taking a letter from me. But had he met them before meeting me, he would certainly have obliged them by not delivering your letter at all.[d] 4. But I am surprised that in your present letter you have not given any indication of receiving my letter, either: and although I examine the matter from every angle, I am unable to discover the reason. That Eumathius[e] has arrived among you is proved by Iphicrates'[f] letter now to hand, but for him to have arrived and not delivered it I think

[d] As a sophist himself, Leontius would be well aware of the possible devices Libanius' rivals might use to reduce his standing.

[e] Pedagogue of Anatolius, son of the Armenian Adamantius; *BLZG* 135 (ii).

[f] Armenian, father of Libanius' pupil Maximus; *BLZG* 187. The passage indicates the time of writing to be after the start of the school session beginning in autumn 359.

ἔχειν,[1] ὑπὲρ οὗ πολλοὺς καὶ καλοὺς διῆλθε λόγους
καὶ πρὸς ὃν δεῖν ἐπιστέλλειν οὐκ ἀνῆκε λέγων,
ὥστ' ἐγὼ μὲν πολλάκις ἠρόμην ὃν ἦγε νέον, εἰ
τέθνηκεν ὁ παιδαγωγός, οὐ γὰρ ἂν ἐδόκει μοι ζῶν
τοῦτο ἁμαρτεῖν, τοῦ δὲ λέγοντος, ὡς περίεστιν,
ἀπορῶν οὐ πέπαυμαι.   5. φράσον οὖν, εἴτ'
ἔλαβες εἴτε μή· τῷ μὲν γὰρ ἡσθήσομαι,[2] τὸ δ'
ἀντίγραφά σοι τῶν πρώτων ποιήσει πέμπειν.

[1] ἔχειν F   εἶχεν Wolf (Mss.).
[2] σοι after ἡσθήσομαι Wolf (Mss.), del. F.

46. Ἀνατολίῳ

1. Τὸ μὲν τοὺς σοφιστὰς διασύρειν εἰωθός σοι
καὶ παλαιόν, ἔδει δὲ καὶ τὴν Πυθίαν τοῦτο παθεῖν,
ὅπως σοι τὰ πρέποντα τῷ νέῳ πράττηται σχήματι. λέγουσιν οὖν σοι καὶ οἱ σοφισταὶ καὶ ἡ Πυθία·
μὴ παύσαιο διασύρων ἃ τιμᾶν ἄξιον. 2. ἐγὼ
δὲ φιλεῖσθαι μὲν ὑπὸ σοῦ πιστεύων καὶ ἐπέστελλον καὶ ἐπήγγελλον εὖ παθεῖν οὐδὲν αἰτῶν
ὑπεραῖρόν σου τὴν δύναμιν, ἀλλ' οἷα πολλὰ καθη-
μέραν ἔσπειρες ἀξίοις τε ὁμοίως καὶ μὴ τοιούτοις·

[a] Written in autumn 359, this continues the war of
words begun in *Letter* 40. The tone has progressed from
that of serio-comic badinage to one of injured *amour
propre*.

makes no sense, since he spoke long and feelingly on the matter and never stopped telling me whom I ought to write to. In consequence I have frequently enquired of the lad he brought here[g] whether his attendant was dead, for I could not conceive that he would be so remiss if he were alive. He tells me that he is still alive, and so I am completely at a loss. 5. Tell me, then, whether you have received it or not: if so, I shall be pleased; if not, the first consequence will be the despatch of a copy to you.[h]

[g] Anatolius: *BLZG* 69 (v); contrast *PLRE* 61 (7).

[h] For Libanius' copy books of his letters cf. *Epp.* 1307.3, 1218.

46. To Anatolius[a]

1. To rail at sophists is a habit of yours, and an old one, too. The Pythia also should have had the same experience, for your behaviour to fit your new station. So both sophists and the Pythia[b] have this to say to you: do not stop railing at what you should respect. 2. In the confidence that I had your friendship, I started to write to you and solicit a favour from you, in this requesting nothing beyond your powers but merely the kind of thing you have daily scattered broadcast to people deserving and undeserving alike. But, instead of supporting me,

[b] A covert reference to Plat. *Prot.* 343b and the Pythian mottoes of γνῶθι σεαυτόν and μηδὲν ἄγαν, both of which Anatolius has ignored.

ἐπεὶ δὲ ἀντὶ τοῦ συμπρᾶξαι γράμμα ἡμῖν ἔπεμψας
παιδιᾶς γέμον, καιρὸν ἥκειν ἡγησάμην τοῦ μήτε
ὑπὲρ χάριτος μήτ' ἄλλως ἐπιστέλλειν.   3. καὶ
διαφυγόντος μὲν τὴν νόσον ἥσθην οὐχ ἧττον αὐτοῦ
τοῦ διαπεφευγότος, ἐξῆν δέ που καὶ ἄνευ τοῦ γράφειν ἥδεσθαι, καὶ οὐχ ὅστις οὐκ ἔγραφεν, οὗτος
οὐδὲ ἥδετο, ἀλλ' ὥσπερ ἐν τοῖς γεγραφόσιν ὅτι
ἥσθησαν ἦν ἴσως εὑρεῖν τὸν οὐχ ἡσθέντα, οὕτως
ἐνῆν καὶ μετὰ σιγῆς ἡσθῆναι.   4. σὺ δὲ ἐδέου
κόλακος, ἀλλ' οὐχ ἡδομένου διὰ φιλίαν. ἀγνοεῖν
δὲ λέγων ᾧ τοῦ γράφειν ἐπαυσάμην, ὕβρει δευτέρᾳ τὴν προτέραν παρέρχῃ τότε μὲν οὐκ ἄξιον
ἡγησάμενος φροντίδος, νῦν δὲ οὐδ' ὅτι μου κατη-
μέλησας εἰδώς.   5. καὶ πρᾶγμα πέπονθας οὐκ
ἀλλότριον τῆς ἐξουσίας. οἱ γὰρ ἐπὶ λαμπρᾶς τῆς
τύχης ὑμεῖς οὐδὲ ἀδικεῖν οὓς ἀδικεῖτε ἡγεῖσθε
νομίζοντες προσήκειν ὑμῖν μὲν ὑβρίζειν, ἐκείνοις
δὲ πανταχοῦ προσκυνεῖν.   6. ὁρᾷς ὅτι κρεῖττον
ἦν σοι μὴ κινεῖν τὸν ἀνάγυρον; νῦν δὲ ἐπιθυμήσας

---

c In the interval of some months Anatolius had suffered
an illness from which he had recovered. He complains that
he had received no note of commiseration from Libanius.

you sent me a letter that was full of persiflage, and so I judged the time had come for me not to write, whether for favour or for any other reason. 3. And though I was no less pleased at your recovery from illness than you, who actually had recovered, it was possible, I presume, to feel pleasure even without writing: if one does not write it does not follow that one is not pleased either.[c] Among those who have written to express their pleasure you might perhaps find one who felt none, and similarly, one might feel pleasure and yet be silent. 4. What you needed was someone to flatter you, not someone to be pleased because of your friendship. And when you say that you do not know why I stopped writing, you outdo the earlier injury with another. Then you did not regard me as worthy of a moment's thought, now you do not even realize that you have neglected me.   5. Your attitude is not uncommon to your position: you people who enjoy such exalted fortune do not even appreciate the injustice you inflict on your victims: you think it proper for you to throw your weight about and for them everywhere to kow-tow to you.   6. Don't you see that it would pay you not to stir up a hornet's nest?[d] As things are, in your desire to loose my

[d] Cf. Aristoph. *Lys.* 68 and scholiast, *Paroem. Gr.* 1.46. Ancient scholars thought that ἀνάγυρος must have been a foul-smelling plant, but it was actually the name of a vengeful ghostly hero; see Aristophanes, Ἀνάγυρος frr. 41–66 Kassel-Austin), *Zenob.* 4:204.

μοι λῦσαι τὴν σιωπὴν ἐπὶ σαυτὸν ἔλυσας καὶ
ῥεχθὲν ἔγνως καὶ ταῦτα οὐκ ἂν νήπιος, ἀλλ' οὐδὲ
Ὀδυσσέως λειπόμενος ἐν δόλοις. 7. Ὀπτάτῳ
δὲ πέμψας μὲν χρυσίον ἐπαινῇ παρ' ἡμῶν, ὅτι δὲ
αὐτὸν ἐλπίζων τῷ χρυσίῳ ποιήσειν ῥητορικὸν
ἑκατὸν στατῆρας ἔπεμψας ἐξὸν χιλίους, οὐκ
ἐπαινῇ· εἰ γὰρ οὓς ἔπεμψας οὐ μικρὸν δύνανται,
μᾶλλον ἂν ὠφέλεις ἀπὸ πλειόνων. ἀλλὰ καὶ
τοῦτο τὸ μικρὸν παρ' ἡμῖν τε κεῖται[1] καὶ ἡ
δαπάνη κατὰ λόγον χωρεῖ.

[1] μέγα inser. after τε F (S Vi): om. Wolf (other Mss.).

---

[e] Homer Il. 17.32.
[f] Cf. BLZG 227 (iii), Petit, Étudiants 144, 146. The
Scholiast makes the guess that he is Anatolius' son.

47. Ἀνατολίῳ

1. Σὺ μὲν παρεκάλεις με πρὸς παρρησίαν ὡς
πᾶν οἴσων ὅ τι ἂν ἐξ ἐμοῦ λέγηται, Αἰσχύλος δὲ
ἀποτρέπει λέγων μὴ δεῖν τοὺς ἥττους θρασυστο-
μεῖν. ἀλλὰ καὶ Εὐριπίδης φησίν, ὡς οἱ μεγάλα
πνέοντες, περὶ ὑμῶν δή που λέγων, πικρῶς
φέρουσι λόγους παρ' ἐλαττόνων κρείσσονας. ὅμως

---

[a] Libanius' last surviving letter to Anatolius before his

silence, you have loosed it upon yourself and realize what you have done, especially as you are no fool,[e] but are inferior in guile not even to Odysseus himself.   7. For sending money to Optatus,[f] you receive praise from us, but you get no praise for sending him a mere hundred staters[g] in the expectation of making him proficient in rhetoric with it, when you could have sent a thousand. If the cash you sent is of no little effect, you would be more help with more. However, even this pittance is deposited with us, and the spending of it goes according to plan.

Rather, he is in receipt of subsistence from him in the way that Letoius subsidised needy students (*Ep.* 550, *Letter* 22).

[g] Stater = *solidus* (cf. *Or.* 1.61).

47. To Anatolius[a]

1. You used to bid me be frank, professing that you would put up with anything I say, but Aeschylus deters me.[b] He says that lesser mortals should not be bold of tongue. Moreover, Euripides says that men of might, obviously meaning you, resent powerful arguments presented by inferiors.[c]

death in office in 360. Anatolius had replied to the previous letter and the correspondence had taken a less heated tone.

[b] Aesch. *Suppl.* 203.

[c] Eurip. *Andr.* 188.

δέ, ἐπειδὴ τῶν ἀμοιβαίων ἐπιθυμεῖς, σοί τε χαριοῦμαι καὶ τοῖν ποιηταῖν, τοῖς μὲν οὐ πάντα εἰπών, σοὶ δὲ οὐ πάντα κρύψας. 2. πρῶτον μὲν οὖν περὶ τοῦ μέτρου τῶν γραμμάτων ἐκεῖνο λέγω, ὅτι σὺ μὲν τῶν ἐμῶν τὴν βραχύτητα δυσχεραίνεις, ἐγὼ δὲ τῶν σῶν τὸ μῆκος. τὸ μὲν οὖν ἐμὸν ἡ Σπάρτη παραμυθεῖται, καὶ σὺ προσείρηκας Λακωνικὴν τὴν ἐπιστολήν, τῆς δὲ σῆς φλυαρίας εἰπὲ τοὺς ἡγεμόνας· ἀλλ᾽ οὐκ ἂν ἔχοις πλὴν εἰ τὸν ἀκριτόμυθον τὸν ἐπὶ τῆς ἐκκλησίας τῶν Ἀχαιῶν κλάοντα. 3. τὴν δὲ ἀρχήν σοι λήγειν καὶ πάνυ πείθομαι. φαίνῃ γὰρ ὑπὸ μὲν τοῦ λυπεῖσθαι παραπαίειν, ὑπὸ δὲ τοῦ παραφρονεῖν τοιαῦτα γράφειν. ἕως δὲ οὐ προσεδόκησας τῆς ἀρχῆς τὸ τέλος, ἐσωφρόνεις. ταυτὶ δὲ ἔγραφες ὄντως ἀγρυπνῶν, οὐ γὰρ ἦν καθεύδειν ὑπὲρ τῆς ἐξουσίας τρέμοντα. 4. Ἰουλιανὸς δὲ τῶν μὲν πρώτων παρ᾽ ἡμῖν οὐκ ἦν, ἐγένετο δ᾽ ἂν τῶν πρώτων, εἰ μὴ τὸ μὲν πρῶτον ἐν ὀρχουμένῃ πόλει διήγαγεν, ἔπειτα παρ᾽ ἡμῶν ὡς τάχιστα ἀπεπήδησεν, ἐπειδὴ οὐ κακός γε ἐπεφύκει πρὸς λόγους, ἴσως δὲ καὶ

---

[d] Cf. *Ep.* 399.2.

[e] Thersites: Homer *Il.* 2.246–269.

[f] He had been prefect since early 357. An average term

However, since you are eager for a reply, I will defer
to you and to this pair of poets, to them by not telling all, to you by not concealing all. 2. First then,
with regard to the length of our letters, I have this
much to say; you resent the brevity of mine,[d] I the
tediousness of yours. For mine, then, Sparta provides encouragement: even you have dubbed the
epistolary style "Laconic." But tell me: who are the
patterns for this nonsense of yours? None, save him
of unbridled tongue who wept in the assembly of the
Achaeans.[e] 3. I am quite convinced that your
office is nearing its end.[f] It seems that your foolish-
ness springs from your annoyance, and the writing
of such a letter from craziness. While ever you did
not look forward to the end of your prefecture,
you kept control of yourself. This letter of yours
was written in a state of insomnia, for you could
not sleep a wink for worrying about your position.
4. Julianus[g] was not one of my first-class students.
He could have been first-class, had he not first spent
his time in a city of revelry[h] and then decamped
from me as quickly as he could, for he was not at all
bad in his aptitude for oratory. Probably he cast

is three years or more at this time.

[g] *BLZG* 192 (ix), *PLRE* 470 (9): one of the pupils who
followed Libanius from Constantinople to Antioch. He
then, to Libanius' disgust, began a career as a minor
official.

[h] Constantinople, as usual, the target of Libanius'
scorn; e.g., *Or.* 1.76.

αὐτῶν ὧν ἀφῖκτο φέρων ἀπέβαλε τοὺς πλείους,
ὡς συνεγένετό σοι. 'ἐσθλῶν μὲν γὰρ ἀπ' ἐσθλά,'
τὸ δὲ ἐχόμενον ἀφίημι σὴν χάριν. 5. δοκεῖ δέ
μοι κἀκείνῃ παροξυνθῆναι γενέσθαι στρατιώτης·
ἑώρα τὸν ὕπατον τὸν ἀεροβατοῦντα καὶ μέγα
φθεγγόμενον καὶ περιφρονοῦντα τοὺς θεοὺς τοῖς
μὲν ἄλλοις ἐπικείμενον, ὑποπεπτωκότα δὲ ἀνθρώποις, ὧν ἀνδράποδα κέκτηται βελτίω. 6.
ἠράσθη οὖν ἰσχύος, ἣν εὗρε σὲ θεραπεύοντα. μὴ
οὖν θαυμάσῃς, εἰ σοῦ μένοντος ἐν τῷ δι' ἐκείνους
δύνασθαι ζηλώσει τὸν Ἰουλιανὸν Ὀπτάτος.

---

i Theognis 35–6: ἐσθλῶν μὲν γὰρ ἀπ' ἐσθλὰ μαθησέαι· ἢν δὲ
κακοῖσιν | συμμίσγῃς, ἀπολεῖς καὶ τὸν ἐόντα νόον. "From good men
you will learn good. Mix with the bad, and you will lose
even the brains you have."

48. Ἰαμβλίχῳ

1. Οὐ μόνον οὐκ ἄχθομαι παρακαλούμενος,
ἀλλὰ καὶ χαίρω προτρέποντος, ὅτι μοι τούτῳ
δηλοῦται τὸ καὶ αὐτὸν ἐνεργὸν εἶναι σέ. 2. τὸ
μὲν οὖν φροντίζειν ὅπως μὴ εἰς ὄνους ἀφ' ἵππων ὅ

---

a Cf. Bouchery p. 158; *Letter* 24; Cameron, "Iamblichus
at Athens," *Athenaeum* (1957): 143–53. Iamblichus, a
much travelled young man, was at this time in Cilicia. The

aside the greater part of the eloquence he brought with him once he became your associate. "Such wood, such chips"—what follows I omit for your sake.[i] 5. It appears to me that he has been encouraged to become a military man from the fact that he saw as consul[j] one who had his head in the clouds, talking big, despising the gods,[k] oppressing other men and cringing before people who are worse than the slaves he owns.   6. So he fell in love with the power which he found you hankering after. Do not be surprised then, when you remain in a position of influence through such as them, to find Optatus copying Julianus.

[j] Datianus, consul 358. Libanius is at his most daring here, in criticising so openly the highest official of the day in a letter to a prefect. He must have been sure of Anatolius' sympathy and discretion.

[k] Aristoph. *Clouds* 225 ff.

48. To Iamblichus[a]

1. So far from being annoyed at your directions, I actually rejoice at your instructions, for it is thus proved that you too are busily engaged.   2. Both your uncle[b] and I approve of your prudence in trying

Comes, Modestus, departing on a tour of inspection, delivers the letter and presents.

[b] Sopater (ii, the correspondent of Libanius), not Libanius' uncle, Phasganius, as Seeck.

τε θεῖος ἐπαινεῖ καὶ ἐγώ, ὀψὲ δὲ τοῦτο ἰδόντες. οἶμαι γὰρ ἤδη τι φοιτᾶν ἡμῖν ἐκεῖθεν, ἐλπίζομεν δὲ αὐτὸ θήσεσθαι διὰ τῶν ἀρχόντων καλῶς. 3. Μοδέστῳ δὲ μέλλοντι νυκτὸς ἐπὶ Κιλικίας δραμεῖσθαι βιβλίον ἑσπέρας εἰσάγω τὰ δῶρα ἐγγράψας, Ὀλύμπιος δὲ οὐκ ἀπῆν. ὁ δὲ τοῖς ἄλλοις ἥδεσθαι φήσας ὡς οὐκ ἔχουσιν ὄγκον διεωθεῖτο τοὔλαιον. ἡμῶν δὲ οὐκ ἀνιέντων ἀνέβη μὲν ὡς ἄμεινον ζητήσων ᾗ χρὴ ποιεῖν, οἷα δὲ ἐν θορύβῳ τῷ περὶ τὴν ἔξοδον, ἀφῃρέθη τὴν περὶ τούτου ψῆφον. ἦν οὖν λοιπὸν ἀναμεῖναι. 4. σοὶ μέντοι μένειν μὲν οὐκ ἔστιν ἐκεῖ, χωρεῖν δὲ ἀνάγκη δεῦρο τοῦ τε μαχέσασθαι πρὸς τὴν ἀπὸ Θρᾴκης εἴσπραξιν καὶ διαφυγεῖν ὅλως βουλήν, ἣ τοῖς μὲν ἀνωνύμοις λυσιτελεῖ, τοὺς δ' οἷα σὺ διαδεξαμένους οὐκ ἂν λαμπροτέρους θείη.

---

[c] "From horses to donkeys," cf. *Ep.* 71.2, *Or.* 62.61: a favoured proverb of Libanius and others. See *Paroem. Gr.* 1.41. The reference is to Themistius' summons to join the Senate (cf. §4, below). The ἄρχοντες, the officials at court, can be persuaded to drop the matter.

to avoid buying a pig in a poke,[c] though we are late in observing it for what it is. I think that we shall have some fresh development from there soon, but we hope to settle it all right through the governors. 3. As Modestus was due to leave for Cilicia during the night, I took a letter to him in the evening, listing the presents in it. Olympius[d] was with me, too. Modestus said that he was pleased with the rest, since they were not too bulky, but he objected to the oil. We persisted, and he went upstairs to find a better way of doing it, but, as was to be expected in the usual hustle and bustle of his departure, he failed to decide this matter. The upshot, then, was for it to wait.   4. However, you cannot wait there: you must come here to contest the demands from Thrace[e] and to keep quite clear of the Senate. That position profits nonentities, but it could never increase the renown of people with an inheritance like yours.[f]

[d] Libanius' lifelong friend, who also found himself in Themistius' net.

[e] Constantinople, and the demand for an entry fee on joining the Senate. He was to rely upon the praetorian prefect in Antioch.

[f] Iamblichus' grandfather was the foremost Neoplatonist of the day, Sopater i (cf. Eunap. *V.S.* 462–3, Cameron in *Athenaeum* 35:143–53).

49. Μοδέστῳ

1. Μικροῦ τὸν δεσμὸν ἀπορρήξας, ὁ δέ ἐστι νέοι καὶ τέχνη καὶ τὰ τοῦ διδάσκειν κακά, μετὰ τῶν βελτίστων τουτωνὶ τῶν ἑλκομένων ἧκον· τοσοῦτος ἐμέ τε καὶ τὴν πόλιν ἔσεισε φόβος. ἔστι γὰρ οὖν ἄνθος τῆς πόλεως ἡ τούτων οἰκία. 2. λογιζόμενοι δέ, τίς ἦν ὁ καλῶν καὶ παρ' ὃν ἥξουσι, πείθειν εἴχομεν ἡμᾶς αὐτούς, ὡς ἄρα αὐτοὺς δέχεται λιμήν, οὐ σκόπελος. ὥστε ἀνεπνέομεν πρὸς ἀλλήλους λέγοντες· 'τί δ' ἂν γένοιτο κακὸν ἀπὸ τοῦ καλοῦ Μοδέστου;' καλὸν δὲ εἶναί σε τοῖς τε ὅλοις πειθόμεθα καὶ μάλιστά γε δὴ τούτοις αὐτοῖς ὧν τὰ παρόντα μέρος. 3. πρᾶγμα γὰρ παραλαβών, ὃ πεσὸν[1] εἰς χεῖρας ἄρχοντος τέρψιν τινὰ τὸ κακῶς ποιεῖν ποιουμένου πολλὴν ἂν ἤγειρε[1] φλόγα, γαλήνην ἀπέφηνας[1] τὴν προσδοκωμένην ζάλην τοῖς μὲν δοὺς ἀναβάλλεσθαι, τοὺς δὲ ὅλως ἀπαλλάξας ἐπί τε τοὺς ὀρφανοὺς οὐκ ἐάσας ἁρπαγὴν κωμάσαι. 4. σὺ καὶ τὴν τούτων οὓς νῦν ἔχεις ἀδελφὴν ἐδάκρυσάς τε ἀγομένην καὶ ηὔξω

---

[1] ὃ πεσὸν ... ἂν ἤγειρε ... ἀπέφηνας F, conj. Seeck (p. 354)   ὁ παῖς ... ἀνήγειρε ... ἀποφήνας Wolf (Mss.).

49. To Modestus[a]

1. I nearly tore off the fetters imposed by my pupils, my profession and the troubles of teaching and accompanied these excellent people who have been arrested, such was the fear that shook both the city and myself. Their family, you see, is the flower of the city. 2. But, upon considering who it was who issued the summons and before whom they were proceeding, we were able to persuade ourselves that they would find a refuge, not a reef. So we breathed again, as we told each other, "What harm could there be from the noble Modestus?" That you are noble we are convinced by your general conduct and in particular by this very incident, of which the present matter forms part. 3. For you inherited a case which, had it fallen into the hands of a governor who took some pleasure in injustice, would have caused a great conflagration, but instead you revealed the expected tempest to be a calm: to some you granted a remand, others you cleared completely, so allowing no orgy of looting to be perpetrated against their fatherless children. 4. You shed tears at the arrest of the sister of those

[a] Modestus presided over the treason trials held at Scythopolis (Amm. Marc. 14.12.6 ff), in which many of the notables of Antioch and elsewhere were involved. Libanius here offers pleas for some of them. The letter was evidently written before the death of his uncle, and is to be dated to the early winter of 359/60.

τε ἡμῖν ἀποσωθῆναι καὶ τάχα οὐκ ἀτυχήσεις. γενοῦ δὴ καὶ τούτοις ἀνθ᾽ Ἑρμιόνος καὶ τὴν γνώμην ἣν ἐνεστήσω νόμισον νόμον. τοὺς μὲν γὰρ ἄλλους ἀλλοτρίοις παραδείγμασι παιδεύομεν, σὺ δὲ ἂν τοῖς σοῖς ἀκολουθήσῃς, πάνθ᾽ ἡμῖν εὖ κείσεται. 5. πολλαχόθεν δέ μοι τῶν ἀνδρῶν μέλει καὶ μὴ πᾶν ὑπὲρ αὐτῶν ποιοῦντι λόγος οὐκ ἔσται. φιλίαν τε γὰρ ἐκ πατέρων δεδέγμεθα δίκαιά τε προσγεγένηται μείζω. τῷ μὲν γὰρ Ἀντιόχῳ πάλαι συμφοιτῶν νῦν υἱὸν ἐν μουσείοις τρέφω μόνον ὄντα αὐτῷ, τῷ δ᾽ Ἀρσενίῳ συνεφοίτων μὲν καὶ αὐτῷ πρεσβύτερος νέῳ, γενομένῳ δὲ ἀνδρὶ δι᾽ ἀρετὴν τρόπων εἰς τὰ μάλιστα χρῶμαι, καὶ νῦν ἃ πρὸς τοὺς ἄλλους ἀπόρρητά μοι, ῥητὰ πρὸς τοῦτον. 6. περὶ δὲ αὖ τοῦ τρίτου τί μεῖζον εἴποιμ᾽ ἂν ἢ ὅτι τοιούτους ἀδελφοὺς οὐ καταισχύνει κεκτημένος μὲν μικρά, τῷ μὴ πολλὰ δὲ οὐ λυπούμενος, ἡσυχίαν τιμῶν καὶ τὸ τοῖς φίλοις εἶναι βέβαιος ἀσκῶν; 7. τούτους ἡμῖν, ὦ θρέμμα

---

[b] Cf. Letter 82.2, Paroem. Gr. 1.38. The temple of Demeter and Persephone in Hermione was a place of refuge.

who are now haled before you and prayed that she might be saved for us, and perhaps your prayers will not be unsuccessful. Be then to these also as a tower of strength,[b] and deem the resolution which you have formed to have the force of law. We teach others by the example of other people, but if you follow your own, all will be well with us. 5. I have many grounds for my concern for the men, and there will be no excuse if I do not do all I can for them. The friendship between us we inherited from our fathers, and their claims have become more and greater, for long ago I was a fellow pupil of Antiochus,[c] and now I have his only son[d] as my pupil at school; I was also at school with Arsenius,[e] though a little his senior, and now that he has become a man, he is one of my closest associates because of the excellence of his character, and now what I keep secret from others is no secret from him. 6. Moreover, with regard to the third what more need I say than that he is no disgrace to such brothers, since though his possessions are small, he is not upset that they are not great, he respects the quiet life, and schools himself to be true to his friends. 7. Send them back to us unscathed, o

[c] *BLZG* 76 (ii), *principalis* of Antioch.

[d] *BLZG* 90 (iii).

[e] *BLZG* 90 (ii). The names of the other brother (§ 6) and of the sister (§ 4) are not known.

Δίκης, ἀπαθεῖς τε καὶ ταχέως ἀπόπεμπε τῇ τε ἄλλῃ φυλάξας καὶ τῷ μὴ τοῖς κυσὶν ἐκδοῦναι.

50. Μοδέστῳ

1. Σὲ μὲν εἴη τὰ εἰωθότα ποιεῖν, ταῦτα δέ ἐστι νόμους τε βεβαιοῦν καὶ σῴζειν πόλεις καὶ μισεῖν συκοφάντας καὶ βοηθεῖν ἀδικουμένοις · ἡμῖν δέ, ὡς μὲν ὁ κοινὸς λόγος, καὶ τὰ κοινὰ βλάπτεται, εἰ δὲ τοῦτο μεῖζον τοῦ ἀληθοῦς, ἀλλ' ἐκεῖνό γε οὐ ψεῦδος, ὅτι τήν γε ἡμετέραν οἰκίαν ἀπολώλεκεν ἡ τελευτὴ τοῦ θείου.   2. τέθνηκεν, ὦ θεοί, τέθνηκεν ὁ πάντα ἄριστος Φασγάνιος, ὃν σὺ μάλιστα ἀνθρώπων ᾐδέσθης καὶ ὑφ' οὗ μάλιστα ἀνθρώπων ἐθαυμάσθης καὶ περὶ οὗ μάλιστα ἀσθενοῦντος ἐφρόντισας.   3. ἐγὼ μὲν οὖν εὐξαίμην ⟨ἂν⟩[1] ἐπ' ἐκείνῳ τὴν αὐτὴν εὐθὺς ἐλθεῖν, ἐπεὶ δὲ τετήρημαι λύπῃ καὶ δάκρυσιν, εἰς μίαν ὁρῶ παραμυθίαν, σέ τε καὶ τὴν σὴν δύναμιν. ὧν νῦν τε ἀπολαύομεν ἀπόντος καὶ δῆλον ὡς μειζόνως, ἡνίκα ἂν ἔλθῃς, ἀπολαυσόμεθα.

[1] ⟨ἂν⟩ inser. F.

offspring of Justice, and quickly; protect them in all
else, and especially by refusing them to be given to
the dogs for burial.[f]

[f] Cf. Soph. *Ajax* 830.

50. To Modestus

1. You, I trust, are engaged on your normal
activities, namely the confirmation of laws, the
preservation of cities, hatred of slander, and assistance to the victims of wrongdoing.[a] For me, however, our commonweal suffers as does our common
report; and if this seems an exaggeration, certainly
it is no lie that our household has been ruined by
the death of my uncle.   2. Phasganius, alas, the
peerless Phasganius is dead[b]—he, whom of all men
you most respected, who of all men most admired
you and of whom, in his illness, you took most
thought.   3. I could pray to travel the same road
straight after him, but since I am beset by grief and
tears, I look to but one consolation, yourself and
your influence. This I now enjoy in your absence:
clearly I shall enjoy it even more when you arrive
here.

[a] Modestus is still engaged upon the treason trials at
Scythopolis, as in the previous letter.
[b] Cf. *Or.* 1.117 ff, where Libanius reveals the deep distress that the death of Phasganius, together with that of
his mother, caused him in the next two years. Cf. also
Letter 64.